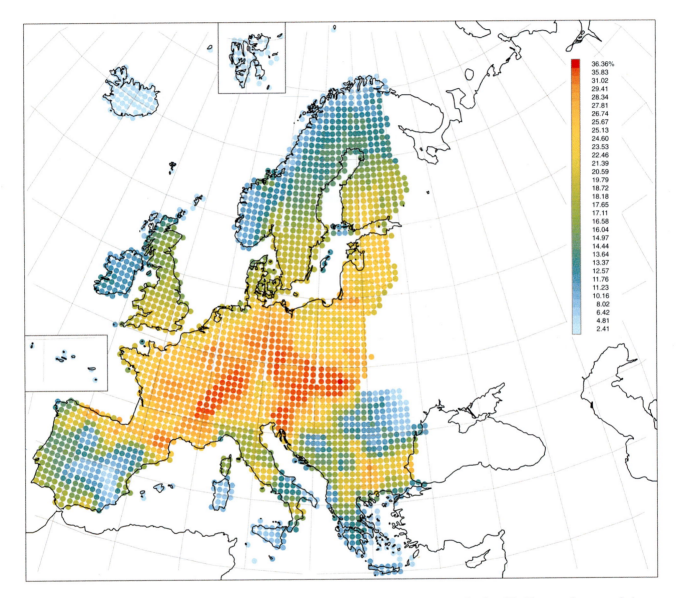

Figure 1 Species richness of mammals across Europe. This illustrative map was prepared using Worldmap software and shows species richness (number of species per grid square) with one level of smoothing. The entire atlas dataset has been used, including introduced species. There are some differences between the *Atlas Flora Europaea* UTM grid used by this software and the one used in the Atlas, particularly around the south-eastern borders of Europe and also in the treatment of some island groups.

THE ATLAS OF
EUROPEAN
MAMMALS

In memory of

François G. de Beaufort (1936–1995)
Director, Secretariat de la Faune et de la Flore, 1979–1989.
First President of the *Societas Europaea Mammalogica.*

THE ATLAS OF EUROPEAN MAMMALS

by A. J. Mitchell-Jones, G. Amori, W. Bogdanowicz,
B. Kryštufek, P. J. H. Reijnders, F. Spitzenberger, M. Stubbe,
J. B. M. Thissen, V. Vohralík & J. Zima

T & A D
POYSER
NATURAL
HISTORY

This book is printed on acid-free paper.

Illustrations © the Artists

© 1999 by ACADEMIC PRESS

First published in 1999 by T & AD Poyser Ltd
24-28 Oval Road, London NW1 7DX

Academic Press
24-28 Oval Road, London NW1 7DX, UK
http://www.hbuk.co.uk/ap/

Academic Press
525 B Street, Suite 1900, San Diego, California 92101-4495, USA
http:/www.apnet.com

ISBN: 0-85661-130-1

A catalogue for this book is available from the British Library

Typeset by Hedgehog, Worcestershire, UK
Printed by Midas Printing Ltd, Hong Kong

99 00 01 02 03 9 8 7 6 5 4 3 2 1

8/00

Contents

Editorial Committee

Editor-in-Chief

Anthony J. Mitchell-Jones (English Nature, UK)

Regional co-ordinators

Anthony J. Mitchell-Jones (English Nature, Peterborough, UK) – Western and northern Europe
Friederike Spitzenberger (Natural History Museum, Vienna, Austria) – Central and south-eastern Europe

Data co-ordinator

Johan B. M. Thissen (National Reference Centre for Nature Management, Wageningen, The Netherlands)

Species account editors

Giovanni Amori (CNR, Centro Genetica Evoluzionistica, Rome, Italy) – Lagomorpha, Rodentia
Wiesław Bogdanowicz (Museum & Institute of Zoology, Warsaw, Poland) – Chiroptera
Boris Kryštufek (Natural History Museum, Ljubljana, Slovenia) – Rodentia, Insectivora
Peter J. H. Reijnders (Institute for Forestry and Nature Research, Wageningen, The Netherlands) – Pinnipedia
Friederike Spitzenberger (Natural History Museum, Vienna, Austria) – Insectivora
Michael Stubbe (Martin-Luther University, Halle, Germany) – Carnivora
Jan Zima (Academy of Sciences and Charles University, Prague, Czech Republic) – Artiodactyla
Vladimír Vohralík (Charles University, Prague, Czech Republic)

Published by Academic Press on behalf of the *Societas Europaea Mammalogica*

Country co-ordinators

Albania	M. Vlašín & P. Koutný (Veronica, Brno, Czech Republic); C. Prigioni (University of Pavia, Italy)
Austria	F. Spitzenberger (Natural History Museum, Vienna).
Belgium	R. Libois (University of Liège); E. van der Straeten (University of Antwerp).
Bosnia & Herzegovina	B. Kryštufek (Slovenian Museum of Natural History, Ljubljana, Slovenia).
Bulgaria	P. Benda (National Museum, Prague, Czech Republic); G. Markov (Institute of Zoology BAS, Sofia); V. Vohralík (Charles University, Prague, Czech Republic).
Croatia	N. Tvrtković (Croatian Natural History Museum, Zagreb); B. Kryštufek (Slovenian Museum of Natural History, Ljubljana, Slovenia).
Czech Republic	M. Anděra (National Museum, Prague); J. Zima (Academy of Sciences & Charles University, Prague).
Denmark	T. Asferg (National Environmental Research Institute, Kalø).
Estonia	T. Maran (Tallinn Zoo).
Faeroe Islands	D. Bloch (Museum of Natural History, Tórshavn).
Finland	H. Henttonen (Finnish Forest Research Institute, Vantaa).
France	P. Haffner & H. Maurin (Muséum National d'Histoire Naturelle, Paris).
Germany	P. Boye (Bundesamt für Naturschutz, Bonn); R. Hutterer (Museum A. Koenig, Bonn); M. Stubbe (Martin-Luther University, Halle).
Greece	G. Catsadorakis (WWF, Athens); O. von Helversen (University of Erlangen, Germany); V. Vohralík (Charles University, Prague, Czech Republic).
Hungary	G. Csorba (Hungarian Mammalogical Society, Budapest)
Iceland	P. Hersteinsson (University of Iceland, Reykjavik)
Ireland	T. Hayden (University College Dublin).
Italy	G. Amori (CNR, Centro Genetica Evoluzionistica, Rome); C. Prigioni (University of Pavia).
Kaliningrad Region, Russia	G. Grishanov & V. Beliakov (University of Kaliningrad)
Latvia	V. Pilāts (Gauja National Park, Sigulda).
Lithuania	L. Balčiauskas (Institute of Ecology, Vilnius).
Luxembourg	E. Engel (Musée National d'Histoire Naturelle, Luxembourg).
Macedonia	B. Kryštufek (Slovenian Museum of Natural History, Ljubljana, Slovenia); S. Petkovski (Macedonian Museum of Natural History, Skopje).
Malta	J. J. Borg (Malta Bat Group, Rabat).
The Netherlands	J. B. M. Thissen (National Reference Centre for Nature Management, Wageningen).
Norway	P. Shimmings & A-H. Rønning (Norwegian Zoological Society, Oslo).
Poland	W. Bogdanowicz (Museum & Institute of Zoology PAS, Warsaw); B. W. Wołoszyn (Institute of Animal Systematics & Evolution PAS, Kraków).
Portugal	M. L. Mathias & M. G. Ramalhinho (University of Lisbon); M. J. Cabral (Institute for Nature Conservation, Lisbon)
Romania	D. Murariu (Natural History Museum, Bucharest); I. Coroiu (Babes-Bolayi University, Cluj-Napoca)
Slovakia	A. L. G. Dudich (Technical University in Zvolen); M. Uhrin (Muránska National Park); M. Žilinec (Institute of Forest Ecology, Zvolen).
Slovenia	B. Kryštufek (Slovenian Museum of Natural History, Ljubljana).
Spain	L. J. Palomo (SECEM & University of Málaga); F. González (SECEMU, Oviedo).
Sweden	I. Ahlén & L. Hansson (Swedish University of Agricultural Sciences, Uppsala); K. Fredga (Uppsala University).
Switzerland	S. Capt (Centre Suisse de Cartographie, Neuchâtel); F. Saucy (University of Fribourg).
Turkey	C. Kurtonur & B. Özkan (Trakya University, Edirne).
United Kingdom	A. J. Mitchell-Jones (English Nature, Peterborough); H. R. Arnold (Environmental Information Centre, Huntingdon); W. I. Montgomery (The Queen's University of Belfast).
Yugoslavia	B. Kryštufek (Slovenian Museum of Natural History, Ljubljana, Slovenia); M Paunović (Natural History Museum in Belgrade).

Artists

P. Barrett, Z. Bihari, E. Hazebroek, U. Iff, T. P. McOwat, J. Mikuletič, F. Müller, M. Nāzāreanu, R. Lindsay, D. Ovenden, V. Ree, D. Roth, P. Twisk, V. Zadražil

Authors of species accounts

G. Amori, M. Anděra, F. M. Angelici, M. Apollonio, R. C. van Apeldoorn, H. Baagøe, K. Bauer, J. Benzal, S. Bertolino, P. Beuving, J. D. S. Birks, S. M. J. M. Brasseur, P. W. Bright, W. Bogdanowicz, S. Broekhuizen, C. M. C. Catto, J. Červený, L. Contoli, A. S. Cooke, M. Cristaldi, I. Currado, M. Delibes, A. C. Entwistle, J. Fa, S. Fajardo, M. G. Filippucci, R. Fons, M. C. Forchhammer, R. García-Perea, L. Gavish, R. Gerell, J. Gisbert, J. Gliwicz, M. Gorgas, A. Guillén, J. Gurnell, L. Hansson, J. Hausser, O. von Helversen, H. Hemmer, M. Homolka, I. Horáček, A. M. Hutson, R. Hutterer, C. Ibáñez, Z. Jakubiec, G. Jones, K. Kauhala, P. Koubek, F. Krapp, Z. A. Krasiński, B. Kryštufek, L. Lapini, S. Lovari, A. Loy, R. Libois, A. Machado Carrillo, M. Macholán, T. Maran, D. Masson, P. J. Mazzoglio, S. Męczyński , W. I. Montgomery, P. A. Morris, K. Nygrén, J. M. Palmeirim, L. J. Palomo, L. Pedrotti, D. Peshev, M. Preleuthner, C. Prigioni, Z. Pucek, E. Pulliainen, A-I. Queiroz, M. G. Ramalhinho, R. D. Ransome, G. Reggiani, P. J. H. Reijnders, E. H. Ries, L. Rodrigues, M. Röhrs, V. V. Rozhnov, J. Rydell, F. Saucy, G. Schlapp, H. W. Schofield, C. Shiel, F. Spitz, F. Spitzenberger, G. Storch, C. Stubbe, M. Stubbe, H-P. B. Stutz, S. Sulkava, F. Tattersall, G. Topál, Z. Urbańczyk, E. Vernier, P. Vogel, V. Vohralík, L. Wauters, U. Weinhold, M. Wolsan, D. Yalden, J. Zima.

Editors of the common names

Luis Pastor Ramos & Johan B. M. Thissen

This atlas should be cited as: Mitchell-Jones, A. J., Amori, G., Bogdanowicz, W., Kryštufek, B., Reijnders, P. J. H., Spitzenberger, F., Stubbe, M., Thissen, J. B. M., Vohralík, V. & Zima, J. (1999) *Atlas of European Mammals*. The Academic Press, London. 496 pp.

Preface

Since the 1992 Rio Conference, decision-makers and the public have both become more conscious of the value that biodiversity has for our future and how its preservation is one of the main challenges for the coming century. Biodiversity cannot be seen any longer as an inconvenience to development. Biodiversity is a fundamental part of the heritage of man and, as such, an important resource for harmonious human development and fulfilment. These ideas were already at the heart of the European Campaign on Nature Conservation that the Council of Europe launched in 1970 and which led, after some inter-governmental work, to the adoption of the Convention on the Conservation of European Wildlife and Natural Habitats (Bern Convention, 1979).

Many Europeans tend to associate the term 'biodiversity' with the conservation of rare and colourful animals and plants in tropical ecosystems, while ignoring the beauty and interest of the wildlife on their own doorstep. European mammals comprise one of those fascinating and varied groups asking for our attention. The populations of many European mammal species have declined progressively and their distribution has shrunk to alarming levels, particularly in central Western Europe where urbanisation and intensive agriculture have left little space for wildlife. To be able to conserve those species and improve the status of mammals, all conservationists need the help and support of the scientific community. Works such as the one you have in your hands are fundamental not just for the improvement of scientific knowledge but for action too. I am deeply honoured to welcome this extraordinary atlas and to congratulate, in the name of all European conservationists, the *Societas Europaea Mammalogica* for the hard work, the professionalism and the enthusiasm of the competent team that has put together this most useful Atlas. My special remembrance goes to the late François de Beaufort, who was at the origin of this initiative and who devoted his whole life to the study of European mammals.

Eladio Fernández-Galiano
Head *ad interim* of the Division of Protection
and Management of the Environment
Council of Europe

Strasbourg, February 1998

History and overview of the project

The European Mammals Atlas, to put **E**uropean **M**ammals on **M**aps (EMMA), was begun at a meeting initiated and hosted by the *Secretariat de la Faune et de la Flore* (now *Service du Patrimoine Naturel)* in the National Museum of Natural History in Paris in 1988 (de Beaufort & Vignon, 1989). At that meeting, invited representatives from a wide range of European countries recognized the valuable contribution such an atlas could make to the development of mammalogy in Europe and agreed that an atlas project should be undertaken. Following the meeting, a new society, the *Societas Europaea Mammalogica,* was set up, primarily as a means of delivering the project, but with a wider remit to improve communication between all European mammalogists. The first President of the Society was François de Beaufort, now deceased.

Work on the Atlas began with the establishment of an Editorial Committee, the development of a species list, agreement on the mapping system to be used and the production of base maps for each country. Regional co-ordinators were appointed, each responsible for promoting and co-ordinating the project in one part of Europe. For each country, one or more country co-ordinators were identified and asked to take on the work of collecting, organizing and submitting the data. The varying stages of development of mammalogy across Europe meant that this task ranged from abstracting data from an existing national database to setting up a complete new national recording system.

To complement the maps, short species accounts in a standard format were commissioned from a wide range of experts and edited by members of the Editorial Committee. These are not intended to replace the much more detailed reviews available in specialist works but give a brief summary of the species and an introduction to the literature. An illustration of each species was also commissioned from a range of European artists to complete a two-page layout for each species.

At a later stage, it was decided to include the common names of all species in a wide range of European languages in order to make the atlas accessible to as wide an audience as possible.

As well as a standard layout for each species, a table is included, giving summary information, such as a complete European mammal species list and the international legal situation and conservation status of each species.

Introduction

Accurate, up to date and detailed distribution maps are a basic resource both for biologists and policy makers. The value of such maps is widely recognized and most European countries have national or regional projects to collect and publish such data, usually arranged by taxonomic group. Despite much work, there remains great variation both within and between countries in the development of mapping projects and there are also great differences in the availability of data for different taxonomic groups. In general, mapping the distribution of birds is most advanced, though mapping vascular plants also has a long history. Despite their wide range of interactions with man and, for some, their value as game species, mammals remain a generally poorly recorded group, probably because of the nocturnal and cryptic habits of most species.

From its conception, this *Atlas* was intended to focus on the current distributions of European mammals using only validated records from defined time periods plotted onto a standard grid. Although a brief account of each species accompanies each map, the atlas is not intended to provide the depth of information that is available in specialist handbooks, notably the recent and comprehensive *Handbuch der Säugetiere Europas* (Niethammer & Krapp, 1978–). Neither is the atlas a field or identification guide comparable with publications such as Macdonald & Barrett (1995). The illustrations are intended to give an impression of the species rather than act as an identification guide.

Intended study area and coverage achieved

At the launch of the project in 1988 (de Beaufort & Vignon, 1989) it was decided to try to cover the same area as the *Atlas Florae Europaeae* as described by Jalas & Suominen (1972). At a meeting in 1992 this was changed to an area that has also been defined recently (1997) by others as the study area of the new project *Fauna Europaea* (A. Legakis, in litt.), although the seas are excluded. The eastern border of this area is the Greek-Turkish border in the Aegean, the north-western shore of the Dardanelles, Sea of Marmara and the Bosphorus, the Black Sea coast of European Turkey, Bulgaria, Romania, the Ukraine and Russia, the Russian border in the Caucasus, the western coast of the Caspian Sea, the Kazakhstan-Russian border, the Ural mountains and the eastern coast of Novaya Zemlya. In the southeast, where the delimitation of Europe is most controversial, the study area excludes Kazakhstan, Armenia, Georgia, Azerbaijan, Asia Minor and Cyprus.

Regrettably, from the vast area of the former Soviet Union, data have been received only from the Baltic States and the Kaliningrad Region, the Russian exclave between Lithuania and Poland. Therefore Russia (except Kaliningrad), Belarus, Ukraine and Moldova are not covered.

In the Atlantic Ocean the study area includes the four archipelagos of the Azores, Madeira, Islas Selvagens and Canary Islands. In the Mediterranean it includes Malta and all islands, which belong to European states, including Gökçeada (European Turkey), but excluding the Spanish islands close to the coast of Morocco, such as the Islas Chafarinas.

In fact the area of coverage is to a large extent the same as in most major European mammal reference books, such as the *Catalogue of the Mammals of Western Europe (Europe exclusive of Russia)* (Miller, 1912), *Zoogdierengids van Europa ten westen van 30° oosterlengte* (van den Brink, 1955, 1978), the *Handbuch der Säugetiere Europas* (Niethammer & Krapp, 1978–) and *The Mammals of Britain and Europe* (Macdonald & Barrett, 1995). A geographically more comprehensive guide to the mammals of Europe is *Säugetiere Europas* (Görner & Hackethal, 1988).

The coverage achieved can be seen in the map of the total number of recorded species per 50 km UTM square (Figure 1). This is in fact a combination of two factors: actual species richness and completeness of recording. The general pattern is one of increasing species richness from north-west to south-east, culminating at the large mountain chains of the Pyrénées, Alps and Carpathians. For the last region this is partly obscured by relative under-recording in Romania. Farther south in Europe, in the Mediterranean region, species richness is rather low, but under-recording is also a factor here.

More information on coverage achieved is given in the Country accounts (page 7).

Grid system

As for all other European species mapping projects (vascular plants: Jalas & Suominen, 1967, 1972–; breeding birds: Hagemeijer & Blair, 1997; amphibians and reptiles: Gasc *et al.*, 1997; projects of the European Invertebrate Survey: Kime, 1990; Svendsen & Fibiger, 1992), the Universal Transverse Mercator (UTM) grid has been used. The use of the UTM grid for mapping of species and its advantages and disadvantages are discussed extensively by Rasmont & André (1989). No advice has been given to the country co-ordinators whether to use the old 'European Data' UTM system, based on the ellipsoid of Hayford, or the universal 'World Geodetic System'. The latter has probably been used in Eastern Europe, whereas the former old system might have been applied in Western Europe. In fact the country co-ordinators were free to use the UTM field maps most commonly used in their country, irrespective of projection parameters. Because the difference between the systems is never more than a few hundred metres, this matter is of minor importance in our continentwide project.

The basic mapping unit is the 50 x 50 km cell (50 km UTM square). For convenience the cells are referred to as 'squares', although some of them are not exactly square.

The standard UTM grid system is based on zones of latitude eight degrees high and longitude six degrees wide. The height of the northernmost row of zones – in our area of coverage only Svalbard – is, however, twelve degrees.

The west–east axis, the width of the squares within the zones, is difficult to manage because the meridians of longitude converge towards the North Pole. Fewer squares can be accommodated within a zone nearer to the pole than towards the equator. To keep the width of as many squares as possible at 50 km some method must be adopted to reduce gradually, in a northwards direction, the number of squares within each zone of the UTM grid. Two seam squares bordering each sixth meridian on either side are diminished towards the pole and at a width of 30 km are merged to one square with a width of 60 km. This one seam square on the top of each sixth meridian is diminished towards the north to be combined at a remaining width of 40 km with the two neighbouring 50 km squares into two new seam squares of 70 km width at either side of the sixth meridian. The width of the squares thus varies between 30 and 70 km. There are some differences between this grid and the one proposed by de Beaufort & Vignon (1989), mainly because the single seam square is

dissolved at a width of about 40 km rather than the 20 km they proposed.

Merging of two seam squares 30 km wide into one of 60 km happens at 46°, 58°, 67° and 79°N and combining of a single seam square 40 km wide and two standard 50–km squares into two new squares at 36°, 49°, 60°, 69° and 80°N. This whole repeating process can be seen on the map of the species number per square (Figure 1). The breeding bird atlas (Hagemeijer & Blair, 1997) has used the same system, except for Svalbard.

The UTM zone system as defined by NATO (UTM-MGRS) deviates from the regular width of six degrees in two areas, both on Norwegian territory. The first deviation is in Svalbard, where the width of zones 33X and 35X is extended on each side with three degrees to a total of not six but twelve degrees: 33X goes from 9°E to 21°E and 35X from 21°E to 33°E. Furthermore 31X is extended to the east and 37X to the west, each by three degrees. The zones 32X, 34X and 36X are skipped. This has been done to accommodate Svalbard, with the exception of the eastern tip of Kvitøya (37X), into only two zones: 33X and 35X. The UTM-MGRS has been followed in this one deviation, because it is much more convenient to have only two rather wide zones for Svalbard rather than four very narrow ones. However, in this *Atlas* an unmodified regular UTM grid has been applied for the coast of Norway between Stavanger and Ålesund west of 6°E (zone 31V), not the UTM-MGRS, which treats this area as if in zone 32V. In the UTM-MGRS in this area, zone 32V is extended to the west into 31V. This second deviation has not been followed in our Atlas, because there is no obvious reason to do so.

Background map of Europe

Level 1 of the third version of the digitized Administrative Regions Pan Europe map (AREU10MV3) of EUROSTAT has been used as a background geographical map. This map has been digitized at a scale of 1:10 000 000 and it is depicted in the *Atlas* at a scale of about 1:25 000 000. The Canary Islands, Madeira and the Islas Selvagens, the Azores and the Spitsbergen archipelago appear as three insets at the left. The map is in Lambert azimuthal projection, with 9°E 48°N as point of origin.

Collection and validation of records

The primary intention of the *Atlas* is to give as accurate a picture as possible of the current distribution of mammals in Europe. Thus, all records shown in this *Atlas* can ultimately be traced back, via a country co-ordinator, to published records or records held on national databases or by individuals. Country co-ordinators were asked not to make assumptions about the occurrence of a species in any particular square. Inevitably, this means that there are blank squares even for common species in well-recorded countries and that for some countries there are large areas where a species almost certainly occurs but there are no records available to us. All atlases suffer from this problem, and we hope that this publication will stimulate interest in mammal recording and lead to an increase in the availability of validated records at the national level. Inevitably too there will be inaccuracies; this is unavoidable given the dynamic nature of mammal populations, changes in taxonomy and the need to collect data over relatively long periods. Species extending their distributional area, such as some rapidly spreading introductions, will be under-represented, whilst declining species are likely to be over-represented. Such problems emphasize the inadequacies of distribution atlases for monitoring mammal populations and confirm that an atlas must be seen as only the first step towards developing regional, national or international monitoring systems for mammals.

One problem for all recording schemes is the impossibility of proving the absence of a species, particularly when a species has declined or disappeared from an area. In many atlases, species are recorded as being present within particular time periods and disappearances must be inferred from the fact that a species was once recorded in an area but is not included in the most up to date category.

In this *Atlas* we have taken the view that arises naturally from our wish to show the current status of species as accurately as possible and takes account of the relatively long period over which records have been collected. In general, species are shown as being present for all areas for which there are positive records within the appropriate time period. However, where thorough and recent surveys have failed to demonstrate the current presence of a species at the time of compilation, we have removed records from the database to reflect this

change. The situation of the otter *Lutra lutra* in The Netherlands provides an excellent example. Otters were widespread, though rare, in The Netherlands until the late 1970s, when the species declined to extinction. Widespread surveys have since confirmed this. If all the post-1970 records of the otter were included on the map, this would give an unrealistic and optimistic picture of the situation and so they have been excluded. Similar changes have been made for other species, with the final decision on inclusion or exclusion being made by the country co-ordinator.

Mapping periods and symbols

● Species present. Based on data collected since 1 January 1970, modified by published data on extinctions to give the current status of the species. Positive records since 1970 are omitted from the map only where more recent detailed surveys have failed to detect the species.

● Presence presumed. Based on data collected before 1970, but where there is no evidence to suggest the species has become extinct.

The species list and taxonomy

The species list for the area of coverage was developed by the Editorial Committee and supplemented by a longer list covering the wider area of Europe (Appendix 1). The latter includes all species currently established and breeding in the wild in the study area of the *Fauna Europaea*, including some vagrants but excluding escaped pets or domestic animals not established in the wild or still dependent on man.

In the maps, we have also excluded the feral goats, descendants of domestic stock, found in some countries of Western Europe because of the possibility of confusion with the true wild goat *Capra aegagrus*. For species, such as *Rangifer tarandus*, which include both truly wild animals as well as semi-domesticated flocks (defined as those which are collected together from time to time for management purposes), we have chosen to show only the distribution of the wild populations, but have included information about the distribution of the semi-domestic herds in the text.

Decisions on the exclusion of records of vagrants have

been left to the country co-ordinator, but with guidance from the Editorial Committee. In general, we have recommended the exclusion of single records or small numbers of records where these are clearly vagrants which are well beyond the main range of the species, but have suggested the inclusion of all records for species known to be expanding their range.

Taxonomic nomenclature for the *Atlas* follows that of Wilson & Reeder (1993) with the very few exceptions described below.

Controversy persists over the specific/subspecific status of the two commensal house mice *Mus (musculus) musculus* Linnaeus, 1758 and *Mus (musculus) domesticus* Schwartz & Schwartz, 1943. Since these two taxa are parapatric and thus hybridize in the zone of sympatry, some authors (e.g. Musser & Carleton, 1993) consider them conspecific. On the other hand, both taxa are clearly recognizable in the majority of their distributional ranges, which gave us a reason to consider them as separate species, rather than mapping their distinct ranges jointly.

Wilson & Reeder (1993) consider *Herpestes auropunctatus* and *H. javanicus* as a single species, *Herpestes javanicus,* but these have been treated here as separate species, as in the *Handbuch* (Krapp, 1993). In fact only *H. auropunctatus* is present in Europe.

A recent Opinion (Opinion 1894) by the ICZN (1998) has ruled that the generic name *Glis* Brisson, 1762 should be conserved, despite the rejection, for nomenclatural purposes, of the work in which it occurs. This results in the correct use of the name *Glis glis* (Linnaeus, 1766) rather than *Myoxus glis* (Linnaeus, 1766).

Microtus bavaricus (König, 1962), which was described from Garmisch-Partenkirchen in Bavaria, Germany, remains the least known European mammal. Since no specimens have been collected since June 1962, the only known population of *M. bavaricus* is presumed extinct and the species is thus not included in this atlas.

Sokolov & Tembotov (1989) published records of *Neomys schelkovnikovi* to the north of the Caucasus, i.e. in Europe. However, recent work by Kryštufek *et al.* (1998) has demonstrated that *N. fodiens* does not occur in Asia Minor and that the specific name *teres* Miller, 1908 predates *schelkovnikovi,* so these shrews should

correctly be referred to as *Neomys teres* Miller, 1908.

The nomenclature of the wild ancestors of domesticated species presents a particular problem. In this atlas, we have followed the policy advocated by Corbet (1978), by adopting the earliest valid name based upon a non-domesticated form. Thus the wild sheep has been included as *Ovis ammon* rather than *Ovis aries* and *Capra aegagrus* has been used in preference to *Capra hircus* for the wild goat.

The spelling of the specific names of some species differs slightly from that adopted by Wilson & Reeder (1993) and is considered to meet all the requirements of the current International Code of Zoological Nomenclature. For all these exceptions, *Mustela eversmanii* and a number of bats (Bogdanowicz & Kock, 1998), the original description of the species has been inspected by either the species account author or the editor for the group.

Species ranges

The mobility of mammals and the limitations of presence/absence mapping create many difficulties for atlas compilers as there is no easy way of defining or indicating the 'normal' range of a species or specifying which records lie outside that range; a single record of a species can be sufficient to show the presence of that species in a 50 km UTM square. For example there are some species, such as *Lemmus lemmus,* which expand their range from time to time, either regularly or irregularly, and others which are so poorly recorded that their normal range is not well defined. Nevertheless, we believe that we have achieved an acceptable balance between showing the normal range for the majority of species while allowing for changes in distribution. Where there are difficulties over this approach, we have included some notes in the species account indicating the changes that occur.

Species accounts

Each map is accompanied by a brief account in a standard layout prepared by a specialist. The accounts consist of a number of sections:

Distribution. A succinct description of the species' world (if appropriate) and European distribution, with comments on endemism, former distribution, extinctions or reintroductions. Place names are either widely recognized English names or are taken from the *Times World Atlas.*

Geographic variation. Reference may be made to known variation within the species, island forms, clines or the existence of named subspecies.

Habitat. A short description of the broad ecological requirements of the species and critical factors affecting its distribution.

Population status. Any information about abundance or changes in abundance, together with information about typical population densities or sizes.

International legal and conservation status. Whether the species is included in international conventions or directives and whether the species has an IUCN classification of *Lower Risk – near threatened* or worse. IUCN classifications of *Lower Risk – least concern* and *Not Threatened* are not included. International conventions are the Convention on the Conservation of Natural Habitats and of Wild Fauna and Flora (Bern Convention), the Convention on the Conservation of Migratory Species of Wild Animals (Bonn Convention), the Convention on International Trade in Endangered Species of Wild Fauna and Flora (CITES) and the International Convention for the Regulation of Whaling (ICRW). Status under the EU Directive on the Conservation of Natural Habitats and of Wild Fauna and Flora (Habitats Directive) and EU Regulation No 338/97 on the Protection of Species of Wild Fauna and Flora by Regulating Trade Therein is also included.

Other information. May include any other points of interest, such as significant threats, exploitation, pest status, or whether the species is considered a vector of disease.

Common Names

Each species account is accompanied by the common name of the species in 33 European languages

	English
AL	Albanian
BG	Bulgarian
CZ	Czech
DE	German
DK	Danish
EE	Estonian
ES	Spanish (Castilian)
FI	Finnish
FO	Faeroese
FR	French
GR	Greek
HR	Croatian
HU	Hungarian
IR	Irish
IS	Icelandic
IT	Italian
LT	Lithuanian
LU	Luxembourgish
LV	Latvian
MK	Macedonian
MT	Maltese
NL	Dutch
NO	Norwegian
PL	Polish
PT	Portogese
RO	Romanian
RU	Russian
SE	Swedish
SI	Slovenian
SK	Slovakian
TR	Turkish
YU	Serbian

Country Accounts

The EMMA project operated through a network of country co-ordinators, who undertook the data collection, validation and submission. These country co-ordinators, often working in partnership, accepted the responsibility for the quality of the data and retained final control over the data that were used for the atlas. As part of their task, country co-ordinators were also asked to prepare a short account giving general information about the way in which the data were collected, including information about data sources or national *Atlas* projects. In addition, they were asked to comment on the extent of data coverage for the country in question and any special features of the data. These accounts also provide an opportunity to acknowledge the help that has been provided by a wide range of mammalogists and institutions across Europe, without whom this project would not have been possible.

Albania
M. Vlašín, P. Koutný and C. Prigioni

The data collection for Albania has been co-ordinated separately by Mojmír Vlašín and Petr Koutný from the Czech Republic and Claudio Prigioni from Italy. Knowledge of Albanian mammals is very poor and fragmented and a national atlas project does not exist.

Five expeditions were made by Vlašín and Koutný to collect data, primarily on small mammals and bats; one of these was supported by the Ministry of Environment of the Czech Republic and the University of Tirana. In the field, a variety of methods was used, including trapping, netting, searching caves and using bat detectors as well as inspecting dead mammals on roads.

Small mammal data have also been collected from trapping by F. Bego, F. Lamani and A. Zilio. Information on some carnivores and game species has been obtained from the General Directorate of Forestry Economy of Albania as well as from the literature and by inspecting furs in local markets. Further data about bats were drawn from the literature (Hanák *et al.*, 1961; Lamani, 1970). For the otter, the distribution is based on field survey by Prigioni *et al.* (1986) and subsequent observations (Prigioni, 1990–92, unpubl.).

Data were also obtained from published and unpublished reports about the environmental situation in the country (Atkinson *et al*, 1990; TEI & ELC, 1992),

from the collections of Tirana Museum, personal observations in the field and from the observations of naturalists, foresters and gamekeepers. In addition, a number of zoologists, including Vladimír Hanák, Marcel Uhrin, Ivan Horáček and Jan Zima, contributed some unpublished data.

Austria
F. Spitzenberger

The data on the distribution of mammals in Austria were collected almost exclusively by members of the staff of the Mammal Department of the Natural History Museum in Vienna and by amateurs associated with this department.

Kurt Bauer started systematic faunistic research in Austria in the late 1950s with a detailed study of the mammal fauna of the Lake Neusiedl area. Funded by a grant of the Austrian Science Fund, Barbara Herzig-Straschil trapped small mammals in all parts of Austria between 1975–1980. Her samples were enlarged by material collected for several dissertations (riverine forests in Lower Austria – Spitzenberger, Steiner; *Spermophilus citellus* – Herzig-Straschil; bats in Vorarlberg – Baschnegger; Lake Neusiedl area – Hoi-Leitner; *Mus spicilegus* – Willenig, Unterholzner; mountains in Styria – Stuhlmeier; farmland in Lower Austria – Götz) and by bat observations in caves in winter and lofts in summer by Anton Mayer and other amateurs. The analysis of owl pellets provided approximately 4000 distributional data points for Austrian mammals.

Systematic investigations of house-dwelling bats were carried out in Carinthia (1985–1990), southern Styria (1991–1995 – together with Peter Sackl) and Burgenland and Vorarlberg (1996–97) by F. Spitzenberger. Research on forest-dwelling bats has just begun in Salzburg.

The following curators of Provincial Museums kindly gave access to their collections and allowed the use of their data: Karl Adlbauer (Graz); Gerhard Aubrecht (Linz); Erich Kreissl (†) (Graz); Margit Schmid (Dornbirn); Erich Steiner (St., Pölten); Eberhard Stüber (Salzburg).

Data on game species and predators were collected partly with the help of hunters' associations (Lower Austria, Carinthia), partly taken from literature.

All data are recorded on the basis of 1 x 1 geographic minute. They are managed in a databank situated in the Mammal Department of the Natural History Museum of Vienna. The actual number of data items is 83 000, consisting of 30 000 voucher specimens, 11 000 bat observations and 8 000 records taken from the literature.

Funded by a grant from the Ministry of Environment, a Mammal Fauna of Austria is currently being produced. The work will be finished in 1999.

Belgium
R. Libois and E. van der Straeten

Nearly all small mammal data are based on barn owl pellet analyses performed either by Asselberg (1971), Van der Straeten (1972) or Libois (1984). The results of specific studies on the yellow-necked mouse *Apodemus flavicollis* (Van der Straeten & Van der Straeten, 1977) and on the *Soricinae* (Mys *et al.*, 1985; Libois, 1986) are also included.

The data for bat species are regularly recorded by a team of volunteers associated with the Royal Institute of Natural Sciences in Brussels. The provisional atlas they produced was taken as the basis of the bat mapping for the present work (Fairon *et al.*, 1982). Moreover, for Flanders, data compilation has been done by A. Lefevre.

Data for other species (lagomorphs, ungulates, carnivores and easily recognizable rodents and insectivores such as hedgehog, mole, red squirrel, dormice or muskrat) were collected by means of an inquiry addressed to a naturalist network (AVES ornithological society) and to the members of the Nature and Forest administration. The results were published as a report on the threatened mammals of southern Belgium (Libois, 1982). Updated data are to be found in Libois (1993). The data were recorded in a 1 km UTM square when possible, in a 5 km square otherwise. Most of these data consist of direct sightings or of signs (footprints, dens, scats, etc.). When a species was considered as rare (otter, badger, dormice) or difficult to identify with certainty (otter, wildcat, dormice in some cases), field studies were undertaken and only their positive results were taken into account. For Flanders, especially, L. Wauters provided data for *Sciurus vulgaris, Tamias sibiricus* and *Capreolus capreolus*. The otter distribution follows Metsu & Van Den Berge (1987).

Bosnia & Herzegovina, Croatia, Macedonia, Slovenia and the Federal Republic of Yugoslavia
B. Kryštufek

In January 1992, when the members of the EMMA Committee met in Vienna in order to organize mapping of European mammals according to countries, the Socialist Federal Republic of Yugoslavia (SFRY) no longer existed. Regardless of the new political reality, we all agreed that the mapping had to be undertaken for the entire territory of the former Yugoslavia. Further developments proved this decision to be correct as the decay of the SFRY, which started in June 1991, was followed in different regions by military conflicts and civil war, which were particularly severe and long-lasting in Bosnia and Herzegovina. The following independent states are now descendants of the SFRY: Bosnia and Herzegovina, Croatia, Macedonia, Slovenia and the Federal Republic of Yugoslavia.

Within the European framework, SFRY was the top hot-spot in biodiversity, which is reflected also in the mammalian fauna. As a part of the Balkans it bridges the faunas of Europe and Asia Minor; in addition, it was an important Pleistocene refuge, where numerous mammals survived as relics, as well as evolved into endemic forms: *Talpa stankovici, Dinaromys bogdanovi, Microtus felteni,* and *Microtus thomasi,* besides numerous chromosomal races of mole rats *Nannospalax leucodon* and subspecies of other mammals, which are known only from restricted areas of the Balkan Peninsula.

Although the beginnings of mammal research dated back to the pre-Linnean period in some of the former SFRY countries (e.g. Slovenia), modern mammalogical work started after WWI, with the arrival of the Russian zoologist Vladimir E. Martino to the Kingdom of Yugoslavia. Inspired by Miller's Catalogue on European Mammals, he started collecting voucher specimens all over Yugoslavia. One of his first discoveries was the finding of the relict vole, now known as *Dinaromys bogdanovi,* in the karst of Montenegro. Martino inspired the next generation of Yugoslav mammalogists (particularly B. Petrov and the late Đ. Mirić), who organized a strong mammalogical centre in Belgrade, which was, in the post-WWII period, engaged mainly in small mammal research. In the post-war period, Mrs Beatrice Đulić studied mammals, mainly bats, from

Zagreb, which thus became the second centre of mammal research in the former SFRY. Extensive research collections of voucher specimens resulted from these activities, some of which appear to have been lost in recent years. Seven or so decades of intensive field work, supported by karyological analyses, resulted in a considerable accumulation of data, which enabled us to prepare reliable distribution maps for *The Atlas of European Mammals*. This holds particularly for insectivores and rodents, but much less so for bats.

Yugoslavian mammalogy used to be nearly always associated only with academic centres (universities, institutes and museums), which provided highly reliable information, but which finally turned out to be one of its great disadvantages, namely the difficulty of mapping a highly diverse and predominantly mountainous territory by only a few professionals. In other words, Yugoslav mammalogy had no amateur tradition. On the other hand, game species (including all lagomorphs, carnivores, and ungulates, but also several rodents), were for the last 50 years under the surveillance of forestry professionals, who acted mainly as game biologists. Unfortunately, there was hardly any communication between zoologists and foresters and for that reason there are many gaps in the distribution maps of game mammals. Even for species or in regions, where distributions seem to be mapped in detail, the level of reliability is much lower for game species than it is for small mammals.

Although *The Atlas of European Mammals* attempts to provide an up to date and recent picture of the distribution of European mammals, this was difficult to achieve for the entire territory of SFRY. Information for parts of Croatia, and particularly for the entire area of Bosnia and Herzegovina, should be regarded as historical (before 1991), rather than recent, as far as big game is concerned. Besides the direct destruction of game, military operations resulted in the possession of firearms by an uncontrolled number of people. In some regions, the situation regarding game species is thus likely to be much worse than it was five or six years ago.

Of the four co-ordinators, Boris Kryštufek mapped insectivores, bats, lagomorphs, and rodents for the entire territory of SFRY, and the remaining groups (carnivores, ungulates) for Slovenia and Bosnia & Herzegovina. Nikola Tvrtković provided records for carnivores and ungulates in Croatia and completed the ranges for the remaining groups living in this territory. Milan Paunović and Svetozar Petkovski contributed maps of carnivores and ungulates for FRY and Macedonia, respectively. Preparation of the final maps was done by Boris Kryštufek, who also takes responsibility for the data compilation statement for these countries.

Bulgaria
P. Benda, G. Markov and V. Vohralík

The main sources of small mammal data (Insectivora and Rodentia) were published records. Altogether, 198 publications containing distributional data about Bulgarian mammals were examined. In addition, numerous unpublished records gathered by V. Vohralík and his colleagues and students during the last 17 years in Bulgaria were included; voucher specimens are stored in collections of the Department of Zoology, Charles University, Prague (DZCHU).

Some problems arose with species which have been recognized only in recent years. That is why in *Mus domesticus* and *M. macedonicus* mostly records based either on voucher specimens or on biochemically proven materials were used. Older records from the literature were included only when a detailed morphological description enabling their unequivocal identification was available. In *Mus musculus* and *M. spicilegus* only data supported by electrophoresis or DNA and Y chromosome analyses were used. In *Microtus arvalis* and *M. rossiaemeridionalis* only records supported by karyotype were included. Many *Neomys fodiens* records given in the literature had to be omitted due to obvious confusion with *N. anomalus*. Therefore, the distribution of the former species is based only on specimens stored in DZCHU, published records supported by measurements or records published by highly experienced mammalogists.

The maps for the Chiroptera were compiled from 76 publications containing distributional data. In addition, numerous unpublished data gathered by the staff, students and co-workers of DZCHU were included. Bats were recorded mostly by netting organized by Vladimír Hanák, Ivan Horáček and Jaroslav Červený between 1975 and 1988. Voucher specimens are stored in the DZCHU.

The data for Lagomorpha, Carnivora and Artiodactyla

have been compiled by Georgy Markov from the data bank of the Bulgarian Forest Ministry. The data come from two main sources; those gathered on the territories of the state hunting areas and those which come from the territories managed by the Union of Bulgarian Hunters and Fishermen. Data about game species and predators are collected in the same way in each area. The game species in these territories are subject to long-term monitoring and numbers are counted every spring and autumn. Basic information about predators is collected from observations and registrations of all shot animals in every hunting area by game experts. The distribution of Lagomorpha, Carnivora and Artiodactyla is presented in the *Atlas* on the basis of systematic information about their presence on the territory of Bulgaria during the last ten years.

Czech Republic
M. Anděra and J. Zima

Many different sources of data were used to obtain an actual distributional status of all the species of Czech mammals. Most of the small mammal records have been compiled from the literature and completed by the unpublished collection data of scientific institutions (especially the Department of Zoology, National Museum-Natural History, Prague; Institute of Landscape Ecology, Czech Academy of Science, Brno; Department of Zoology, Faculty of Natural Sciences, Charles University, Prague). These data have been mostly based either on trapped animals or on owl pellets but visual observations have been accepted for some larger species (e.g. squirrel, souslik, beaver, dormice). Data for bats have been substantially completed by unpublished observations and ringing records of the members of the Czech Bat Conservation Trust.

The basic source of records of game species (and also of certain others – e.g. hamster, squirrel) consisted of questionnaires completed by members of the Czech-Moravian Gamekeepers Union and forest districts of the state forest service (the Czech Forests).

The national co-ordinators wish to express their gratitude to the many people who have assisted in preparing the Czech contribution. I. Horáček (Prague) took part in the compilation of the data for bats and P. Koubek (Brno) for ungulates. Their help is greatly appreciated.

Special thanks are due also to Z. Bárta, V. Bejček, B. Beneš, L. Bufka, Z. Buřič, J. Červený, P. Eleder, J. Flousek, B. Franěk, J. Gaisler, I. Grulich, V. Hanák, V. Hanzal, M. Homolka, J. Hudeček, J. Chytil, M. Jóža, P. Koutný, J. Krátký, J. Malý, P. Miles, V. Mrlík, J. Obuch, Z. Rumler, Z. Řehák, J. Sklenář, P. Skřivan, K. Studená, J. Šafář, P. Šapovaliv, A. Toman, Z. Vitáček, M. Vlašín, J. Wagner, K. Weidinger, R. Zajíček, V. Zavadil, P. Zbytovský and J. Zukal. In addition, many of other professional mammalogists and collaborators have made their records available for this work.

Denmark
T. Asferg

Information on the presence of Danish mammals has been obtained from a number of sources, *e.g.* museum collections, field projects (published and unpublished data), status surveys, and game bag records.

The maps for Denmark have been prepared by:

Hans Baagøe, Zoological Museum, University of Copenhagen: all *Chiroptera* species, *Muscardinus avellanarius, Neomys fodiens, Martes foina.*

Thomas Secher Jensen, Institute of Biological Sciences, Dept. of Zoology, University of Aarhus: *Clethrionomys glareolus, Microtus agrestis, M. arvalis, Micromys minutus, Apodemus agrarius, A. flavicollis, A. sylvaticus, Mus musculus, Sicista betulina.*

Jens Lodal, Danish Pest Infestation laboratory: *Talpa europaea, Rattus rattus, R. norvegicus, Arvicola terrestris.*

Aksel Bo Madsen, National Environmental Research Institute, Department of Landscape Ecology: *Erinaceus europaeus, Lepus europaeus, Oryctolagus cuniculus, Lutra lutra, Cervus elaphus, C. nippon, Dama dama, Sus scrofa.*

Tommy Asferg, National Environmental Research Institute, Department of Landscape Ecology: *Sciurus vulgaris, Vulpes vulpes, Meles meles, Mustela erminea, M. nivalis, M. putorius, M. vison, Martes martes, Phoca vitulina, Halichoerus grypus, Capreolus capreolus.*

Estonia

T. Maran

The basic data for EMMA in Estonia came from the initiative of the Estonian Theriological Society (ETS) to collect data for the Atlas of Estonian Mammals. The work was initiated in the early 1980s and continued until 1992. The data were organized on a 10 x 10 km UTM grid and were divided into categories according to their 'quality': trap record, animal observed, tracks recorded, observation by other persons, questionnaire, etc. Most of the records on the distribution of small mammals rely on trapping evidence, whereas data on game originate from official game censuses, direct observations and special questionnaires.

The main people involved in data collection were Uudo Timm, Mati Masing, Andrei Miljutin, Peeter Ernits, Kaarel Roht and Tiit Maran. Considerable assistance was provided by more than 30 interested naturalists. All the activities were conducted on a voluntary basis. The data in every specified region were collected during week-long theriological field-schools arranged by the ETS. These schools were held annually for nine years (1981–1989) and turned out to be the most effective way to collect data as well as to provide training for volunteers.

In the middle of the 1990s the data were updated and special contributions were made by Tiit Maran (European mink), Mati Masing and Lauri Lutsar (bats, small mammals, hedgehogs and others), Uudo Timm (small mammals, including dormice and flying squirrel), Ivar and Mart Jüssi (seals) and others. The final database contains more than 10 000 records on the distribution of mammals in Estonia.

The data compilation was done by Tiit Maran in close co-operation with Mati Masing and Uudo Timm. Technical and financial assistance during the whole project has been kindly provided by Tallinn Zoo and the Estonian Hunters Society.

Faroe Islands

D. Bloch

In the Faroe Islands, the data collection for EMMA has been done by Dorete Bloch from the Faroese Museum of Natural History.

The number of mammal species in the Faroes is low, except for the marine mammals and Cetacea are not included in this *Atlas*. Moreover, all terrestrial mammals in the Faroes are introduced or commensal. Therefore, it has not been a hard task to compile data for EMMA.

Finland

H. Henttonen

The data collection for EMMA in Finland has been co-ordinated by Heikki Henttonen and Asko Kaikusalo. The Finnish Forest Research Institute has kindly supported this work.

Most small mammal data are based on Asko Kaikusalo's personal work over a 30-year period. Furthermore, we thank the Zoological Museum, University of Oulu (Kalevi Heikura) and the Zoological Museum, University of Turku (Esa Lehikoinen) for their kind help. In addition, a great number of mammalogists (too many to mention here) have made their records available. Probably more than 99% of the records of small mammals in Finland have been included here. Almost all the data have been based on trapped animals. Visual observations have been accepted for Norway lemmings *Lemmus lemmus*. The characteristic feeding signs of the wood lemming *Myopus schisticolor*, when observed by an experienced mammalogist, have been accepted. Some data from owl pellets have been included when the material certainly comes from the breeding period of owls and the territory is not too close to the grid border. WWF specialist groups on garden dormouse *Eliomys quercinus* (Ilkka Koivisto and Asko Kaikusalo) and flying squirrel *Pteromys volans* (Päivi Eronen and Jouni Paakkonen) have been helpful.

The data compilation for bats has been done by Olli Haukkovaara in co-operation with Juhani Lokki and Torsten Stjernberg. Knowledge of Finnish bats is still locally restricted and will probably expand in future.

Data for game species and large predators have mostly been compiled by Kaarina Kauhala from the data bank of the Game Division, Finnish Game and Fishery Research Institute. The data come from two main sources. First, Finland has an extensive game monitoring system based on permanent game triangles. Each side of a triangle is 3 km. The basic Finnish map grid (10 x 10 km, scale 1: 20 000) can contain one game triangle. Altogether about 1500 triangles have been located, and the number of triangles counted each year is over 1000. Consequently, almost all 50 x 50 km EMMA grids contain several, some of them up to 25 game triangles. The triangles are censused twice a year. Three observers walk (late summer) or ski (February – early March, a few days after a fresh snow fall) the base line and 20 m on each side. In late summer, visual observations and in winter both visual observations and snow tracks are counted. Altogether, this makes more than 20 000 km of game census annually. The game data included show those grids where a species has been observed in 1988-1995. Second, the Game Division has a network of long-term contact persons (about 500) who annually collect information from their local game association and report to the Division. In addition to the data bank, we have been helped by game experts on specific species: Ilpo Kojola on wild forest reindeer *Rangifer tarandus fennicus,* Erik S. Nyholm on large predators and Risto Sulkava on otter *Lutra lutra.* Harto Lindén, the head of the Game Division, has actively supported EMMA work. The long-term work of WWF specialist groups on the European mink *Mustela lutreola* (Heikki Henttonen), arctic fox *Alopex lagopus* (Asko Kaikusalo) and seals (Martti Soikkeli and Tero Sipilä) has been extremely helpful. Additional important information has been obtained from Jukka Lahtinen and Olli Haukkovaara.

France
P. Haffner and H. Maurin

Up to 1995, the task of compiling data for the EMMA project was co-ordinated by François de Beaufort (Secrétariat de la Faune et de la Flore, Muséum National d'Histoire Naturelle, Paris). When he died, Hervé Maurin and Patrick Haffner (Service du Patrimoine Naturel, Muséum National d'Histoire Naturelle, Paris) took over and were put in charge of co-ordination at the national level.

Work on collecting data on mammals started as early as 1978, with a view to preparing distribution maps. Most of the work was done by a network of observers from the Société Française pour l'Etude et la Protection des Mammifères (SFEPM) (French Society for the Study and Protection of Mammals). All data were computerized by the Secrétariat de la Faune et de la Flore (which was renamed Service du Patrimoine Naturel in 1995), which was then headed by François de Beaufort. An Atlas for France was published in 1984. A preliminary

compilation of French data for the EMMA project was based on these data.

Between 1996 and 1997, a major revision was undertaken in order to correct and verify the French maps for the EMMA project. The SFEPM and the Office National de la Chasse (ONC) (National Hunting Office) were put in charge. The SFEPM mobilized its network of observers, using its local agents to co-ordinate the work. As for the ONC, it received help from its Centres Nationaux d'Etudes et de Recherches Appliquées (CNERA) (National Centres for Applied Studies and Research), i.e. CNERA Deer-Wild Boar, CNERA Mountain fauna, CNERA Small and sedentary animals in lowlands, CNERA Predators and pests. Validation for insectivores and rodents was co-ordinated by Stéphane Aulagnier (SFEPM), while Didier Masson (SFEPM) undertook the same task for bats. Jacques Trouvilliez, and later Yves Tachker (ONC) co-ordinated validation for carnivores, lagomorpha and ungulates. Numerous data – many of them so far unpublished – collected between 1985 and 1996 for regional inventories or special programmes were compiled.

The co-ordinators would like to thank those individuals or organisations who contributed to this work of compiling data : M. Barataud, E. Bas, G. Baumgart, P. Bayle, A. Butet, G. Coppa, S. Dubie, B. Durieux, G. Faggio, L. Gavory, P. Giosa, M.-O. Guth, M. Harouët, G. Issartel, J.-M. Joly, C. Joulot, F. Leugé, P. Lustrat, C. Maizeret, P. Medard, D. Michelat, D. Monfort, F. Neri, P. Orsini, P. Pénicaud, F. Poitevin, J.-B. Popelard, O. Prévost, V. Ridoux, R. Rosoux, S. Roué, M. Salotti, F. Schwaab, J.-M. Serveau, D. Sirugue, Y. Tupinier, J.-P. Urcun, Charente Nature, Conservatoire-Etude des Ecosystèmes de Provence/Alpes du sud, Coordination Mammalogique du Nord de la France, Centre Ornithologique Rhône-Alpes Isère, Centre Ornithologique Rhône-Alpes Savoie, Centre Permanent d'Initiation à l'Environnement des Pays de l'Oise, Deux-Sèvres Nature, Erminea, Groupe Chiroptères Rhône-Alpes, Groupe d'Etude et de Protection des Mammifères d'Alsace, Groupe Mammalogique Breton, Groupe Mammalogique Lorrain, Groupe Mammalogique Normand, Groupe Mammifères du Limousin, Groupe Naturaliste de Franche-Comté, Groupe Ornithologique Nord, Groupe de Recherche et d'Etude pour la Gestion de l'Environnement, Ligue pour la Protection des Oiseaux Auvergne, Naturalistes Orléanais, Nature Cher, Nature et Recherche, Océanopolis, Parc National du Mercantour, Parc Naturel

Régional du Morvan, Picardie Nature, SEPANSO, section mammalogique de la Société d'Etude et de Protection de la Nature en Bretagne; as well as ONC agents, with special thanks to : F. Biadi, B. Boiseaubert, J.-J. Camarra, M. Catusse, F. Léger, Y Léonard, Y. Magnani, S. Marchandeau, P. Migot, D. Mouron, R. Péroux et P. Rouland.

The co-ordinators would also like to thank the hundreds of mammalogists, amateurs or professionals, who collected data as part of the local or national inventories, thus improving the quality of the results published in the *Atlas*.

Germany
P. Boye, R. Hutterer and M. Stubbe

The data collection for EMMA in Germany started shortly after the German unification process. As a consequence of the historical circumstances, the work has been co-ordinated separately for former West Germany by Peter Boye and Rainer Hutterer, and for former East Germany by Michael Stubbe.

Compilation of the data for western Germany was complicated by the political subdivision into ten Federal Länder. In most of them, regional mapping projects had been implemented by governmental, scientific or private initiatives. A complete regional mammal atlas existed only for Schleswig-Holstein; the remaining area had to be covered by numerous partial faunas. In fact, the complete published and unpublished literature, as far as available, has been surveyed for reliable records of mammals.

Unpublished data collections have been an essential source for some regions. Special support was offered by the Ministry of Environment Baden-Württemberg (Landesanstalt für Umweltschutz), which provided a complete set of distribution maps of the mammals of Baden-Württemberg, the Bayerisches Landesamt für Umwelt, which provided data of their species conservation programme, Museum Alexander Koenig, for distribution maps of Rhineland mammals, and the Gesellschaft für Naturschutz und Ornithologie Rheinland-Pfalz. A large number of individual mammalogists provided further records. We are grateful to all these persons and institutions.

A full coverage of all squares could not be accomplished. No, or very few, data were available for certain regions in Hessen, north-western Niedersachsen and the alpine foreland of Bavaria. Bats are better recorded than other small mammals. Most carnivores and artiodactyls (which are under hunting law in Germany) are poorly recorded, although their general distribution is known. Only species of special interest to nature conservation (e.g. otter, wildcat, ibex, but also raccoon) are well documented in their occurrence.

The data for eastern Germany were based mainly on a project co-ordinated by Michael Stubbe in collaboration with a large number of East German colleagues. Preliminary results were published in 1994 by Michael and Annegret Stubbe.

The data compilation by Stubbe was integrated into a research project funded by the Federal Agency for Nature Conservation. The same institution supported Boye's contribution to EMMA.

Greece
G. Catsadorakis, O. von Helversen and V. Vohralík

The compilation of data for the Carnivora and Artiodactyla, made by G. Catsadorakis, was based mainly on a number of papers published in *Biologia Gallo-Hellenica* and was completed with additional unpublished data from several people.

Information about the distribution of these two orders in Greece was very scanty until the mid-1980s. At that time Prof. J. Matsakis, Professor of Animal Ecology, University of Athens, undertook a project 'A Survey of the Fauna of Greece', part of a larger project funded by the Ministry of Agriculture. Prof. Matsakis recognised the importance of updated surveys for these species and, with his enthusiasm and help, a number of small surveys were completed. Most of these were later published in a special issue of *Biologia Gallo-Hellenica* devoted to the mammals of Greece and the results were put onto 1:500 000 maps.

The most detailed data about the distribution of the monk seal *Monachus monachus* came from the Society for the Protection of the Monk Seal (MOm). The map for the red fox *Vulpes vulpes* has been verified for the islands, but it is considered to be present everywhere on the mainland. The weasel *Mustela nivalis* is also considered to be present everywhere in mainland Greece. Its distribution on the islands is not detailed, though it is present on almost all the larger islands. The same is true for beech marten *Martes foina* and badger *Meles meles,* though their presence is better documented. Western and marbled polecat *Mustela putorius* & *Vormela peregusna* and pine marten *Martes martes* are very rare and confined to northern Greece. Most work on the distribution of the otter *Lutra lutra* was done in the early 1980s by S. M. Macdonald and C. F. Mason and was complemented by the observations of many Greek workers. The brown bear's *Ursus arctos* range was known from many sources.

The following people contributed to the preparation of the maps, either through personal communication or through their published works: P. Adamakopoulos and T. Adamakopoulos (bear, chamois, wild cat), D. Bousbouras (fallow deer), G. Giannatos (jackal), V. Hatzirvassanis (wolf, chamois), Y. Ioannidis (jackal, fallow deer), Th. Kominos and M. Panagiotopoulou (lynx), H. Papaioannou (chamois), K. Poirazidis (red deer), A. I. Sfougaris (wild goat).

The following people provided data through personal communications, mainly about the distribution of the Lagomorpha, but for the other two orders as well: D. Bousbouras, M. Malakou, Ch. Malakos, M. Mylonas, K. Paragamian, K. Papakonstantinou, K. Poirazidis.

Maps of small terrestrial mammals (Insectivora and Rodentia) were prepared by V. Vohralík, mostly from published records. Altogether, 113 original papers containing distribution data were surveyed and all Greek localities given in the *Handbuch der Säugetiere Europas* were checked. In some particular cases *(Erinaceus, Myocastor, Rattus norvegicus)* unpublished records by V. Vohralík and personal information by Greek zoologists were also used.

Some problems arose with species that have been recognized only in recent years. That is why published records of *Mus musculus spicilegus* were considered as those of *Mus macedonicus,* and records of *Mus musculus brevirostris* and *M. m. praetextus* as those of *Mus domesticus.* All published records of *Microtus arvalis* were ascribed to *M. rossiaemeridionalis* because the presence of the former species in Greece has not been confirmed by karyotype (for more details see Vohralík and Sofianidou 1992).

Data on bats have been compiled by Otto von Helversen. Most of the data are unpublished records collected in the last 30 years, complete up to 1995. Bats were captured with mist-nets; visual and acoustical records (e.g. of *Tadarida teniotis)* are also included for animals that could be identified with certainty. Additional data have been contributed by K. G. Heller, K. Paragamian, H. Pieper, A and C. Liegl, R. Weid and others. Knowledge of the distribution of bats in Greece is certainly incomplete, but probably better than for the adjacent south-east European countries.

Hungary
G. Csorba

The data collection for the Hungarian mammal distribution maps was financially supported by the Ministry of Environment and Regional Policy and the Hungarian Natural History Museum and was co-ordinated by Gábor Csorba on behalf of the Hungarian Mammalogical Society (HMS). The computerized data-processing was done by Gábor Rácz.

During the preparation of the maps the main sources were:

A questionnaire circulated among the members of HMS to which a great number of professional and amateur mammalogist contributed; a variety of signs (tracks, feeding remains, sightings, trapped animals) have been accepted according to the species in question.

The owl-pellet analyses database of the Hungarian Natural History Museum, where the majority of the data derived from the work of Egon Schmidt.

The computerized database of the holdings of the Mammal Collection, Hungarian Natural History Museum. The joint database of the Hungarian Bat Research Society and Bat Protection Foundation which cover almost the whole territory of Hungary and is based mainly on the research work done in the last seven years; the data were compiled by Dávid Csanádi.

The distribution map of otter based on the work of Ildikó Kemenes and the national survey organized by Pál Gera of the Foundation for Otters.

Data for game species and several carnivore species have been compiled by Sándor Csányi and László Szemethy of University of Agricultural Sciences, Department of Wildlife Biology and Management from the Game Management Database and the questionnaires sent regularly to hunting companies; this work is continuously supported by the Ministry of Agriculture.

In the case of the wolf and lynx, important additional information has been provided by Tamás Lapos and Ádám Szabó. In addition, data published in scientific periodicals, reports and hunting magazines have also been included.

Iceland
P. Hersteinsson

Most of the commensal rodent *(Rattus norvegicus* and *Mus domesticus)* data are based on interviews with vermin control officers in various parts of Iceland. The data on the only free-living rodent, *Apodemus sylvaticus,* are based on work by Karl Skirnisson, as well as interviews with vermin control officers and a large number of farmers. Visual identification of individuals trapped by these sources was deemed sufficient.

Data on the occurrence of *Alopex lagopus* and *Mustela vison* are based on hunting statistics compiled by the Wildlife Management Institute of Iceland. Data on the distribution of *Rangifer tarandus* are based on work done by Skarphedinn Thorisson as well as surveys co-ordinated by the Wildlife Management Institute. Data on the breeding distribution of seals are based on surveys done by Erlingur Hauksson of the Fisheries Research Institute of Iceland.

Republic of Ireland and Northern Ireland
T. Hayden and W. I. Montgomery

The distribution maps for mammals in the Republic of Ireland and Northern Ireland are derived from research carried out or published between 1992 and 1997. The main sources of data were the National Bat Survey: Bats in Ireland (1994), and the Badger and Habitat Survey of Ireland (1994) and Northern Ireland (1994), during which data on other species were also collected. These were supplemented by data from ongoing research and surveys in the National Parks and Wildlife Service; the Irish Deer Society; the Northern Ireland Deer Society; the Irish Wildlife Trust; the Ulster Wildlife Trust; the Mammal Research Group; Department of Zoology, University College Dublin; the School of Biology and Biochemistry, The Queen's University Belfast; the Department of Zoology, Trinity College Dublin; the Department of Zoology, University College Galway; the Department of Zoology and Animal Ecology, University

College Cork, the Department of the Marine, the Central Fisheries Board, the Salmon Research Agency, Coillte Teoranta and Forestry Service of Northern Ireland. The distributional data for bats is incomplete. Four species, initially identified on the basis of echolocating calls, have been added to the list since 1995 although their range throughout the whole island has not yet been established.

Italy
G. Amori and C. Prigioni

The data collection for Italy has been co-ordinated by Giovanni Amori and Claudio Prigioni, who in 1990 promoted the Italian Mammal Atlas Project (P.A.M.I.). Several mammalogists have assisted with the project, providing their personal data and their help in bibliographic and museum research. The collection of the data has been made according to specific instructions and the records have been checked by specialists of the different mammal groups in order to verify their reliability. About 90% of the records have been obtained from the literature; the remainder being original data collected in recent years by field survey. The data included in EMMA have been drawn from P.A.M.I.

Small mammal data have mostly been compiled by Gaetano Aloise, Marco Cantini and Paolo De Bernardi who also gathered records made available by many mammalogists.

For bats, current knowledge is very poor. We have mainly considered data from the literature and provided by the Italian Association for the Conservation of Bats (Bruno Zava and Carlo Violani).
The data compilation for lagomorphs has been done mainly by Francesco M. Angelici.

For the carnivores we have taken into account data regarding the finding of dead animals, feeding remains near dens (e.g. red fox *Vulpes vulpes),* trapping, visual observations (e.g. stoat *Mustela erminea* and weasel *Mustela nivalis),* identification of tracks and signs (e.g. badger *Meles meles* and otter *Lutra lutra).* For the ungulate distributions the same evidence with the addition of vocalizations was accepted.

Kaliningrad Region, Russia
V. V. Beliakov and G. P. Grishanov

The data submitted were gathered by Drs V. V. Beliakov

and G. P. Grishanov of the Zoology Department, University of Kaliningrad during fieldwork conducted continuously since 1964.

Latvia
V. Pilāts

The data collection both for the Latvian mammal atlas and for EMMA has been co-ordinated by Valdis Pilāts.

In 1991, the project 'Atlas of Latvian Mammals' began, serving as a good starting point to join EMMA. The collection of data for the atlas was carried out in two main ways; through a summary of all published and unpublished material as well as the distribution of questionnaires. The questionnaire survey was launched in 1991, mostly through the assistance of volunteers. Altogether more than 50 volunteers, both amateurs and professional zoologists, contributed to the survey.

Most of the data for small mammals (voles, mice and shrews) were kindly presented by Tatjana Zorenko. In turn most of those data were obtained by trapping done by the National Environmental Health Centre during 1951–1987 as well as by Egons Tauriņš during 1942–1956.

The data compilation for bats has been done by Gunārs Pētersons with the assistance of Viesturs Vintulis. Bat records in summer roots and hibernating sites as well as those obtained by bat detector were used.

Records of other small and medium-sized non-game mammals (e.g. dormice, hedgehogs, flying squirrel *Pteromys volans)* originated mostly from visual observations. All such data were carefully evaluated by experts.

A great part of the data (mostly visual observations) on Red List species, particularly on brown bear *Ursus arctos,* were collected by Juris Lipsbergs.

Data for 17 game species were obtained from Latvian Forest Service statistics (starting from 1923) and have been mostly compiled by Māris Lielkalns. The surveys for game statistics were done by foresters in areas supervised by them. The accuracy of those surveys depends on the species involved: large mammals are fairly well recorded but small species are quite often missed. Mārtiņš Balodis, Gunārs Skriba, Jānis Ozoliņš and Aivars Ornicāns as local experts on beaver, red deer

and otter respectively have also contributed to the data compilation.

Lithuania
L. Balčiauskas

In the period 1995–1997, the project group 'Ecological diversity of Lithuania' and the Biodiversity Database were the main data sources.

Before the first dataset was compiled, the Lithuanian Foundation for Science and Studies grant-aided a project 'Application of information systems to the analysis of biodiversity of terrestrial vertebrates', which enabled the sending of questionnaires to Lithuanian naturalists. About 80 reliable answers were returned. The number of names is too great to include here, but the help of J. Auglys, V. Jusys, M. Jankauskienė, M. Kirstukas, V. Lopeta, V. Malinauskas, V. Mačiulis and V. Naruševičius gave a great input to the atlas. Also, in 1996-1997 the foundation 'Ecologia' gave financial support for the publication of the Lithuanian National Atlas of mammals, amphibians and reptiles.

The small mammal dataset is based mostly on data from L. Balčiauskas, R. Juškaitis and R. Mažeikytė, with help from many naturalists in the province. Literature sources were also analysed, but we cannot hope that more than a fraction of possible data are included. Almost all data were from trapped mammals, with some from owl pellet analysis. Most of the dormice data were supplied by R. Juškaitis.

Data on bats are mainly from the leading Lithuanian specialists D. H. Pauža and N. Paužienė, with contributions from A. Gudaitis, A. Balbierius and V. Jusys. Knowledge of Lithuanian bats is still restricted but in recent years investigations on bats were performed in five Lithuanian districts.

A. Ulevičius supplied most of the beaver data and a made a major input to the small carnivores dataset. Data on the large predators are from the questionnaires and from the Biodiversity Database. Game species data are from the questionnaires and a compilation from official census data made by L. Balčiauskas. As the game expert, R. Baleišis helped with the most of ungulate species.

L. Balčiauskienė input most computer data, and E. Budrys performed the most complicated Biodiversity Database queries.

Luxembourg

E. Engel

The data for bats are based on 6 years' work by Christine Harbusch, Jacques Pir and Edmeé Engel and data for small mammals are based on 6 years' work by Claudine Junck. The results of these projects, which were initiated by the Natural History Museum, are in press.

Data compilation for the wildcat was done by Marc Moes during a study initiated by the Administration des Eaux et Forêts, Service de la Conservation de la Nature. Data for the Mustelidae were collected by Adil Bagli *(Mustela putorius)* and Laurent Schley and Schauls Michel *(Meles meles).*

Malta

J. J. Borg

The data collection for the Maltese Islands was co-ordinated by John J. Borg of the Malta Bat Group.

The data for the Algerian hedgehog *Atelerix algirus* and weasel *Mustela nivalis* are based on 20 years of work by several persons and include observations of living specimens as well as counts of road kills. Data on micro-mammals from Gozo are based mainly on remains from barn owl pellets by Joe Sultana (1971), Stephen Schembri & Richard Cachia-Zammit (1979), J. J. Borg and R. Cachia-Zammit (1988 and 1994), while a trapping programme for shrews was carried out in Gozo in 1990 by Peter Vogel (Switzerland), Patrick J. Schembri, Mark Borg and J. Sultana, and in Malta between 1995–1997 by J. J. Borg and Michael Gatt. Data for *Apodemus sylvaticus* are based on a study carried out by Charles Savona-Ventura in the early 1980s and later by J. J. Borg, including also data on the house mouse. For the occurrence of rabbits *Oryctolagus cuniculus,* farmers and ferret-using hunters were interviewed along with direct observations by several persons. The data on bats have been compiled and published by J. J. Borg with contributions by Carlo Violani (University of Pisa, Italy) and Bruno Zava (Italian Bat Group, Palermo, Italy).

The Netherlands

J. B. M. Thissen

Data collection for The Netherlands has been done by Johan Thissen, the former co-ordinator of the second national mammal atlas project. The National Reference Centre for Nature Management of the Ministry of Agriculture, Nature Management and Fisheries has kindly supported this work. Sim Broekhuizen has helped in finding common Dutch names.

The first atlas of the mammals of the Netherlands was published by Van Wijngaarden *et al.* (1971), covering the period 1946–1970. Most of the data for the current work have been taken from the second national atlas, which covers the period 1970–1988 (Broekhuizen *et al.,* 1992), including data from an earlier specific bat atlas focusing on the period 1970–1984 (Glas, 1986). For this second atlas all records were primarily judged by the kind of observation: sightings, catches, finds or traces. Sightings and traces of shrews and mice were not accepted; sightings of bats only if at close range in roosts. Remains in pellets and faeces have been included. The information on bats has been updated using the new bat atlas (Limpens *et al.,* 1997), which focuses on the distribution in summer in the period 1986–1993, using mainly bat detector records. Recent local extinctions and new additional published and unpublished data have been taken into account up to the year 1997.

Vagrants, e.g. raccoon dog, animals which probably have been transported passively, e.g. greater noctule, and populations in enclosures, e.g. mouflon, have been excluded from the European Atlas.

Norway, Svalbard and Jan Mayen

P. Shimmings and A. H. Rønning

A large part of the data has been taken from the National Mammal Atlas Project (Pattedyratlas) database. The project was initiated in 1993 and is based on records from 1980 onwards. Records from before 1980 have been taken mainly from the literature as well as from correspondence with field workers.

The extent of coverage varies greatly on the Norwegian mainland, with relatively few records from sparsely populated areas (such as in the north) and where there are few active field workers (parts of the west coast, mid-Norway as well as in the north). Records are also sparse from areas of the country where the National Mammal Atlas Project has no regional co-ordinator.

Coverage of Svalbard is considered to be rather poor, particularly for seals. This can be partly explained by the fact that the national co-ordinator was not asked to include observations from Svalbard as part of the EMMA project until July 1996. This meant that there was little time to collect data. The same problem applies to Jan Mayen, which has been little visited by naturalists and for which there are no resident mammals.

The distribution of *Erinaceus europaeus* is well documented, and is largely based on data collected as part of a national questionnaire, the results of which have recently been published (Johansen, 1995), but knowledge of the distribution of most *Sorex* species is considered to be patchy. For example, *S. araneus* and *S. minutus* are almost certainly found throughout the mainland, and the gaps are likely to be the result of lack of information.

There are few people working on bats in Norway, although mapping of distribution has progressed considerably in the last ten years or so. The sibling species *Myotis brandtii* and *M. mystacinus* are very poorly mapped due to difficulty in separating these, both in the field and in the hand. The distribution of *M. daubentonii* and *Pipistrellus pipistrellus* is believed to have been well mapped, particularly in the south-east.

Knowledge of lagomorphs for the country is considered to be good, with *Lepus timidus* (the only indigenous species) occurring throughout the country.

There is a paucity of records for *Arvicola terrestris* which probably occurs along much of the west and southern coast. *Microtus rossiaemeridionalis* is the only rodent species occurring on Svalbard, and is found only in one 50 km square (other populations appear to have died out). Similarly, *Rattus norvegicus* undoubtedly has a wider distribution than the data suggest. Data is presented for *Mus musculus* only although it has been suggested that *M. domesticus* may occur along the coast from Agder to Troms (no studies have been undertaken to investigate this in greater detail). Maps showing the distribution range of *Apodemus flavicollis* and *A. sylvaticus* have recently been published (Lura *et al.*, 1995), and fit in well with the data presented for EMMA. For other rodents we have reasonably good knowledge of species distribution, given the lack of observers in some parts of the country.

The only regular occurrence of *Canis lupus* is in the south-east of the country near the Swedish border. Records from the south-west of the country have been omitted from the datafiles (squares MK1, MK3, and ML4), as it is certain that there are no longer resident wolves in that area. Occasional observations have been made in other parts of the country of wandering individuals – only those from Finnmark in the north are included, as there are a number of records from there. Records are lacking for *Alopex lagopus* in some parts of Norway where it is known to occur, particularly in mid-Norway. The same is true for *Ursus arctos,* the males of which can wander considerable distances. The occurrence of *Mustela putorius* is poorly documented, with the only confirmed records being in the south-east. For other carnivores the data present a good picture of the general distribution of the various species.

For Pinnipedia, only *Phoca vitulina* and *Halichoerus grypus* occur regularly and breed on islands along the coast of mainland Norway. *Odobenus rosmarus* and *P. groenlandica* can occur anywhere along the coast during invasion years, when both species can wander from their normal arctic quarters. Other seal species are considered accidental along the mainland coast and are therefore not included in the dataset. Records of the occurrence of pinnipeds from Svalbard are considered to be far from complete, with the exception of *P. vitulina.*

Dama dama has only been recorded naturalised in one area of south-east Norway, in Østfold county. The range of *Cervus elaphus* is currently expanding northwards. Numbers of both *Alces alces* and *Capreolus capreolus* have increased in recent years. Gaps in the data are due mainly to a lack of information received, although both are absent from parts of western Norway. Only herds of *Rangifer tarandus* within the current range of wild stock are included, thereby excluding the semi-domesticated herds in the north. In addition *R. t. platyrhynchus* is confined to Svalbard. *Ovibos moschatus* is found in one small area, although individuals can roam considerable distances.

Poland
W. Bogdanowicz and B. W. Wołoszyn

Research on the mammalian fauna of Poland has a long tradition reaching back to the first half of the 18th century. Nevertheless, only quite recently has the distributional status of all the mammal species been verified, summarized and substantially updated. The gap has been filled by the *Atlas of Polish Mammals,* edited by Pucek and Raczyński (1983). It was based on the UTM 10 km x 10 km grid and included findings from pellets, trapping, shooting, direct observations of mammals and their activities in the field, institutional and private collections, as well as from questionnaires and an extensive review of the literature. The basic source of information consisted of the original material collected chiefly between 1961 and 1975 and housed in the Mammal Research Institute, Polish Academy of Sciences (PAS), Białowieża.

Many different sources of information were used to obtain an actual range of mammals at the national scale. Most records have been compiled from the literature and completed by the unpublished material of scientific institutions (especially Mammal Research Institute PAS and Institute of Animal Systematics and Evolution PAS, Cracóv). Information on the mammals of central Poland has been updated thanks to field work done by Janusz Markowski and Janusz Hejduk (both University of Łódź – see also Markowski & Hejduk, in press). The compilation of data for bats was based mainly on a number of papers published in *Biuletyn Centrum Informacji Chiropterologicznej, Przegląd Przyrodniczny* and *Przegląd Zoologiczny,* and completed by several professional and amateur chiropterologists, including Andrzej L. Ruprecht (retired; previously Mammal Research Institute PAS) and Krzysztof Kasprzyk (University of Toruń). In the case of seals, most of the valuable information has been provided by Krzysztof E. Skóra and Iwona Kuklik (both University of Gdańsk).
Technical work was done by Ludmiła Szuma, Agnieszka Maciejewska, Katarzyna Daleszczyk and Elwira Szuma (all Mammal Research Institute PAS Białowieża). Kazimierz Kowalski (Institute of Animal Systematics and Evolution PAS Kraków), Tomasz Kokurewicz (Academy of Agriculture, Wrocław) and Przemysław Rachowiak (University of Poznań) kindly helped in finding common Polish names.
The data collection has been summarized and the project co-ordinated by Wiesław Bogdanowicz (Museum and Institute of Zoology PAS, Warsaw) and Bronisław W. Wołoszyn (Institute of Animal Systematics and Evolution PAS Kraków).

Portugal
M. L. Mathias, M. G. Ramalhinho and M. J. Cabral

The data collection for Portugal has been co-ordinated by Maria da Luz Mathias, Maria da Graça Ramalhinho and Maria João Cabral, with the assistance of Margarida Santos-Reis.

In the difficult task of data compilation for EMMA we had help from many specialists who filled the gaps in our database, updating it to the end of 1997.

Most of the records available on small mammals in Portugal, probably nearly 90%, have been gathered by Maria da Luz Mathias and Maria da Graça Ramalhinho over the past 20 years. Thanks are due to António Mira, João São José, Paula Rebelo, Ana Luisa Costa and Jorge Prudêncio (Faculty of Sciences, Lisbon) for information on small mammals in general and also to Ana Isabel Queirós and Henrique Carvalho (Nature Conservation Institute, Lisbon) for making available data on the Pyrenean desman and the southern water vole respectively. Data on the occurrence of all the species listed for Portugal were based on trapping, owl pellets and carnivore scats. Visual observations have been included only for the red squirrel.

Nearly 70% of the Portuguese bat fauna is composed of threatened species, which are consequently very localised and not abundant. Moreover, for most of this century, very few mammalogists have been interested in bats. So, as it is for many other countries, knowledge of Portuguese bats is still scarce. Data available and included here are mostly based on the personal work of Jorge Palmeirim (Centre for Environmental Biology, Faculty of Sciences of Lisbon), Luisa Rodrigues, Ana Rainho, Cláudia Franco and Sara Bicho (Nature Conservation Institute, Lisbon).

The data compilation for lagomorphs has been done by Maria da Luz Mathias. Information concerning these and other game species, carnivores (red fox, genet and Egyptian mongoose) and artiodactyls (red deer, fallow deer, roe deer and wild boar), came mainly from two sources; reported deaths during the hunting season and records from game associations.

Most of the data on Portuguese carnivores were made available by Margarida Santos-Reis and Francisco Petrucci-Fonseca (Centre for Environmental Biology, Faculty of Sciences of Lisbon), Ana Ferreira, Alberto

Carvalho, José Pedro Tavares (Faculty of Sciences, Lisbon) as well as by Luis Palma (lynx) (University of Algarve), Anabela Trindade (otter), Paulo Carmo, Luis Moreira and Inês Barroso (wolf), Margarida Fernandes, Helena Ceia, Pedro Sarmento, Luis Roma and Paula Abreu (lynx, genet, fox, Egyptian mongoose, wildcat, polecat, beech marten) (Nature Conservation Institute, Lisbon). These data were based on live-trapping, visual observations, game records, tracks and other signs of presence.

The present status of cervids in the wild is worth mentioning here. The occurrence of red deer and fallow deer is nowadays mostly restricted to special confined areas, some of which are game reserves. Very few populations of these species occur in the wild. On the contrary, although reduced, the range of the roe deer in the wild extends over the most northern part of the country. Here we have included only data concerning occurrence in the wild, made available by Maria João Cabral, Paulo Carmo and Inês Barroso (Nature Conservation Institute, Lisbon).

We thank the Bocage Museum (University of Lisbon), the Centre for Environmental Biology and the Nature Conservation Institute for having supported this work.

Romania
D. Murariu and I. Coroiu

The geographical position of Romania, halfway between the North Pole and Equator and half way between the Atlantic Ocean and the Ural Mountains, as well as the significant zonal aspects of the climate on the one hand and the lack of a team of scientists working only on mammals on the other hand, presented significant difficulties for the collection of data for the European Mammals Atlas.

References to Romanian mammals extend back to the 17th century. Various foreign travellers who visited Romania were impressed and wrote about the richness of the game species, such as wolves, foxes, wild boar, bears and deer. The first lists were published only after 1920 (Simionescu, 1920; Calinescu, 1931). More systematic studies started in the second half of the 20th century (Dumitrescu *et al.* 1962–63; Simionescu 1965; Hamar, 1967; Popescu and Baru, 1979).

Unfortunately, these specialists are retired or even passed away. However, their publications and the personal experience of the national co-ordinator, D. Murariu, together with annual field trips and discussions with local people in villages all over the country allowed the compilation of distribution maps for every mammal species reported from Romania.

For some game species as well as for some small mammals, Ion Coroiu and Victoria Banaru completed the draft maps, with a particular emphasis on the Danube Delta, Western Carpathians and Retezat National Park. Their data were based on additional literature and collected and observed specimens. Those valuable contributions are very much welcomed.

Nevertheless, the Romanian mammalian literature correlated with data from Bucharest's Museum of Natural History collections, with the co-ordinator's personal notes and in some cases (e.g. for *Alces alces*) reports in daily papers or *in verbis,* proved later with a trophy donated by local hunters (e.g. Mr. Sidorenko from Saint George/Sfântu Gheorghe village in the Danube Delta) were instrumental in preparing the distribution data.

Slovakia
A. L. G. Dudich, M. Uhrin and M. Žilinec

The data collection for EMMA in Slovakia has been co-ordinated by Alexander L. G. Dudich. Most of the small mammal data are based on field work of the former staff of the Research Station of the Slovak Academy of Sciences in Staré Hory (Head: Andrej Štollmann). Available data from most regional museums of former Czechoslovakia have been used. Most of the data have been from trapped animals, but visual observations have been accepted for the mole and red squirrel. Data from owl pellets have been included if data from trapped animals were not available.

Bat records were collected by Marcel Uhrin. Most data on bats are based on literature records and original observations of the compilers in collaboration with members of the Bat Protection Group (Slovak Environmental Agency).

The data for ungulate game species were compiled by Milan Žilinec and carnivore game species by A. L. G. Dudich from the official hunting statistics which are based on the annual game counts on 31st March in each hunting area as well as on hunters' personal observations of game, throughout the year. The data compilation for otter *Lutra lutra*, chamoix *Rupicapra rupicapra* and marmot *Marmota marmota* was organized by Peter Urban with Dr Ján Kadlečík. The records of the otter result from the project 'European otter and its conservation in Slovakia', which was carried out by a group of specialists and volunteers. Data on the marmot come from the databank of the Administrations of Tatra National Park and Low Tatras National Park as well as from game management statistics. Almost all data on the chamois *R. rupicapra* come from organized counts of this species or from official game management statistics.

Spain
L. J. Palomo and F. González

The Atlas of Mammals in Spain (excluding bats) is a project carried out by the Spanish Society for the Conservation and Study of Mammals (SECEM). This project, started in 1992, is based on the UTM 10 km x 10 km grid and includes, at present, more than 50 000 records. A variety of sources have been used to obtain distribution data. The majority of records were compiled from the literature; 325 publications, including regional and local atlases, were examined, providing more than 60% of the records. That information was supplemented with unpublished collection data from scientific institutions (Universities and Museums) and questionnaires completed by the staff of Natural and National Parks. In addition, numerous unpublished records, based on visual observations, trapped or shot animals or owl-pellets, donated by members of SECEM and collaborators were accepted, after verification by a species specialist.

The study area (data were available for one sixth of the Iberian Peninsula, together with the Balearic and Canary islands) is not uniformly sampled. The bibliographic origin of most records, and therefore the impossibility of guiding their collection, is the reason for the existence of large areas without records. This situation is not so evident when the 50 km UTM squares are employed (95% covered). Data for the Canary Islands were gathered in collaboration with Dr R. Hutterer (Museum A. Koenig, Bonn).

For bats, the maps have been prepared with information extracted from the data bank of the Regional Atlas of Bats of Spain (ARQE), a project developed by the Spanish

Society for Conservation and Study of Bats (SECEMU). Records have been compiled by specialists of the SECEMU, who reviewed all information in their work areas, without new surveys. Data compilation was begun in 1994 and will be finished in 1998. For this reason, the maps do not show unpublished records or records without a precise location in UTM co-ordinates. Despite these limitations, the maps are the most complete reference currently available in the UTM grid system about the distribution of the 27 bat species recorded in Spain.

Data distribution throughout the country is very irregular, since some regions have never been sampled or the sampling work is new and still unpublished, or has not been reviewed. The use of bat detectors for distribution surveys is still very restricted and almost all the data relate to captured individuals.

Sweden
I. Ahlén, L. Hansson and K. Fredga

The data collection for Sweden, except for bats, was co-ordinated by Lennart Hansson and Karl Fredga.

There has not been any countrywide inventory of mammal distributions in Sweden. Therefore, we have relied on the expertise of people that have recently done ecological or genetical research in the field on the various species. Distribution maps have been prepared by such experts and subsequently scrutinized by the co-ordinators. For a few species it was impossible to find any real experts and the co-ordinators have then prepared those maps in addition to the treatment of species for which they have personal knowledge.

The following persons have thus been involved in the compilations:

Henrik Andrén *(Sciurus vulgaris)*, Anders Angerbjörn *(Alopex lagopus, Lepus timidus)*, Lena Berg *(Muscardinus avellanarius)*, Göran Cederlund *(Capreolus capreolus)*, Kjell Danell *(Ondatra zibethicus)*, Bodil Enoksson *(Micromys minutus)*, Robert Franzén *(Canis lupus, Gulo gulo, Lynx lynx, Ursus arctos)*, Karl Fredga (Soricidae, *Erinaceus europaeus, Microtus oeconomus, Myopus schisticolor, Mustela nivalis* and *M. erminea)*, Rune Gerell *(Mustela vison, Oryctologus cuniculus)*, Lennart Hansson (Rodentia, except as indicated elsewhere, *Talpa europaea)*, Göran Hartman *(Castor fiber)*, Björn Helander *(Halichoerus grypus)*, Tero

Härkönen *(Phoca hispida* and *P. vitulina)*, Fredrik Karlsson *(Alces alces)*, Sten Lavsund *(Cervus elaphus)*, Erik Lindström *(Martes martes, Meles meles, Vulpes vulpes)*, Nils G. Lundh *(Ovibos moschatus)*, Gunnar Markgren *(Nyctereutes procyonoides)*, Torsten Mörner *(Lepus europaeus)*, Peter Mortenson *(Lutra lutra)*, Bo Thelander *(Dama dama, Mustela putorius, Sus scrofa)*.

Data collection for the bats was co-ordinated jointly by Ingemar Ahlén and Rune Gerell. Ingemar Ahlén prepared the maps of *Myotis dasycneme, M. myotis, M. bechsteinii, Pipistrellus nathusii, Eptesicus serotinus, Nyctalus leisleri, Barbastella barbastellus,* and *Plecotus austriacus* while Rune Gerell prepared the maps of *Myotis nattereri, M. mystacinus, M. brandtii, M. daubentonii, Eptesicus nilssonii, Pipistrellus pipistrellus, Nyctalus noctula, Vespertilio murinus,* and *Plecotus auritus.* For the first group, the rare species, all known observations were referred to 50 km UTM squares, while the second group, the common species with continuous distribution, was indicated with filling the squares up to the known distribution border plus the single isolated occurrences discovered outside the continuous range. The very late request for material for the project (June 1997) with need of almost immediate answer made this necessary for Sweden.

Switzerland
S. Capt and F. Saucy

The data for EMMA in Switzerland have been contributed by Francis Saucy. The data collected for the Swiss Atlas of Mammals have been used after translation into UTM co-ordinates. Published in 1995 by the Swiss Society for Wildlife Biology under the direction of Jacques Hausser (Hausser, 1995), the Swiss national atlas is the result of the joint efforts of several hundred biologists and collaborators. For each of the 90 species treated, a short description is given in German, French and Italian. Using an original modelling approach of the habitat (scale: 1 km^2), two-colour maps show the potential and actual distribution of the species, as well as the locations of the observations used in the model. Initiated by Jean-Denis Bourquin and completed by F. Saucy, the database (more than 200 000 records) has been transferred to the Centre Suisse de Cartographie de la Faune in Neuchâtel, where it is administered by Simon Capt.

For the EMMA atlas, only observations recorded after 1970 have been used. The Swiss territory covers only 33 squares of the EMMA grid, among which only 8 are not shared with a neighbouring country. Therefore, in spite of gaps in the distribution of several species at the national level, the coverage is certainly excellent at the European scale.

For bats, the data of local observers have been compiled and transmitted by Hans-Peter Stutz and Pascal Moeschler. Based on recent observations, they give accurate maps in most cases. Data collection for small mammals has been co-ordinated by André Meylan for rodents, by J. Hausser and Peter Vogel for insectivores, by Albert Keller and Marco Salvioni for lagomorphs and by Claude Mermod for small carnivores. Data from various collections in universities and museums (mostly based on trapping records and analyses of owl pellets) have been used. In several cases, maps need to be improved at the national scale. Peter Lueps and Simon Capt have co-ordinated the data collection for large carnivores. Radiotelemetry data have been used in the case of the lynx *Lynx lynx.* For ungulates (co-ordination: Augustin Krämer and Hansjoerg Blankenhorn), hunting statistics, as well as visual observations provided by national and cantonal wildlife services have been utilized.

Turkey
C. Kurtonur and B. Özkan

The compilation of data for Turkish Thrace mammals has been performed by Cengiz Kurtonur in co-operation with Beytullah Özkan and Tansel Türkyilmaz. These data are based mainly on the Thracian mammals collection of Cengiz Kurtonur, which is kept in the Zoological Museum of Istanbul University, and also on the Thracian mammals collection of Beytullah Özkan and Tansel Türkyilmaz at Trakya University, Edirne. In addition, the following have helped to complete the work: Salih Doğramacı and Haluk Kefelioglu from Ondokuz Mayis University (Insectivora, Rodentia), Irfan Albayrak (Chiroptera) and Erkut Kivanç (Rodentia) from Ankara University. We would like to thank Boris Kryštufek from the Slovenian Museum of Natural History for providing additional information.

United Kingdom

A. J. Mitchell-Jones and H. R. Arnold

The British mammal records were collected mainly under the auspices of the Mammal Society, in co-operation with the Biological Records Centre, Institute of Terrestrial Ecology, Monks Wood. The recording scheme began in 1965, and was then organized by Dr Gordon Corbet. A similar scheme to record deer was set up in 1967 by the British Deer Society, organized by Michael Clarke. An atlas for Great Britain, based on the 10 km squares of the British National Grid and including more than 115 000 records was published in 1993 (Arnold, 1993). Data for Northern Ireland were collected in close co-operation with the co-ordinator for the Republic of Ireland.

Sight records were accepted for most species, except for bats, though many small mammal records were from trapped animals.

Several single species surveys were carried out during the recording period (often funded by organizations such as the Vincent Wildlife Trust and the Nature Conservancy Council and its successors) for such species as harvest mouse, dormouse, water vole, otter, badger and pine marten and these have all added substantially to the database. In many cases, the recent surveys have been used to establish areas from which species have recently disappeared.

Seal records were mainly collected and collated by the Natural Environment Research Council's Sea Mammal Research Unit at Cambridge. Many bat records came from databases maintained by English Nature, with some additional information from the Bat Conservation Trust and many individuals. We are grateful for all their help.

In many cases, the maps were updated and checked with the help of national or local experts, including Roger Long (Jersey), Pat Costen (Guernsey) and Ed Pooley (Isle of Man).

Species that are rapidly changing their distribution are particularly difficult to map and we are grateful for the help that we have received for the polecat *Mustela putorius* from Johnny Birks.

Editorial work on the Atlas was generously supported by the Nature Conservancy Council and its successor, English Nature.

Acknowledgements

At the request of the Atlas project, the National Reference Centre for Nature Management *(IKC Natuurbeheer)* in the Netherlands, part of the Ministry of Agriculture, Nature Management and Fisheries, put the data management for *The Atlas of European Mammals* in their work programme for the period 1994–1997. Building on their experience with the European breeding bird atlas (Hagemeijer & Blair, 1997), *IKC* staff members Peter Frigge, Johan Thissen and Bart Looise have done most of this work. Peter Frigge's role has been of vital importance, designing and maintaining the database and writing all computer programs, including automatic mapping procedures. *IKC* has financed the central data entry by paying a commercial firm for the processing of records submitted on paper maps. During her traineeship at the *IKC* in 1997 Patricia Beuving has accurately completed most of the final database corrections. Part of this work was done by Marcel Huijser of the Dutch-Belgian Mammal Society.

The European Topic Centre on Nature Conservation, the Institute for Terrestrial Ecology and the European Bird Census Council have been of great help in developing the project, especially the grid system. In particular, Marc Roekaerts, Sophie Condé, Dorian Moss, Simon Wright and Ward Hagemeijer have given crucial advice, information and computer files.

Many people have helped the Editorial Committee with their work during the ten years of the project. We would particularly like to thank T. Asferg, P. Boye, G. Csorba, L. Gjerde, P. Haffner, T. Hayden, H. Henttonen, R. Libois, M. L. Mathias, L. J. Palomo, C. Prigioni, F. Saucy and B. Wołoszyn for their help at meetings of the Committee.

List of Species Described

Marsupialia

Macropus rufogriseus	(Desmarest, 1817)	Red-necked wallaby

Insectivora

Atelerix algirus	(Lereboullet, 1842)	Algerian hedgehog
Erinaceus concolor	Martin, 1838	Eastern hedgehog
Erinaceus europaeus	Linnaeus, 1758	Western hedgehog
Sorex alpinus	Schinz, 1837	Alpine shrew
Sorex araneus	Linnaeus, 1758	Common shrew
Sorex caecutiens	Laxmann, 1788	Masked shrew
Sorex coronatus	Millet, 1828	Millet's shrew
Sorex granarius	Miller, 1910	Spanish shrew
Sorex isodon	Turov, 1924	Taiga shrew
Sorex minutissimus	Zimmermann, 1780	Least shrew
Sorex minutus	Linnaeus, 1766	Pygmy shrew
Sorex samniticus	Altobello, 1926	Appenine shrew
Neomys anomalus	Cabrera, 1907	Miller's water shrew
Neomys fodiens	(Pennant, 1771)	Water shrew
Crocidura canariensis	Hutterer, López-Jurado & Vogel, 1987	Canary shrew
Crocidura leucodon	(Hermann, 1780)	Bi-coloured white-toothed shrew
Crocidura osorio	Molina & Hutterer, 1989	Osorio shrew
Crocidura russula	(Hermann, 1780)	Greater white-toothed shrew
Crocidura sicula	Miller, 1900	Sicilian shrew
Crocidura suaveolens	(Pallas, 1811)	Lesser white-toothed shrew
Crocidura zimmermanni	Wettstein, 1953	Cretan white-toothed shrew
Suncus etruscus	(Savi, 1822)	Pygmy white-toothed shrew
Galemys pyrenaicus	(E. Geoffroy, 1811)	Pyrenean desman
Talpa caeca	Savi, 1822	Blind mole
Talpa europaea	Linnaeus, 1758	Common mole
Talpa occidentalis	Cabrera, 1907	Iberian mole
Talpa romana	Thomas, 1902	Roman mole
Talpa stankovici	V. Martino & E. Martino, 1931	Balkan mole

Chiroptera

Rhinolophus blasii	Peters, 1866	Blasius' horseshoe bat
Rhinolophus euryale	Blasius, 1853	Mediterranean horseshoe bat
Rhinolophus ferrumequinum	(Schreber, 1774)	Greater horseshoe bat
Rhinolophus hipposideros	(Bechstein, 1800)	Lesser horseshoe bat
Rhinolophus mehelyi	Matschie, 1901	Mehely's horseshoe bat
Myotis bechsteinii	(Kuhl, 1817)	Bechstein's bat
Myotis blythii	(Tomes, 1857)	Lesser mouse-eared bat
Myotis brandtii	(Eversmann, 1845)	Brandt's bat
Myotis capaccinii	(Bonaparte, 1837)	Long-fingered bat
Myotis dasycneme	(Boie, 1825)	Pond bat
Myotis daubentonii	(Kuhl, 1817)	Daubenton's bat
Myotis emarginatus	(E. Geoffroy, 1806)	Geoffroy's bat
Myotis myotis	(Borkhausen, 1797)	Greater mouse-eared bat
Myotis mystacinus	(Kuhl, 1817)	Whiskered bat
Myotis nattereri	(Kuhl, 1817)	Natterer's bat

Pipistrellus kuhlii	(Kuhl, 1817)	Kuhl's pipistrelle
Pipistrellus maderensis	(Dobson, 1878)	Madeira pipistrelle
Pipistrellus nathusii	(Keyserling & Blasius, 1839)	Nathusius' pipistrelle
Pipistrellus pipistrellus	(Schreber, 1774)	Common pipistrelle
Pipistrellus savii	(Bonaparte, 1837)	Savi's pipistrelle
Nyctalus azoreum	(Thomas, 1901)	Azorean bat
Nyctalus lasiopterus	(Schreber, 1780)	Greater noctule
Nyctalus leisleri	(Kuhl, 1817)	Leisler's bat
Nyctalus noctula	(Schreber, 1774)	Noctule
Eptesicus bottae	(Peters, 1869)	Botta's serotine
Eptesicus nilssonii	(Keyserling & Blasius, 1839)	Northern bat
Eptesicus serotinus	(Schreber, 1774)	Serotine
Vespertilio murinus	Linnaeus, 1758	Parti-coloured bat
Barbastella barbastellus	(Schreber, 1774)	Barbastelle
Plecotus auritus	(Linnaeus, 1758)	Brown long-eared bat
Plecotus austriacus	(J. B. Fischer, 1829)	Grey long-eared bat
Plecotus teneriffae	Barrett-Hamilton, 1907	Tenerife long-eared bat
Miniopterus schreibersii	(Kuhl, 1817)	Schreibers' bat
Tadarida teniotis	(Rafinesque, 1814)	European free-tailed bat

Primates

Macaca sylvanus	(Linnaeus, 1758)	Barbary ape

Lagomorpha

Lepus capensis	Linnaeus, 1758	Cape hare
Lepus castroviejoi	Palacios, 1977	Broom hare
Lepus corsicanus	de Winton, 1898	Corsican hare
Lepus europaeus	Pallas, 1778	Brown hare
Lepus granatensis	Rosenhauer, 1856	Iberian hare
Lepus timidus	Linnaeus, 1758	Mountain hare
Oryctolagus cuniculus	(Linnaeus, 1758)	Rabbit
Sylvilagus floridanus	(J. A. Allen, 1890)	Eastern cottontail rabbit

Rodentia

Sciurus anomalus	Güldenstaedt, 1785	Persian squirrel
Sciurus carolinensis	Gmelin, 1788	Grey squirrel
Sciurus vulgaris	Linnaeus, 1758	Red squirrel
Callosciurus erythraeus	(Pallas, 1779)	Pallas's squirrel
Callosciurus finlaysonii	(Horsfield, 1824)	Thailand tree squirrel
Atlantoxerus getulus	(Linnaeus, 1758)	Barbary ground squirrel
Marmota marmota	(Linnaeus, 1758)	Alpine marmot
Spermophilus citellus	(Linnaeus, 1766)	European souslik
Spermophilus suslicus	(Güldenstaedt, 1770)	Spotted souslik
Tamias sibiricus	(Laxmann, 1769)	Siberian chipmunk
Pteromys volans	(Linnaeus, 1758)	Russian flying squirrel
Castor canadensis	Kuhl, 1820	American beaver; Canadian beaver
Castor fiber	Linnaeus, 1758	Eurasian beaver
Cricetus cricetus	(Linnaeus, 1758)	Common hamster
Cricetulus migratorius	(Pallas,1773)	Grey hamster

Mesocricetus newtoni	(Nehring, 1898)	Romanian hamster
Myopus schisticolor	(Lilljeborg, 1844)	Wood lemming
Lemmus lemmus	(Linnaeus, 1758)	Norway lemming
Clethrionomys glareolus	(Schreber, 1780)	Bank vole
Clethrionomys rufocanus	(Sundevall, 1846)	Grey-sided vole
Clethrionomys rutilus	(Pallas, 1779)	Red vole
Dinaromys bogdanovi	(Martino, 1922)	Balkan snow vole
Arvicola sapidus	Miller, 1908	Southern water vole
Arvicola terrestris	(Linnaeus, 1758)	Water vole
Ondatra zibethicus	(Linnaeus, 1766)	Muskrat
Microtus agrestis	(Linnaeus, 1761)	Field vole
Microtus arvalis	(Pallas, 1778)	Common vole
Microtus cabrerae	Thomas, 1906	Cabrera's vole
Microtus duodecimcostatus	de Sélys-Longchamps, 1839	Mediterranean pine vole
Microtus felteni	Malec & Storch, 1963	Balkan pine vole
Microtus gerbei	(Gerbe, 1879)	Pyrenean pine vole
Microtus guentheri	(Danford & Alston, 1880)	Guenther's vole
Microtus lusitanicus	(Gerbe, 1879)	Lusitanian pine vole
Microtus multiplex	(Fatio, 1905)	Alpine pine vole
Microtus oeconomus	(Pallas, 1776)	Root vole
Microtus rossiaemeridionalis	Ognev, 1924	Sibling vole
Microtus savii	(de Sélys-Longchamps, 1838)	Savi's pine vole
Microtus subterraneus	(de Sélys-Longchamps, 1836)	Common pine vole
Microtus tatricus	Kratochvil, 1952	Tatra vole
Microtus thomasi	(Barrett-Hamilton, 1903)	Thomas's vole
Chionomys nivalis	(Martins, 1842)	Snow vole
Meriones tristrami	Thomas, 1892	Tristram's jird
Spalax graecus	Nehring, 1898	Balkan mole rat
Nannospalax leucodon	(Nordmann, 1840)	Lesser mole rat
Micromys minutus	(Pallas, 1771)	Harvest mouse
Apodemus agrarius	(Pallas, 1771)	Striped field mouse
Apodemus alpicola	Heinrich 1952	Alpine mouse
Apodemus flavicollis	(Melchior, 1834)	Yellow-necked mouse
Apodemus mystacinus	(Danford & Alston, 1877)	Rock mouse
Apodemus sylvaticus	(Linnaeus, 1758)	Wood mouse
Apodemus uralensis	(Pallas, 1811)	Pygmy field mouse
Rattus norvegicus	(Berkenhout, 1769)	Brown rat
Rattus rattus	(Linnaeus, 1758)	Black rat; Ship rat
Mus domesticus	Schwartz & Schwartz, 1943	Western house mouse
Mus macedonicus	Petrov & Ružić, 1983	Balkan short-tailed mouse
Mus musculus	Linnaeus, 1758	Eastern house mouse
Mus spicilegus	Petényi, 1882	Steppe mouse
Mus spretus	Lataste 1883	Algerian mouse
Acomys minous	Bate, 1906	Cretan spiny mouse
Glis glis	(Linnaeus, 1766)	Fat dormouse; Edible dormouse
Muscardinus avellanarius	(Linnaeus, 1758)	Common dormouse
Eliomys quercinus	(Linnaeus, 1766)	Garden dormouse
Dryomys nitedula	(Pallas, 1778)	Forest dormouse
Myomimus roachi	(Bate, 1937)	Mouse-tailed dormouse
Sicista betulina	(Pallas, 1779)	Northern birch mouse

Sicista subtilis	(Pallas, 1773)	Southern birch mouse
Hystrix cristata	Linnaeus, 1758	Crested porcupine
Myocastor coypus	(Molina, 1782)	Coypu

Carnivora

Canis aureus	Linnaeus, 1758	Golden jackal
Canis lupus	Linnaeus, 1758	Wolf
Alopex lagopus	(Linnaeus, 1758)	Arctic fox
Vulpes vulpes	(Linnaeus, 1758)	Red fox
Nyctereutes procyonoides	(Gray, 1834)	Raccoon dog
Ursus arctos	Linnaeus, 1758	Brown bear
Ursus maritimus	Phipps, 1774	Polar bear
Procyon lotor	(Linnaeus, 1758)	Raccoon
Mustela erminea	Linnaeus, 1758	Stoat
Mustela eversmanii	Lesson, 1827	Steppe polecat
Mustela lutreola	(Linneus, 1761)	European mink
Mustela nivalis	Linnaeus, 1766	Weasel
Mustela putorius	Linnaeus, 1758	Western polecat
Mustela vison	Schreber, 1777	American mink
Vormela peregusna	(Güldenstaedt, 1770)	Marbled polecat
Martes foina	(Erxleben, 1777)	Beech marten; Stone marten
Martes martes	(Linnaeus, 1758)	Pine marten
Gulo gulo	(Linnaeus, 1758)	Wolverine
Meles meles	(Linnaeus, 1758)	Badger
Lutra lutra	(Linnaeus, 1758)	Otter
Genetta genetta	(Linnaeus, 1758)	Common genet
Herpestes auropunctatus	Hodgson, 1836	Small Indian mongoose
Herpestes ichneumon	(Linnaeus, 1758)	Egyptian mongoose
Felis silvestris	Schreber, 1775	Wildcat
Lynx lynx	(Linnaeus, 1758)	Lynx
Lynx pardinus	(Temminck, 1827)	Iberian lynx; Pardel lynx
Odobenus rosmarus	(Linnaeus, 1758)	Walrus
Phoca groenlandica	Erxleben, 1777	Harp seal
Phoca hispida	Schreber, 1775	Ringed seal
Phoca vitulina	Linnaeus, 1758	Common seal; Harbour seal
Halichoerus grypus	(Fabricius, 1791)	Grey seal
Erignathus barbatus	(Erxleben, 1777)	Bearded seal
Monachus monachus	(Hermann, 1779)	Mediterranean monk seal
Cystophora cristata	(Erxleben, 1777)	Hooded seal

Artiodactyla

Sus scrofa	Linnaeus, 1758	Wild boar
Muntiacus reevesi	(Ogilby, 1839)	Reeves' muntjac
Axis axis	(Erxleben, 1777)	Axis deer
Dama dama	(Linnaeus, 1758)	Fallow deer
Cervus elaphus	Linnaeus, 1758	Red deer
Cervus nippon	Temminck, 1838	Sika deer
Odocoileus virginianus	(Zimmermann, 1780)	White-tailed deer
Alces alces	(Linnaeus, 1758)	Elk; Moose
Rangifer tarandus	(Linnaeus, 1758)	Reindeer

Hydropotes inermis	Swinhoe, 1870	Chinese water deer
Capreolus capreolus	(Linnaeus, 1758)	Roe deer
Bison bonasus	(Linnaeus, 1758)	European bison
Rupicapra pyrenaica	Bonaparte, 1845	Southern chamois
Rupicapra rupicapra	(Linnaeus, 1758)	Alpine chamois
Ovibos moschatus	(Zimmermann, 1780)	Musk ox
Capra aegagrus	Erxleben, 1777	Wild goat
Capra ibex	Linnaeus, 1758	Alpine ibex
Capra pyrenaica	Schinz, 1838	Spanish ibex
Ammotragus lervia	(Pallas, 1777)	Barbary sheep
Ovis ammon	(Linnaeus, 1758)	Mouflon

THE SPECIES ACCOUNTS

Mapping periods and symbols

● Species present. Based on data collected since 1 January 1970, modified by published data on extinctions to give the current status of the species. Positive records since 1970 are omitted from the map only where more recent detailed surveys have failed to detect the species.

● Presence presumed. Based on data collected before 1970, but where there is no evidence to suggest the species has become extinct.

Macropus rufogriseus (DESMAREST, 1817)

E. Hazebroek

Distribution

World: Australasian; eastern Australia from central Queensland to South Australia and Tasmania. Introduced to New Zealand (South Island), Great Britain and Germany, though now extinct in Germany.
Europe: small feral populations readily establish themselves in western Europe, but seem ephemeral; currently only present in Great Britain.

Geographic variation

Mainland Australian race *M. rufogriseus banksianus* Quoy & Gairnard, 1825 breeds throughout the year; Tasmanian race *M. r. rufogriseus* has seasonal breeding, and it is this race that has been introduced elsewhere.

Habitat

A scrub wallaby, lying up in bushy cover during the day, but emerging to feed in more open areas at dusk. Feeds mainly on dwarf shrubs, e.g. *Calluna* sp., *Vaccinium* spp., and grasses, but also browses shrubs.

Population status

Widespread and patchily common in its native Australian range; considered a forest pest, and subject to intensive control in New Zealand. In Europe, small feral populations of up to 70 have established themselves at four sites in Britain, one in the Channel Isles (UK), one on the Isle of Man (UK) and one in Germany (now Poland), for 20–50 years, but two have died out and one is barely viable. Captive/park populations thrive, and are likely to continue to found feral populations, but their long-term survival seems doubtful.

International legal & conservation status

None.

Other information

Ecologically, this species is comparable with *Lepus* and *Capreolus* in its feeding, habits and habitat; in Britain it certainly coexists with *Lepus*, but *Capreolus* is absent from areas where it occurs, so relationships are uncertain, although an incompatibility between *Capreolus* and *Macropus* was suspected in Germany. Possibly ill-adapted to the fragmented European landscape; vulnerable to road traffic, to recreational disturbance, and to competition from sheep.

Literature

Niethammer (1963)
Ronseveil *et al.* (1991)
Warburton & Sadleir (1990)
Yalden (1991)

D. W. Yalden

© Societas Europaea Mammalogica

Macropus rufogriseus

Atelerix algirus (Lereboullet, 1842)

T. P. McOwat

Algerian hedgehog

AL	-	LT	-
BG	Алжирски таралеж	LU	Algereschen Kéisécker
CZ	Ježek alžírský	LV	-
DE	Wanderigel	MK	-
DK	Spansk pindsvin	MT	Qanfud tal-Ferq
EE	-	NL	Trekegel
ES	Erizo moruno	NO	Algeripiggsvin
FI	Vaeltajasiili	PL	Jeż algierski
FO	-	PT	-
FR	Hérisson d'Algérie	RO	-
GR	-	RU	Алжирский ёж
HR	Jež selac	SE	Spansk igelkott
HU	Mediterrán sün	SI	Alžirski jež
IR	-	SK	Jež alžírsky
IS	-	TR	-
IT	Riccio algerino	YU	-

Distribution

World: North Africa from Mauritania to Libya, eastern coast of the Iberian Peninsula, Djerba, Malta, Ibiza, Formentera, Canary and Balearic Islands. Probably introduced to Europe and many islands by man.

Europe: confined to some localities on the Mediterranean coasts of Spain, the Canary Islands and Malta; seems to be extinct in France.

Geographic variation

Four subspecies have been described, one of them (*A. algirus vagans* Thomas, 1901) from Europe (Menorca). Three subspecies are currently recognized as valid: *A. a. algirus* (Lereboullet, 1842), characterized by large size, on the African mainland, Malta and Canary islands; *A. a. vagans*, smaller in size, on the Balearic islands and *A. a. girbaensis* (Vesmanis, 1980), small and confined to Djerba and possibly the adjacent Tunisian mainland. Many island populations exhibit a high degree of colour variation.

Habitat

Prefers lowlands and hills up to 400 m, but in Morocco it can reach 900 m (High Atlas). Prefers dry habitats, but may be quite common in grassland environments, farmlands, fields, meadows, gardens and various agroecosystems, showing, however, a clear preference for scrub vegetation areas. Has been found to be common in the vicinity of human settlements on Formentera.

Population status

In Europe the species must be considered very rare, perhaps everywhere allochthonous; frequent only on the Canary Islands and Malta.

International legal & conservation status

Bern Convention, Appendix II.
EU Habitats & Species Directive, Annex IV.

Literature

Corbet (1988)
Fayard *et al.* (1984)
Holz & Niethammer (1990c) – review

L. Lapini

© Societas Europaea Mammalogica

Atelerix algirus

Erinaceus concolor Martin, 1838

M. Năzăreanu

An electrophoretic study of allozymic variability seems to indicate that two species of eastern *Erinaceus* (*E. concolor* Martin, 1838 with *terra typica* in Trabzon, Turkey and *E. roumanicus* Barrett-Hamilton, 1900 with *terra typica* in Gageni, Romania) may occur together in Western Anatolia. If this were proved to be true, the correct name of European eastern hedgehogs would have to be reconsidered.

Distribution

World: Eastern Europe and Asia Minor, Israel, north Iran and north-west Iraq, east to west coast of the Caspian Sea and to the River Ob.
Europe: north-east Italy (the entire Trentino-Alto Adige and Eastern Friuli-Venezia Giulia), Slovenia and the entire Balkan Peninsula, southern and eastern Austria, Czech Republic, Poland, the Baltic Republics and Russia. Widely distributed on Adriatic and Greek islands. Narrow overlapping zones with *E. europaeus* in north-east Italy, west Slovenia (Nova Gorica district), central Austria, Czech Republic, Poland and northern Russia.

Geographic variation

Six subspecies have been described from the European part of its range, from which *E. concolor nesiotes* Bate, 1906 and *E. c. rhodius* Festa, 1914 are clearly distinguishable from the mainland subspecies, but their respective ranges and systematic value are not yet clear.

Habitat

Prefers lowlands and hills up to 300–800 m, but may be present on the mountain slopes up to 1400 m in the Eastern Alps and Taurus mountains. Prefers urban and suburban habitats and agricultural land to natural vegetation. Here it selects scrub vegetation areas at the borders of large forests. The Eastern hedgehog also maintains these environmental preferences on eastern Adriatic coasts, being usually quite common also in karst environments.

Population status

This hedgehog has no serious conservation problems, but in areas with a cold climate it may be naturally rare. The main cause of mortality of the Eastern hedgehog is probably starvation during hibernation mainly in the first winter. Locally, road mortality may be a limiting factor of its population density.

International legal & conservation status

None.

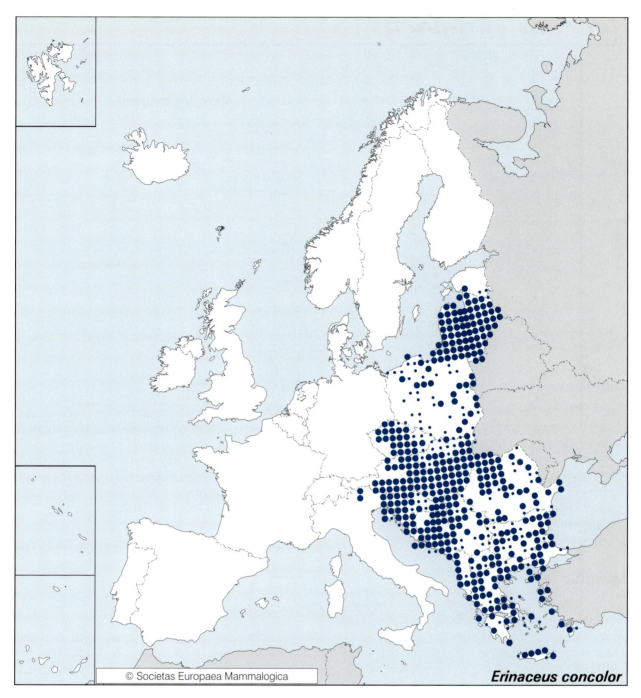

© Societas Europaea Mammalogica

Erinaceus concolor

Literature

Filippucci & Lapini (1988)
Filippucci & Simson (1996)
Holz & Niethammer (1990a) – review
Lapini (1989)
Lapini *et al.* (1996)

L. Lapini

Erinaceus europaeus Linnaeus, 1758

V. Ree

Distribution

Endemic to Europe. From south-western and central Scandinavia (introduced to Finland), Britain and Ireland, the Iberian Peninsula to Italy, western Slovenia, central and western Austria, western Poland and in the northern Baltic region east to the Urals. Present also on Mediterranean Islands (Corsica, Sardinia, Elba, Sicily), on most of the French Atlantic islands as well as on British islands (autochthonous and introduced). For zones of sympatric occurrence with *E. concolor* see that species.

Geographic variation

Seven geographic races have been described, but their status is still uncertain. A preliminary allozymic study of some of these races suggests the validity of *E. erinaceus europaeus* Linnaeus, 1758 and *E. e. italicus* Barrett-Hamilton, 1900, while *E. e. hispanicus* Barrett-Hamilton, 1900 might even be a full species.

Habitat

Prefers lowlands and hills up to 400–600 m, but is also locally present on mountains, exceptionally up to 1500–2000 m (Alps and Pyrénées). Seems to be more common in suburban than in rural areas. Locally very abundant in orchards, vineyards and gardens. Outside cultivated land it prefers marginal zones of forests, particularly ecotonal scrub and grass vegetation. In the Mediterranean region it maintains these environmental preferences, but is usually less common in dry habitats.

Population status

The species has no serious conservation problems, but in the northern parts of its range and at higher altitudes it may be relatively rare. This may be due to the climate. Road mortality may locally diminish its population density, but the principal cause for mortality of this hedgehog is probably starvation during hibernation, particularly during its first winter.

International legal & conservation status

Bern Convention, Appendix III.

Other information

May hybridize in captivity with *Erinaceus concolor*, but in nature no genetic introgression between these two *Erinaceus* species, which are separated by a genetic distance of about one million years, has been found.

Literature

Filippucci & Lapini (1988)
Filippucci & Simson (1996)
Holz & Niethammer (1990b) – review
Lapini (1989)
Lapini *et al.* (1996)
Petrov (1989)

L. Lapini

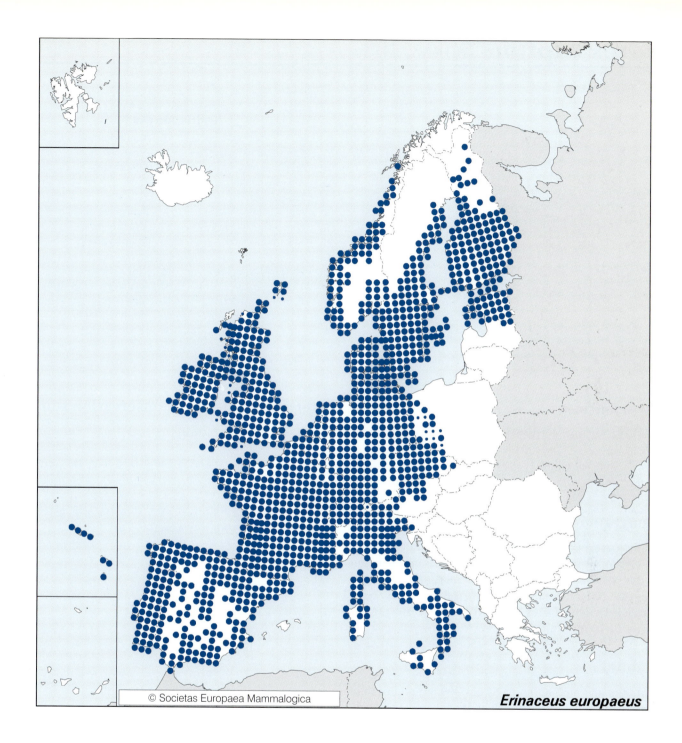

© Societas Europaea Mammalogica

Erinaceus europaeus

Sorex alpinus SCHINZ, 1837

M. Năzăreanu

Distribution

Endemic to Europe. Disjunct distribution areas in the Alps, Balkans, Carpathians and several isolated mountains in Germany. Probably extinct in the Pyrénées, in the first decades of this century, and the Harz.

Geographic variation

Several subspecies described, but their validity has not been confirmed recently. Small-sized animals of the Eastern Alps surrounded by populations of larger animals; clinal increase of tail length from west to east. Three karyotypic forms known from the Western Alps, Swiss Jura and central Europe.

Habitat

Montane and alpine; ranging from 200 m to more than 2500 m altitude. At lower elevations linked to cool and humid environments like small brooks in deep, densely vegetated shady ravines. In forests in moist, shady places under mossy rocks and logs. At higher elevations tending to more open habitats where it lives in holes and crevices in rocky ground and under stone walls.

Population status

Still widespread but local in the Alps; small peripheral relict populations threatened by habitat loss through forest clearing and destruction of brooks and small rivers.

International legal & conservation status

Bern Convention, Annex III.

Literature

Dannelid (1994)
Lukáčǒvá *et al.* (1996)
Spitzenberger (1990c) – review

F. Spitzenberger

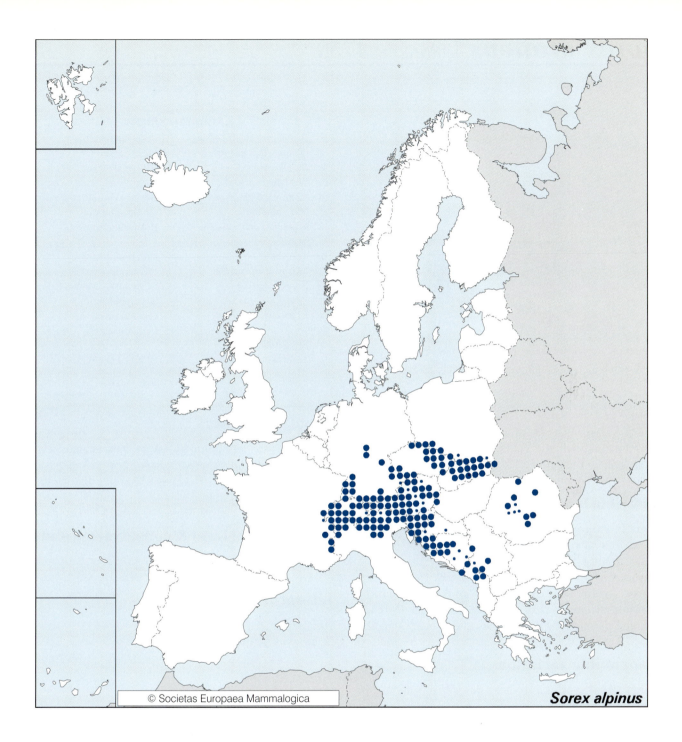

© Societas Europaea Mammalogica

Sorex alpinus

Sorex araneus LINNAEUS, 1758

P. Barrett

Similar in appearance to *Sorex coronatus, S. granarius* and *S. samniticus*. In small overlap zones it can be distinguished by skull characters and karyotype from these species.

Distribution

World: Palaearctic north to the Arctic coast and eastwards to Lake Baikal except for dry steppe and desert zones.
Europe: widely distributed, but absent from Ireland, Outer Hebrides, Shetland, most of France, Mediterranean zone including southern Balkans. Isolated populations in Pyrénées and Massif Central.

Geographic variation

About 19 subspecies have been described from Europe. However, status of most of them is uncertain. High degree of chromosomal variation due to Robertsonian translocations. Diploid number of chromosomes varies between 18–30. Around 50 karyotypic races are currently recognized within the distribution range.

Habitat

Prefers moist and cool habitats with dense vegetation cover. Highest densities in riverine forests and reed beds, but occurs in all kinds of forests, rock crevices and even in sand dunes. From sea level to 2480 m altitude.

Population status

One of the most abundant shrew species. Densities vary between 1–50 individuals/ha according to season and habitat. Local declines because of habitat disturbances and pesticides possible.

International legal & conservation status

Bern Convention, Appendix III.

Literature

Hausser *et al.* (1990)
Zima *et al.* (1996)

M. Anděra

42

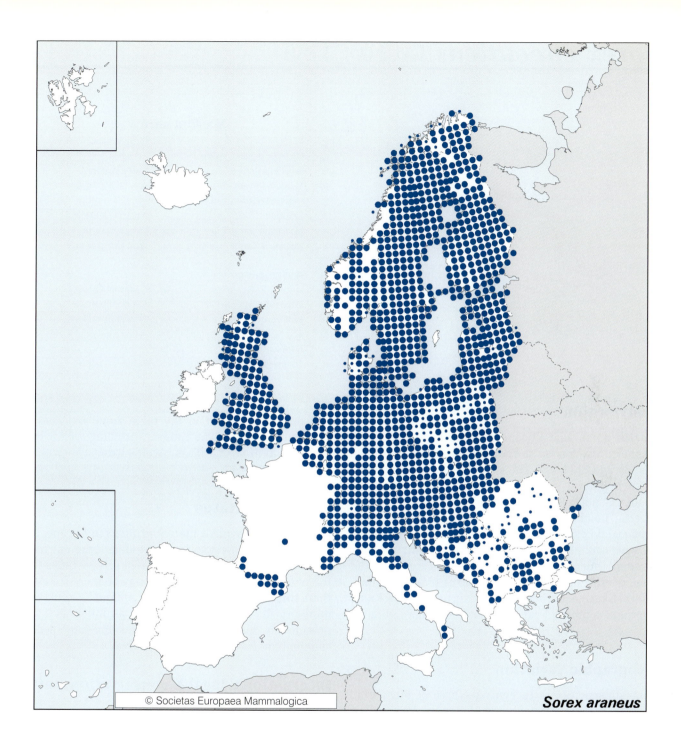

© Societas Europaea Mammalogica

Sorex araneus

43

Sorex caecutiens LAXMANN, 1788

T. P. McOwat

Masked shrew

AL	-	LT	Laplandijos kirstukas
BG	Средна кафявозъбка	LU	-
CZ	Rejsek prostřední	LV	Vidējais cirslis
DE	Maskenspitzmaus	MK	-
DK	Lapspidsmus	MT	-
EE	Laane-karihiir	NL	Noordse spitsmuis
ES	Musaraña careta	NO	Lappspissmus
FI	Idänpäästäinen	PL	Ryjówka średnia
FO	-	PT	-
FR	Musaraigne masquée	RO	-
GR	-	RU	Средняя бурозубка
HR	Laponska rovka	SE	Lappnäbbmus
HU	Laxmann-cickány	SI	Borealna rovka
IR	-	SK	-
IS	Lappasnjáldra	TR	-
IT	Toporagno di Laxmann	YU	-

Distribution

World: north-east Europe and northern Asia from northern Sweden up to the Chukchi Peninsula, Kuril Islands and Sakhalin. The southern border runs from eastern Poland through central Ukraine, southern Bashkiria, north Kazakhstan, the mountains of southern Siberia, north Mongolia, north-east China, Korea to Japan (Hokkaido, Honshu, Shikoku).
Europe: confined to the northern parts. From northern Sweden, Norway, Finland, Estonia, eastern Poland (Białowieża Forest), northern Belarus (Polock region), central Ukraine, European Russia, up to the lower Kama river and southern Urals. Not recorded from Lithuania or Latvia.

Geographic variation

Four subspecies are recognized, three of them from Europe: *S. caecutiens pleskei* Ognev, 1921, *S. c. lapponicus* Melander, 1942 and *S. c. karpinskii* Dehnel, 1949. *S. c. karpinskii* is probably isolated in Białowieża Forest and differs from the others by larger body size and tail length, as well as the pattern of unicuspids, decreasing in size from first to fourth. Size proportion of unicuspids exhibits geographic variation. Complex clinal variation of cranial characters.

Habitat

Similar habitat preference to *Sorex araneus,* but confined to wetter places. Mainly in coniferous, mixed and deciduous forest in the taiga zone; but also in different habitats of the tundra, including willow and birch scrub in river valleys. Avoids extensive swamps and peat bogs.

Population status

Generally less frequent than *S. araneus* in Europe, but its proportions increase in a latitudinal gradient from south to north. In Białowieża Forest it is 35 times less frequent than *S. araneus,* but it may be more frequent than this species in northern Lapland. Population numbers fluctuate between years as much as 1:10, presumably due to winter conditions and interspecific competition. No regular cycle observed.

International legal & conservation status

Bern Convention, Appendix III.

Other information

Adult males of *S. c. karpinskii* have a pleasant smell of 'chypre', which differentiates them from other shrew species producing musk.

Literature

Borowski & Dehnel (1952)
Dehnel (1949)
Dolgov (1985)

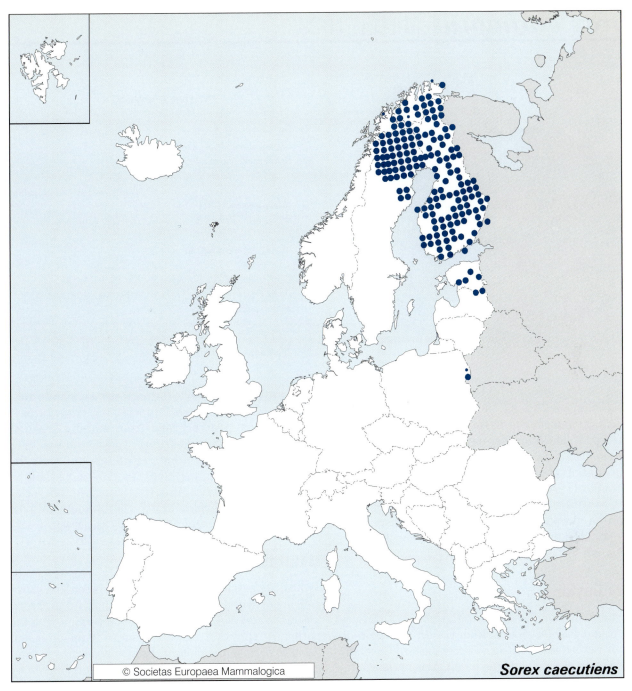

© Societas Europaea Mammalogica

Sorex caecutiens

Ivanter (1975)
Pucek (1992)
Sulkava (1990a) – review

Z. Pucek

Sorex coronatus MILLET, 1828

P. Twisk

Millet's shrew

AL	-	LT	-
BG	-	LU	Schabrackenspëtzmaus
CZ	Rejsek západoevropský	LV	-
DE	Schabrackenspitzmaus	MK	-
DK	-	MT	-
EE	-	NL	Tweekleurige bosspitsmuis
ES	Musaraña de Millet	NO	-
FI	Ranskanpäästäinen	PL	Ryjówka Milleta
FO	-	PT	-
FR	Musaraigne couronnée	RO	-
GR	-	RU	-
HR	Zapadnoeuropska šumska rovka	SE	Millets näbbmus
		SI	Atlantska gozdna rovka
HU	Millet-cickány	SK	-
IR	-	TR	-
IS	-	YU	-
IT	Toporagno di Millet		

Very similar to *S. araneus,* although clearly recognizable by its karyotype (2N = 22, NF = 44 in females). Several biochemical and genetic diagnostic markers have been described, of which urinary pepsines are probably the most useful for simple identification. Morphological determination is usually possible, but complex and geographical variation in size requires *ad hoc* analyses in different areas. The lack of clear and constant diagnostic morphological characters explains why in many publications this species is not distinguished from *S. araneus.*

Distribution

Endemic to Europe. Parapatric to *S. araneus* and largely to *S. granarius.* Distributed from Galicia and León on the northern coast of Spain to north-eastern Germany and western Austria. Limited by the Alps in the south-east and partially replaced by *S. araneus* in mountains above 800–1200 m, as well as in wet areas in the eastern and northern part of its distribution. In the south it is largely absent from the Mediterranean zone. Present on Jersey, but absent from the coastal dunes and polders of the Netherlands.

S. coronatus is apparently expanding its range to the detriment of *S. araneus* in recent times. This seems to be linked to climatic change.

Geographic variation

The largest *S. coronatus* are found along the Alps and in southern Germany; morphological clines lead to smaller individuals both to the north-west and the south-west. Uniformly dark individuals (*santonus* – morphotypes) are recorded from marshy areas of Charente, south-western France. They live in sympatry with normal three-coloured individuals and show the typical *S. coronatus* karyotype, so they should not be assigned a subspecific status. Otherwise two subspecies described: *S. c. euronotus* Miller, 1901 in south-western France and *S. c. fretalis* Miller, 1909 on Jersey.

Habitat

Typical *Sorex* habitats, with thick vegetation just above soil level; woods, hedges, abandoned or unmown meadows and marshes. Where in competition with the parapatric species *S. araneus*, limited to the drier and warmer parts of the biotope. Frequently excluded from gardens and the periphery of human settlements by *Crocidura russula.*

Population status

As with every species of *Sorex,* population numbers of *S. coronatus* are limited in intensively cultivated areas.

International legal & conservation status

Bern Convention, Appendix III.

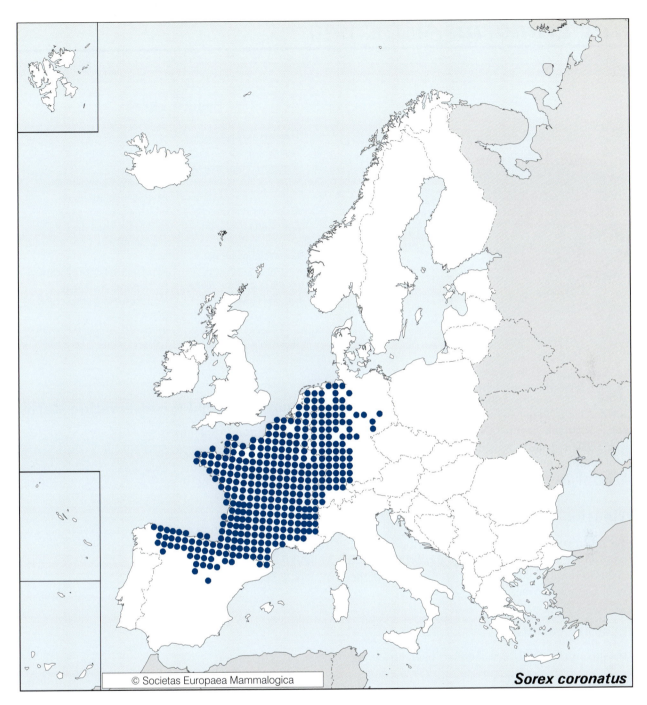

© Societas Europaea Mammalogica

Sorex coronatus

Literature

Butet & Leroux (1993)
Butet & Volobouev (1995)
Genoud (1982)
Hausser (1990) – review
Loch (1977)
López-Fuster & Ventura (1996)
Neet & Hausser (1990, 1991)

J. Hausser

Sorex granarius MILLER, 1910

T. P. McOwat

Spanish shrew

AL	-	LU	-
BG	Испанска кафявоэъбка	LV	-
CZ	Rejsek iberský	MK	-
DE	Iberische Waldspitzmaus	MT	-
DK	-	NL	Iberische bosspitsmuis
EE	-	NO	Spansk spissmus
ES	Musaraña ibérica	PL	Ryjówka pirenejska
FI	Espanjanpäästäinen	PT	Musaranho-de-dentes-vermelhos
FO	-		
FR	Musaraigne ibérique	RO	-
GR	-	RU	Пиренейская бурозубка
HR	Iberska šumska rovka	SE	Spansk näbbmus
HU	Spanyol cickány	SI	Iberijska gozdna rovka
IR	-	SK	-
IS	-	TR	-
IT	Toporagno iberico	YU	-
LT	-		

Genetically very closely related to *Sorex araneus*. Characteristic karyotype supposedly ancestral to the *S. araneus – arcticus* group (2N = 38, NF = 40–42 in females). Clear-cut morphological identification needs the use of complex multivariate analysis. Slightly smaller than *S. coronatus*.

Distribution

Endemic to Europe: Iberian species, distributed from the Tagus river to Galicia and eastwards along the Sierras de Gredos and de Guadarrama. Absent from the plateau of Castilla la Vieja.

Geographic variation

A decreasing north–south size cline has been observed.

Habitat

Woods, scrub, stream shores and screes, from the Atlantic coast up to 2000 m in the mountains. Limited to areas in which the mean annual rainfall is above 600 mm, suggesting an altitudinal segregation within areas of overlap with *S. coronatus*.

Population status

Unknown.

International legal & conservation status

Bern Convention, Appendix III.

Literature

Catzeflis *et al.* (1982)
Gisbert *et al.* (1988)
López-Fuster & Ventura (1996)
Taberlet *et al.* (1994)
Volobouev & Catzeflis (1989)
Wójcik & Searle (1988)

J. Hausser

© Societas Europaea Mammalogica

Sorex granarius

49

Sorex isodon Turov, 1924

T. P. McOwat

Taiga shrew

AL	-	LT	Užbaikalės kirstukas
BG	Източносибирска	LU	-
	кафявозъбка	LV	Austrumsibīrijas cirslis
CZ	Rejsek tajgový	MK	-
DE	Taigaspitzmaus	MT	-
DK	Taigaspidsmus	NL	Grauwe spitsmuis
EE	Must-karihiir	NO	Taigaspissmus
ES	Musaraña siberiana	PL	Ryjówka równozębna
FI	Korpipäästäinen	PT	-
FO	-	RO	-
FR	Musaraigne sombre	RU	Равнозубая бурозубка
GR	-	SE	Taiganäbbmus
HR	Sibirska rovka	SI	Temna rovka
HU	Fenyőcickány	SK	-
IR	-	TR	-
IS	-	YU	-
IT	Toporagno oscuro		

Because of the rather small differences from the common shrew *S. araneus, S. isodon* was detected in northern Europe rather late: Finland, 1949; Norway, 1968 and Sweden, 1977. The taxonomic position of the Taiga shrew has been changing and unclear until the 1970–1980s, when it was still called *S. centralis* Thomas, 1911 or *S. sinalis* Thomas, 1912.

Distribution

World: from Scandinavia in the west through Siberian coniferous forests to the Pacific coast and Sakhalin Island.
Europe: more or less continuously distributed from eastern Finland to northern Russia. Isolated records from the Scandinavian peninsula consist of single specimens from a few places in central Sweden and Norway. The occurrence in Scandinavia is obviously only imperfectly known. The distribution greatly resembles that of *S. minutissimus*, but is more restricted.

Geographic variation

Four subspecies have been described (based on colour, size and form of the skull), one of them from Europe (*S. isodon ruthenus* Stroganov, 1936 from central Russia), but true extent of geographic variation still only partly known.

Habitat

Mostly in old and moist mixed or spruce forests with a thick moss layer and dense undergrowth of grasses and herbs, often along small brooks or rivers or the edges of peat bogs. Sometimes also on moist field-forest edges, on abandoned fields and yards with dense meadow vegetation.

Population status

Occurs mostly in small local populations in densely covered habitats; obviously always rare in Europe. In northern Europe and also in north-western Siberia the percentage of this species is generally less than 1% of all *Sorex* captures with snap traps and pitfall traps. In the most suitable habitats in eastern Finland, representation in the total catch was 3 – 13%. Many local populations declining because the preferred habitats are being altered by forestry and drainage.

International legal & conservation status

Bern Convention, Appendix III.

Literature

Corbet (1978)
Dolgov (1985)
Hoffmann (1971, 1987)
Ivanter (1975)
Skarén (1972)
Sulkava (1990b) – review

S. Sulkava

Sorex isodon

51

Sorex minutissimus ZIMMERMANN, 1780

P. Twisk

Because of its small size, this species was not detected in Finland and Scandinavia until the 1950s or 1960s.

Distribution

World: northern Palaearctic from Scandinavia through the Siberian coniferous forests to the Pacific coast and Sakhalin and Hokkaido islands. Northernmost populations in Siberian forest tundra and southernmost in mixed forests (European Russia) and forest steppes (southern Siberia).

Europe: continuous distribution includes central and northern Russia, most of Finland and northern Scandinavia. Isolated records in southern Norway. Probably more widespread in central Scandinavia than currently known.

Geographic variation

All European populations probably belong to the nominate subspecies, in spite of the fact that two others (*S. minutissimus neglectus* Ognev, 1921 and *S. m. karelicus* Stroganov, 1949) have been described from western Russia. Subspecies described from Siberia are based on variation of colour (light in northern and southernmost populations) and weight (lowest in forest tundra).

Habitat

Different habitats in forests and peat bogs. The preferred forest habitats are mostly fresh or moist, spruce dominated and with a thick moss layer, but it is often also found in dry pine forests and open clear-cuts. Common habitats also include boggy brook valleys and moist peatland margins. In central Finland (Oulu district) found to be common on open and pine-growing bogs with many peaty hummocks. There, several tens of individuals have been caught with pitfall traps on open peat bog and identified in the pellets of the Northern shrike *Lanius excubitor,* which often breeds on pine-growing bog.

Population status

Populations obviously stable, but densities compared to other shrew species (*S. araneus, S. minutus* and in north-east Europe also *S. caecutiens*) probably always low. It is seldom caught in standard small mammal traps. In pitfall traps it comprises only 1–2% of the catch. Draining of peat bogs may reduce local populations, but forest cutting seems not to cause decreases.

International legal & conservation status

Bern Convention, Appendix III.

Literature

Corbet (1978)
Judin (1964)
Skarén (1972)
Sulkava (1990c) – review

S. Sulkava

© Societas Europaea Mammalogica

Sorex minutissimus

Sorex minutus Linnaeus, 1766

M. Năzăreanu

Pygmy shrew

AL	-	LU	Kleng Spëtzmaus
BG	Малка кафявозъбка	LV	Mazais cirslis
CZ	Rejsek malý	MK	Мала ровка
DE	Zwergspitzmaus	MT	-
DK	Dværgspidsmus	NL	Dwergspitsmuis
EE	Väike-karihiir	NO	Dvergspissmus
ES	Musaraña enana	PL	Ryjówka malutka
FI	Vaivaispäästäinen	PT	Musaranho-anão-de-dentes-vermelhos
FO	-		
FR	Musaraigne pygmée	RO	Chiţcanul-pitic
GR	Νανομυγαλίδα	RU	Малая бурозубка
HR	Mala rovka	SE	Dvärgnäbbmus
HU	Törpecickány	SI	Mala rovka
IR	Dallóg fraoigh	SK	Piskor malý
IS	Dvergsnjáldra	TR	Cüce sivriburun
IT	Toporagno nano	YU	Мала ровчица
LT	Kirstukas nykštukas		

Distribution

World: Eurasia, from Portugal to Lake Baikal in Siberia.
Europe: most of Europe except for southern Iberia, the Mediterranean coasts and islands, and the Atlantic islands north of Scotland. The species is common in the British Isles as well as in Scandinavia and central Europe. South of the Alps, in southern France, on the Iberian Peninsula and in the Balkans the pygmy shrew is confined to higher altitudes, where its distribution becomes patchy. Pygmy shrews easily colonize islands by active dispersal or passive transport and are thus found temporarily on many islands in northern Europe.

Geographic variation

Pygmy shrews vary markedly in size from north to south, isolated populations in Spain, Italy and Greece being largest. Exceptional karyotypes have been found on the islands Öland and Gotland. Isolated populations in southern Europe need careful study in order to assess their degree of isolation and taxonomic status.

Habitat

The pygmy shrew occurs in a wide range of habitats, depending on latitude and elevation. Dunes and heathlands are common habitats along the North Atlantic coasts, while swamps and meadows are frequently used throughout its continental range. In southern Europe, montane forests up to 1700 m become more important.

Population status

Common in suitable habitats throughout its range. Particularly in swamps it may be the dominant small mammal species and even outnumber the common shrew *S. araneus*. Like most shrews, however, it depends on the presence of moist habitats with a rich plant cover and supply of invertebrates.

International legal & conservation status

Bern Convention, Appendix III.

Literature

Fredga *et al.* (1995)
Hutterer (1990) – review

R. Hutterer

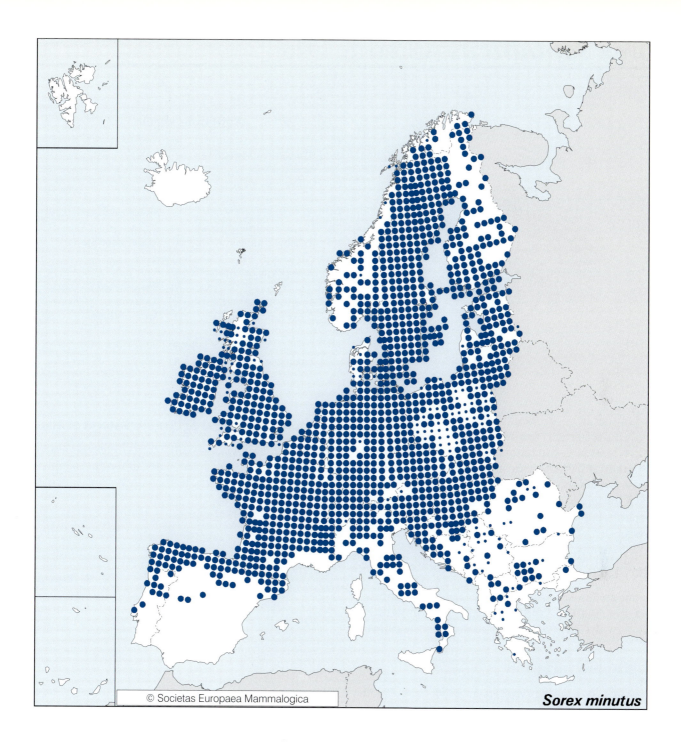

© Societas Europaea Mammalogica

Sorex minutus

Sorex samniticus ALTOBELLO, 1926

T. P. McOwat

Very similar to *S. araneus* from which it was only recently distinguished. Totally acrocentric karyotype (2N = 52, NF = 52). Chromosomal comparison and mitochondrial DNA analysis suggest that *S. samniticus* could be a relict species of the ancestral lineage leading to the *S. araneus* – *S. arcticus* group. Morphologically, this species can be recognized by the shape of its upper incisors.

Distribution

Endemic Italian species. Appenines south to Calabria. Exact distribution, and especially its competitive relations with *Crocidura* representatives, poorly known.

Geographic variation

Subspecies *S. s. garganicus* Pasa, 1951 from Monte Gargano is reported to be slightly smaller than nominate form.

Habitat

Mostly along rivers in mountainous areas between 300 and 1160 m altitude. Replaced by *S. araneus* at higher altitudes. One locality of syntopy with *S. araneus* at Pescaserolli, Abbruzzi (1160 m).

Population status

Unknown.

International legal & conservation status

Bern Convention, Appendix III.

Literature

Dannelid (1989, 1994)
Graf *et al.* (1979)
Pasa (1951)
Taberlet *et al.* (1994)

J. Hausser

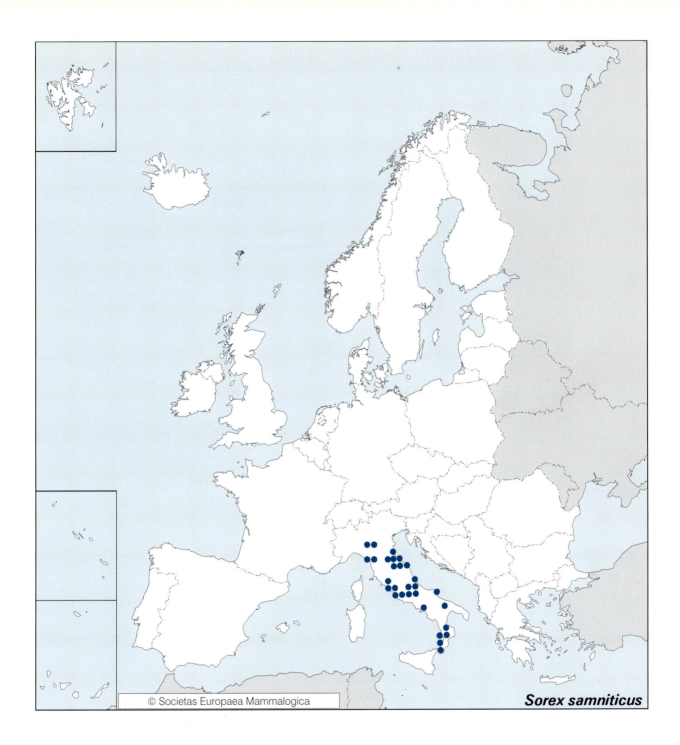

© Societas Europaea Mammalogica

Sorex samniticus

Neomys anomalus Cabrera, 1907

M. Năzăreanu

Similar to the water shrew *Neomys fodiens*, but generally smaller in sympatric populations. Fur less dense, fringes of stiff hair on tail and legs less well developed.

Distribution

World: continental Europe between 37° and 55°N and Asia Minor.
Europe: patchy distribution in the Mediterranean and temperate parts of Europe east to the river Don. Formerly more widespread, ranging to the North Sea in Holocene times.

Geographic variation

North to south directed clines of decreasing body size, but increasing length of tail, hind foot and skull. Five subspecies have been described from Europe, but only *N. anomalus soricoides* Ognev, 1908 from Białowieża seems to be clearly definable.

Habitat

Eutrophic riparian vegetation of still freshwater bodies, bogs and slow-flowing brooks and rivers from lowlands to 1850 m altitude. Its ecological habits seem to be strongly influenced by competition with the larger *Neomys fodiens*. Where the latter is missing, *N. anomalus* adopts aquatic habits and increases in size. In low mountains *N. anomalus* inhabits the upper reaches of rivers and keeps to shallow bodies of waters and bogs. In the Alps both species can coexist at brooks in the montane and submontane zone. When food is scarce, *N. anomalus* can also feed in terrestrial habitats.

Population status

Relict character of distribution and constant habitat loss through drainage of wetlands and destruction of riparian habitats make this species very vulnerable. Densities vary in reaction to varying competition with *N. fodiens*. In the absence of *N. fodiens* it attains high densities locally. Low water tables and drying out of riparian vegetation favour *N. anomalus*.

International legal & conservation status

Bern Convention, Appendix III.

Literature

Spitzenberger (1990a) – review

F. Spitzenberger

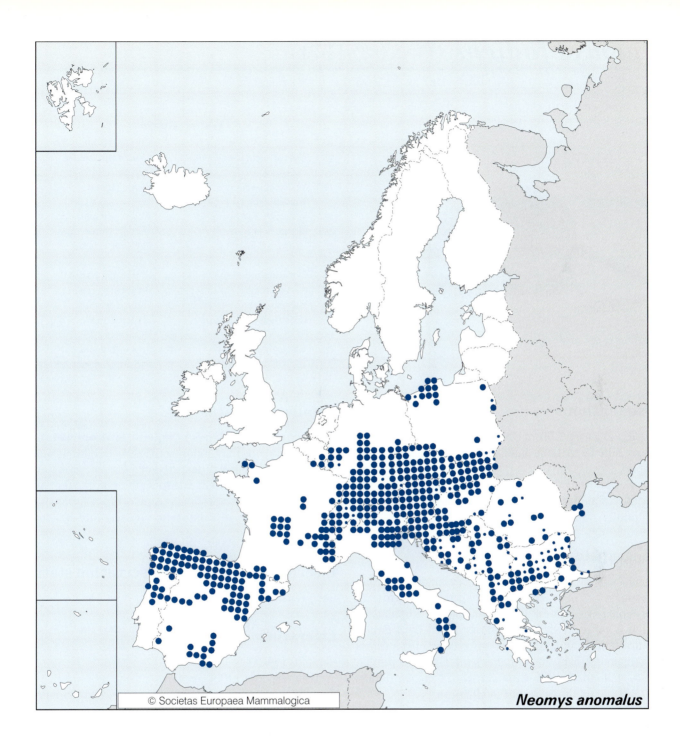

Neomys anomalus

© Societas Europaea Mammalogica

Neomys fodiens (PENNANT, 1771)

P. Twisk

	Water shrew		
AL	-	LT	Vandeninis kirstukas
BG	Голяма водна эемеровка	LU	Waasserspëtzmaus
CZ	Rejsec vodní	LV	Ūdenscirslis
DE	Wasserspitzmaus	MK	Водна ровка
DK	Vandspidsmus	MT	-
EE	Vesimutt; Tava-vesimutt	NL	Waterspitsmuis
ES	Musgaño patiblanco	NO	Vannspissmus
FI	Vesipäästäinen	PL	Rzęsorek rzeczek
FO	-	PT	-
FR	Crossope aquatique	RO	Chiţcanul-de-apă
GR	Νερομυγαλίδα	RU	Водяная кутора
HR	Vodena rovka	SE	Vattennäbbmus
HU	Közönséges vízicickány	SI	Povodna rovka
IR	-	SK	Dulovnica vodná
IS	Vatnasnjáldra	TR	Su sivriburunu
IT	Toporagno acquatico	YU	Водена ровчица

Distribution

World: Palaearctic. From Britain and Arctic Scandinavia across Siberia to Lake Baikal, Far East and Sakhalin Island.
Europe: southern European border runs along the Cantabrian mountains, the Pyrénées, Alps, Abruzze and mountains of the Balkan Peninsula.

Geographic variation

In spite of fairly high levels of genetic variation between populations, only little geographic variation in morphology except for the north Spanish population, which is large in size and characterized by a dental feature. This population is recognized by most authors as a distinct subspecies *N. fodiens niethammeri* Bühler, 1963, while the British water shrew *N. f. bicolor* (Shaw, 1791) does not deserve subspecific rank.

Habitat

The most aquatic of the European shrews. All kinds of riparian and littoral habitats, such as marine shores, lakes and rivers, but also swamps, humid woodland, wet meadows and even fields in the northern parts of its range. In the south confined to mountainous areas (attaining 2500 m above sea level in the Alps) living along fast-flowing mountain brooks and small rivers, in riverine forests and reedbeds of lakes.

Population status

Well adapted to all kinds of aquatic environment, but local populations may suffer from loss of habitat through drainage of wetlands, destruction of river banks and shortage of suitable food due to water acidification and water pollution with pesticides and fertilizers. Densities fluctuate strongly in relation to seasons and between years.

International legal & conservation status

Bern Convention, Appendix III.

Literature

Catzeflis (1984)
Spitzenberger (1990b) – review

F. Spitzenberger

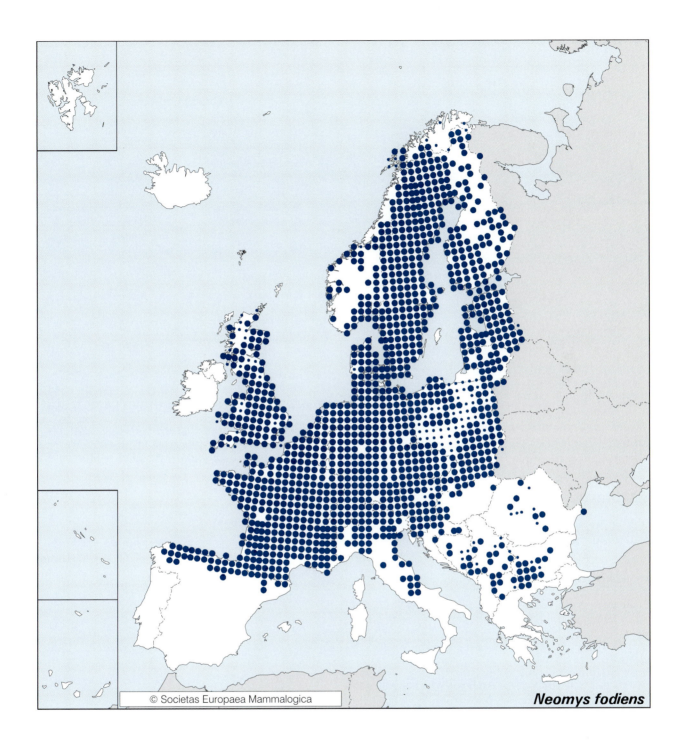

Neomys fodiens

Crocidura canariensis Hutterer, López-Jurado & Vogel, 1987

P. Twisk

Canary shrew

AL	-	LU	-
BG	-	LV	-
CZ	Bělozubka kanárská	MK	-
DE	Kanarenspitzmaus	MT	-
DK	-	NL	Canarische spitsmuis
EE	-	NO	-
ES	Musaraña canaria	PL	Zębiełek kanaryjski
FI	Kanarianpäästäinen	PT	Musaranho-de-dentes-brancos das Canárias
FO	-		
FR	Crocidure des Canaries	RO	-
GR	-	RU	-
HR	Kanarska rovka	SE	-
HU	Kanári-cickány	SI	Kanarska belozoba rovka
IR	-	SK	-
IS	-	TR	-
IT	Crocidura delle Canarie	YU	-
LT	-		

It has been argued, on the basis of a mandibular study, that *C. canariensis* should be treated as a subspecies of *C. sicula*. However, other biological and morphological information support its specific status. A revision of the entire group is required.

Distribution

Endemic to the eastern Canary Islands. Occurs on Fuerteventura, Lobos, Lanzarote and Mt. Clara.

Geographic variation

The shrews of Mt. Clara are larger and paler than the shrews living on the other islands.

Habitat

Canary shrews live in barren lava fields which are locally called 'malpaís', and in other rocky areas. They live also in nearby gardens and agricultural land. On Mt. Clara, they occur in coastal sand dunes.

Population status

Appears to be common in Fuerteventura and Lanzarote, based on the analysis of barn owl pellets. Large portions of its principal habitat, the malpaís, have been destroyed in the past. Other portions remain within nature reserves. The species is now extinct on Graciosa and Alegranza, from which the islands Holocene fossils are known.

International legal & conservation status

Bern Convention, Appendix II.
EU Habitats & Species Directive, Annex IV.
IUCN Red List, Vulnerable.

Literature

Hutterer *et al.* (1992)
Sarà (1996)

R. Hutterer

© Societas Europaea Mammalogica

Crocidura canariensis

Crocidura leucodon (Hermann, 1780)

M. Năzăreanu

Bi-coloured white-toothed shrew

AL	Hundegjati barkebardhe	LU	Feldspëtzmaus
BG	Белокоремна белозъбка	LV	Baltkrūtainais baltzobcirslis
CZ	Bělozubka bělobřichá	MK	Полска ровка
DE	Feldspitzmaus	MT	-
DK	Markspidsmus	NL	Veldspitsmuis
EE	Põllukarilik	NO	Markspissmus
ES	Musaraña bicolor	PL	Zębiełek białawy
FI	Kenttäpäästäinen	PT	-
FO	-	RO	Chiţcanul-de-câmp;
FR	Crocidure leucode		Cârticioara
GR	Χωραφομυγαλίδα	RU	Белобрюхая белозубка
HR	Dvobojna rovka	SE	Fältnäbbmus
HU	Mezei cickány	SI	Poljska rovka
IR	-	SK	Bielozúbka bielobruchá
IS	Akursnjáldra	TR	Tarla sivriburunu
IT	Crocidura ventre bianco	YU	Пољска ровчица
LT	Dvispalvis baltadantis kirstukas		

Distribution

World: Europe and western Asia from north-west France to the Caspian Sea, from 5°W to 55°E and 35° to 53°N.

Europe: absent from a large part of southern France, the Iberian Peninsula and apparently from all major Mediterranean islands except Lesbos. Western and northern border in the Netherlands and Germany fluctuating owing to habitat deterioriation and competition with the common white-toothed shrew *C. russula,* which is the same size and weight.

Geographic variation

Two subspecies are currently recognized: *C. leucodon leucodon* (Hermann, 1780) and *C. l. narentae* Bolkay, 1925. Their respective ranges are not completely understood. A long corridor comprising the Alps, western Austria, Bohemia and western Poland seems to separate a northern and southern population in Europe. This separation runs through the presumed range of the nominate subspecies, but it is not established whether this affects diversification at the subspecific level.

Habitat

In central Europe and in Italy, *C. leucodon* is found mainly in open country, particularly in agricultural landscapes. It is tolerant of even less cover than the two other *Crocidura* species that occur in the same area. At the northern edge of its range, it tends to associate with urban areas, including gardens and even houses. This trend is particularly marked in Poland, where the species is rare in small towns and villages and more common in larger towns. In western France, it is found in moist habitats with thick cover, together with *Sorex minutus* and *Neomys fodiens.* In the Balkans and in Asia Minor it occurs also in mountains, frequenting moist localities such as rocky screes, banks of rivers and brooks as well as stone walls.

Population status

Seems to be decreasing or at least temporarily fluctuating, especially at the northern and western borders of its range. As its preferred habitat is open rural country, it is affected by intensive agriculture (pesticides, loss of cover and food as a consequence of large-scale monocultures and the clearing of agriculturally unproductive land).

International legal & conservation status

Bern Convention, Appendix III.

Literature

Krapp (1990) – review

F. Krapp

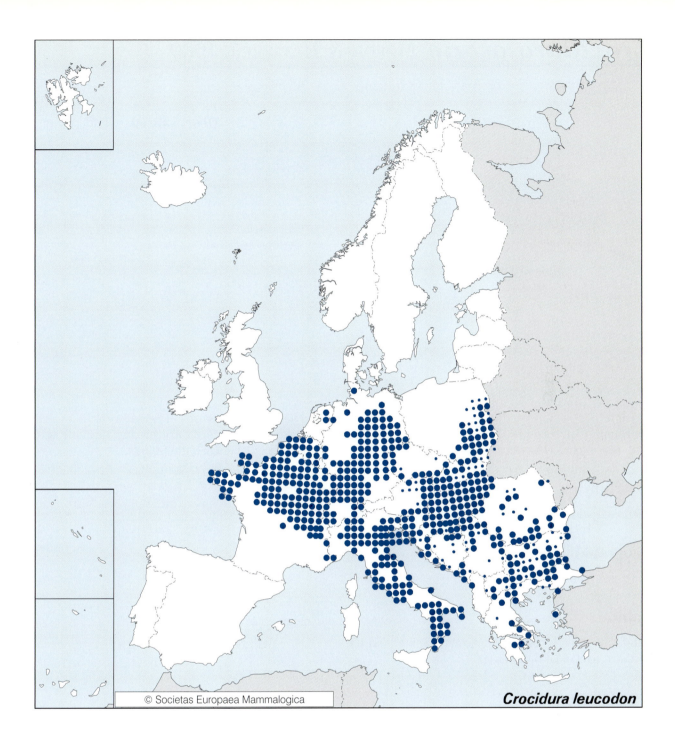

© Societas Europaea Mammalogica

Crocidura leucodon

Crocidura osorio Molina & Hutterer, 1989

T. P. McOwat

Osorio shrew			
AL	-	IT	-
BG	-	LT	-
CZ	Bělozubka malá	LU	-
DE	Osorio-Spitzmaus	LV	-
DK	-	MK	-
EE	-	MT	-
ES	Musaraña de Osorio	NL	-
FI	Osorionpäästäinen	NO	-
FO	-	PL	Zębiełek Osorio
FR	Crocidure de la Grande Canarie	PT	-
		RO	-
GR	-	RU	-
HR	Planinska kanarska rovka	SE	-
		SI	-
HU	Osorio-cickány	SK	-
IR	-	TR	-
IS	-	YU	-

C. osorio is closely related to *C. russula* but differs in the number of chromosomes, morphology, ecology, vocalization, and behaviour.

Distribution

Endemic to the Canary island of Gran Canaria, Spain.

Geographic variation

None observed.

Habitat

Humid evergreen forest and degraded habitats in the northern part of Gran Canaria.

Population status

Undetermined. The species is not common throughout its range. A recent census of the species (O. Molina, pers. comm.) has shown again that it is restricted to the northern and most humid part of the island.

International legal & conservation status

Bern Convention, Appendix III.
IUCN Red List, Vulnerable.

Other information

Since its discovery in Gran Canaria, two specimens have been found in the suburbs of Santa Cruz, the capital of Tenerife. These records are presumably due to the frequent traffic between the islands.

Literature

Hutterer *et al.* (1992)
Molina & Hutterer (1989)

R. Hutterer

© Societas Europaea Mammalogica

Crocidura osorio

Crocidura russula (HERMANN, 1780)

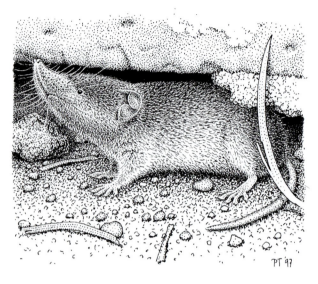

P. Twisk

Many Asiatic and African populations previously assigned to *C. russula* actually represent other species. Animals from central and eastern Europe, Asia Minor and Israel must be considered as *C. suaveolens* according to allozyme and karyotype analyses.

Distribution

World: Palaearctic including North Africa (Tunisia, Algeria and Morocco).
Europe: Iberian Peninsula, France, some Atlantic and Channel islands, Benelux states, Germany, western Switzerland and western Austria. Also on some Mediterranean islands: Ibiza, Sardinia and Pantelleria. Missing from the British Isles and absent south of the Alps.

Geographic variation

Many subspecies have been described, but biochemical studies showed a remarkable genetic uniformity. Only *C. russula ichnusae* Festa, 1912 from Sardinia and *C. r. yebalensis* Cabrera, 1913 from North Africa seem to be valid.

Habitat

In the northern part of its range and at higher altitudes it is mainly associated with human settlements, living in gardens and houses. Commensalism more pronounced during winter, when, specially in mountainous habitats, territoriality is lost. In the Mediterranean region it occurs in a great variety of habitats, but seems to prefer open or semi-open grasslands, cultivated areas, low shrubs, as well as ecotone formations and, above all, old terraces with dry stone walls.

Population status

Quite common and well distributed all over its range. Can reach high densities and, in the Mediterranean region, is often the dominant prey species in the barn owl's diet. Due to its synanthropic habits, can suffer from the use of insecticides and other toxic chemicals.

International legal & conservation status

Bern Convention, Appendix III.
Fully protected in some countries.

Literature

Catalan *et al.* (1988)
Genoud & Hutterer (1990) – review
Hutterer (1993)
Sarà *et al.* (1990)

M. G. Ramalhinho, R. Libois and R. Fons

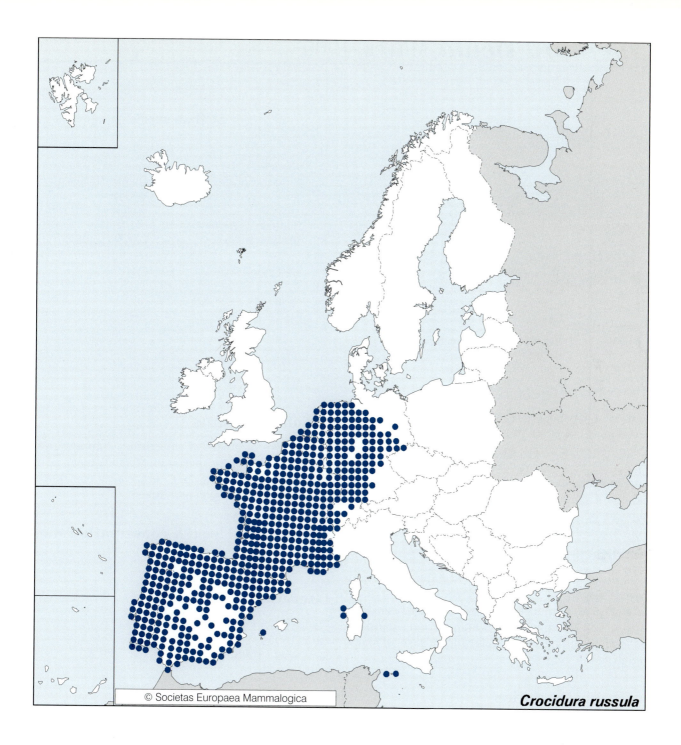

© Societas Europaea Mammalogica

Crocidura russula

69

Crocidura sicula Miller, 1900

T. P. McOwat

Sicilian shrew

AL	-	LU	-
BG	-	LV	-
CZ	Bělozubka sicilská	MK	-
DE	Sizilienspitzmaus	MT	Ġurdien Geddumu Twil
DK	-		ta' Għawdex
EE	-	NL	Siciliaanse spitsmuis
ES	Musaraña de Sicilia	NO	-
FI	Sisilianpäästäinen	PL	Zębiełek sycylijski
FO	-	PT	-
FR	Crocidure de Sicile	RO	-
GR	-	RU	-
HR	Sicilijanska rovka	SE	-
HU	Szicíliai cickány	SI	Sicilska belozoba rovka
IR	-	SK	-
IS	-	TR	-
IT	Crocidura siciliana	YU	-
LT	-		

Status as independent species proved by its particular karyotype of 2N = 36, NF = 56. Before chromosomal recognition, this shrew was variously assigned to *C. russula, C. suaveolens* and *C. leucodon*. A similar karyotype is shown also by *C. canariensis*. Genetic analyses of Moroccan species are needed to understand the origin of these two island shrews.

Distribution

Endemic to the Sicilian-Maltese archipelago and at present found on Sicily, the Egadi Islands (e.g., Favignana, Marettimo, Levanzo), Ustica, and Gozo. May be extinct on Malta, where it is known from subfossils. The fossil material from the Ghar Dalam cave on Malta belongs to the same species.

Geographic variation

Owing to their smaller size in comparison with the nominate subspecies of Sicily, the populations of Gozo (*C. sicula calypso* Hutterer, 1991) and of the Egadi Islands (*C. s. aegatensis* Hutterer, 1991) have been described as geographic races.

Habitat

Based on owl pellet analyses, *C. sicula* inhabits suburban and agricultural land as well as open scrubland. In summer, its association with humid habitats is obvious.

Population status

Much lower numbers in comparable trapping results than other *Crocidura* species on Mediterranean islands (*C. russula* on Pantelleria, *C. suaveolens* on Crete and Lesbos and *C. leucodon* on Lesbos).

International legal & conservation status

Bern Convention, Appendix III.

Literature

Maddalena *et al.* (1990) – review
Sarà (1996)
Sarà *et al.* (1990)
Vogel (1988)

P. Vogel

© Societas Europaea Mammalogica

Crocidura sicula

Crocidura suaveolens (PALLAS, 1811)

Z. Bihari

Lesser white-toothed shrew

AL	Hundegjati i vogel	LT	Mažasis baltadantis
BG	Малка белозъбка		kirstukas
CZ	Bělozubka šedá	LU	Gaardespëtzmaus
DE	Gartenspitzmaus	LV	Mazais baltzobcirslis
DK	Havespidsmus	MK	Градинарска ровка
EE	Väikekarilik; Kodumutt	MT	-
ES	Musaraña de campo	NL	Tuinspitsmuis
FI	Kotipäästäinen	NO	Hagespissmus
FO	-	PL	Zębiełek karliczek
FR	Crocidure des jardins	PT	Musaranho-pequeno-de-
GR	Κηπομυγαλίδα		dentes-brancos
HR	Poljska rovka	RO	Chiţcanul-de-grădină
HU	Keleti cickány	RU	Малая белозубка
IR	-	SE	Trädgårdsnäbbmus
IS	-	SI	Vrtna rovka
IT	Crocidura minore	SK	Bielozúbka krpatá
		TR	Bahçe sivriburunu
		YU	Вртна ровчица

Allozyme and karyotype analyses demonstrated that shrews from Corsica, eastern Europe, Asia Minor and Israel previously considered as *C. russula* are in fact *C. suaveolens*.

Distribution

World: Palaearctic south of the 54th parallel from the Atlantic coast to Japan (Tsushima island). Known from Israel and Saudi Arabia, Asia Minor and the Caucasus, Kara-Kum and Kyzyl-Kum deserts as far as Lake Balkhash (Kazakhstan), southern Kyrgyzstan, North and South Korea, Taiwan, lowlands of north-eastern China between Shanghai and Beijing.
Europe: north-west of the Iberian Peninsula, western France (including some Atlantic and Channel islands) and from southern France to Italy and the Balkans, and to central and eastern Europe north to Poland. On most of the eastern Mediterranean islands and on Menorca, Corsica, Elba and Capraia.

Geographic variation

Morphologically and biochemically polymorphic. Size variation on the continent is obviously independent from genetic relationships. Several subspecies, many of them from islands, have been described, mainly due to their large size, but their status is not clear. Electrophoretic data indicate, that *Crocidura suavolens cypria* Bate, 1904 from Cyprus is biochemically more distant from Turkish populations than is the case with *C. s. caneae*

Miller, 1909 from Crete. *C. s. enezsizunensis* (Heim de Balsac & Beaufort, 1966) from the isle of Sein is probably extinct and replaced by *C. russula*.

Habitat

In north-eastern Europe and at higher altitudes synanthropic (houses, gardens and parks) especially in winter. In western and southern Europe occurs in a wide variety of habitats. Avoids dense forests, but is abundant in hedges, vineyards, olive groves, in coastal sand dunes and may also occur around boulders in mountainous areas. In the Mediterranean region in dry (old terraces with stone walls and in low maquis scrub) and wet places with dense vegetation. Found at altitudes between sea level and 1600 m but is quite rare above 1000 m.

Population status

Not very common in the western part of its range and much less abundant than *C. russula* when sympatric. Seems to have been replaced by *C. russula* owing to competitive exclusion mainly on small islands, but also in many continental places. May suffer from the use of insecticides and other toxic chemicals in agricultural areas.

International legal & conservation status

Bern Convention, Appendix III, but *C. s. caneae* is on Appendix II as *C. s. ariadne*.

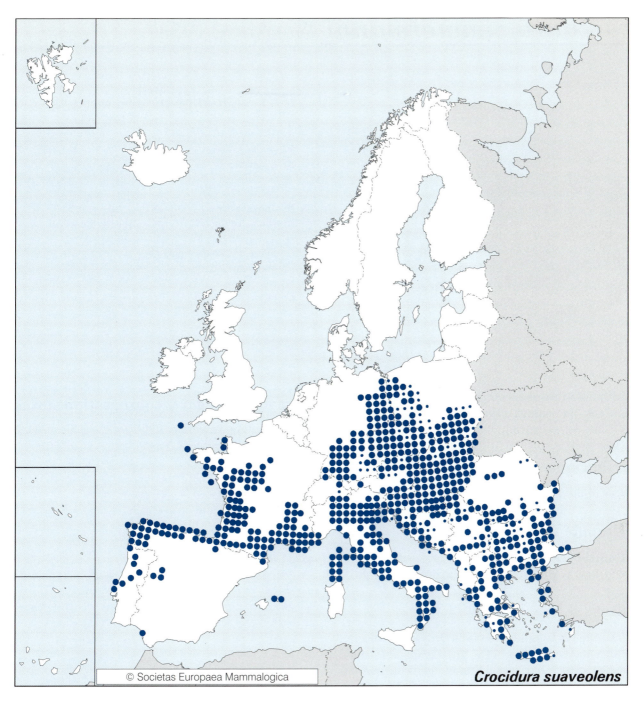

© Societas Europaea Mammalogica

Crocidura suaveolens

Literature

Cosson *et al.* (1996)
Ingelög *et al.* (1993)
Vlasák & Niethammer (1990) – review

R. Libois, M. G. Ramalhinho & R. Fons

Crocidura zimmermanni Wettstein, 1953

T. P. McOwat

Originally described as subspecies of *C. russula*, but now recognized as separate species on the basis of morphology, karyology and faunal history.

Distribution

Endemic to the island of Crete.

Geographic variation

No subspecies described; indications of size differences between central and western populations were found.

Habitat

Judging from the trapping sites (Ídhi Óros – type locality at 1400 m and Lévka Óri at 1150 m), this species seems to exist in rather harsh conditions (snow in winter, drought in summer). But the analysis of owl pellets collected at altitudes of 140–830 m revealed that this species also exists at low altitudes.
Syntopic with *C. suaveolens* at the type locality.

Population status

Seems to be very local and rare. 19 049 mammal remains from pellets of the barn owl *Tyto alba* contained only 150 *C. zimmermanni* but 2147 *C. suaveolens*.

International legal & conservation status

Bern Convention, Appendix III.
IUCN Red List, Vulnerable.

Literature

Pieper (1990) – review
Reumer (1986)
Vesmanis & Kahmann (1978)
Vogel (1986)

P. Vogel

© Societas Europaea Mammalogica

Crocidura zimmermanni

Suncus etruscus (SAVI, 1822)

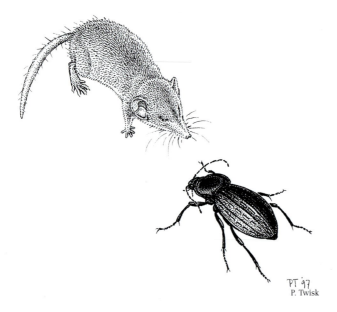

PT 97
P. Twisk

Distribution

World: southern Palaearctic from Portugal and Morocco to Arabia, Asia Minor, Caucasus, Turkmenistan, Tajikistan. Reported also from the Himalayas and south-west China (province of Yunnan), but small *Suncus* from southern India probably belong to a different species. Occurs also in savannahs and on mountains south of the Sahara. Small *Suncus* from Madagascar and the Comoros sometimes referred to as *S. madagascariensis* (Coquerel, 1848) may belong to *S. etruscus*.
Europe: restricted to the Mediterranean basin (including many islands).

Geographic variation

Sardinian specimens described as *S. etruscus pachyurus* Küster, 1835 are larger than those from southern Europe. A clinal variation is reported in Spain, specimens from the north being larger than those of the south.

Habitat

Confined to areas with mean July temperatures not less than 20°C. Prefers extensively used or abandoned olive groves and vineyards with old dry stone walls and stone-piles, but occurs also in low maquis shrub and open forests of Mediterranean oaks and pines. Sometimes in marsh areas. Avoids sand dunes, dense forests and intensively cultivated land, but found in gardens and even in old towns. Vertical distribution from the coast to more than 1000 m above sea level.

Population status

Unknown in most of its range. Much less common than *Crocidura russula* in trapping experiments and as barn owl prey. In Istria up to 74 times less common than *C. suaveolens,* but in the Marismas del Guadalquivir 14 times more common. Sensitive to insecticides and herbicides.

International legal & conservation status

Bern Convention, Appendix III.

Literature

Fons (1975a, b)
Libois (1984)
Lipej & Kryštufek (1992)
Rey & Landin (1973)
Spitzenberger (1990d)

R. Libois & R. Fons

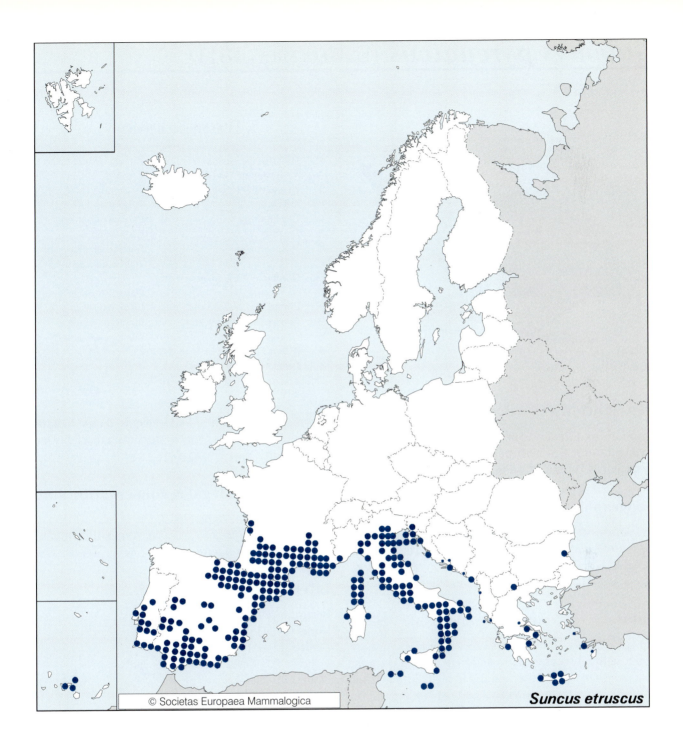

© Societas Europaea Mammalogica

Suncus etruscus

Galemys pyrenaicus (E. GEOFFROY, 1811)

D. Ovenden

Pyrenean desman

AL	-	LU	-
BG	Пиринейски вихохул	LV	Pireneju vihuhols
CZ	Vychuchol pyrenejský	MK	-
DE	Pyrenäen-Desman	MT	-
DK	Desman	NL	Pyreneese desman
EE	Piisammutik	NO	Pyreneisk desman;
ES	Desmán ibérico		Bisamspissmus
FI	Vesimaamyyrä	PL	Wychuchoł pirenejski
FO	-	PT	Toupeira-de-água
FR	Desman des Pyrénées	RO	-
GR	-	RU	Пиренейская выхухоль
HR	Pirenejska vodenkrtica	SE	Bisamnäbbmus
HU	Pireneusi pézsmacickány	SI	Pirenejski vihulj
IR	-	SK	Dezman pyrenejský
IS	Bísamsnjáldra	TR	-
IT	Desman dei Pirenei	YU	-
LT	-		

Distribution

Endemic to Europe: northern part of the Iberian Peninsula and isolated mountains in central Spain, occurring in Portugal, Spain, Andorra and France.

Geographic variation

Two subspecies have been described *(G. pyrenaicus pyrenaicus* and *G. p. rufulus* (Graells, 1897)), but their status is not clear. Desmans from the Pyrénées *(G. p. pyrenaicus)* seem to differ in size from other populations.

Habitat

Aquatic member of the mole family. Prefers fast-running water, with low temperature and high oxygen content. Occurs also in middle reaches and in high altitude lakes of the French Pyrénées as well as near the sea shore. Can survive in some moderately polluted watercourses. Vertical distribution: 5 –1800 m.

Population status

Probably in regression in most of the distribution area. Locally abundant only in regions influenced by Atlantic climate in the north-west of the Iberian Peninsula and on the French side of the Pyrénées. Densities of 6.15 ind./km of a watercourse in the Cordillera Cantábrica and 2.85 ind./km in the Navarro Pirineos were reported.

Main threats are water abstraction (particularly in watercourses characterized by low water-level in summer), pollution, destruction of riparian vegetation and the construction of hydroelectric dams. Incidental capture in fish nets is a locally important mortality factor (e.g. in north-east Portugal).

International legal & conservation status

Bern Convention, Appendix II.
EU Habitats & Species Directive, Annex II & Annex IV.
IUCN Red List, Vulnerable.

Literature

Bertrand (1993)
Nores (1991)
Queiroz *et al.* (1996)

A. I. Queiroz

© Societas Europaea Mammalogica

Galemys pyrenaicus

Talpa caeca SAVI, 1822

T. P. McOwat

Blind mole

AL	Urithi i verber	LT	-
BG	Сляпа къртица	LU	-
CZ	Krtek slepý	LV	-
DE	Blindmaulwurf	MK	Слеп крт
DK	Blind muldvarp	MT	-
EE	-	NL	Blinde mol
ES	Topo ciego	NO	Blind moldvarp
FI	Sokkokontiainen	PL	Kret ślepy
FO	-	PT	Toupeira-cega
FR	Taupe aveugle	RO	Cârtiţa-mică
GR	Τυφλασπάλακας	RU	Слепой крот
HR	Patuljasta krtica	SE	Blind mullvad
HU	Mediterrán vakond	SI	Sredozemski krt
IR	-	SK	Krt slepý
IS	Blindvarpa	TR	Akdeniz köstebeği
IT	Talpa cieca	YU	Слепа кртица

Distribution

Endemic to southern Europe: western Alps, the Apennines and the Balkans, between the Neretva river (Herzegovina) and the Gulf of Corinth (Greece). Records for the Romanian Carpathians require further support. Small blind moles with a caecoidal pelvis from European Turkey and south-eastern Bulgaria were recently ascribed to *T. levantis* Thomas, 1906, but this needs to be confirmed. Altitudinal distribution in the Alps between 200 and 1800 m and in the Balkans from sea level up to 2000 m, but only 18% of Balkan records are from below 1000 m.

Geographic variation

Balkan populations differ from the Alpine ones in the fundamental number of chromosome arms (NF = 68 and 70 respectively). Size is highly variable, the smallest moles in the Balkans coming from the area of sympatry with *T. europaea* or *T. stankovici* (both larger). Three subspecies reported from the Apennines and the Alps. Four Balkan subspecies were recently reduced to two.

Habitat

Deciduous woodlands, meadows and pastures. In karstic areas, restricted to places with deep soil, e.g. small fields at the bottom of dolines. In the Balkans, where it is sympatric with *T. europaea,* the latter species populates wetter places with deep soil, while the smaller *T. caeca* is displaced onto dryer, rockier ground.

Population status

Not known, but may be common locally. Distribution sporadic in karstic areas.

International legal & conservation status

None.

Literature

Kryštufek (1994)
Niethammer (1990a) – review
Simionescu (1971)
Vohralík (1991)

B. Kryštufek

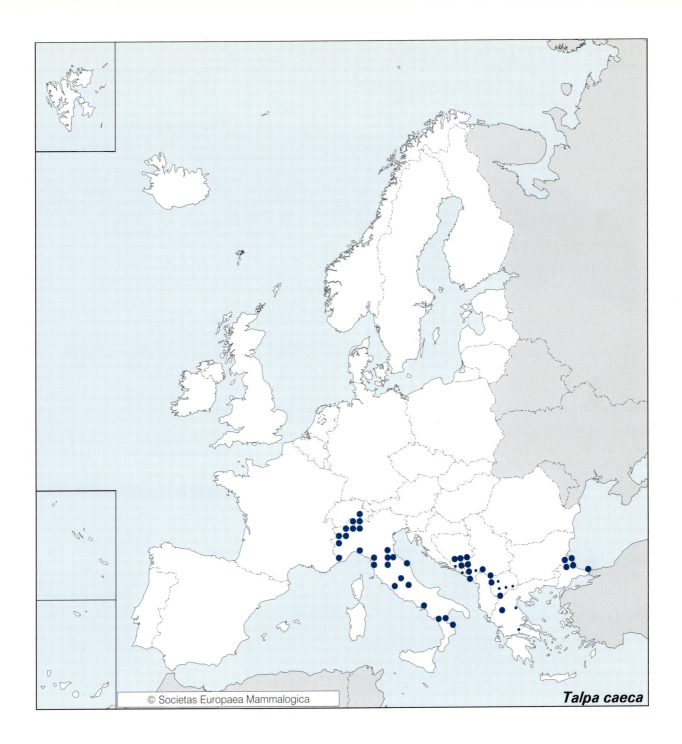

© Societas Europaea Mammalogica

Talpa caeca

Talpa europaea LINNAEUS, 1758

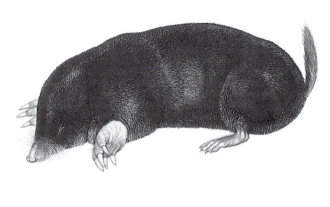

P. Barrett

Common mole

AL	Urithi	LT	Kurmis
BG	Обикновенна къртица	LU	Maulef
CZ	Krtek obecný	LV	Kurmis
DE	Maulwurf	MK	Обичен крт
DK	Muldvarp	MT	Talpa
EE	Mutt; Tava-mutt	NL	Mol
ES	Topo europeo	NO	Moldvarp
FI	Maamyyrä	PL	Kret
FO	Moldvørpa	PT	Toupeira-europeia
FR	Taupe d'Europe	RO	Cârtiţă
GR	Ασπάλακας	RU	Обыкновенный крот
HR	Europska krtica	SE	Mullvad
HU	Közönséges vakond	SI	Navadni krt
IR	-	SK	Krt podzemný
IS	Moldvarpa	TR	Avrupa köstebeği
IT	Talpa europea	YU	Европска кртица

Distribution

World: from the Pyrénées and Great Britain east to the rivers Ob and Irtysh.

Europe: widely distributed, but missing from Ireland, large parts of the Iberian peninsula, the southern Apennines, south Balkans and Scandinavia, where it occurs only in Denmark, south Sweden and Finland. Abundant on many islands in the Baltic Sea and around the British coast, but absent from most North Sea islands and all Mediterranean islands except Cres (north Adriatic).

Geographic variation

Size highly variable and usually decreasing with altitude. Significant interpopulation variability in the number of premolars, with supernumerary or missing teeth in the maxilla and mandible. The large number of described subspecies is frequently reduced to two, *T. europaea europaea* and *T. e. frisius* Müller, 1776, which differ in mean rostral breadth.

Habitat

A burrowing species, present in most habitats where the soil is deep enough to allow tunnelling. Common in periodically flooded meadows, agricultural grassland, arable land, and in deciduous woodland but rare in coniferous forests. Uncommon on stony, sandy, permanently waterlogged and acid soils. From sea level up to 1000 m in Scotland and 2400 m in the Alps.

Population status

Common in suitable habitats, with fairly stable populations. Population densities up to 16 per hectare.

International legal & conservation status

None.

Other information

The mole is commonly considered to be a pest of agricultural and amenity land and is widely persecuted. In some countries it is hunted intensively for its fur. About 250 000 skins were traded annually in Poland before 1960, but the species is no longer hunted there.

Literature

Niethammer (1990b) – review
Pucek (1981)

B. Kryštufek

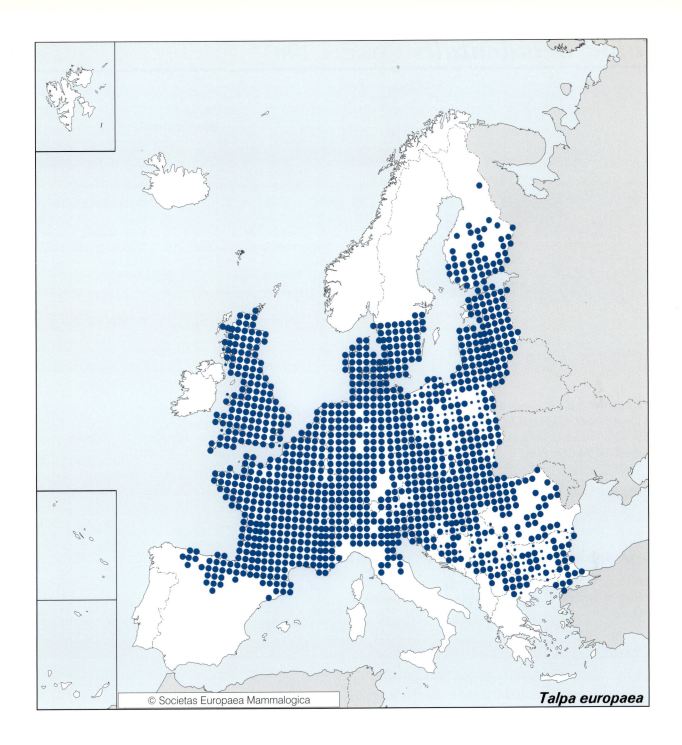

© Societas Europaea Mammalogica

Talpa europaea

Talpa occidentalis Cabrera, 1907

T. P. McOwat

Because of morphological similarity previously regarded a subspecies of *Talpa caeca*, but genetically so different from all other members of the genus *Talpa* that it has been given specific rank.

Distribution

Endemic to Portugal and Spain.

Geographic variation

Size variation throughout the range is related to ecological factors. Geographic variation has not been reported.

Habitat

Strictly fossorial species, living permanently in subterranean tunnel systems. In the wetter parts of the Iberian peninsula widely distributed in meadows; in the south increasingly confined to mountain areas up to 1300 m above sea level. Diet seems to consist mainly of earthworms.

Population status

Common throughout its range.

International legal & conservation status

None.

Iberian mole

AL	-	LU	-
BG	-	LV	-
CZ	Krtek iberský	MK	-
DE	Spanischer Maulwurf	MT	-
DK	-	NL	Iberische blinde mol
EE	-	NO	-
ES	Topo ibérico	PL	Kret zachodni
FI	Pyreneidenkontiainen	PT	Toupeira; Toupeira de Cabrera
FO	-		
FR	Taupe ibérique	RO	-
GR	Ρωμαϊκός ασπάλακας	RU	-
HR	Iberska krtica	SE	-
HU	Ibériai vakond	SI	Iberijski krt
IR	-	SK	-
IS	-	TR	-
IT	Talpa occidentale	YU	-
LT	-		

Literature

Filippucci *et al.* (1987)
Jimenez *et al.* (1984)
Niethammer (1990c) – review

A. Loy

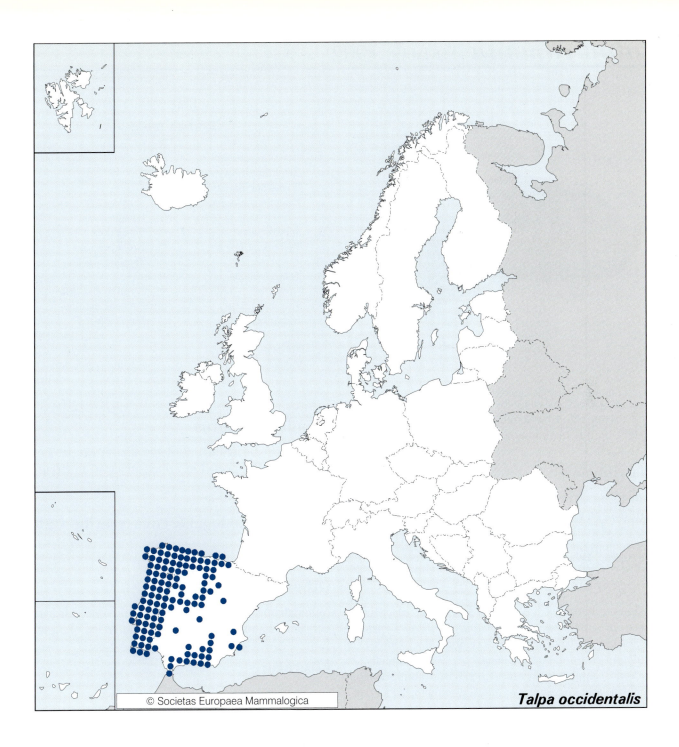

© Societas Europaea Mammalogica

Talpa occidentalis

Talpa romana THOMAS, 1902

T. P. McOwat

Roman mole

AL	-	LT	-
BG	Голямозъба къртица	LU	-
CZ	Krtek římský	LV	-
DE	Römischer Maulwurf	MK	-
DK	Romersk muldvarp	MT	-
EE	-	NL	Romeinse mol
ES	Topo romano	NO	Romersk moldvarp
FI	Italiankontiainen	PL	Kret apeniński
FO	-	PT	Toupeira-romana
FR	Taupe romaine	RO	-
GR	-	RU	Крупнозубый крот
HR	Talijanska krtica	SE	Romersk mullvad
HU	Római vakond	SI	Debelozobi krt
IR	-	SK	-
IS	Sólvarpa	TR	-
IT	Talpa romana	YU	Крупноэуба кртица

Differs from *Talpa europaea*, with which it is parapatric in Italy, mainly in skull and teeth proportions.

Distribution

Endemic to central and southern Italy. Never found in Sardinia and probably extinct in Sicily (last record 1885). Reports of an isolated population from southern France (Var region) need further confirmation.

Geographic variation

Various subspecies have been described, essentially based on skull size: *Talpa romana montana* Cabrera, 1925 from Abruzzo and Molise regions, the extinct *T. r. aenigmatica* Capolongo & Panasci, 1976 from Sicily, *T. r. adamoi* Capolongo & Panasci, 1976 from south-central Calabria, and *T. r. brachycrania* Capolongo & Panasci, 1976 from Lucania. More recent studies revealed that size follows a clinal variation, from northern large-sized specimens to southern small ones, suggesting the need of an accurate revision of the geographic variability.

Habitat

Strictly fossorial and territorial, lives permanently underground in individual tunnel systems. Found in a variety of habitats, from open fields to dense forests. Occurs from sea level to an altitude of about 2000 m.

Population status

Appears to be widespread across its range. Local declines are suspected in areas subjected to intensive field cultivation.

International legal & conservation status

None.

Other information

Although now recognized as endemic species, still legally persecuted and included in the national list of pests.

Literature

Capanna (1981)
Capolongo & Panascì (1976)
Filippucci *et al.* (1987)
Loy *et al.* (1996)
Niethammer (1990d) – review

A. Loy

© Societas Europaea Mammalogica

Talpa romana

Talpa stankovici V. Martino & E. Martino, 1931

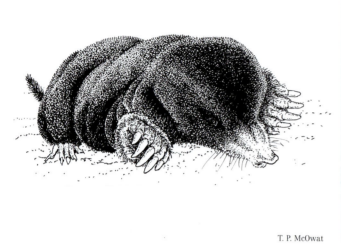

T. P. McOwat

Balkan mole

AL	Urithi i Stankovicit	LT	-
BG	-	LU	-
CZ	Krtek balkánský	LV	-
DE	Balkan-Maulwurf	MK	Реликтен крт
DK	-	MT	-
EE	-	NL	Balkan mol
ES	Topo de los Balcanes	NO	-
FI	Balkaninkontiainen	PL	Kret bałkański
FO	-	PT	-
FR	Taupe des Balkans	RO	-
GR	Βαλκανικός ασπάλακας	RU	-
HR	Balkanska krtica	SE	-
HU	Balkán-vakond	SI	Balkanski krt
IR	-	SK	-
IS	-	TR	-
IT	Talpa dei Balcani	YU	Балканска кртица

Described as a subspecies of *Talpa romana* and treated as such until recently, when allozyme and morphometric studies confirmed its independent specific status.

Distribution

Endemic to Europe. Restricted to the Balkans west of the River Vardar (Axios): southern Montenegro, western Macedonia, north-eastern Greece and probably Albania. Single island record from Corfu.

Geographic variation

Fundamental number of chromosomal arms variable (NF = 66 or 64). Altitude does not affect size in Macedonian populations. Two subspecies are recognized, based mainly on size.

Habitat

Open habitats, from sandy beaches at sea level up to high mountain pastures above the timber line. Avoids dry skeletal soils, which limits its distribution in the lowlands. Lives in sympatry with *T. caeca* but not with *T. europaea*. Altitudinal range from sea level up to 2200 m in Macedonia and 2300 m in Greece.

Population status

Not known, but may be locally abundant.

International legal & conservation status

None.

Literature

Filippucci *et al.* (1987)
Kryštufek (1994)
Niethammer (1990e) – review

B. Kryštufek

© Societas Europaea Mammalogica

Talpa stankovici

Rhinolophus blasii PETERS, 1866

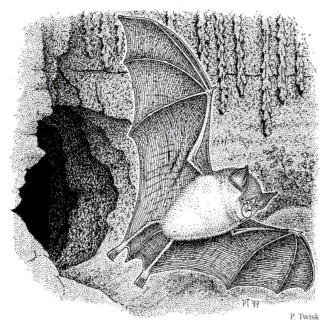

P. Twisk

Blasius' horseshoe bat

AL	Lakuriqnate hundepatkua i Blasiusit	IT	Ferro di cavallo di Blasius
		LT	-
BG	Средиземноморски подковонос	LU	Blasius-Huffeisennues
		LV	-
CZ	Vrápenec Blasiův	MK	Бласиев потковичар
DE	Blasius-Hufeisennase	MT	-
DK	Blasius' hesteskonæse	NL	Blasius' hoefijzerneus
EE	-	NO	Blasiushesteskonese
ES	Murciélago dálmata de herradura	PL	Podkowiec Blasiusa
		PT	-
FI	Blasinhevosenkenkäyökkö	RO	Liliacul-lui-Blasius
FO	-	RU	Средиземноморский подковонос
FR	Rhinolophe de Blasius		
GR	Ρινόλοφος του Blasius	SE	Blasius hästskonäsa
HR	Blazijev potkovnjak	SI	Blasijev podkovnjak
HU	Blasius-patkósdenevér	SK	-
IR	-	TR	-
IS	-	YU	Средоэемни потковичар

Distribution

World: from south-eastern Europe to the Caucasus, Kopet-Dag and Pakistan; the Near East; Africa, from the Mediterranean coast across Ethiopia and Eritrea, south to Transvaal.

Europe: restricted to south-western Romania and the Balkans. Found also on adjacent islands, including Crete.

Geographic variation

Four subspecies are currently recognized. Only the nominate form in Europe (extends as far east as Iran).

Habitat

Mediterranean and sub-Mediterranean woodlands. Roosting sites in Europe and Asia in natural or man-made caves; *Rhinolophus euryale* seems to be its most frequent associate in the Balkans. Summer colonies also in attics in the northern part of the range (Romania).

Population status

Not known, but probably the rarest European horseshoe bat. Presumably extinct in the north-western part of its historical distribution area (Istria, Karst of Trieste). Decrease documented also in Romania.

International legal & conservation status

Bern Convention, Appendix II.
Bonn Convention, Appendix II.
EU Habitats & Species Directive, Annex II & Annex IV.
IUCN Red List, Lower Risk – near threatened.

Other information

Human disturbance and loss of caves are the main threats. Endangered by fumigation of caves with organochlorine pesticides in Israel.

Literature

Koopman (1994)
Kryštufek & Đulić (in press) – review
Kryštufek & Petrov (1989)
Stebbings & Griffith (1986)

B. Kryštufek

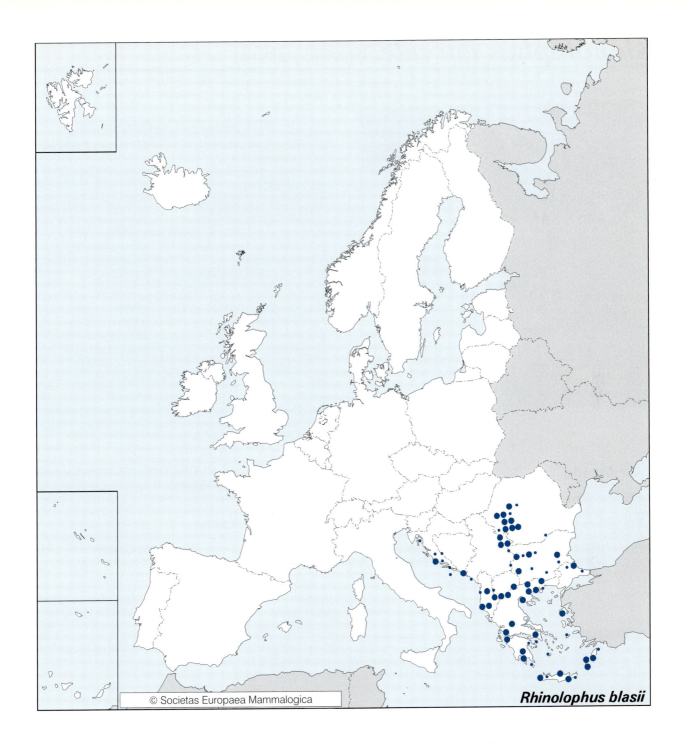

© Societas Europaea Mammalogica

Rhinolophus blasii

91

Rhinolophus euryale Blasius, 1853

P. Twisk

Distribution

World: Palaearctic; north-western Africa (Morocco to Tunisia), southern Europe, Near Orient to Turkmenia and Iran.

Europe: southern part of the continent, north to central France, southern Slovakia and western Romania. Present on large Mediterranean islands, but absent on the Balearics.

Geographic variation

Four subspecies recognized; only the nominate form in Europe.

Habitat

Roosts throughout the year in caves and artificial underground shelters, rare in buildings. Nursing colonies large, most often from 50 to 400 females, usually located below 1000 m altitude. Frequently found in clusters with *Rhinolophus ferrumequinum, Myotis emarginatus,* and *Miniopterus schreibersii* during the breeding season, and with *R. ferrumequinum* during hibernation. Sex ratio in colonies about 1:1 during the whole year, which is very uncommon in European bats. Preys on moths and other insects within or near vegetation, preferring areas with at least some bush and arboreal cover. Sedentary, short range movements between breeding and hibernation roosts. Longest recorded movement 134 km.

Population status

Population decline of about 70% observed in France between 1940 and 1980. All of the 83 colonies studied disappeared or showed critical decrease due to uncontrolled ringing, speleological disturbance in caves, and intensive usage of organochlorine pesticides. A slow recovery noticed between 1980 and 1987. A large population decline reported from Slovakia, although some colonies of 100–200 remain.

International legal & conservation status

Bern Convention, Appendix II.
Bonn Convention, Appendix II.
EU Habitats & Species Directive, Annex II & Annex IV.
IUCN Red List, Vulnerable.

Other information

Total protection of all of the cave roosts is urgently required. In some areas of southern Iberia, its dropping piles are used as fertilizer.

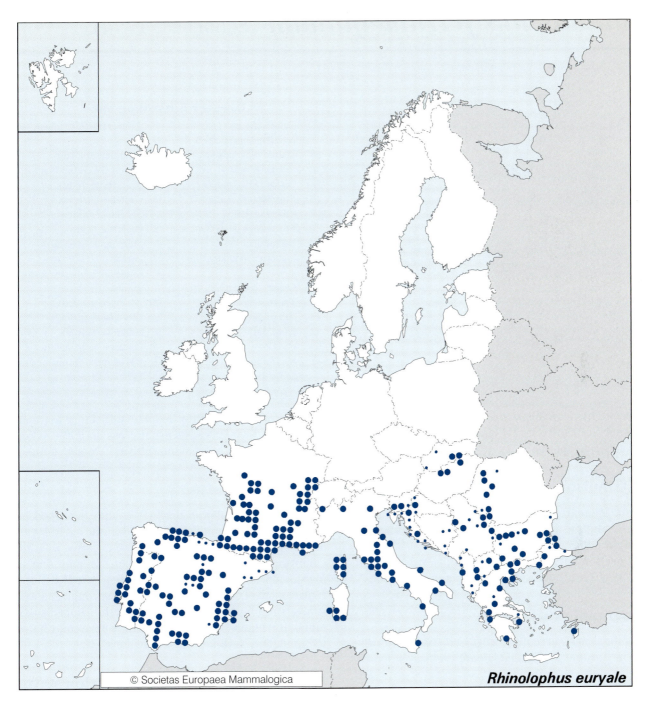

© Societas Europaea Mammalogica

Rhinolophus euryale

Literature

Brosset *et al.* (1988)
Brosset & Caubère (1959)
Schober & Grimmberger (1989)
Stebbings & Griffith (1986)

C. Ibáñez

Rhinolophus ferrumequinum (Schreber, 1774)

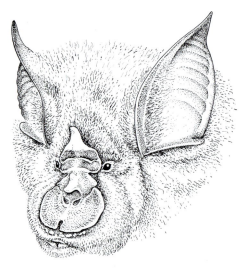

T. P. McOwat

Greater horseshoe bat

AL	Lakuriqnate hundepatkua i madh	LU	Grouss Huffeisennues
BG	Голям подковонос	LV	-
CZ	Vrápenec velký	MK	Голем потковичар
DE	Große Hufeisennase	MT	Farfett il-Lejl tan-Nagħla Kbir; Rinolofu Kbir
DK	Stor hesteskonæse	NL	Grote hoefijzerneus
EE	Suur-sagarnina	NO	Stor hesteskonese
ES	Murciélago grande de herradura	PL	Podkowiec duży
FI	Isohevosenkenkäyökkö	PT	Morcego-de-ferradura-grande
FO	-	RO	Liliacul-cu-nas-potcoavă-mare
FR	Grand rhinolophe		
GR	Τρανορινόλοφος	RU	Большой подковонос
HR	Veliki potkovnjak	SE	Stor hästskonäsa
HU	Nagy patkósdenevér	SI	Veliki podkovnjak
IR	-	SK	Podkovár stíhlokrídly
IS	Skeifublaka	TR	Büyük nal burunlu yarasa
IT	Ferro di cavallo maggiore	YU	Велики потковичар
LT	-		

Rhinolophus ferrumequinum nippon Temminck, 1835 from northern and central China, Korea, and Japan may be a separate species.

Distribution

World: Palaearctic; temperate Eurasia from Britain to Japan, south to north-western Africa, Palestine, Iran, Pakistan and northern India.
Europe: southern and central Europe, also south and west Wales and south-western England.

Geographic variation

Six subspecies currently recognized, with two occurring in Europe: *R. ferrumequinum creticus* Iliopoulou-Georgudaki & Ondrias, 1986 (Crete) and *R. f. ferrumequinum* (remainder of European range and north-western Africa). Size clines occur, with larger specimens found in warmer climates.

Habitat

Requires warm caves, mines or attic roosts for summer births and development of young, adjacent to grazed permanent pastures and deciduous woodland. In mountains usually below 800 m altitude, rarely up to 2000 m. Mean temperature (minimum 10°C) in April and May is crucial since it determines birth timing and population levels. Hunts mainly beetles and moths at low levels over grass and in woodland or its edges by hawking or perch feeding. Sedentary. Distance between summer and winter roosts usually less than 20–30 km. Longest recorded movement 180 km.

Population status

Documented population declines in the UK, based on long-term ringing studies, occurred in the early 1960s and 1980s and were probably due to negative weather conditions. The loss of insect food supplies due to insecticide use or changes in farming practices, and replacement of deciduous trees by conifers, either slowed recovery or made it impossible. Finally the loss of disused mines and human disturbance in caves have contributed to population declines in some regions.

International legal & conservation status

Bern Convention, Appendix II.
Bonn Convention, Appendix II.
EU Habitats & Species Directive, Annex II & Annex IV.
IUCN Red List, Lower Risk – conservation dependent.

Other information

Changes in habitat use may affect the larger *R. ferrumequinum* and smaller *R. hipposideros* differently. Declines in the former's populations seem to be linked to increases in the latter in south-west England.

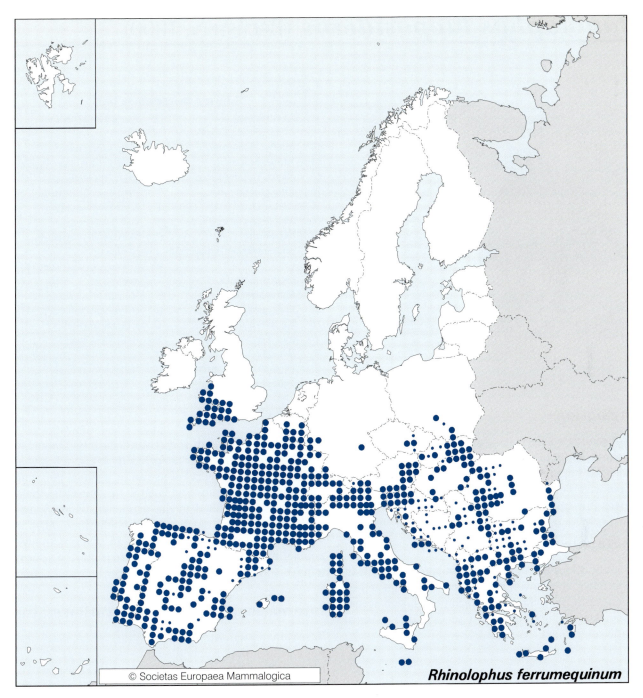

© Societas Europaea Mammalogica

Rhinolophus ferrumequinum

Literature

Horáček (1984)
Kryštufek (1993)
Ransome (1989, 1990)
Ransome & McOwat (1994)

R. D. Ransome

Rhinolophus hipposideros (BECHSTEIN, 1800)

P. Twisk

Distribution

World: mainly western Palaearctic, from Ireland east to Kashmir, south to north-western Africa, and through western Arabia to Ethiopia and Sudan.
Europe: widely distributed through western, central, and southern Europe.

Geographic variation

Taxonomic allocation of several populations is unclear, and from two up to seven subspecies are recognized by different authors. Evidence of variation in size across Europe, which may be related to variation in local climatic conditions.

Habitat

Originally roosted in caves throughout the year, now more frequently roosts in buildings during the summer months. Makes extensive use of night roosts, which are often small outbuildings or caves. Recorded from sea level up to 2000 m altitude. Forages within or along the edges of broadleaf deciduous woodland and riparian vegetation. Where habitat is fragmented, hedgerows and other linear landscape features, such as tree lines, are important commuting routes and foraging areas. Preys mainly on Diptera, Lepidoptera, and Neuroptera. Sedentary; winter and summer roosts usually within 5–10 km. Longest recorded movement 153 km.

Population status

Although widespread, many authors have reported population declines over the past fifty years, notably in the more northern parts of its range, such as Belgium, Luxembourg, Germany and Poland. In some cases these declines have resulted in the extinction of previously healthy populations, such as in the Netherlands (1983). Vulnerable across most of its present range, although populations in areas where roosts are protected appear to have stabilized or started to recover.

International legal & conservation status

Bern Convention, Appendix II.
Bonn Convention, Appendix II.
EU Habitats & Species Directive, Annex II & Annex IV.
IUCN Red List, Vulnerable.

Other information

Conspicuous in both summer and winter roosts, and thus highly sensitive to intentional or unintentional disturbance. Dereliction or renovation of old buildings may also result in the loss of suitable roosting sites. Removal of continuous linear landscape features may isolate colonies from potential foraging areas.

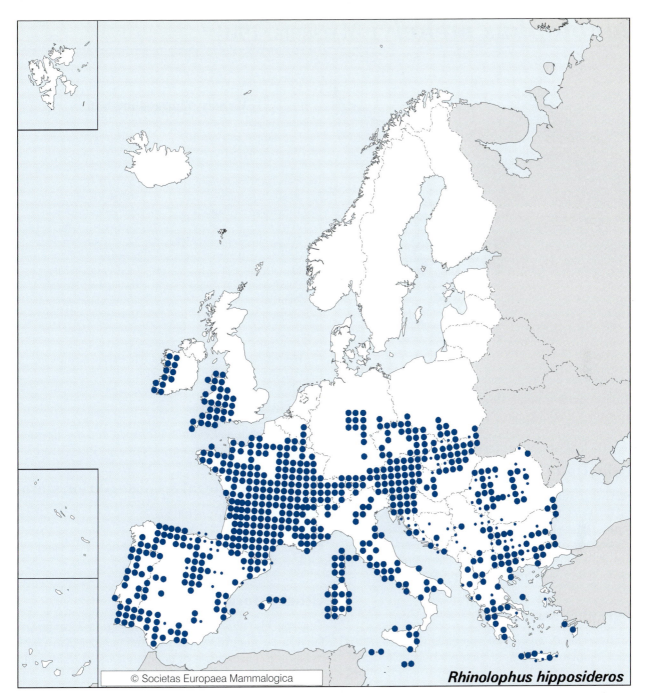

© Societas Europaea Mammalogica

Rhinolophus hipposideros

Literature

Beck (1995)
Kokurewicz (1990)
Koopman (1994)
Pir (1996)
Roer (1984)
van Vliet & Mostert (1997).

H. W. Schofield

97

Rhinolophus mehelyi Matschie, 1901

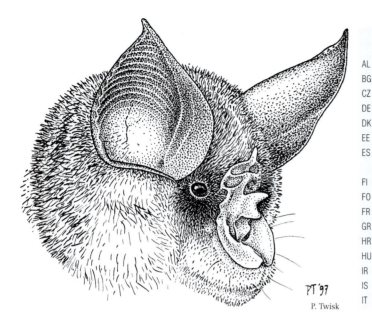

PT '97
P. Twisk

Confusion with morphologically similar species, particularly *R. euryale,* has obscured its range in certain regions.

Distribution

World: North Africa and southern Europe through Asia Minor to Transcaucasia and western Iran.
Europe: the range probably discontinuous, with populations in central and southern Iberia, southern France, Balkan peninsula, south-eastern Romania, the Caucasus, and some large Mediterranean islands.

Geographic variation

The subspecies *R. mehelyi carpetanus* Cabrera, 1904 (Iberian peninsula) and *R. m. tunetae* Deleuil & Labbé, 1955 (northern Africa) are not accepted by most authors. The species is, therefore, considered to be monotypic.

Habitat

Exclusively a cave-dwelling bat associated with Mediterranean and sub-Mediterranean climates. During parturition it is often found in dense colonies shared with other species, such as *Myotis myotis, M. blythii,* and *Miniopterus schreibersii.* Hibernates in less dense, sometimes large colonies, which may also include individuals of other species. Roosting requirements vary throughout the year, forcing it to make migrations between roosts. Movements of up to 90 km recorded. Foraging behaviour unknown.

Population status

Seems to be almost extinct in France and has declined in various parts of its range.

International legal & conservation status

Bern Convention, Appendix II.
Bonn Convention, Appendix II.
EU Habitats & Species Directive, Annex II & Annex IV.
IUCN Red List, Vulnerable.

Other information

The species' dependence on underground cavities of fairly large dimensions restricts the number of available roosts and concentrates its populations. Disturbance and roost damage are the most serious threats.

Literature

DeBlase (1972)
Kowalski *et al.* (1986)
Strinati & Aellen (1958)

L. Rodrigues & J. M. Palmeirim

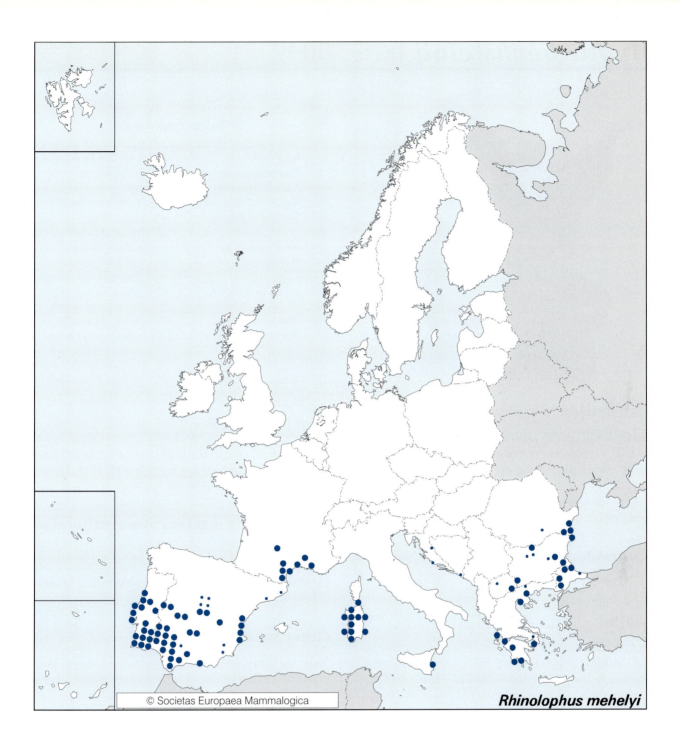

© Societas Europaea Mammalogica

Rhinolophus mehelyi

Myotis bechsteinii (KUHL, 1817)

D. Roth

Bechstein's bat

AL	Lakuriqnate veshmiu i Bechsteinit	LT	Bechšteino peléausis
BG	Бехщайнов нощник	LU	Bechstein-Flëntermaus
CZ	Netopýr velkouchý	LV	Lielausainais naktssikspārnis
DE	Bechsteinfledermaus	MK	Долгоушест ноћник
DK	Bechsteins flagermus	MT	-
EE	-	NL	Bechsteins vleermuis
ES	Murciélago de Bechstein	NO	Bechsteinflaggermus
FI	Korvasiippa	PL	Nocek Bechsteina
FO	-	PT	Morcego-de-Bechstein
FR	Murin de Bechstein	RO	Liliacul-cu-urechi-late
GR	Μυωτίδα του Bechstein	RU	Длинноухая ночница
HR	Velikouhi šišmiš	SE	Bechsteins fladdermus
HU	Nagyfülű denevér	SI	Veliki navadni netopir
IR	-	SK	Netopier vel'kouchý
IS	-	TR	Büyük kulaklı yarasa
IT	Vespertilio di Bechstein	YU	Дугоухи вечерњак

Distribution

World: western and central Europe and Asia Minor to the Caucasus and northernmost Iran.
Europe: from the Iberian Peninsula east to the Ukraine and Moldova. Local populations in southern England, Wales, southern Sweden, and Bornholm mark the northern border of the range.

Geographic variation

None known.

Habitat

Recorded up to 1800 m altitude. The real distribution is very insular, depending on the presence of suitable habitats. Largely restricted to natural, mainly deciduous, forests with a high proportion of old trees; also found in orchards and parks. Highest population density observed in stands of mature beeches and oaks with environmental forestry. Hunts mainly in forests and forest edges, also gleaning its prey from vegetation and the ground. Catches Lepidoptera, Diptera, Planipennia, and also non-flying Arthropoda. In winter found only in very low numbers in underground localities; it may also hibernate in hollow trees. Apparently sedentary; longest recorded movement 35 km.

Population status

Considered rare nearly everywhere, common only in optimal habitats and then its population density may reach 10 ind./km². Increasing number of records and extending range are probably mainly due to more intensive field research. There is no evidence of changes in numbers of a well known population in Northern Bavaria for the last 15 years.

International legal & conservation status

Bern Convention, Appendix II.
Bonn Convention, Appendix II.
EU Habitats & Species Directive, Annex II & Annex IV.
IUCN Red List, Vulnerable.

Other information

Bird- and bat-boxes are fairly readily accepted, but the protection and wise use of natural old forests is especially important. Lives in separated maternity groups of high genetic relatedness: young females remain in the group, whereas males emigrate.

Literature

Baagøe (in press a) – review
Kerth *et al.* (1995)
Schlapp (1990)
Wolz (1993)
Zuchuat & Keller (1995)

G. Schlapp

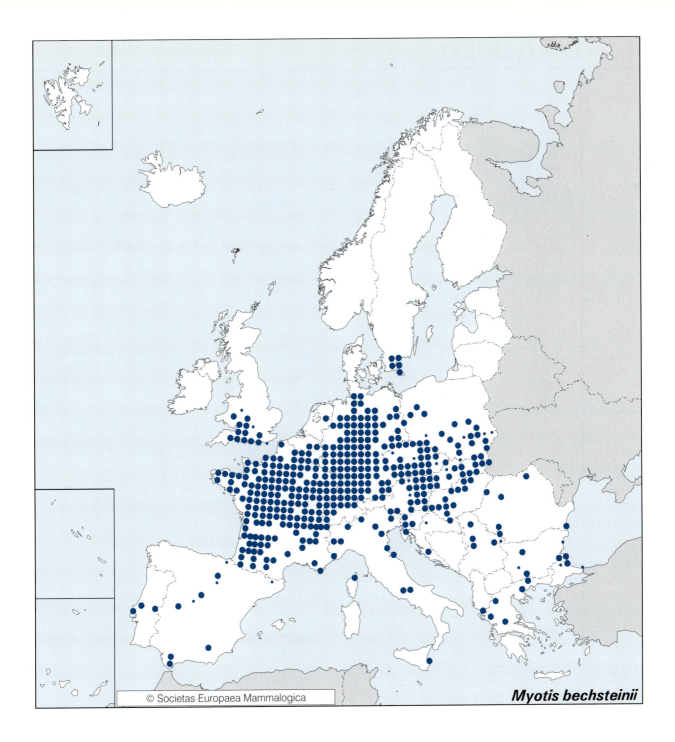

Myotis bechsteinii

© Societas Europaea Mammalogica

Myotis blythii (TOMES, 1857)

Z. Bihari

Lesser mouse-eared bat

AL	Lakuriqnate veshmiu i vogel	LU	-
BG	Остроух нощник	LV	-
CZ	Netopýr východní	MK	Остроушест ноќник
DE	Kleines Mausohr	MT	Farfett il-Lejl Widnet il-Ġurdien
DK	Lille museøre		
EE	Teravkõrv-lendlane	NL	Kleine vale vleermuis
ES	Murciélago ratonero mediano	NO	Liten musøre
		PL	Nocek ostrouszny
FI	Hiirenkorvasiippa	PT	Morcego-rato-pequeno
FO	-	RO	Liliacul-mic-cu-urechi-de-şoarece
FR	Petit murin		
GR	Μικρομυωτίδα	RU	Остроухая ночница
HR	Oštrouhi šišmiš	SE	Mindre musöra
HU	Hegyesorrú denevér	SI	Ostrouhi netopir
IR	-	SK	Netopier ostrouchý
IS	-	TR	Fare kukali küçük yarasa
IT	Vespertilio minore	YU	Мали мишоухи вечерњак
LT	-		

A sibling species to *Myotis myotis,* but on average smaller, with a shorter and narrower ear with a narrow rounded tip, relatively longer tibia, and generally greyer fur.

Distribution

World: Palaearctic; southern Europe and Asia east to the Himalayas – the very sporadic records farther to the east are rather doubtful.
Europe: northern border reaching roughly 46-48°N, close to 50°N in the Czech Republic and Slovakia; south to Sicily and Greece. Also Malta (J. Borg, in litt.).

Geographic variation

Up to six subspecies distinguished, with two of them probably occurring in Europe: *M. blythii oxygnathus* (Monticelli, 1885) (southern Europe) and the rather controversial *M. b. lesviacus* Iliopoulou-Georgudaki, 1984 (Lesbos island off Anatolia). In continental Europe increasing in size from west to east.

Habitat

A very gregarious species of Asiatic origin, ecologically linked to semi-arid warm and open habitats. In Europe prefers regions with not too dense tree and scrub cover; also in limestone areas and in areas of human settlements. Recorded up to 1000 m altitude. During summer, besides the usually preferred cave roosts, also in warm attics in the north. Very occasionally in tree holes. Winter roosts in caves and mines with a temperature of 6–12°C. Feeds preferentially on orthopterans hunted in open grass habitats. Occasional migrant; longest recorded movement 600 km.

Population status

A large decline since the 1950s is striking and easily seen in several areas, including central Europe, Israel and even central Asia.

International legal & conservation status

Bern Convention, Appendix II.
Bonn Convention, Appendix II.
EU Habitats & Species Directive, Annex II & Annex IV.

Other information

Protection of caves and other roosts necessary. Killed during remedial timber treatment.

Literature

Arlettaz *et al.* (1997)
Benda & Horáček (1995b)
Schober & Grimmberger (1989)
Spitzenberger (1996)
Stebbings & Griffith (1986)

G. Topál

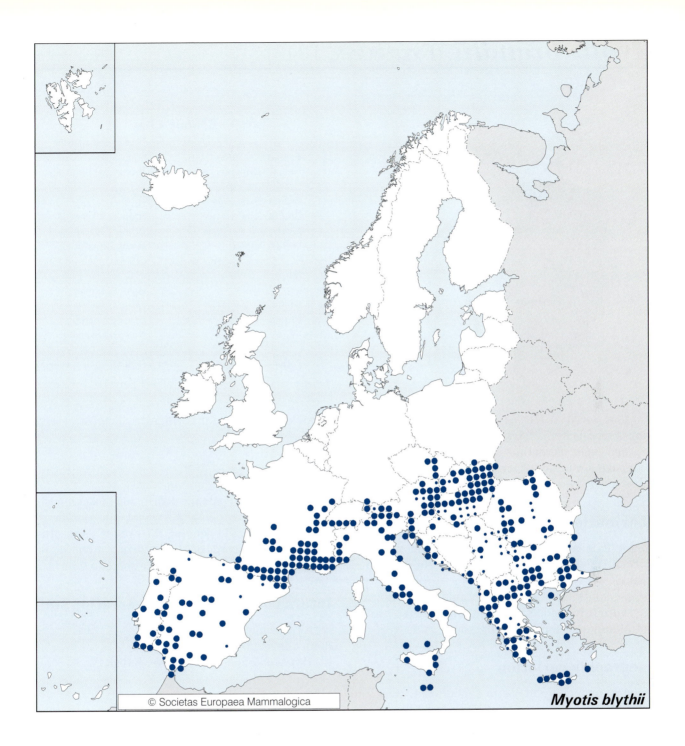

Myotis blythii

Myotis brandtii (EVERSMANN, 1845)

P. Twisk

Brandt's bat

AL	-	LT	Branto peléausis
BG	Брандтов нощник	LU	Grouss Baartflёntermaus
CZ	Netopýr Brandtův	LV	Branta naktssikspārnis
DE	Große Bartfledermaus	MK	-
DK	Brandts flagermus	MT	-
EE	Brandti lendlane	NL	Brandts vleermuis
ES	Murciélago de Brandt	NO	Brandtflaggermus
FI	Isoviiksisiippa	PL	Nocek Brandta
FO	-	PT	-
FR	Murin de Brandt	RO	-
GR	-	RU	Ночница Брандта
HR	Brandtov šišmiš	SE	Brandts fladdermus
HU	Brandt-denevér	SI	Brandtov netopir
IR	-	SK	Netopier Brandtov
IS	-	TR	-
IT	Vespertilio di Brandt	YU	Велики бркати вечерњак

First discovered in Europe in 1958. Recognized as a distinct species from *Myotis mystacinus* in 1970. Ears, face, and flight membranes brownish, lighter base to inner edge of ear, dorsal fur usually light-brown, penis club-shaped at end.

Distribution

World: Palaearctic; across Eurasia from southern Scotland, England, and eastern France to Korea and Japan.
Europe: mainly northern (to 65°N) and central Europe; absent from Ireland. Reaching south-eastern France, central Italy, and Bulgaria in the south.

Geographic variation

Three subspecies currently recognized; only the nominate form in Europe (east to western Siberia).

Habitat

More frequent than *M. mystacinus* in woodland and water areas, less often in human settlements. Recent altitudinal range from sea level to 1800 m; subfossil remains found up to 2020 m in the Alps. Summer roosts nearly always in buildings and bird- and bat-boxes. Nursery colonies usually monospecific, composed of 20–120, sometimes up to 350 females. Forages at low to medium height. Catches mainly Lepidoptera and Diptera. Hibernates mostly in caves and mines, frequently in joint clusters with *M. mystacinus* and *M.*

daubentonii. Occasional migrant; longest recorded movement 230 km.

Population status

Probably rare and patchily distributed in south-eastern and central Europe, widespread and common in northern Europe. In general, the ratio of its records to the number of records of *M. mystacinus* increases from the west to the east, and from the south to the north.

International legal & conservation status

Bern Convention, Appendix II.
Bonn Convention, Appendix II.
EU Habitats & Species Directive, Annex IV.

Other information

Colonies known to have declined substantially in Wales owing to remedial timber treatment. Also endangered by habitat modification and loss of caves.

Literature

Gerell (1987)
Koopman (1994)
Řehák & Beneš (1996)
Schober & Grimmberger (1989)
Taake (1992)
Zingg & Arlettaz (1995)

R. Gerell

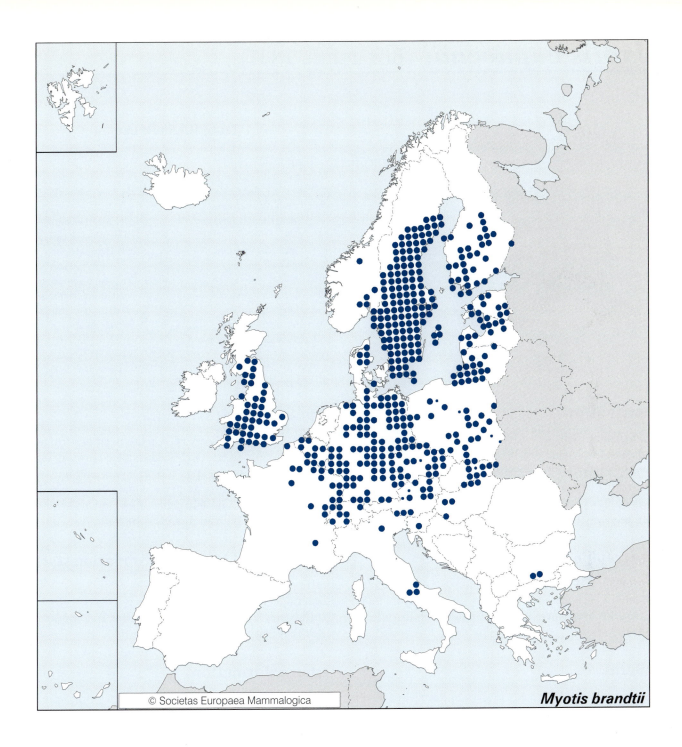

© Societas Europaea Mammalogica

Myotis brandtii

Myotis capaccinii (Bonaparte, 1837)

P. Twisk

Long-fingered bat

AL	Lakuriqnate veshmiu gishtgjate	LT	-
BG	Дългопръст нощник	LU	-
CZ	Netopýr dlouhonohý	LV	-
DE	Langfußfledermaus	MK	Долгопрст ноћник
DK	Capaccinis flagermus	MT	-
EE	-	NL	Capaccini's vleermuis
ES	Murciélago patudo	NO	Capacciniflaggermus
FI	Pitkäsormisiippa	PL	Nocek długopalcy
FO	-	PT	-
FR	Murin de Capaccini	RO	Liliacul-cu-degete-lungi
GR	Ποδαρομυωτίδα	RU	Средиземная ночница
HR	Dugonogi šišmiš	SE	Capaccinis fladdermus
HU	Hosszúlábú denevér	SI	Dolgonogi netopir
IR	-	SK	-
IS	-	TR	Uzun ayaklı yarasa
IT	Vespertilio di Capaccini	YU	Дугопрсти вечерњак

Distribution

World: north-western Africa, southern Europe, and south-western Asia.
Europe: eastern coast of Iberia and the low Ebro basin, southern France, Italy, Balkan Peninsula, north to northern Italy and Romania. Most large Mediterranean islands.

Geographic variation

Two subspecies are currently recognized: *M. capaccinii capaccinii* (France and Italy) and the noticeably paler *M. c. bureschi* (Heinrich, 1936) (Bulgaria to the east and south).

Habitat

Summer and winter roosts always in natural caves or in artificial but still cave-like underground shelters. Nursery colonies of 100–1000 females, usually in warm caves not far from water bodies. Typically clusters together with other species, mainly *Miniopterus schreibersii, Myotis myotis,* and *M. blythii.* Hunts over ponds or quiet streams, sometimes trawling. May interact with *M. daubentonii*, since one of these species is normally rare or absent where the other is common. Migration not well known; bats are away from breeding roosts in winter, probably in short-range displacements. Scattered individuals found in crevices inside caves in winter.

Population status

Greatly endangered. Very rare in the northern fringe of the distribution. Extinct in Switzerland. At present eight breeding colonies are known from Spain and only one from France. As many as five colonies disappeared in Spain during the last ten years. Rare but widespread and locally abundant in the eastern Mediterranean.

International legal & conservation status

Bern Convention, Appendix II.
Bonn Convention, Appendix II.
EU Habitats & Species Directive, Annex II & Annex IV.
IUCN Red List, Vulnerable.

Other information

The low abundance of most populations and specific habitat requirements make this species highly endangered by any negative influence. Populations reduced in numbers by loss of hunting areas owing to draining, channelling, and pollution of lowland rivers and water bodies. Very vulnerable to human disturbance and loss of scarce cave roosts.

Literature

Blanco & González (1992)
Đulić (1989)

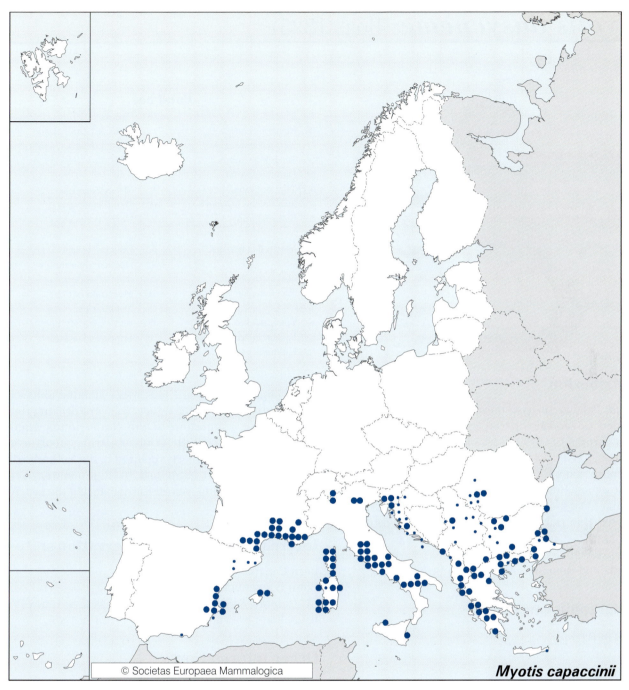

© Societas Europaea Mammalogica

Myotis capaccinii

Harrison & Bates (1991)
Médard & Guibert (1990)
Pandurska (1996)
Stebbings (1988)

A. Guillén

Myotis dasycneme (Boie, 1825)

PT 97
P. Twisk

Pond bat

AL	-	LU	Grouss
BG	Езерен нощник		Waasserflëntermaus
CZ	Netopýr pobřežní	LV	Dīķu naktssikspārnis
DE	Teichfledermaus	MK	-
DK	Damflagermus	MT	-
EE	Tiigilendlane	NL	Meervleermuis
ES	Murciélago lagunero	NO	Damflaggermus
FI	Lampisiippa	PL	Nocek łydkowłosy
FO	-	PT	-
FR	Murin des marais	RO	Liliacul-de-iaz
GR		RU	Прудовая ночница
HR	Močvarni šišmiš	SE	Dammfladdermus
HU	Tavi denevér	SI	Močvirski netopir
IR	-	SK	Netopier pobrežný
IS	Tjarnablaka	TR	-
IT	Vespertilio dasicneme	YU	Барски вечерњак
LT	Kūdrinis peléausis		

Distribution

World: Palaearctic from the Netherlands and southern Sweden to central Siberia; an isolated record from Manchuria.

Europe: breeding colonies in the Netherlands, northern Germany, Denmark, southern Sweden, Poland, Belarus, Baltic region, Russian Plain (north up to St. Petersburg), Ukraine, Moldova, south-eastern Slovakia, and north-western Hungary. In winter more or less regular in regions quite distant from breeding areas (e.g., Belgium, central Germany, and central Slovakia). Exceptional in Croatia and Romania. Absent from British Isles.

Geographic variation

None observed.

Habitat

Regions rich in stagnant waters and riparian vegetation (e.g., lowland river basins and canals). Recorded from sea level up to 1000 m altitude. Summer roosts in lofts and cavity walls of buildings, probably also in hollow trees. Some populations apparently entirely isolated during the breeding season. Most winter records from underground spaces; may also use other hibernacula, such as hollow trees. Regular seasonal migrations up to 330 km.

Population status

Ranks among the rarest bat species in Europe. A total world population in the 1980s was estimated to be ca. 6000 individuals. This figure was underestimated because the population of the Netherlands alone oscillates around 8000-10000. A strong decline in breeding colonies formerly reported in the Netherlands seems not to have happened. A slight increase in numbers observed in central Europe during the last 10 years.

International legal & conservation status

Bern Convention, Appendix II.
Bonn Convention, Appendix II.
EU Habitats & Species Directive, Annex II & Annex IV.
IUCN Red List, Vulnerable.

Other information

Owing to its islet-like distribution, low abundance of local populations, and strict habitat requirements, it may be greatly endangered by any negative influence, including extensive changes in landscape structures (e.g., water drainage and stream regulations).

Literature

Horáček & Hanák (1989)
Mostert (1997)
Sluiter *et al.* (1971)
Stebbings & Griffith (1986)

I. Horáček

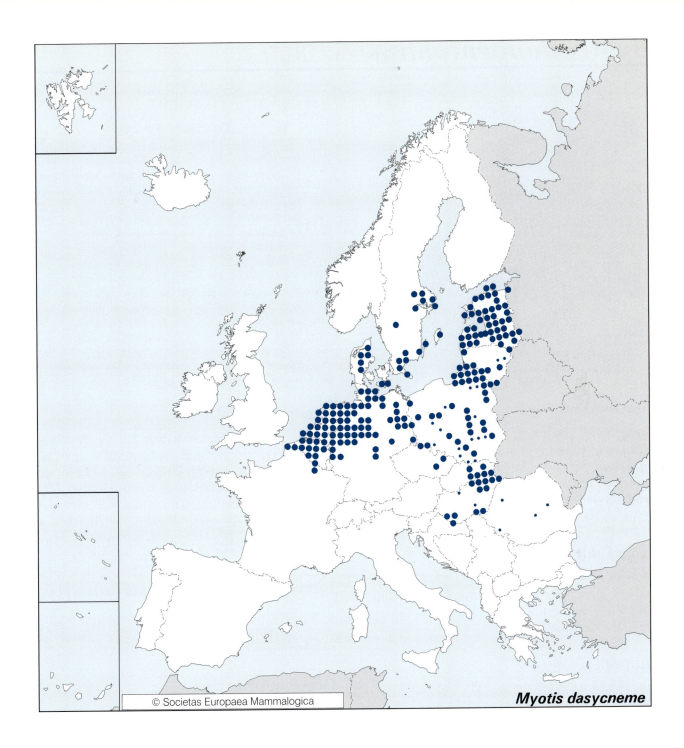

Myotis dasycneme

Myotis daubentonii (KUHL, 1817)

D. Roth

Daubenton's bat

AL	Lakuriqnate veshmiu i Daubentonit	LT	Vandeninis peléausis
BG	Воден нощник	LU	Waasserflëntermaus
CZ	Netopýr vodní	LV	Ūdeņu naktssikspārnis
DE	Wasserfledermaus	MK	Воден ноћник
DK	Vandflagermus	MT	-
EE	Veelendlane	NL	Watervleermuis
ES	Murciélago de ribera	NO	Vannflaggermus
FI	Vesisiippa	PL	Nocek rudy
FO		PT	Morcego-de-água
FR	Murin de Daubenton	RO	Liliacul de apă
GR	Μυωτίδα του Daubenton	RU	Водяная ночница
HR	Riječni šišmiš	SE	Vattenfladdermus
HU	Vízi denevér	SI	Obvodni netopir
IR	Ialtóg daubentóin	SK	Netopier vodný
IS	Vatnablaka	TR	Su yarasası
IT	Vespertilio di Daubenton	YU	Водени вечерњак

Distribution

World: from western Europe to eastern Siberia, Manchuria, Sakhalin, Kamchatka, the Kurile Islands, Hokkaido, Korea and eastern China. Also southern China (including Tibet) and north-eastern India.
Europe: from Portugal and Ireland to the Urals and from central Scandinavia to southern Italy and northern Greece.

Geographic variation

Three subspecies currently recognized, but only the nominate form in Europe. Individuals from the northern part of the range in the western Palaearctic are larger than those from the south.

Habitat

Associated with lakes, ponds, and streams, but also regularly hunts in deciduous and mixed forests. Summer shelters mostly in hollow trees, sometimes in buildings, under bridges, in bird- and bat-boxes, rock crevices, and nest tunnels of sand martins *Riparia riparia*. Hibernates in caves or abandoned forts and mines, often in cellars and concrete bunkers in large cities. The upper altitudinal limit usually within 400–700 m in summer, and 300–1100 m in winter. Consumes a diversity of Diptera (mainly non-biting midges – Chironomidae), Lepidoptera, Hemiptera, Trichoptera, Ephemeroptera, and Coleoptera. Dispersal season dominated by short-range flights (1–88 km); longest recorded movement 260 km.

Population status

One of the most abundant bats in Europe. Populations have increased in size in many parts of the range, perhaps due to favourable climatic changes. Some eutrophication might also be beneficial (more chironomids). A density above 1 ind./km^2 recorded in the Bohemian pond region in the Czech Republic, and ca. 2.4 ind./km^2 in north-eastern Scotland, near the northern limit of its distribution.

International legal & conservation status

Bern Convention, Appendix II.
Bonn Convention, Appendix II.
EU Habitats & Species Directive, Annex IV.

Other information

Main threats are disturbance in hibernation and loss of roosts. Killed by vandals, especially while hibernating. Nursery roosts in buildings threatened by remedial timber treatments. In Russia, considered to be an important factor in limiting the focus of malaria and tularemia.

Literature

Bogdanowicz (1994) – review
Corbet & Hill (1992)
Kokurewicz (1995)
Kuzjakin (1950)
Mitchell-Jones *et al.* (1989)

W. Bogdanowicz

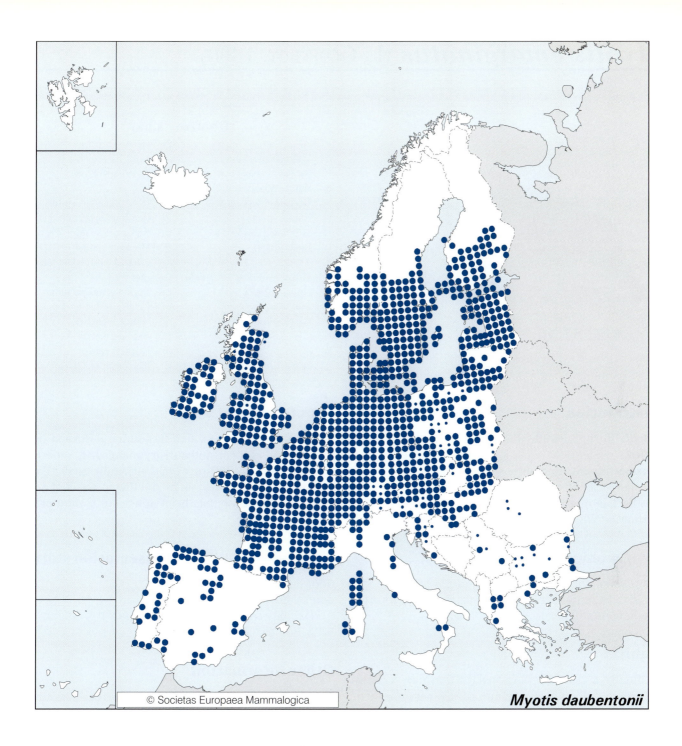

© Societas Europaea Mammalogica

Myotis daubentonii

Myotis emarginatus (E. Geoffroy, 1806)

D. Roth

Geoffroy's bat

AL	-	LU	-
BG	Трицветен нощник	LV	-
CZ	Netopýr brvitý	MK	Тробоен ноћник
DE	Wimperfledermaus	MT	-
DK	Geoffroys flagermus	NL	Ingekorven vleermuis
EE	Käharlendlane	NO	Geoffroyflaggermus
ES	Murciélago orejirroto	PL	Nocek orzęsiony
FI	Ruskosiippa	PT	Morcego-lanudo
FO	-	RO	Liliacul-cu-urechi-răscroite
FR	Murin à oreilles échancrées	RU	Трёхцветная ночница
GR	Πυρρομυωτίδα	SE	Geoffroys fladdermus
HR	Riđi šišmiš	SI	Vejicati netopir
HU	Csonkafülű denevér	SK	Netopier brvitý
IR	-	TR	Kirpikli yarasa
IS	-	YU	Шиљоухи вечерњак
IT	Vespertilio smarginato		
LT	-		

Distribution

World: Europe, south-west and central Asia, North Africa.

Europe: mainly southern, south-eastern and central Europe. Absent from the northern part of the continent. Northern border at a line between the Netherlands and southern Poland. Also the Crimea and the Caucasus.

Geographic variation

Only the nominate subspecies recognized in Europe and Africa. Subspecific allocations of some Asiatic populations still uncertain.

Habitat

Originally a cave-dwelling species that has recently adapted to buildings as summer roosts, particularly in the northern parts of its distribution. Overwinters in caves, galleries, and cellars. Prefers karstic areas as well as warm regions with parks, gardens and water reservoirs. Maternity colonies mainly confined to elevations between 200–500 m. Recorded up to 1800 m altitude in caves. Frequently in joint colonies with horseshoe bats. No specialized feeding strategy. Preys mainly on spiders, dipterans, and moths (including caterpillars), usually picking them off branches or off the ground. Predominantly sedentary, movements usually within 40 km (longest recorded 160 km).

Population status

Numerous populations live in southern Europe (the Balkans and France), and nursery colonies are reported containing up to 500 or even 1000 individuals. Rare and patchily distributed in northern areas. Local increase in numbers has been noticed in certain parts of central Europe.

International legal & conservation status

Bern Convention, Appendix II.
Bonn Convention, Appendix II.
EU Habitats & Species Directive, Annex II & Annex IV.
IUCN Red List, Vulnerable.

Other information

May be threatened locally by damaging the roost sites, both in summer and winter.

Literature

Beck (1995)
Koopman (1994)
Spitzenberger & Bauer (1987)
Zukal (1994)

J. Červený

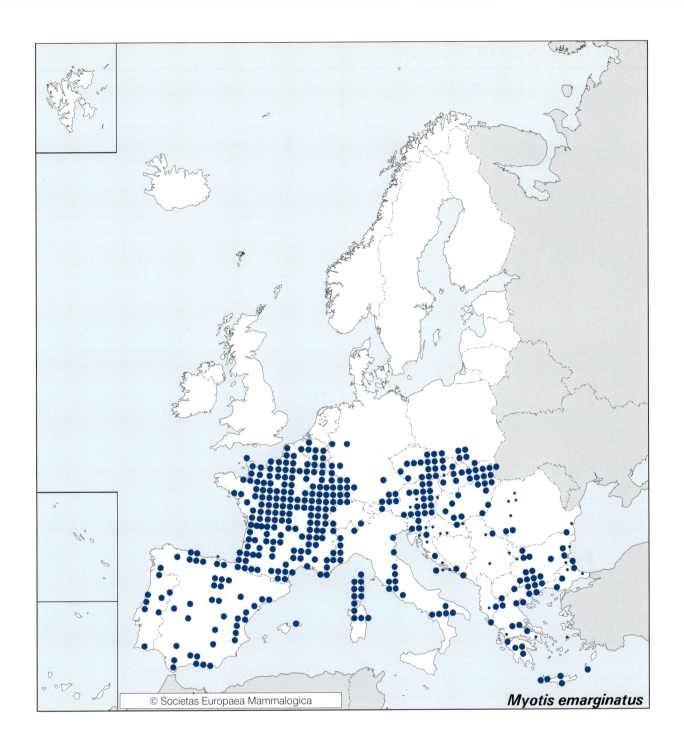

© Societas Europaea Mammalogica

Myotis emarginatus

Myotis myotis (Borkhausen, 1797)

Z. Bihari

Greater mouse-eared bat

AL	Lakuriqnate veshmiu i madh	LU	Grouss Flëntermaus
BG	Голям нощник	LV	Lielais naktssiksparnis
CZ	Netopýr velký	MK	Голем ноћник
DE	Großes Mausohr	MT	Farfett il-Lejl Widnet il-Ġurdien Kbir
DK	Stor museøre		
EE	Suurlendlane	NL	Vale vleermuis
ES	Murciélago ratonero grande	NO	Stor musøre
		PL	Nocek duży
FI	Jättiläissiippa	PT	Morcego-rato-grande
FO	-	RO	Liliacul-mare-cu-urechi-de-şoarece
FR	Grand murin		
GR	Τραυομυωτίδα	RU	Большая ночница
HR	Veliki šišmiš	SE	Större musöra
HU	Közönséges denevér	SI	Navadni netopir
IR	-	SK	Netopier veľký
IS	Músablaka	TR	Fare kulaklı büyük yarasa
IT	Vespertilio maggiore	YU	Велики мишоухи вечерњак
LT	Didysis peléausis		

Distribution

World: through western Eurasia from the Iberian Peninsula to the Ukraine, Turkey, Israel, Lebanon, and Syria; also North Africa.

Europe: throughout, but excluding Iceland, British Isles, and most of Scandinavia, except for one vagrant in southern Sweden. One vagrant individual also caught in Latvia, which is the northernmost record ever observed. In the south including the Balearic Islands, Corsica, Sardinia, and Sicily.

Geographic variation

Subspecific or sometimes even specific allocation of some Mediterranean and Asian populations is still unclear and controversial. Three subspecies accepted, but only the nominate form currently recognized in Europe. In the western Palaearctic increasing in size from west to east.

Habitat

In the south originally and currently residing the full year in caves and mines. In northern areas an extremely synanthropic species forming nursery colonies in buildings, mostly in attics. Maternity roosts are most frequently situated in lowland regions, usually below 600 m. Hibernates in caves, mines, and cellars, rarely in bridges. Sometimes in mixed colonies with the sibling species *M. blythii*. Hunts in forest-rich landscapes inside forests and on adjoining cultivated but open areas. Preys on large insects (mainly Coleoptera) which are often gleaned from the ground. Occasional migrant; longest recorded movement 390 km.

Population status

Widespread and regionally abundant. In the European Palaearctic the populations have stabilized at lower levels after a drastic decline from the 1950s to the 1970s. Now increasing in numbers in nursery colonies and hibernation quarters. An attempted colonization of southern England in the 1950s had failed by the 1990s.

International legal & conservation status

Bern Convention, Appendix II.
Bonn Convention, Appendix II.
EU Habitats & Species Directive, Annex II & Annex IV.
IUCN Red List, Lower Risk – near threatened.

Other information

Remedial timber treatment in buildings and disturbance in nursery and hibernation sites are probably the main threats.

Literature

Arlettaz *et al.* (1997)
Benda & Horáček (1995a)

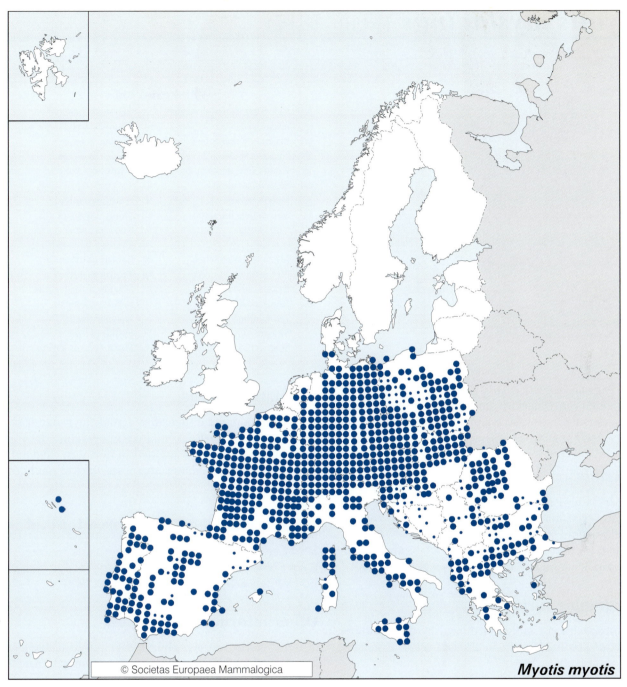

© Societas Europaea Mammalogica

Myotis myotis

Graf *et al.* (1992)
Petersons (1995)
Spitzenberger (1996)
Stutz (1989)

H-P. B. Stutz

Myotis mystacinus (KUHL, 1817)

D. Roth

Whiskered bat

AL	Lakuriqnate veshmiu me mustaqe	LT	Ūsuotasis peléausis
BG	Мустакат нощник	LU	Kleng Baartflëntermaus
CZ	Netopýr vousatý	LV	Bārdainais naktssikspārnis
DE	Kleine Bartfledermaus		
DK	Skægflagermus	MK	Мустаѣест нођник
EE	Habelendlane	MT	-
ES	Murciélago bigotudo	NL	Baardvleermuis
FI	Viiksisiippa	NO	Skjeggflaggermus
FO	-	PL	Nocek wąsatek
FR	Murin à moustaches	PT	Morcego-de-bigodes
GR	Μουστακονυχτερίδα	RO	Liliacul-mustăcios
HR	Brkati šišmiš	RU	Усатая ночница
HU	Bajuszos denevér	SE	Mustaschfladdermus
IR	Ialtóg ghiobach	SI	Brkati netopir
IS	Skeggblaka	SK	Netopier fúzatý
IT	Vespertilio mustacchino	TR	Bıyıklı yarasa
		YU	Мали бркати вечерњак

A sibling species with *Myotis brandtii*. Ears, face, and flight membranes blackish, no lighter base to inner edge of ear, dorsal fur grey-brown to black-brown, penis not club-shaped at end.

Distribution

World: mainly Palaearctic; from Ireland, northern Iberia and Morocco to Korea and Japan, also the western Himalayas and southern China.
Europe: widely distributed, north to 64°N; absent from northern Scotland and Denmark (except Bornholm).

Geographic variation

Six subspecies currently recognized by most authors; only the nominate form in Europe (east at least to Transcaucasia).

Habitat

Recorded from sea level to 1920 m altitude. Not so obviously associated with woodland and water as *M. brandtii,* most often in gardens, parks, and riparian habitats. Roosts in buildings and bird- and bat-boxes in summer, and mostly in caves, mines and cellars in winter. Forages at low and medium height, usually 1.5–6 m above the ground. Prey consists mainly of Diptera, Arachnida, and Lepidoptera, and can be caught on the wing or picked off branches or off the ground. Occasional migrant; longest recorded movement 240 km.

Population status

Increasing population densities across the range from the south to the north. A minimum population density of about 1.5 ind./km² estimated in northern England, based on counting in maternity roosts. Rare in southern Europe and Ireland.

International legal & conservation status

Bern Convention, Appendix II.
Bonn Convention, Appendix II.
EU Habitats & Species Directive, Annex IV.

Other information

Most threatened by chemical remedial timber treatments. Needs specific protection of nursery roosts and hibernacula.

Literature

Beck (1995)
Corbet & Hill (1992)
Gerell (1987)
Jones *et al.* (1996)
Schober & Grimmberger (1989)
Taake (1992)

R. Gerell

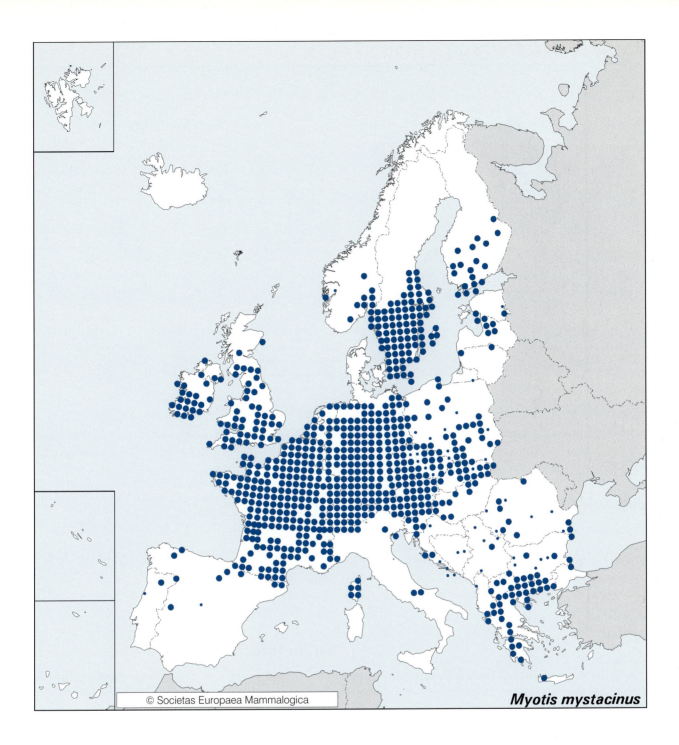

Myotis mystacinus

© Societas Europaea Mammalogica

Myotis nattereri (KUHL, 1817)

D. Roth

Distribution

World: from Portugal and Ireland to the Urals, Near East, and Turkmenia; also north-western Africa.
Europe: widely distributed, up to 63°N in Sweden.

Geographic variation

Two subspecies are currently recognized: *M. nattereri nattereri* (Europe to the Urals, Near East, Morocco and Algeria) and *M. n. tschuliensis* Kuzyakin, 1935 (Transcaucasia, Iraq, Turkmenistan). In the western Palaearctic generally increasing in size from west to east.

Habitat

Predominantly a woodland bat. Altitudinal range from sea level to 2000 m; most localities in central Europe between 300–700 m. Summer roosts in buildings, hollow trees, and bat-boxes, sometimes in cracks under bridges; hibernacula most often in caves, cellars, and mines. Most significant foraging habitats are woodland edges, parkland, roadside vegetation, and sheltered areas of water. Diet mainly composed of dipteran flies (Diptera), but beetles (Coleoptera), harvestmen (Opiliones), spiders (Araneae), and caterpillars (Lepidoptera larvae) are also important. May feed opportunistically on many different arthropods (size range 1–15 mm) at latitudes of 57°N or higher. Prey is gleaned from vegetation or caught in flight. Sedentary; longest recorded movement 90 km.

Population status

Widespread throughout the UK to northern Scotland. Nevertheless, the species appears to be rare over large areas of Europe, especially in the south. The summer population of the Netherlands is estimated at 1500–3000 adult individuals. Density about 0.04 ind./km² in western Bohemia, the Czech Republic.

International legal & conservation status

Bern Convention, Appendix II.
Bonn Convention, Appendix II.
EU Habitats & Species Directive, Annex IV.

Other information

Threatened by loss of roosts, especially by remedial timber treatment. Requires specific protection of nursery roosts and hibernacula.

Literature

Benda & Horáček (1995b)
Boye *et al.* (1990)
Horáček & Hanák (1984)
Hůrka (1989)
Limpens & Feenstra (1997)
Swift (1997)

W. Bogdanowicz

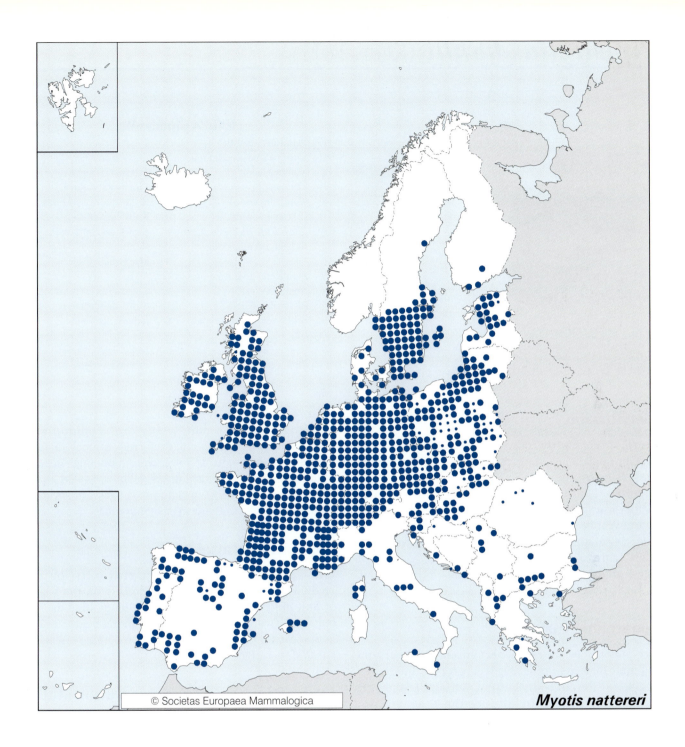

Myotis nattereri

Pipistrellus kuhlii (Kuhl, 1817)

P. Barrett

Distribution

World: from the Iberian Peninsula east to 93°E in Southern Asia; most of Africa; also the Canary and Cape Verde Islands.

Europe: southern and western Europe; the northernmost localities known from north-western and central France, Switzerland, Austria, Hungary, southern Bulgaria, southern Ukraine, and south-western Russia. A few vagrants recorded in Great Britain. Assumed to reach south-west Germany on at least four occasions (D. Kock, pers. comm.).

Geographic variation

Five subspecies currently recognized, but only the nominate form in Europe. Slight geographic differences. In general the individuals from Adriatic islands are smaller than those inhabiting the neighbouring mainland.

Habitat

Exhibits one of the highest degrees of synanthropy among bats, being either common or abundant in urban areas. Associated with relatively warm lowland basins and lower mountain areas. The upper altitudinal range usually within 585–645 m in Italy, and below 1000 and 1450 m in France and Spain, respectively. Typically hunts over street lamps, but also in open areas with no artificial lights, or over porches, sometimes inside buildings. Catches mainly Diptera, Lepidoptera, Trichoptera, and Hemiptera. Preferred summer shelters are crevices on and in old and modern buildings. Readily utilizes bat-boxes in rural areas. Winter roosts, as far as is known, in crevices in cliffs and cellars. Shows great interest in exploring new areas. Sedentary.

Population status

Widespread and common, particularly in the Mediterranean area. Population density on the island of Rab in Croatia was estimated to be as high as 730 ind./km². Over 10 ind./km² at elevations below 600 m in the Greater Caucasus. Increasing in numbers in many parts of its range.

International legal & conservation status

Bern Convention, Appendix II.
Bonn Convention, Appendix II.
EU Habitats & Species Directive, Annex IV.

Other information

Banning the use of toxic chemicals in buildings would be the most effective conservation measure. Subject to persecution, particularly when it enters buildings in September and October in groups of 5 to 400 individuals. A mass kill with organochlorine insecticides reported from Israel.

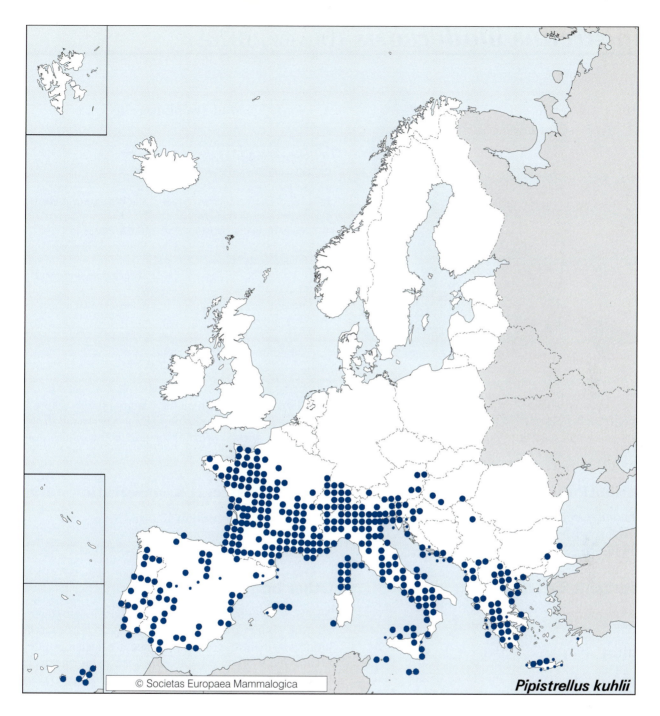

© Societas Europaea Mammalogica

Pipistrellus kuhlii

Literature

Beck (1995)
Bogdanowicz (in press) – review
Gaisler (1994)
Makin & Mendelssohn (1989)
Vernier (1993, 1995)

E. Vernier & W. Bogdanowicz

Pipistrellus maderensis (Dobson, 1878)

P. Twisk

Madeira pipistrelle

AL	-	LT	-
BG	Мадейрски прилеп	LU	-
CZ	Netopýr makaronéský	LV	-
DE	Madeira-Zwergfledermaus	MK	-
DK	-	MT	-
EE	-	NL	Madeira dwergvleermuis
ES	Murciélago de Madeira	NO	-
FI	Madeiranpikkulepakko	PL	Karlik maderski
FO	-	PT	Morcego da Madeira
FR	Pipistrelle de Madère	RO	-
GR	-	RU	Мадейрский нетопырь
HR	Madeirski šišmiš	SE	-
HU	Madeira-törpedenevér	SI	Madejrski mali netopir
IR	-	SK	-
IS	-	TR	-
IT	Pipistrello di Madeira	YU	-

A geographically isolated form with no completely clear taxonomic status. Regarded as a valid species by most authors, although sometimes suggested to be conspecific with *Pipistrellus kuhlii*.

Distribution

World and Europe: very limited; only Madeira and four of the Canary Islands: Tenerife, La Gomera, La Palma, and El Hierro.

Geographic variation

None known.

Habitat

Associated with areas of human settlement, also in woodlands, then most frequently in pine forests. Altitudinal range from sea level to 2150 m on the Canary Islands, preferring lowlands on Madeira. Hunts small flying insects (Lepidoptera, Diptera, and Coleoptera) at low or medium height, around street lamps and over water surfaces. Breeds in cracks of buildings. As summer roosts and mating sites it also uses hollow trees and bird- or bat-boxes. Found in crevices in rocks and bridges in winter.

Population status

Not well known as there are no historical data on its population size. Not threatened on Madeira. The most abundant bat species in all the Canary Islands where it is recorded. Although the population decreased in the 1950s after aerial spraying for pest control, it is now likely to be increasing.

International legal & conservation status

Bern Convention, Appendix II.
Bonn Convention, Appendix II.
EU Habitats & Species Directive, Annex IV.

Other information

A regional programme for the protection of bats started on the Canary Islands in 1993. Soon afterwards hundreds of bat-boxes were erected in selected wooded areas. Some other roosts have been protected from human disturbance. The extensive use of agricultural pesticides is perhaps the greatest threat on the Canary Islands.

Literature

Benzal & Fajardo (1994)
Benzal & Izquierdo (1993)
Corbet (1978)
Mathias (1988)
Trujillo (1991)

S. Fajardo & J. Benzal

© Societas Europaea Mammalogica

Pipistrellus maderensis

Pipistrellus nathusii (KEYSERLING & BLASIUS, 1839)

T. P. McOwat

Distribution

World: confined to Europe, Asia Minor, and Transcaucasia.
Europe: from Iberia to the Urals, north to Scotland, south-eastern Sweden, and extreme southern Finland. Two, most probably ship-assisted individuals, also recorded in Iceland.

Geographic variation

No subspecies. In Europe shows a slight tendency to increase in size (as defined by forearm length) from west to east.

Habitat

Parkland as well as mixed and pine forests, often riparian habitats. Although associated with lowland basins, recorded up to 2200 m altitude in the Alps. Preferred summer roosts are hollow trees, bat- and bird-boxes, also wooden churches, and residential buildings. Winter roosts usually in crevices in cliffs, hollow trees, and cracks in buildings. Typically hunts along rides, paths, and woodland edges, and also over water. Preys on small to medium-sized flying insects, mainly non-biting midges of the family Chironomidae. Highly migratory, most migrations in a NE–SW direction. Several movements over 1000 km, with the longest flight being 1905 km.

Population status

Patchily distributed and assumed to be rare in most European countries. This estimation is probably biased due to the use of inappropriate census methods. Certainly commoner in many areas than so far realized and increasingly found in bird- and bat-boxes placed in woodland. About 50000–100000 adult individuals assumed to occur in late summer and early autumn in the Netherlands. Locally abundant in Latvia, where 24 nursery colonies averaging 70 females each were recorded in 1990. A nursery colony of over 100 individuals has recently been discovered in Northern Ireland (J. M. Russ, J. K. O'Neill & W. Montgomery, in litt.). Density below 1 ind./km² in the Greater Caucasus.

International legal & conservation status

Bern Convention, Appendix II.
Bonn Convention, Appendix II.
EU Habitats & Species Directive, Annex IV.

Other information

Endangered by loss of hollow trees and remedial timber treatment in buildings. Feeding mainly on chironomids and because of that may be affected by changes in water quality.

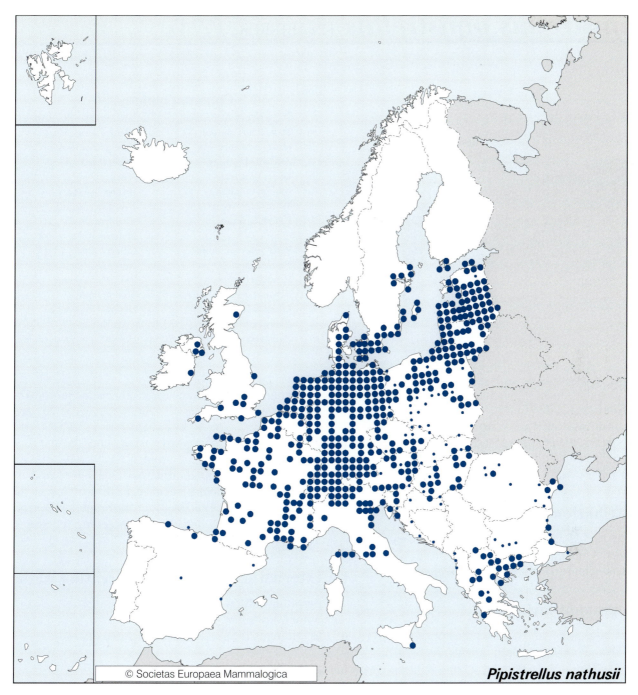

© Societas Europaea Mammalogica

Pipistrellus nathusii

Literature

Beck (1995)
Lina & Rheinhold (1997)
Petersen (1994)
Petersons (1990)
Rachwald (1992)
Rakhmatulina (1996)

W. Bogdanowicz

125

Pipistrellus pipistrellus (Schreber, 1774)

P. Twisk

Recent studies have shown that *P. pipistrellus* exists as two forms with different echolocation calls and extensive genetic divergence. These are clearly cryptic species (45 kHz and 55 kHz cryptic species). General statements in the text refer to studies where the two species have not been separated.

Distribution

World: Palaearctic; most of Europe, some parts of south-western Asia and northern Africa.
Europe: widely distributed south of about 63–64°N.

Geographic variation

Pipistrellus p. mediterraneus Cabrera, 1904 described as a subspecies from Spain may be the 55 kHz cryptic species. The 55 kHz bats occur in northern, western and southern Europe, with 45 kHz bats more abundant in central Europe. The two cryptic species are sympatric in the UK, Switzerland, and southern Denmark.

Habitat

Feeds in a wide range of habitats including farmland, open woodland, over lakes and even in urban areas. Often patrols tree lines. The 55 kHz bats are more associated with riparian habitats in the UK than are 45 kHz bats. The 55 kHz pipistrelles feed mainly on chironomids and ceratopogonids, while 45 kHz bats eat mainly psychodid and anisopodid Diptera. Roosts mainly in buildings, though sometimes hibernates in caves in continental Europe.

Population status

Widespread and abundant across its range. Numbers in UK nursery colonies seem to have declined in the past 20 years. Status in other European countries unclear. Population densities for breeding females in northern Britain about 5 ind./km².

International legal & conservation status

Bern Convention, Appendix III.
Bonn Convention, Appendix II.
EU Habitats & Species Directive, Annex IV.

Other information

Populations may have declined in some areas through poisoning by remedial timber treatment chemicals. Residues of organochlorine pesticides found in maternity colonies in Germany. A population in an industrial area of Sweden declined while a rural population maintained numbers over the same time period. Drainage and water pollution were believed to be the major causes of the decline. Both cryptic species are negatively affected by the addition of treated sewage effluent to rivers.

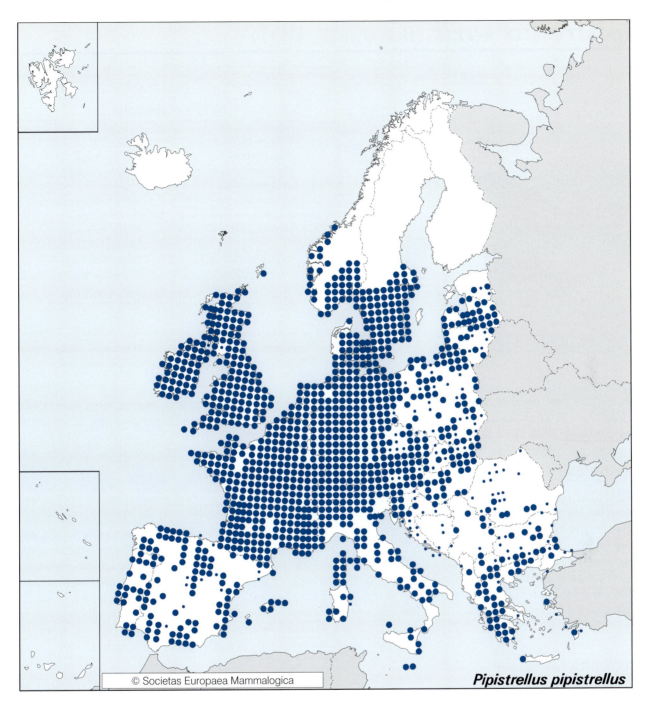

© Societas Europaea Mammalogica

Pipistrellus pipistrellus

Literature

Avery (1991)
Barratt *et al.* (1997)
Boyd *et al.* (1988)
Gerell & Lundberg (1993)
Harris *et al.* (1995)
Jones & van Parijs (1993)

G. Jones

Pipistrellus savii (Bonaparte, 1837)

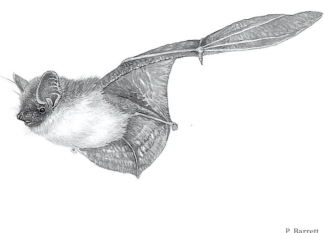

P. Barrett

	Savi's pipistrelle		
AL	Pipistreli i Savit	LT	-
BG	Кожовиден вечерник	LU	-
CZ	Netopýr Saviův	LV	-
DE	Alpenfledermaus	MK	Савиев лилјак
DK	Savis flagermus	MT	-
EE	Alpi nahkhiir	NL	Savi's dwergvleermuis
ES	Murciélago montañero	NO	Saviflaggermus
FI	Alppipikkulepakko	PL	Karlik Saviego
FO	-	PT	Morcego de Savii
FR	Vespère de Savi	RO	Liliacul-de-munte
GR	Βουνονυχτερίδα	RU	Кожановидный нетопырь
HR	Primorski šišmiš	SE	Alpfladdermus
HU	Alpesi törpedenevér	SI	Savijev netopir
IR	-	SK	-
IS	-	TR	-
IT	Pipistrello di Savi	YU	Планински слепи мишић

Generic status controversial, and recent morphological and biochemical analyses plead for an independent genus *(Hypsugo)* from the true *Pipistrellus*.

Distribution

World: Palaearctic; from southern Europe and north-western Africa to Mongolia; possibly to Japan and Burma, if some oriental forms are conspecific. Also Canary and Cape Verde islands.
Europe: widespread in Mediterranean and sub-Mediterranean regions, including most islands. North to south-eastern France, central Switzerland, Austria, Hungary, and south-eastern Romania. A few vagrants recorded from Great Britain.

Geographic variation

Up to six subspecies distinguished, but some of them may be specifically distinct. Only the nominate subspecies recognized in Europe. Large individual variability in fur coloration, even within the same population.

Habitat

Typically an inhabitant of rocky areas, from sea-level up to more than 2000 m (Alps, Pyrénées, Sierra Nevada). Frequently found in the same regions as the crag martin *Ptyonoprogne rupestris*. Roosts mainly in crevices in cliffs, sometimes in buildings (e.g., in cracks in walls, behind shutters) or under the bark of trees; rarely noticed in caves. Forages in open spaces along cliffs, over wooded slopes, mountain pastures, stretches of water or above lighted villages. Preys mainly on Lepidoptera, Diptera, Hymenoptera, Neuroptera, and Hemiptera.

Population status

Until recently considered rare, if not extinct, in many countries. This estimation was probably biased owing to the use of inappropriate census methods such as searching underground sites. Mist netting and acoustic detection with the help of a bat detector show its omnipresence in all suitable environments, at least in France, Switzerland, and Spain. One of the most common bats in towns of northern Italy.

International legal & conservation status

Bern Convention, Appendix II.
Bonn Convention, Appendix II.
EU Habitats & Species Directive, Annex IV.

Other information

Remedial timber treatment in buildings may constitute a threat.

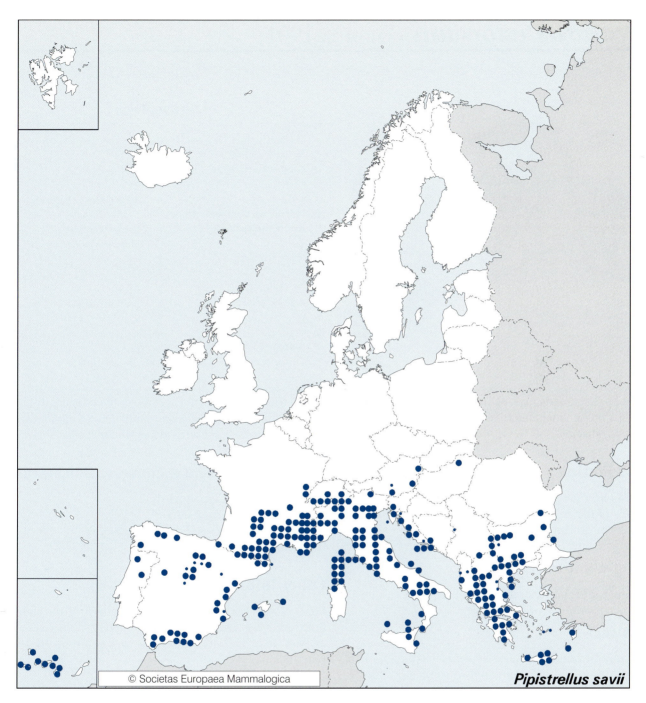

© Societas Europaea Mammalogica

Pipistrellus savii

Literature

Arlettaz *et al.* (1993)
Beck (1995)
Horáček & Hanák (1986)
Ruedi & Arlettaz (1991)
Spitzenberger (1997a)
Zingg (1988)

D. Masson

Nyctalus azoreum (THOMAS, 1901)

PT 97 P. Twisk

It has been included in *N. leisleri* by many authors, but recent studies concluded that it should be regarded as a separate species.

Distribution

World and Europe: restricted to the eastern and central islands of the Azores. It has not been recorded on the westernmost islands, Flores and Corvo.

Geographic variation

No geographic variation has been described.

Habitat

Probably the microchiropteran species that forages most often during daytime. Commonly observed hunting in bright light, especially during the afternoon. However, it is still clearly a predominantly nocturnal animal, since the levels of activity recorded at night are many times higher than those recorded during daytime. During this period seems to be particularly active in the elevated areas, inland. At night hunts mostly around street lights in villages, which are in general located on the coast. Known to roost in narrow spaces in buildings, although it is also likely to use other types of shelters.

Population status

Fairly abundant, reaching much higher densities than its larger continental counterpart, *N. leisleri,* probably due to the absence of pipistrelles on the islands. But in spite of its abundance, the very limited and fragmentary range makes this endemic species vulnerable.

International legal & conservation status

Bern Convention, Appendix II.
Bonn Convention, Appendix II.
EU Habitats & Species Directive, Annex IV.
IUCN Red List, Vulnerable.

Other information

Land cover changes and the substitution of the light bulbs on street lamps by energy efficient bulbs, which attract less insects, could pose problems to its populations.

Literature

Moore (1975)
Palmeirim (1991)
Speakman & Webb (1993)

J. M. Palmeirim

© Societas Europaea Mammalogica

Nyctalus azoreum

Nyctalus lasiopterus (SCHREBER, 1780)

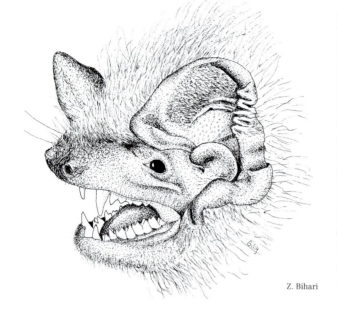

Z. Bihari

Greater noctule

AL	-	LT	Didysis nakviša
BG	Голям вечерник	LU	-
CZ	Netopýr obrovský	LV	Milzu vakarsikspārnis
DE	Riesenabendsegler	MK	Голем вечерник
DK	Stor brunflagermus	MT	-
EE	Hiidvidevlane	NL	Grote rosse vleermuis
ES	Murciélago nóctulo grande	NO	Riseflaggermus
FI	Jättiläislepakko	PL	Borowiec olbrzymi
FO	-	PT	Morcego-arborícola-gigante
FR	Grande noctule	RO	Liliacul-mare-de-amurg
GR	Μεγάλος νυχτβάτης	RU	Гигантская вечерница
HR	Veliki večernjak	SE	Jättefladdermus
HU	Óriás-koraidenevér	SI	Veliki mračnik
IR	-	SK	Netopier východný
IS	-	TR	Büyük akşamcı yarasa
IT	Nottola gigante	YU	Велики ноћник

Nyctalus aviator (Thomas, 1911) from Japan, China, and Korea was thought to be a subspecies of *N. lasiopterus,* but now it is recognized as a separate species.

Distribution

World: Palaearctic, from the Atlantic coast of Europe (Portugal, Spain, and France) to Iran and the Ust-Urt plateau in Uzbekistan; from north Africa to Poland and the Gor'kij region in Russia. One record (by some due to passive transportation – J. B. M. Thissen, pers. comm.) also from the Netherlands.

Europe: partially known. Mainly Mediterranean in western Europe; as far north as 55°N and even beyond this latitude in eastern Europe. Absent from the northern part of the continent.

Geographic variation

None known.

Habitat

Occupies mixed forests, mainly with deciduous trees, and large parks in southern and western Europe. Associated with oak and oak-hornbeam forests in the Ukraine and Russia. Relatively regular in willow and poplar woodlands along river valleys during migrations. Nursery roosts and hibernacula in hollows of old trees, less common in buildings. Preys on large moths and beetles high over open areas or above tree tops.

Population status

Unknown. Up to now recorded in about 120–130 localities in Europe. In southern Spain 57 bats were ringed in three different localities of the same area from 1989 to 1993. In the Sierra de Gredos and the city of Seville (Spain) two groups composed respectively of 3 and 12 bats have been found in hollow trees since 1979. In eastern Europe, further east fewer greater noctules are found. Rare in north Africa, with only a few scattered records.

International legal & conservation status

Bern Convention, Appendix II.
Bonn Convention, Appendix II.
EU Habitats & Species Directive, Annex IV.
IUCN Red List, Lower Risk – near threatened.

Other information

Loss of deciduous woodlands, parklands, and hollow trees are probably the greatest threat. Reduction in number of large insects may also be affecting populations.

Literature

Ibáñez *et al.* (in press) – review
Kuzjakin (1980)
Maeda (1983)

J. Benzal

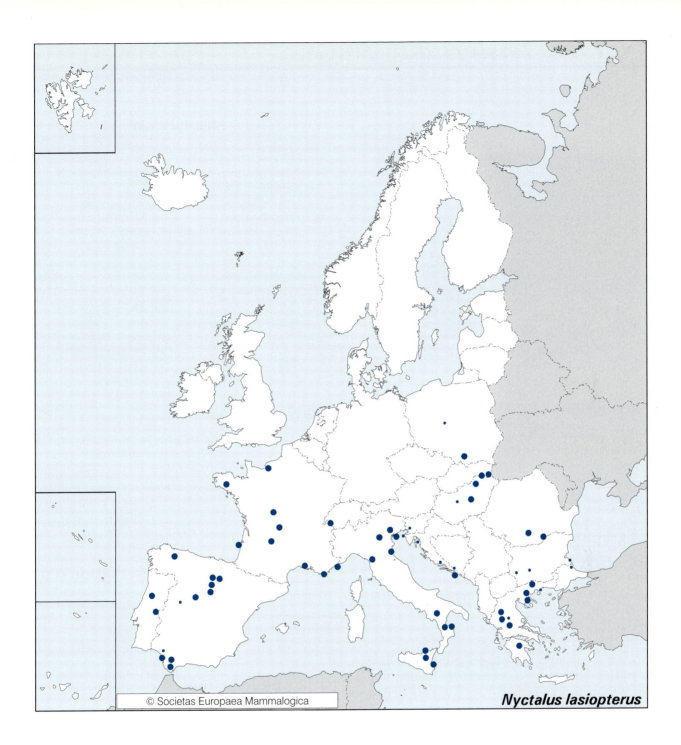

Nyctalus lasiopterus

© Societas Europaea Mammalogica

133

Nyctalus leisleri (Kuhl, 1817)

D. Roth

Leisler's bat

AL	-	LU	-
BG	Лайслеров вечерник	LV	Mazais vakarsikspārnis
CZ	Netopýr stromový	MK	Шумски вечерник
DE	Kleinabendsegler	MT	-
DK	Leislers flagermus	NL	Bosvleermuis
EE	Väikevidevlane	NO	Leislerflaggermus
ES	Murciélago nóctulo pequeño	PL	Borowiec Leislera; Borowiaczek
FI	Metsäisolepakko		
FO	Leislers flogmús	PT	Morcego-arborícola-pequeno
FR	Noctule de Leisler		
GR	Μικρονυχτοβάτης	RO	Liliacul-mic-de-amurg
HR	Mali večernjak	RU	Малая вечерница
HU	Szőröskarú koraidenevér	SE	Leislers fladdermus
IR	Ialtóg leisléir	SI	Gozdni mračnik
IS	-	SK	Netopier stromový
IT	Nottola di Leisler	TR	Küçük akşamcı yarasa
LT	Mažasis nakviša	YU	Мали ноћник

Distribution

World: from western Europe to south-western Asia, east to 79° 40´ E in Uttar Pradesh, India. Also north-western Africa.

Europe: throughout, except Iceland, Denmark, Norway, most of Sweden, Finland, Estonia and northern Russia.

Geographic variation

Two currently recognized subspecies, *N. leisleri leisleri* and *N. l. verrucosus* Bowdich, 1825; the latter smaller than the former and geographically isolated to Madeira.

Habitat

Although considered a tree-roosting species in Europe, in Ireland nursery roosts are chiefly located in attic spaces of buildings. There are no records of hibernacula from Ireland. Elsewhere hibernation is thought to be in hollow trees, buildings, and occasionally in rock crevices. Foraging is mainly concentrated over open areas. There may be marked differences in the diet between countries. In Ireland and England, Diptera of the suborders Nematocera and Cyclorrhapha are by far the most significant prey, but Coleoptera, Trichoptera, and Lepidoptera are also important. Limited data from Germany indicate that Lepidoptera, Nematocera, and Neuroptera may, at least locally, be important food items (C. Shiel, unpubl.). Generally migratory; longest recorded movement 1245 km – from Russia to Turkey.

Population status

Ireland is generally considered to be the stronghold of its world distribution. Initial investigations suggest that the Irish population is stable, with nursery colonies of up to 100 individuals relatively common. Elsewhere considered to be vulnerable, although a greater interest in bats notably increased the number of records in Iberia, Britain, France, Germany, and Greece.

International legal & conservation status

Bern Convention, Appendix II.
Bonn Convention, Appendix II.
EU Habitats & Species Directive, Annex IV.
IUCN Red List, Lower Risk – near threatened.

Other information

As Leisler's is Ireland's largest bat it does not appear to suffer competition from any other bat species (e.g., noctule). This may explain its relative success and abundance there. The main threat to this species in Ireland is the exclusion of nursery colonies from buildings.

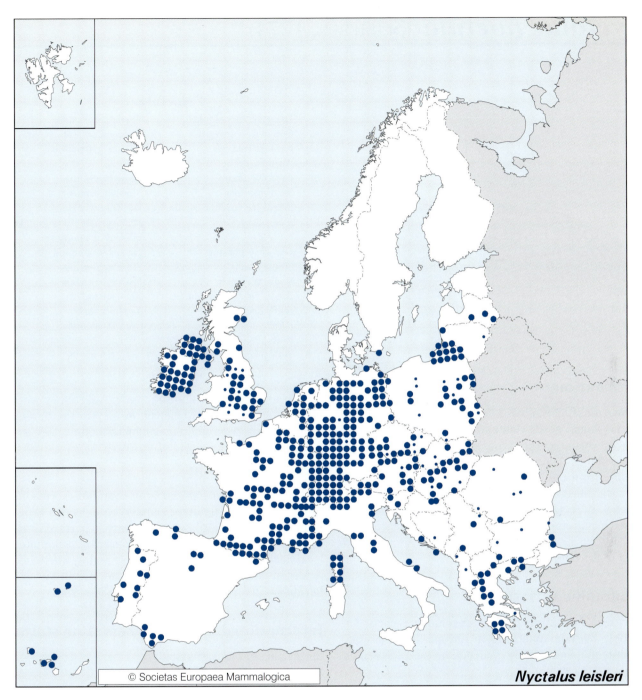

© Societas Europaea Mammalogica

Nyctalus leisleri

Literature

Bates & Harrison (1997)
Bogdanowicz & Ruprecht (in press) – review
Hanák & Gaisler (1983)
Palmeirim (1991)
Schober & Grimmberger (1989)
Sullivan *et al.* (1993)

C. Shiel

Nyctalus noctula (SCHREBER, 1774)

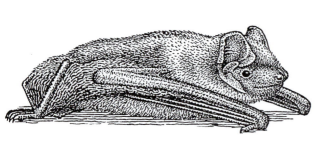

P. Twisk

Noctule

AL	Lakuriqnate noktule	LU	Bëschflëntermaus
BG	Обикновен вечерник	LV	Rūsganais vakarsikspārnis
CZ	Netopýr rezavý	MK	Лисест вечерник
DE	Abendsegler	MT	Noktula
DK	Brunflagermus	NL	Rosse vleermuis
EE	Suurvidevlane	NO	Storflaggermus
ES	Murciélago nóctulo común	PL	Borowiec wielki
FI	Isolepakko	PT	Morcego-arborícola-grande
FO	-	RO	Liliacul-de-amurg
FR	Noctule commune	RU	Рыжая вечерница
GR	Νυχτοβάτης	SE	Stor fladdermus
HR	Rani večernjak	SI	Navadni mračnik
HU	Közönséges koraidenevér	SK	Netopier hrdzavý
IR	Ialtóg noctúil	TR	Akşamcı yarasa
IS	Húmblaka	YU	Средњи ноћник
IT	Nottola comune		
LT	Rudasis nakviša		

Distribution

World: most of Europe and Asia to south-western Siberia, China, north Vietnam, and Taiwan, doubtfully Malaysia. Also recorded from Africa. Assumed to have reached Mozambique on at least one occasion.
Europe: from the Iberian Peninsula to the Urals and Caucasus. Several bat-detector records from Ireland (I. Ahlén & H. J. Baagøe, pers. comm.). In Sweden the northern limit coincides with the *limes norrlandicus* (60-61°N), which marks the transition from the broad-leaved forest to the boreal coniferous forest.

Geographic variation

At present, five subspecies are presumably recognized, but only the nominate form in Europe. It is possible, however, that there is more than one species represented in this complex.

Habitat

Altitudinal range from sea level to 1923 m in the Alps. The species originally used trees throughout the year and rock crevices for hibernation, but has now adopted buildings, particularly for hibernation in central Europe. Forages mainly over lakes, ponds, meadows, and marshland, usually in the vicinity (<10 km) of the roosting site. Preys preferentially on Trichoptera, Diptera, Lepidoptera, and Coleoptera. Low winter temperatures govern the need for southerly, frequently mass migration in autumn. In spring, only females are known to migrate back to the region where they were born, while males are believed to stay in the mating area. Longest recorded movement 1600 km.

Population status

In general still widespread and abundant across its range. In optimal habitats, population densities range from 30 to 80 ind./km². Now quite rare in parts of Great Britain, particularly in agricultural areas. Documented local declines in the Netherlands are mainly attributed to loss of wetlands. Regarded as vulnerable in Sweden because of the rapid destruction of hollow trees.

International legal & conservation status

Bern Convention, Appendix II.
Bonn Convention, Appendix II.
EU Habitats & Species Directive, Annex IV.

Other information

May be subject to some illegal persecution. The availability of tree holes may limit populations, and bat-boxes are readily used. In Germany, found with a concentration of organochlorine residues which may cause chronic diseases.

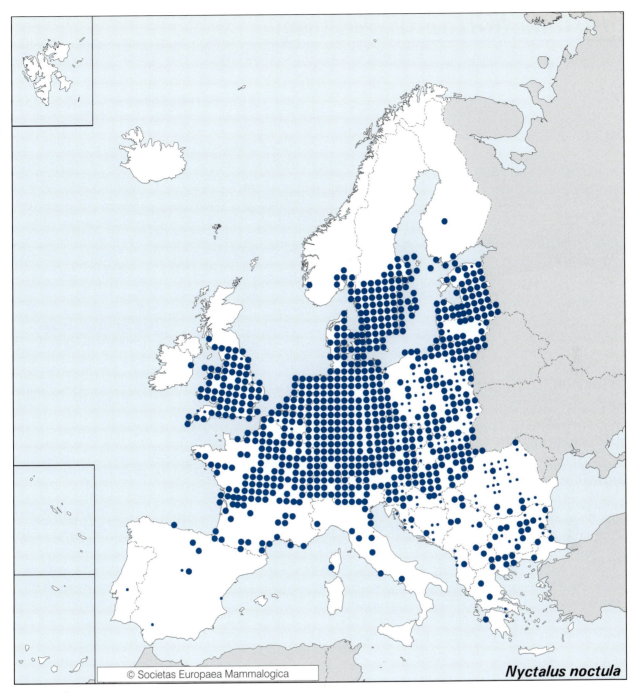

© Societas Europaea Mammalogica

Nyctalus noctula

Literature

Ahlén & Gerell (1989)
Boonman *et al.* (1997)
Corbet & Hill (1992)
Gaisler *et al.* (1979)
Gloor *et al.* (1995)
Scharenberg (1992)

W. Bogdanowicz

Eptesicus bottae (Peters, 1869)

T. P. McOwat

Distribution

World: from the island of Rhodes in Europe, Asia Minor, Egypt, and Arabia to Pakistan and north-western China. *Europe:* currently recorded only from Rhodes.

Geographic variation

Several subspecies in Asia but in Europe only *E. bottae anatolicus* Felten, 1971 (east to south-western Iran).

Habitat

In Rhodes and southern Anatolia confined to coastal plains below about 200 m above sea level. Day roosts in narrow crevices between stones or bricks in the ceilings and walls of ruins, other buildings and, presumably, rock-faces.

Population status

The species is reasonably widespread but probably never abundant. Seems to be fairly common on Rhodes.

International legal & conservation status

Bern Convention, Appendix II.
Bonn Convention, Appendix II.
EU Habitats & Species Directive, Annex IV.

Literature

Felten (1971)
Hanák & Gaisler (1971)
Helversen (in press)
Nader & Kock (1990)
Spitzenberger (1994)

O. von Helversen

© Societas Europaea Mammalogica

Eptesicus bottae

Eptesicus nilssonii (KEYSERLING & BLASIUS, 1839)

V. Ree

Northern bat

AL	-	LT	Šiaurinis šikšnys
BG	Северен кожовиден прилеп	LU	-
CZ	Netopýr severní	LV	Ziemeļu sikspārnis
DE	Nordfledermaus	MK	Обичен северник
DK	Nordflagermus	MT	-
EE	Põhja-nahkhiir	NL	Noordse vleermuis
ES	Murciélago de huerta norteño	NO	Nordflaggermus
		PL	Mroczek pozłocisty
FI	Pohjanlepakko	PT	-
FO	-	RO	Liliacul-nordic
FR	Sérotine de Nilsson	RU	Северный кожанок
GR	-	SE	Nordisk fladdermus
HR	Sjeverni noćnjak	SI	Severni netopir
HU	Északi késeidenevér	SK	-
IR	-	TR	-
IS	Norðleðurblaka	YU	Северни поноћњак
IT	Serotino di Nilsson		

Distribution

World: Palaearctic, from central Europe to Japan.
Europe: mainly northern and central Europe. The only bat that reaches the Arctic circle.

Geographic variation

Subspecific status very unclear; from two to six subspecies currently recognized by different authors. Only the nominate form in Europe.

Habitat

Associated with uplands in the south and with areas of human habitation, particularly in the north. Altitudinal range between 200–2000 m above sea level. Colonies nearly always in houses in summer. In winter, mostly in houses and cellars. Catches only flying insects, mainly small dipterans (30–80% by volume), but also moths, dung-beetles and insects that fly over water. Feeds in open places, along edges of woodlands, over lakes and rivers and also near street lamps in built up areas. No long-range migration recorded; longest known movement 115 km.

Population status

No evidence for population decline in Europe. Widespread and common over much of its range, increasing in some areas. Most abundant bat in the north. Population density in Scandinavia decreases with increasing latitude, being about five times higher at 57°N than in a similar landscape at 65°N.

International legal & conservation status

Bern Convention, Appendix II.
Bonn Convention, Appendix II.
EU Habitats & Species Directive, Annex IV.

Other information

Being a house bat, it may be subject to some persecution by house owners, but since colonies are small, serious problems are relatively uncommon.

Literature

Hanák & Horáček (1986)
Koopman (1994)
Rydell (1992, 1993)-review
Rydell *et al.* (1994)
Zukal & Gaisler (1989)

J. Rydell

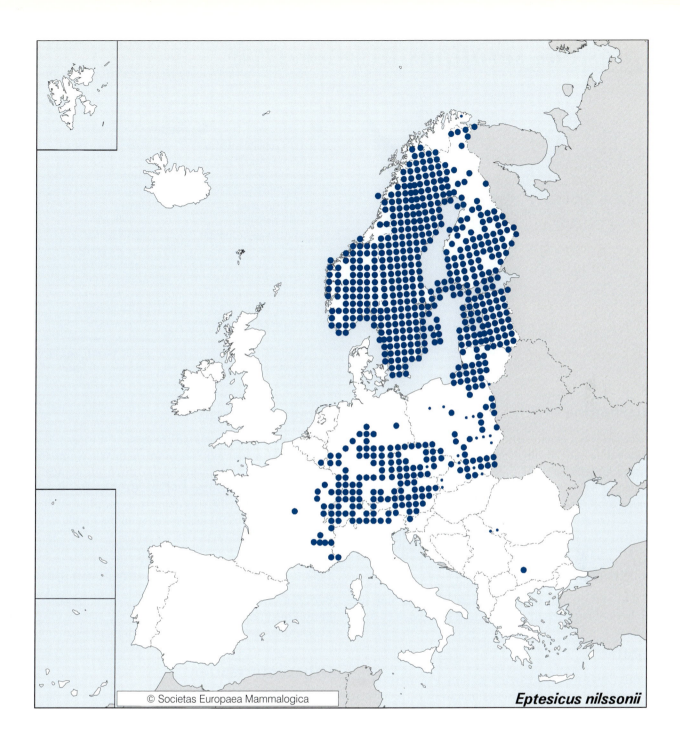

© Societas Europaea Mammalogica

Eptesicus nilssonii

Eptesicus serotinus (Schreber, 1774)

Z. Bihari

Serotine

AL	Lakuriqnate serotine	LT	Vėlyvasis šikšnys
BG	Късновечерен прилеп	LU	-
CZ	Netopýr večerní	LV	Platspārnu sikspārnis
DE	Breitflügelfledermaus	MK	Ширококрилен северник
DK	Sydflagermus	MT	Serotin
EE	Hilis-nahkhiir	NL	Laatvlieger
ES	Murciélago de huerta	NO	Sørflaggermus
FI	Etelänlepakko	PL	Mroczek późny
FO	-	PT	Morcego-hortelão
FR	Sérotine commune	RO	Liliacul-cu-aripi-late
GR	Τρανονυχτερίδα	RU	Поздний кожан
HR	Kasni noćnjak	SE	Sydfladdermus
HU	Közönséges késeidenevér	SI	Pozni netopir
IR	-	SK	Netopier pozdný
IS	Síðblaka	TR	Geniş kanatlı yarasa
IT	Serotino comune	YU	Велики поноћњак

Distribution

World: Europe, North Africa, Near East, central Asia, east to China and Taiwan. Northern Indomalayan region. **Europe:** absent from Ireland, northern Britain, most of Sweden, Norway, Finland and Estonia. Found throughout the rest of Europe, including some Mediterranean islands. One record also from the Canary Islands.

Geographic variation

Several extralimital subspecies accepted, but only the nominate form currently recognized in Europe.

Habitat

Highly synanthropic with summer roosts most commonly in buildings, occasionally trees, where it forms maternity colonies of *ca.* 20–60 individuals (up to 100 +). Winter roosts in buildings, underground sites in small numbers, particularly in south-eastern Europe. Hunts in varying habitats, including parkland, hedgerows, woodland edge, white streetlights and gardens, and unimproved pastures. Preys mainly on chafer beetles in spring and early summer, and dung beetles in autumn, also moths, tipulids and other small dipterans, hemipterans, and hymenopterans. Recorded up to 900 m in summer, and 1 100 m in winter. Generally sedentary; longest recorded movement 330 km.

Population status

Population probably stable in most of Europe. Some evidence of recent expansion in Denmark. Some local declines recorded with perceived threat to population owing to loss of pasture and increase in use of cattle antihelminthic drugs reducing the number of dung beetles. Also problems associated with maintenance and renovation of buildings.

International legal & conservation status

Bern Convention, Appendix II.
Bonn Convention, Appendix II.
EU Habitats & Species Directive, Annex IV.

Other information

The bat species with the highest incidence of rabies-related virus in mainland Europe.

Literature

Baagøe (1986)
Beck (1995)
Brass (1994)
Catto *et al.* (1994)
Koopman (1994)
Robinson & Stebbings (1994)

C. M. C. Catto & A. M. Hutson

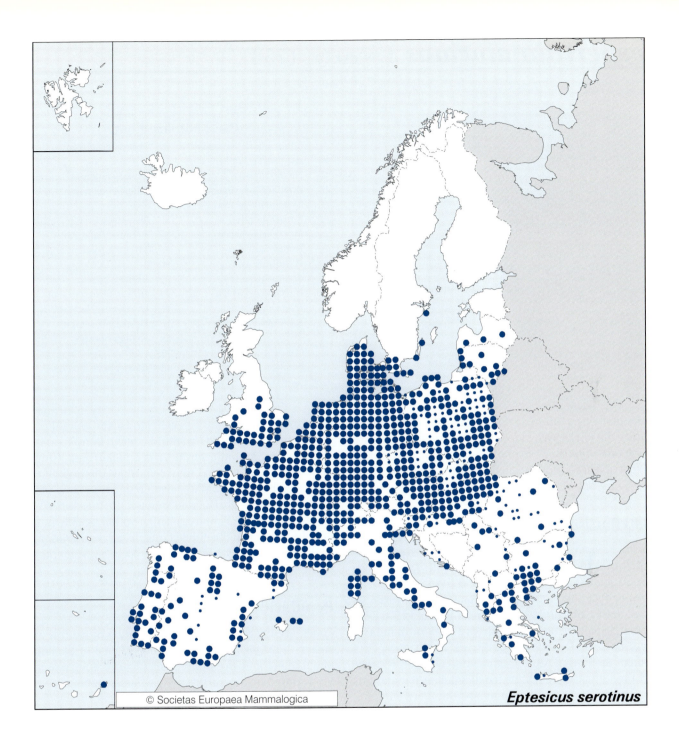

Eptesicus serotinus

Vespertilio murinus LINNAEUS, 1758

D. Roth

Linnaeus' description lacks detail, and in the 19th century the name was widely, but erroneously used also for *Myotis myotis*. To avoid this confusion some 20th century authors have argued for and used the name *Vespertilio discolor* Kuhl, 1817.

Distribution

World: Palaearctic. North to northern Russia, east to Manchuria and the Ussuri Region, south to northern Iran, Afghanistan, and northern Pakistan.
Europe: distributional border difficult to specify exactly for all areas, but probably northern Russia (55–61°N), southern Sweden, southern Norway, eastern Denmark, north-eastern Germany, south-west to France, east through the Italian Alps, south-east to northern Greece and the Caucasus. Perhaps small satellite populations or migrants in the Netherlands and southern Finland. Westernmost records of breeding: eastern Denmark, north-eastern and south-western Germany and Switzerland. Numerous vagrants found far outside the normal range as far as the Faroes.

Geographic variation

Two subspecies are recognized: *V. murinus ussuriensis* Wallin, 1969 (south-eastern Siberia, Korea, north-eastern China) and *V. m. murinus* (remainder of range).

Habitat

Typically forages at 10–40 m height, in straight flight in the open air over many different landscape types. Feeds on beetles and moths around street lamps in late summer and autumn, but insects smaller than 10 mm (dipterans, aphids, etc.) may constitute the bulk of the food at all seasons. Maternity colonies in low, often modern, and well-insulated houses. In Russia also in hollow trees and nest boxes. Hibernation usually in tall buildings, often in big cities. Long distance migration in eastern and central Europe, but local movements in Denmark.

Population status

Considered rare or vulnerable in much of central and eastern Europe, but there is no evidence of declining populations and the number of records is increasing. Very abundant in north-east Zealand, Denmark, and common and perhaps spreading in southern Sweden.

International legal & conservation status

Bern Convention, Appendix II.
Bonn Convention, Appendix II.
EU Habitats & Species Directive, Annex IV.

Other information

V. murinus has a characteristic low frequency (down to 10 kHz) display sound heard in towns in the autumn, most often around large buildings used as winter roosts. Nurseries sometimes cause problems in Danish one family houses.

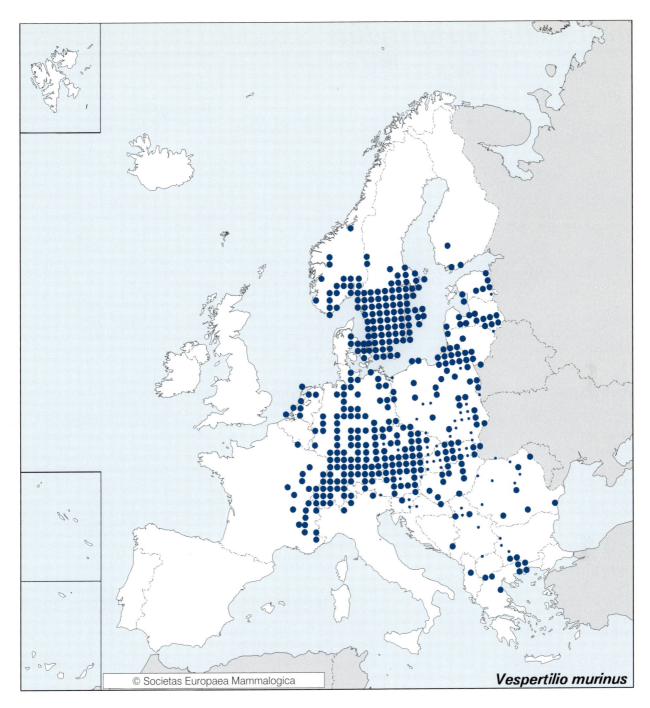

© Societas Europaea Mammalogica

Vespertilio murinus

Literature

Baagøe (in press b) – review
Baagøe & Bloch (1994)
Rydell & Baagøe (1994) – review

H. J. Baagøe

Barbastella barbastellus (SCHREBER, 1774)

T. P. McOwat

Distribution

World: from the north of the Iberian Peninsula to the Caucasus and from southern Scandinavia and Latvia to some, Mediterranean islands and Morocco; also Canary Islands.

Europe: throughout, except Iceland, Northern Ireland, Scotland, most of Scandinavia, Estonia and much of southern Europe. A single bat-detector record from Ireland (I. Ahlén, pers. comm).

Geographic variation

None known.

Habitat

Probably prefers upland and forest habitats. In Austria known localities range from 170 m to 1990 m altitude but are concentrated in the submontane and montane belt. Recorded at 2260 m in the Pyrenean mountains. Hunts over water, along forest edges, and in parks. Roosts in hollow trees and buildings. Diet includes mainly microlepidopterans and small dipterans. Nursery colonies often found behind window shutters. Hibernates in caves, bunkers, tunnels or cellars, especially in cold places; usually solitary or in small groups but occasionally in large tight clusters of several hundred individuals. Appears to make reasonably long flights (up to 290 km), but data about regular migrations are lacking.

Population status

Little known. Seems to be one of the rarest bats in western Europe. Endangered in several countries, including Germany, Switzerland, France, and Belgium. Probably extinct in the Netherlands (1994). A population decrease has been reported in most of its European range. The population density is probably much higher in central Europe (Bavaria, Bohemia, Slovakia, Poland), where winter colonies of several hundred bats are found. Most records come from winter periods and there have been few summer observations.

International legal & conservation status

Bern Convention, Appendix II.
Bonn Convention, Appendix II.
EU Habitats & Species Directive, Annex II & Annex IV.
IUCN Red List, Vulnerable.

Other information

May be subject to some illegal persecution. Very sensitive to disturbance and this factor, together with the loss of roosts and food, is probably causing a major population decrease. Protecting key sites and creating new roosts would be the most important conservation measures.

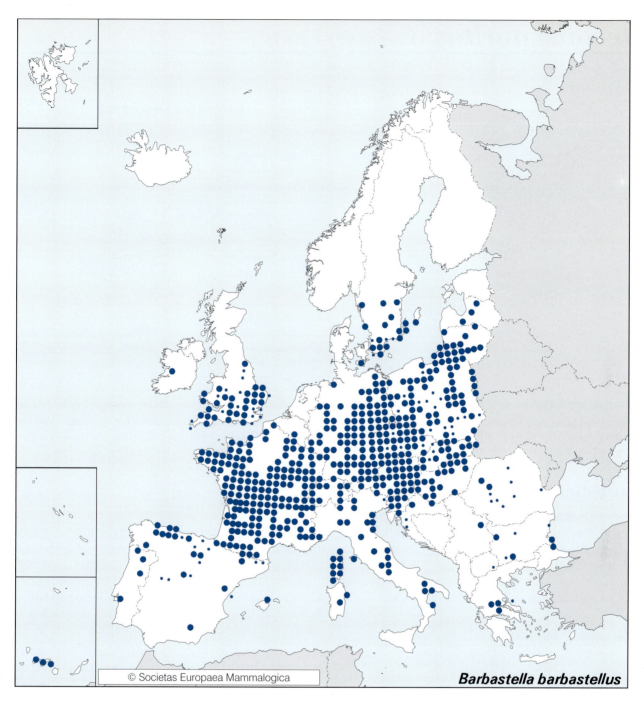

© Societas Europaea Mammalogica

Barbastella barbastellus

Literature

Hollander & Limpens (1997)
Richarz (1989)
Rydell & Bogdanowicz (1997) – review
Spitzenberger (1993)
Stebbings (1988)
Urbańczyk (1990)

Z. Urbańczyk

Plecotus auritus (Linnaeus, 1758)

R. Lindsay

Brown long-eared bat

AL	Lakuriqnate veshgjate	LV	Garausainais sikspārnis;
BG	Дългоух прилеп		Brūnais garausainis
CZ	Netopýr ušatý	MK	Ушест лилјак
DE	Braunes Langohr	MT	-
DK	Langøret flagermus	NL	Grootoorvleermuis
EE	Suurkõrv; Pruun-suurkõrv	NO	Langøreflaggermus
ES	Murciélago orejudo dorado	PL	Gacek brunatny
FI	Korvayökkö	PT	Morcego-orelhudo-
FO	-		castanho
FR	Oreillard roux	RO	Liliacul-urecheat-brun
GR	Ωτονυχτερίδα	RU	Бурый ушан
HR	Sjeverni dugouhi šišmiš	SE	Långörad fladdermus
HU	Barna hosszúfülű-denevér	SI	Rjavi uhati netopir
IR	Ialtóg fhadcluasach	SK	Netopier svetlý
IS	Langeyrnablaka	TR	Kahverengi uzun kulaklı
IT	Orecchione comune		yarasa
LT	Rudasis ausylis	YU	Смеђи дчгочхи лиљак
LU	Laangouer-Flёntermaus		

Similar in appearance to *Plecotus austriacus*, but generally smaller and its pelage is a browner colour; thumb usually over 6 mm, thumb claw long (2.5–3.0 mm) and pointed.

Distribution

World: Palaearctic, from the British Isles through Europe; disjunct distribution across Asia, with populations occurring in Mongolia, south-east Siberia, north-west China, and Japan.
Europe: widespread; as far south as southern Portugal, Italy, and Greece, and as far north as 63–64°N.

Geographic variation

Of the two currently recognized European subspecies, *P. auritus auritus* has a broad distribution in temperate and a large part of meridional Europe, whereas *P. a. begognae* de Paz, 1994 is practically limited to the centre of the Iberian Peninsula. Morphometrically, *P. a. begognae* is larger than the nominate form.

Habitat

Generally a woodland species, but will also hunt around isolated trees in parks and gardens. Lepidoptera and Diptera are the preferred prey and are often gleaned from foliage. Appears to forage in the vicinity of the roost, generally within 1 km. Uses the roof spaces of houses, barns, and churches, as well as tree holes in summer. Often roosts in older, wood-lined buildings, which are situated close to woodland. Hibernates in caves, mines, buildings, and trees. Highest nursery roost 1660 m (Switzerland), otherwise up to 2000 m, but usually below that. Considered to be sedentary; longest recorded movement 66 km.

Population status

In summer distributed in many small colonies, with little interchange between them. Generally abundant in northern Europe, but rare in more southern countries. In central Europe (western Bohemia) summer population density about 0.1 ind./km². Evidence of local population declines in the Netherlands, and some suggestion of historical declines in north-eastern Scotland.

International legal & conservation status

Bern Convention, Appendix II.
Bonn Convention, Appendix II.
EU Habitats & Species Directive, Annex IV.

Other information

Vulnerable to inappropriate pesticide applications within roosts. Bat-boxes may provide important roosts for this species.

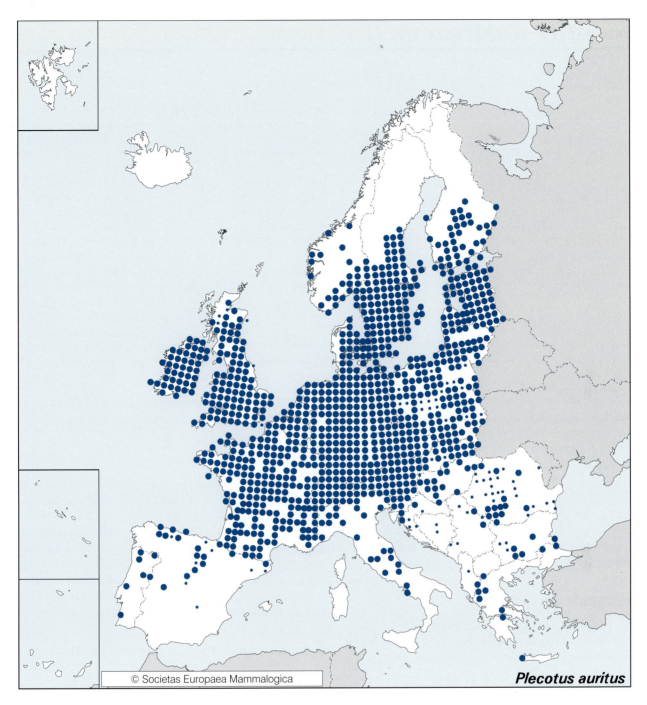

© Societas Europaea Mammalogica

Plecotus auritus

Literature

Entwistle *et al.* (1996, 1997)
Heise & Schmidt (1988)
Hůrka (1989)
Jansen & Buys (1997)
Olsen *et al.* (1996)

A. C. Entwistle

Plecotus austriacus (J. B. Fischer, 1829)

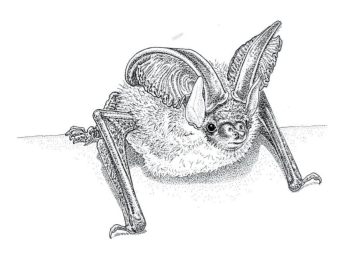

R. Lindsay

Grey long-eared bat

AL	Lakuriqnate veshgjate i hirte	LT	Pilkasis ausylis
BG	Сив дългоух прилеп	LU	Gro Laangouer-Flëntermaus
CZ	Netopýr dlouhouchý	LV	Pelēkais garausainis
DE	Graues Langohr	MK	Сив ушест лилјак
DK	Grå langøret flagermus	MT	Farfett il-Lejl Widnejħ Kbar
EE	Hall-suurkõrv	NL	Grijze grootoorvleermuis
ES	Murciélago orejudo gris	NO	Grå langøreflaggermus
FI	Harmaakorvayökkö	PL	Gacek szary
FO	-	PT	Morcego-orelhudo-cinzento
FR	Oreillard gris	RO	Liliacul urecheat cenuşiu
GR	Μεσογειακὴ ωτονυχτερίδα	RU	Серый ушан
HR	Juzni dugouhi šišmiš	SE	Grå långörad fladdermus
HU	Szürke hosszúfülű-denevér	SI	Sivi uhati netopir
IR	-	SK	Netopier sivý
IS	-	TR	Gri uzun kulaklı yarasa
IT	Orecchione meridionale	YU	Сиви дчгочхи љиљак

Distribution

World: from Iberia and North Africa, north to southern England, eastwards throughout mainland Europe, except for Denmark and most of Scandinavia, to Mongolia, western China and the Himalayas. Also the Cape Verde islands.
Europe: from Portugal in the west and southern England, The Netherlands, northern Germany and northern Poland in the north, to south-west Belarus, the Ukraine and the Caucasus in the east, and Italy and Greece in the south. Also present on Madeira

Geographic variation

Many extralimital names. Of the two currently recognized European subspecies, *P. austriacus austriacus* has a broad distribution in temperate and a large part of meridional Europe, whereas *P. a. kolombatovici* Đulić, 1980 is geographically most probably limited to the Adriatic coast and islands of the former Yugoslavia. Morphometrically, *P. a. kolombatovici* is smaller than the nominate form.

Habitat

In central Europe, associated with lowland basins and open agricultural landscapes. Common in both small settlements and large towns, where it occupies various spaces in buildings. In southern Europe, inhabits a great variety of open and semi-covered areas in the subxerothermic country and roosts primarily in rocky cavities. Hibernates in buildings, caves, mines, and trees. Diet dominated by Lepidoptera (Noctuidae and Hepialidae). Sedentary, longest recorded movement 62 km.

Population status

Relatively numerous in the Mediterranean and Transcaucasia and in the regions south of its northern border, including central Germany at about 50–52°N. In western Bohemia in the Czech Republic, summer population density was estimated to be around 0.1 ind./km². A density of up to 5 ind./km² has been recorded in the old residential quarters and garden areas of Brno. A decline in the 1970s in the northern part of its range has been attributed to cooler weather conditions.

International legal & conservation status

Bern Convention, Appendix II.
Bonn Convention, Appendix II.
EU Habitats & Species Directive, Annex IV.

Other information

Vulnerable to remedial timber treatment. In Germany, found to be contaminated with residues of organochlorine insecticides, and seems to suffer badly from poisoning by wood preserving chemicals used during the renovation of buildings.

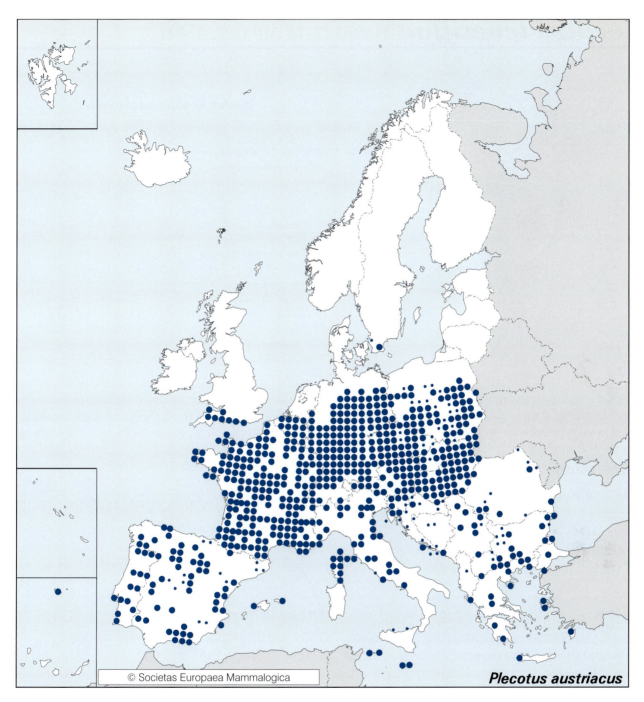

© Societas Europaea Mammalogica

Plecotus austriacus

Literature

Braun (1986)
Corbet & Hill (1992)
Gaisler (1979)
Horáček *et al.* (in press) – review
Hůrka (1989)
Strelkov (1988)

W. Bogdanowicz

151

Plecotus teneriffae Barrett-Hamilton, 1907

P. Twisk

Previously listed frequently either within *Plecotus auritus* or within *P. austriacus,* but now regarded as a valid species by most authors.

Distribution

World and Europe: very limited; only three of the Canary Islands: Tenerife, La Palma, and El Hierro.

Geographic variation

None known.

Habitat

Associated mostly with woods and scrubland, preferring pine forests of *Pinus canariensis* to mixed or laurel forests. Altitudinal range from 170 m up to 2300 m. Roosts solitary or in small clusters in the outer areas of caves (volcanic tubes) and water mines, sometimes in buildings and in crevices of bridges, both in summer and winter. To date only one nursery colony of 61 bats recorded in a cave. Never found in tree holes or in bat- or bird-boxes. Hunts mainly by gleaning insects from foliage; also observed to prey on flying insects inside caves or water mines. Diet dominated by noctuid moths.

Population status

Not well known as there are no historical data. On the largest of the Canary Islands (Tenerife) more abundant on the northern than on the southern slopes. The population declined in the 1950s after aerial fumigations for pest control, but it is now likely to be increasing. Although it is fairly abundant in the archipelago, the very limited range makes it vulnerable.

International legal & conservation status

Bern Convention, Appendix II.
Bonn Convention, Appendix II.
EU Habitats & Species Directive, Annex IV.
IUCN Red List, Vulnerable.

Other information

A regional programme for bat protection started on the Canary Islands in 1993. By 1994 18 caves occupied by *P. teneriffae* had been protected from human disturbance.

Literature

Benzal & Fajardo (1994)
Benzal & Izquierdo (1993)
Ibáñez & Fernández (1985)
Koopman (1993)
Trujillo (1991)

J. Benzal & S. Fajardo

© Societas Europaea Mammalogica

Plecotus teneriffae

Miniopterus schreibersii (Kuhl, 1817)

P. Barrett

The taxonomy of non-European populations is unclear, with one author even suggesting that *M. schreibersii* is actually a complex of allopatric species. This view is not widely accepted and we do not follow it here. The genus *Miniopterus* is often placed in its own family, Miniopteridae, separated from the Vespertilionidae.

Distribution

World: present in most Old World tropical and sub-tropical regions, from southern Eurasia to Africa, Australia, and the Solomon Islands.
Europe: southern Europe, from Iberia to the Caucasus.

Geographic variation

The European population is morphologically very uniform and only the nominate subspecies is recognized on this continent. Elsewhere, the situation is still poorly studied.

Habitat

A colonial species that roosts almost exclusively in caves and mines throughout the year, often forming colonies of several thousand individuals. Isolated individuals or small groups are sometimes found in other types of shelters, such as attics. The roost climatic requirements vary throughout the year and individuals are known to migrate up to 550 km in search of roosts appropriate to each season. Parturition colonies and non-breeding individuals often occupy different roosts. During the nursing season the females are highly philopatric, returning to give birth in the roosts where they were born.

Population status

Although there are still some very large colonies, the species has declined markedly. This decline is particularly evident in the northern part of the European range, from Romania to France. In other areas, the species also seems to be declining due to human disturbance, closure of roosts, and insecticide applications.

International legal & conservation status

Bern Convention, Appendix II.
Bonn Convention, Appendix II.
EU Habitats & Species Directive, Annex II & Annex IV.
IUCN Red List, Lower Risk – near threatened.

Other information

Since most of its population is concentrated in a few roosts, these should be protected. However, care should be taken since there is evidence that these bats do not tolerate grilles placed at the entrance of their roosts.

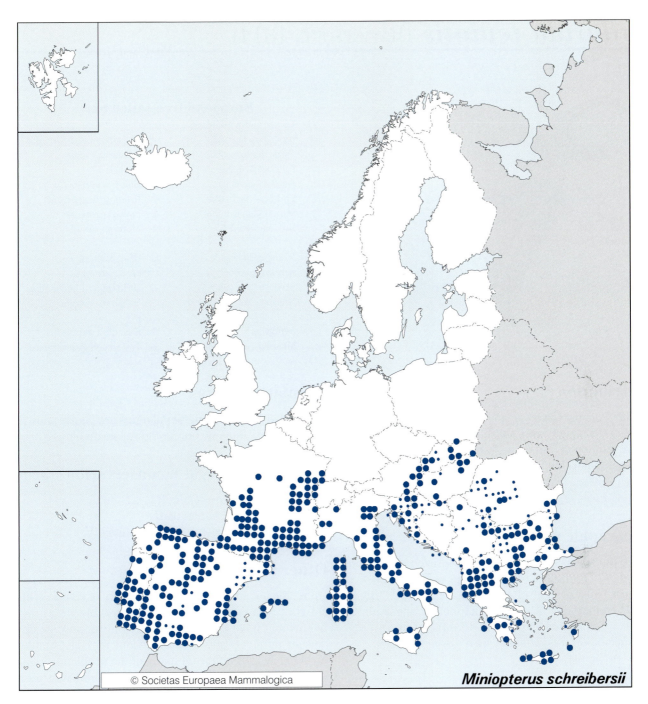

© Societas Europaea Mammalogica

Miniopterus schreibersii

Literature

Bernard & Bester (1988)
Maeda (1982)
Palmeirim & Rodrigues (1995)
Richardson (1977)
Serra-Cobo & Balcells (1991)
van der Merwe (1973)

L. Rodrigues

Tadarida teniotis (Rafinesque, 1814)

P. Twisk

Distribution

World: from the Canary Islands through northern Africa, southern Europe, and southern palaearctic Asia to Japan, southern China and Taiwan.
Europe: mainly Mediterranean region, north to southern France, Switzerland, southern Croatia and Bulgaria. Also in the Caucasus.

Geographic variation

Three subspecies are currently recognized: *T. teniotis rueppellii* (Temminck, 1826) (Egypt and Arabia), *T. t. teniotis* (west of Central Asia) and *T. t. insignis* (Blyth, 1861) (remainder of range). Taxonomic allocation of some populations from Asia is uncertain and the subspecies *T. t. insignis* may be a distinct species.

Habitat

Open habitat, roosting in fissures and hollows in rock outcrops, quarries, and sea cliffs. Also sometimes in artificial structures, including bridges, water towers, cathedrals, and other tall buildings. Altitudinal range from sea level to 2300 m. A high and fast-flying aerial hawker, emerging late and returning early, using low frequency echolocation calls to avoid detection by tympanate moths. Colonies usually small, from 5 to 50, sometimes up to 130 individuals (J. Benzal, in litt.). Winter behaviour poorly known, but activity recorded in winter in Malta (J. Borg, pers. comm.) and Switzerland. Probable short-range or partial migrant.

Population status

Detailed distribution and populations are poorly known; generally low density, but no figures available.

International legal & conservation status

Bern Convention, Appendix II.
Bonn Convention, Appendix II.
EU Habitats & Species Directive, Annex IV.

Other information

Difficulties of study (e.g., inaccessibility of roosts, wide ranging foraging behaviour and possible migratory behaviour) have resulted in little information on this species until recently. This behaviour may also render it relatively immune from many of the problems facing bats, although quarrying has been identified as a problem in some areas. More research is urgently required.

Literature

Arlettaz (1990, 1995)
Corbet & Hill (1992)
Koopman (1994)
Rydell & Arlettaz (1994)
Yoshiyuki (1989)

A. M. Hutson

156

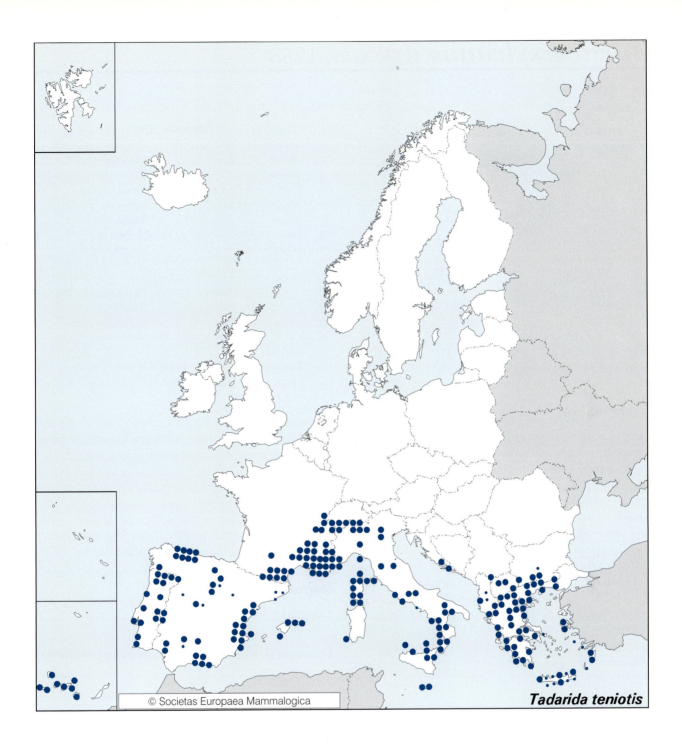

© Societas Europaea Mammalogica

Tadarida teniotis

157

Macaca sylvanus (Linnaeus, 1758)

E. Hazebroek

	Barbary ape		
AL	Majmun Makak	LT	Magotas
BG	Магот	LU	Berberaf
CZ	Magot	LV	Ziemeļāfrikas makaks
DE	Magot	MK	Макак магот
DK	Magot; Berberabe	MT	Xadina ta' Barbarija
EE	Magot	NL	Magot
ES	Mona de Berbería	NO	Berberape
FI	Magotti	PL	Makak magot
FO	-	PT	Macaco de Gibraltar
FR	Magot	RO	-
GR	-	RU	Варварийская обезьяна
HR	Bezrepi magot	SE	Berberapa
HU	Berber makákó	SI	Berberska opica
IR	-	SK	Makak magot
IS	Serkjaapi	TR	-
IT	Bertuccia	YU	-

Distribution

World: Palaearctic region of north Africa but primarily restricted to high mountains in Morocco (Rif region, Moyen Atlas, Haut Atlas) and Algeria (Djurdjuras, Kabylies). Confined to fragmented populations throughout its current range.

Europe: formerly widespread throughout Europe during Pleistocene times but probably became extinct due to anthropogenic pressures. There is no evidence of remnant populations surviving into historic times anywhere in Europe. However, an introduced population has been maintained on the Rock of Gibraltar, with the first animals likely to have originated from an importation in the early 1740s. There are reports of at least three other introductions of monkeys from Morocco to Gibraltar; the last of which (1939–1943) gave rise to the current population in Gibraltar.

Geographic variation

No subspecies recognized. However, recent studies have indicated clear genetic differences between Algerian and Moroccan populations.

Habitat

The species is found in a variety of habitat types in north Africa, ranging from dry Mediterranean scrub, oak *(Quercus suber, Q. ilex)* woodlands to high-altitude coniferous forests (fir and cedar). In Gibraltar, the species uses the Rock's cliff systems and more open areas, and will occasionally penetrate the more extensive thick matorral vegetation which covers most of the upper Rock. Some troops of monkeys are known, more so in the past, to enter the town areas on the lower slopes of the Rock. A sub-population of monkeys is well-habituated to humans and spends most of its active time along tourist-frequented roads on the upper Rock in wait for food handouts. This has had detrimental consequences on the health of the monkeys, and has increased the risk of monkey bites to people.

Population status

140–150 monkeys in six troops.

International legal & conservation status

IUCN Red List, Vulnerable.
CITES, Appendix II. EC 338/97, Annex B.

Other information

The monkeys of Gibraltar are not affected by habitat destruction, illegal poaching or by any other major threat typical of wild populations. The population does need, however, to be managed scientifically in order to ensure its long-term viability (genetic and demographic) on the Rock. Despite their importance, the Barbary apes on Gibraltar have been cared for by the British Army (1915–1957), later by the Gibraltar Regiment (1957–1992) and presently by a tourism-based private company (since 1992) with the sole aim of feeding the animals and offering *ad hoc* veterinary assistance. Problems relating

© Societas Europaea Mammalogica

Macaca sylvanus

to the impact of tourists, the unmonitored demographic and genetic condition of the populations and the consequences of an uncontrolled increase in numbers exceeding the area's carrying capacity, need urgent resolution.

Literature

Fa (1981, 1984, 1992)
Fa & Lind (1996)
Martin & von Segesser (1996)

J. E. Fa

159

Lepus capensis LINNAEUS, 1758

T. P. McOwat

Distribution

World: throughout Africa in non-forested areas. According to some authors, the species occurs also from the Middle East to China.
Europe: present only on Sardinia.

Geographic variation

Many subspecies have been recognized. *L. capensis mediterraneus* Wagner, 1841 is present on Sardinia.

Habitat

A wide ranging species occurring in a variety of biotopes in Africa, including desert and steppe areas, grasslands and mountain valleys up to 4000 m. The Sardinian subspecies is found throughout the island.

Population status

No estimates are available for the Sardinian population. Nevertheless a general decrease in numbers has been suspected in the recent past, even if it is considered locally common.

International legal & conservation status

Bern Convention, Appendix III.

Other information

In Italy the Sardinian hare is considered a game species. Captive breeding projects are carried out for restocking purposes.

Literature

Corbet (1978)
Spagnesi & Trocchi (1992)

F. M. Angelici

Lepus capensis

Lepus castroviejoi PALACIOS, 1977

D. Ovenden

Distribution

Endemic to the Iberian Peninsula. It occurs in the highlands of the Cantabrian Mountains (northern Spain), on a narrow fringe 230 km long by 25–40 km wide.

Geographic variation

A monotypic species.

Habitat

Lives mainly in mountain broom and heathlands, between 1000 and 1900 m. Also found in clearings of mixed deciduous forest.

Population status

Relatively abundant within its restricted range, except in the east. Present status unknown, apparently suffering a decline.

International legal & conservation status

Bern Convention, Appendix III (as part of *L. capensis sensu lato*).
IUCN Red List, Vulnerable.

Other information

Game species. Potential overhunting in the eastern part of its range. It needs protection due to its restricted range.

Literature

Palacios (1976)
Palacios & Meijide (1979)
Palacios & Ramos (1979)

R. García-Perea & J. Gisbert

© Societas Europaea Mammalogica

Lepus castroviejoi

Lepus corsicanus DE WINTON, 1898

D. Ovenden

Formerly considered a subspecies of *L. europaeus,* but recently recognized as a valid species on the basis of genetics morphometrics and morphological characters. Morphologically similar to *Lepus castroviejoi.*

Distribution

Endemic to central and southern Italy, including Sicily. The precise distribution is still not fully known. Introduced to Corsica around the 16th century, but probably extinct by the 1990s (R. Péroux, in litt.).

Geographic variation

A monotypic species.

Habitat

Very similar to that of *L. europaeus* but occurs also in the Mediterranean maquis. Due to competition between the two species, the remaining populations of *L. corsicanus* are now restricted to the mountainous areas of the peninsula and in lowlands and hills where the density of introduced brown hares is low. In Sicily, the species can occur also in the lowlands. Vertical range from sea level to 2000 m.

Population status

Uncertain. It probably suffered severe contraction due to hunting and competition with restocked *L. europaeus.*

International legal & conservation status

Bern Convention, Appendix III (as part of *L. capensis sensu lato).*

Other information

Game species because for Italian law still considered conspecific with *L. europaeus.* Captive breeding projects to safeguard this species are being carried out in Italy and Sicily.

Literature

Palacios (1996)
Vigne (1992)

F. M. Angelici

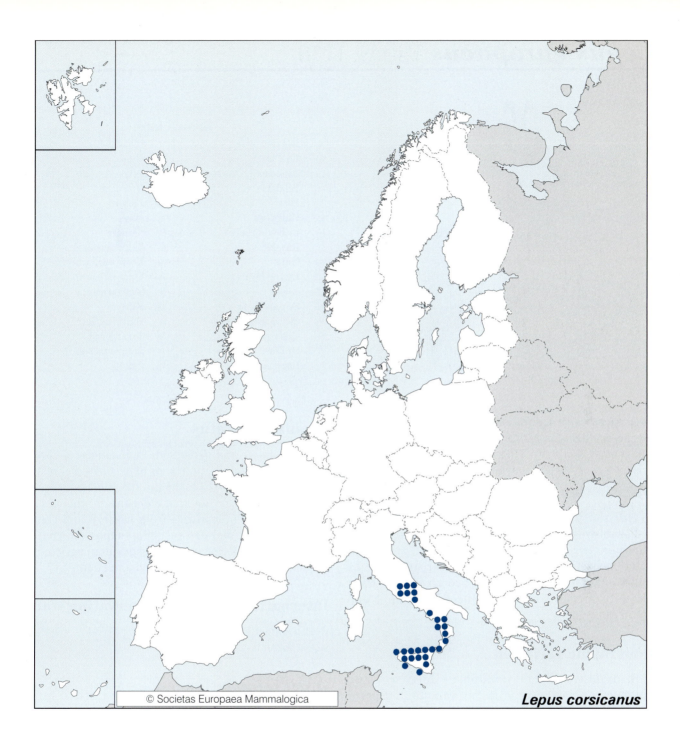

© Societas Europaea Mammalogica

Lepus corsicanus

Lepus europaeus PALLAS, 1778

F. Müller

Now specifically separated from similar but smaller species occurring in Africa, Iberia, southern Italy, Sicily and central Asia.

Distribution

World: from western Europe to west Siberian lowlands and south-west Asia (Iran).
Europe: throughout Europe except northern Scandinavia, northern Russia, the Iberian peninsula south of Cantabria and the Ebro river and most Mediterranean islands. Introduced to Ireland and southern Sweden.

Geographic variation

High mobility and occupation of dominant and continuous habitats result in low variation observed among mainland populations. However, several subspecies are recognized in Europe differing mainly in size and colour pattern. Geographic variation obscured by translocations.

Habitat

Temperate open woodland, farmland with pastures and grassland, steppes. Prefers flat country, occurring up to 1500 m in the mountains. Woods, scrub and hedges are used as resting sites.

Population status

Mainly solitary and dispersed, with ranges of several tens or, exceptionally, hundreds of hectares. Population densities vary from 0.2 to 0.7 ind./ha. Most populations considered secure. However, a decline in numbers has been recorded in countries from western and central Europe in recent decades, resulting supposedly from the extensive use of fertilizers and pesticides in agriculture, as well as heavy agricultural mechanization.

International legal & conservation status

Bern Convention, Appendix III (as part of *L. capensis sensu lato).*

Other information

Important game species in most countries. In areas of sympatric occurrence, it may occasionally hybridize with the mountain hare *Lepus timidus,* but the hybrids are sterile.

Literature

Angermann (1983)
Flux & Angermann (1990) – review
Hartl *et al.* (1993)
Pielowski & Pucek (1976)
Schneider (1978) – review
Zörner (1981) – review

M. Homolka & J. Zima

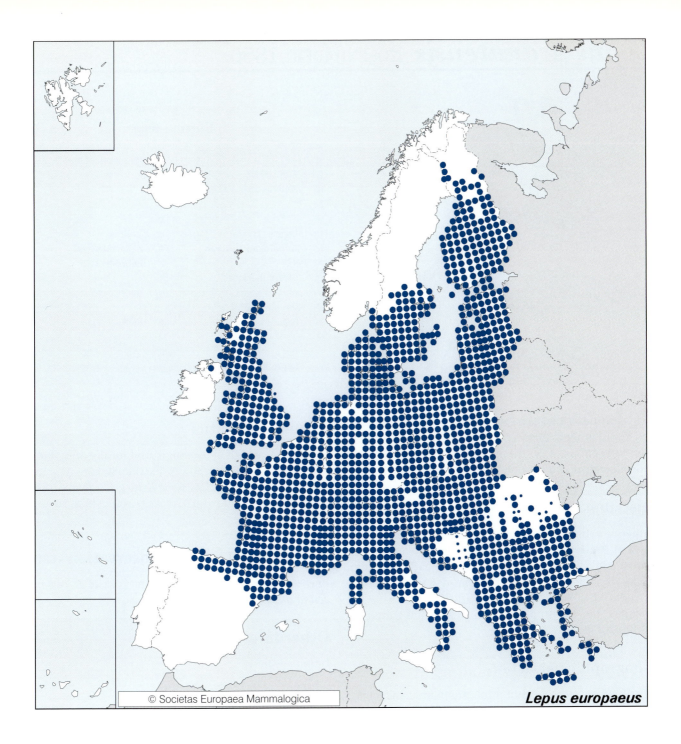

© Societas Europaea Mammalogica

Lepus europaeus

Lepus granatensis ROSENHAUER, 1856

D. Ovenden

Originally described as a species, it has been considered for decades as a form of *Lepus capensis*. It is now recognized as a valid species on the basis of morphological and genetic traits.

Distribution

Endemic to the Iberian-Balearic area. Its range includes most of the Iberian Peninsula (excluding the north-east and north centre), and Mallorca (Balearic Islands). Formerly on Ibiza (Balearic Islands), now extinct. Introduced to southern France and Corsica in recent decades, but no proof of established populations (R. Péroux, in litt.).

Geographic variation

Three subspecies, including the nominate subspecies, are recognized: *L. granatensis gallaecius* Miller, 1907 from Galicia and Asturias (north-west Spain), *L. g. granatensis* from the remainder of the Iberian Peninsula, and *L. g. solisi* Palacios and Fernandez, 1992 from Mallorca.

Habitat

The species occurs in a variety of habitats, from humid mountain forests (north-west of its range) to dry culture lands (central Spain) or dunes (Mediterranean coastal areas). In Mallorca, it appears in dry crops and thickets. It can be found from sea level to 1900m.

Population status

Common in much of its range, and locally abundant in central and southern Spain. Extremely rare or extinct in western Galicia and western Asturias, as well as north to the Ebro river. Rare on Mallorca, extinct in the western mountains.

International legal & conservation status

Bern Convention, Appendix III (as part of *L. capensis sensu lato).*

Other information

Game species.

Literature

Palacios (1978)
Palacios (1983)
Palacios & Fernandez (1992)
Palacios & Meijide (1979)

R. Garcia-Perea & J. Gisbert

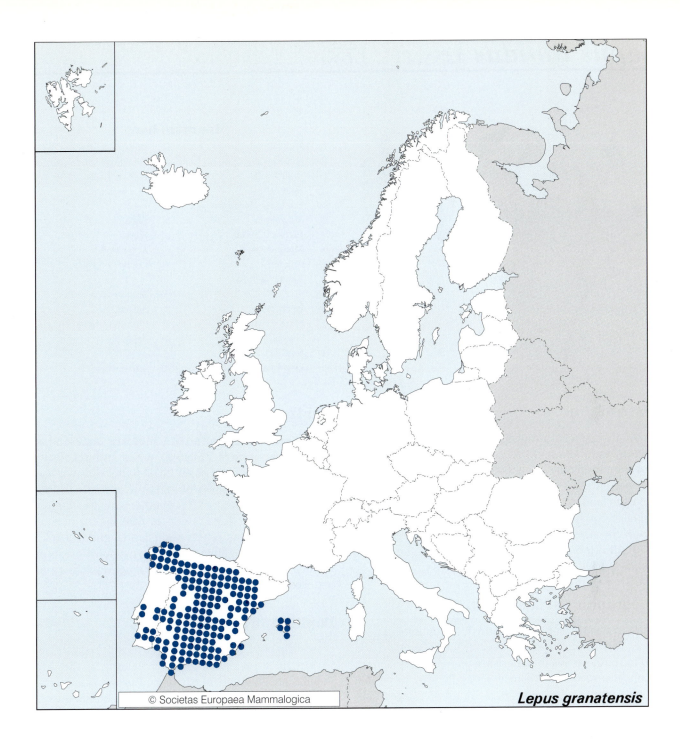

© Societas Europaea Mammalogica

Lepus granatensis

169

Lepus timidus Linnaeus, 1758

ED '97 Hazebroek

Mountain hare

AL	-	LT	Baltasis kiškis
BG	Снежен заек	LU	Polarhues
CZ	Zajíc bělák	LV	Baltais zaķis
DE	Schneehase	MK	Бел зајак
DK	Snehare; Nordhare	MT	-
EE	Valgejänes	NL	Sneeuwhaas
ES	Liebre variable	NO	Hare
FI	Metsäjänis	PL	Zając bielak
FO	Snjóhara	PT	Lebre-variável
FR	Lièvre variable	RO	-
GR	-	RU	Заяц-беляк
HR	Bijeli zec	SE	Skogshare
HU	Havasi nyúl	SI	Planinski zajec
IR	Giorria	SK	Zajac belák
IS	Snæhéri	TR	-
IT	Lepre variabile	YU	Алпски зец

Distribution

World: throughout the northern Palaearctic from Ireland to Hokkaido. According to some authors, North American arctic hares also belong to this species.
Europe: on the continent from Fennoscandia and the Baltic (including north-east Poland and Belarus) through northern Russia. Occurs also in Ireland and Scotland and in the Alps. Introduced into northern England (*c.* 1870), the Hebrides, Shetland, Orkney and the Faeroe Islands (1854).

Geographic variation

White in winter and greyish brown in summer in most areas. The Irish race is yellowish brown also in winter, and in southern Sweden there are populations (perhaps a subspecies) that are partly or totally grey in winter. North European hares seem to be a little larger than the more southern ones, and Scottish hares smaller than the others. Alpine hares seem to be lighter and have relatively longer ears. Six subspecies have been described from Europe and 11 others from Asia. Craniologically the subspecies of Scotland (*L. timidus scoticus* Hilzheimer, 1906) and the Alps (*L. t. varronis* Miller, 1901) are near each other, but far from the larger Irish subspecies (*L. t. hibernicus* Bell, 1837), which is more like the nominate subspecies of N. Europe. *L. t. kozhevnikovi* Ognev, 1929 of central Russia is yellow-brown in summer.

Habitat

In Scotland on heather moors, montane grassland and open forests above 250–300 m, in Ireland also on lowland pastures and open fields (where brown hares are still absent). In the Alps mostly at altitudes of 1500–3000 m, in summer to 3700 m (above the tree line) and in winter lower down (even to 600 m). In northern Europe also on the coasts and islands, and in Lapland up to treeless fells. Most numerous in young forests and bushes at the edges of fields, bogs, clearings and watercourses.

Population status

Long term population trends have mostly been stable in recent decades, perhaps decreasing in the Alps. Populations fluctuate in Northern Europe with 4 or 7–8 year cycles. In Scotland and in northern Russia the cycle length is mostly 10 years. Sometimes deep population crashes are caused by tularaemia (a bacterial disease), and local retreats by dominating brown hares (e.g., in southern Sweden and in Ireland). Densities generally 1–10 hares/km² (e.g., in Scotland and Finland), but in local optimum habitats up to 200–300 hares/km². In Finland the annual hunting bag was 175000–950000 hares in 1980–93.

International legal & conservation status

Bern Convention, Appendix III.
EU Habitats & Species Directive, Annex V.

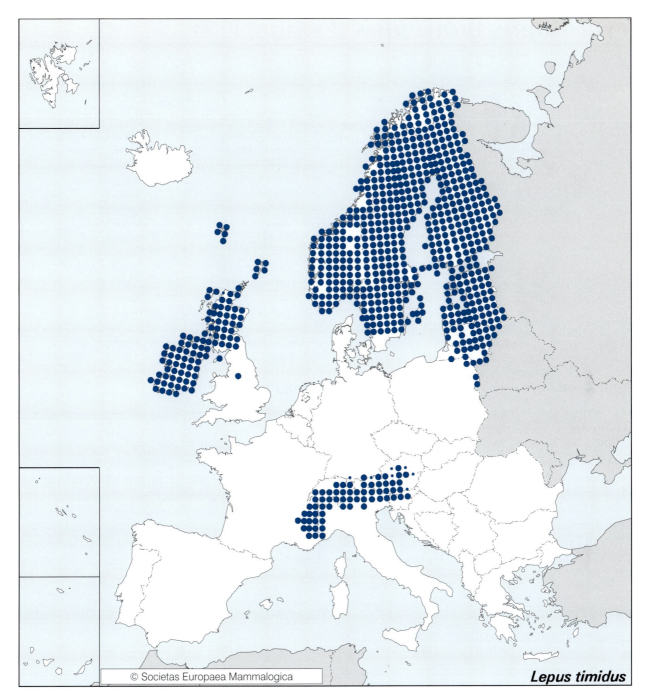

© Societas Europaea Mammalogica

Lepus timidus

Other information

At the day resting place (lair) mountain hares often, especially in snowy situations, make burrows or short tunnels, but they lie (sleep) outside, near the opening of the tunnel.

Literature

Baker *et al.* (1983)
Bergengren (1969)
Danilov *et al.* (1996)
Hewson (1995)

Niethammer (1963)
Pulliainen & Tunkkari (1987)
Sulkava (1989)

S. Sulkava

171

Oryctolagus cuniculus (Linnaeus, 1758)

J. Mikuletič

Distribution

World: western Palaearctic except most of Fennoscandia. Introduced to all continents except Antarctica.

Europe: original range limited to Iberia. By introductions, which started as early as the Roman period, and natural spread, the rabbit came to western and central Europe and to certain parts of southern and eastern Europe. Now north to Shetland, southern Sweden and Gotland, east to the north coast of the Black Sea. Very localized in the Balkans, mainly on Greek islands.

Geographic variation

No subspecies are recognized on the mainland of Europe. However, certain populations on Atlantic and/ or western Mediterranean islands are considered separate subspecies on the basis of small size and paler colour. Three genetically distinct lineages were found in Spain, southern France, and northern Africa, respectively.

Habitat

Grassland and meadows with sandy soils, surrounded by woodland, scrub, hedges or rocks which provide cover. Avoids higher altitudes, coniferous woodland, and cold or humid habitats.

Population status

At higher densities forms stable colonies comprising up to 20 adults. The population density usually varies from 0.5 to 10, exceptionally 25–100, individuals per hectare. European populations crashed due to myxomatosis in the 1950s, and the virus may still affect numbers in certain areas. Populations on Atlantic and Mediterranean islands, subspecies *O. c. huxley* (Haeckel, 1874), may be endangered. Domesticated forms of the rabbit occur worldwide, but there is poor information about the admixture of domestic strains in natural populations.

International legal & conservation status

None.

Other information

Important game animal in areas where common. Digs deep burrows; large groups build a complicated system of underground tunnels.

Literature

Bobak (1970) – review
Gibb (1990)
Hardy *et al.* (1995)
Monnerot *et al.* (1994a)
Monnerot *et al.* (1994b)

M. Homolka & J. Zima

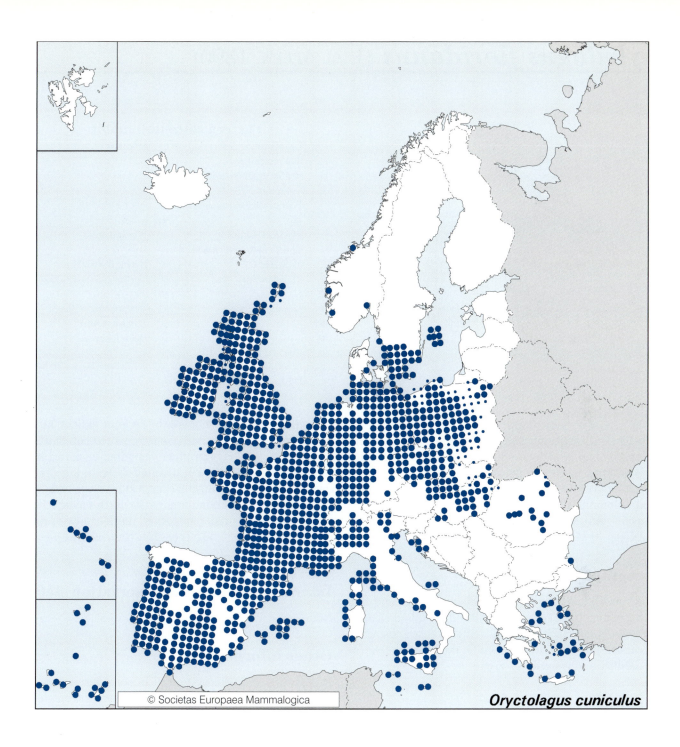

© Societas Europaea Mammalogica

Oryctolagus cuniculus

173

Sylvilagus floridanus (J. A. ALLEN, 1890)

D. Ovenden

Eastern cottontail rabbit

AL	Lepuri i Florides	IT	Silvilago
BG	Флоридски заек	LT	-
CZ	Králík východoamerický	LU	-
DE	Östliches	LV	-
	Baumwollschwanzkaninchen	MK	-
DK	-	MT	-
EE	Florida sooküülik	NL	Floridakonijn
ES	Conejo de cola de algodón	NO	-
	de Florida	PL	Królik florydzki
FI	Floridanjänis	PT	Coelho-cauda-de-algodão
FO	-	RO	-
FR	Lapin de Floride	RU	Флоридский кролик
GR	-	SE	Bomullskanin
HR	-	SI	Belorepi kunec
HU	Floridai nyúl	SK	-
IR	-	TR	-
IS	Ullskotta	YU	-

Distribution

World: from extreme southern Canada through the eastern and south-eastern USA (with disjunct populations in New Mexico, Texas and Arizona) to Mexico, parts of Yucatan, Venezuela, western Costa Rica and Colombia.
Europe: introduced to France, where now extinct, and northern Italy.

Geographic variation

The species has been subdivided in various geographic races of uncertain systematic value. The Italian eastern cottontails cannot be ascribed to any of these subspecies because there is no information on their morphological variability and geographic origin.

Habitat

The eastern cottontail prefers dry areas, and avoids densely forested habitats. It lives in farmland, fields, meadows, stone walls overgrown with brush and the borders of forested areas as well as along edges of marshes. In northern Italy the species is only locally common, and is particularly associated with scrub areas along river-beds and railway-escarpments.

Population status

The species has been introduced to France and Italy for hunting. In France it seems to be recently extinct, but in northern Italy it still survives in fragmented populations. In this area the first introductions dated back to 1966. In north-west Italy the populations show an increasing density and their expansion occurs along river-beds and road and railway embankments. In north-eastern Italy there is another small population, but it is located on a small lagoon island and it is entirely controlled by private game-managers.

International legal & conservation status

None.

Other information

In Italy the Eastern cottontail is considered a game species, but it should be eradicated to prevent local competition with the brown hare. The major attractions to hunters of this little lagomorph are its great productivity, its immunity to myxomatosis and also its quick zigzag running.

Literature

Chapman *et al.* (1980)
Doria (1991)

L. Lapini

Sylvilagus floridanus

Sciurus anomalus GÜLDENSTAEDT, 1785

T. P. McOwat

Distribution

World: Transcaucasia, Turkey, Iraq, Syria, Lebanon, Israel, Jordan, and Iran.
Europe: confined to the vicinity of Istanbul (where introduced in 1964) and two Aegean islands: Lesbos (Greece) and Gökçeada (Turkey).

Geographic variation

Three subspecies described, *S. anomalus anomalus, S. a. syriacus* Ehrenberg, 1828 and *S. a. pallescens* (Gray, 1867), but their validity uncertain. Colour variations are found throughout its distribution. The dorsum is chestnut-grey to grizzled grey, the underparts vary from strong rusty colour to buff-yellow with auburn-brown on the flanks and outerparts of the legs. The tail is mainly grey-brown with red variations and a black band around the rim. Diploid number of chromosomes is 40 and the fundamental number of chromosomal arms varies between 74 and 76.

Habitat

Mainly in mixed and deciduous forests. Avoids strictly coniferous forests.

Population status

Very few individuals have been seen in Israel. Unofficial reports claim a dangerous decline in population size in Lebanon and Syria in the last few decades. A population decline was noted in Jordan at the beginning of this century. No other formal information concerning its population status is available from other countries. Reproduction can occur throughout the year with two to three peaks. The number of young per litter varies from one to seven.

International legal & conservation status

EU Habitats & Species Directive, Annex IV.
Bern Convention, Appendix II.
IUCN Red List, Lower Risk – near threatened.

Other information

Hunted for sport and food in various parts of its distribution. Very little commercial importance because of its low fur value. Can cause damage to commercial walnut crops.

Literature

Harrison & Bates (1991)
Hecht-Markou (1994)
Koprowski & Gavish (in press) – review
Özkan (1995)

L. Gavish & J. Gurnell

Sciurus anomalus

177

Sciurus carolinensis GMELIN, 1788

ED '97

E. Hazebroek

Grey squirrel

AL	-	LT	Pilkoji voverė
BG	Каролинска катерица	LU	-
CZ	Veverka popelavá	LV	Pelēkē vāvere
DE	Grauhörnchen	MK	-
DK	Grå egern	MT	-
EE	Hallorav	NL	Grijze eekhoorn
ES	Ardilla gris	NO	Gråekorn
FI	Harmaaorava	PL	Wiewiórka szara
FO	-	PT	Esquilo-cinzento
FR	Ecureuil gris	RO	-
GR	-	RU	Каролинская белка
HR	Američka vjeverica	SE	Grå ekorre
HU	Szürke mókus	SI	Siva veverica
IR	Iora glas	SK	-
IS	Gráíkorni	TR	-
IT	Scoiattolo grigio	YU	-

Distribution

World: native to south-eastern Nearctic; introduced to South Africa (1900), Australia (*c.* 1900, now extinct) and Europe.
Europe: introductions are from USA and Canada to Great Britain (several times with several translocations, 1876–1929), Ireland (1913 from England) and Italy (1948 to Piedmont, south Torino from USA and to Liguria, Genova Nervi in 1966 from USA).

Geographic variation

Five subspecies recognized in North America. Exhibit a size cline in North America that follows Bergmann's rule, with body mass increasing from south to north. Black squirrels occur in north-eastern part of range (Canada).

Habitat

Mainly broad-leaved forests, hedgerows, parks and gardens.

Population status

Introduced into Great Britain and Italy. Common within range; range expansion continues in both countries where it is replacing the red squirrel *Sciurus vulgaris.* Densities vary considerably, depending mainly on tree seed availability; range 1 to 8 ind./ha.

International legal & conservation status

None

Other information

In Britain and Italy it is a pest of forestry because it strips the bark from trees, especially broad-leaved. Important game animal in North America, sometimes hunted for sport or to control locally in Great Britain.

Literature

Currado *et al.* (1987)
Flyger & Gates (1982)
Gurnell (1996)
Gurnell & Pepper (1988, 1993) – reviews
Steele & Weigl (1993)

J. Gurnell & L. Wauters

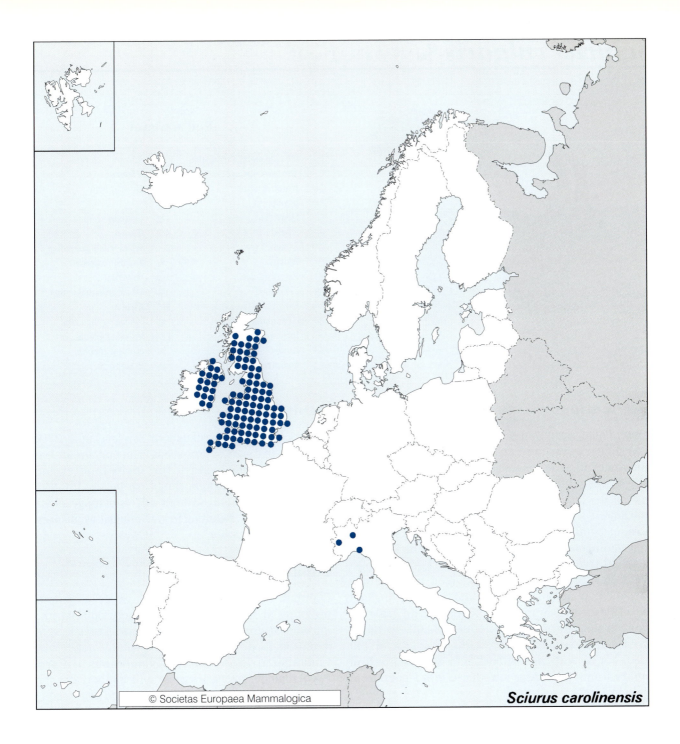

© Societas Europaea Mammalogica

Sciurus carolinensis

Sciurus vulgaris LINNAEUS, 1758

U. Iff

Red squirrel

AL	Ketri	LT	Paprastoji vovere
BG	Обикновена катерица	LU	Kaweechelchen
CZ	Veverka obecná	LV	Vāvere
DE	Eichhörnchen	MK	Верверица
DK	Egern	MT	-
EE	Orav; Tava-orav	NL	Eekhoorn
ES	Ardilla roja	NO	Ekorn
FI	Orava	PL	Wiewiórka pospolita
FO	Íkorni	PT	Esquilo-vermelho
FR	Ecureuil roux	RO	Veveriţa
GR	Σκίουρος	RU	Обыкновенная белка
HR	Europska vjeverica	SE	Ekorre
HU	Közönséges mókus	SI	Navadna veverica
IR	Iora rua	SK	Veverica stromová
IS	Rauðíkorni	TR	Avrupa sincabı
IT	Scoiattolo comune	YU	Веверица

Distribution

World: Palaearctic from British Isles in the west, south to Mediterranean, the Caucasus (where introduced), southern Urals and Altai mountains in central Mongolia, to north-east China. Found on Sakhalin Island off east coast of Russia and most northerly Japanese island of Hokkaido.

Europe: common throughout Europe. Introductions from continental Europe to Britain in the 19th and 20th centuries have led to mixed populations. Extinct in most of southern Britain except for island populations; scattered populations in central and northern England and Wales; still common in Scotland and Ireland. Denmark: introductions in the 19th and 20th centuries have led to mixed populations. Portugal: absent for 400 years, but recently moved back into northern part of country from Spain. Also introduced into Lisbon from Spain in 1993.

Geographic variation

Up to 40 subspecies have been described, although taxonomic positions uncertain. Very variable coat colour. Dorsal colour ranges from grey to red, brown and black. The colour of the tail, feet and ear tufts may be the same or may contrast with the back. Distinct red, brown and black colour morphs can be found. Some populations bimorphic or trimorphic. The distribution of morphs tends to be stable except where introductions have occurred, such as in Britain and Denmark.

Habitat

Forests, parks and gardens from sea-level up to 2200 m (tree line) in the Alps. Tree seeds from both broad-leaved and conifer species are the main food resource throughout their range; fungi are locally important. Forest fragmentation strongly affects demography and genetic diversity, resulting in lower densities, dispersion and genetic variation.

Population status

Common throughout most of its range. Populations declining in Britain where it is being replaced by the introduced grey squirrel *Sciurus carolinensis;* similar situation in northern Italy, especially near Torino. Endangered in Britain and vulnerable in Europe. Population density varies geographically and also shows large annual fluctuations in response to tree seed crop availability. Densities vary from 0.1 to 1.5 ind./ha. A series of years with poor tree seed crops may lead to a population decline. At high densities (*c.* 1/ha.) reproduction and emigration are density-dependent.

International legal & conservation status

Bern Convention, Appendix III.
IUCN Red List, Lower Risk – near threatened.

Other information

Hunted for fur, food or sport in parts of its range. Can be a pest locally when population densities are high

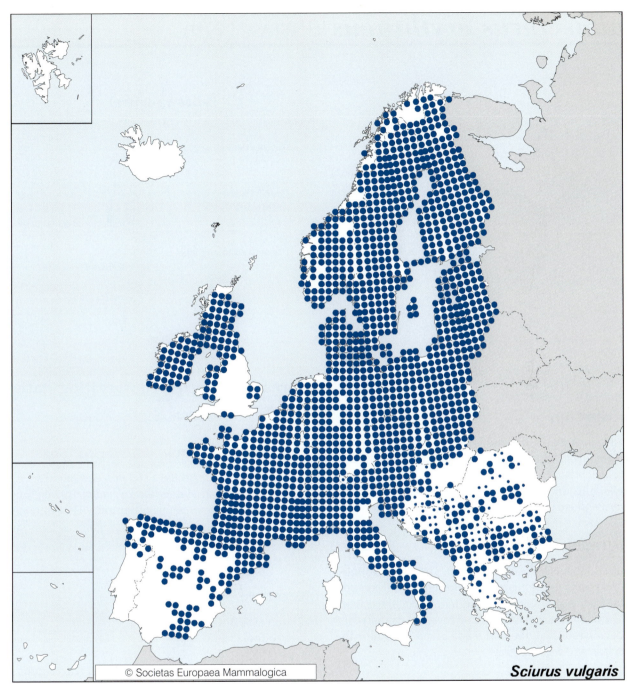

Sciurus vulgaris

© Societas Europaea Mammalogica

because it strips the bark from conifer trees, or feeds heavily on conifer buds.

Literature

Currado *et al.* (1987)
Degn (1973)
Gurnell (1987) – review
Wauters *et al.* (1994)
Wauters & Lens (1995)
Witalfsky (1978) – review

J. Gurnell & L. Wauters

181

Callosciurus erythraeus (Pallas, 1779)

P. Barrett

	Pallas's squirrel		
AL	-	LT	-
BG	-	LU	-
CZ	Veverka Pallasova	LV	-
DE	-	MK	-
DK	-	MT	-
EE	Pune-kabeorav	NL	-
ES	Ardilla de Pallas	NO	-
FI	-	PL	Wiewiórka pręgobrzucha
FO	-	PT	-
FR	Ecureuil à ventre rouge	RO	-
GR	-	RU	Желтолапая белка
HR	-	SE	-
HU	Csinos tarkamókus	SI	Veverica lepotka
IR	-	SK	-
IS	-	TR	-
IT	-	YU	-

Includes *C. flavimanus* (Geoffroy St Hilaire, 1831).

Distribution

World: throughout the Indochinese biogeographical subregion from Bhutan to Taiwan and on the Malayan peninsula.
Europe: introduced to Cap d'Antibes (Alpes-Maritimes) in France in early 1970s.

Geographic variation

About 25 subspecies are recognized. The Cap d'Antibes squirrel seems to belong to *C. erythraeus erythrogaster* from the parts of Assam and Myanmar (Burma) between the Brahmaputra and Chindwin rivers. The colour of its back is olive-brown; the underside is red and the chin, neck, legs and feet are grey.

Habitat

Forests, parks and garden. In Europe found in localized areas, abundant in gardens at Cap d'Antibes.

Population status

Now more than 100 Cap d'Antibes squirrels at densities higher than *S. vulgaris.* Frequently only one offspring in each litter (females have only two pairs of nipples) but they breed all year round.

International legal & conservation status

None.

Other information

Habits and behaviour similar to other tree squirrels. Cap d'Antibes squirrels are larger than *S. vulgaris,* weighing 340–460 g, and they do not have ear tufts. They damage garden trees by bark stripping and gnaw telephone cables. There are no natural predators in the gardens at Cap d'Antibes.

Literature

Jounanin (1990)
Moore & Tate (1965)
Nowak (1991)

J. Gurnell & L. Wauters

Callosciurus erythraeus

© Societas Europaea Mammalogica

Callosciurus finlaysonii (HORSFIELD, 1824)

P. Barrett

	Thailand tree squirrel		
AL	-	LT	-
BG	-	LU	-
CZ	Veverka Finlaysonova	LV	-
DE	-	MK	-
DK	-	MT	-
EE	-	NL	-
ES	Ardilla de Indochina	NO	-
FI	-	PL	-
FO	-	PT	-
FR	-	RO	-
GR	-	RU	Белка Финлайсона
HR	-	SE	-
HU	-	SI	-
IR	-	SK	-
IS	-	TR	-
IT	Scoiattola di Finlayson	YU	-

Includes *C. ferrugineus* (F. Cuvier, 1829)

Distribution

World: Myanmar (Burma) east of the Irrawaddy River, Thailand (except in the south-west and on the Peninsula), southern Indochina.
Europe: introduced to one locality in Italy (Acqui Terme – Alessandria).

Geographic variation

Sixteen subspecies have been recognized. *C. finlaysonii bocourtii* (Milne-Edwards, 1867) is the subspecies introduced to Italy from central Thailand.

Habitat

This is an arboreal squirrel found in many habitats. It lives in open woods, coconut plantations, and dense forests. In Acqui Terme it lives in a public park on conifer and broadleaf trees.

Population status

High density, increasing, but still restricted to 2 ha of the park.

International legal & conservation status

None.

Other information

Two pairs illegally introduced about 15 years ago. The Italian hunting law (1992) authorizes control interventions on introduced species. This species is a pest of conifer and broadleaf trees for its bark-stripping activity all the year round. Interactions with native animal species are unknown.

Literature

Corbet & Hill (1992)
Lekagul & McNeely (1988)
Moore & Tate (1965)

I. Currado, S. Bertolino & P. J. Mazzoglio

Callosciurus finlaysonii

185

Atlantoxerus getulus (Linnaeus, 1758)

P. Barrett

Distribution

World: native to North Africa: Morocco, Grand and Middle Atlas south to Agadir and north edge of Sahara, north-west Algeria.
Europe: introduced to Fuerteventura, Canary Islands.

Geographic variation

Monotypic species.

Habitat

The species is well adapted to stony environments, mountain slopes and open country, but also a wide array of agricultural habitats, where its presence is favoured by stone walls where it can seek refuge. It does not enter irrigated fields.

Population status

Initial rapid growth resulted in *c.* 200000 or even more individuals but was followed by a considerable reduction of its numbers. However, the squirrel is now more evenly distributed throughout the entire island.

International legal & conservation status

None.

Other information

The species was first introduced to the Canary Islands in 1965 as a single mating pair from North Africa. It does not seem to provoke any serious economic or ecological damage. The eradication of this species is now quite impossible; nevertheless every attempt has been made to prevent its dispersion to other islands of the Archipelago.

Literature

Machado Carrillo (1985)

G. Amori & A. Machado Carrillo

© Societas Europaea Mammalogica

Atlantoxerus getulus

Marmota marmota (LINNAEUS, 1758)

E. Hazebroek

Distribution

Endemic to Europe. The present range covers an Alpine core region extending from south-eastern France to Lower Austria. Several marginal isolates exist in the Pyrénées, Massif Central, Jura, Vosges, the Black Forest, the Apennines, Slovenian Alps, High Tatras and Romanian Carpathians. During the Pleistocene, marmots occupied a large area in the plains of Europe, but had to recede to higher altitudes at the end of the glaciation. Autochthonous populations descending from these postglacial colonizers still inhabit the Alpine core region of France, Switzerland, Italy, western Austria, Berchtesgaden in Germany and the High Tatras. The other populations originate from reintroductions (the Carpathians) or introductions.

Geographic variation

Two subspecies are distinguished: the nominate one populates the Alps, while *M. marmota latirostris* Kratochvíl, 1961, is endemic to the High Tatras. A mixed population in the Lower Tatras has resulted from introductions of both subspecies.

Habitat

In the Alps, alpine meadows and open pasture at altitudes from 600 to 3200 m; in the Pyrenean mountains between 1600 and 2400 m above sea level. Forests are generally avoided. Marmots mostly live on middle slopes facing the south, colonies are located on alluvial ground (soft and deep soil) as well as on rocky ground (hard and thin soil with outcropping rocks or total absence of grass). The preferred region consists of the zone 400–600 m above the local timber line.

Population status

The nominate subspecies, which is abundant in the Alpine core region, has been the source for the majority of introductions. The marginal populations, especially the isolates outside the Alps, may be endangered (e.g., in the case of the introduced populations of the Jura, the risks of extinction were considered to be high; in Germany the alpine marmot is quoted to be potentially threatened).

Genetic investigations revealed reduced levels of protein variation (2 out of 50 loci were found to be polymorphic) in all the populations studied so far in the eastern range of the distribution area; this is ascribed to a severe bottleneck in the eastern populations. The subspecies *M. m. latirostris* is rare and endangered and therefore under strict protection (Slovakia, Poland).

Population densities are reported to range between 23.8 to 36.4 marmots/100 ha (Gran Paradiso) and 40 to 80 marmots/100 ha (Tessin).

International legal & conservation status

Bern Convention, Appendix III.

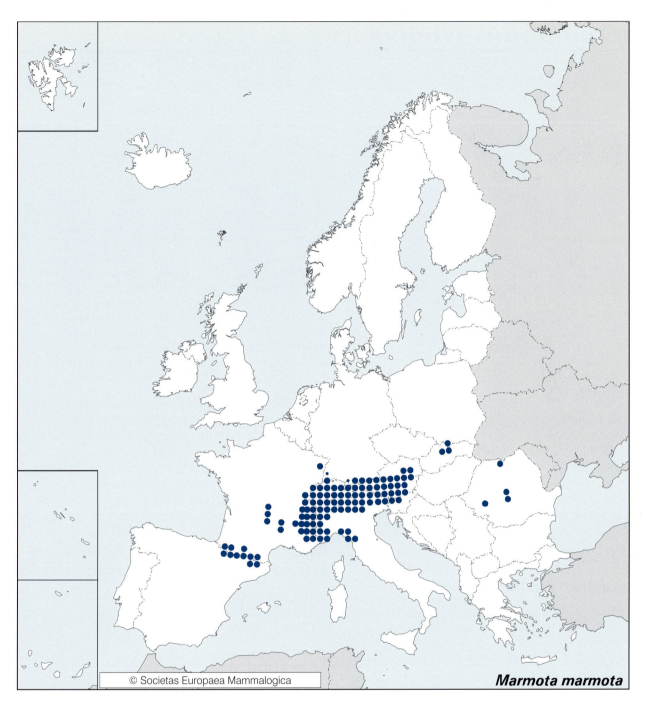

© Societas Europaea Mammalogica

Marmota marmota

Other information

Marmots have been exploited for food, fat and fur. The fat is still used as medicine, but nowadays marmots are mainly hunted for trophies. In some regions (e.g., France) the burrows dug by marmots are thought to interfere with agricultural activities (e.g., national park of the Vanoise, France).

Literature

Arnold (1990)
Bassano *et al.* (1992)
Bibikov (1996)
Krapp (1978a) – review
Le Berre *et al.* (1996)
Preleuthner *et al.* (1995)

M. Preleuthner

Spermophilus citellus (Linnaeus, 1766)

Z. Bihari

Distribution

Endemic to Europe. Range in two main parts, divided by the Carpathians. One part includes the Pannonian basin and adjacent plains of the Czech Republic, Austria, Hungary, Slovakia, western Romania and Yugoslavia; the other is to the south and east of the Carpathians in Southern Romania, Bulgaria, Thrace, Moldavia and Ukraine. Small peripheral isolates in southern Poland, Slovakia, eastern Germany, Macedonia and northern Greece.

Geographic variation

The validity of eight subspecies, which were based on slight differences in colour, size and skull shape, was not confirmed in a comprehensive review of the species. Shape of baculum subject to categorical interpopulation variation. Marginal isolated populations are phenetically most divergent, with *S. citellus karamani* (Martino & Martino, 1940) from the Jakupica Mts. (central Macedonia) being most distinct.

Habitat

Short-grass steppe, natural or anthropogenic, on well drained soil, from sea level up to 2500 m.

Population status

Serious decline reported from many parts of the range, particularly from the Pannonian Plain, with some marginal isolates becoming extinct this century (e.g., in Germany and Poland). Although there are still large stable populations throughout the species' range, fragmentation already seems to be critical. The main threat is the transformation of steppe into arable land and the abandonment of grazing, resulting in tall grass meadows where the souslik cannot survive. Population densities between 18 and 48 ind./ha reported for suitable habitats in Yugoslavia; mountain pastures of eastern Serbia support between 5 and 14 ind./ha.

International legal & conservation status

Bern Convention, Appendix II.
EU Habitats & Species Directive, Annex II & Annex IV.
IUCN, Vulnerable.

Literature

Kryštufek (1996)
Kryštufek & Hrabě (1996)
Męczynski (1985)
Ružić (1978) – review
Stubbe & Stubbe (1994)

B. Kryštufek

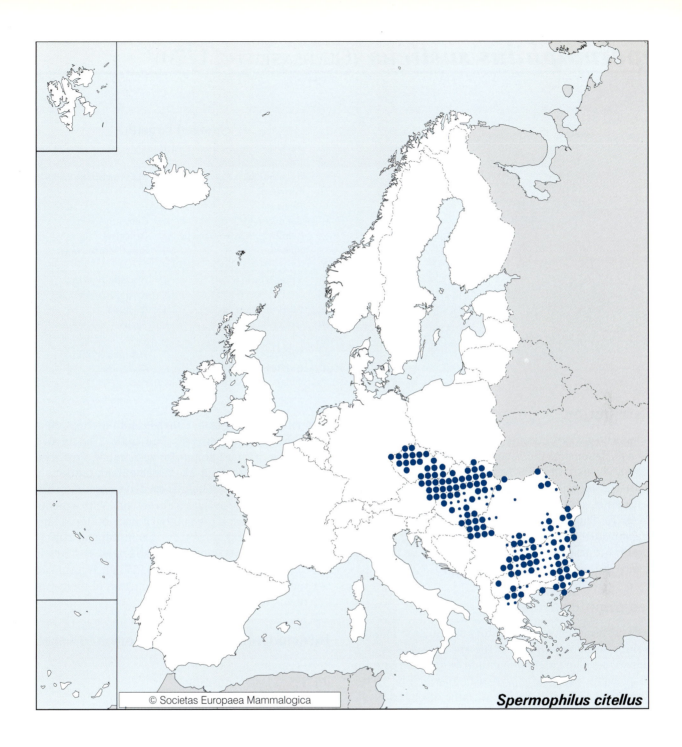

© Societas Europaea Mammalogica

Spermophilus citellus

Spermophilus suslicus (GÜLDENSTAEDT, 1770)

T. P. McOwat

Distribution

Endemic to eastern Europe, where range from the Volga River in the east to the River Wieprz in south-eastern Poland. The majority of its range is in the southern parts of Russia as well as in Ukraine and Moldova. The westernmost locality is near the city of Lublin (51° 12´N, 22° 40´E). The Polish population is probably an isolate, not connected to the range in Ukraine. Another western isolate, occurring in Belarus, is limited to the area between 52° 50´N, 25° 40´E and 53°40´N, 27° 20´E.

Geographic variation

Five subspecies have been distinguished, based mainly on the coloration and size of the specimens as well as skull shape. The Polish population is included into the subspecies *S. suslicus volhynensis* (Reschetnik, 1946), first described from Volhynia, Ukraine. Its status needs confirmation.

Habitat

Steppes, fallow fields, pastures, road and field margins. It prefers open and rather flat areas covered with low graminous vegetation, e.g. intensively grazed or mown pastures.

Population status

The distribution area and population size are not well known in the east. In the last few decades sousliks have become completely extinct in some areas (e.g., the north-eastern part of Wyżna Lubelska-Lublin Upland) and much reduced in others. The main reason is the conversion of their habitats for agriculture, forestry and urbanization, as well as direct extermination. The number of colonies has decreased considerably in Poland, where the species is threatened with extinction. In southern Russia, the southern distributional border had shifted northwards by the middle of the 19th century, and the spotted souslik was replaced by *Spermophilus pygmaeus* (Pallas, 1779). Hybridization between the two species at the junction of their ranges has been recorded.

International legal & conservation status

Bern Convention, Appendix II.
IUCN Red List, Vulnerable.

Other information

It can be maintained in captivity, which makes it a suitable experimental animal, particularly in hibernation research. It was used also in studies of interferons. The spotted souslik may be a carrier of tularemia.

Spermophilus suslicus

© Societas Europaea Mammalogica

Literature

Denisov (1961)
Denisov *et al.* (1969)
Gromov *et al.* (1965)
Kandefer-Szerzeń *et al.* (1994)
Męczyński (1991)
Pyatrouski (1958)

S. Męczyński

Tamias sibiricus (Laxmann, 1769)

U. Iff

Distribution

World: from northern European Russia across Asia as far as China and Hokkaido (Japan).

Europe: recent immigrant from Siberia, now advanced as far as Russian Karelia. Also introduced to western Europe, where isolated populations are present in Belgium, Germany, The Netherlands, Switzerland and Italy. Since introductions are from escaped pets, it is likely that the species has been introduced to some other European countries as well.

Geographic variation

Four subspecies are currently recognized, although the majority of geographical variation is clinal. East Asian populations are the most variable. Specimens introduced to Europe presumably represent the subspecies *T. sibiricus lineatus* (Siebold, 1824) which populates the Far East. Autochthonous populations of northern European Russia belong to the nominate subspecies.

Habitat

Woodland with bushy understorey. Introduced populations established mainly in parks and in towns.

Population status

Common in its natural range, but little information is available about its population status in Europe. The only information is from northern Italy: near Verona the population was estimated at 100 individuals, and in Belluno at about 1000.

International legal & conservation status

None.

Literature

Amori & Gippoliti (1995)
Dal Farra *et al.* (1996)
Krapp (1978b) – review

G. Amori

© Societas Europaea Mammalogica

Tamias sibiricus

Pteromys volans (Linnaeus, 1758)

P. Barrett

Distribution

World: northern Palaearctic, from Finland and western Russia through Siberian coniferous forest zone to the Pacific coast. Of the Pacific islands, occurs on Sakhalin and Hokkaido.

Europe: the westernmost population covers the southern half of Finland. The northernmost breeding forest patches are between 65°N and the arctic circle. Few records in the easternmost parts of the Baltic States. The most south-western records are from Belarus.

Geographic variation

Seven subspecies described from the Palaearctic, two of them from Europe. Flying squirrels of Finland and northern Russia belong to the nominate subspecies, which is characterized by a pure silver-grey back and tail, a character particularly conspicuous in winter fur. The other European subspecies, *P. volans ognevi* Stroganov, 1936, has a yellowish tinge in its silver-grey parts. It lives in the most south-western parts of the species range, i.e. to the south-west of Moscow and Novgorod.

Habitat

Prefers mature mixed forests with about half the trees being spruces and the tree canopy coverage amounting to 60–90%. Large aspen, alder and birch trees are important for food, and trunks with woodpecker holes for nests. Suitable forests should not be fragmented with open clearings, because flying squirrels are unwilling to cross open areas on the ground. Occasionally occurs close to human habitations and may have nests in nesting boxes or even in buildings.

Population status

Most populations in decline because of a decrease in the area of old mixed forests. Some local populations in western and southern Finland still fairly stable, but as a whole the species has declined strongly there since the 1940s. Still widespread but rare in Russian Karelia, but more common in St Petersburg region. A rough estimate is 45000 pairs for Finland and 35000 for St Petersburg region in the early 1990s.

International legal & conservation status

Bern Convention, Appendix II.
EU Habitats & Species Directive, Annex II* & Annex IV.
IUCN Red List, Lower Risk – near threatened.

Other information

Feeds in winter mainly on catkins of *Alnus* and *Betula*. Catkins are also stored in autumn as heaps in various holes and on branches of old spruces. Summer diet includes mainly leaves of deciduous trees, especially *Alnus*.

© Societas Europaea Mammalogica

Pteromys volans

Literature

Hokkanen & Fokin (1997)
Hokkanen, *et al.* (1982)
Kaikusalo (1993)
Sulkava (1978) – review
Sulkava & Sulkava (1993)

S. Sulkava

197

Castor canadensis KUHL, 1820

J. Mikuletič

Distribution

World: distributed throughout North America, where it is indigenous and widely reintroduced; introduced to Argentina and Europe.

Europe: currently present in Finland, Russia and Austria. Introduced from New York state (from a population that was itself the result of a reintroduction from Canada and Wyoming) into Finland in 1937 and later translocated to eastern and northern parts of the country. Emigrated east from Finland into Russia, where first detected in 1952 in Karelia. Translocated from Karelia to the Amur basin, and in 1977 to Kamchatka. Introduced to Austria in 1953. Also introduced to Poland (1926), Ukraine (1943) and France (1975), but these populations have since become extinct. There are reports of commercial fur farms in Europe. Mixed populations of *C. canadensis* and *C. fiber* occur on the Danube close to Vienna, but are not shown on the map as individuals have not recently been identified to the species level.

Geographic variation

Twenty-four subspecies recognised in North America, but no information about which are present in Europe.

Habitat

Lakes, swamps, streams, rivers and ditches where they have year-round access to water and woody vegetation. Comparisons in Russia suggest that Canadian beavers are more likely to build dams and lodges than the European species. In North America it can live at altitudes up to 3400 m.

Population status

Widely reintroduced throughout North America, where the population is generally stable and increasing. In North America, densities vary widely reaching 0.76 colonies per km².

In Europe, range and abundance expanded rapidly in Karelia and south-eastern Finland between the 1960s and 1980s. Much of the Finnish Canadian beaver population results from an introduction of just two pairs.

C. canadensis is an undesirable exotic in Europe. Little is known of the potential for competitive interaction between the two *Castor* species, but the presence of the Canadian species appears to be detrimental to the European one. At sites in Finland (but not in Poland or Ukraine), where both species were released, *C. canadensis* apparently displaced *C. fiber*.

International legal & conservation status

None.

Other information

In their native habitat, Canadian beavers are a keystone species which significantly modify the structure and dynamics of aquatic environments at the landscape level; these alterations may persist for centuries.

© Societas Europaea Mammalogica

Castor canadensis

In North America, particularly Canada, *C. canadensis* is a commercially very important furbearer, but when fur prices are low animals are also harvested at public expense for damage control.

In Finland, Canadian beavers damage forestry through flooding conifers and raising the water table. There is a short open hunting season in Finland, but their dams and lodges are protected.

Literature

Danilov (1995)
Ermala (1995)
Jenkins & Busher (1979)
Lahti & Helminen (1974)
Larson & Gunson (1983)

F. Tattersall

Castor fiber LINNAEUS, 1758

F. Müller

Distribution

European beavers once occurred throughout Europe and Asia, but habitat loss and over-hunting drastically reduced their range. By the early 20th century only five isolated sites remained in Europe; on the Rhône in France, the Elbe in Germany, southern Norway, areas of the Neman River and Dnepr Basin (Belarus) and Voronezh (Russia). Remnants also in Siberia and China. Since then beavers have been widely reintroduced, most recently to The Netherlands, Croatia and Hungary. They are now scattered across Europe and into western Siberia. Small populations in China and Mongolia. Mixed populations of *C. fiber* and *C. canadensis* occur on the Danube close to Vienna, but are not shown on the map as individuals have not recently been identified to the species level.

Geographic variation

There is no clear consensus regarding the number of subspecies, and many reintroduced populations were founded with beavers from a mixture of origins. Nonetheless, at least four subspecies are recognized in Europe: *C. fiber galliae* Geoffroy, 1803 from the Rhône; *C. fiber albicus* Matschie, 1907 from the Elbe; *C. fiber fiber* from Scandinavia; and *C. fiber vistulanus* Matschie, 1907 from Eastern Europe. Some *C. fiber vistulanus* have black rather than brown fur, but subspecies definitions are based mainly on cranial measurements. Three more subspecies in Asia.

Habitat

Lakes, swamps, streams, rivers and ditches where they have year-round access to water and woody vegetation. Although generally a woodland animal, they can live on farmland and even in quiet urban areas. Prefer lowland areas, but some introductions at approximately 500 m above sea level have persisted.

Population status

By the early 20th century the world population was only *c.* 1200 individuals but now there are almost half a million, of which 350000 in Europe. Recovery has been a result of continuing protection, reintroductions and translocations. Generally densest populations in countries with oldest reintroduced populations and large areas of suitable habitat (e.g., Latvia). Densities are roughly 0.2 colonies per km^2 in stable populations, but territory size varies with habitat quality.

International legal & conservation status

Bern Convention, Appendix III.
EU Habitats & Species Directive, Annex II & Annex IV (excluding Finnish and Swedish populations, which are on Annex V).
IUCN Red List, Lower Risk – near threatened.

Other information

Beavers have a major impact on their environment

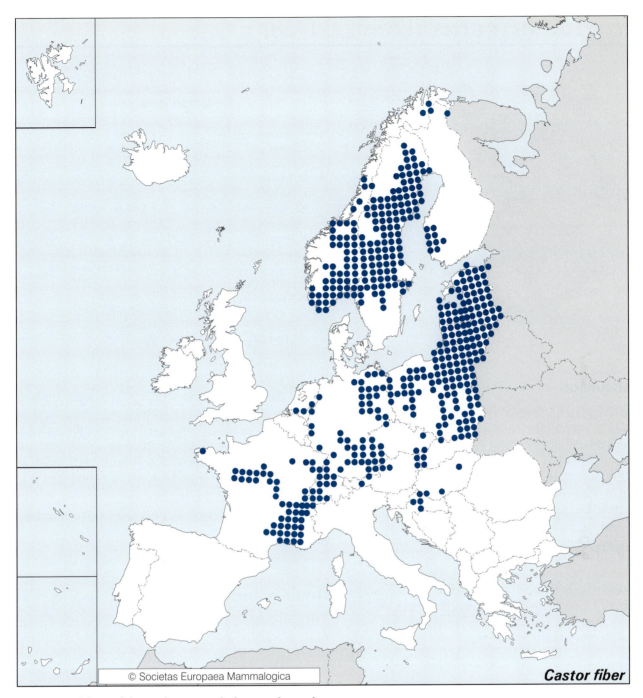

© Societas Europaea Mammalogica

Castor fiber

through building of dams, burrows, lodges and canals, but the extent to which they construct these depends on local hydrology, geology, climate and food availability. Can damage crops, roads and trees through feeding and flooding, but in general should be considered a key-stone species in riparian habitats.

Among reintroduced populations, most mortality results from interference by man, particularly car accidents. In some countries beavers are treated as a game animal, with closed seasons and protection for dams. *C. fiber* and *C. canadensis* cannot interbreed, but the American species might outcompete the native European beaver in areas of overlap.

Literature

Heidecke (1986)
Macdonald *et al.* (1995)
Nolet (1997)
Nolet & Rosell (1998)

F. Tattersall

Cricetus cricetus (LINNAEUS, 1758)

Z. Bihari

Common hamster

AL	-	LT	Paprastasis žiurkėnas
BG	Обикновен хомяк	LU	Hamster
CZ	Křeček polní	LV	Eiropas kāmis
DE	Feldhamster	MK	Крчок
DK	Hamster	MT	-
EE	Hamster	NL	Hamster
ES	Hámster común	NO	Hamster
FI	Hamsteri	PL	Chomik europejski
FO	Hamstur	PT	-
FR	Grand hamster	RO	Hârciog; Căţelul-pământului
GR	-	RU	Обыкновенный хомяк
HR	Veliki hrčak	SE	Hamster
HU	Közönséges hörcsög	SI	Veliki hrček
IR	-	SK	Skrečok pol'ný
IS	Hamstur	TR	Hamster
IT	Criceto comune	YU	Хрчак

Distribution

World: Palaearctic, from western Europe across Russia and Kazakhstan to the Jenissej, between 5° and 95°E and 44°and 59°N.
Europe: from The Netherlands, Belgium, France (Alsace) and Germany in the west to Russia in the east. From Russia in the north to Slovenia, Croatia, Yugoslavia and Bulgaria in the south.

Geographic variation

Two subspecies are accepted, the eastern hamster *C. cricetus cricetus* and the western *C. c. canescens* Nehring, 1899 from Belgium, the Netherlands and adjacent Germany. A third, *C. c. nehringi* Matschie, 1901 is considered invalid. In addition to the common wild colour type, melanistic and leucistic individuals are known.

Habitat

Farmland with heavy layers of loam and loess soil up to 400 m. High humidity and a stony substrate do not meet the demands of a hamster habitat. It is found in nearly every crop such as wheat, rye, oats, barley, corn and sugar beet. *Medicago* and *Trifolium* fields are of importance as population refuge. Occasionally in hedges, gardens and meadows.

Population status

Threatened in western Europe. Spring population density there is low, between 0.5 – 3/ha. Local extinction has taken place in various countries (e.g., Belgium, The Netherlands, France, Germany). Viable populations are assumed in eastern Europe but exact data are not available. Outbreaks occurred locally until 1974 at 10–20 year intervals with densities up to 800/ha.

International legal & conservation status

Bern Convention, Appendix II.
EU Habitats & Species Directive, Annex IV.

Other information

Still persecuted as a farmland pest and trapped for fur trade in eastern Europe. Between 1950–1970 millions of furs from the German Democratic Republic were exported. Hunting statistics for these years already show a steady decline of trapped individuals. Although hunting hamsters became less profitable in the late 1960s, the species was trapped until 1989. In other western European countries the hamster was of less economic value.

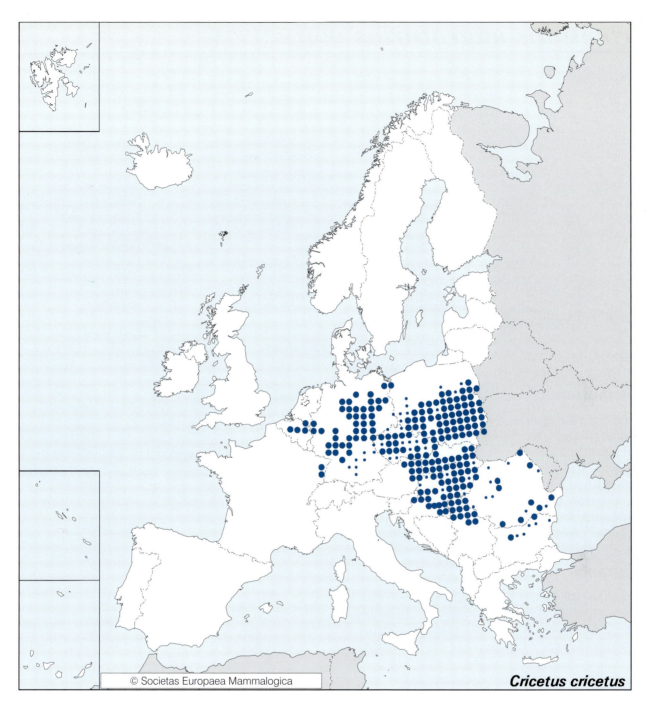

© Societas Europaea Mammalogica

Cricetus cricetus

Literature

Kramer (1956)
Nechay *et al.* (1977) – review
Niethammer (1982b)
Petzsch (1952)
Vogel (1936)
Wendt (1984)

U. Weinhold

Cricetulus migratorius (PALLAS, 1773)

M. Năzăreanu

Distribution

World: from Mongolia and western China in the east through Central Asia, to eastern Europe. Southern border passes from Kashmir through Pakistan, Iran, Iraq, Syria, Israel and Turkey to the Aegean Sea.
Europe: from Transcaucasia, south European Russia and Ukraine to north-west Romania. Isolated populations known from south-eastern Bulgaria, European Turkey and south-eastern Greece.

Geographic variation

Twenty-five subspecies have been described, mostly according to size and colour differences. Mountain forms are bigger, eastern are paler. The subspecific status of Balkan populations is uncertain and needs revision.

Habitat

Exhibits considerable habitat plasticity. Prefers steppes and stony places covered with sparse vegetation. Common in fields and dry pastures. Inhabits also deserts and semideserts. In Central Asia and Transcaucasia often synanthropic. Vertical range from sea level (Bulgaria, Romania) to 4300 m (Pamir Mts.).

Population status

Population densities in Ukraine, Russia and Central Asia are much lower than those in voles and mice; population outbreaks are rare. Its occurrence in the Balkans is only sporadic.

Literature

Bašenina (1951)
Flint (1966)
Niethammer (1982a) – review

V. Vohralík

© Societas Europaea Mammalogica

Cricetulus migratorius

Mesocricetus newtoni (Nehring, 1898)

M. Năzăreanu

Romanian hamster

AL	-	LT	-
BG	Черногърд хомяк	LU	-
CZ	Křeček Newtonův	LV	Ņūtona kāmis
DE	Rumänischer Goldhamster	MK	-
DK	-	MT	-
EE	-	NL	Roemeense hamster
ES	Hámster rumano	NO	Rumensk gullhamster
FI	Romanianhamsteri	PL	Chomik Newtona
FO	-	PT	-
FR	Hamster de Newton	RO	Hamsterul-românesc
GR	-	RU	Хомяк Ньютона
HR	Bugarski hrčak	SE	Rumänsk hamster
HU	Dobrudzsai aranyhörcsög	SI	Balkanski zlati hrček
IR	-	SK	-
IS	-	TR	Avurtlak
IT	Criceto di Romania	YU	-

Distribution

Endemic to the eastern Balkans where it inhabits lowlands along the right bank of the lower Danube in Romania and Bulgaria.

Geographic variation

Monotypic species without apparent geographic variation.

Habitat

Prefers barren ground, dry steppe and *Medicago* fields. Present also in cereals, vineyards and gardens. Restricted to lowlands below 460 m.

Population status

Uncommon throughout its range, population outbreaks only local and rare.

International legal & conservation status

Bern Convention, Appendix II.
IUCN Red List, Vulnerable.

Literature

Christov (1985)
Hamar & Schutowa (1966)
Markov (1960)
Niethammer (1982d) – review

V. Vohralík

© Societas Europaea Mammalogica

Mesocricetus newtoni

Myopus schisticolor (Lilljeborg, 1844)

D. Ovenden

Wood lemming

AL	-	LT	Miškinis lemingas
BG	Китайски цокор	LU	-
CZ	Lumík lesní	LV	Meža lemings
DE	Waldlemming	MK	Шумски леминг
DK	Skovlemming	MT	-
EE	Metslemming	NL	Boslemming
ES	Léming de bosque	NO	Skoglemen
FI	Metsäsopuli	PL	Leming leśny
FO	-	PT	-
FR	Lemming de forêt	RO	-
GR	-	RU	Лесной лемминг
HR	Šumski leming	SE	Skogslämmel
HU	Erdei lemming	SI	Gozdni leming
IR	-	SK	-
IS	Skógarlæmingi	TR	-
IT	Lemming delle foreste	YU	-

Distribution

World: northern Palaearctic, from central Scandinavia through Finland, northern and central Russia to the Pacific coast and to Sakhalin island.

Europe: westernmost populations are found in the westernmost autochthonous spruce forests of south-eastern Norway. It is common in central and northern Sweden. Finland is patchily populated and the species is absent from northern Lapland (to the north of spruce forests) and from south-western coastal areas. In Russia, occurs through entire Karelia south to central Russia, where the most south-western population lives *c.* 300 km west of Moscow.

Geographic variation

Five subspecies, mainly distinguished by the extent of the brown patch on the back, have been described from the Palaearctic region. In Europe only the nominate subspecies, with a round brown patch on the lower back. The subspecies *M. schisticolor vinogradovi* Scalon & Rajewski, 1940 from around the Urals has brown colour on the whole back from the base of the tail to the head.

Habitat

Permanent breeding habitats are old spruce-dominated forests with very thick moss layer (*Hylocomium, Pleurozium, Dicranum,* and *Ptilium* species). Moist parts of forests and even pine-bogs with high dwarf-shrubs and moss-hummocks are preferred in summer. At high population density also in dry forests and in winter even in clear-cuts. Local migrations have often been recognized because of dead animals on the roads. In winter, feeds almost exclusively on mosses *(Pleurozium, Dicranum* and *Hylocomium),* but summer diet includes also grasses. In autumn it stores mosses under trunks and stones as heaps of up to 2–3 litres.

Population status

Population densities often stay very low for decades. Weak increases in density are observed during peak years of *Clethrionomys* species. High population densities and small-scale migrations are probable, but irregular and often at very long intervals, e.g. in 1910, 1957–1958 and 1963 in northern Finland. Populations in Fennoscandia are generally decreasing because of extensive logging in old spruce forests, which are the species main habitat.

International legal & conservation status

IUCN Red List, Lower Risk – near threatened.

Other information

The sex-ratio is female-biased (75% females : 25% males), because half the X-chromosomes behave in a way that allows XY-individuals to develop as females. The sex-ratio of young can be 50% : 50% or 75% : 25%, but all-female offspring were also recorded. Scandinavia has been colonized by wood lemmings after the Ice Age

© Societas Europaea Mammalogica

Myopus schisticolor

from the north-east, resulting in limited diversity of mitochondrial DNA due to a founder effect.

Literature

Fedorov *et al.* (1996)
Gromov & Polyakov (1992)
Kalela (1963)
Niethammer & Henttonen (1982) – review
Sulkava *et al.* (1996)

S. Sulkava

209

Lemmus lemmus (Linnaeus, 1758)

D. Ovenden

Norway lemming

AL	Lemingu	LT	Norveginis lemingas
BG	Норвежки леминг	LU	-
CZ	Lumík norský	LV	Kalnu lemings
DE	Berglemming	MK	Леминг обичен
DK	Lemming	MT	-
EE	Norra lemming	NL	Berglemming
ES	Léming de tundra	NO	Lemen
FI	Tunturisopuli	PL	Leming właściwy
FO	Læmingi	PT	Leming-da-tundra
FR	Lemming des toundras	RO	-
GR	-	RU	Норвежский лемминг
HR	Planinski leming	SE	Fjällämmel
HU	Közönséges lemming	SI	Skandinavski leming
IR	-	SK	Lumík
IS	Læmingi	TR	-
IT	Lemming comune	YU	Леминг

Lemmus lemmus is fairly closely related to Asian species or subspecies of the brown lemming *(L. amurensis, L. sibiricus, L. chrysogaster,* and *L. novosibiricus).*

Distribution

Endemic to Fennoscandia and the Kola peninsula of Russia, including at least the larger islands. During migration individuals can reach the Baltic and agricultural areas in central Fennoscandia.

Geographic variation

No evident geographic variation.

Habitat

Fennoscandian alpine and subarctic areas. Often in bogs and mires in summer and on dry, open ridges in winter. During peak numbers, it can overconsume local food resources, particularly certain moss species. During migrations, it can be found in forest areas, on frozen lakes and on agricultural land. Large accumulations of lemmings are found at river forks and lake margins during migration and many individuals drown while attempting to cross rivers.

Population status

Strongly fluctuating populations or cyclic dynamics. Fairly regular 3–4 year cycles in southern part of range, particularly in south Norway, more irregular outbreaks (once a decade or less) in northern parts. Shows peak numbers in a region at the same time as vole populations. Some suspicion of recently declining numbers in Swedish range owing to rare occurrences of high numbers and large-scale migrations during last 20–30 years; however, not supported for other parts of the range. Heavy reindeer grazing in Sweden supposed to negatively affect numbers but no conclusive evidence.

International legal & conservation status

None.

Other information

Of no economic importance, except as a tourist attraction to Fennoscandian mountains.

Literature

Jennersten (1995) – review
Kalela (1961)
Kalela & Koponen (1971)
Oksanen & Oksanen (1992)
Stenseth & Ims (1993) – review
Tast (1982a) – review

L. Hansson

© Societas Europaea Mammalogica

Lemmus lemmus

Clethrionomys glareolus (SCHREBER, 1780)

T. P. McOwat

	Bank vole		
AL	-	LU	Rout Bëschmaus
BG	Горска полевка	LV	Meža strupaste; Rūsganā
CZ	Norník rudý		mežstrupaste
DE	Rötelmaus	MK	Лисеста полјанка
DK	Rødmus	MT	-
EE	Leethiir; Tava-leethiir	NL	Rosse woelmuis
ES	Topillo rojo	NO	Klatremus
FI	Metsämyyrä	PL	Nornica ruda
FO	-	PT	-
FR	Campagnol roussâtre	RO	Şoarecele-scurmǎtor-de-
GR	Δασοσκαπτοποντικός		pǎdure
HR	Riđa voluharica	RU	Рыжая полёвка
HU	Vöröshátú erdeipocok	SE	Skogssork
IR	Vól bruaigh	SI	Gozdna voluharica
IS	Bakkastúfa	SK	Hrdziak lesný
IT	Arvicola rossastra	TR	Kızıl sırtlı fare
LT	Rudasis pelėnas	YU	Риђа волухарица

Distribution

World: Western Palaearctic forest belt, from British Isles to Lake Baikal. Also in northern Asia Minor.
Europe: north to the Arctic circle, south to northern Spain, mountains of Italy, and the Balkans. Presence in Ireland probably results from recent introduction. Common on the islands off the Atlantic and Baltic coasts, but absent from Mediterranean islands.

Geographic variation

Considerable and complex variation of size, relative tail length, skull proportions, dental pattern and colour has led to the description of more than 30 subspecies. A revision and interpretation is still missing. Marginal populations as well as mountain forms tend to be larger with relatively longer tails than those in central and north European lowlands. Light-coloured forms live in the south-east and in the lowlands of Central Europe, dark forms in north-east Europe and Britain and some in mountains. Interpopulation variability in the Y chromosome, which is either acrocentric or metacentric, shows no clear geographic pattern.

Habitat

All types of forests from sea level to 2400 m altitude. Prefers densely covered clearings and margins of moist deciduous and mixed forests. Highest densities on banks of brooks and in riverine forests accompanying rivers and streams. In deforested areas with high general humidity also in parks, gardens and hedgerows, even grasslands. In the south, restricted to montane forests.

Population status

Very common in large parts of Europe. Densities vary between 6–12 ind./ha and 50–100 ind./ha Bank vole populations show multiannual fluctuations which may be cyclic or noncyclic.

International legal & conservation status

None.

Literature

Petrusewicz (1983)
Viro & Niethammer (1982) – review

F. Spitzenberger

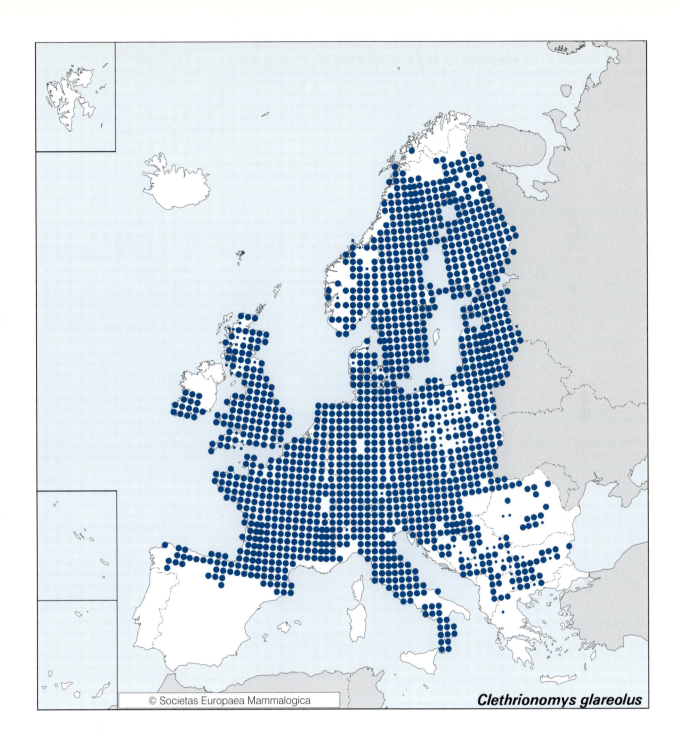

Clethrionomys glareolus

© Societas Europaea Mammalogica

Clethrionomys rufocanus (Sundevall, 1846)

T. P. McOwat

Grey-sided vole

AL	-	LT	Rudnugaris pelėnas
BG	Червеносива горска полевка	LU	-
CZ	Norník šedavý	LV	Austrumu mežstrupaste
DE	Graurötelmaus	MK	-
DK	Gråsidemus	MT	-
EE	Mägi-leethiir	NL	Rosgrijze woelmuis
ES	Topillo de Sundevall	NO	Gråsidemus
FI	Harmaakuvemyyrä	PL	Nornica szaroruda
FO	-	PT	-
FR	Campagnol de Sundevall	RO	-
GR	-	RU	Красно-серая полёвка
HR	Sivoriđa voluharica	SE	Gråsiding
HU	Deres erdeipocok	SI	Siva gozdna voluharica
IR	-	SK	-
IS	Grásiđa	TR	-
IT	Arvicola di Sundevall	YU	-

Distribution

World: northern Palaearctic, from western Scandinavia through northern Russia to the Pacific coast (including islands of Sakhalin, Hokkaido, and Rishiri), and in central Asia (Altai and Mongolia).
Europe: common in Norway (except south-western coastal areas, but present on the mountains of southern Norway), and in central and northern Sweden. In Finland, restricted to the northern third, although in the east occurs in Russian Karelia as far south as Lake Ladoga.

Geographic variation

Of six subspecies, as described in the northern Palaearctic area (based mainly on colour), only the nominate form (relatively dark) is found in Europe.

Habitat

Different types of forests, i.e. dry and moist coniferous as well as birch forests on lowlands and on the slopes of fells. Prefers stony (rocky) places with many natural holes. Also on dry peat-bogs and above the timber-line on fells among shrubs. In the coniferous forest area also in clearings. In the southern parts of the distribution in Finland often in river valleys with stony slopes, and, on the other hand, on tops and slopes of some southern fells (possibly for microclimatical reasons).

Population status

A common species in northern Fennoscandia (from northern Norway to Kola peninsula), often most abundant at the coniferous tree line and in subarctic birch forests. Its occurrence is scattered, although widespread in Russian Karelia. Long-term population trend is obviously stable, but populations fluctuate strongly (relative density in Finnish Lapland from less than one to 10–20 ind. per 100 trap nights). Peaks at 4–5 years intervals were observed in Finnish Lapland between 1955 and 1983. The peak years 1982–83 were simultaneous in several areas, especially in coniferous forests, but since then the yearly changes have been slight and irregular.

International legal & conservation status

None.

Other information

Feeds mostly on vegetative parts of plants, green grasses and herbs; in autumn it feeds on berries and in winter on dwarf shrubs (especially *Vaccinium myrtillus* and *V. uliginosum*).

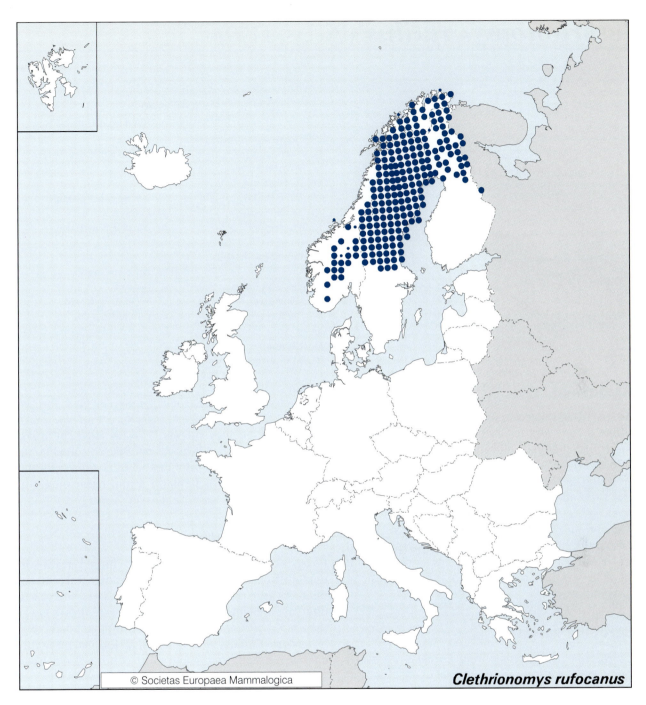

© Societas Europaea Mammalogica

Clethrionomys rufocanus

Literature

Gromov & Polyakov (1992)
Henttonen & Viitala (1982) – review
Henttonen *et al.* (1987)
Sulkava (1996)
Viitala (1977)

S. Sulkava

Clethrionomys rutilus (PALLAS, 1779)

P. Twisk

Distribution

World: northern Holarctic, where it occurs in subarctic birch forest zone and in northern parts of coniferous forests, from Scandinavia through Siberia to the Pacific coast (between 43° and 73°N), Sakhalin and Hokkaido (Japan), and in the northern parts of North America (Alaska and Canada).

Europe: restricted to northernmost Norway, Sweden, Finland and Russia. In Finland also an isolated area in the eastern part of the country. In north-western and central European Russia the species is sparse but widespread much more to the south than in Fennoscandia.

Geographic variation

Ten subspecies, as described from Eurasia, are based mainly on colour differences. Some taxonomists accept, however, only six subspecies. The subspecies, *C. rutilus rossicus* Dukelsky, 1928, lives in continental Europe from Scandinavia to Ural Mts. The nominate race, which is a rich red, lives in western Siberia. In addition, Siivonen (1967) has tentatively described a new subspecies *(C. r. finmarchicus)* from the island of Nord-Fuglöy (northern Norway) as being slightly larger and darker than the mainland form. Several subspecies also exist in North America.

Habitat

Prefers productive (eutrophic or mesotrophic) forests, rich in grasses and herbs (especially Scrophulariaceae).

Common in northern European subarctic birch forests. In coniferous zone occurs in mossy spruce forests; unlike other *Clethrionomys* species it avoids clear-cut areas. Habitat selection may be restricted also by competition, since the species is overdominated by *C. rufocanus* and *Microtus* species. In Lapland found occasionally in buildings.

Population status

Long-term population trend obviously stable in northernmost Europe, but populations fluctuate in numbers as in other northern voles with 4–5 years peak intervals. Densities in Finland have been always lower than in *C. rufocanus*. More southern populations (e.g. in eastern Finland and in Russian Karelia) probably decreasing with increasing clear-cutting of old fresh spruce forests.

International legal & conservation status

None.

Other information

In autumn stores seeds, especially of Scrophulariaceae; may transport in its mouth 50–60 seeds of *Melampyrum* at once.

© Societas Europaea Mammalogica

Clethrionomys rutilus

Literature

Gromov & Polyakov (1992)
Henttonen & Peiponen (1982) – review
Ivanter (1975)
Oksanen & Henttonen (1996)
Siivonen (1967)

S. Sulkava

Dinaromys bogdanovi (Martino, 1922)

T. P. McOwat

	Balkan snow vole		
AL	Miu i Bogdanovit	LU	-
BG	Югославска полевка	LV	-
CZ	Hraboš skalní	MK	Високопланинска
DE	Bergmaus		полјанка
DK	Nehrings bjergmus	MT	-
EE	-	NL	Bergmuis
ES	Topillo de Nehring	NO	Europeisk fjellmus
FI	Balkaninlumimyyrä	PL	Nornik bałkański
FO	-	PT	-
FR	Campagnol de Martino	RO	-
GR	-	RU	Югославская полёвка
HR	Dinarski voluhar	SE	Bergsork
HU	Őspocok	SI	Dinarska voluharica
IR	-	SK	-
IS	-	TR	-
IT	Arvicola dei Balcani	YU	Динарска волухарица
LT	-		

The only living representative of the genus *Dinaromys*, having no close relationship with any other living arvicolid. Although originally described as a member of *Chionomys,* it was long considered to be the only surviving species of the fossil genus *Dolomys* Nehring, 1898.

Distribution

Endemic to the Balkans: the Dinaric Alps of Croatia, Bosnia and Herzegovina, Montenegro and Kosovo, as well as the Šara-Pindus mountains of western Macedonia. Undoubtedly present in Albania, and possibly also in Greece.

Geographic variation

Eight subspecies, as described until now, can be restricted into two groups, represented by *D. bogdanovi bogdanovi* and *D. b. grebenscikovi* (Martino, 1935) and differing in the structure of the first lower molar. Electrophoretic analysis, based on 28 proteins, suggests deep genetic differences between the two. Karyotype is stable.

Habitat

Rock dweller, restricted to limestone areas with well developed karst phenomena, mainly deep fissures or small caverns with a stable microclimate. The majority of records are from stone piles on meadows above the tree line, rarely from the forests. Sympatric with *Chionomys nivalis* on the margin of the distribution area. Competition between the two rock-dwelling voles not well understood but may present a threat to *D. bogdanovi*. Altitudinal range from sea level to 2200 m.

Population status

Relict form, not known outside the karst of the western Balkans. Distribution sporadic as a result of island type habitats. Local demes could be quite small and thus vulnerable to extinction. However, the majority of the range is in inaccessible areas, and thus not directly threatened by man. North-western range reduced since the Upper Pleistocene onwards.

International legal & conservation status

IUCN Red List, Lower Risk – near threatened.

Literature

Kryštufek (1991)
Petrov & Todorović (1982) – review

B. Kryštufek

Dinaromys bogdanovi

Arvicola sapidus Miller, 1908

T. McOwat

Similar in size and habits to the aquatic form of *A. terrestris,* but differs in morphological characters (skull, baculum) and chromosomal number *(A. sapidus* : 2N = 40; *A. terrestris* : 2N = 36).

Distribution

Endemic to south-western Europe, i.e., Portugal, Spain and France. Sympatry with *A. terrestris* is not well known, but probably restricted merely to fossorial populations of *A. terrestris* in central France, the Pyrénées and northern Iberian peninsula.

Geographic variation

Two subspecies are recognized: a dark form, *A. sapidus tenebricus* Miller, 1908, in the northern part of the distribution range (France, northern Spain) and a paler morph, *A. s. sapidus,* in the rest of the Iberian peninsula.

Habitat

Always associated with water (streams, marshes). Occurs mostly along slowly flowing streams with abundant vegetation from sea level up to 1600 m in the Alps, 2000 m in the Pyrénées and 2300 m in the Sierra Nevada. Swims well and digs its burrows in river banks. Diet is mainly herbivorous, with occasional animal items.

Population status

Apparently under threat in many areas. Limited to wetlands and streams where banks and riparian vegetation have not been altered. Population fluctuations are not known, but highest densities probably do not exceed 5 ind./100 m of river bank. Not known to cause damage to crops.

International legal & conservation status

IUCN Red List, Lower Risk – near threatened.

Literature

Reichstein (1982a) – review
Ventura *et al.* (1989)

F. Saucy

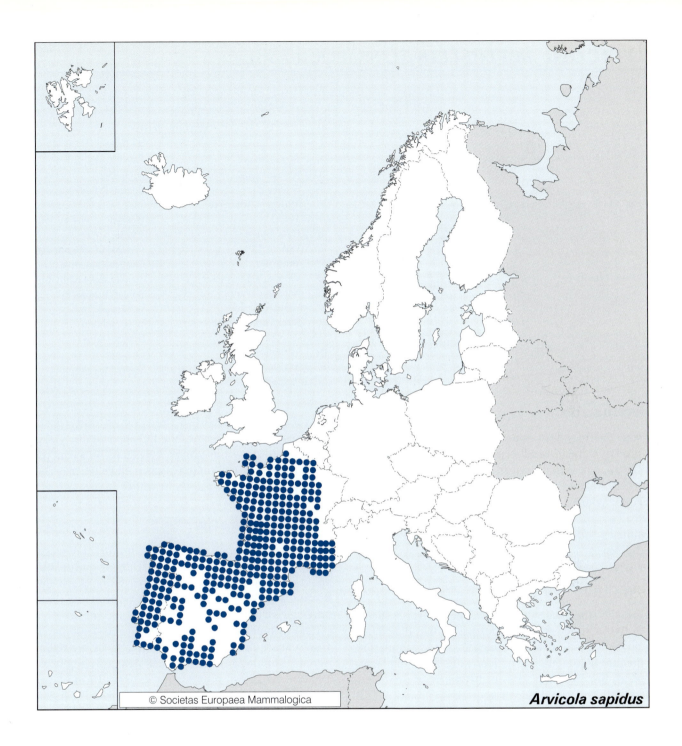

© Societas Europaea Mammalogica

Arvicola sapidus

Arvicola terrestris (LINNAEUS, 1758)

M. Năzăreanu

Distribution

World: Palaearctic species ranging from Great Britain to the Lena Basin in Siberia. Extends from the Arctic circle to Lake Baikal, north of the Aral Sea, northern Iran and Near East.

Europe: widely distributed, but absent from Ireland, western and southern France, southern Iberian peninsula, southern Greece and from highest elevations in the Alps.

Geographic variation

At least 36 subspecies described. A polymorphic species with two distinct ecological forms: widely distributed aquatic populations and isolated fossorial populations in the mountains (the Carpathians, the Alps, the Massif Central, the Pyrénées and in the north of Spain and Portugal). The two differ in body mass (aquatic: 150–300 g; fossorial: 60–150 g), in fur colour (from black to pale brown with dark morphs most common in aquatic populations), in social behaviour, mating system and use of space. Fossorial voles have more protruding incisors.

Habitat

Aquatic forms populate rivers, streams, lakes, marshes, forests and wet areas both in the lowlands and in the mountains. Water quality and cover seem important. Individuals from aquatic forms can also colonize temporarily drier habitats where they behave like typical fossorial morphs. Fossorial populations occur in dry or mesic grasslands (meadows, pastures and occasionally in wooded areas) where they live in underground burrows similar to those of the European mole. The diet is mainly herbivorous. Water voles feed on aerial parts of plants (mostly in summer), as well as on tree roots, rhizomes, bulbs and tubers in winter.

Population status

Aquatic populations apparently under threat in western Europe (Britain, Italy, the Netherlands) due to water pollution, loss of habitat or mink predation (L. Nieder & R. van Apeldoorn, pers. comm.). Fossorial populations undergo strong and periodic fluctuations (5–8-year cycles) with densities ranging between 0–1000 ind./ha. They can then cause severe damage in grasslands. Aquatic populations rarely reach densities higher than 100 ind./ha in wet habitats (or approx. 15 ind./100 m of river bank) except when they colonize dry habitats where they behave like fossorial populations. In some parts of Europe, aquatic forms can cause serious damage in orchards (even at low or moderate abundance) and in crops during exceptional outbreaks.

International legal & conservation status

None.

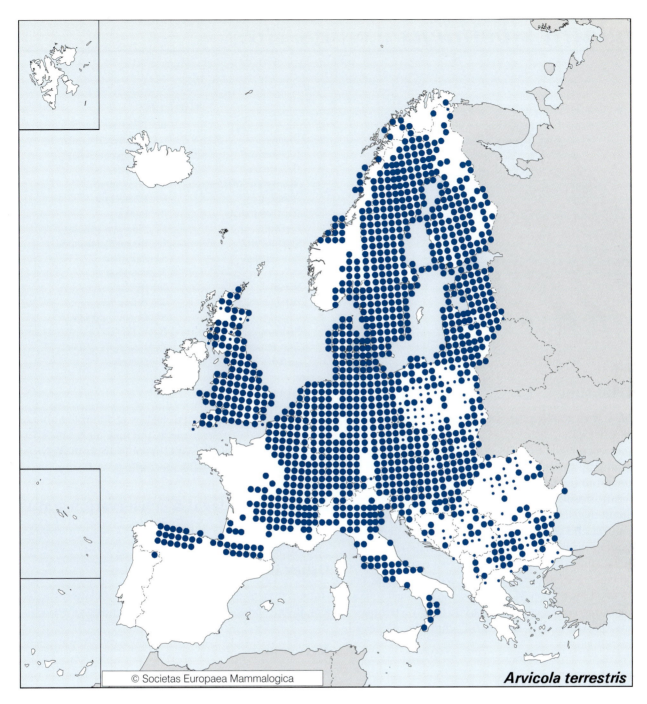

© Societas Europaea Mammalogica

Arvicola terrestris

Literature

Boyce (1991)
Morel & Meylan (1970)
Reichstein (1982b) – review
Saucy (1994)
Strachan & Jefferies (1993)
Ventura & Gosàlbez (1989)

F. Saucy

223

Ondatra zibethicus (Linnaeus, 1766)

U. Iff

Muskrat			
AL	-	LU	Bisamrat
BG	Ондатра	LV	Ondatra; Bizamžurka
CZ	Ondatra	MK	Бизамска полјанка
DE	Bisamratte	MT	-
DK	Bisamrotte; Moskusrotte	NL	Muskusrat
EE	Ondatra	NO	Bisamrotte
ES	Rata almizclera	PL	Piżmak
FI	Piisami	PT	Rato-almiscarado
FO	Moskusrotta	RO	Bizamul; Sobolanul-mirositor
FR	Rat musqué		
GR	-	RU	Ондатра
HR	Bizam	SE	Bisam
HU	Pézsmapocok	SI	Pižmovka
IR	-	SK	Ondatra pižmová
IS	Bísamrotta; Moskusrotta	TR	-
IT	Topo muschiato	YU	Бизамски пацов; Ондатра
LT	Ondatra		

Distribution

World: native to Nearctic, where common in most of North America.

Europe: introduced to Bohemia in 1905, from where it has gradually spread. The spread was also assisted by escapes from fur farms (France, Belgium, Poland) and deliberate introductions (Finland, Russia, Lithuania). Two main distribution areas in Europe now, in western and central and in north-eastern Europe, respectively. Widespread in western Europe from northern France to central and eastern Europe (Black Sea coast). Present also in eastern Fennoscandia and northern Russia, but absent from the British Isles, most of the Mediterranean, western and southern Scandinavia. The distribution pattern may still change because of continuing dispersal and introductions.

Geographic variation

No subspecies recognized in Europe, although clinal variation in skull dimensions occurs. The probable ancestor of European populations was the nominate subspecies from eastern Canada.

Habitat

Lives always by fresh water, still or flowing. Banks of ponds, lakes, rivers and canals with rich riparian vegetation, and in marshes. Penetrates along streams even in mountains. In winter, builds a lodge of grass and reeds with several chambers.

Population status

Common species. Normal densities in suitable habitats 1–2 breeding pairs per hectare, but may increase to 50–60 individuals in peak years. In some areas (e.g., Great Britain) exterminated after becoming established.

International legal & conservation status

None.

Other information

Hunted for fur. Because of burrowing activity regarded as a pest in ponds and other constructions on rivers.

References

Akkermann (1975a, b, c)
Doude van Troostwijk (1976)
Hoffmann (1958) – review
Niethammer (1963)
Pietsch (1982) – review
Willner *et al.* (1980) – review

J. Zima

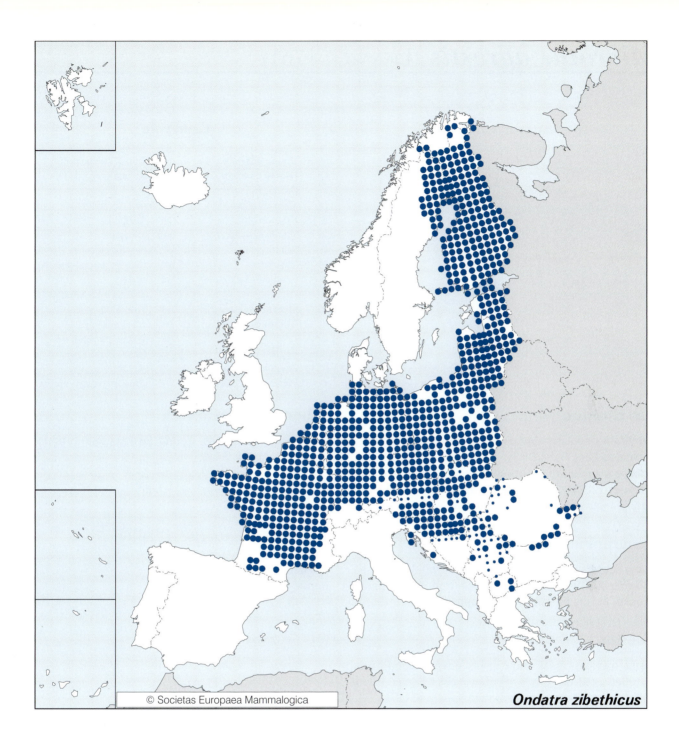

© Societas Europaea Mammalogica

Ondatra zibethicus

Microtus agrestis (Linnaeus, 1761)

T. P. McOwat

Field vole

AL	-	LU	Kleng Wullmaus
BG	Тъмна полевка	LV	Tumšā strupaste;
CZ	Hraboš mokřadní		Krūmāju strupaste
DE	Erdmaus	MK	-
DK	Markmus	MT	-
EE	Niidu-uruhiir	NL	Aardmuis
ES	Topillo agreste	NO	Markmus
FI	Peltomyyrä	PL	Nornik bury
FO	Hagamús	PT	Rato-do-campo-de-rabo-
FR	Campagnol agreste		curto
GR	-	RO	Şoarecele de pământ
HR	Livadna voluharica	RU	Тёмная полёвка
HU	Csalitjáró pocok	SE	Åkersork
IR	-	SI	Travniška voluharica
IS	Engjastúfa	SK	Hraboš močiarny
IT	Arvicola agreste	TR	-
LT	Pievinis pelėnas	YU	Ливадска волухарица

Distribution

World: Palaearctic species, ranging from western Europe to Lake Baikal.
Europe: throughout the continent, except Ireland, southern Europe, the lowlands of central and most of south-eastern Europe and northernmost Russia.

Geographic variation

About seven subspecies are considered valid in Europe, differing in the body size, coat coloration and dental pattern, particularly in the first upper molar.

Habitat

Moist habitats with rich grass cover, woodlands, marshes, peat-bogs, wet meadows, river banks. Builds underground burrow system with spherical nest.

Population status

Common within the distribution range, except in marginal areas in western and central Europe where it may be locally rare. The population density fluctuates markedly with a cycle of approximately four years.

International legal & conservation status

None.

Other information

Can damage pastures, young forestry plantations or orchards in peak years.

References

Hansson (1982)
Krapp & Niethammer (1982) – review
Myllymäki (1970, 1977)
Reichstein (1958/59)
Stenseth (1977)

J. Zima

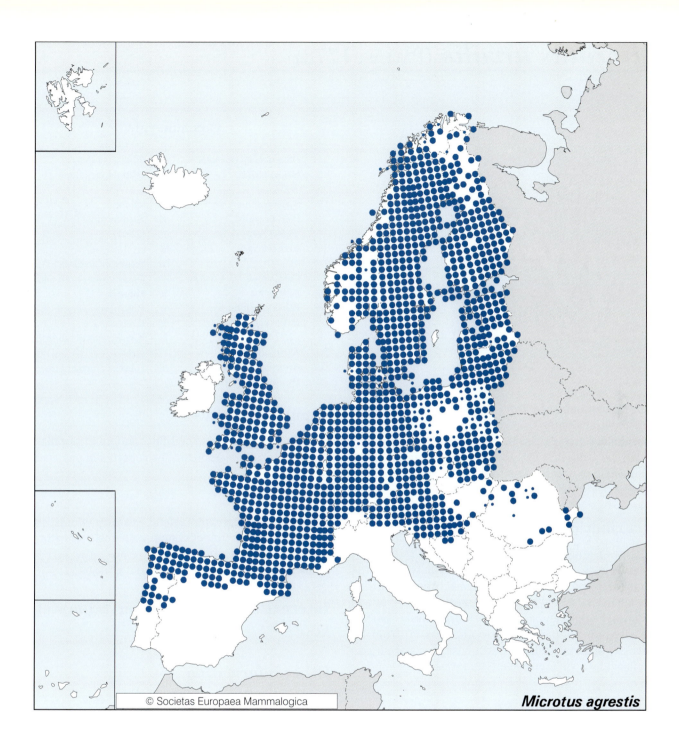

© Societas Europaea Mammalogica

Microtus agrestis

227

Microtus arvalis (PALLAS, 1778)

P. Barrett

Common vole

AL	-	LU	Feldmaus
BG	Обикновена полевка	LV	Lauku strupaste
CZ	Hraboš polní	MK	Обична полјанка
DE	Feldmaus	MT	-
DK	Sydmarkmus	NL	Veldmuis
EE	Põld-uruhiir	NO	Sørmarkmus
ES	Topillo campesino	PL	Polnik
FI	Kenttämyyrä	PT	-
FO	-	RO	Şoarecele de câmp
FR	Campagnol des champs	RU	Обыкновенная полёвка
GR	Αρουραίος	SE	Fältsork
HR	Poljska voluharica	SI	Poljska voluharica
HU	Mezei pocok	SK	Hraboš poľný
IR	-	TR	Kısa kuyruklu adi tarla faresi
IS	Akurstúfa		
IT	Arvicola campestre	YU	Пољска волухарица
LT	Paprastasis pelėnas		

Can be distinguished from other sympatric voles by shorter and lighter coat, less hairy ears, and tooth morphology. Sympatric *(M. rossiaemeridionalis* Ognev, 1924) or parapatric *(M. obscurus* (Eversmann, 1841)) sibling species can be safely differentiated only by karyological examination.

Distribution

European endemic species. Continuous range from Atlantic coast of France to central Russia with isolated populations on the Iberian peninsula. Absent from the British Isles (except Orkney Islands), Mediterranean, most of Fennoscandia, and northern Russia. Eastern distribution limits in Ukraine and Russia, from the Dniester River towards the north-east. In eastern Russia replaced by a sibling species, *M. obscurus*.

Geographic variation

More than 20 subspecies recognized in Europe. The status of most of them is questionable. Insular populations confined to certain Atlantic islands (Yeu, Guernsey, Orkney Islands) deserve particular interest, and some of them have been described as separate subspecies (e.g., *M. arvalis orcadensis* Millais, 1904, characterized by large body size). However, no karyotypic differences have yet been reported between insular and mainland populations.

Population status

Common, with pronounced fluctuations in population density. More than 1000 ind./ha reported in peak years.

Habitat

Open cultivated agricultural land, grazed pastures, short meadows. Builds tunnel system with nests and storage chambers. Tunnels connected by surface runways. Feeds mainly on green parts of plants and grasses.

International legal & conservation status

None.

Other information

Serious pest of agriculture. It may be a vector of various diseases.

Literature

Kratochvíl (1959) – review
Niethammer & Krapp (1982) – review
Sokolov & Bashenina (1994) – review
Stein (1958) – review

J. Zima

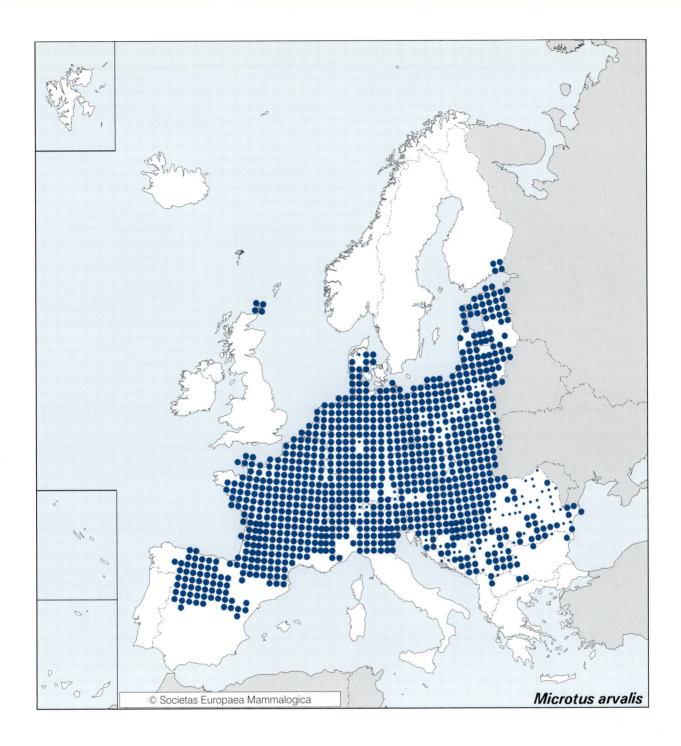

Microtus arvalis

Microtus cabrerae Thomas, 1906

T. P. McOwat

Distribution

Endemic to the Iberian Peninsula. Although records are widely scattered across the peninsula, the actual distribution area is fragmented.

Geographic variation

Two subspecies are usually recognized: *M. cabrerae cabrerae* and *M. c. dentatus* Miller, 1910. Morphological differences between them are negligible, however, which makes their validity questionable.

Habitat

Pastures and fields close to surface water. Humid slopes and foothills with a Mediterranean climate at altitudes between 500 to 1000 m are preferred habitats, while regions with high summer temperatures are avoided. Summer activity is mainly restricted to underground galleries.

Population status

Small colonies are subject to strong annual fluctuations. Because of the fragmented distribution, populations are small and isolated. Farming practices during recent decades have presumably reduced its range and accelerated the fragmentation. Distribution area decreased since the Pleistocene, with subfossil (Holocene) records outside the actual range.

International legal & conservation status

Bern Convention, Appendix II.
EU Habitats & Species Directive, Annex II & Annex IV.
IUCN Red List, Lower Risk – near threatened.

Literature

Ayarzaguena & López-Martínez (1976)
Niethammer (1982e) – review
Ventura *et al* (1998)

L. J. Palomo

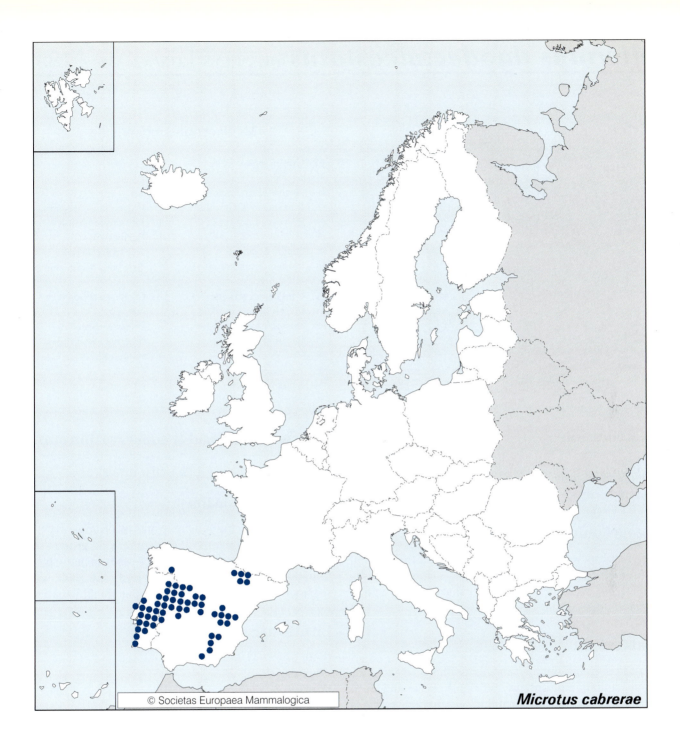

© Societas Europaea Mammalogica

Microtus cabrerae

Microtus duodecimcostatus DE SÉLYS-LONGCHAMPS, 1839

P. Twisk

Mediterranean pine vole

AL	-	LU	-
BG	Средиземноморска полевка	LV	-
		MK	-
CZ	Hraboší středomořský	MT	-
DE	Mittelmeer-Kleinwühlmaus	NL	Provençaalse woelmuis
DK	Provence-markmus	NO	Provencemarkmus
EE	-	PL	Darniówka śródziemnomorska
ES	Topillo cavador		
FI	Välimerentunnelimyyrä	PT	Rato-cego-mediterrânico
FO	-	RO	-
FR	Campagnol provençal	RU	Средиземноморская полёвка
GR	Ρυγχοσκαπτοποντικός		
HR	Sredozemni voluharić	SE	Provence-gransork
HU	Ibériai pocok	SI	Sredozemska kratkouha voluharica
IR	-		
IS	-	SK	-
IT	Arvicola iberica	TR	-
LT	-	YU	-

Distribution

Endemic to the western Mediterranean area of Europe. Widely distributed throughout the Iberian Peninsula (except north-west) and south-east France.

Geographic variation

Seven subspecies have been described on the basis of colour and size. The species is now considered as monotypic, regardless of the fact that interpopulation variation does occur.

Habitat

Most fossorial of the Iberian voles with preferences for open habitats and ground sufficiently loose and deep for digging. In wide areas of the Iberian Peninsula it is the only representative of the genus *Microtus*. Altitudinal distribution ranges from sea level to 2250 m in the Sierra Nevada. Restricted to the Mediterranean climate area, it tolerates more adverse temperatures and drought than other *Microtus* species.

Population status

Populations stable with no cyclic fluctuations over the years. Since it is an agricultural pest at higher densities (up to 400/ha) it is controlled in some areas. Control measures can drastically affect local populations.

International legal & conservation status

None.

Other information

Intensive burrowing activity results in a complex system of galleries and burrows. Feeds mainly on grasses and herbaceous plants, occasionally also on fruit trees. Reproduction proceeds throughout the year, with seasonal variations resulting in population fluctuations.

Literature

Niethammer (1982f) – review
Winking (1976)
Winking & Niethammer (1970)

L. J. Palomo

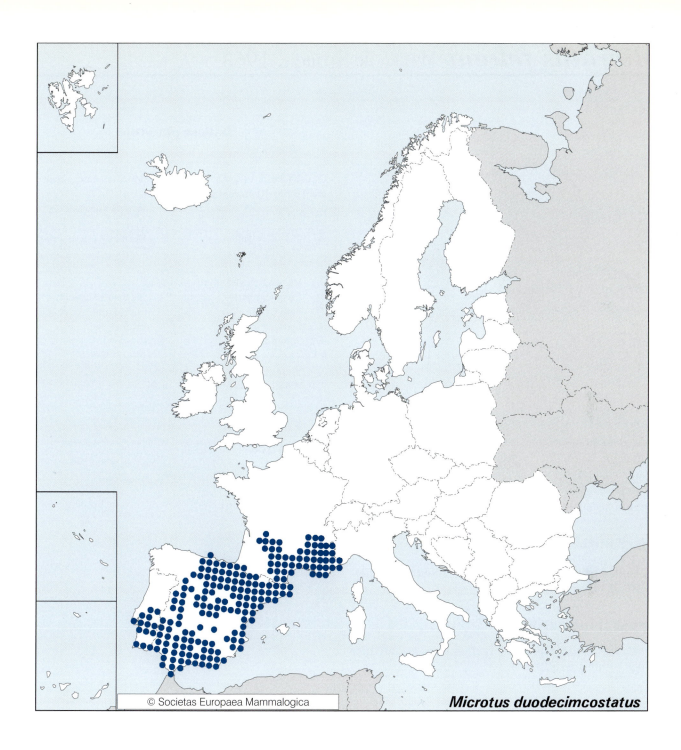

© Societas Europaea Mammalogica

Microtus duodecimcostatus

Microtus felteni Malec & Storch, 1963

T. P. McOwat

Balkan pine vole

AL	Miu i Feltenit	LU	-
BG	-	LV	-
CZ	Hrabošík Feltenův	MK	Фелтенова полјанка
DE	Felten-Kleinwühlmaus	MT	-
DK	-	NL	Felten's woelmuis
EE	-	NO	-
ES	Topillo de Felten	PL	Darniówka macedońska
FI	Makedonianmyyrä	PT	-
FO	-	RO	-
FR	Campagnol de Felten	RU	-
GR	Ρυγχοσκαπτοποντικός του Felten	SE	Makedonsk gransork
		SI	Makedonska kratkouha voluharica
HR	Feltenov voluharić		
HU	Felten-pocok	SK	-
IR	-	TR	-
IS	-	YU	-
IT	Arvicola della Macedonia		
LT	-		

Described as a subspecies of *M. savii,* but later raised to specific level, due to different karyotype. Recently again considered a subspecies of *M. savii* from which it is morphologically indistinguishable. This step, however, was not accepted by all authors.

Distribution

Endemic to the Balkans: southern Serbia, Macedonia, northern Greece, and Albania.

Geographic variation

Specimens from Macedonia larger on average than their Greek counterparts.

Habitat

Mainly mountainous forests, exceptionally also on cultivated land in the lowland. Vertical range between 360 and 2050 m above sea level. Only exceptionally syntopic with *M. subterraneus.*

Population status

Little known and rare species throughout its range. No evidence of population decline.

International legal & conservation status

IUCN Red List, Lower Risk – near threatened.

Literature

Niethammer (1982g) – review
Petrov (1992)
Petrov *et al.* (1976)

B. Kryštufek

© Societas Europaea Mammalogica

Microtus felteni

Microtus gerbei (Gerbe, 1879)

T. P. McOwat

	Pyrenean pine vole		
AL	-	LU	-
BG	-	LV	-
CZ	Hrabošík pyrenejský	MK	-
DE	Pyrenäen-Kleinwühlmaus	MT	-
DK	-	NL	Pyreneese woelmuis
EE	-	NO	-
ES	Topillo de Gerbe	PL	Darniówka pirenejska
FI	Pyreneidentunnelimyyrä	PT	-
FO	-	RO	-
FR	Campagnol des Pyrénées	RU	-
GR	-	SE	-
HR	Pirenejski voluharić	SI	Pirenejska kratkouha
HU	Pireneusi pocok		voluharica
IR	-	SK	-
IS	-	TR	-
IT	Arvicola dei Pirenei	YU	-
LT	-		

This species is also known under the name *M. pyrenaicus* (de Sélys-Longchamps, 1847), which is now considered as *nomen dubium*.

Distribution

Endemic to the western Mediterranean area of Europe: Central and south-west France north to the Loire, the Pyrénées and the eastern Cantabrian Mountains.

Geographic variation

Four subspecies, as described on the basis of colour and skull shape, are very weakly differentiated.

Habitat

The Pyrenean pine vole is a fossorial species, inhabiting pastures and cultivated fields. In the Pyrénées, and other mountain regions, it is semi-fossorial, living in grasslands and along rocky woodland borders. Preferred regions have less than 1000 mm rainfall and average annual temperatures below 15–16°C. It is found at altitudes up to 2000 m in the Pyrénées.

Population status

Densities in central France locally up to 100 ind./ha; despite this, the species is not considered to be an agricultural pest.

International legal & conservation status

None.

Literature

Gosálbez (1987)
Krapp (1982c) – review (as *M. pyrenaicus)*

L. J. Palomo

Microtus gerbei

237

Microtus guentheri (DANFORD & ALSTON, 1880)

P. Twisk

Guenther's vole

AL	-	LT	-
BG	Гюнтерова полевка	LU	-
CZ	Hraboš Güntherův	LV	-
DE	Levante-Wühlmaus	MK	Медитеранска полјанка
DK	Guenthers markmus	MT	
EE	-	NL	Mediterrane veldmuis
ES	Topillo de Guenther	NO	Middelhavsmarkmus
FI	Isokenttämyyrä	PL	Nornik anatolski
FO	-	PT	
FR	Campagnol méditerannéen	RO	
GR	Αρουραίος της Ανατολικής	RU	Полёвка Гюнтера
	Μεσογείου	SE	Östlig medelhavssork
HR	Levantinska voluharica	SI	Anatolska voluharica
HU	Levantei pocok	SK	-
IR	-	TR	Tarla faresi
IS	-	YU	Средоземна волухарица
IT	Arvicola di Günther		

The taxonomy of the *M. socialis* (Pallas, 1773) group, to which *M. guentheri* belongs, is not definitely agreed. Of the three species as currently recognized, *M. guentheri* is characterized by large size, robust skull and also by its karyotype (2N = 54).

Distribution

World: if *M. irani* Thomas, 1921 is accepted as a valid species, then *M. guentheri* is restricted to Anatolia and south-eastern Balkans. Otherwise, the range includes also Israel, Syria, and Lebanon, with an isolate in Libya. *Europe:* fragmented range includes Turkish Thrace, northern and eastern Greece, southern Bulgaria, Macedonia and southern Serbia. Exceptionally occurs also on islands (St Thomas (Bulgaria) and Lesbos).

Geographic variation

Three subspecies as currently recognized from Europe, are based on differences in average size. However, interpopulation variation of phenetic characters is weakly expressed, as is slight divergence of European populations from the western Anatolian ones. Karyotype stable among European populations.

Habitat

Dry meadows and pastures with sparse vegetation on well drained soil. Locally syntopic with *M. rossiaemeridionalis*. European localities from lowlands, e.g., in Macedonia between 150 and 500 m above sea level.

Population status

Sporadic in Europe, but locally common. Populations undergo large fluctuations with severe declines. This gives the impression of local extinctions, which, however, are not documented in the Balkans. High population densities reported from the Asiatic range; e.g., at peak over 500 holes were reopened per hectare. Over a million and half hectares were infested in Turkey in the plague year 1931. No such large-scale population peaks occur in Europe.

International legal & conservation status

IUCN Red List, Lower Risk – near threatened.

Literature

Bodemheimer (1949)
Niethammer (1982h) – review

B. Kryštufek

Microtus guentheri

© Societas Europaea Mammalogica

Microtus lusitanicus (GERBE, 1879)

T. P. McOwat

Lusitanian pine vole

AL	-	LU	-
BG	Иберийска полевка	LV	-
CZ	Hrabošík iberský	MK	-
DE	Iberien-Wühlmaus	MT	-
DK	-	NL	Baskische woelmuis
EE	-	NO	-
ES	Topillo lusitano	PL	Darniówka iberyjska
FI	Lusitaniantunnelimyyrä	PT	Rato-cego
FO	-	RO	-
FR	Campagnol basque	RU	Иберийская полёвка
GR	-	SE	Västiberisk gransork
HR	Iberski voluharić	SI	Luzitanska kratkouha
HU	Baszk pocok		voluharica
IR	-	SK	-
IS	-	TR	-
IT	Arvicola di Portogallo	YU	-
LT	-		

Distribution

Endemic to Europe, where restricted to a small area in the north-western triangle of the Iberian Peninsula; of marginal occurrence also in south-west of France.

Geographic variation

Although several subspecies have been described, cranial and biometric evidence hardly justifies any further division of the species. Specimens from central Portugal, ascribed to the nominate subspecies, seem to differ from the remainder *(M. lusitanicus mariae* Forsyth Major, 1905). Karyotype is variable with several pericentric inversions being involved.

Habitat

Burrows in deep soil, mainly on grasslands, pastures and cultivated fields; also stays close to small stone walls. It is less fossorial than *M. duodecimcostatus,* with which it is sympatric in the central part of the Iberian Peninsula. Altitudinal range is between sea level and 2000 m (Sierra de Gredos).

Population status

No multiannual cyclic fluctuations recorded so far. Reproduction continues throughout the year.

International legal & conservation status

None.

Other information

Pest of orchards and vegetable crops. Control measures can affect local populations.

Literature

Niethammer (1982i) – review
Winking (1976)

L. J. Palomo

Microtus lusitanicus

241

Microtus multiplex (FATIO, 1905)

T. P. McOwat

Alpine pine vole

AL	-	LU	-
BG	-	LV	-
CZ	Hrabošík Fatiův	MK	-
DE	Alpen-Kleinwühlmaus	MT	-
DK	Fatios markmus	NL	Fatio's woelmuis
EE	-	NO	Alpemarkmus
ES	Topillo de Fatio	PL	Darniówka alpejska
FI	Alppitunnelimyyrä	PT	-
FO	-	RO	-
FR	Campagnol de Fatio	RU	Кустарниковая полёвка
GR	-	SE	Alpgransork
HR	Alpski voluharić	SI	Ilirska kratkouha
HU	Alpesi pocok		voluharica
IR	-	SK	-
IS	-	TR	-
IT	Arvicola di Fatio	YU	Велика волухарица
LT	-		

Distribution

Endemic to Europe. From the eastern Massif Central in France, across the Alps to the western Dinaric Alps and Istria; isolates in the Toscanian and Ligurian Apennines, Bosnia (where its scope is not well understood owing to confusion with *Microtus subterraneus),* northern Croatia, and western Serbia.

Geographic variation

Composed of two karyotypic forms, the western (2N = 48, NF = 54) and the eastern (2N = 46, NF = 52), with little known zone of parapatric occurrence in the Italian Alps. The eastern form sometimes considered as an independent species *M. liechtensteini* (Wettstein, 1927). Several subspecies, described on the basis of conventional taxonomic characters, have not yet been confirmed by other data sets.

Habitat

It prefers clearings and small meadows with lush herbs rather than mature forests. In the mountains also in the dwarf (knee) pine, and on the coast in dry meadows and along hedgerows. Vertical range from sea level in Istria to 2800 m in the Alps. Rarely sympatric with *M. subterraneus.* Lack of data on the coexistence of these two closely related species.

Population status

Locally common. No population decline recorded.

International legal & conservation status

None.

References

Krapp (1982a) – review
Storch & Winking (1977)

B. Kryštufek

© Societas Europaea Mammalogica

Microtus multiplex

243

Microtus oeconomus (Pallas, 1776)

PT 97   P. Twisk

Distribution

World: Holarctic species, ranging from Alaska in the east through northern Asia as far as China, Mongolia and the steppe zone in the south and north-western Europe in the west.

Europe: main range from northern Fennoscandia and north-eastern Germany in the west throughout Poland, Belarus and northern and central European Russia. Along western and southern borders in Europe isolated (relict) populations exist in The Netherlands, southern Norway and central Sweden, the Finnish Baltic coast and Austria, Slovakia and Hungary. Historical distribution included also the North Sea coast of Germany and Stockholm, where it is now extinct.

Geographic variation

Six subspecies are described in European part of the distribution area: *M. oeconomus arenicola* (de Sélys-Longchamps, 1841) (The Netherlands), *M. oe. ratticeps* (Keyserling and Blasius, 1841) (Russia), *M. oe. medius* (Nilsson, 1844) (Norway), *M. oe. stimmingi* (Nehring, 1899) (near Brandenburg), *M. oe. mehelyi* Ehik, 1928 (Hungary), *M. oe. finmarchicus* Siivonen, 1967 (Norway, Vesterál islands). The normal chromosome number of the species is 2N = 30, but polymorphism is known from Norway (2N = 31 and 32).

Habitat

Root voles prefer moist to wet vegetation with high plant coverage. Important habitat types are flooded shores or lakes, banks of rivers and brooks, open bogs, eutrophic peatlands and wet meadows. Voles migrate before winter (seasonal migration) into drier parts or other habitat types like grassy meadows or even houses.

On the island of Texel (The Netherlands) where other vole species do not occur (but *Microtus agrestis* has been recently introduced) the species inhabits also dry habitat types like road verges and dunes. Competition with other rodent species occurs (especially *Microtus agrestis* and *M. arvalis*).

Population status

The range contracts at the western and southern borders in Europe (e.g., Poland). Isolated populations in particular are decreasing (Hungary, Austria, Slovakia, The Netherlands) and are threatened. In The Netherlands competitive exclusion in combination with deterioration of root vole habitats seems to play a role. Elsewhere, populations are stable and the species is not endangered. Low densities in spring (4/ha, April) are known from The Netherlands, higher densities in summer from Norway (123/ha) and Poland (130/ha). Cyclic fluctuations occur in Fennoscandia.

International legal & conservation status

Bern Convention, Appendix III.
EU Habitats & Species Directive, Annex II*
(*M. oe. arenicola* only), Annex IV (*M. oe. arenicola* & *M. oe. mehelyi*).
IUCN Red List, Lower Risk – near threatened.

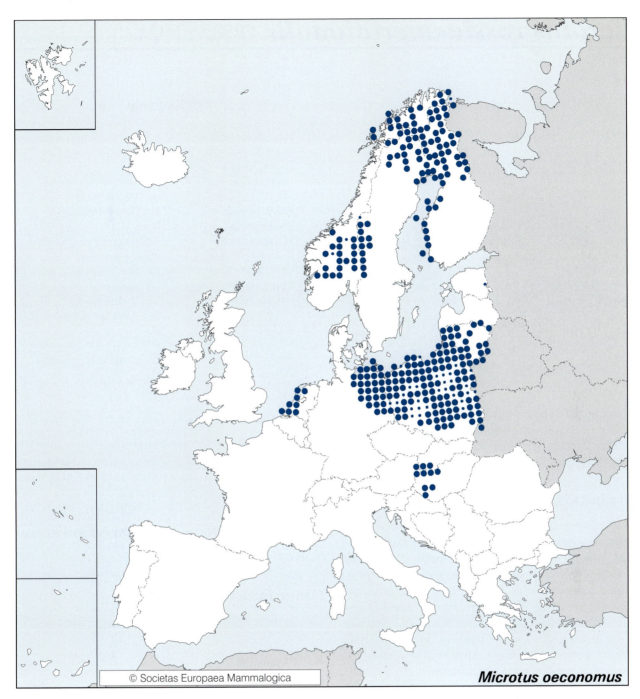

© Societas Europaea Mammalogica

Microtus oeconomus

Other information

Populations can reach pest densities and cause damage in continuous man-made habitat (grassland, coniferous forest).

Literature

Jorga (1971)
Kostian (1970)
Ligtvoet & van Wijngaarden (1994)
Sałata-Piłacińska (1990)
Tast (1982b)-review
van Wijngaarden & Zimmerman (1965)

R. C. van Apeldoorn

Microtus rossiaemeridionalis Ognev, 1924

T. P. McOwat

Morphologically quite similar to *Microtus arvalis,* but slightly larger and with distinctly different karyotype. Synonyms include *Microtus subarvalis* Meyer, Orlov & Skholl, 1972, and *M. epiroticus* Ondrias, 1966.

Distribution

World: Palaearctic species; south-eastern and eastern Europe, Asia Minor, Siberia eastwards almost to Lake Baikal. Absent from the Caucasus, tundra zone, and steppe-desert areas north of the Caspian Sea.
Europe: range includes Balkan peninsula, lowlands adjacent to the Black Sea; eastern Europe from Ukraine and Belarus, extending to the Baltic region and southern Finland in the north and the Urals in the east. Certain areas of occurrence were apparently settled by accidental introductions (e.g., Svalbard).

Geographic variation

A number of subspecies with mostly unclear status described within *M. arvalis sensu lato.*

Habitat

Agricultural lands, windbreaks, meadows, light forests. In southern parts of the range prefers humid habitats along rivers and lakes.

Population status

Common. Populations exhibit annual fluctuations in numbers. The peak densities, reported from Macedonia, can be extremely high, and up to 200000 burrow openings per hectare were reported.

International legal & conservation status

None.

Other information

Can become a serious agricultural pest in peak years.

References

Král *et al.* (1980)
Malygin (1983) – review
Petrov & Ružič (1982) – review
Sokolov & Bashenina (1994) – review

J. Zima

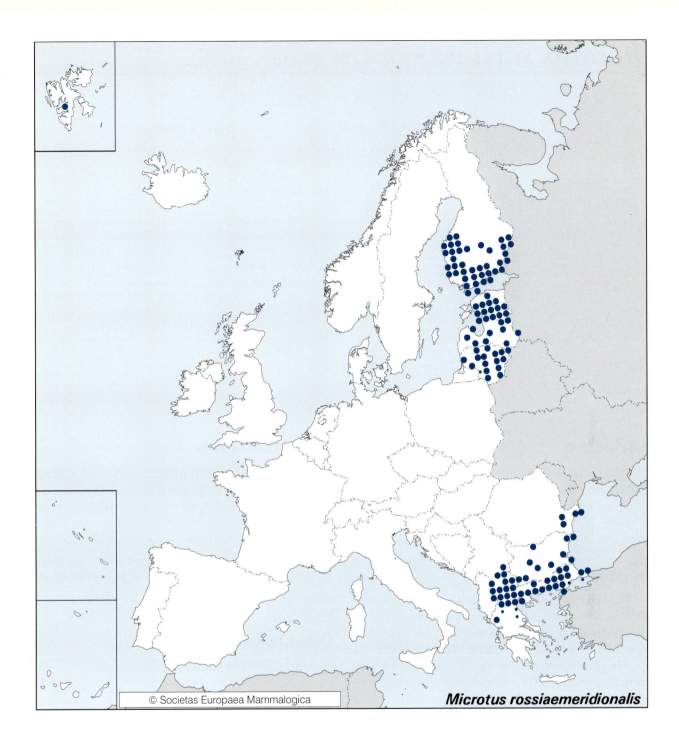

© Societas Europaea Mammalogica

Microtus rossiaemeridionalis

Microtus savii (DE SÉLYS-LONGCHAMPS, 1838)

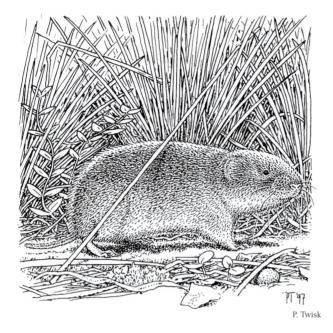
P. Twisk

Distribution

European endemic: Italian peninsula, where absent from the north-east and other marginal areas, but including South Tessin (Switzerland) and Sicily; its occurrence on the island of Elba has not been confirmed. Marginal occurrence in south-east France.

Geographic variation

Two subspecies are recognized in addition to the nominate one: the smaller *M. savii nebrodensis* (Minà-Palumbo, 1868) was described from Sicily; the very short-tailed *M. s. brachycerus* von Lehmann, 1961 for Calabria, but this was also recently suggested as a separate species. The X-chromosome shape and size are variable, particularly in the southernmost part of the area. Local variations recorded along the main Italian peninsula (e.g., size increase towards the Latium region).

Habitat

Widespread in the majority of terrestrial ecosystems, being absent from high mountains (particularly in the northernmost part of the area), some very sandy or rocky areas, densely wooded or poorly drained biotopes. Well adapted to cultivated and even urbanized lands. Altitudinal range from sea level to 2000 m.

Population status

One of the dominant species in small mammal communities; key prey for many predatory reptiles, birds and mammals. Despite periodic outbreaks observed in some populations of cultivated areas, no important and steady long-term trend has been observed.

International legal & conservation status

None.

Other information

Locally considered as an agricultural pest.

Literature

Contoli (1980) – review
Galleni *et al.* (1994)
Galleni *et al.* (1998)
Krapp (1982d) – review
Niethammer (1981)
Salvioni (1986) – review
Santini (1974)

L. Contoli

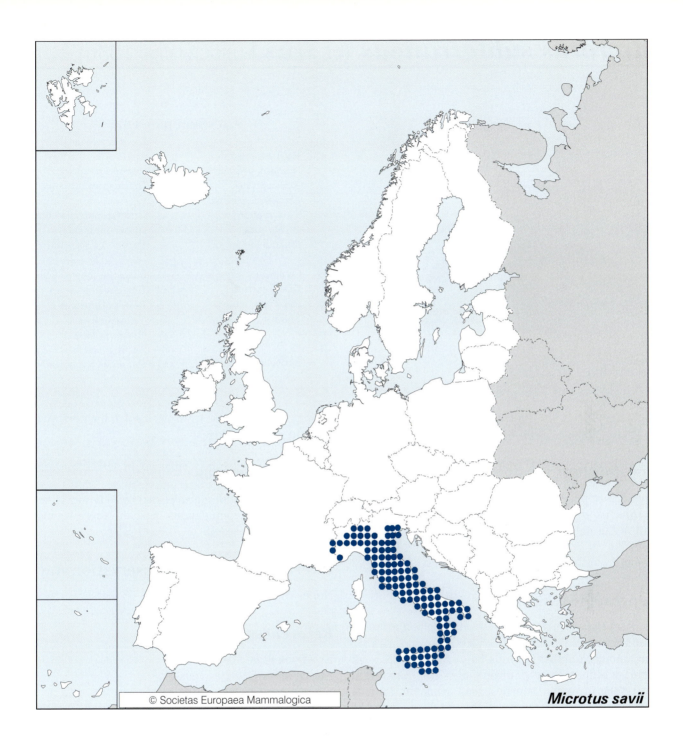

© Societas Europaea Mammalogica

Microtus savii

Microtus subterraneus (DE SÉLYS-LONGCHAMPS, 1836)

P. Barrett

Populations from the Balkans, previously ascribed to *M. majori* Thomas, 1906 belong to *M. subterraneus*.

Distribution

World: Europe and western Anatolia.
Europe: from the Atlantic coasts of France, across central Europe to Ukraine, as far east as the river Don; an isolate in Estonia and near St Petersburg (Russia). Absent from the Mediterranean coast and islands.

Geographic variation

Two karyotype forms recognized, differing in the diploid number of chromosomes, but having a stable fundamental number of arms NF = 60. The 2N = 52 form, which locally contains also an autosomal pericentric inversion, is widespread, while the 2N = 54 race is of marginal occurrence. In addition, a number of subspecies have been diagnosed on size, tooth peculiarities and colour. Largest size attained in the Balkans.

Habitat

Highly tolerant as regards habitat, occurring from dry or marshy meadows in the lowlands to alpine pastures; also rocky habitats above the timber line, as well as broadleaf and coniferous woodland. Its distribution probably more restricted by the presence of other voles, particularly competing semifossorial species, than by habitat. Vertical range from sea level in the north-west, to 2300 m in the Alps.

Population status

Common and viable species throughout much of its range. Although populations oscillate, there seems to be no long-term trend.

International legal & conservation status

None.

References

Kryštufek *et al.* (1994)
Niethammer (1982j) – review
Sablina *et al.* (1989)

B. Kryštufek

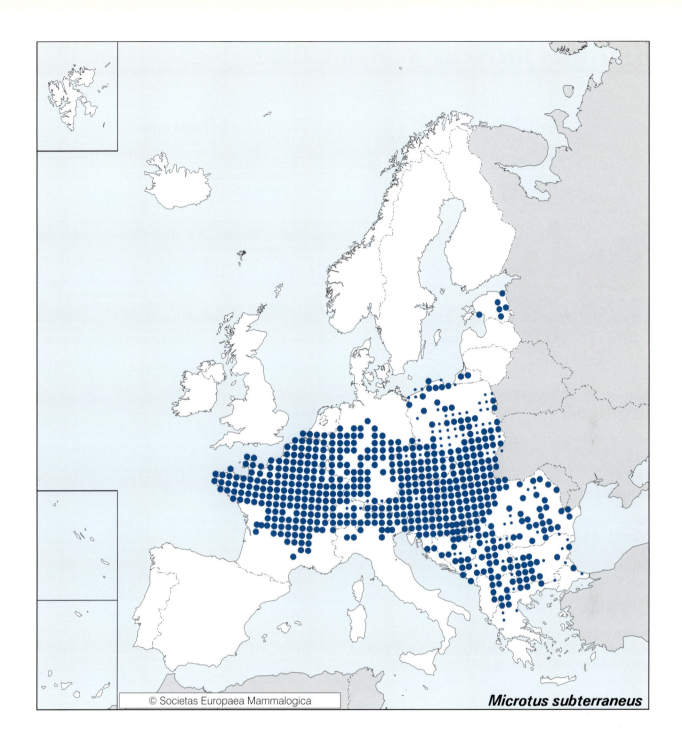

© Societas Europaea Mammalogica

Microtus subterraneus

Microtus tatricus Kratochvíl, 1952

P. Twisk

Distribution

Endemic to the Carpathians of Slovakia, Poland, Ukraine, and Romania.

Geographic variation

Two subspecies are recognized, the nominate one in the Western Carpathians and *M. tatricus zykovi* (Zagorodnyuk, 1989) in the Eastern Carpathians, respectively.

Habitat

Montane spruce forests with deep soil layer, montane meadows along streams, humid rocky habitats at altitudes from 800 to 2350 m.

Population status

Insular distribution pattern with many isolated populations. Population numbers not exactly known, but there are no signs of density decrease or range restriction.

International legal & conservation status

Bern Convention, Appendix II.
IUCN Red List, Lower Risk – near threatened.

Other information

A rare rodent with restricted range in Europe.

Literature

Flousek *et al.* (1985)
Kowalski (1960)
Kratochvíl (1970)
Niethammer (1982k) – review
Zagorodonyuk (1989)
Zagorodnyuk & Zima (1992)

J. Zima

Microtus tatricus

253

Microtus thomasi (Barrett-Hamilton, 1903)

T. P. McOwat

Thomas's vole

AL	Miu i Thomasit	LT	-
BG	Томасова полевка	LU	-
CZ	Hrabošík balkánský	LV	-
DE	Balkan-Kurzohrmaus	MK	-
DK	-	MT	-
EE	-	NL	Thomas' woelmuis
ES	Topillo de Thomas	NO	Balkanmarkmus
FI	Balkanintunnelimyyrä	PL	Darniówka bałkanska
FO	-	PT	-
FR	Campagnol de Thomas	RO	-
GR	Σκαπτοποντικός του Thomas	RU	Полёвка Томаса
		SE	Balkangransork
HR	Balkanski voluharić	SI	Balkanska kratkouha voluharica
HU	Thomas-földipocok		
IR	-	SK	-
IS	-	TR	-
IT	Arvicola di Thomas	YU	Црногорска волухарица

Although originally described as an independent species, it was mainly considered as a race of *Microtus duodecimcostatus*. Its specific status has been reconfirmed by karyotype analysis. Analysis of molar pattern variation suggests that similarities between *M. duodecimcostatus* and *M. thomasi* are more likely to be due to convergence than to phyletic proximity.

Distribution

Endemic to the south-western Balkans, where it occurs from the Neretva River (Herzegovina), across Montenegro and mainland Greece to Peloponessos. Probably also in Albania. Of the islands, only on Euboea.

Geographic variation

Kratochvíl (1971) recognized two species, besides *M. thomasi* also *M. atticus* (Miller, 1910) from Attika. This opinion was not accepted and *atticus* is generally considered a subspecies. Karyotype highly polymorphic; the four allopatric chromosomal races established until now differ in the diploid number of chromosomes (range 40 to 44) and the fundamental number of chromosomal arms (range 42 to 46).

Habitat

Most fossorial of the Balkan *Microtus* voles, so its distribution restricted to deeper soil. Open habitats are preferred; in Herzegovina and Montenegro meadows and pastures on limestone, occasionally also cultivated areas; in Greece high mountain pastures. Vertical range from 40 to 1700 m.

Population status

Localized, but common locally. In one karst field in Herzegovina the autumn density at the beginning of reproduction estimated at 383 ind./ha.

International legal & conservation status

IUCN Red List, Lower Risk – near threatened.

References

Brunet-Lecomte & Nadachowski (1994)
Giagia-Athanasopoulou *et al.* (1995)
Kratochvíl (1971)
Niethammer (1982l) – review
Petrov & Živković (1972)

B. Kryštufek

© Societas Europaea Mammalogica

Microtus thomasi

Chionomys nivalis (MARTINS, 1842)

U. Iff

On the basis of fossil records and genetic differentiation, *Microtus* and *Chionomys* can be considered as separate genera.

Distribution

World: from south-western Europe to the Caucasus, Turkey, Israel, Lebanon, Syria, and Iran.
Europe: restricted to the mountain or rocky regions of Spain, south-eastern France, the Alps, the Apennines, the Balkans, and the Carpathians of Slovakia, Romania, Poland and Ukraine. Of the islands, present only on Euboea.

Geographic variation

The snow vole, with its fragmented distribution, is considered to be a glacial relict. Due to its discontinuous distribution, several subspecies have been described but their validity is still discussed and should be carefully assessed. At the end of the Würm glaciation, the western Alps were recolonized by the south-western populations and the central Alps were populated by glacial relict populations with immigrants from eastern Europe. The existence of these two groups of populations is supported by biochemical data.

Habitat

C. nivalis is linked to the mountain tops above the tree-line between 1000 and 4700 m, but in some areas could be found also at lower altitudes in woodless and rocky biotopes.

Population status

Common in suitable habitat. No evidence of cycling populations. No population decline recorded.

International legal & conservation status

Bern Convention, Appendix III.
IUCN Red List, Lower Risk – near threatened.

Literature

Chaline & Graf (1988)
Filippucci *et al.* (1991)
Graf (1982)
Krapp (1982b) – review (as *Microtus nivalis*)
Kryštufek (1990)
Kryštufek & Kovačić (1989)

G. Amori

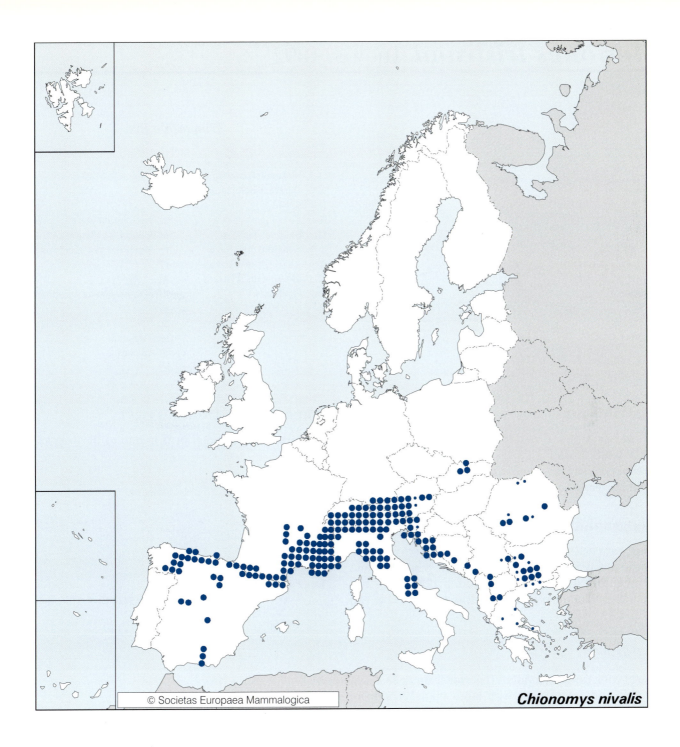

© Societas Europaea Mammalogica

Chionomys nivalis

Meriones tristrami THOMAS, 1892

T. P. McOwat

Distribution

World: Asia Minor, Middle East, Transcaucasia and north-western Iran.
Europe: of very marginal occurrence, being restricted to the Aegean Island of Kos.

Geographic variation

Four subspecies are recognized in Arabia, which differ in size and colour; desert forms are the palest. Diploid number of chromosomes is stable (2N = 72) but fundamental number of autosomal arms varies between 70 and 89.

Habitat

Use of wide range of habitats reported from Arabia, but deserts and dry steppes with more than 100 mm of annual precipitation are preferred. Although resistant to adverse temperatures it does not go above 1550 m in Lebanon. However, it reaches up to 2000 m in Transcaucasia.

Population status

One of the most common jirds of the Middle East and Turkey. Populations fluctuate significantly, and in some years it may become a pest.

International legal & conservation status

None.

Other information

In Transcaucasia and Iran it is one of the vectors of plague.

Literature

Ejgelis (1980)
Harrison & Bates (1991)
Kefelioğlu (1997)
Pavlinov *et al.* (1990)
Pieper (1966)

B. Kryštufek & V. Vohralík

© Societas Europaea Mammalogica

Meriones tristrami

Spalax graecus NEHRING, 1898

T. P. McOwat

Balkan mole rat

AL	-	LU	-
BG	-	LV	-
CZ	Slepec polní	MK	-
DE	Bukowinische Blindmaus	MT	-
DK	Østlig blindmus	NL	Oostelijke blindmol
EE	-	NO	Østlig blindmus
ES	Rata-topo de Bukovina	PL	Ślepiec grecki
FI	Romaniansokkohiiri	PT	-
FO	-	RO	Cartofarul-mare; Orbetele-răsăritean
FR	Spalax de Bukovine		
GR	-	RU	Буковинский слепыш
HR	-	SE	Östlig blindmus
HU	Bukovinai földikutya	SI	Karpatsko slepo kuže
IR	-	SK	-
IS	-	TR	Kör fare
IT	Spalace ungherese	YU	-
LT	-		

Distribution

Endemic to Europe, where it is restricted to a small area around Černovcy (Ukraine) and Romania (Suceava, Craiova, Transylvania and the lower Danube valley).

Geographic variation

The population from Craiova is ascribed to a distinct subspecies *S. graecus istricus* Mehely, 1909, which is considered by some authors to be an independent species.

Habitat

Steppes; also small fields and orchards. During winter and early spring the animals aggregate; for the rest of the year they are more evenly dispersed.

Population status

Little known species with small and fragmented distribution area. Population density mainly 1–3 ind. ha, up to 23 ind./ha.

International legal & conservation status

Bern Convention, Appendix II.
IUCN Red List, Vulnerable.

Literature

Bannikov & Sokolov (1985)
Savić (1982b) – review
Topachevskii (1969) – review

B. Kryštufek

© Societas Europaea Mammalogica

Spalax graecus

Nannospalax leucodon (Nordmann, 1840)

Z. Bihari

Lesser mole rat

AL	Miu urith	LU	-
BG	Сляпо куче	LV	-
CZ	Slepec malý	MK	Слепо куче
DE	Westblindmaus	MT	-
DK	Vestlig blindmus	NL	Westelijke blindmol
EE	-	NO	Vestlig blindmus
ES	Rata-topo occidental	PL	Ślepiec mały
FI	Unkarinsokkohiiri	PT	-
FO	-	RO	Cartofarul-mic; Orbetele-apusean
FR	Spalax occidental		
GR	Μικροτυφλοποντικός	RU	Малый слепыш
HR	Sljepaš	SE	Västlig blindmus
HU	Nyugati földikutya	SI	Zahodno slepo kuže
IR	-	SK	Slepec
IS	-	TR	Kör fare
IT	Spalace romeno	YU	Слепо куче
LT	-		

The genus is in need of a comprehensive taxonomic review. Limits of *N. leucodon* against *N. nehringi* (Satunin, 1898), a species of Asia Minor, Armenia and Georgia, are not well defined, consequently making its scope uncertain. Mole rats from east Aegean islands of Greece and Turkey might represent *N. nehringi*, as the karyotype race from the island of Lesbos (2N = 38, NF = 74) occurs also on the western coast of Anatolia.

Distribution

World: south-east Europe and perhaps north-west Anatolia.
Europe: from southern Ukraine in the north to Peloponnesos in the south. Westernmost records from Bosnia and Hungary; eastern border runs along the western Black Sea coast. Distribution area focused in the Balkan countries: Bosnia and Herzegovina, Yugoslavia, Macedonia, Greece, Bulgaria and European Turkey.

Geographic variation

Enormous variation in size, colour, osteological and dental characters and particularly so in chromosomes, resulted in the recognition of a plethora of names, many of them hardly meeting the most basic requirements of the International Code of Zoological Nomenclature. Twenty-two chromosomal forms recognized so far, with the diploid number varying between 38 and 62, and fundamental number of chromosomal arms between 74

and 96. *Nannospalax leucodon,* as understood here, is undoubtedly an aggregate of several allopatric or parapatric species. However, in the absence of a comprehensive taxonomic revision, it is safer to avoid splitting.

Habitat

Steppes, meadows and pastures, from sea level to 2400 m. Deep, loose and well drained soil is preferred, while it avoids forests, swamps and marshes. Also absent from rocky substrates. Ploughed soil and extensive cultivated fields are generally not populated, although it is doing well on mosaics of pastures and small fields, as well as in orchards.

Population status

Considerable retreat of western border in historical times documented on the Pannonian Plain; local extinctions followed cultivation. A less drastic decrease documented also in other segments of the distributional range, e.g., in Attica and southern Pannonia. On the other hand, there are still many areas supporting viable populations. The superspecies *leucodon* is thus not threatened, but some of the chromosomal forms have very restricted areas and are thus likely to be vulnerable to extinction. Population densities generally from 1 to 13 ind./ha, but higher values also reported (23 ind./ha). Reproduction is slow; the average number of young per litter between 2 and 4.

© Societas Europaea Mammalogica

Nannospalax leucodon

International legal & conservation status

IUCN Red List, Vulnerable.

Other information

Where common, this mole rat is considered a pest to agriculture and is persecuted as such. However, since it is generally removed by ploughing, extensive control measures are rarely undertaken. In some areas its bite is considered by local people to be poisonous and thus harmful to cattle.

Literature

Savić (1982a) – review
Savić & Soldatović (1984)
Topachevskii (1969) – review

B. Kryštufek

Micromys minutus (PALLAS, 1771)

P. Twisk

Harvest mouse

AL	-	LT	Pelė mazylė
BG	Малка мишка	LU	Kleng Feldmaus
CZ	Myška drobná	LV	Pundurpele
DE	Zwergmaus	MK	Цуцест глушец
DK	Dværgmus	MT	-
EE	Pisihiir	NL	Dwergmuis
ES	Ratón espiguero	NO	Dvergmus
FI	Vaivaishiiri	PL	Badylarka
FO	-	PT	-
FR	Rat des moissons	RO	Soarecele-pitic
GR	Νανοποντικός	RU	Мышь-малютка
HR	Patuljasti miš	SE	Dvärgmus
HU	Törpeegér	SI	Pritlikava miš
IR	-	SK	Myš drobná
IS	Dvergmús	TR	Hasat faresi
IT	Topolino delle risaie	YU	Патуљасти миш

Distribution

World: from the Oriental region (Assam and Myanmar) throughout the Palaearctic, where it ranges from western Europe to Japan.

Europe: eastern and central Europe as far west as north-west Spain and England (locally in Wales and Scotland). Missing from Norway and the majority of Sweden; reaches 66°N in Finland. Absent also from the Alps, and the majority of Italy, while it is of local appearance in the Balkans.

Geographic variation

Sixteen subspecies described from Europe are poorly defined except *M. minutus danubialis* Simionescu, 1974 from the Danube delta which seems to be characterized by larger skull measurements. Size is larger also in other Balkan populations from southern Bulgaria, Macedonia and northern Greece.

Habitat

Mainly lowlands but exceptionally attaining 1700 m in southern European mountains. Original habitat probably reedbeds; in humid north-west European climates also in fields and gardens; in drier parts of its range more strongly linked to aquatic environment like wetlands, open parts and fringes of humid forests, weedy road ditches, rice fields and only very rarely in corn fields.

Population status

Many local populations have declined because of loss or alteration of habitat, such as drainage, drying out or degradation of wetlands and large-scale intensification of agriculture eliminating ditches, damp grassy patches and weeds in fields. In northern Germany density varied between 6.2 and 25.4 ind./ha, depending on habitat.

International legal & conservation status

IUCN Red List, Lower Risk – near threatened.

Literature

Böhme (1978b) – review
Jüdes (1981)
Spitzenberger (1986) – review

F. Spitzenberger

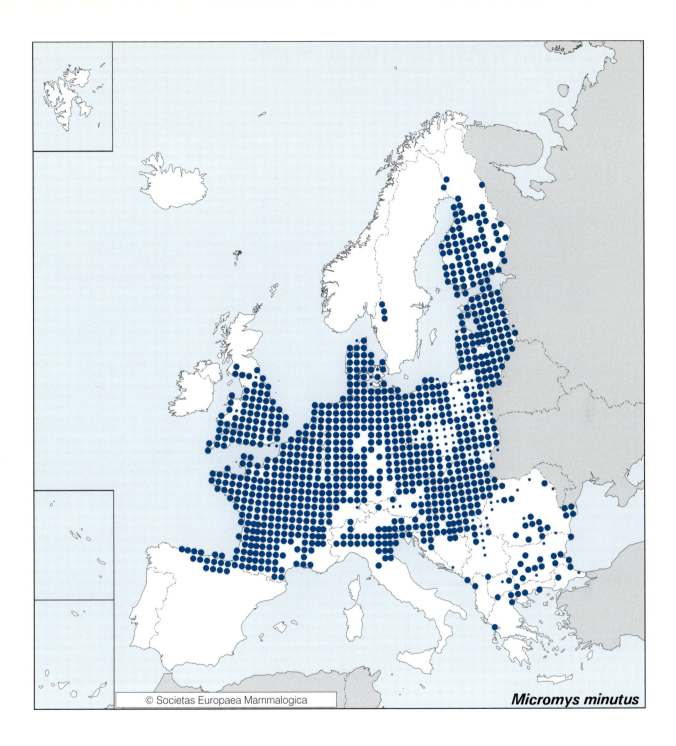

Micromys minutus

© Societas Europaea Mammalogica

265

Apodemus agrarius (PALLAS, 1771)

M. Năzăreanu

Striped field mouse

AL	-	LT	Dirvinė pelė
BG	Полска мишка	LU	-
CZ	Myšice temnopásá	LV	Svītrainā klaidoņpele
DE	Brandmaus	MK	Блатски глушец
DK	Brandmus	MT	-
EE	Juttselg-hiir	NL	Brandmuis
ES	Ratón listado	NO	Brannmus
FI	Peltohiiri	PL	Mysz polna
FO	-	PT	-
FR	Mulot rayé	RO	Şobolanul-de-câmp
GR	Αγροποντικός	RU	Полевая мышь
HR	Prugasti poljski miš	SE	Brandmus
HU	Pirók erdeiegér	SI	Dimasta miš
IR	-	SK	Ryšavka tmavopása
IS	Brandmús	TR	Çizgili orman faresi
IT	Topo selvatico dorso striato	YU	Пругасти миш

Distribution

World: extensive range, which includes Palaearctic and Oriental regions, is in two portions. The western isolate includes central and eastern Europe, the Caucasus, parts of Kazakhstan, Kyrghyzstan, and Siberia west of Lake Baikal, with adjacent regions of Mongolia and China. The eastern isolate covers southern parts of the Russian Far East, Manchuria, Korea, and China south to approximately 25°N; also Taiwan.

Europe: southern Finland in the north, central Germany, Denmark and north-eastern Italy in the west and Balkan countries (Macedonia, Greece, Turkish Thrace) in the south. Distributional border unstable, with many marginal isolates. Recently recorded in Austria, possibly as a result of range expansion.

Geographic variation

Southern populations in Europe tend to be larger and, particularly along the southern border, also darker. Four subspecies were described from Europe (exclusive of Russia), but genetic distance analysis of biochemical data failed to recognize distinct geographic races. Size differences seem to result from non-genetic, environmental adaptations. Additional subspecies were described from Russia, the Caucasus, Korea, China and Taiwan. Characteristic mid-dorsal stripe is lost in some Chinese populations.

Habitat

Primarily lowlands, although it can go up to 1750 m in southern Europe (e.g., Macedonia). Preferred habitats are fringes of forests, grassland, corn fields, gardens, marshes, reedbeds, urban parks. In winter sometimes comes into barns and human settlements. Seems to be a relatively recent inhabitant of urban green areas, where it may predominate in the small mammal community.

Population status

Very abundant in the Far East; significantly less in the European part of its range. Known to produce irregular population outbreaks, however for the last 30 years no such outbreaks have been reported in central Europe. Density varies greatly among habitats, between 5 and 50 ind./ha; in central Europe densities are lowest in forests and highest in rich urban green areas. Abundance increases nearly tenfold during population outbreaks.

International legal & conservation status

None.

Other information

During population peaks considered harmful to corn crops.

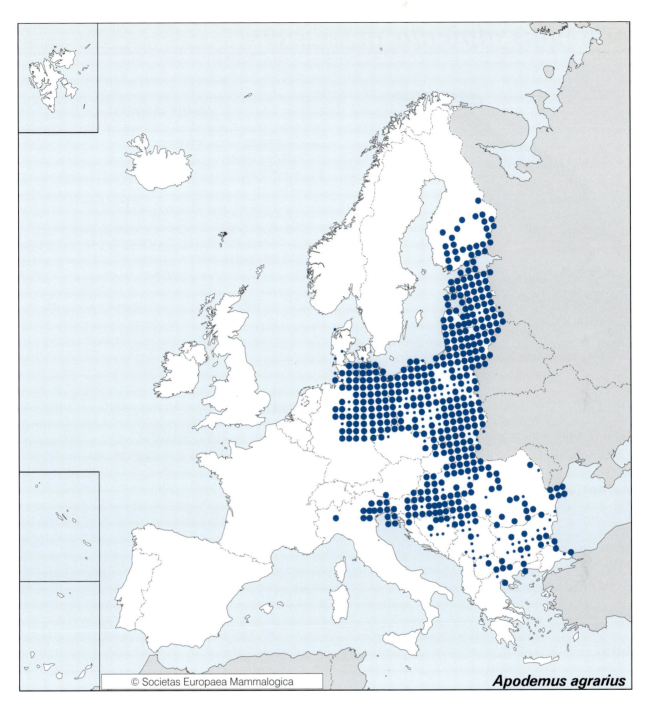

© Societas Europaea Mammalogica

Apodemus agrarius

Literature

Andrzejewski & Wrocławek (1961)
Andrzejewski *et al.* (1978)
Böhme (1978a) – review
Hille & Meinig (1996)
Spitzenberger (1997b)

J. Gliwicz & B. Kryštufek

Apodemus alpicola HEINRICH, 1952

P. Twisk

Alpine mouse			
AL	-	LT	-
BG	Алпийска горска мишка	LU	-
CZ	Myšice alpská	LV	-
DE	Alpenwaldmaus	MK	-
DK	-	MT	-
EE	-	NL	Alpenbosmuis
ES	Ratón alpino	NO	-
FI	Alppimetsähiiri	PL	Mysz alpejska
FO	-	PT	-
FR	Mulot alpestre	RO	-
GR	-	RU	-
HR	Alpski miš	SE	-
HU	Alpesi erdeiegér	SI	Alpska belonoga miš
IR	-	SK	-
IS	-	TR	-
IT	Topo selvatico alpino	YU	-

Originally considered a subspecies of *A. flavicollis* yet was shown to occur syntopically with *A. flavicollis* and *A. sylvaticus* and is morphologically and biochemically distinct.

Distribution

Endemic to Europe, where it is confined to the Alps of France, Switzerland, Germany, Italy, and Austria. In Austria, restricted to the northern and central Alps.

Geographic variation

Unknown.

Habitat

Prefers a combination of debris and rocks, water and grassy spots, mostly in the montane woodland zone. Recorded 550–2000 m above sea level.

Population status

Abundant in suitable habitats.

International legal & conservation status

IUCN Red List, Data deficient.

Literature

Spitzenberger & Englisch (1996)
Storch & Lütt (1989)
Vogel *et al.* (1991)

G. Storch

© Societas Europaea Mammalogica

Apodemus alpicola

Apodemus flavicollis (Melchior, 1834)

P. Barrett

Yellow-necked mouse

AL	Miu gusheverdhe i pyllit	LT	Geltonkaklė pelė
BG	Жълтогърла горска мишка	LU	Giel Bëschmaus
		LV	Dzeltenkakla klaidoŋpele
CZ	Myšice lesní	MK	Жолтогрлест шумски глушец
DE	Gelbhalsmaus		
DK	Halsbåndmus	MT	-
EE	Kaelushiir	NL	Grote bosmuis
ES	Ratón de collar	NO	Stor skogmus
FI	Metsähiiri	PL	Mysz leśna
FO	-	PT	-
FR	Mulot à collier	RO	Şoarecele gulerat
GR	Κρικοποντικός	RU	Желтогорлая мышь
HR	Šumski miš	SE	Större skogsmus
HU	Sárganyakú erdeiegér	SI	Rumenogrla miš
IR	-	SK	Ryšavka lesná
IS	Kragamús	TR	Orman faresi
IT	Topo selvatico collo giallo	YU	Жутогрли миш

Distribution

World: western Palaearctic; Europe, Near East.
Europe: more northern on mainland Europe than *A. sylvaticus*, in Finland and Sweden north to 64°N. East to the Urals. Limited distribution in the west and south; absent from western France and much of the Iberian Peninsula. Absent from most offshore islands, including Iceland, Ireland, The Balearics, Sardinia, Corsica, Sicily and Cyprus, but occurs on several Adriatic and Aegean islands. Present in Great Britain, where its current distribution is restricted to the south.

Geographic variation

Larger in north and west of range with a complete, yellow, pectoral collar evident in all individuals including juveniles. Smaller body size and incomplete pectoral collar in south and east.

Habitat

Regarded as primarily a species of mature deciduous woodland although known from other habitats including other deciduous woodland types and coniferous forest. More montane in habitat in southern part of range, though in the Balkans and western Anatolia the species is common in the lowlands but avoids extensive cultivated land. Annual population cycle as in *A. sylvaticus* with similar peak and minimum densities. No convincing evidence of multiannual cycles in abundance.

Population status

Widespread and abundant across its range. Human impacts only on a limited scale. No recent change in status but evidence of contraction of range in Britain associated with removal of original deciduous woodland for agriculture. Densities even in mature deciduous woodland generally low though occasionally reaching 60 ind./ha in Great Britain; more frequently part of mixed species communities in deciduous forest of over 100 ind./ha in eastern Europe.

International legal & conservation status

None.

Other information

An important prey species of mammalian carnivores and owls in woodlands and forests. Ecologically important consumer of tree and other seeds; opportunistically significant predator of invertebrates. Not usually a pest in agriculture although may cause problems in stores. Carrier of a number of zoonotic pathogens including hantavirus.

Literature

Flowerdew *et al.* (1985)
Montgomery (1985)
Niethammer (1978a) – review

W. I. Montgomery

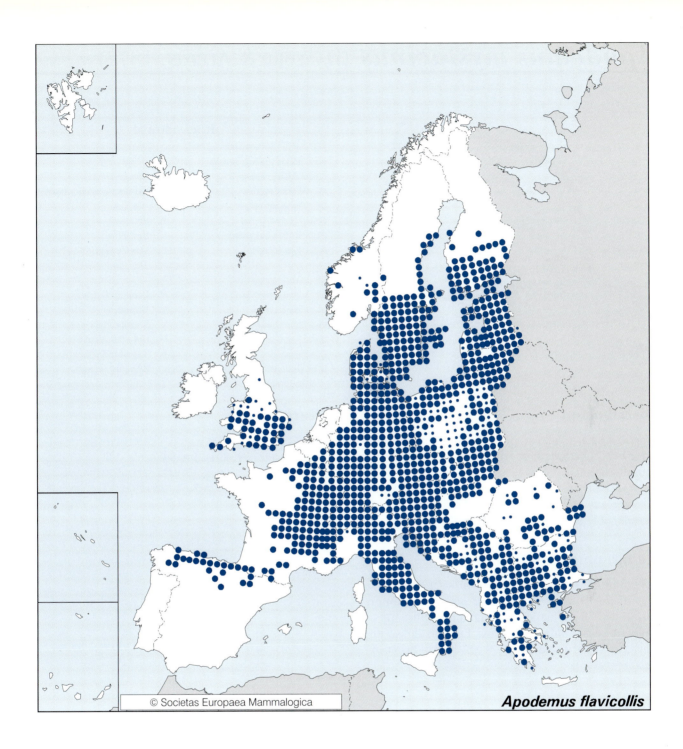

© Societas Europaea Mammalogica

Apodemus flavicollis

271

Apodemus mystacinus (Danford & Alston, 1877)

P. Twisk

Rock mouse

AL	Miu i shkembit	LT	-
BG	Планинска мишка	LU	-
CZ	Myšice krasová	LV	-
DE	Felsenmaus	MK	Шумски глушец камењар
DK	Klippemus	MT	-
EE	-	NL	Rotsmuis
ES	Ratón balcánico	NO	Bergmus
FI	Kalliohiiri	PL	Mysz wąsata
FO	-	PT	-
FR	Mulot rupestre	RO	-
GR	Βραχοποντικός	RU	Горная мышь
HR	Krški miš	SE	Klippmus
HU	Szirti erdeiegér	SI	Kraška miš
IR	-	SK	Ryšavka fúzatá
IS	-	TR	Kaya faresi
IT	Topo selvatico greco	YU	Крашки миш

Distribution

World: western Palaearctic, from south-east Europe to Near East, north to west Caucasus, east to north Iraq, south to Israel.
Europe: restricted to the southern and western Balkans. Also various Aegean and Ionian islands; of the Adriatic islands, only on Korčula and Mljet.

Geographic variation

Five named subspecies. Anatolian *(A. mystacinus mystacinus)* and European *(A. m. epimelas* (Danford & Alston, 1877)) populations are dentally distinct and most likely represent different species. Eastern and southern Aegean island populations with molar structure of *mystacinus* type.

Habitat

Prefers rock and rock debris that are rich in crevices and show some cover of grasses and scrubs. Typical rock dweller. Recorded on the Balkan peninsula from sea level to 1620 m.

Population status

Abundant in suitable habitats. No evidence of decline in Europe.

International legal & conservation status

None.

Literature

Kock *et al.* (1972)
Niethammer (1978b) – review
Storch (1977)

G. Storch

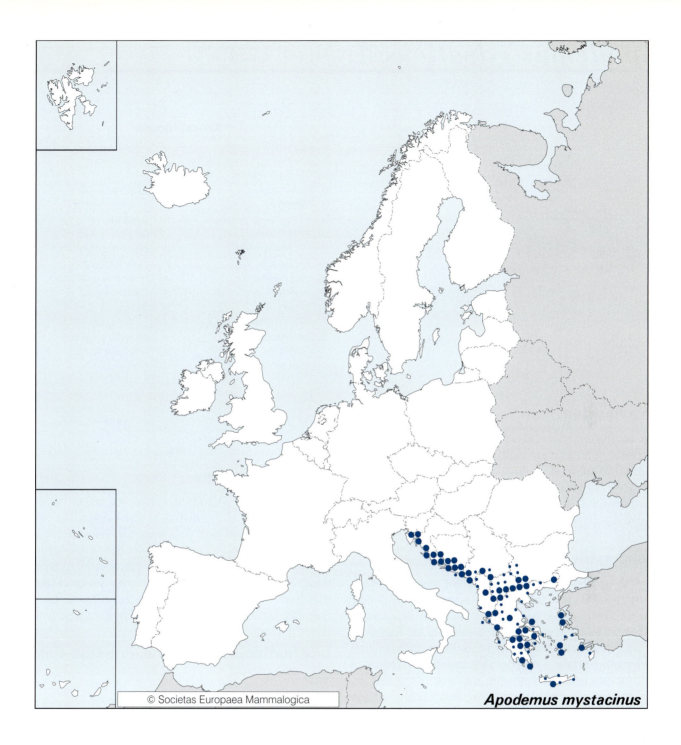

© Societas Europaea Mammalogica

Apodemus mystacinus

Apodemus sylvaticus (LINNAEUS, 1758)

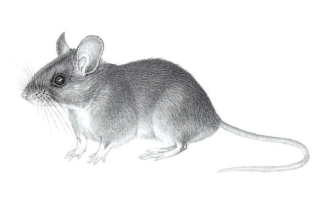

P. Barrett

Distribution

World: Europe, Asia Minor and parts of north Africa.
Europe: widespread in Europe, from the Iberian peninsula to westernmost Russia. As far north as Iceland, southern Norway and Sweden. In the Mediterranean it is found on the majority of islands, including Sardinia, Corsica, Sicily and Crete.

Geographic variation

Numerous island forms described but most, especially around the British Isles, do not warrant sub-specific status. Others such as *A. sylvaticus dicrurus* (Rafinesque, 1814) on Sicily may be valid. Tendency for forms on smaller islands to be larger than those on the mainland or larger islands. Considerable pelage variation in colour, pectoral stripe and white tail tip but no discernible geographic patterns. Polymorphic at the molecular level even where dealing with island populations.

Habitat

Extremely variable, including suburban areas or inner city areas where parkland or railway embankments are available, agricultural land, oldfields, riparian habitats, moors, forestry plantations and woodlands of all kinds. Geographic variation in habitat use with western populations associated with diverse habitats and eastern ones with woodland edge habitats and, in the extreme east, steppeland. Present as one of the most common small mammals under the more arid conditions of Mediterranean habitats.

Population status

Widespread and abundant across its range. Human impacts only on a limited scale associated with agrochemicals and lead pollution. No recent change in status. Peak annual densities in woodland may exceed 50 ind./ha in heavy mast years while lows may be less than 1 ind./ha. Peak densities may be greater in woodland adjacent to arable fields or lower in, for example, sand dunes. No evidence of multiannual cycles.

International legal & conservation status

None.

Other information

An important prey species of mammalian carnivores and owls. Ecologically important consumer of tree and other seeds; opportunistically significant predator of invertebrates. Intensively studied. Not usually a pest in agriculture although may cause problems through seed removal of pulses and other crops in fields and greenhouses. Carrier of a number of zoonotic pathogens, including hantavirus, louping ill virus and spirochaetes but not regarded as a major threat to health of either man or domestic animals.

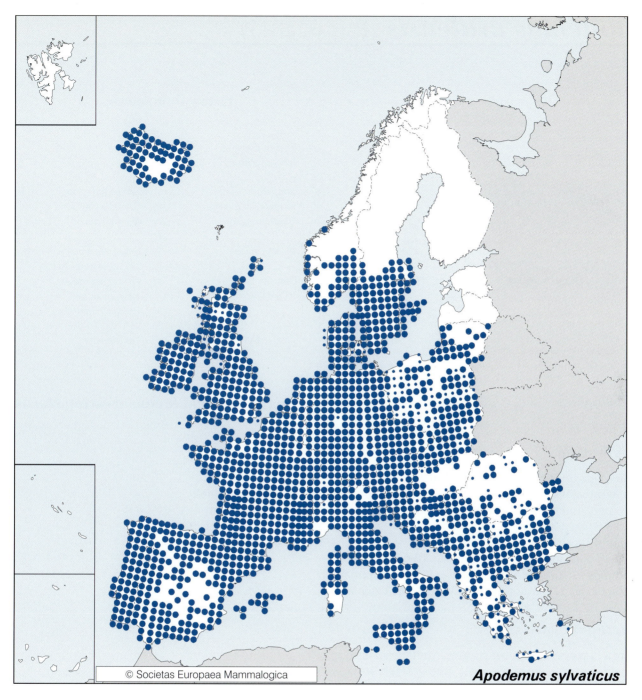

© Societas Europaea Mammalogica

Apodemus sylvaticus

Literature

Flowerdew *et al.* (1985)
Flowerdew (1991)
Mezhzherin & Lashkova (1992)
Niethammer (1978c) – review
Wilson *et al.* (1993)

W. I. Montgomery

Apodemus uralensis (PALLAS, 1811)

T. P. McOwat

Pygmy field mouse

AL	-	LT	-
BG	-	LU	-
CZ	Myšice malooká	LV	Meža klaidoņpele
DE	Zwergwaldmaus	MK	-
DK	-	MT	-
EE	Metshiir	NL	Kleine bosmuis
ES	Ratón de campo enano	NO	Dvergskogmus
FI	Uralinmetsähiiri	PL	Mysz zielna
FO	-	PT	-
FR	Mulot pygmée	RO	Şoarecele mic de pădure
GR	-	RU	Малая лесная мышь
HR	Stepski miš	SE	Dvärgskogsmus
HU	Kislábú erdeiegér	SI	Ravninska miš
IR	-	SK	Ryšavka malooká
IS	-	TR	-
IT	Topo selvatico pigmeo	YU	Пољки миш

In Europe usually cited under *Apodemus microps* Kratochvil & Rosicky, 1952.

Distribution

World: Palaearctic, from central Europe, northern Anatolia and Baltic States east to east Kazakhstan, north-west China, and Altai Mts. (Mongolia). Limits in Central Asia not well understood.
Europe: from the Czech Republic in the west through southern Poland, north-eastern Austria and the Pannonian Plain, south to Bulgaria. From Romania through Ukraine and Russia, north to Latvia and Estonia.

Geographic variation

About a dozen named subspecies, though specific allocations of several Asiatic subspecies need corroboration. No subspecies recognized from the European part of its range.

Habitat

In Europe, cultivated land, open dry country, and humid riparian forest. In Turkey, Ukraine and Transcaucasia mainly along brooks and streamlets in wooded areas, often with dense cover of shrubs.

Population status

A patchy, colony-like distribution was observed in parts of its range.

International legal & conservation status

None.

Literature

Filippucci *et al.* (1996)
Mezhzherin & Zagorodnyuk (1989)
Musser & Carleton (1993)
Vorontsov *et al.* (1992)

G. Storch

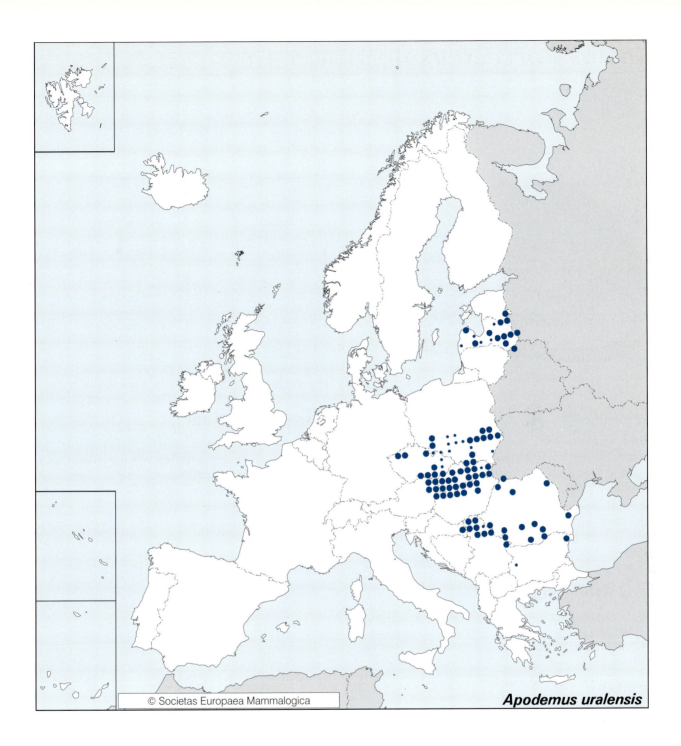

© Societas Europaea Mammalogica

Apodemus uralensis

Rattus norvegicus (BERKENHOUT, 1769)

P. Twisk

Distribution

World: a native of north-east Asia but now cosmopolitan. *Europe:* throughout Europe, but sporadically in sparsely inhabited areas, namely parts of Fennoscandia. Not as widespread in the Mediterranean region as farther north. Although some records of brown rat in Europe date back to the Middle Ages, its permanent and widespread diffusion occurred at the time of the Industrial Revolution (17th–18th century).

Geographic variation

Beside the nominate subspecies occurring in Europe, *R. norvegicus caraco* (Pallas, 1779) is recognized for Asia.

Habitat

Being a good swimmer, it inhabits river banks and sewerage systems. Where synanthropic, it is linked to the waste and refuse water produced by man (store houses, animal farms, etc.); occurs also in crop fields near water.

Population status

Common. It is considered a pest.

International legal & conservation status

None.

Other information

Like the black rat, *R. norvegicus* is responsible for much damage to buildings, facilities and food-stuffs, as well as the spreading of pathogens such as leptospirosis, hantavirus, rickettsiosis, borreliosis and many others hazardous to man and animals.

Literature

Becker (1978a) – review
von Dirk (1976)

G. Amori & M. Cristaldi

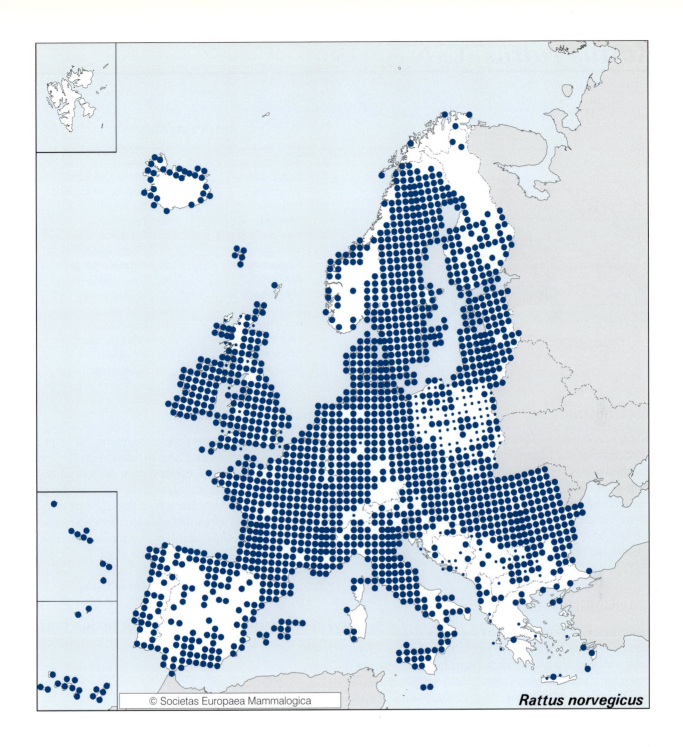

© Societas Europaea Mammalogica

Rattus norvegicus

Rattus rattus (Linnaeus, 1758)

P. Twisk

Distribution

World: presumably native to South-East Asia and after the postglacial period widespread worldwide as a result of human activities.

Europe: present in most European countries with the exception of Fennoscandia, where it is now extinct, except for one site in Denmark. In the British Isles confined to a few ports and islands. Sporadic in the Pannonian Plain and Poland; probably extinct in Slovakia.

Geographic variation

Three different colour morphs have been described: 'rattus' (all black), 'frugivorus' (brown above and white below with a sharp demarcation line) and 'alexandrinus' (brown back and pale grey below). Many subspecies have been described from Asia. Two chromosomal forms exist. The Asian type is characterized by the diploid number 2N = 42, while the Oceanic (or the European) type possesses the diploid set of 38 (or rarely 40) chromosomes.

Habitat

Highly commensal in Atlantic and continental Europe. In Mediterranean countries, particularly on islands, also occurs outdoors around human settlements as well as in the countryside and agricultural areas. It can build nests in trees and the upper part of buildings.

Population status

Very common in Mediterranean countries. The species showed great declines and local extinctions in the British Isles, where its presence is now limited to sea ports and two offshore islands, and in central and eastern European countries where river ports along Danube are possible ways of access and spreading as in Hungary and adjacent regions. After a decline almost to extinction, the black rat has recovered in The Netherlands since about 1968, finding a new biotope in modern piggeries; a similar change has been reported from eastern Germany.

International legal & conservation status

None.

Other information

The black rat is considered a pest, causing severe damage to stored food and crops. It has been a very important vector of diseases, especially for plague epidemics in past centuries. Nevertheless, nowadays *Rattus norvegicus* is a more efficient vector of diseases. Viral, bacterial and protozoal diseases are the most dangerous for man.

Literature

Becker (1978b) – review
Jabir *et al.* (1985)
Yosida (1980) – review

G. Amori & M. Cristaldi

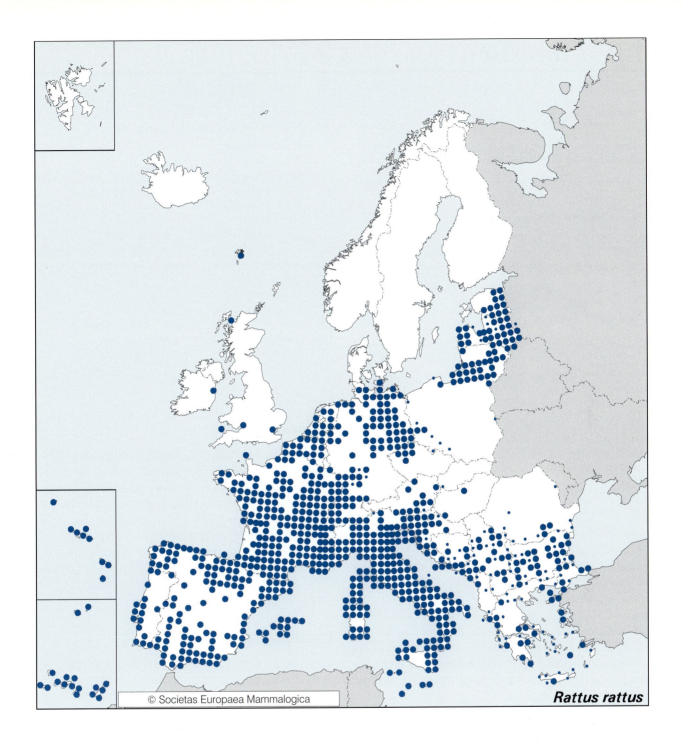

Rattus rattus

Mus domesticus SCHWARZ & SCHWARZ, 1943

E Hazebroek

ED '97.

Regarded as a subspecies of *M. musculus* by some authors while others treat it as a distinct species. It includes also the tobacco mouse *M. poschiavinus* Fatio, 1869.

Distribution

World: western and southern Europe, Asia from Turkey to Iran and southwards to North Africa. Through its close association with humans it has colonized both Americas, Africa south of the Sahara, northern Australia and oceanic islands.

Europe: restricted to western and southern parts of the mainland, Mediterranean islands, the British Isles and Faroe Islands. Its range abuts that of *M. musculus* in central and south-eastern Europe, where these taxa form a narrow hybrid zone stretching from the Jutland Peninsula to Bulgaria.

Geographic variation

Three subspecies, *M. domesticus domesticus, M. d. brevirostris* Waterhouse, 1837, and *M. d. praetextus* Brants, 1827, have been usually recognized yet both morphological and genetic analyses have not substantiated these taxa to be distinct units. About 35 different karyotypic races have been hitherto described with a decreased number of chromosomes owing to Robertsonian fusions.

Habitat

House mice are ecologically highly opportunistic animals but weak competitors. Typically, they are strictly commensal yet are also able to live outdoors. They occur in an immensely wide range of habitats including such extremities as coal mines and frozen meat stores. Some populations have undergone a secondary feralization and colonized various outdoor habitats such as agricultural lands, sand dunes, salt marshes, sea-bird cliffs, grasslands, and roadside verges with bushes. It avoids woodlands and extremely dry areas.

Population status

Common, except in some extreme habitats (e.g., mountains). Reproduction is rapid, with the average number of young per litter about 5–7; up to three litters per year outdoors, in ricks and in buildings throughout the year. Population size and density are highly variable but indoor populations are generally smaller yet of higher densities. Large irregular population outbreaks were recorded in the USA and Australia. Maximal density of outdoor populations about 60 ind./ha; extreme cases: 875 mice per hectare were recorded during a plague in Australia, whilst a density as high as 70000 animals per hectare was found in a chicken barn in USA.

International legal & conservation status

None.

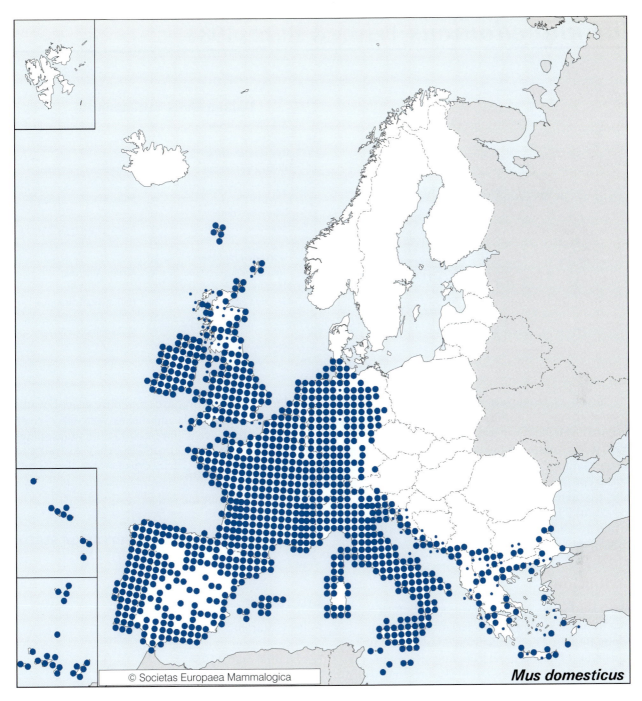

© Societas Europaea Mammalogica

Mus domesticus

Other information

This species is a significant pest, inflicting economic wastage by destroying and contaminating stored foods and crops and causing other kinds of damage as well. It is also a vector of diseases transmittable to man (e.g., leptospirosis, salmonellosis), though less important than rats. It has also contributed substantially to the genome of most laboratory mouse strains.

Literature

Auffray *et al.* (1990)
Belkhir *et al.* (1991)
Berry (1981) – review
Sage *et al.* (1993)

M. Macholán

Mus macedonicus PETROV & RUŽIĆ, 1983

T. P. McOwat

Balkan short-tailed mouse

AL	Miu i maqedonise	LT	-
BG	-	LU	-
CZ	Myš makedonská	LV	-
DE	Balkan-Hausmaus	MK	Македонски глушец
DK	-	MT	-
EE	-	NL	Macedonische huismuis
ES	Ratón macedónico	NO	-
FI	Makedoniankotihiiri	PL	Mysz domowa bałkańska
FO	-	PT	-
FR	Souris de Macédoine	RO	-
GR	Μακεδονικός ποντικός	RU	Мышь Аббота
HR	Makedonski kućni miš	SE	-
HU	Macedón egér	SI	Balkanska hišna miš
IR	-	SK	-
IS	-	TR	Makedonya ev faresi
IT	Topolino della Macedonia	YU	-

Also referred as *M. abbotti* Waterhouse, 1838, or *M. tataricus* Satunin, 1908. Yet since the type specimen of *M. abbotti* from Trabzon was found to be a juvenile individual showing morphological features typical for commensal mice this name was rejected. Similarly, *M. tataricus* appeared to be conspecific with *M. musculus*. Finally, the name *M. spretoides,* which is sometimes used, should be abandoned as a *nomen nudum.* Frequently confused with the genetically and morphologically close *M. spicilegus.*

Distribution

World: Asia Minor, Transcaucasia, Middle East as far east as Iran and southwards to Israel and Jordan.
Europe: Balkan Peninsula from Macedonia to the European part of Turkey and from Bulgaria south of the Stara Planina Mts. to Greece; found also on some Aegean islands (Samothraki, Chios, Lesbos, Samos). Sympatric but not syntopic with *M. domesticus.*

Geographic variation

The level of genetic and morphological variation is very low.

Habitat

Limited mostly to the Mediterranean climatic zone and (in Europe) to altitudes lower than 500 m. Reported from a wide range of habitats: grain fields, roadside vegetation, crop fields, dry shrubby places, bushy banks, sand dunes beaches, orchards and olive groves, wadis, humid patches with reeds and rushes along lakes, rivers and canals, etc. It avoids forests and human dwellings.

Population status

Common throughout the range.

International legal & conservation status

None.

Literature

Auffray, Marshall *et al.* (1990)
Auffray, Bouvier *et al.* (1990)
Bonhomme *et al.* (1984)
Milishnikov *et al.* (1989)
Sage (1981) – review
Vohralík & Sofianidou (1987)

M. Macholán

Mus macedonicus

Mus musculus LINNAEUS, 1758

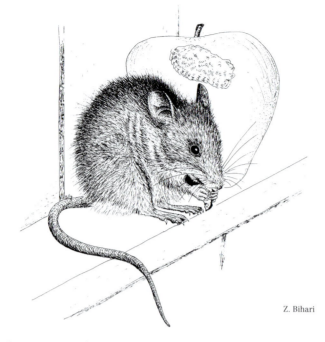

Z. Bihari

Sometimes referred to as *M. musculus musculus* (see the *M. domesticus* account for details).

Distribution

World: Palaearctic, from northern and central Europe to the Far East, including northern China; missing from some northernmost extremities of Eurasia.
Europe: Fennoscandia, central and eastern Europe, Iceland (P. Hersteinsson, pers. comm.) and islands in the Baltic Sea. It meets with *M. domesticus* along *c.* 1200-km hybrid zone from Denmark through central Europe and the Balkans to Bulgaria; another zone of contact of the two taxa is in the Caucasus region.

Geographic variation

A varied number of subspecies were recognized depending on the author. However, those taxa have not been substantiated to be distinct units according to morphological and genetic analyses. Karyotypically much more stable than *M. domesticus*. Mitochondrial DNA less variable than in *M. domesticus*.

Habitat

Similar to that of *M. domesticus*. Commensal, yet it occurs also outdoors. Some populations live in agricultural lands, meadows and shrublands during mild seasons but overwinter in buildings, hay stacks and straw ricks. They have been reported from rocky outcrops along the northern Arctic coast, 50 km from the nearest human dwellings. Like *M. domesticus*, this species avoids woodlands.

Population status

Common except under ecological extreme conditions (higher mountains, deserts and semi-deserts, northern parts of Eurasia). This species has a rapid reproductive rate, with 1–12 (exceptionally up to 14) embryos per litter; the average number of young per litter is 5–9. Outside buildings usually not very numerous; population size and density is similar to *M. domesticus* but irregular outbreaks are extremely rare.

International legal & conservation status

None.

Other information

As with *M. domesticus,* this species is a significant pest, inflicting economic wastage by destroying and contaminating stored foods and crops and causing other kinds of damage as well. It is also a vector of diseases transmittable to man (e.g., leptospirosis, salmonellosis), though less important than rats. It has contributed substantially to the genome of most laboratory mouse strains.

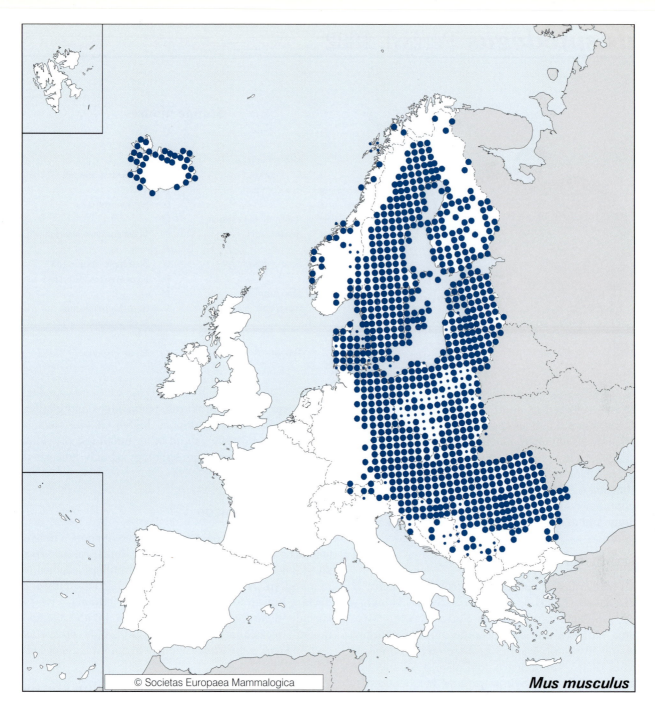

© Societas Europaea Mammalogica

Mus musculus

Literature

Boursot *et al.* (1993)
Kotenkova & Bulatova (1994) – review
Kutcheruk (1994)
Prager *et al.* (1996)
Sage (1981)
Zima *et al.* (1990)

M. Macholán

Mus spicilegus PETÉNYI, 1882

Z. Bihari

Steppe mouse

AL	-	LT	-
BG	-	LU	-
CZ	Myš panonská	LV	-
DE	Ährenmaus	MK	Степски домашен глушец
DK	-	MT	-
EE	-	NL	Steppenmuis
ES	Ratón de las estepas	NO	-
FI	Arokotihiiri	PL	Mysz domowa południowa
FO	-	PT	-
FR	Souris des steppes	RO	Şoarecele-de-mişună
GR	-	RU	Курганчиковая мышь
HR	Miš humkaš	SE	-
HU	Güzü egér	SI	Stepska hišna miš
IR	-	SK	Myš panónska
IS	-	TR	-
IT	Topolino delle steppe	YU	Миш хумкаш

Sometimes referred to as *M. hortulanus* Nordmann, 1840, but since the type specimen described from a garden in Odessa appeared to be *M. musculus* this name is no longer valid. *M. spicilegus* is frequently confused with *M. musculus,* which is morphologically very similar. It is characterized by gathering a pile of seeds above a nest chamber with a network of tunnels and covering it with a mound of soil.

Distribution

Known from Europe only, namely from the vicinity of Lake Neusiedl (Austria), southern Slovakia, Hungary, Serbia, Bulgaria north of the Stara Planina Mts., Romania, Moldova and Ukraine (as far north as Kharkov) till Rostov (Russia). A small and isolated population occurs in Ulcinj, Montenegro, and also in Albania and in north-west Greece. Sympatric and frequently also syntopic with *M. musculus.*

Geographic variation

The level of geographic variability is low. The Ulcinj population was found to be morphologically distinct from other *M. spicilegus* populations.

Habitat

Natural steppe grasslands and agrocoenoses mostly not higher than 200 m above sea level; grain fields, disturbed vegetation surrounding agricultural lands, open habitats along river courses, orchards, wood edges and glades, thin pine woods, sandy steppes, higher alluvial islets. It avoids human dwellings and other buildings; previous records of this species from buildings actually concerned *M. musculus*.

Population status

Common in suitable habitats yet with reduction of native steppe patches and changes in agricultural practices this species is likely to face a decline in numbers, especially in marginal areas. There are usually 1–20 mounds per hectare but up to 60–100 in suitable habitats. Five to six individuals (but sometimes up to 14) inhabit a single mound. Occasional syntopic occurrence of *M. musculus* and *Apodemus sylvaticus* within a mound was recorded.

International legal & conservation status

IUCN Red List, Lower Risk – near-threatened.

Other information

Where numerous, it might be regarded as an agricultural pest.

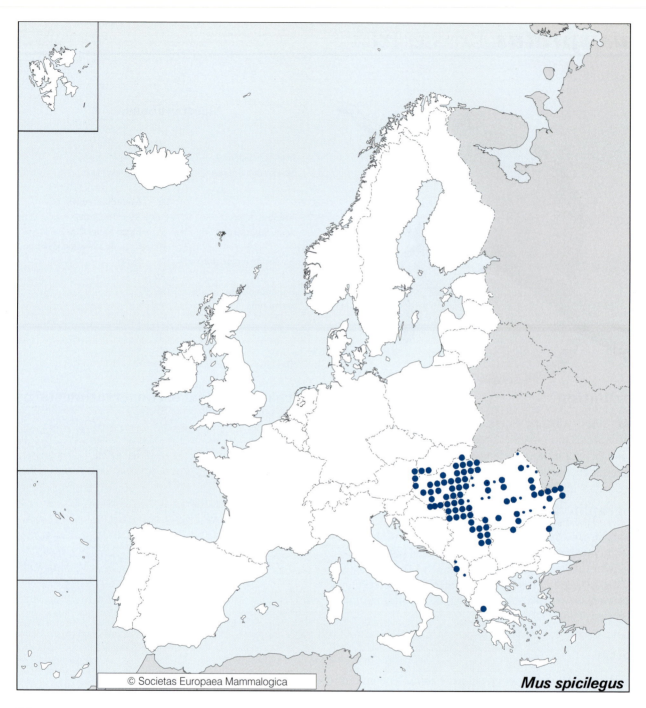

© Societas Europaea Mammalogica

Mus spicilegus

Literature

Gerasimov *et al.* (1990)
Kryštufek & Macholán (1998)
Macholán & Vohralík (1997)
Pisareva (1948) – review
Sage (1981)

M. Macholán

Mus spretus LATASTE, 1883

P. Twisk

Algerian mouse

AL	-	LT	-
BG	-	LU	-
CZ	Myš středozemní	LV	-
DE	Heckenhausmaus	MK	-
DK	-	MT	-
EE	-	NL	Algerijnse muis
ES	Ratón moruno	NO	Algerihusmus
FI	Algeriankotihiiri	PL	Mysz algierska
FO	-	PT	Rato-das-hortas; Ratinho-ruivo
FR	Souris d'Afrique du Nord	RO	-
GR	-	RU	-
HR	Zapadnomediteranski kućni miš	SE	-
HU	-	SI	Pirenejska hišna miš
IR	-	SK	-
IS	-	TR	-
IT	Topolino algerino	YU	-

Distribution

World: south-western Europe and North Africa from Morocco to Libya.
Europe: occurs in southern France, Iberian Peninsula and the Balearic Islands.

Geographic variation

In general, this species exhibits a low level of genetic variation. Furthermore, French and Spanish populations have lower diversity of mitochondrial DNA than African ones, suggesting that the European mice have undergone a bottleneck in population size during the colonization of Europe.

Habitat

Limited to the Mediterranean climatic zone. It occurs in countryside below 1 000 m, such as grasslands, maquis, and woodlands adjacent to corn fields. This species avoids buildings except for a few cases from Spain. Sympatric but not syntopic with *M. domesticus*.

Population status

Common throughout the range. Reproduction almost during the whole year, with two peaks, in April and August; mean litter size 5–6. Population densities *ca*. 3–12 ind./ha (average 7.6 ind./ha).

International legal & conservation status

None.

Literature

Boursot *et al.* (1985)
Cassaing & Croset (1985)
Sage (1981) – review
Vargas *et al.* (1991)

M. Macholán

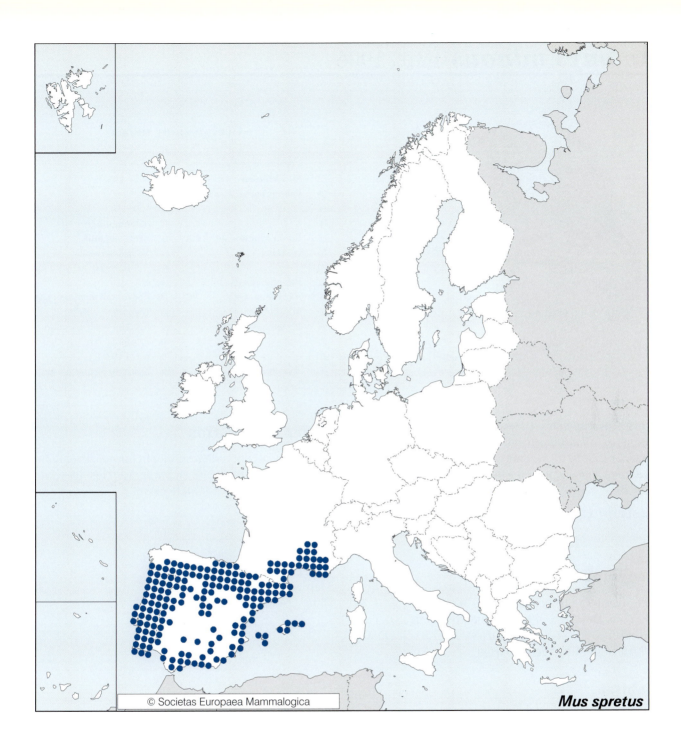

© Societas Europaea Mammalogica

Mus spretus

Acomys minous BATE, 1906

P. Twisk

Previously considered a subspecies of other *Acomys* species (*A. dimidiatus* (Cretzschmar, 1826), *A. cahirinus* (Desmarest, 1819)). Separate species status is based on particular karyotype and isolated distribution.

Distribution

Endemic to the island of Crete.

Geographic variation

Two distinct chromosome races described (2N = 38, NF = 66 and 2N = 49, NF = 68, respectively). Their distribution pattern is, however, not clear, and hybridization has been reported.

Habitat

Dry rocky scrub on hillsides, rocky crevices. May enter houses, especially in winter. Avoids higher altitudes (above 500–600 m). Omnivorous, with prevalence of vegetable food.

Population status

Not exactly known, but it may be common in suitable habitats. There are no recent reports of apparent population declines.

International legal & conservation status

IUCN Red List, Vulnerable.

Other information

Considered a rare rodent species in Europe. Evolutionary relationships to other *Acomys* species in eastern Mediterranean are not quite clear.

Literature

Dieterlen (1963)
Dieterlen (1978) – review
Matthey (1963)
Zimmermann *et al.* (1953)

J. Zima

© Societas Europaea Mammalogica

Acomys minous

Glis glis (LINNAEUS, 1766)

Z. Bihari

Distribution

World: Europe, northern Asia Minor, the Caucasus, and north-western Iran.
Europe: southern and central part of the mainland, from northern Spain to the River Volga. Northernmost records are from the Baltic States, and the southernmost from the island of Crete. Introduced also to England. Found on many Mediterranean islands.

Geographic variation

Approximately eight subspecies recognized currently, based on differences in size and coloration. Doubtful that all are valid. The smallest populations come from central Europe and southern Balkans, and the largest from the Dinaric Alps and Italy. Karyotype is stable.

Habitat

Deciduous and mixed forests of beech, oak and chestnut. Highest population densities on karstic substrate, with underground spaces suitable for hibernation. On the Mediterranean coast also maquis and shrubland on rocky ground. Frequently enters huts and houses. It is found from sea level to the upper limit of deciduous trees; in central Europe rarely above 1000 m (highest record from 1400 m); in the south up to 2000 m.

Population status

Common in the south, where considered to be pest to forestry and agriculture at peak densities. Rare throughout central Europe and probably threatened along the northern border of its range. Population densities around 5 ind./ha in central Europe, but higher values (20–22 ind./ha) are also reported. Densities probably higher in southern Europe.

International legal & conservation status

Bern Convention, Appendix III.
IUCN Red List, Lower Risk – near-threatened.

Other information

It was bred in captivity for food in ancient Rome. In Slovenia, where it was a commodity species from the 13th century onwards, it was an important source of meat, fat and extra money (by selling skins) for poor peasants. Hunting was taxed throughout its history. Tradition of hunting still strong, although without commercial motivations. Similar attitude known also in Croatia and Italy. Covered by game act in Slovenia and Croatia.

Literature

Carpaneto & Cristaldi (1995)
Jurczyszyn (1995)
Storch (1978c) – review

B. Kryštufek

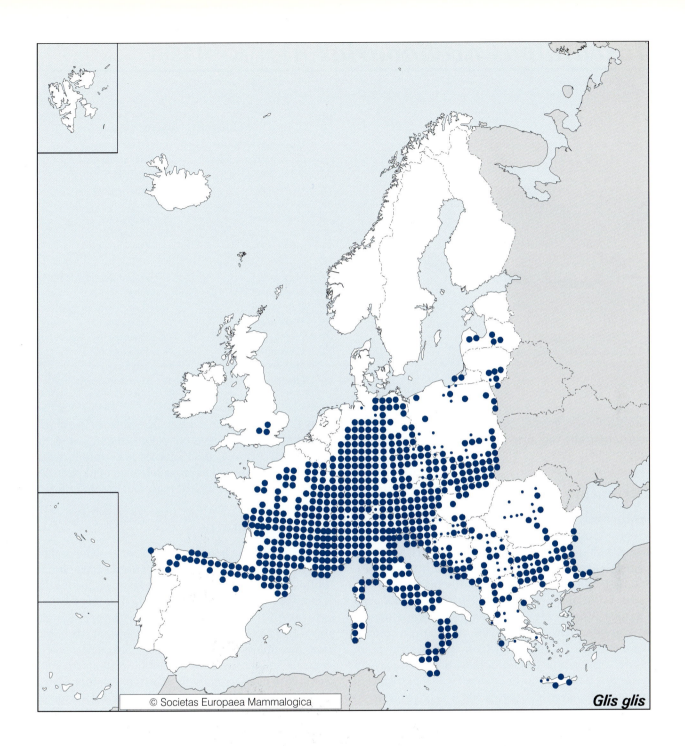

© Societas Europaea Mammalogica

Glis glis

295

Muscardinus avellanarius (Linnaeus, 1758)

M. Năzăreanu

Common dormouse

AL	Gjumashi i lajthise	LU	Hieselmaus
BG	Лешников сънливец	LV	Mazais susuris; Lazdu susuris
CZ	Plšík lískový		
DE	Haselmaus	MK	Полв лешникар
DK	Hasselmus	MT	-
EE	Pähklinäpp	NL	Hazelmuis
ES	Muscardino	NO	Hasselmus
FI	Pähkinähiiri	PL	Orzesznica
FO	-	PT	-
FR	Muscardin	RO	Pârşul-de-alun; Pârşul-roşu
GR	Βουνομυωξός		
HR	Puh orašar	RU	Орешниковая соня
HU	Mogyorós pele	SE	Hasselmus
IR	-	SI	Podlesek
IS	Heslimús	SK	Plch lieskový
IT	Moscardino	TR	Fındık faresi
LT	Lazdyninė miegapelė	YU	Пух лешникар

A monospecific genus, closely allied to *Glis,* with characteristically very prehensile feet and finely ridged teeth.

Distribution

World: western Palaearctic, mainly Europe but including northern Anatolia.

Europe: widespread from the Mediterranean to southern Sweden, eastward to Russia (about latitude 50°E), excluding Iberia. Island populations occur in Great Britain, Corfu and Sicily. Local distribution is affected by habitat fragmentation, resulting in range attrition. For example, over the last 100 years, the common dormouse has disappeared from half its range in England, and is now absent in most northern parts of the country, including areas where it was found only 30 years ago. Similar processes are likely to have occurred elsewhere in northern Europe, but historical data are generally lacking.

Geographic variation

Five subspecies are recognized, but all are essentially rather similar in appearance.

Habitat

Mixed deciduous forest, especially the forest edge and understorey shrubs (including hedgerows in farmland and secondary growth). *Muscardinus* is an arboreal sequential specialist feeder, eating flowers, insects and fruits as each become seasonally available in summer. It is not normally active on the ground. Thus, a high diversity of arboreal food sources is essential. Nearer the core of its range, a broader selection of habitats may be used, including broadleaf regrowth in conifer forests.

Population status

Even in favourable habitats, population density probably does not usually exceed 10 adults per hectare, but few studies have been made. In unfavourable habitats, density may be only half this figure. Thus small isolated habitat patches are likely to support minimal populations, which are vulnerable to stochastic extinction unless habitat patches are linked by woodland strips or hedgerows. The common dormouse is highly sensitive to climate, both directly (bad weather restricts feeding activity and results in facultative torpor, compromising reproductive potential) and indirectly through the effects of sunshine and temperature on ripening and availability of vital food supplies. Climate is likely to be limiting at geographical and altitudinal extremes of range; elsewhere population density is probably limited by density dependent factors, especially as males are strongly territorial in the breeding season.

International legal & conservation status

Bern Convention, Appendix III.
EU Habitats & Species Directive, Annex IV.
IUCN Red List, Lower Risk – near-threatened.

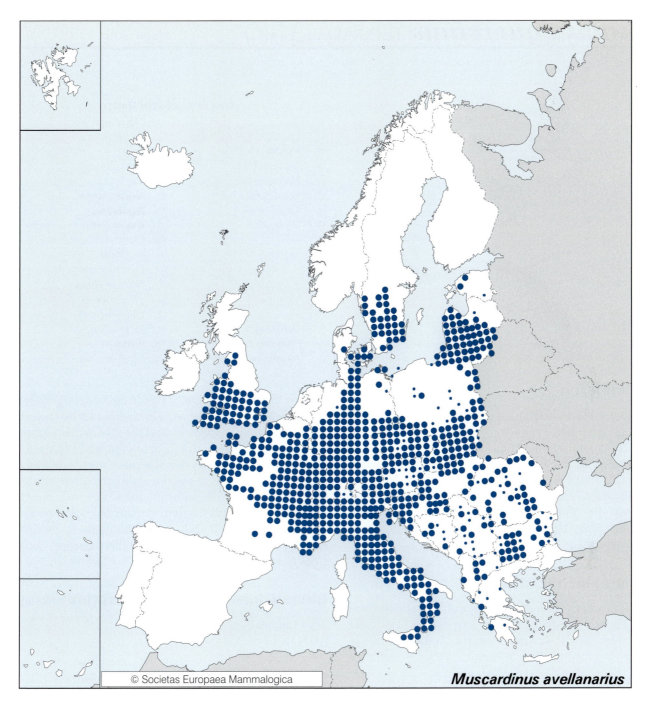

© Societas Europaea Mammalogica

Muscardinus avellanarius

Other information

The dormouse is not a significant disease carrier, rarely carries ectoparasites and has no significant effect on human economic interests. It was formerly popular as a pet, but this is now illegal in many countries.

Literature

Bright & Morris (1996)
Corbet (1978)
Storch (1978d) – review

P. A. Morris

Eliomys quercinus (LINNAEUS, 1766)

U. Iff

Garden dormouse

AL	-	LU	Gaardeschléifer
BG	Градински съпливец	LV	Dārza susuris
CZ	Plch zahradní	MK	-
DE	Gartenschläfer	MT	-
DK	Havesyvsover	NL	Eikelmuis
EE	Lagrits; Oravhiir	NO	Hagesyvsover
ES	Lirón careto	PL	Żołędnica
FI	Tammihiiri	PT	Leirão; Rato-dos-pomares
FO	-	RO	Pârşul-de-stejar; Pârsul-de-ghindă
FR	Lérot	RU	Садовая соня
GR	-	SE	Trädgårdssovare
HR	Vrtni puh	SI	Vrtni polh
HU	Kerti pele	SK	Plch záhradný
IR	-	TR	Meşe faresi
IS	Garðsvæfla	YU	Вртни пух
IT	Topo quercino		
LT	Ąžuolinė miegapelė		

Distribution

European endemic: from western Europe to the Urals. Actually confined to western Europe with scattered populations in the east. Limited to Dalmatia in the Balkan Peninsula. Absent from the British Isles and Iceland. Roman record in England probably results from introduction. Present on numerous Mediterranean islands: Formentera, Majorca, Menorca, Corsica, Sardinia, Sicily, Lipari, Krk, Brač, Hvar, Ščedro, Korčula, and Lastovo.

Geographic variation

Nine subspecies grouped in two morphotypes: *quercinus* and *lusitanicus*. Four distinct karyotypes have been described: 2N = 48 (Iberian Peninsula, Italian Peninsula, Balkan Peninsula), 2N = 50 (central Europe, Sardinia), 2N = 52 (central-eastern Alps), and 2N = 54 (western Alps). No correspondence exists between karyotypes and morphotypes.

Habitat

Not strictly arboreal, it is often found on the ground in scrub and especially among rocks and stone walls. Mainly found in woodland, both deciduous and coniferous, but it also occurs in orchards and gardens. It can reach 2000 m in the Alps and Pyrénées.

Population status

In recent decades this species has declined in central-eastern Europe and disappeared from areas of former occurrence. Rare in Latvia, Lithuania and in eastern Germany. Extensive regression of the area of distribution during this century in the Czech Republic. The species is considered extinct in the Slovakian part of western Carpathians. It disappeared from the continental parts of Croatia. Population densities can reach 30–50 ind./ha. Reproduction, starting from the second year, occurs once (rarely twice) annually in central Europe, more frequently twice in southern Europe. Litter sizes range between 1 and 9, mostly 4 to 6 young.

International legal & conservation status

Bern Convention, Appendix III.
IUCN Red List, Vulnerable.

Literature

Filippucci & Kotsakis (1995)
Filippucci, Civitelli & Capanna (1988)
Kryštufek & Kraft (1997)
O'Connor (1986)
Storch (1978b) – review

M. G. Filippucci

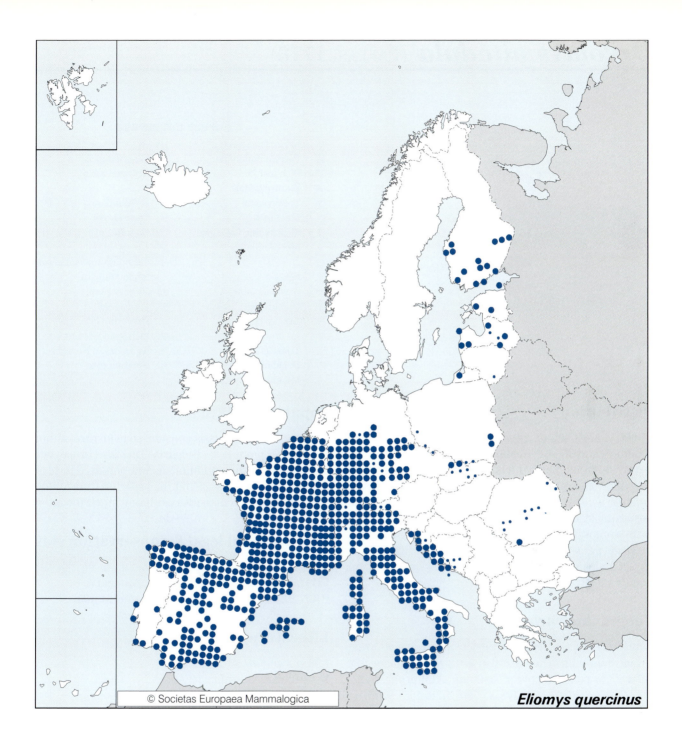

© Societas Europaea Mammalogica

Eliomys quercinus

Dryomys nitedula (PALLAS, 1778)

P. Barrett

Distribution

World: mainly the deciduous woodland zone between 10°–90°E, and 30°–60°N. Many isolates on the periphery, mainly in Israel, central Iran, Afghanistan, Turkestan, Tien Shan and Sinkiang.
Europe: widespread on the Balkan peninsula. The westernmost localities are from eastern Switzerland, the northernmost from Latvia and vicinity of Kazan (Russia), the easternmost just west of the Urals, and southernmost from Calabria and Peloponnesos. Does not occur on islands.

Geographic variation

Numerous subspecies described from extensive area, ten of them with type localities in Europe. Subspecific differences concern colour, size and skull proportions. Electrophoretic analysis confirmed genetic differentiation among the European populations. Karyotype is stable.

Habitat

Wide range of habitats populated in Europe with no clear preferences: wood-steppes (Thrace), Mediterranean evergreen shrubs (Montenegro), broad-leaved, mixed and coniferous forests (mainly in the mountains), dwarf pine and piles of rocks (alpine meadows). From the sea coast up to 2300 m above sea level. Nowhere syntopic with *Eliomys quercinus*.

Population status

In Europe west of Russia considered to be rare, although there are regions (e.g., Bulgaria, Turkish Thrace) where it is common. No population decline reported until now. Populations up to 23–25 ind./ha reported from Moldova; central European densities probably much lower.

International legal & conservation status

Bern Convention, Appendix III.
EU Habitats & Species Directive, Annex IV.
IUCN Red List, Lower Risk – near-threatened.

Literature

Filippucci *et al.* (1995)
Kryštufek & Vohralík (1994)
Lozan (1970)
Storch (1978a) – review

B. Kryštufek

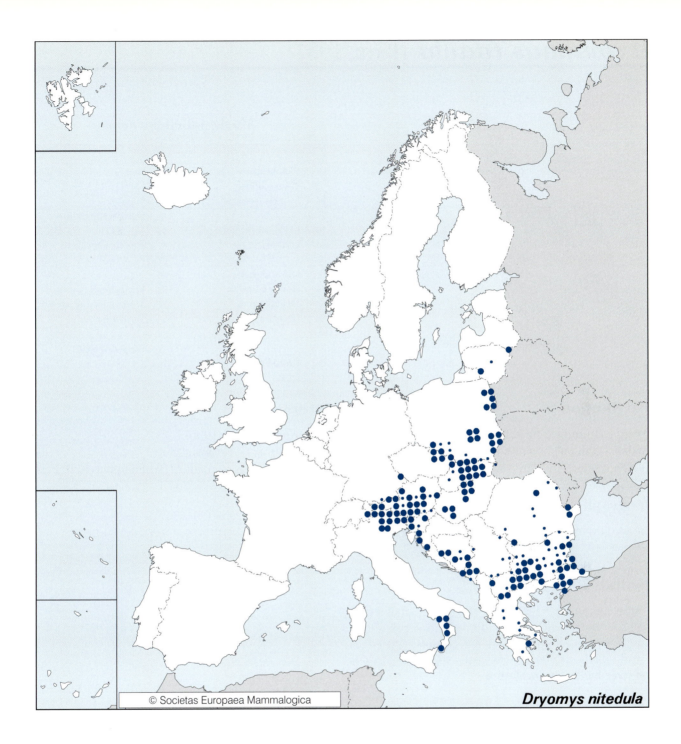

© Societas Europaea Mammalogica

Dryomys nitedula

Myomimus roachi (BATE, 1937)

T. P. McOwat

Distribution

World: easternmost Balkan peninsula and Asia Minor.
Europe: confined to south-east Bulgaria and Turkish Thrace, but may be present in Greek part of Thrace.

Geographic variation

The Bulgarian populations are attributed to the subspecies *M. roachi bulgaricus* Rossolimo, 1976.

Habitat

A little known species. More terrestrial than other dormice. Occurs in dry woodland and scrub. Open country where trees or bushes are grouped, e.g. edges of grain fields, orchards, vineyards, vegetable gardens and river banks, are preferred.

Population status

Information about this species is scarce and its presence is known only for few localities. It is relatively widespread in Turkish Thrace.

International legal & conservation status

Bern Convention, Appendix II & Appendix III.
IUCN Red List, Vulnerable.

Literature

Kurtonur & Özkan (1990)
Storch (1978e) – review

M. G. Filippucci & D. Peshev

Myomimus roachi

303

Sicista betulina (Pallas, 1779)

M. Nāzāreanu

Northern birch mouse

AL	-	LT	Beržinė sicista
BG	Горска скоклва мишка	LU	-
CZ	Myšivka horská	LV	Meža sicista
DE	Waldbirkenmaus	MK	-
DK	Birkemus	MT	-
EE	Kasetriibik	NL	Berkenmuis
ES	Ratón listado nórdico	NO	Bjørkemus
FI	Koivuhiiri	PL	Smużka
FO	-	PT	-
FR	Siciste des bouleaux	RO	Șoarecele de mesteacăn
GR	-	RU	Лесная мышовка
HR	Šumski skočimiš	SE	Buskmus
HU	Északi szöcskeegér	SI	Severna brezova miš
IR	-	SK	Myšovka horská
IS	Birkimús	TR	-
IT	Sminto betulino	YU	-

The taxonomy of birch mice is still unsettled. Populations from the Kursk Region and northern slopes of the Caucasus are characterized by 2N = 44 (NF = 50) and are recently recognized as *Sicista strandi* Formozov, 1931. The distribution of this birch mouse is not well studied yet. It probably reaches from the Dnieper river in Ukraine up to the Volga river, an area previously included in the range of *S. betulina, sensu lato*. The information in this account concerns the chromosome form (2N = 32, NF = 60) for which the specific name *Sicista betulina* is preserved.

Distribution

World: forest and steppe-forest zones and mountain forests of Europe and Asia to Transbaikalia. Localities from the Ussuri Region are considered doubtful.
Europe: from Schleswig-Holstein (Germany), Denmark, and Norway to the east. Isolated populations in Schleswig-Holstein, Denmark, Norway (up to 63°N), Sweden, and from the Alps to the Carpathians document the relict character of the recent species distribution in northern and central Europe. The northern border of the more compact European range includes Finland, Karelia, southern banks of Onega Lake, Archangelsk, lower Mezen' and Pechora rivers up to north Urals. The south-western border of the range includes eastern Poland, Czech Republic, southern Germany, Austria, the Carpathians, northern Ukraine (Lvov, Kiev), Voronezh Region to north Kazakhstan.

Geographic variation

Existing data indicate that the 32 chromosome form is rather monomorphic in coloration and body and skull size, at least in its European range. *S. betulina taigica* Stroganov and Potapkina, 1950 from the Tomsk Region (Siberia) seems to be well distinguished by a black back stripe three times broader than in the nominate subspecies. Subspecific classification needs more studies with modern taxonomic techniques.

Habitat

The birch mouse occupies a variety of habitats: birch and spruce forests, alder and spruce thickets, pine bog forests, swampy meadows, young tree stands, sedge growths, moist and bushy clearings, including alpine meadows and fields bordering forests.

Population status

Usually rare but in some habitats could be quite frequent, composing up to 14% of all small mammals caught. Trapping index changes from 0.6 to 7.1%. Changes in population density from year to year are not greater than 10 times and are dependent on mortality owing to wintering conditions rather than on stable reproduction. No cyclic fluctuations have been observed.

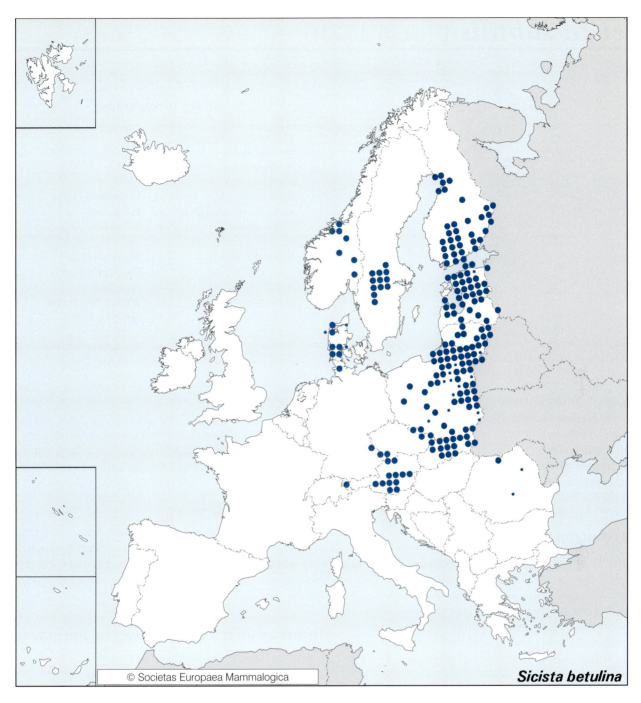

Sicista betulina

International legal & conservation status

Bern Convention, Appendix II.
EU Habitats & Species Directive, Annex IV.
IUCN Red List, Lower Risk – near threatened.

Literature

Hable & Spitzenberger (1989)
Ivanter (1975)
Pucek (1982a) – review
Sokolov *et al.* (1987, 1989)

Z. Pucek

Sicista subtilis (Pallas, 1773)

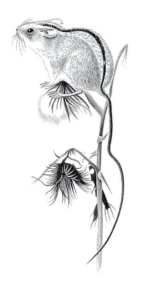

M. Năzăreanu

Taxonomic content not well understood. The subspecies *S. s. severtzovi* Ognev, 1935 from southern Russia (Voronezh Oblast', Kamennaya Steppe) and Ukraine has recently been recognized as a separate species by its distinctive karyotype (2N = 18–20, NF = 26–28). Further documentation is needed to establish the specific status and distribution of this form.

Distribution

World: Palaearctic; from central Europe through southern Russia and northern Kazakhstan to north-western China and the Altai Mts. in Mongolia.
Europe: from the Pannonian Plain and south-eastern Poland through Romania, northern Bulgaria, Ukraine (Kremenets, Luck), and southern Russia (Voronezh Region, Kuybyshev, Orsk) as far north as 53°–55°N. Extinct in Austria.

Geographic variation

Polytypic species; pelage darker in northern populations. Karyotype polymorphic (2N = 24–26, NF = 39–46) due to two (*S. subtilis vaga* (Pallas, 1779), *S. s. sibirica* Ognev, 1935) or three *(S. s. subtilis)* structural chromosome rearrangements. Five subspecies are recognized, of which three are represented in European fauna, with *severtzovi* being provisionally treated as a distinct species.

Habitat

Generally eurytopic species, more frequently occurring in steppes and open woodlands, grasslands, agrocenoses and the margins of cultivated fields and in shelter belts.

Population status

No exact data available. It is usually rare, but may constitute up to 25% of all rodents caught in north Kazakhstan. It is less abundant in northern ranges compared with the southern one. No visible population trends observed.

International legal & conservation status

Bern Convention, Appendix II.
IUCN Red List, Lower Risk – near-threatened.

Literature

Flint (1960)
Pucek (1982b) – review
Sokolov *et al.* (1986, 1987)

Z. Pucek

© Societas Europaea Mammalogica

Sicista subtilis

Hystrix cristata LINNAEUS, 1758

U. Iff

Distribution

World: North Africa from Morocco to Egypt; south of Sahara from Senegal to Ethiopia and north Tanzania. Italy.
Europe: the Italian peninsula south of the Po valley and Sicily.

Geographic variation

Several subspecies are recognized. The nominate form was described for Italy.

Habitat

Mediterranean maquis, abandoned fields, bushy areas and arid and rocky terrain. It is distributed from sea level up to more than 1500 m.

Population status

In Italy the range is expanding northward and the population density is increasing, probably because of legal protection. In Sicily the species is widespread and the population density seems to be stable.

International legal & conservation status

Bern Convention, Appendix II.
EU Habitats & Species Directive, Annex IV.
IUCN Red List, Lower Risk – near-threatened.

Other information

Many authors believe that the crested porcupine was introduced into Italy, probably by the Romans. Fossil and subfossil records indicate its occurrence in Italy and adjoining countries at least since the Upper Pleistocene. In spite of legal protection, it is still illegally hunted for food.

Literature

Amori & Angelici (1992)
Mohr (1965)
Niethammer (1982c) – review

G. Amori & F. M. Angelici

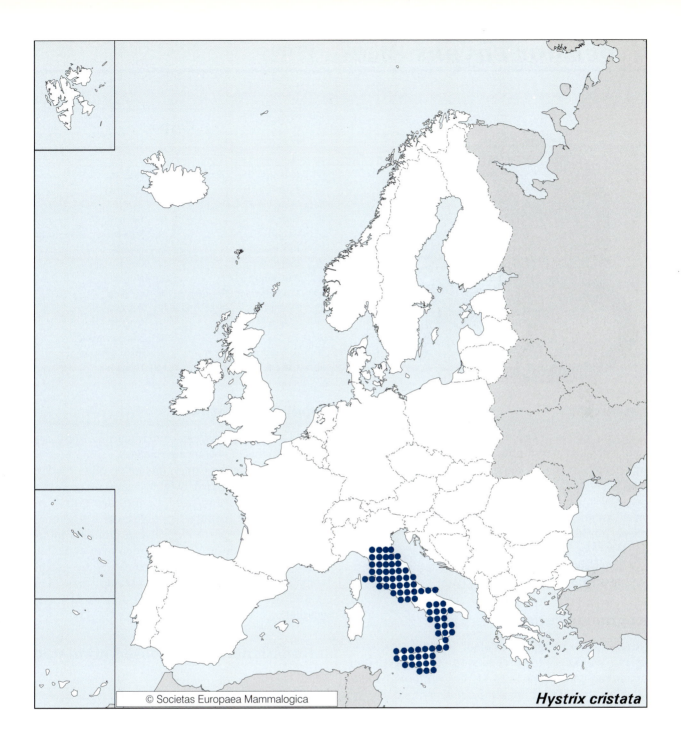

© Societas Europaea Mammalogica

Hystrix cristata

Myocastor coypus (Molina, 1782)

U. Iff

Coypu

AL	Nutria	LT	Nutrija
BG	Нутрия	LU	-
CZ	Nutrie	LV	Nūtrija
DE	Nutria	MK	Нутрија
DK	Sumpbæver; Bæverrotte	MT	-
EE	Nutria	NL	Beverrat
ES	Coipú	NO	Sumpbever; Beverrotte
FI	Rämemajava	PL	Nutria
FO	Bævurrotta	PT	Coipu
FR	Ragondin	RO	Nutria
GR	Μυοκάστορας, Νούτρια	RU	Нутрия
HR	Nutrija	SE	Sumpbäver
HU	Nutria	SI	Nutrija
IR	-	SK	Nutria riečna
IS	Bjórrotta	TR	Su maymunu
IT	Nutria	YU	Нутрија

Distribution

World: indigenous to South America, where it occurs in sub-tropical Argentina, Uruguay, Paraguay, the southern part of Brazil, south-eastern Bolivia, Peru and Chile. Introduced to North America, Europe, the Middle East, Africa, Japan and the Asiatic part of the former Soviet Union.
Europe: introduced in the 1920s for fur production; since then feral populations established in many countries. Particularly common in France, Germany and Italy; recently eradicated from Great Britain.

Geographic variation

Five subspecies recognized. Colour varieties selected in captive stocks. Where recorded, the subspecies introduced to Europe was *M. coypus bonariensis* (Commerson, 1805), from northern Argentina.

Habitat

Adapted to a semi-aquatic mode of life, coypus inhabit rivers, streams, lakes, wetlands, natural and artificial ponds; preferred areas have emergent or succulent vegetation along the banks. Almost exclusively herbivorous, they feed on a broad range of aquatic and semi-aquatic plants. Coypus dig complex burrow systems into the banks of waterways, or build surface nests in waterside vegetation or in shallow water.

Population status

A rapid increase in numbers and range followed escapes from fur-farms or deliberate releases.

Outside its native range, the coypu often reaches a remarkable population density, causing damage to crops, to drainage systems and to native plants. As a consequence, introduced populations are generally considered to be pests. Reduced in numbers in some parts of their natural range through over-exploitation or eradication. Seasonal fluctuations in the northern hemisphere range from less than 1 to more than 24 ind./ha and are generally ascribed to periods of freezing weather.

International legal & conservation status

None.

Other information

Exploited for fur and meat in South America, North America and Russia. It carries various infections transmittable to animals, and in some cases to man: leptospirosis, salmonellosis, pasteurellosis, botulism, some viral and fungal infections, and parasitic infections such as toxoplasmosis.

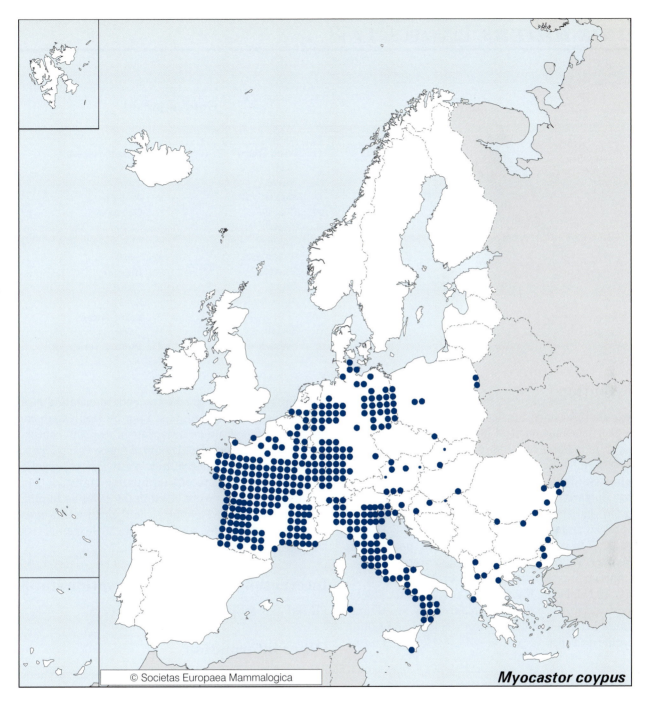

© Societas Europaea Mammalogica

Myocastor coypus

Literature

Doncaster & Jouventin (1989)
Gosling (1989)
Gosling & Skinner (1984)
Niethammer (1963)
Reggiani *et al.* (1993)
Stubbe (1982b) – review
Woods *et al.* (1992) – review

G. Reggiani

Canis aureus LINNAEUS, 1758

V. Zadražil

Distribution

World: south-eastern Europe, Asia Minor, the Middle East, the Caucasus, central and southern Asia to Sri Lanka and Thailand. Northern and eastern Africa, south to Nigeria and Tanzania.

Europe: resident in the Caucasus, Turkish Thrace, Greece, Bulgaria, Albania, the eastern Adriatic coast and Romania. Extirpated in the 1960s in Macedonia, but reappeared there by the end of the 1980s. Spread recently into Serbia and established permanent populations. Vagrants frequent in Hungary and Slovenia, also appearing occasionally in north-eastern Italy, Austria and Slovenia. Known from many islands, at least some of which were recently colonized by swimming. Altitudinal range mainly between sea level and 600 m in southern Greece.

Geographic variation

Several subspecies described from Europe, but their validity is questionable. Dalmatian jackals have a more robust skull than Bulgarian ones.

Habitat

Maquis and shrubland on the coast; shrubs, woods and reeds inland. Habitats are frequently influenced by humans. Permanent populations established in wolf-free areas.

Population status

Distributional border fluctuates with alternating local extinctions and colonizations. Step by step expansion documented for Dalmatian jackals in the 20th century, probably as a result of wolf control measures in former Yugoslavia. Colonization of new areas also reported in Bulgaria. According to official hunting statistics, 14.6 jackals per 100 km^2 were killed in the 1983/84 hunting season in northern Dalmatia. The jackal is the most common canid in this area as only 9.3 foxes per 100 km^2 were killed in the same period.

International legal & conservation status

EU Habitats & Species Directive, Annex V.

Other information

Persecuted as a pest of small game, domestic animals, vegetables, fruit and grapes. Its fur has no commercial value, at least in Dalmatia.

Literature

Demeter & Spassov (1993)
Ioannides & Giannatos (1991)
Kryštufek *et al.* (1997)
Kryštufek & Tvrtković (1990a, b)

B. Kryštufek

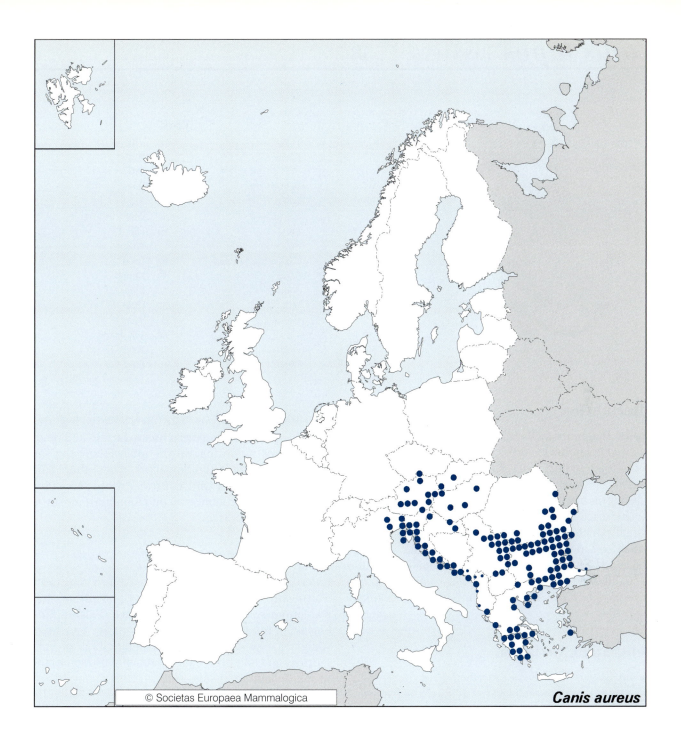

© Societas Europaea Mammalogica

Canis aureus

Canis lupus Linnaeus, 1758

V. Zadražil

Distribution

World: Holarctic; in Eurasia from south-western and north-western Europe through Russia and central Asia (in the south to northern Arabia and India) to the coast of the Pacific Ocean. North America: Alaska, Canada, parts of the northern USA and an isolated population in Mexico. **Europe:** originally throughout Europe. Now only isolated or small populations in the Iberian and Italian peninsula, French Alps and Fennoscandia. Widespread throughout Russia (except a large area around Moscow), the Baltic States, Belarus, northern Ukraine, eastern Poland, Slovakia, Romania and the mountains of the Balkan peninsula.

Geographic variation

Six subspecies have been described from Europe, but only two of them are realistic: the nominate subspecies, *Canis lupus lupus* the 'timber wolf', from Fennoscandia to southern Europe and along the coniferous forest zone to Siberia, and *C. l. albus* Kerr, 1782, the light-coloured 'tundra wolf' which lived in northernmost Russia and perhaps also Fennoscandia. The 'timber wolf' includes the isolated southern populations, although Spanish wolves are slightly smaller and have a red-brown tinge in the fur colour. About 30 'tundra wolves' existed in the 1960s, but by the 1980s there was only a mixed population with the 'timber wolf'.

Habitat

Mainly in the wide open woodlands and mountains. In the northern coniferous zone often on large bog areas, and in Lapland and northern Russia on fells and tundra. Roaming or migrating wolves often follow the same routes along ridges and bog areas, where there is less snow. In southern and central Europe nowadays, because of persecution, only on mountains, mostly at a height of 600–2400 m.

Population status

Exterminated long ago in most western and central European countries. Many recent populations fairly stable and some have even increased (Poland, Spain, Slovakia), but some small populations are endangered (Bulgaria, Sweden). Mountain populations of Spain, Portugal and Italy are isolated, probably also some others in the Balkan peninsula. In the 1990s about 300–400 individuals in Portugal, 2000 in Spain, 400–500 in Italy, 1000 in former Yugoslavia and 200–300 in Greece. A few are roaming in Norway, about 45–50 in Sweden and 150 in Finland. From the large population in Romania (2500, mainly in the Carpathians) about 700 are killed anually.

International legal & conservation status

Bern Convention, Appendix II.
EU Habitats & Species Directive, Annex II* & Annex IV, except Finnish populations, Spanish populations north of Duero and Greek populations north of the 39th parallel, Annex V.
CITES, Appendix II (reservation by Switzerland). EC 338/ 97, Annex A (except Spanish populations north of Duero

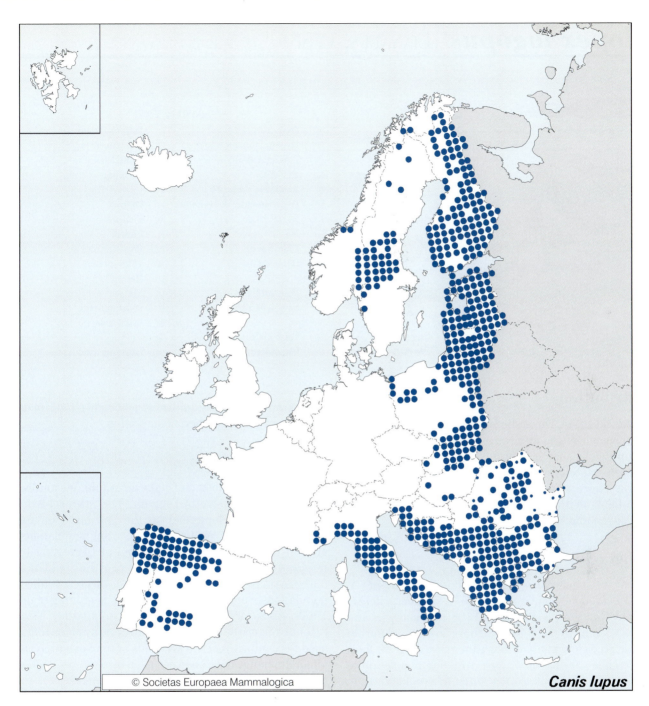

© Societas Europaea Mammalogica

Canis lupus

and Greek populations north of the 39th parallel, which are Annex B).

IUCN Red List, Vulnerable (Italy only), Lower Risk – conservation dependent (Spain and Portugal only).

Other information

A territorial species, which lives in packs. The size of the territories varies usually between 700 and 1500 km². In Europe, packs consist of usually fewer than 15 individuals but may comprise 20 or more in Canada and Alaska. Hunting tactics developed for catching cervids; domestic animals are also killed.

Literature

Bibikov (1988)
Bjärvall (1983)
Blanco *et al.* (1992)
Hell (1990)
Peters (1993)
Pulliainen (1974, 1980, 1985)
Sörensen *et al.* (1986)
Voskar (1983)

S. Sulkava & E. Pulliainen

Alopex lagopus (Linnaeus, 1758)

E. Hazebroek

Arctic fox

AL	Delphra polare	LT	Poliarinė lapė
BG	Песец; Полярна лиснuа	LU	Polarfuuss
CZ	Liška polární	LV	Polārlapsa
DE	Eisfuchs	MK	Поларна лисица
DK	Polarræv; Fjeldræv	MT	-
EE	Polaarrebane; Jäärebane	NL	Poolvos
ES	Zorro ártico	NO	Fjellrev
FI	Naali	PL	Piesiec
FO	Fjallarevur	PT	Raposa-árctica
FR	Renard polaire	RO	Vulpe-polara
GR	-	RU	Песец
HR	Polarna lisica	SE	Fjällräv
HU	Sarki róka	SI	Polarna lisica
IR		SK	Líška polárna
IS	Tófa; Melrakki	TR	-
IT	Volpe artica	YU	Поларна лисица

Distribution

World: Holarctic. The arctic fox inhabits the tundra zone of northern Eurasia and North America.
Europe: fells of the Scandinavian mountain range (Sweden and Norway), the tundra coast of northernmost Norway, northernmost European Russia and Finnish Fjeld-Lapland (Enontekiö and Utsjoki). Also on Iceland, Jan Mayen and Svalbard.

Geographic variation

Seven subspecies are recognized, two of them, *A. lagopus lagopus* (continent) and *A. l. spitzbergenensis* Barrett-Hamilton & Bonhote, 1898 (Spitsbergen and Novaya Zemlya), in Europe. There are two different colour phases: white and blue, the percentage of their occurrence varying very much from one population to another. The blue-phase fox tends to predominate in island populations, such as Iceland (67%).

Habitat

The arctic fox is closely associated with particular tundra habitats, i.e. its traditional breeding burrow systems, but may wander hundreds of kilometres in the High Arctic regions or even deep into the taiga zone in order to avoid malnutrition in the absence of acceptable food. The arctic fox eats all kinds of meat and other animal matter ranging from lemmings, other small rodents and birds (and their eggs) to all kinds of carrion available on the sea coast or left as food remains by polar bears, wolves and other predators. It also finds food from herbivores that have died of starvation.

Population status

The arctic fox has been one of the most valuable natural resources of the arctic regions. The status of the populations has depended on the one hand on the availability of food resources for breeding populations, and on the other hand on the level of harvesting by trappers in relation to the productivity of the population (i.e. sustainable use). For instance, the original Finnish populations were overharvested at the beginning of the 1900s, thus almost destroying the population. Most recently the traditional breeding burrow systems (often used for centuries) of the arctic fox of the Scandinavian Mountain Range have been occupied by red foxes, *Vulpes vulpes,* excluding their original inhabitants.

International legal & conservation status

Bern Convention, Appendix II.
EU Habitats & Species Directive, Annex II* & Annex IV.

Other information

The arctic fox possesses the ability to produce large litters (up to 18 cubs) when there is plenty of food available, and to use resorption of embryos or foetuses if food appears scarce. The arctic fox has been domesticated. This blue fox industry plays a major role besides the American mink in the worldwide fur trade.

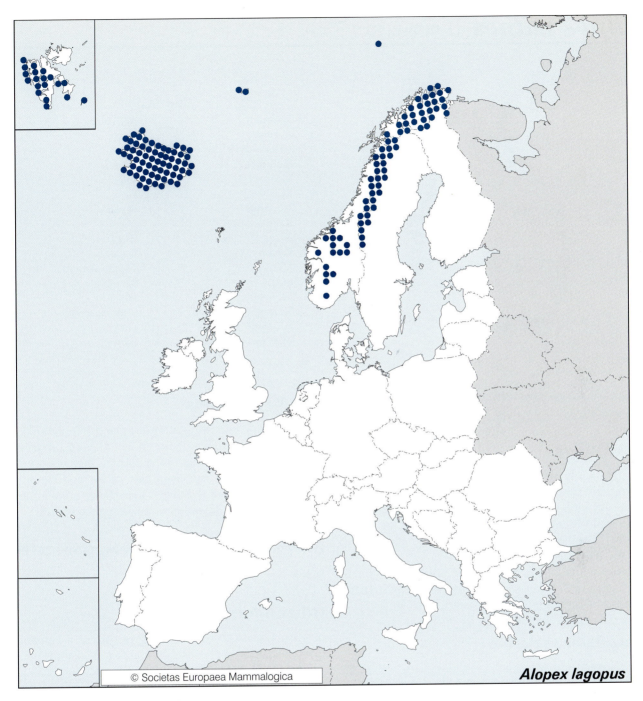

© Societas Europaea Mammalogica

Alopex lagopus

Literature

Pulliainen (1965, 1993a)

E. Pulliainen

Vulpes vulpes (Linnaeus, 1758)

V. Zadražil

The red fox is the best investigated canid species in Europe and one of the most important fur animals.

Distribution

World: mainly Holarctic. Large area throughout the Palaearctic from north-western Africa to China and Japan. Arabian penisula, north of Indian subcontinent, Sikkim and Bhutan. North America without the Arctic Islands. Introduced to Australia, various Pacific islands and the USA.
Europe: whole of Europe, except Crete and smaller Greek islands, Balearic Islands, Malta, Elba, Lipari, Outer Hebrides, Orkney, Shetland, Faroes and Iceland.

Geographic variation

Many subspecies, some of them without clear scientific diagnosis. In Europe not more than four or five subspecies (*V. vulpes vulpes, V. v. ichnusae* Miller, 1907, *V. v. silacea* Miller, 1907, *V. v. anatolica* Thomas, 1920, *V. v. hellenica* Douma-Petridou & Ondrias, 1980). A revision would be useful.

Habitat

The red fox is found in all types of forests and open landscapes; also very adaptable to urban and suburban ecosystems and feeding conditions. Vertical distribution up to 3000 m; limits of reproduction not well investigated.

Population status

Stable populations everywhere. Spring population in Europe (without Russia) between 750000 and 1 million. In some countries greater fluctuations in population dynamics in connection with vole cycles and climatic conditions. In central Europe increasing populations through oral immunization of foxes against rabies.

International legal & conservation status

None.

Other information

In most European countries the red fox is a valuable quarry species and considered a pest of useful game animals. At present there is no important international fur market, and, in reaction to the rabies oral immunization as well as lack of hunting rewards, populations are increasing everywhere, also in human settlements. The pressure on protected species such as ground-breeding birds can be significant (e.g., in Germany). Main diet is small mammals, seasonally, but also omnivorous. In some regions the red fox is an important vector of rabies, trichinosis and echinococcosis (*Echinococcus multilocularis*). Social regulation of density only in non-exploited population structures. Maximum age 12 years; high reproduction rate with rapid population turnover.

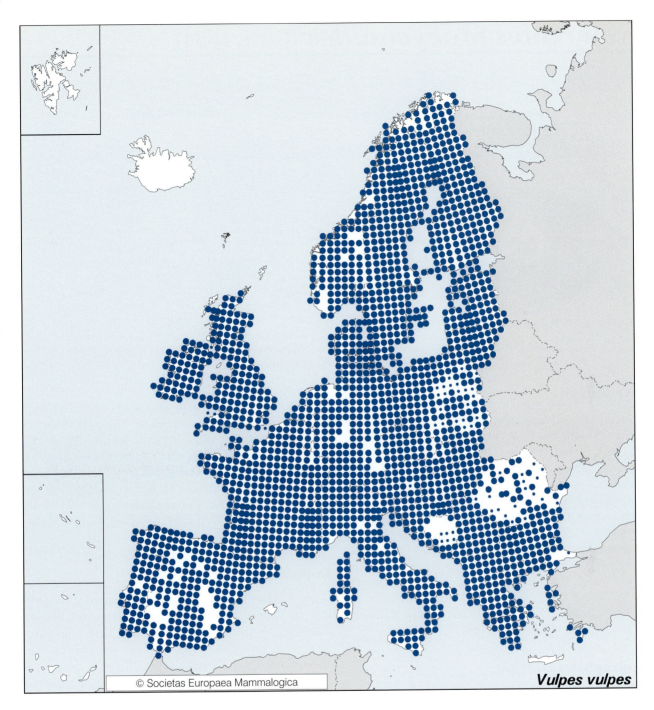

© Societas Europaea Mammalogica

Vulpes vulpes

Literature

Labhardt (1990)
Macdonald (1987)
Stubbe (1982a)
Stubbe (1989b)
Wandeler & Lüps (1993)

M. Stubbe

Nyctereutes procyonoides (Gray, 1834)

U. Iff

	Raccoon dog		
AL	-	LU	-
BG	Енотовидно куче	LV	Jenotsuns
CZ	Psík mývalovitý	MK	Раконовидно куче
DE	Marderhund	MT	-
DK	Mårhund	NL	Wasbeerhond
EE	Kährikkoer; Kährik	NO	Mårhund
ES	Perro mapache	PL	Jenot
FI	Supikoira	PT	Cão-mapache
FO	-	RO	Câinele enot
FR	Chien viverrin	RU	Енотовидная собака
GR	-	SE	Mårdhund
HR	Kunopas	SI	Rakunasti pes
HU	Nyestkutya	SK	Psík medviedikovitý
IR	-	TR	-
IS	Marðarhundur	YU	Ракунолики пас;
IT	Cane procione		Ракунопас
LT	Usūrinis šuo		

Distribution

World: the original distribution of the raccoon dog covers large areas of the Far East: many parts of China, Korea, south-east Russia, north-east Indochina and Japan. Russians introduced the species (more than 9000 individuals) mainly to European parts of the former Soviet Union between 1929 and 1955.

Europe: since its introduction to the Ukraine, Belarus, Russia and Latvia, the raccoon dog has colonized many European countries and is today found in Russia, Belarus, Moldova, Ukraine, Finland, Sweden, the Baltic States, Poland, Germany, Romania, Bulgaria, Hungary and Serbia. Raccoon dogs are occasionally seen in Norway, Denmark, The Netherlands, France, Switzerland, Austria, Slovenia and Bosnia.

Geographic variation

The raccoon dog consists of several subspecies. The Japanese raccoon dog or 'tanuki' may even be a distinct species; it differs in many respects, e.g. as to its chromosome number, from the other subspecies. In Europe, however, there is only one subspecies *N. procyonoides ussuriensis* Matschie, 1908, which was introduced from the far east (Amur – Ussuri region) to European Russia.

Habitat

The raccoon dog is very adaptable and lives in a variety of habitats. It prefers the proximity of water and is often found along lake and river shores and in other damp places. It is found in both deciduous and coniferous forests, but most often in moist forests with much undergrowth and possible den sites. Because the raccoon dog is dormant in winter, the length of the summer is critical to it. When the summer is very short the young, in particular, have difficulties in accumulating enough fat before the winter and are not able to survive the long winter. Thus, the northern limit of the distribution is determined by climate.

Population status

Since the 1950s the population has increased rapidly (e.g., in Finland, the Baltic States and Poland). In some countries (e.g., Finland and Latvia), the population peaked in the mid-1980s and has slightly declined thereafter. Thus, after a rapid increase phase the population has stabilized, at least in the eastern part of its European distribution. The raccoon dog may, however, still be spreading westwards in Europe.

International legal & conservation status

None.

Other information

In Europe, the raccoon dog is considered a pest that has an effect on native fauna. However, this is often exaggerated. The raccoon dog is truly omnivorous and the majority of its diet consists of small mammals, frogs, lizards, fish, insects, plants and carrion. It may cause

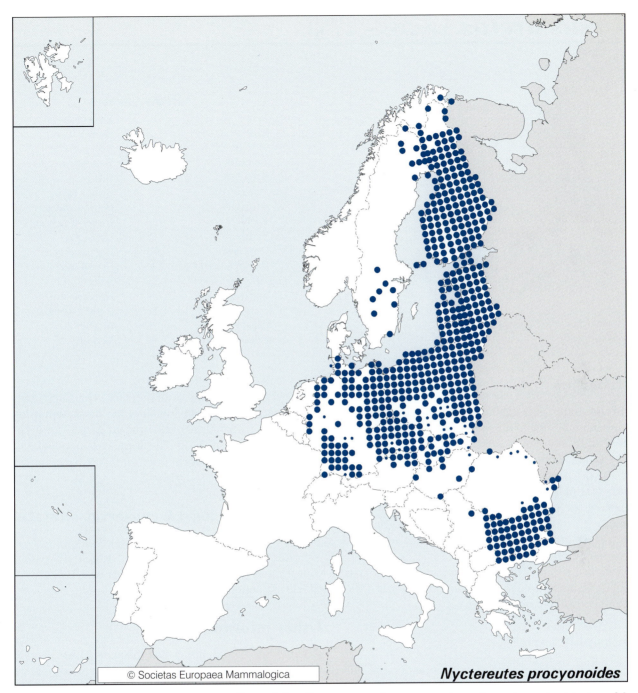

© Societas Europaea Mammalogica

Nyctereutes procyonoides

damage to native fauna only occasionally and locally. The raccoon dog seems to have found a vacant niche in Europe; no severe competiton has been observed with native carnivores. At least in northern Europe, both the raccoon dog and the badger *M. meles,* with which the raccoon dog might compete most severely, are dormant in winter. This may reduce competition for food, because food is abundant in summer but scarce in winter.

The raccoon dog is also an important vector of rabies; in Poland and the Baltic states it is the most important after the red fox *V. vulpes,* and in Finland it was the most important during the epidemics in 1988–1989. The raccoon dog also carries trichinosis and sarcoptic mange and may be an important vector of these parasites.

Literature

Helle & Kauhala (1991)
Kauhala (1992,1996a, b)
Kauhala *et al.* (1993)
Niethammer (1993)
Nowak (1993)

K. Kauhala

Ursus arctos Linnaeus, 1758

V. Zadražil

Brown bear

AL	Ariu	LT	Rudasis lokys
BG	Кафява мечка	LU	Bronge Bier
CZ	Medvěd hnědý	LV	Brūnais lācis
DE	Braunbär	MK	Кафеава мечка
DK	Brun bjørn	MT	Ors
EE	Pruunkaru	NL	Bruine beer
ES	Oso pardo	NO	Bjørn; Brunbjørn
FI	Karhu	PL	Niedźwiedź brunatny
FO	Bjørn	PT	Urso
FR	Ours brun	RO	Urs; Urs-brun
GR	Καστανή αρκούδα	RU	Бурый медведь
HR	Mrki medvjed	SE	Björn
HU	Barna medve	SI	Rjavi medved
IR	-	SK	Medved' hnedý
IS	Skógarbjörn	TR	Ayı; Boz ayı
IT	Orso bruno	YU	Медвед

Distribution

World: Holarctic. Throughout the Palaearctic mainland from western Europe to the Far East and Japan. Extinct in the British Isles, much of Western Europe, European Russia, China, Korea and south Japan. North America: north Mexico, Rocky Mountains, north and north-west Canada and Alaska.

Europe: restricted to mountain ranges (Cantabrian Mts., Pyrénées, Abruzze, eastern Alps, Dinaric Alps, Balkans, Carpathians and Caucasus), with lowland forests occupied only in northern Russia, Fennoscandia, Estonia and Latvia. On the verge of extinction in the western Pyrénées. Reintroduced to the central Pyrénées in 1996, but not yet included on the map.

Geographic variation

Polymorphic species with taxonomic situation not fully determined at present. Seven to eleven subspecies are recognized with large differences in body size and fur colour.

Habitat

Forest zones of the Palaearctic and Nearctic but inhabits also tundra, steppes, edges of deserts. In areas of dense human population, restricted to higher, inaccessible mountain areas.

Population status

Estimates over the last 50 years show an almost 100%

increase in the European population. The Carpathian population of 7500 individuals is the most numerous, then the Balkan population of 3000 and the Scandinavian one of 1000. The Scandinavian population constitutes the western part of the Euro-Siberian continuous range.

International legal & conservation status

Bern Convention, Appendix II.
EU Habitats & Species Directive, Annex II* (except Finnish and Swedish populations), Annex IV.
CITES, Appendix II, EC 338/97, Annex A.

Other information

A game species in many countries and also illegally hunted. Causes damage to agriculture: oat crops, domestic animals and beehives. Synanthropization a serious problem, especially in areas of heavy tourist traffic (national parks), though attacks on people exceptional. Usually lives singly. The brown bear is omnivorous, eating berries, roots and leaves, also small and big game, carrion and fish. Body mass of new-born young 350–500 g; adults in Europe up to 450 kg. No true hibernation but winter rest with body temperature 3–4° below normal.

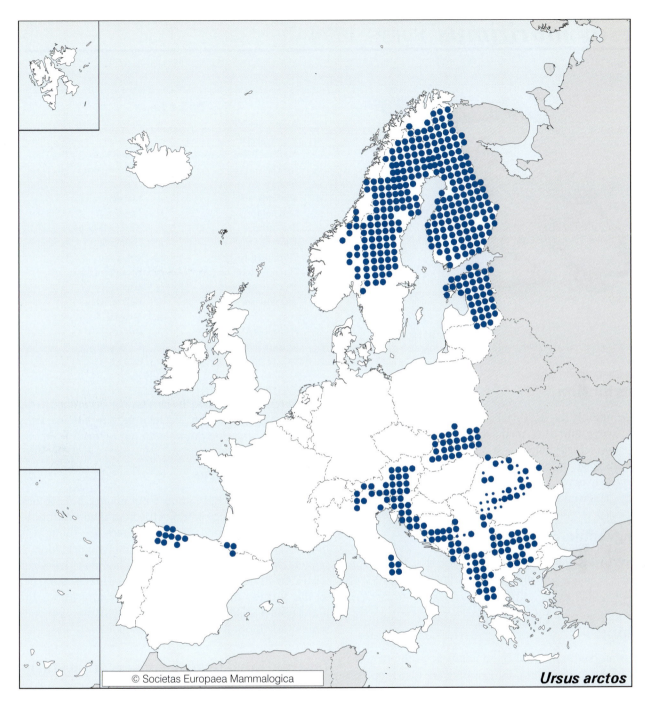

© Societas Europaea Mammalogica

Ursus arctos

Literature

Jakubiec (1993)
Sörensen (1990)

Z. Jakubiec

Ursus maritimus PHIPPS, 1774

V. Zadražil

Polar bear

AL	Ariu i bardhe	LT	Baltasis lokys
BG	Бяла мечка	LU	Äisbier
CZ	Medvěd lední	LV	Ledus lācis
DE	Eisbär	MK	Бела мечка
DK	Isbjørn	MT	-
EE	Jääkaru	NL	IJsbeer
ES	Oso polar	NO	Isbjørn
FI	Jääkarhu	PL	Niedźwiedź polarny
FO	Hvítabjørn	PT	Urso-polar
FR	Ours polaire	RO	Urs-polar
GR	Πολική αρκούδα	RU	Белый медведь
HR	Polarni medvjed	SE	Isbjörn
HU	Jegesmedve	SI	Beli medved
IR	-	SK	Medved' l'adový
IS	Hvítabjörn	TR	Buz ayısı
IT	Orso polare	YU	Бели медвед

Distribution

World: mainly the drift-ice zone of the Arctic Ocean but also throughout the Arctic Basin, even close to the geographic north pole.
Europe: large populations are found on the islands of Svalbard (Norway), Franz Joseph's Land and Novaya Zemlya (Russia).

Geographic variation

Today *Ursus maritimus* is considered a monotypic species, which is split into several large populations with limited exchange.

Habitat

The preferred habitat of the polar bear is the drift-ice zone of the Arctic ocean, though they are also found on the coastal areas and islands of the region. Generally in the summer, the edge of the drift-ice forms the southern border of the region where this species lives. The main food of the polar bear is seal (90%), primarily ringed seals *Phoca hispida* together with bearded seals *Erignathus barbatus,* harp seals *Phoca groenlandica* and hooded seals *Cystophora cristata.* Also included in the diet are young or weak musk-oxen and reindeer, young birds and carrion of stranded whales, fish and invertebrates. Vegetation, such as seaweed, grass, berries and other fruits may also be eaten. It has been observed that the polar bear resorts to cannibalism, catching weak or young individuals of its own species if the opportunity arises. *Ursus maritimus* is a true hibernator, leaving the drift-ice zone in December to dig holes in the snow and ice around the coasts. Only pregnant or lactating animals do not hibernate.

Population status

Despite detailed observations from planes, helicopters, satellites and drift-ice stations the population cannot be accurately determined. However, there are thought to be between 7000 and 20000 specimens worldwide. It is believed that this will remain stable provided strict local and international protection continues. Contrary to the former theory of circumpolar migration, the population is split into several main populations between which only limited exchange takes place.

International legal & conservation status

Bern Convention, Appendix II.
CITES Appendix II. EC 338/97, Annex B.
Hunting by local people using traditional methods in the exercise of their traditional rights is allowed.
IUCN Red List, Lower Risk – conservation dependent.

Other information

Based on average size, the polar bear is the largest existing terrestrial carnivore. Unlike other species of bear, the soles of the feet of the polar bear are covered with fur and there are short webs between the toes. The animal is perfectly protected against cold and heat by its white fur on black skin. The thick layer of fat beneath

© Societas Europaea Mammalogica

Ursus maritimus

the skin causes the bear to have a density of less than 1, so that even dead specimens cannot sink. One of the consequences of strict protection of the polar bear has been an increase in average life-span to 17–19 years.

Literature

Gorgas (1993) – review
Kurt *et al.* (1988)
Larsen (1980)
Uspensky (1989)
Vibe (1982)

M. Gorgas

Procyon lotor (Linnaeus, 1758)

E. Hazebroek

Raccoon

AL	-	LT	Meškėnas
BG	Американски енот	LU	Wäschbier
CZ	Mýval severní	LV	Jenots
DE	Waschbär	MK	Ракун
DK	Vaskebjørn	MT	-
EE	Pesukaru	NL	Wasbeer
ES	Mapache	NO	Vaskebjørn
FI	Pesukarhu	PL	Szop pracz
FO	Tváttarbjørn	PT	Mapache; Ratão-lavadeiro;
FR	Raton laveur		Guaxinim
GR	Ρακούν	RO	-
HR	Rakun	RU	Енот
HU	Ёszak-amerikai	SE	Tvättbjörn
	mosómedve	SI	Rakun
IR	-	SK	Medvedík čistotný
IS	Þvottabjörn	TR	-
IT	Orsetto lavatore	YU	Ракун

Distribution

World: Originally a North American species, occurring from the prairie provinces of Manitoba and Saskatchewan (56°N) and Alberta (58°N) in Canada, in the USA except for parts of the Rockies and deserts, south to Mexico and the southern states of central America perhaps as far as northern Columbia.

Europe: In 1934 two pairs of *Procyon* were released in the forest district of Vöhl in Hessen, Germany. Before and after 1945 farmed animals escaped at various places in central Europe. The subsequent increase in distribution is well documented. The species was also introduced into the former Soviet Union from 1936 onwards, where it was actively acclimatized at 26 localities in Belarus, Azerbaijan, Dagestan, Uzbekistan and the area of Krasnodar. From Germany, the species migrated to the Benelux States, France, Switzerland, Austria and the Czech Republic. Some individuals have also been found in Poland, Hungary, Denmark and Slovakia.

Geographic variation

In north and central America 25 subspecies have been described, with *P. lotor hirtus* Nelson & Goldman, 1930 being the most widespread and *P. l. marinus* Nelson, 1930 the most restricted (Florida Keys). The origin of the animals introduced into Europe for fur farming is unknown and its taxonomic status has not been investigated in Eurasia.

Habitat

The species uses a wide variety of habitats. Woodland with old trees and holes near to lakes and rivers is preferred. *Procyon lotor* also settles in suburban ecosystems with parks and gardens.

Population status

Range and density in the whole European distribution area is increasing. Population density in preferred habitats is 1–2 ind./100 ha, but can be even higher in suburban habitats.

International legal & conservation status

None.

Other information

Animals accummulate large fat deposits in the autumn (up to 2.5 kg) for the inactive winter months. The species is a vector for rabies.

Literature

Hall & Kelson (1959)
Heptner & Naumov (1974)
Lutz (1984)
Niethammer (1963)

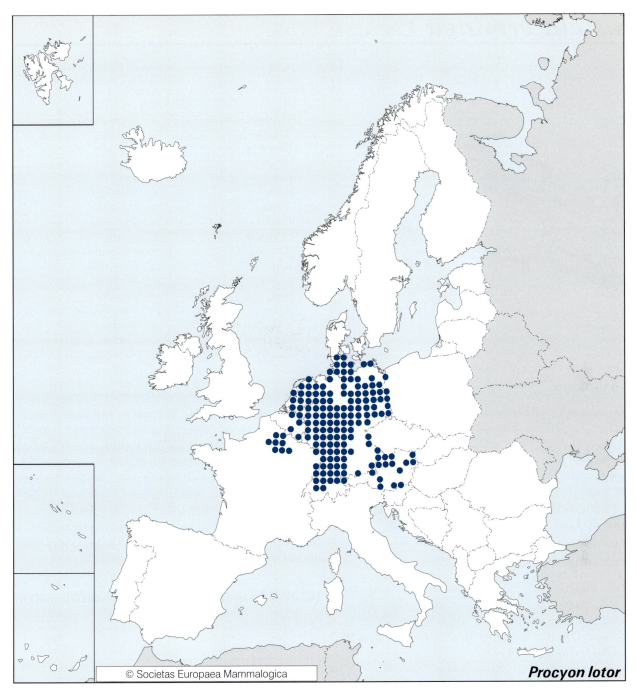

© Societas Europaea Mammalogica

Procyon lotor

Pavlov *et al.* (1973)
Röben (1975, 1976)
Stubbe (1975, 1990,1993c)

M. Stubbe

Mustela erminea LINNAEUS, 1758

F. Müller

Distribution

World: very wide circumpolar distribution, inhabiting central and northern Europe, Asia, northern North America, and north-eastern Greenland. Naturalized in New Zealand.

Europe: throughout Europe with the exception of the Mediterranean zone and some north Atlantic islands. Naturalized on the island of Terschelling (NL), but has recently died out.

Geographic variation

In North America nine and in Eurasia 20 subspecies are recognized. In Europe not more than three subspecies are accepted: *Mustela erminea erminea, M. e. hibernica* (Thomas & Barrett-Hamilton, 1895) and *M. e. minima* Cavazza, 1912.

Habitat

The stoat occupies a wide range of habitats. It is a rodent specialist in its food biology, and is thus more at home in habitats rich with rodent populations. The most preferred habitats are coniferous and mixed forests, but the species is also found in tundra, boundaries of fields and meadows, shrubby river banks and lakeshores. The stoat also inhabits the summits of fells and mountains up to 3000 m.

Population status

Formerly the stoat was hunted for its white winter fur.

For example, in Finland during the 1930s a total of 30000 pelts was sold. Nowadays the status of the population is more dependent on the general structure of the habitat (many built habitats are no longer acceptable) and the abundance of its most favoured food items (lemmings, voles and/or mice). The farther north the stoat lives, the more the abundance of its prey populations and its own populations fluctuate from year to year. In the absence of small rodents, stoats tend to withdraw, if possible, to refuges with some food to await the reappearance of the next peak of their prey.

International legal & conservation status

Bern Convention, Appendix III.

Other information

The stoat is a terrestrial predator but it can also climb and swim. It may pursue water voles in their burrows as well as field voles in their tunnels inside the snow cover. In fact, the stoat may disappear for days into this subnivean life when the ground is covered by deep snow.

Literature

King (1989)
Pulliainen (1981)
Reichstein (1993a)
Stubbe & Stubbe (1997)

E. Pulliainen

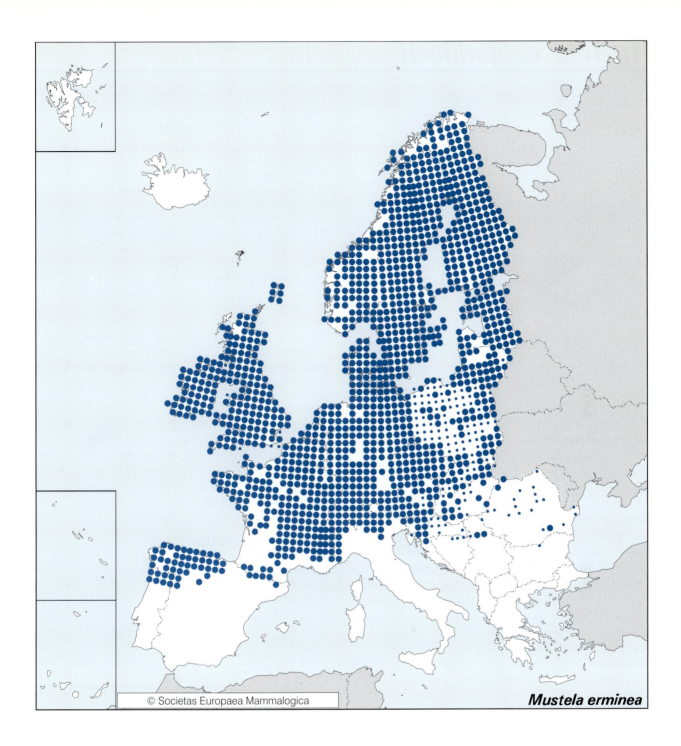

© Societas Europaea Mammalogica

Mustela erminea

Mustela eversmanii LESSON, 1827

M. Năzăreanu

Steppe polecat

AL	-	LT	-
BG	Степен пор	LU	-
CZ	Tchoř stepní	LV	Stepes sesks
DE	Steppeniltis	MK	Степски твор
DK	Steppeilder	MT	-
EE	Stepituhkur	NL	Steppenbunzing
ES	Turón de la estepa	NO	Steppeilder
FI	Arohilleri	PL	Tchórz stepowy
FO	-	PT	-
FR	Putois des steppes	RO	Dihor-de-stepă
GR	-	RU	Степной хорёк
HR	Stepski tvor	SE	Stäppiller
HU	Molnárgörény	SI	Stepski dihur
IR	-	SK	Tchor stepný
IS	Steppuvísla	TR	-
IT	Puzzola delle steppe	YU	Степски твор

Likely conspecific with the Nearctic *Mustela nigripes* Audubon & Bachman, 1851. Presumably hybridizes introgressively with *Mustela putorius*.

Distribution

World: Palaearctic, from central and eastern Europe and northwestern Georgia through southern Russia, Kazakhstan, northern Turkmenistan, Uzbekistan, northern Tadzhikistan, and Kyrgyzstan to Mongolia and western, central, and northeastern China. Maximum range, extending from the Pyrénées to Alaska, achieved in the late Pleistocene.

Europe: represented by two major populations separated by the Carpathians: the western population (subspecies *M. eversmanii hungarica* (Éhik, 1927)) restricted to the Czech Republic, eastern Austria, southern Slovakia, Ukraine south of the Carpathians, Hungary, northern Yugoslavia, and western Romania; the eastern population (nominate subspecies) distributed in northern Bulgaria, southern Romania, Moldova, Ukraine east and north of the Carpathians, south-eastern Poland, southern European Russia, and Kazakhstan, continuous with the main Asian distribution of the species.

Geographic variation

Six subspecies recognized, including two in Europe (see above).

Habitat

Steppes, semi-deserts, grasslands, and cultivated fields; often in association with colonies of sousliks. Occurs in Europe up to 1000 m above sea level and in Asian high mountains up to 2500 m.

Population status

Still rather numerous, particularly in southern European Russia and Kazakhstan, though unevenly spaced and abundant across its range, with unstable population densities, strongly depending on food resources (primarily rodents). Capable of spreading and colonizing new areas rapidly.

International legal & conservation status

Bern Convention, Appendix II.

Other information

Hunted for pelts. Karyotype, with 2N = 38, differs from *Mustela putorius* with 2N = 40. The steppe polecat digs burrows by itself or uses the dens of prey species or other carnivores.

Literature

Heptner *et al.* (1967)
Wolsan (1993)

M. Wolsan

© Societas Europaea Mammalogica

Mustela eversmanii

Mustela lutreola (LINNAEUS, 1761)

F. Müller

As a result of its similar appearance, the European mink is often confused with the American mink *Mustela vison* introduced to Europe at the beginning of the 20th century. The basic distinguishing feature is a wide white area around the upper lip of the European mink, which is absent on the American mink, though, infrequently, small spots of white also occur on the upper lip of the American mink. Despite this similarity, the European mink is only distantly related to the American mink; its close appearance is the result of convergence to a semi-aquatic life-style. Its closest relatives are the European polecat *Mustela putorius* and Siberian weasel *Mustela sibirica*.

Distribution

Endemic to Europe. Historically widespread in continental Europe, from the Urals to northern Spain and from the Caucasus to central Finland. There are no historical data on the presence of European mink in Portugal, Italy, Belgium, Denmark, Sweden and Norway. Since the middle of the 19th century, the European mink has suffered from a serious decline: first because of habitat loss and later owing to competition with the American mink. To date fragmented remnant populations still exist in northern Spain, western France, Latvia, Estonia, Belarus, central regions of European Russia and the Danube delta in Romania. In 1981–1989 the European mink was introduced onto two islands in the Kuril Islands (Kunashir and Iturup) in the Russian Far East. The introduction has been reported to be unsuccessful.

Geographic variation

Various subspecies have been described since the early 1900s. However, due to the continuous nature of the distribution, the variation in species seems to be of clinal nature and, thus, without any taxonomic value. The most distinctive population was in the Caucasus (probably now extinct).

Habitat

The European mink has specific habitat requirements. Being a semi-aquatic carnivore, it typically inhabits small rapid-current streams or rivers with lush riparian vegetation. It can seldom be found in marshes, lakes or larger rivers. There are no records of the European mink living on the sea coast.

Population status

Since the mid-19th century, the species has suffered from a major decline and has become extinct in most European countries. It is estimated that to date its range has dwindled to less that 20% of the original. The decline of the species continues at an accelerating rate.

International legal & conservation status

Bern Convention, Appendix II.
EU Habitats & Species Directive, Annex II & Annex IV.
IUCN Red List, Endangered.

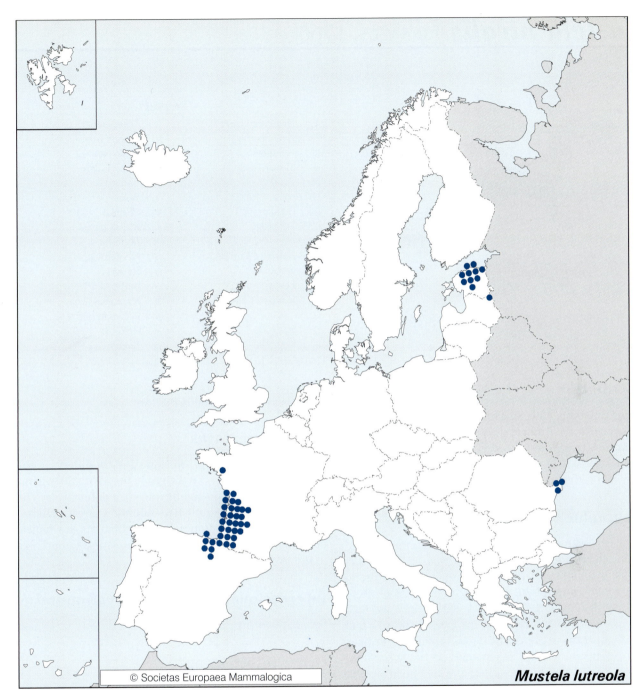

Mustela lutreola

© Societas Europaea Mammalogica

Other information

A European Breeding Programme (EEP) for a self-sustaining captive population of the European mink was initiated by the European Mink Conservation and Breeding Committee (EMCC) in 1992. At the end of 1996, 64 specimens were kept in 10 zoos.

Literature

Heptner *et al.* (1967)
Maran (1992, 1996)
Maran & Henttonen (1995)
Novikov (1939)
Shvarts & Vaisfeld (1993)
Sidorovich *et al.* (1995)
Stubbe (1993d) – review
Youngman (1982)

T. Maran

Mustela nivalis LINNAEUS, 1766

F. Müller

Distribution

World: Holarctic. A broad circumpolar distribution from northern North America via Asia into Europe and northern Africa. Naturalized in New Zealand.
Europe: the whole of mainland Europe, Great Britain, many Mediterranean islands and the Azores.

Geographic variation

There are two (or even three) subspecies in Europe and two in North America. The pygmy weasel, *M. nivalis nivalis,* is found in northern Fennoscandia and Russia, whereas the range of the common or least weasel, *M. n. vulgaris* Erxleben, 1777, covers central and western Europe (south of the range of the pygmy weasel) and the Mediterranean zone. The weasels of the latter area may constitute a third subspecies *M. n. boccamela* Bechstein, 1800. Specimens of the northern pygmy weasel are white in winter coat and smaller than the more southern common weasels, which are brown in winter. Weasels of the Alps and other high mountains are also white in winter.

Habitat

This small carnivore accepts a wide range of habitats from fields and meadows, and river- and lake-shores to different kinds of forests and mountain zones. It can even be found in the desert conditions of southern Russia. It is essential that there is enough food and shelter available. If there is a scarcity of food, these solitary weasels tend to seek a refuge with some prey for survival over the poor period.

Population status

The pygmy weasel is the smallest member of the Carnivora, its maximum weight being about 80 g. Thus it has had little or no significance in the fur trade. The population size is mainly dependent on the abundance of food and shelter. Population fluctuations are typical of this small rodent specialist. They are most remarkable in the northern part of its range.

International legal & conservation status

Bern Convention, Appendix III.

Other information

The pygmy weasel is adapted to produce as many offspring as possible when food is abundant and so has no delayed implantation like some larger mustelids. Thus it can produce two litters during the course of one summer. The first litter is born in April–May and the second in July–August. It can live for long periods inside the snow cover and even produce offspring there, if the local vole or lemming population is abundant.

Literature

King (1989)
Pulliainen (1981)
Reichstein (1993b)

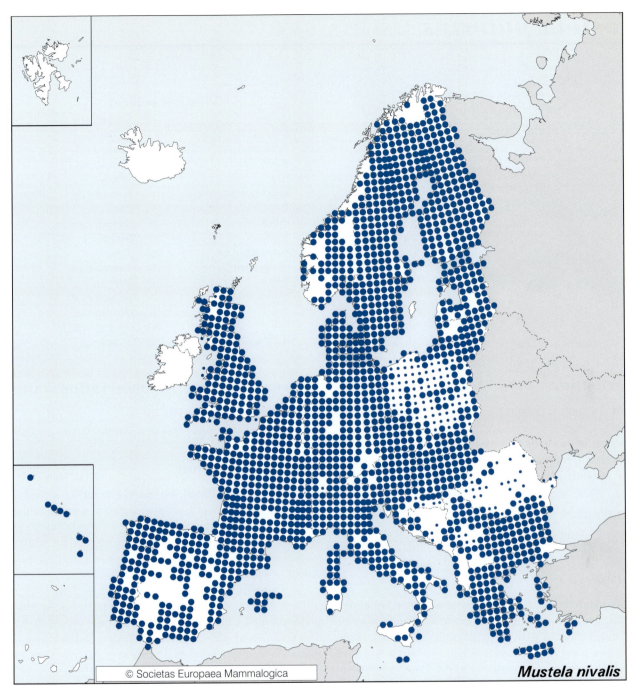

© Societas Europaea Mammalogica

Mustela nivalis

Stubbe & Stubbe (1998)

E. Pulliainen

335

Mustela putorius Linnaeus, 1758

F. Müller

Distribution

World: European endemic; most of Europe west of the Urals.
Europe: widespread, but absent from northern Scandinavia, Ireland, Mediterranean islands and much of the Balkans and eastern Adriatic coast.

Geographic variation

Variability slight and no subspecies currently recognized.

Habitat

Found in all lowland habitats, especially woodlands, sand dunes, forest fringes and river valleys. Wetlands used in association with predation on amphibians. High altitudes avoided. Often associated with human settlements such as farmsteads and village margins in winter. In central Europe frequency was closely connected with density of common hamster *Cricetus cricetus* in former times.

Population status

Evidence of recent range expansion northwards, eastwards and southwards in eastern part of range, perhaps associated with land-use change and milder winters. Currently recovering from near-extinction in Great Britain, and spreading in response to diminished trapping pressure. Recent declines reported in Switzerland, Germany and Denmark. Population density often low (1/1000 ha) and rarely exceeds 5–10/1000 ha in best habitats.

International legal & conservation status

Bern Convention, Appendix III.
EU Habitats & Species Directive, Annex V.

Other information

Formerly widely hunted for sport, fur and as a pest of game and poultry. Now partly protected and only a minor quarry in most countries. Accidental road casualties and secondary rodenticide poisoning are significant causes of mortality. Recognized by some agriculturalists as a useful predator of rabbits, rats and hamsters.

Cross-breeding with feral domesticated form (ferret) *Mustela furo* may produce individuals with generally paler pelage or patches of pale fur on throat and feet. Feral populations of *M. furo* established in many areas, especially on islands (e.g., Mediterranean, northern Britain, Isle of Man (UK), Texel (NL), Azores), where they may resemble *M. putorius* closely. Hybridization with European mink *Mustela lutreola* occasionally reported for Finland, Karelia and Moscow region.

Literature

Blandford (1987)
Jensen & Jensen (1972)
Stubbe (1989c)
Weber (1988)

J. Birks

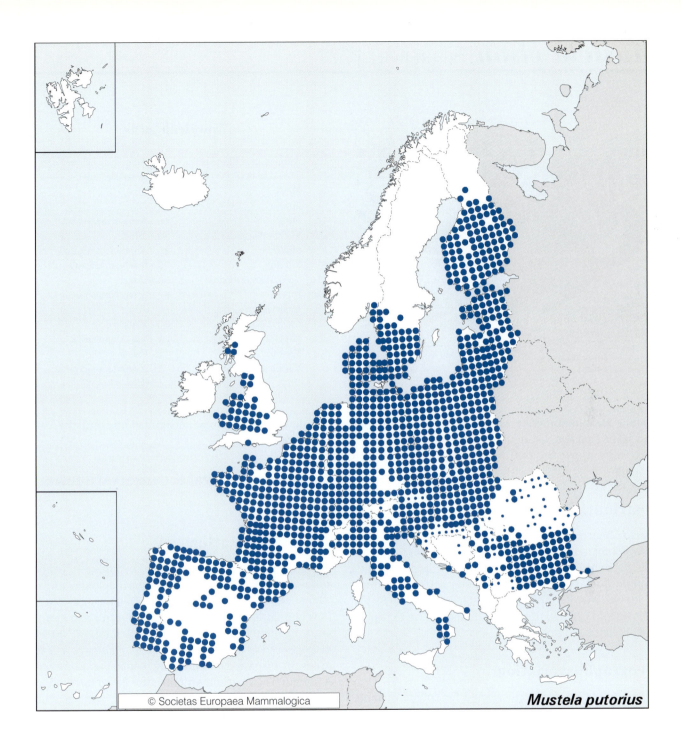

Mustela putorius

Mustela vison SCHREBER, 1777

E. Hazebroek

American mink

AL	-	LT	Kanadinė audinė
BG	Американска норка	LU	Amerikaneschen Nerz
CZ	Norek americký	LV	Amerikas ūdele
DE	Mink	MK	-
DK	Mink	MT	-
EE	Mink	NL	Amerikaanse nerts
ES	Visón americano	NO	Mink
FI	Minkki	PL	Norka amerykańska
FO	Minkur	PT	Visão-americano
FR	Vison d'Amérique	RO	Vizon
GR	Βιζόν	RU	Американская норка
HR	Američka vidrica; Vizon	SE	Mink
HU	Amerikai nyérc	SI	Mink
IR	Minc Mhericánach	SK	Norok americký
IS	Minkur	TR	Vizon
IT	Visone americano	YU	Америчка видрица; Визон

Similar in appearance to European mink *M. lutreola*. Can sometimes be distinguished in the field by the lack of a white upper lip, but this character is not wholly reliable.

Distribution

World: Nearctic; most of north America.
Europe: introduced, mostly by escapes from fur farms. Mink farming was mostly in north-west Europe and mink populations are now spreading south from northern Europe and west from Russia. Also in Iceland, the British Isles and an isolated population in Spain. The European area is increasing rapidly.

Geographic variation

Farmed populations were selected for colour variants. Most wild populations have reverted to wild-type colour, but especially in Germany black mutants (standard mink) are found.

Habitat

Prefers rivers, lakes and coasts, but will cover long distances away from water. A generalist predator whose diet is opportunistic.

Population status

Spreading and colonizing new areas rapidly. The first escapes occurred during the 1920s (Finland), but wild populations did not expand significantly until the 1950s and 1960s.

International legal & conservation status

None.

Other information

Hunted for pelts in Scandinavia. Considered harmful to some native species such as sea-bird colonies and the water vole *Arvicola terrestris*. Believed harmful to water fowl populations, but little evidence for this at a national scale. In many areas the European mink *M. lutreola* disappeared before the arrival of *M. vison*, but in other areas *M. vison* is competitively displacing *M. lutreola*. A potential competitor with the otter *Lutra lutra,* though data from the UK shows that *L. lutra* can recolonize areas already occupied by *M. vison*.

Literature

Corbet (1980)
Linn & Birks (1989)
Marchant *et al.* (1990)
Strachan & Jefferies (1993, 1996)
Stubbe (1993e) – review

EMMA committee

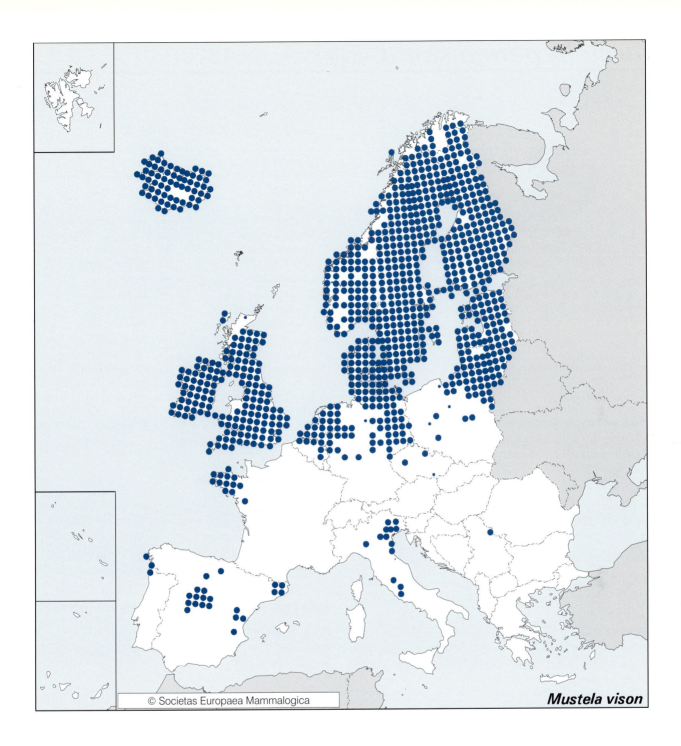

© Societas Europaea Mammalogica

Mustela vison

Vormela peregusna (GÜLDENSTAEDT, 1770)

V. Zadražil

Similar in size to steppe polecat *Mustela eversmanii* but with a distinctive coloration. The colour of the back is bright and mottled, consisting of black, yellow and white areas and spots; ventral part black; a contrasting black and white facial mask. When frightened the animal demonstrates a characteristic behaviour, i.e. it throws its tail over its back and growls.

Distribution

World: Palaearctic, steppes and deserts of south-east Europe, Caucasus, Central Asia, Middle East, northern China and Mongolia.
Europe: south of European Russia (Volga-Don confluence, North Caucasus), south Ukraine, Bulgaria, Romania (Dobrudja), Serbia, Macedonia, Turkish Thrace and north-eastern Greece.

Geographic variation

Taxonomy needs revision. Many forms have been described, but in Europe only the nominate subspecies seems valid. Actual taxonomic structure of the marbled polecat is based on variation of the coloration.

Habitat

Prefers deserts and steppes. Specialized predator, eating mainly desert and steppe rodents (ground squirrels, gerbils). In central Asia very usual trophic relation with *Rhombomys opimus*. Mutual aid between hunting marbled polecat and fox has been described. Critical factor affecting distribution is destruction of natural steppe and desert habitats.

Population status

During the last 100-200 years the northern margin of its range has receded southwards in the Balkans and Ukraine, but at present in European Russia the marbled polecat is recorded at the northern limits of its historic range.

International legal & conservation status

Bern Convention, Appendix II.
IUCN Red List, Vulnerable (European subspecies *V. p. peregusna* only).

Other information

Reproduction is poorly known; marbled polecat has delayed implantation. Juvenile females (before opening the eyes) can be successfully fertilized by adult males (Korneev, pers. comm.). Not hunted for pelts. Predator of rodents, which are vectors of disease. A potential competitor with *Mustela eversmanii*.

Literature

Ben David (1988)
Chotolchu *et al.* (1989)
Heptner *et al.* (1967)
Iljin *et al.* (1996)

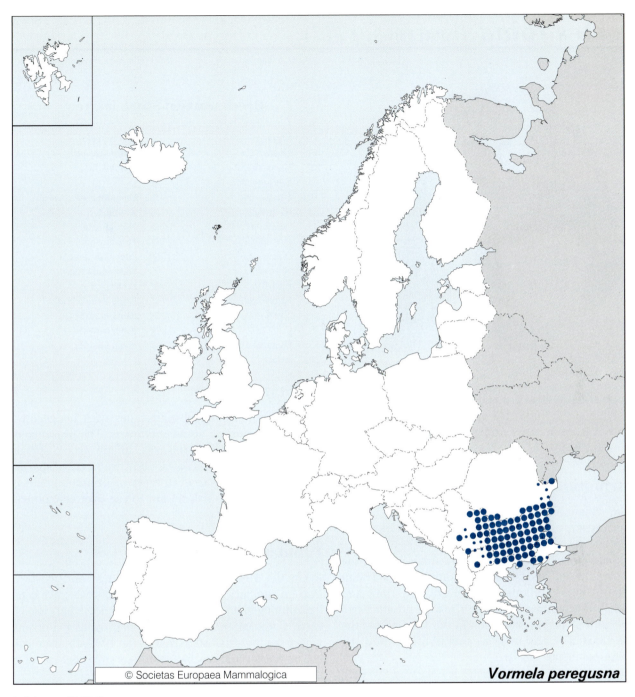

© Societas Europaea Mammalogica

Vormela peregusna

Robinson (1996)
Simak (1997)
Sludsky (1964)

V. V. Rozhnov

Martes foina (ERXLEBEN, 1777)

D. Roth

Beech marten; Stone marten

AL	Kunadhja gushebardhe; Shqarthi	LT	Akmeninė kiaunė
BG	Белка	LU	Steemarder
CZ	Kuna skalní	LV	Akmeņu cauna
DE	Steinmarder	MK	Куна белка
DK	Husmår	MT	-
EE	Kivinugis	NL	Steenmarter; Fluwijn
ES	Garduña	NO	Steinmår
FI	Kivinäätä	PL	Kuna domowa
FO	Márur	PT	Fuinha
FR	Fouine	RO	Jderul-de-piatră
GR	Κουνάβι	RU	Каменная куница
HR	Kuna bjelica	SE	Stenmård
HU	Nyest	SI	Kuna belica
IR	-	SK	Kuna skalná
IS	Hús mörður	TR	Kaya sansarı
IT	Faina	YU	Куна белица

Because of the similar size and great variation in colour and shape of the throat bib of the pine martin *Martes martes* it is sometimes difficult to separate the two species in the field.

Distribution

World: Palaearctic, roughly in the European broad-leaved forest zone and the south Asian steppe zone. The connection goes through the north side of the Caucasus, the Elburz Mountains south of the Caspian Sea and the mountains of Afghanistan to the mountains of Tien Shan and the Altai Mountains in the north and Tibet and probably the mountains of the Chinese provinces of Shensi and Shansi in the south. In the Middle East the beech marten is absent from southern Iran and the Arabian peninsula.
Europe: missing from the British Isles, Norway, Sweden, Finland and northern Russia. The north-eastern border goes roughly from Tallin via Moscow to Rostow. In the Mediterranean, missing from the islands of Mallorca, Corsica, Sardinia, Sicily, some of the smaller Aegean islands and Cyprus.

Geographic variation

Several subspecies are described from the Asian distribution areas as well as from the Balkans and Mediterranean islands. Currently only six subspecies are recognized.

Habitat

Mountains, agricultural landscapes with hedgerows, woodlots, suburban areas and towns. The presence of cavities, such as rock fissures, hollow trees, spaces between hay and straw bales, cavity walls, crawl spaces, cavities under roofs or even burrows or animal dens is essential. Rivers which do not freeze over are natural barriers.

Population status

From the 1960s and 1970s in central and western Europe numbers have increased and habitats have been (re)colonized, including suburban and urban areas. Clearly this phenomenon started in central Europe, where numbers had stabilized by the 1980s. In the north of The Netherlands recolonization is still progressing to the west at about 5 km per year on average.

International legal & conservation status

Bern Convention, Appendix III.

Other information

Beech martens invading suburban habitats sometimes cause inconvenience from the smell of droppings and rotting prey, leaking urine, noise and damage to roofs and insulation materials. A new and spreading phenomenon since the second half of the 1980s is frequent damage to cars caused by biting electrical cables, hoses and insulating materials. This probably

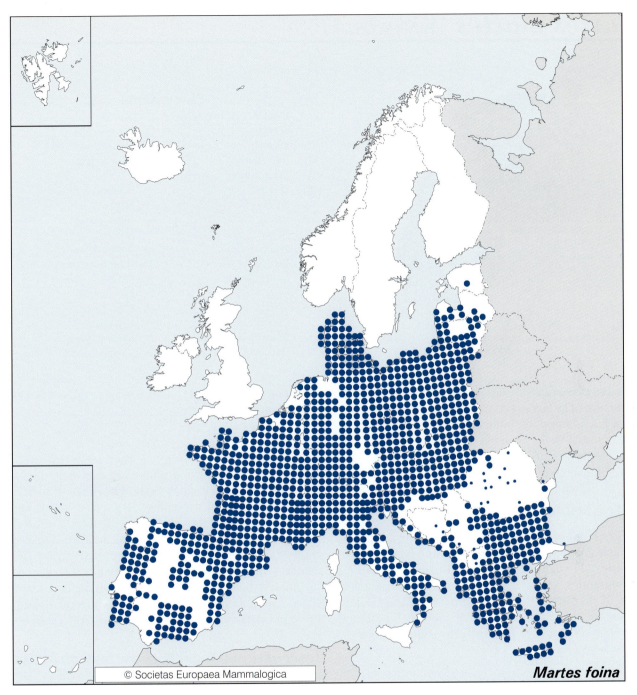

Martes foina

© Societas Europaea Mammalogica

started in northern Switzerland and has spread or jumped to parts of Germany, Austria and Hungary and the south of The Netherlands.

Literature

Corbet (1978)
Douma-Petridou (1984)
Heptner *et al.* (1974)
Kugelschafter *et al.* (1984/85)
Stubbe (1989a)

S. Broekhuizen

Martes martes (LINNAEUS, 1758)

U. Iff

Similar in appearance to the beech marten *Martes foina*. Distinguished by larger ears and smaller patch of cream-yellow fur on throat, the latter being white and extending farther ventrally in *M. foina*. Anatomical differences include concave third premolar (convex in *M. foina)* and smaller baculum in *M. martes*.

Distribution

World: Palaearctic. Europe, westernmost Siberia, Caucasus, Asia Minor, northern Iraq and Iran.
Europe: throughout mainland Europe, including Fennoscandia. Absent from parts of the Low Countries, most of Iberia and Greece. Formerly widespread in Britain, now confined to the north. Patchily distributed in Ireland. Occurs in the Balearic Islands, Corsica, Sardinia and Sicily.

Geographic variation

Animals from eastern part of range said to be smaller. Some poorly differentiated subspecies.

Habitat

Broad-leaved and coniferous forest, and scrub. Avoidance of non-forest habitats, especially by breeding adults. Appears to reach higher densities in forests with incomplete canopy cover, which have more vigorous field and understorey layers; these tend to support higher density of prey for pine martens. Occurs in scrub habitats in western Ireland and the Balearics, that elsewhere would be occupied by *M. foina*. Also in areas with small woodlands.

Population status

Remains widespread and abundant, especially in the more northern and eastern parts of its range. However, trapping, incidental poisoning, forest destruction and fragmentation may have led to a long-term decline in much of Europe, though historical data are lacking. Harvests in Russia now 80% lower than earlier this century. Has declined in The Netherlands. Persecution in the last century resulted in extinction in most of Britain. Population in Scotland currently recovering, those in England and Wales may be virtually extinct.

International legal & conservation status

Bern Convention, Appendix III.
EU Habitats & Species Directive, Annex V.

Other information

Hunted or trapped for fur in some parts of its range. In countries where protected still subject to persecution, often incidental to control of other carnivores.

Literature

Ebersbach & Stubbe (1996)
Grakov (1993)
Langley & Yalden (1977)

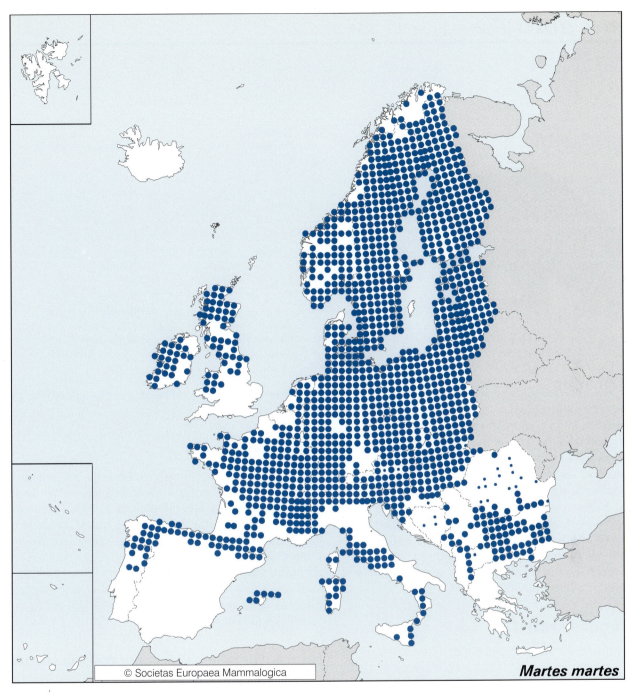

© Societas Europaea Mammalogica

Martes martes

Müskens & Broekhuizen (1986)
Ognev (1931)
Stubbe (1993a) – review

P. W. Bright

Gulo gulo (Linnaeus, 1758)

U. Iff

Distribution

World: Holarctic. Originally a Eurasian species which migrated from Asia across the Bering Strait into North America during the mid-Pleistocene era. Still occurs in northern boreal forests and tundra throughout this zone and even on the massive high mountain ranges to the south of it. In Eurasia regarded as a representative of Arctic-Siberian faunatype.

Europe: historical distribution covered the northern half of Europe to present Germany and Poland in the south. Nowadays occurs only in the mountainous parts of Norway, Sweden and Finland, easternmost Finland and the northernmost regions of Russia.

Geographic variation

The wolverine of the North American continent regarded even as separate species, *Gulo luscus* Linnaeus 1758, or as its own subspecies *Gulo gulo luscus,* differing from the nominate subspecies of the Eurasian continent. Owing to the great mobility of the species, subspecies formation otherwise possible only in isolation on large islands, such as *Gulo gulo vancouverensis* Goldman, 1935 on Vancouver Island, North America.

Habitat

Boreal coniferous, deciduous and mixed forests as well as different kinds of bogs, on mountain ranges from the sea coast through taiga forests to subalpine and alpine regions; on tundra of continents and High Arctic islands. As a poor hunter it is largely dependent on the prey caught by other large predators and the availability of other carrion.

Population status

Populations have generally decreased for various reasons (malnutrition, fur trade, killing as a pest animal and unintentional killing by poisons laid out for foxes and other fur-bearers). However, on the Scandinavian mountain range the population has increased due to protection measures and this increase has resulted in recolonization of former ranges in Finnish Fjeld-Lapland. The population has also increased in eastern Finland (Kainuu and Northern Karelia) owing to protection measures.

International legal & conservation status

Bern Convention, Appendix II.
EU Habitats & Species Directive, Annex II* & Annex IV.
IUCN Red List, Vulnerable.

Other information

Reintroduction is possible only by capture and release, since the species seldom breeds in captivity. In the 1990s wolverines have been caught in Enontekiö, Finnish Fjeld-Lapland, and released in west-central parts of the country. So far, introduced individuals have survived in these new areas.

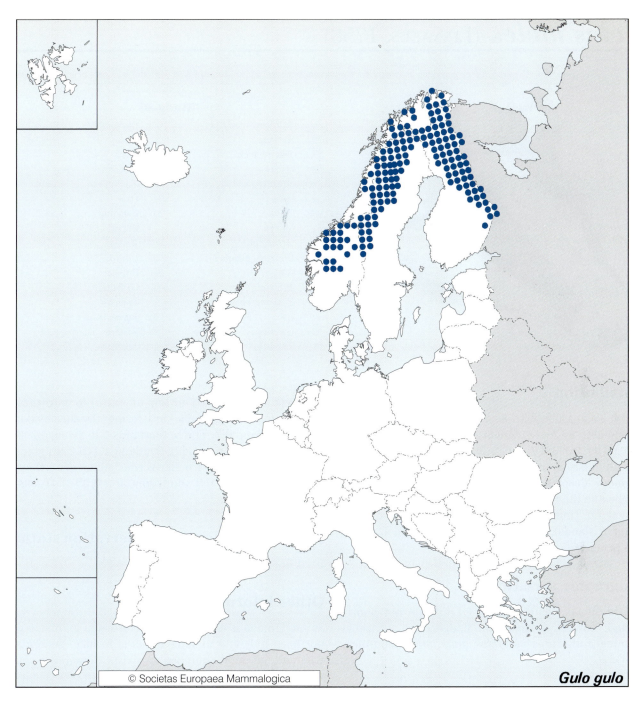

© Societas Europaea Mammalogica

Gulo gulo

Literature

Heptner & Naumov (1974)
Kurtén (1968)
Pulliainen (1988, 1993b) – review

E. Pulliainen

Meles meles (Linnaeus, 1758)

V. Zadražil

Badger			
AL	Baldosa; Vjedulla	LT	Barsukas
BG	Язовец	LU	Duess
CZ	Jezevec lesní	LV	Āpsis
DE	Dachs	MK	Јазовец
DK	Grævling	MT	-
EE	Mäger	NL	Das
ES	Tejón	NO	Grevling
FI	Mäyrä	PL	Borsuk
FO	Grevlingur	PT	Texugo
FR	Blaireau européen	RO	Bursuc
GR	Ασβός	RU	Барсук
HR	Jazavac	SE	Grävling
HU	Eurázsiai borz	SI	Jazbec
IR	Broc	SK	Jazvec lesný
IS	Greifingi	TR	Porsuk
IT	Tasso	YU	Јазавац

Distribution

World: Palaearctic with a part of the Oriental region (south-eastern China); absent from North Africa. West to east from Ireland to Japan, North to south from arctic Finland to Israel, Iran, Afghanistan, Tibet and China.
Europe: widespread and common throughout mainland Europe and the British Isles. On Mediterranean islands present on Tinos and probably Siphnos and Andros (Aegean islands), Crete and Rhodes; not on Balearic archipelago.

Geographic variation

Several subspecies described for Europe but poorly defined. Nowadays the Asiatic badgers are separated by some authorities as *Meles anakuma* (Temminck, 1884).

Habitat

Deciduous and mixed woods, coniferous woods, hedges, scrub, riverine habitat, prevailing agricultural land, suburban areas and urban parks. In alpine or mountainous areas the species occasionally occurs at 1600–1700 m. Set systems are complex and generally covered by fairly thick vegetation; their distribution varies in relation to soils and landscape.

Population status

Population is probably stable over much of the range. A decrease in numbers has occurred on agricultural land because of the destruction of suitable habitats. Population density (adults/km²): former Czechoslovakia 0.1–0.6; Poland 0.7; The Netherlands 1.0; Sweden 2.4–3.2; East Germany 2.0–4.0; Scotland 1.1–6.2; England 4.7–19.7; France 0.5–1.6. In riverine habitat of northern Italy the density is 0.9 adults/km² and 0.05–0.47 sets/km².

International legal & conservation status

Bern Convention, Appendix III.

Other information

Some damage is caused to cereal crops (e.g., maize in northern Italy and in some areas of France) generally when a high population density exists. Sometimes sets with connecting tunnels in open fields can be a hazard for tractors or heavy machinery; in addition, sets located on the banks of irrigated canals can compromise their stability.

The badger is a vector of bovine tuberculosis, but the incidence of this disease has become very low today (e.g., 0.02% in Britain). It is an indirect target in campaigns to control rabies by killing foxes. In some European countries road traffic is an important mortality factor.

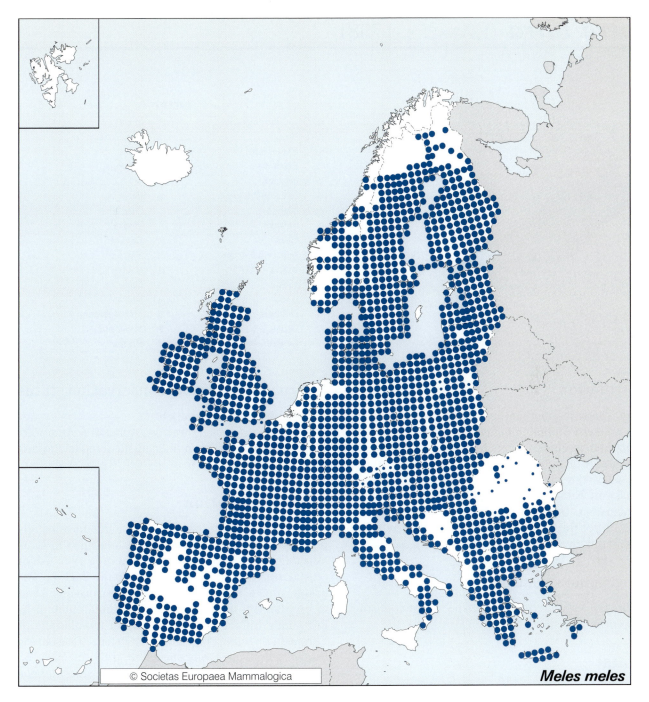

© Societas Europaea Mammalogica

Meles meles

Literature

Henry *et al.* (1988)
Long & Killingley (1983)
Lüps & Wandeler (1993) – review
Masseti (1995)
Stubbe *et al.* (1998)

C. Prigioni

Lutra lutra (Linnaeus, 1758)

U. Iff

Otter

AL	Lunderza; Lutra	LT	Ūdra
BG	Видра	LU	Fëschotter
CZ	Vydra říční	LV	Ūdrs
DE	Fischotter	MK	Видра
DK	Odder	MT	-
EE	Saarmas; Udras	NL	Otter
ES	Nutria	NO	Oter
FI	Saukko	PL	Wydra
FO	Otur	PT	Lontra
FR	Loutre d'Europe	RO	Vidră
GR	Βίδρα	RU	Выдра
HR	Vidra	SE	Utter
HU	Közönséges vidra	SI	Vidra
IR	Dobharcú	SK	Vydra riečna
IS	Otur	TR	Su samuru
IT	Lontra	YU	Видра

Distribution

World: Palaearctic but reaching into the Oriental region. From western Europe to Indonesia; North Africa.
Europe: Formerly widespread throughout Europe, but has declined in central and northern Europe. Absent from all Mediterranean islands except Corfu, Lesbos, Chios and Euboea (Greece). Probably extinct in Liechtenstein, The Netherlands and Switzerland. Many reintroduction or restocking projects including Switzerland, Sweden, Great Britain and Spain.

Geographic variation

Ten subspecies are recognized, but not well investigated. Differences very small.

Habitat

Rivers, streams, lakes, wetlands and coasts. Water quality and productivity are important. The importance of bankside vegetation for cover may depend on the strength of the population.

Population status

Population crash in most of Europe in the 1960s and 1970s, probably because of toxic chemicals exacerbated by hunting and habitat loss. Good populations remain in Portugal, Ireland, Greece, Scotland and the northern Russian Taiga. Now some natural recovery in Finland and Great Britain. Population estimates: Finland 1000, western France 250–400, Italy 130, Germany 500–1000.

International legal & conservation status

Bern Convention, Appendix II.
EU Habitats & Species Directive, Annex II & Annex IV.
CITES, Appendix I (Reservation by Russian Federation).
EC 338/97, Annex A.

Other information

Formerly hunted for fur or sport, but now widely protected. Regarded as a pest by fish farmers in some areas. Road accidents and incidental capture in fish or crustacean traps are important mortality factors. The acidification of rivers and lakes and the consequent loss of productivity may be important. Contamination by PCBs may influence the recovery of populations. A European Breeding Programme (EEP) for self-sustaining captive populations was started in 1985. In 1993, 55 out of 60 otter-keepers were included in the studbook and had agreed to co-operate in the EEP. The total captive population is about 200 individuals. Monitoring programmes have been established.

Literature

Foster-Turley *et al.* (1990)
Mason & Macdonald (1986)
Masseti (1995)
Strachan *et al.* (1990)
Stubbe (1989d, 1993b)
Vogt (1994)

C. Prigioni

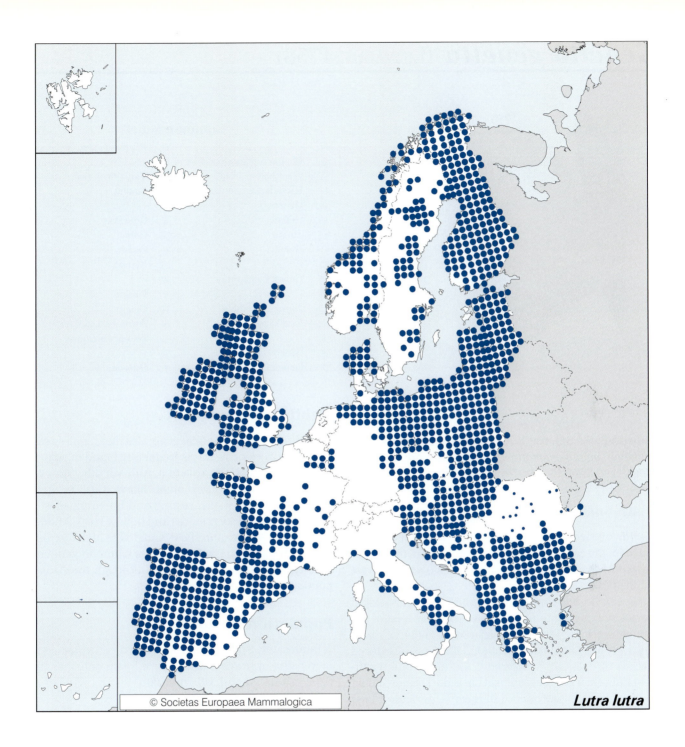

© Societas Europaea Mammalogica

Lutra lutra

Genetta genetta (Linnaeus, 1758)

D. Roth

Common genet

AL	-	LT	Paprastoji geneta
BG	Малка петниста генета	LU	-
CZ	Ženetka tečkovaná	LV	Vidusjūras vivera
DE	Kleinflecken-Ginsterkatze	MK	Генета
DK	Genette	MT	-
EE	Genett	NL	Genetkat
ES	Jineta	NO	Genett
FI	Genetti	PL	Żeneta
FO	-	PT	Geneta
FR	Genette commune	RO	-
GR	-	RU	Генета
HR	Europska cibetka	SE	Genett
HU	Ëszaki petymeg	SI	Severnoafriška ženeta
IR	-	SK	Ženeta obyčajaná
IS	Gínköttur	TR	-
IT	Genetta	YU	Цибетка

The specific status of common genets in Africa, south and east of the Sahara, is not clear. Some authors have included them in *Genetta genetta,* but here we have considered them as *Genetta felina.*

Distribution

World: according to the restricted point of view of Schlawe, the range of *Genetta genetta* covers the north-west of Africa (Morocco, Algeria, Tunisia) and the west of Europe.

Europe: all continental Portugal and Spain and most of France (mainly south of the Loire river and west of the Rhone river). Mediterranean islands of Mallorca, Ibiza and Cabrera (Balearic islands). There are scattered records in Belgium, Switzerland, Germany and north-west Italy. On a zoogeographical basis the species should be considered as introduced in Europe, perhaps a long time ago.

Geographic variation

Four subspecies are commonly recognized in Europe: *G. genetta genetta* (continental Portugal and Spain), *G. g. rhodanica* Matschie, 1902 (France), *G. g. balearica* Thomas, 1902 (Mallorca and Cabrera islands) and *G. g. isabelae* Delibes, 1977 (Ibiza island), but only the last one, very small, can be clearly differentiated from the nominate subspecies.

Habitat

Genetta genetta is a habitat generalist, but requires some vegetal or rocky cover. It is frequently found in riparian habitats, but it is also able to occupy very dry zones. In central Spain it is rarely found above 1200 m and in France 800 m. Usually, resting and breeding sites are established in rocky crevices and hollow trees. Middens (latrines or defaecation sites), situated at high dominant points, are very characteristic. The common genet eats mainly small rodents and birds, although the Balearic populations capture many reptiles.

Population status

A moderately abundant carnivore, whose numbers are increasing in France. In southern Spain densities have been estimated at 0.3-0.7 ind./km².

International legal & conservation status

Bern Convention, Appendix III.
EU Habitats & Species Directive, Annex V.
IUCN Red List, Vulnerable (*G. g. isabelae* only).

Other information

In the past, *Genetta genetta* was frequently trapped because of its fur. It may be killed by other species of carnivores, including lynx, foxes and dogs.

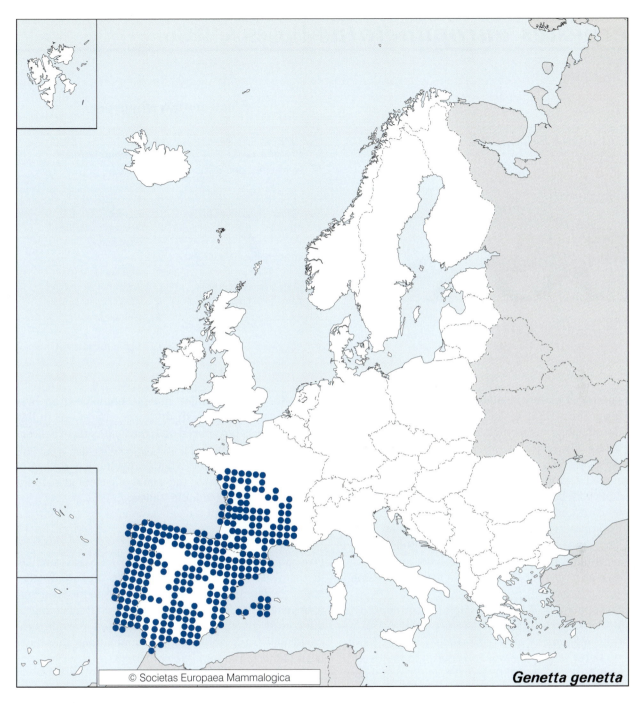

© Societas Europaea Mammalogica

Genetta genetta

Literature

Krapp & Delibes (1993) – review
Livet & Roeder (1987)
Palomares & Delibes (1994)
Palomares *et al.* (1996)
Schauenberg (1966)
Schlawe (1980)
Virgós & Casanovas (1997)

M. Delibes

353

Herpestes auropunctatus Hodgson, 1836

D. Ovenden

This species is closely related to *Herpestes javanicus* (Geoffroy Saint-Hilaire, 1818) from Java, and also considered to be conspecific with it by some authors; in such a case, *javanicus* has priority over *auropunctatus*. Differences involve size, with *H. javanicus* being much larger. Delimitation between the two is obscured in Indochina with large sized mongooses present. Although the sympatric occurrence of *H. auropunctatus* and *H. javanicus* was reported for Malaya, this might result from ignorance of sexual dimorphism in the study on size variability. In this account we have adopted the opinion which restricts *H. javanicus* merely to the island of Java.

The population of *H. auropunctatus* introduced to Europe was in the past incorrectly referred to as *Herpestes ichneumon* or *H. edwardsii* (Geoffroy Saint-Hilaire, 1818). The latter was introduced to Italy, south of Rome, in the early 1950s but the single population evidently become extinct; the last observations are from 1984.

Distribution

World: native to Oriental and marginally to Palaearctic Asia, where it ranges from Iraq and Afghanistan across India and Burma to Indochina. Introduced to many tropical islands (Caribbean, Fiji, Hawaiian, etc.), to Japan, Central and South America, Africa (Tanzania), and Europe.
Europe: the only European population dates to 1910 when specimens purchased in India were introduced to Dalmatia. They were released on the islands of Brač,

Hvar, Korčula, and Mljet, but the population on Brač soon became extinct. In addition, the small Indian mongoose was introduced onto the Peninsula of Pelješac (also Dalmatia), where it is still numerous, and to a single locality in Herzegovina, where it evidently survived as well. An introduction to the island of Golem grad in the Lake of Prespa, Macedonia, failed.

Geographic variation

Five subspecies are currently recognized. Size is smallest in the west and largest in Vietnam and peninsular Malaysia. Populations from arid regions in the west tend to be palest, while those from Assam and Burma appear dark and greyish. Since introduced populations developed from small founder populations they have been subjected to multiple bottlenecks.

Habitat

As a diurnal small carnivore, it seeks shelter in dense cover. In Europe, Mediterranean shrub habitats are preferred.

Population status

Population densities in the Caribbean can be as high as 10/ha. No estimates available from Europe, but the small Indian mongoose is common in Dalmatia.

© Societas Europaea Mammalogica

Herpestes auropunctatus

Other information

Introduced to the island of Mljet in order to exterminate horned vipers *Vipera ammodytes,* which was successful. On the islands the small Indian mongoose is a pest to vegetables, figs, grapes, poultry, and wild fowl. Hunters endeavour, rather unsuccessfully, to exterminate it. Around 1926, mongooses from Mljet Is. were exported to Venezuela. It is thus possible that some South American introductions descend from the Dalmatian population.

Literature

Carpaneto (1990)
Corbet & Hill (1992)
Krapp (1993) – review
Kryštufek & Tvrtković (1992)
Nellis (1989) – review
Tvrtković & Kryštufek (1990)

B. Kryštufek

Herpestes ichneumon (Linnaeus, 1758)

D. Roth

Distribution

World: *Herpestes ichneumon* has mainly an African distribution, being present from the coast of the Mediterranean Sea to the Cape Region in South Africa, but avoiding the extreme deserts and the humid forests. It is also present in the Near East, from Sinai to the south of Turkey, and the Iberian peninsula.

Europe: southern Portugal and south-west Spain. At the beginning of the century it was also present in north-west Iberian Peninsula. On a zoogeographical basis the species should be considered as introduced in Europe, perhaps a long time ago.

Geographic variation

The subspecies *Herpestes ichneumon widdringtonii* Gray, 1842 is the only one present in Europe. It is somewhat bigger and with stronger teeth than the African subspecies.

Habitat

The species occupies Mediterranean maquis, with a clear preference for humid and riparian habitats. It avoids open areas and uses dense thickets and rabbit *Oryctolagus cuniculus* warrens for breeding and resting. In Malaga province *Herpestes ichneumon* has been reported at about 1000 m. In southern Spain, adult mongooses use home ranges of about 3 km² and are diurnal. They are omnivorous, but very young rabbits, taken by digging nests, are an important food.

Population status

The status of the population is unknown, but numbers and probably range have increased in the last 20 years, in Portugal as well as in Spain. In both countries abundance increases from north to south. In some areas of southern Spain densities reach 1.2 ind./km². At present, *Herpestes ichneumon* is considered a pest by hunters, because of its presumed impact on small game species.

International legal & conservation status

Bern Convention, Appendix III.
EU Habitats & Species Directive, Annex V.

Other information

Probably the mongoose range in south-western Europe has undergone fluctuations related to major land-use changes: increased cereal production would reduce the suitable habitat, while set-aside and abandonment of agricultural areas would increase it. Also, the reduction of large predators such as Iberian lynx *Lynx pardinus* and some birds of prey could account for the recent expansion of the mongoose.

© Societas Europaea Mammalogica

Herpestes ichneumon

Literature

Borralho *et al.* (1996)
Delibes (1982)
Delibes & Palomares (1993)
Palomares & Delibes (1993a,b)
Palomares *et al.* (1996)

M. Delibes

Felis silvestris SCHREBER, 1775

F. Müller

Wildcat

AL	Macja e eger	LT	Laukinė katė; Vilpišys
BG	Дива котка	LU	Wёll Kaz
CZ	Kočka divoká	LV	Meža kaķis
DE	Wildkatze	MK	Дива мачка
DK	Vildkat	MT	Qattus Salvaġġ
EE	Metskass	NL	Wilde kat
ES	Gato montés	NO	Villkatt
FI	Metsäkissa	PL	Żbik
FO	Villkattur	PT	Gato-bravo; Gato-cabeçanas
FR	Chat sauvage	RO	Pisică sălbatică
GR	Αγριόγατα	RU	Дикая кошка
HR	Divlja mačka	SE	Vildkatt
HU	Vadmacska	SI	Divja mačka
IR	-	SK	Mačka lesná
IS	Evrópski villiköttur	TR	Yaban kedisi
IT	Gatto selvatico	YU	Дивља мачка

Some earlier authors followed a two-species concept for the European members of *Felis silvestris*, separating some Mediterranean island populations as *Felis libyca*. There is some influence of crossbreeding with domestic cats *Felis catus,* with hybrids sometimes being mistaken for wildcats. Some research problems still exist for the nature of so-called wildcats of Mediterranean islands, where an anthropogenic origin must be assumed.

Distribution

World: Europe south of 52°N and Scotland; throughout Africa, as well as in south-west, south and central Asia (mainly *F. silvestris ornata* Gray, 1830 group) east to western China and Mongolia.
Europe: formerly only absent in Fennoscandia and in the north-east. A massive decline resulted in relict scattered populations. Regional recolonization has started in recent decades and reintroduction programmes have also extended the distribution. The picture is masked by feral cats and by hybridization.

Geographic variation

Members of the *F. silvestris silvestris* group and the (mainly African) *F. s. libyca* Forster, 1780 group live in Europe. The latter is found in Sardinia. South Iberian *silvestris* group cats show some characteristics of their own (*F. s. tartessia* Miller, 1907). The population of Scotland (*F. s. grampia* Miller, 1907) also differs from the mainland ones.

Habitat

The wildcat prefers deciduous forests with dominant oak, followed by beech and mixed forests. The existence of clearings seems to be as important as is the availability of dense shrubby, vegetation and rock crevices, providing the cat with shelter and well-stocked hunting ground. The wildcat is an opportunistic feeder, mainly depending on rodent and lagomorph prey.

Population status

Progressive habitat destruction and hunting pressure resulted in population fragmentation and decline, with a nadir in the first half of the 20th century. Some recovery has been observed in recent decades. Healthy populations are found in France, Germany, the Carpathians, parts of the Iberian peninsula and Italy.

International legal & conservation status

Bern Convention, Appendix II.
EU Habitats & Species Directive, Annex IV.
CITES, Appendix II. EC 338/97, Annex A.
IUCN Red List, Vulnerable (*F. s. grampia* only).

Other information

Snow cover seems to be the most critical factor affecting distribution. A snow layer of more than 20 cm impairs locomotion. Lynx reintroduction programmes may negatively affect wildcat population density, but this is

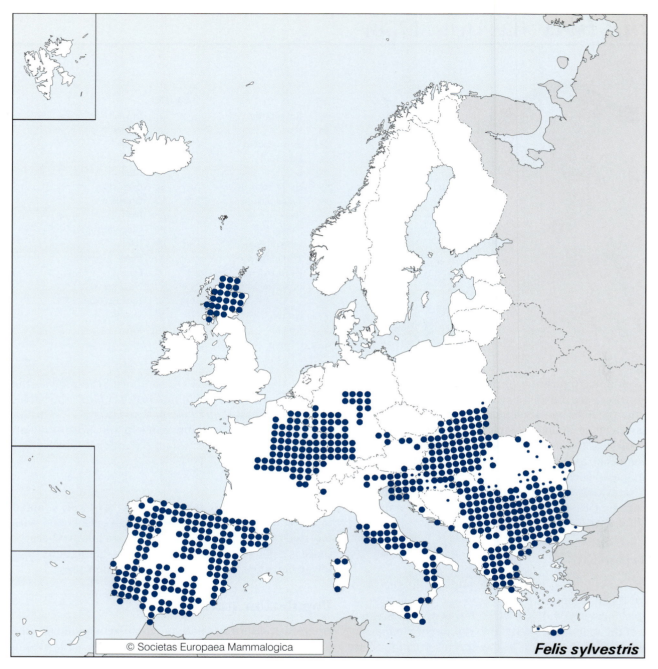

© Societas Europaea Mammalogica

Felis sylvestris

not proved. Control of feral domestic cats is a special problem in wildcat conservation.

Literature

Hemmer (1993a) – review
Piechocki (1990)

H. Hemmer

Lynx lynx (LINNAEUS, 1758)

F. Müller

Lynx

AL	Rreqebulli		LT	Lūšis
BG	Рис		LU	Luuss
CZ	Rys ostrovid		LV	Lūsis
DE	Luchs		MK	Рис
DK	Los		MT	Linċi
EE	Ilves; Tava-ilves		NL	Lynx; Los
ES	Lince europeo		NO	Gaupe
FI	Ilves		PL	Ryś
FO	Geypa		PT	Lince-europeu
FR	Lynx boréal		RO	Râs
GR	Ρῆσος Λύγκας		RU	Рысь
HR	Europski ris		SE	Lo
HU	Közönséges hiúz		SI	Navadni ris
IR	-		SK	Rys ostrovid
IS	Gaupa		TR	Vaşak
IT	Lince		YU	Рис

The evolutionary position of the lynxes is still open to debate. There are reasonable arguments to classify them near the true *Felis* species, but a closer relationship with the pantherines is also possible. Therefore lynxes may be ranked taxonomically as a subgenus *Lynx* within the genus *Felis* or as their own genus *Lynx*. Formerly there was a one-species concept for all lynxes in Europe, but at present authors agree that there are actually two different species: the (northern) lynx *Lynx lynx* and the Iberian or Pardel lynx *Lynx pardinus*.

Distribution

World: from Europe to Siberia and south-west and central Asian mountain regions.
Europe: formerly widely distributed over the forested areas of the mainland, with the exception of the Iberian peninsula. The extinction of the species during recent centuries left populations throughout Scandinavia, in north-eastern Europe, in the Carpathian mountains and in the Balkans. Some lynxes may also have survived in the Pyrénées. New populations have been founded by reintroduction in the Vosges and Jura mountains, in the Alps and in Slovenia and Croatia, using Carpathian lynxes.

Geographic variation

Three population lines are recognizable: the now-extinct lynxes of the western Alps (not to be confused with the modern introduced population), possibly surviving in the Pyrénées (*Lynx lynx spelaens* or even *Lynx spelaens*

(Boule, 1906)), the lynxes of southern Scandinavia, the Carpathians and the Balkans *(Lynx lynx lynx)*; the lynxes of the north-east (*Lynx lynx melinus* (Kerr, 1792)), and a *lynx-melinus* transition zone in the Scandinavian north.

Habitat

The long-legged and large-footed lynx is well adapted to snow cover. In Europe it is clearly associated with forested regions. Dense populations are found wherever there is a good availability of roe deer. Populations have lower densities where hares are the main prey.

Population status

Hunting pressure and habitat destruction resulted in the extinction of the species in all regions with strong anthropogenic landscape conversion. The remaining populations are judged to be mainly stable. Reintroduction programmes produced the problem of acceptance by local human populations.

International legal & conservation status

Bern Convention, Appendix III.
EU Habitats & Species Directive, Annex II & Annex IV (excluding Finnish population).
CITES, Appendix II. EC 338/97, Annex A.

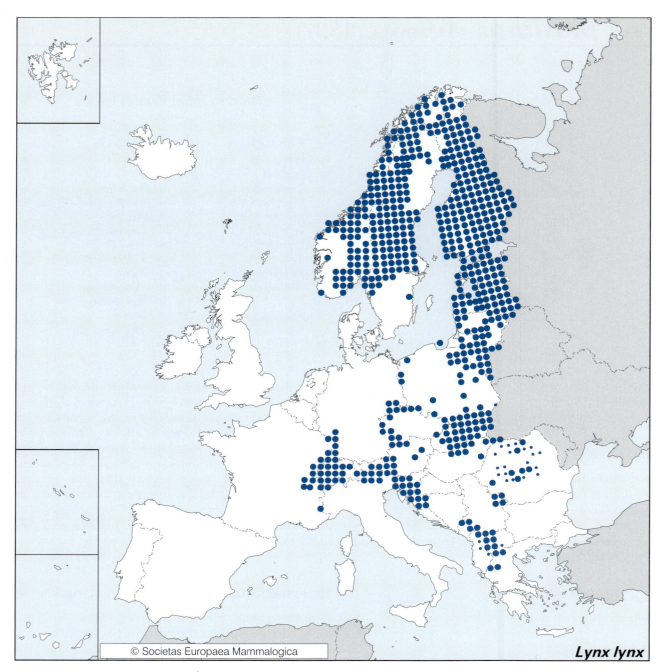

© Societas Europaea Mammalogica

Lynx lynx

Other information

Commercial trapping for furs obviously did not significantly affect the stability of populations in Russia over the last seven decades. Livestock, especially sheep, killing is a factor that must be taken seriously in reintroduction programmes. Wolf and lynx are competing species and wolf conservation impairs lynx density.

Literature

Hemmer (1993b) – review

H. Hemmer

Lynx pardinus (Temminck, 1827)

V. Zadrazil

Iberian lynx; Pardel lynx

AL	-	LT	-
BG	-	LU	-
CZ	Rys pardálový	LV	Ibērijas lūsis
DE	Pardelluchs	MK	-
DK	Pardellos	MT	-
EE	Pürenee ilves	NL	Pardellynx
ES	Lince ibérico	NO	Pantergaupe
FI	Pantteri-ilves	PL	Ryś iberyjski
FO	-	PT	Lince-ibérico; Liberne
FR	Lynx pardelle	RO	-
GR	-	RU	Пиренейская рысь
HR	Iberski ris	SE	Panterlo
HU	Párduchiúz	SI	Iberijski ris
IR	-	SK	Rys škvnitý
IS	Spánargaupa	TR	-
IT	Lince pardina	YU	Иберијски рис

This species has frequently been considered as a subspecies of the Eurasian lynx *Lynx lynx,* but it seems well established that the two are different species.

Distribution

Endemic to Europe. *Lynx pardinus* is found exclusively on the Iberian Peninsula, mainly in southern Spain and Portugal. There are recent dubious records from the northern half of both countries. During the 19th century it was present throughout the Iberian Peninsula. During the Pleistocene it also occupied central Europe.

Geographic variation

No living subspecies have been recognized.

Habitat

The species is very dependent on Mediterranean woodland and maquis thicket, where it finds dense scrub for shelter and abundant rabbits *Oryctolagus cuniculus* for food. Adult individuals are intrasexually territorial all the year round and seasonal changes of habitat and food are very small. The Iberian lynx avoids croplands and tree plantations and as a consequence the suitable habitat is very fragmented.

Population status

During the 1980s, the total world population was estimated at less than 1200 individuals, including subadults but not kittens. There are probably nine distinct subpopulations in Spain, occupying a range of about 11000 km², and three in Portugal, occupying 700 km². These subpopulations are spatially structured as metapopulations and seem to be genetically isolated. Only one of them, in the eastern Sierra Morena and Montes de Toledo, includes more than one hundred individuals. Population numbers have probably decreased strongly in the 1990s as a consequence of an acute reduction of rabbit numbers because of a viral haemorragic disease. The species has been considered by IUCN as the most vulnerable of all the Felidae.

International legal & conservation status

Bern Convention, Appendix II.
EU Habitats & Species Directive, Annex II* & Annex IV.
CITES, Appendix I. EC 338/97, Annex A.
IUCN Red List, Endangered.

Other information

In the past, habitat destruction and direct persecution were the main threats to the species. At present, the decline of lynx numbers is mainly due to habitat loss (and fragmentation) and the decline of its main prey species, the rabbit, owing to myxomatosis, viral haemorragic disease and changes in the landscape. Lynx mortality by human-related causes is also high, although most of the deaths are unintentional (road casualties, captures in traps for foxes and rabbits, etc). Small population size is also a threat: 90% of populations in

© Societas Europaea Mammalogica

Lynx pardinus

areas less than 1000 km² have disappeared since 1960.
Theoretical risks of inbreeding depression and genetic
drift exist.

Literature

Beltrán *et al.* (1996)
Castro & Palma (1996)
Delibes (1980)
Ferreras *et al.* (1992)
Nowell & Jackson (1996)
Rodríguez & Delibes (1990)

M. Delibes

Odobenus rosmarus (Linnaeus, 1758)

E. Hazebroek

Distribution

World: Arctic Atlantic, west to Foxe Basin in Canada and east to the Kara Sea; Arctic Pacific, north to Chukchi Sea; Laptev Sea. The Atlantic walrus is found in two distinct areas, the western and eastern Arctic Atlantic. The latter is mainly European and stretches from eastern Greenland to the Kara Sea.
Europe: Svalbard, Franz Josef Land, Novaya Zemlya and along the Norwegian coast (between 63° and 81°N, seldom south of 70°. Vagrants are occasionally observed on the Atlantic coasts south to the Gulf of Biscay. Prehistoric remains indicate that the species was more widely distributed than at present.

Geographic variation

Two subspecies are commonly recognized: the Atlantic walrus *O. rosmarus rosmarus,* and the Pacific walrus *O. rosmarus divergens* (Illiger, 1815). Anatomical and genetic differences between the two subspecies have been described. A third subspecies, the Laptev walrus *O. rosmarus laptevi* (Chapski, 1940), is not generally accepted.

Habitat

The walrus inhabits Arctic areas with moving pack ice, over shallow water not deeper than 80 m, along continental shelves. It forages in pebble seabeds in search for mainly molluscs and other invertebrates.

Population status

Walrus populations have declined severely owing to over-hunting in the past. The Atlantic subspecies was at the edge of extinction and the Pacific subspecies strongly reduced. In the early 1950s hunting was banned but populations started to recover only after 1970. At present, the east Atlantic population numbers several thousand animals. The Pacific population is estimated to number 230000 animals.

International legal & conservation status

Bern Convention, Appendix II.
IUCN Red List, Data Deficient (*O. r. laptevi,* Laptev walrus, only)

Other information

May be subject to some illegal persecution mainly in Russia. Some hunting licences are still issued in Greenland. When the animals haul out on land or pack ice, extreme gregariousness can be observed.

Literature

Born (1992)
Reijnders *et al.* (1993)
Reijnders *et al.* (1997)

E. H. Ries, S. M.J.M. Brasseur & P. J.H.Reijnders

© Societas Europaea Mammalogica

Odobenus rosmarus

Phoca groenlandica Erxleben, 1777

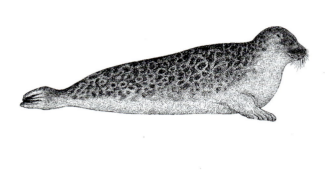

V. Ree

Distribution

World: Three populations of harp seals, with distinct whelping areas, are found in the open Arctic Atlantic. These are the Barents and White Sea (East Ice) population, the Greenland Sea population (West Ice) and the Newfoundland population.

Europe: the range stretches from Iceland, Northern Norway to Svalbard and Arctic Russia, including Novaja Zemlya and Franz Josef Land. Stragglers occasionally occur on the Atlantic coast, south to Brittany. Harp seals are gregarious and follow the ice edge. During the Quaternary glacial periods the species probably occurred farther south. A post-glacial population inhabited the Baltic Sea about 3000 years ago.

Geographic variation

None known.

Habitat

Inhabits the drifting pack ice, migrating south in autumn and north during the summer according to the advancing and retreating ice. Forages opportunistically on a variety of fish and invertebrates. There are two main breeding grounds, in the White Sea and in the Greenland Sea, north of Jan Mayen. The seals concentrate in large rookeries during the breeding season and are widely dispersed thereafter.

Population status

Estimates of harp seal population size and status are inaccurate but several million individuals (2.7–3.5 million) are believed to inhabit the north-eastern Atlantic. Between 1978 and 1984 numerous herds of harp seals invaded the northern coast of Norway every winter and spring. The invasions coincided with periods of very low temperature and extensive ice cover, which resulted in a general westerly migration of animals from the Barents Sea. During 1988 approximately 80000 harp seals drowned along the entire Norwegian coast and this invasion was probably related to a major decline in capelin and cod stocks in the Barents Sea during the preceding years.

International legal & conservation status

Bern Convention, Appendix III.
EU-Directive 83/ 129/EEC, import ban on whitecoat skins. (harp seal pups)
EU Habitats & Species Directive, Annex V.

Other information

Harp seals have been intensively hunted at various times since the end of the 18th century, resulting in marked population declines. Commercial exploitation is mainly concentrated on the white coated pups. The present number of harp seals taken is set by a quota. The general condition of the seal herds seemed to have improved lately and the population increased substantially.

© Societas Europaea Mammalogica

Phoca groenlandica

However, the recent over-fishing of food resources by
man represents a serious danger.

Literature

Kapel (1992b)
Reijnders *et al.* (1993)
Reijnders *et al.* (1997)

E. H. Ries, S.M.J.M. Brasseur &
P.J.H.Reijnders

Phoca hispida SCHREBER, 1775

V. Ree

The species was first described as *Phoca hispida* by Schreber in 1775. Fabricius (1776) called it *Phoca foetida*.

Distribution

World: *Phoca hispida* has a circumpolar distribution throughout the Arctic basin and peripheral seas, including the Bering Sea. In the north-western Atlantic south to Labrador. Isolated populations in the Baltic region.

Europe: *P. hispida* is found along the coasts of northern Europe, north of the Arctic circle and in the Baltic Sea. Isolated populations in Lake Saimaa (Finland) and Lake Ladoga (Russia).

Geographic variation

A total of four subspecies are recognized within Europe, each with their own specific range. The Arctic ringed seal, *P. h. hispida* (Schreber, 1775), the Baltic ringed seal, *P. h. botnica* (Gmelin, 1785) and two freshwater species respectively the Ladoga seal, *P. h. ladogensis* (Nordquist 1899), and the Saimaa seal *P.h. saimensis* (Nordquist 1899). The Baltic, Saimaa and Ladoga ringed seals have been isolated from each other for only 8000-9000 years and about 11000 years from the Arctic ringed seal. Morphological differences are largely attributed to the period of isolation, although environmental factors also influence the rate of differentiation.

Habitat

In general, the seals' distribution changes seasonally, depending on breeding, ice conditions and food availability. All species breed in winter or spring. Pupping habitats are comprised of lairs or cavities on shore-fast or drifting ice covered by a good depth of snow. These cavities protect especially the pups from predators and against the cold and wind. Locations of breeding areas are variable, due to variations in climatic factors. During the summer, small groups or single seals can be found hauled out on the rocks or ice. The seals seem to feed on most available fish species.

Population status

The species is difficult to census because its distribution is large and variable, and because pups are born in lairs. The Arctic ringed seal (6–7 million) is one of the most abundant phocid seals in the world and the population in general is not in danger, though it has been considered that local populations have been over-exploited (in the Eastern Canadian Arctic). The other, much less abundant, subspecies are vulnerable or even endangered. Estimates are: *P. h. botnica*: 3400, *P. h. saimensis*: 200 animals and *P. h. ladogensis*: 5000.

International legal & conservation status

Bern Convention, Appendix III, but *P. h. saimensis* and *P. h. ladogensis* are on Appendix II.
EU Habitats & Species Directive, Annex II *(P. h. botnica)*,

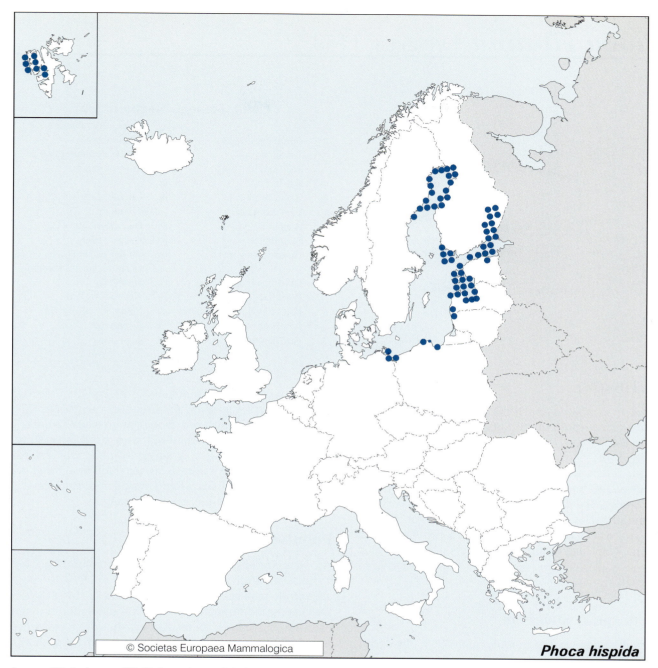

© Societas Europaea Mammalogica

Phoca hispida

Annex II* & Annex IV *(P. h. saimensis),* Annex V.
IUCN Red List, *P. h. botnica* and *P. h. ladogensis*
Vulnerable; *P. h. saimensis,* Endangered.

Other information

The lake-inhabiting species and the Baltic seals are
threatened by a reduction of their lairing possibilities
as humans construct buildings along the shores where
they lair. Pollution is either already a problem or could
become one in these enclosed areas. Locally, competition
for fish exists and seals are accidentally caught. This is
especially a threat to *P. h. botnica* and *P. h. saimensis.*
The latter is also threatened by the artificial lowering of
the water level in Lake Saimaa. Relatively little is known
about *P. h. hispida,* but the population as a whole does
not seem to be threatened. Possible climatic changes
could affect these ice-breeding species as the animals
depend on the stability of the ice and snow for their lairs.

Literature

Helle (1992)
Reijnders *et al.* (1993)
Reijnders *et al.* (1997)

S. M. J. M. Brasseur, E. H. Ries &
P. J. H. Reijnders

Phoca vitulina Linnaeus, 1758

ED '97

E. Hazebroek

Distribution

World: *P. vitulina* is one of the most widely distributed pinnipeds over both longitudinal and latitudinal range (30°N-80°N) and has a practically circumpolar distribution.

Europe: around the British Isles, in the Kattegat/Skagerrak, the south-western Baltic Sea, the Limfjorden, the Wadden Sea and farther south along the North Sea to Brittany. The most northerly distribution is along relatively warm Western Svalbard as a result of the Gulf Stream. They also occur in the waters of Iceland, along the coasts of Norway and on the Murmansk coast of Russia.

Geographic variation

Four sub-species are commonly recognized; the eastern Atlantic harbour seal, *P. v. vitulina* (Linnaeus, 1758), the western Atlantic harbour seal, *P. v. concolor* (DeKay, 1842), the western Pacific harbour seal, *P. v. stejnegeri* (Allen, 1902), and the eastern Pacific harbour seal, *P. v. richardsi* (Grey, 1864). The subspecific distinction of a fifth species, *P. v. mellonae* (Doutt, 1942), is currently under review. *P. v. vitulina* is the only subspecies that occurs in Europe.

Habitat

Harbour seals use a wide variety of coastal habitats including rocky coasts, intertidal rocks on offshore islets, reefs and pebble or sandy beaches. In areas with much human disturbance, seals haul out on tidal sand flats.

As pups swim almost immediately after birth, the seals can use tidal areas even for breeding, providing they are somewhat sheltered from rough seas. Another important criterion for haul-out sites, used for resting, breeding and moulting, is access to deep water. Both inshore and offshore waters are used for foraging. Like most seals, harbour seals seem to feed opportunistically, within relatively distinct feeding habitats.

Population status

An estimate of all *P. vitulina* populations dating from 1989 states 300000–400000 animals. In 1992, the total size of all eastern Atlantic populations of *P. v. vitulina* was estimated to be at least 70000. Since then no total estimates have been made. As over the whole range the population has grown after a dramatic virus epidemic in 1988, it may now well have reached 100000 animals.

International legal & conservation status

Bern Convention, Appendix III.
Bonn Convention, Appendix II (only the Baltic and Wadden Sea populations).
EU Habitats & Species Directive, Annex II, Annex V.

Other information

Overall, *P. vitulina* populations are growing and will be, if not yet, considered competitors of local fisheries. Lack of suitable databases currently hinders ecological research which might well resolve existing controversies.

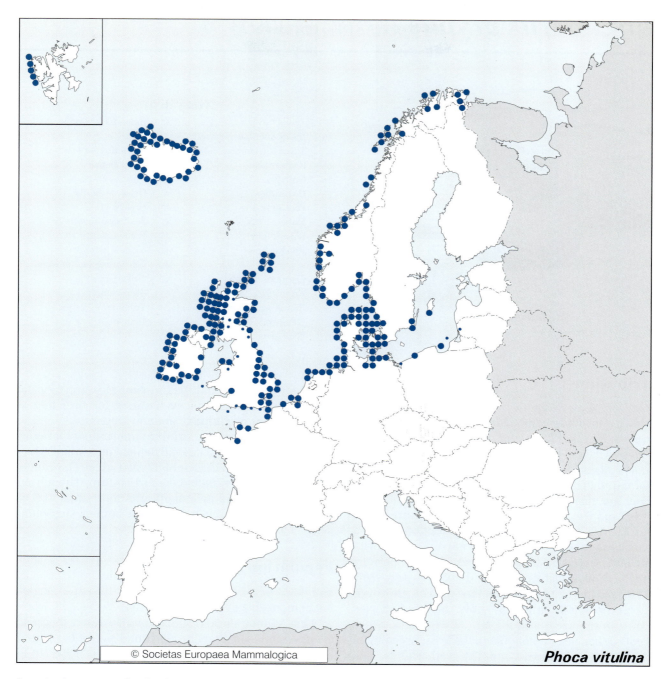

© Societas Europaea Mammalogica

Phoca vitulina

Certain hot spots for high burdens of environmental contaminants overlap with the seals' distribution range (Wadden Sea, Irish Sea, Baltic, and Oslofjord). Some local seal populations are already known to be affected by pollution, and negative effects on the seals' reproductive performance have been demonstrated. Recently, contamination burdens in seals were found to correlate with immune-suppressive characteristics. In this respect, the possibility of a new outbreak of an infectious epidemic still exists. Since harbour seals often live in the vicinity of human settlements, disturbance is one of the factors that could or already does regulate population size, especially in the light of growing populations.

Literature

Reijnders (1992)
Reijnders *et al.* (1993)
Reijnders *et al.* (1997)

S. M. J. M. Brasseur, E. H. Ries &
P. J. H. Reijnders

Halichoerus grypus (FABRICIUS, 1791)

E. Hazebroek

Distribution

World: Grey seals range over the North Atlantic coast. Roughly three stocks can be identified; one in the West Atlantic, one in the Baltic and one in the East Atlantic. The West Atlantic stock ranges from Cape Chidley in the north of Labrador, through Newfoundland, Nova Scotia and the Gulf of St Lawrence to Nantucket.

Europe: the northern border of the East Atlantic stock extends from Iceland to the White Sea. They are found around the British Isles and along the Atlantic and North Sea coasts, down to Brittany in France. The majority (about 80%) breed around the British Isles, especially off the north-west coast of Scotland. Initially grey seals were not considered native of the Wadden Sea. However, recent archeological findings show that this species prevailed in the area until the late Middle Ages. Since the 1950s it has been recolonizing the area, breeding at two locations in Germany and The Netherlands. The range of the Baltic stock includes the Gulfs of Bothnia, Finland and Riga and south to the Gulf of Danzig, extending as far as the border between Poland and Germany, and on the Swedish coast as far as Malmö.

Geographic variation

None known.

Habitat

Breeding sites can be exposed rocky coasts or shelves, shingle or sandy beaches, on grass sites or in caves. In the Baltic and in the Gulf of St Lawrence, grey seals also breed on ice. Intertidal flats in estuaries are used for hauling out, but are not well suited for breeding as newborn pups are initially poor swimmers.

Grey seals generally exhibit opportunistic foraging behaviour. Foraging areas will depend on available prey species, and are therefore highly variable. The ranges of seals were observed to be up to 100 km. Though the maximum recorded dive depth was more than 100 m, most dives seem to reach close to the bottom, suggesting benthic foraging.

Population status

Estimates of population size in the different areas are not comparable as techniques differ.

East Atlantic stock: Over its complete range this stock is either stable or growing. The total size of the British population was estimated to be 111000 in 1997. In its northern range the population is estimated to be over 20000. In the eastern North Sea there are only a few hundred animals.

West Atlantic stock: In 1987 80000-110000 animals.

Baltic stock: Until recently, numbers were dropping. Current numbers are estimated at 5000 animals, indicating a recovery; this could, however, also be due to a change in behaviour of the animals.

International legal & conservation status

Bern Convention, Appendix III.
Bonn Convention, Appendix II (only Baltic Sea population).

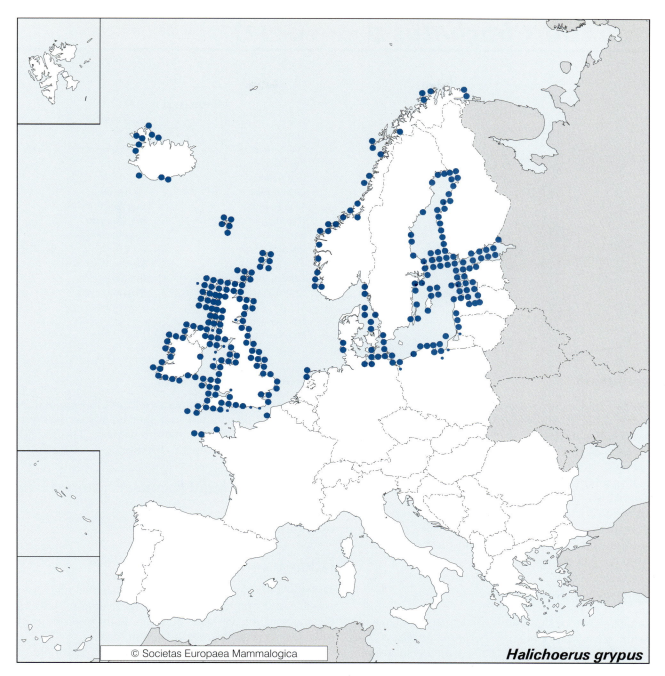

© Societas Europaea Mammalogica

Halichoerus grypus

EU Habitats & Species Directive, Annex II, Annex V.
IUCN Red List, Endangered (only Baltic Sea population).

Other information

Some of the grey seal's prey species are commercially exploited. This has led to controversial public debates about the perceived need for culling programmes to control seal numbers. Lack of suitable databases currently hinders ecological research which might well resolve existing controversies. Concern that the grey seal acts as a vector for the codworm *Pseudoterranova decipiens* has sometimes led to killing. In the Baltic, 15–20% of pups may drown each year in fishing nets, and fertility rates are low as a result of pollution. In highly populated areas disturbance of breeding sites can result in high pup mortality.

Literature

Anderson (1992)
Reijnders *et al.* (1993)
Reijnders *et al.* (1997)

S. M. J. M. Brasseur, E. H. Ries &
P. J. H.Reijnders

Erignathus barbatus (ERXLEBEN, 1777)

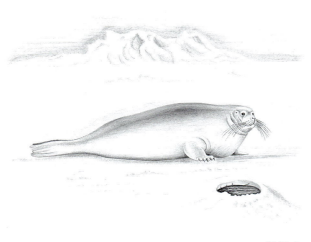

M. Năzăreanu

Distribution

World: the species' distribution is circumpolar with a northern limit at 80°–85°. Arctic Ocean, northern Atlantic south to the Gulf of St Lawrence, northern Pacific as far south as Hokkaido.

Europe: the Atlantic north of Iceland and associated islands, including the Barents and White Seas. Some stragglers found on the Atlantic coasts from the Lofoten Isles down to Portugal. The distribution of breeding and haul-out areas is scattered and not well known. In prehistoric times, the distribution of the bearded seal seems to have been more southerly.

Geographic variation

Two subspecies are commonly recognized, each with its own geographical range: *E. barbatus barbatus* and *E. barbatus nauticus* (Pallas, 1811), which occurs from the Laptev Sea eastwards to the Canadian Arctic.

Habitat

The bearded seal is generally found on pack ice over relatively shallow water, where it forages on bottom-living animals including shrimps, clams, whelks and flat fish. In some areas the animals migrate in relation to the ice cover. These seals are not gregarious and are not found in very large numbers at any one location. As they are associated with drifting ice flows for much of the year, the animals move considerable distances north and south.

Population status

There are no reliable estimates of the total population of this widely distributed seal species but several tens of thousands of animals may be present. The species does not seem to be directly threatened.

International legal & conservation status

Bern Convention, Appendix III.
EU Habitats & Species Directive, Annex V.

Other information

The species is of great importance to coastal indigenous peoples and animals are also caught commercially by Russian sealing vessels. Bearded seals are generally exploited for their strong hides and meat.

Literature

Kapel (1992a)
Reijnders *et al.* (1993)
Reijnders *et al.* (1997)

E. H. Ries, S. M. J. M. Brasseur &
P. J. H. Reijnders

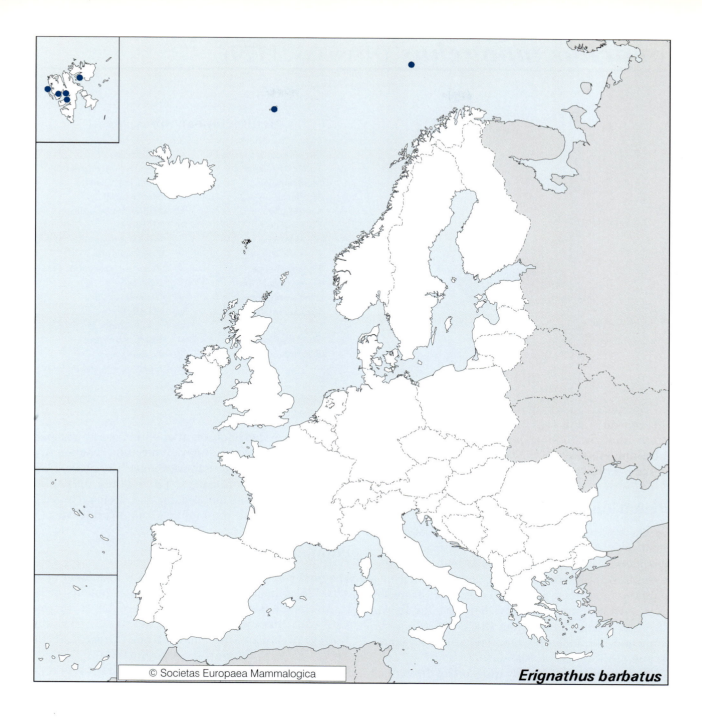

© Societas Europaea Mammalogica

Erignathus barbatus

Monachus monachus (HERMANN, 1779)

M. Năzăreanu

Mediterranean monk seal			
AL	Foka e Mesdheut	LU	-
BG	Белокоремен тюлен	LV	Mūkronis
CZ	Tuleň středomořský	MK	Медитерански монах
DE	Mönchsrobbe	MT	Monka; Bumerin
DK	Munkesæl	NL	Monniksrob
EE	Munkhüljes	NO	Middelhavsmunkesel
ES	Foca monje	PL	Mniszka
FI	Munkkihylje		śródziemnomorska
FO	-	PT	Lobo-marinho
FR	Phoque moine	RO	Foca-cu-burta-albă; Foca-episcop
GR	Μεσογειακή φώκια		
HR	Sredozemna medvjedica	RU	Тюлень-монах
HU	Mediterrán barátfóka	SE	Munksäl
IR	-	SI	Sredozemska medvedjica
IS	Munkaselur	SK	Tuleň mníšsky
IT	Foca monaca	TR	Akdeniz foku
LT	-	YU	Средоземна медведица

Three species of monk seals formerly existed. The Mediterranean monk seal *Monachus monachus,* the Hawaiian monk seal *Monachus schauinslandi* and the Caribbean monk seal *Monachus tropicalis.* The latter species is believed to be extinct.

Distribution

World: the Mediterranean and Black Seas, the Madeiran Archipelago and the north-west coast of Africa.
Europe: populations confined to the Aegean and Ionian Seas, the Desertas Islands and Ponta de São Laurenço on Madeira. Continued presence is recorded from the Adriatic Sea (Croatia and Albania), Sardinia, the Tuscan and Sicilian Islands and in the Black Sea (Bulgaria, Romania and Ukraine). Occasional records from Puglia (Italy) and offshore Italian islands.

This species was formerly widespread throughout the Mediterranean and Black Seas, the north-west coast of Africa down to the 20th parallel and Macronesia including the Azores, Canaries and Madeira. It was severely depleted and disappeared from the French mainland (1930s), Italian mainland and most of Spain (1950s), Andalusia, the Balearics and Tuscan archipelago (1960s), most of Corsica, Sicily, the Egadian Islands and Cyprus in the 1980s.

Geographic variation

Possible separate subspecies status for the monk seals occurring in the Atlantic and in the Mediterranean is currently investigated.

Habitat

Monk seals used to haul out on sandy and rocky beaches; now they are confined to caves with the exception of a very few beaches on the Saharan coast. The caves, often with underwater entrances, have sandy or pebble beaches and are used for breeding and resting. The seals feed on benthic fish communities and invertebrates.

Population status

The total world population is presently estimated to be 320–475 animals. Estimates for major regions of its range were: Aegean Sea (Cyprus, Greece, Libya, Turkey) 120–250, Black Sea (Bulgaria, Romania, Ukraine, Turkey) 10, Ionian Sea (Ionian Islands – Greece) 20–35, Adriatic Sea (Croatia, Albania) 20, Central Mediterranean (Sardinia – Italy) 10, Western Mediterranian (Algeria, Morocco) 20–30, Madeira 20, Sahara coast 100. The latter colony has been recently severely reduced from 300 to 100 animals.

International legal and conservation status

Bern Convention, Appendix II.
Bonn Convention, Appendix I.
EU Habitats & Species Directive, Annex II* & Annex IV.
IUCN Red List, Critically Endangered.
CITES, Appendix I; EC 338/97, Annex A.

Monachus monachus

© Societas Europaea Mammalogica

Other information

The major threat to monk seals used to be deliberate killing by fishermen. This is still considered to occur in the eastern Mediterranean. Other threats are loss of habitat, incidental entanglement and disturbance. Threats from reduction in food supply and diseases should not be ignored. Protected areas with effective control are of fundamental importance to protect this species. A mass mortality recently occurred in the colony at the Saharan coast. Since the middle of May 1997, about 110 seals have been found dead there. The observations of seals in the caves indicated that approximately one third of the world population of this species died within two months. The primary cause is not known, but there is evidence that toxins produced by a dinoflagellate bloom and a viral infection were both involved. The impact of this die-off on the viability of the Atlantic monk seal population is currently being investigated.

Literature

Duguy & Marchessaux (1992)
King (1983)
Reijnders *et al.* (1993)
Reijnders *et al.* (1997)
Ridgway & Harrison (1981)

P. J. H. Reijnders, C. Prigioni,
S. M. J. M. Brasseur & E. R. Ries

Cystophora cristata (Erxleben, 1777)

M. Năzăreanu

The hooded seal is a pelagic species. Because it does not haul out regularly on the coasts, there is no dot map. This atlas does not cover the seas.

Distribution

World: Four separate breeding populations in the North Atlantic, generally divided into two groups: the Greenland Sea stock and the North-west Atlantic stock. The Greenland Sea stock breeds on the 'West Ice' between Jan Mayen and Greenland. The other three breeding sites (North-west Atlantic stock) are in North-American waters: Davis Strait between Greenland and Canada, north of Newfoundland (the 'Front') and the Gulf of St Lawrence.

Europe: The big breeding population of the West Ice, west of Jan Mayen (Greenland Sea stock) can be considered to be European.

After weaning most adult hooded seals migrate to two moulting sites. The North-west Atlantic stock to Denmark Strait between Iceland and Greenland, whereas the Greenland Sea stock moves to an area off north-eastern Greenland at 73–78°N. After moulting, the hooded seals disperse widely in the waters between Iceland, the Faeroes, Svalbard and Greenland.

Stragglers periodically show up on the Norwegian coasts. One single record of reproduction on the Norwegian coast: on the island Otterøya in 1980. Vagrants occur on the Atlantic coasts, down to Portugal; these are usually young animals dispersing.

Geographic variation

None.

Habitat

In the breeding season and during moult hooded seals inhabit the thick drifting ice over deep water of the North Atlantic. Outside these periods also in waters with little or no ice. Adult hooded seals feed on deep water fish such as Greenland halibut *Reinhardtius hippoglossoides*, redfish *Sebastus marinus*, polar cod *Boreogadus saida* and squid *Gonatus fabricii*.

Population status

The estimate for the total hooded seal population is 500000–600000 individuals. This is based on the following pup counts in the different breeding sites: Davis Strait 19000; the Front 82 182; Gulf of St Lawrence >2000; West Ice: 200000.

The populations have declined in size because of heavy hunting pressure. Although catches have been relatively low in the last years, no real recovery seems to have taken place in any of the herds.

International legal and conservation status

Bern Convention, Appendix II.
EU-Directive 83/129/EEC: import ban on blueback seal skins (young hooded seals).

© Societas Europaea Mammalogica

Cystophora cristata

EU Habitats & Species Directive, Annex V.

Other information

Hooded seals have been heavily hunted in the past, mainly in the 'West Ice' and the Gulf of St Lawrence. Up to 100000 individuals used to be killed each year. Hunting quotas have been established since 1974. Reported catches are low now due to market collapse, which resulted from the European Union import prohibition of blueback seal skins.

Literature

Kapel (1992c)
Reijnders *et al.* (1997)

E. H. Ries, P. Beuving, S. S. M. J. Brasseur & P. J. H. Reijnders

Sus scrofa LINNAEUS, 1758

V. Ree

Wild boar

AL	Derri i eger	LT	Šernas
BG	Дива свиня	LU	Wёllt Schwaïn
CZ	Prase divoké	LV	Mežacūka
DE	Wildschwein	MK	Дива свиња
DK	Vildsvin	MT	Hanżir Salvaġġ
EE	Metssiga	NL	Wild zwijn
ES	Jabalí	NO	Villsvin
FI	Villisika	PL	Dzik
FO	Villsvín	PT	Javali
FR	Sanglier	RO	Mistreţ; Porc-sălbatic
GR	Αγριογούρουνο	RU	Кабан
HR	Divlja svinja	SE	Vildsvin
HU	Vaddisznó	SI	Divji prašič
IR	-	SK	Diviak lesný
IS	Villisvín	TR	Yaban domuzu
IT	Cinghiale	YU	Дивља свиња

Distribution

World: Palaearctic, throughout the broad-leaved forest and steppe zones of Europe, Asia and North Africa; Palaeotropical in Asia, east to Greater Sunda Islands.
Europe: widely distributed in western and central Europe, but restricted to mountain areas in Portugal and Spain. Local but in increasing numbers in peninsular Italy, absent in southernmost parts of Greece. Among the Mediterranean islands, native in Corsica and Sardinia only. Disappeared from the British Isles and Scandinavia in the 17th century. Absent from European USSR (except the westernmost and Caucasian parts) before World War II, but then progressively extending northwards and eastwards, up to the Baltic region. Introduced populations in Sweden and Sicily. There are a few escaped individuals in England.

Geographic variation

At least 16 subspecies recognized worldwide, consisting of four geographical groups (Western, Indian, Eastern, and Indonesian). Within the western group, three subspecies are distinguished essentially on the basis of measurements, but appear to be just geographical or ecological variants, with a very low genetic diversity. Two isolated subspecies (*S. scrofa meridionalis* Forsyth Major, 1882 in Sardinia, *S. s. majori* de Beaux & Festa, 1927 in central Italy) have recently been identified as divergent from all other subspecies (including Eurasiatic domestic races) on the basis of the cytochrome B gene.

Wild boar in their whole range are polymorphic regarding their diploid number, with the basic formula with 38 chromosomes (the same as in domestic pig) throughout Asia to east and south-east Europe and Mediterranean islands, and variants with 36 chromosomes due to Robertsonian translocations. Only countries of central and western continental Europe show a majority of individuals with 36 chromosomes.

Habitat

A wide variety of habitats, in the temperate, tropical and equatorial zone. Wild boar seems to be primarily an inhabitant of the temperate broadleaved or tropical monsoon forests, thriving on wild fruit production. Extension into other biomes (taiga, steppe, mediterranean scrubland, open field areas) is always linked with the presence of riparian vegetation, water, and various sheltering habitats. Extension northwards in Russia and Fennoscandia would not have originated through climatic change but rather because of better survival during key periods through additional feeding, decreasing predation or reintroduction.

Population status

Populations increasing in numbers in the entire European range of the species. Particular isolated populations (e.g., *S. s. meridionalis* and *S. s. majori*) are not numerically threatened but deserve attention owing to the risk of hybridization.

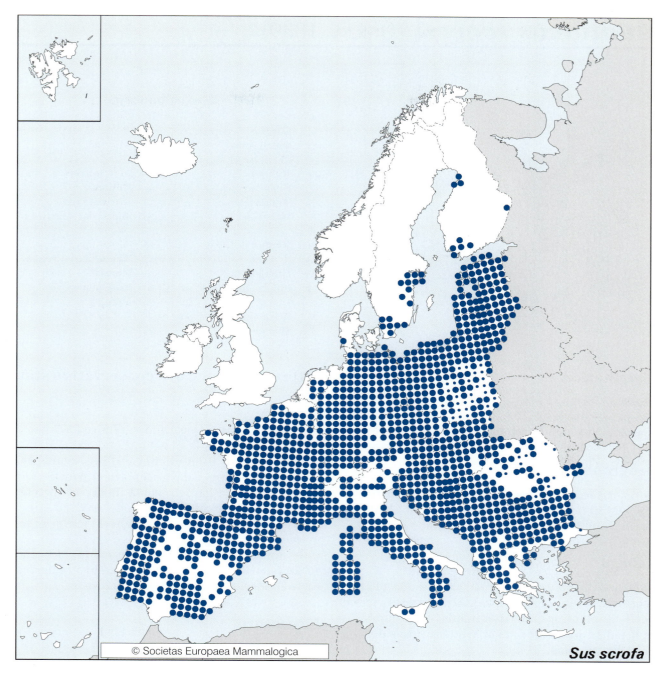

© Societas Europaea Mammalogica

Sus scrofa

International legal & conservation status

Bern Convention, Appendix III (*S. s. meridionalis* (Sardinia) only).

Literature

Bosma *et al.* (1991)
Erkinaro *et al.* (1982)
Fadeev (1981)
Groves (1981)
Oliver (1993, 1995)
Randi (1995)
Randi *et al.* (1996)
Saez-Royuela & Telleria (1986)

F. Spitz

381

Muntiacus reevesi (OGILBY, 1839)

ED '97

E. Hazebroek

Distribution

World: south-east China and Taiwan.
Europe: released and escaped from captivity in Britain, especially England. Introduction to France failed.

Geographic variation

Two subspecies described, *Muntiacus reevesi reevesi* (Ogilby, 1839) being the form on mainland China that was believed to be introduced to Britain.

Habitat

Dense and diverse, such as broadleaved and coniferous woodland, scrub, coppice, overgrown gardens. Spread aided by planting new woodlands. High mortality reported in prolonged, cold winters. Considerable mortality on roads.

Population status

Established in wild since 1920s. Natural rate of spread about 1 km per year with colonization much aided by releases. Pre-breeding population about 40000, being most concentrated in English Midlands. Densities greater than 100/km² recorded. Continuing to increase, especially within current range. Has potential to colonize and spread on parts of European mainland if given further opportunity.

International legal & conservation status

None.

Other information

Sport shooting limited, but culling widespread. Considerable pest, e.g., to coppice regrowth, native ground flora and garden plants. Dense or increasing populations can affect numbers and ranging of *Capreolus capreolus* and numbers of *Hydropotes inermis*.

Introduced *Muntiacus muntjak* (Zimmermann, 1780) reported from wild in one locality in England in early 20th century, but no longer occurs.

Literature

Chapman *et al.* (1993)
Chapman *et al.* (1994a)
Chapman *et al.* (1994b)
Cooke *et al.* (1995)
Cooke *et al.* (1996)
Cooke & Farrell (1995)
Cooke & Lakhani (1996)
Harris *et al.* (1995)

A. S. Cooke

© Societas Europaea Mammalogica

Muntiacus reevesi

Axis axis (ERXLEBEN, 1777)

E D '97   E. Hazebroek

Distribution

World: native to Indian subcontinent, from Nepal and Sikkim to Sri Lanka. Introduced to many parts of the world: Andaman Islands, Australia, Hawaian Islands, South America (Brazil, Argentina, Uruguay), and Texas.
Europe: the only population is restricted to the Brijuni Islands off Istria, Croatia, where introduced before 1916. Introduction to Slovenia from Brijuni stock at the end of 1950s or the beginning of 1960s failed.

Geographic variation

Several subspecific names have been proposed, but their status has not been evaluated. Population from Sri Lanka recognized as a distinct subspecies.

Habitat

Grassland and open forest on Indian subcontinent, while it seldom penetrates into heavy jungle; takes readily to water. On the Brijuni Islands axis deer are parkland game.

Population status

Autochthonous populations not threatened. European population managed. Density of 23/km² reported from central India with home ranges of 500 ha for a male and 180 ha for a female.

International legal & conservation status

None.

Literature

Nowak (1991)
Trense (1989)
Wermmer (1987)

B. Kryštufek

© Societas Europaea Mammalogica

Axis axis

Dama dama (Linnaeus, 1758)

F. Müller

Similar in appearance to the introduced *Cervus nippon* (especially females and yearlings), but can be distinguished by a different design of the rump patch that is clearly black and white, resembling an inverted anchor, and, in mature males, by the large palmate antlers.

Distribution

World: western Palaearctic; originally Turkey and possibly Macedonia. At the end of the last century and at the beginning of the present century introduced to South Africa, Australia, New Zealand, North and South America.
Europe: introduced by Phoenicians to the western Mediterranean and subsequently by Romans and Normans north of the Alps and to the British Isles. Now present in most European countries.

Geographic variation

Apart from wild-type colour, three other coats are common: black, white and 'menil'. The last is a paler version of wild-type, with more pronounced white spots and almost white head, neck and legs.

Habitat

Prefers Mediterranean open woods. Is able to flourish in a very hot and dry climate but is very adaptable to almost all ecological conditions; only alpine regions are definitely not suited for this species.

Population status

Autochthonous populations in Turkey are endangered and a recovery programme has started. Introduced populations all around the world are stable or spreading. It is considered a pest in New Zealand. Fallow deer is a gregarious species and shows a variety of mating systems.

International legal & conservation status

Bern Convention, Appendix III.

Other information

This species was often managed as a park ungulate and its semi-domesticated condition may explain the occurrence of many coat types. Hunting is allowed.

Literature

Chapman & Chapman (1985) – review
Feldhammer *et al.* (1988) – review
Heidemann (1986)
Langbein & Thirgood (1989)

M. Apollonio

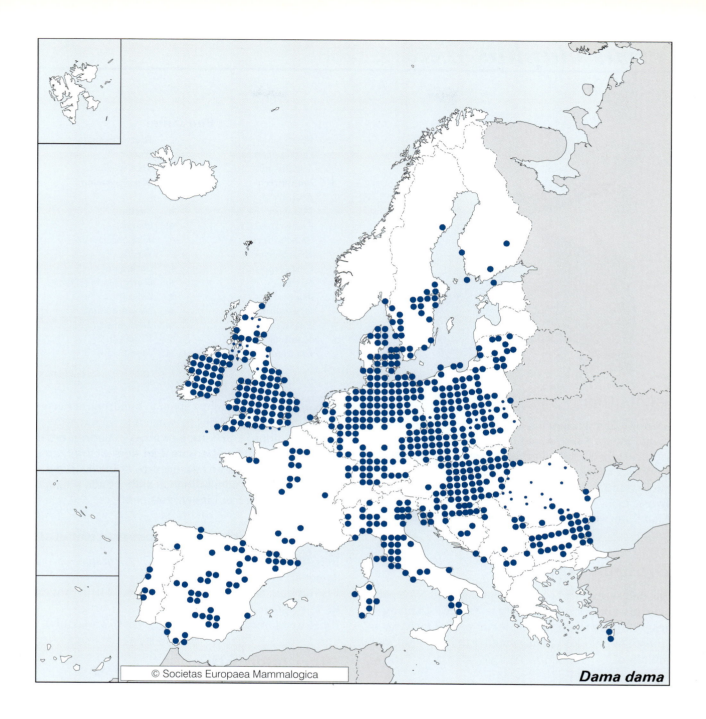

© Societas Europaea Mammalogica

Dama dama

387

Cervus elaphus LINNAEUS, 1758

U. Iff

Distribution

World: Holarctic species occurring in North Africa, Europe, most of the mountain ranges in central Asia, southern Siberia, the Far East, and North America. Introduced to Ireland, Chile, Argentina, Australia and New Zealand.
Europe: most of Europe, except northern Scandinavia, Finland, and certain Mediterranean islands. Extinct in Albania.

Geographic variation

Regarded as a typical polytypic species, with subspecies freely interbreeding to produce fertile offspring. In Europe, distinct subspecies occur particularly on big islands. Their size is usually smaller than in continental populations.

Habitat

Originally lived in open deciduous woodland; now occupies diverse habitats in woodlands, mountain forests, or open moorland. In the Alps and northern Europe moves above the tree line in summer. In Scotland adapted to living outside woodland. Mainly nocturnal; feeds by grazing and browsing. The diet includes heather and conifers in winter.

Population status

Gregarious species, living in herds with sexes separated for most of the year. The home range varies according to season and sex, and may extend to hundreds of hectares. Population density varies between 5 to 45 ind./km².

Populations in Britain, as well as in certain areas of the continent, hybridize with sika deer *Cervus nippon*. Many local populations affected by translocations and introductions of allochthonous individuals originated sometimes even from other continents.

International legal & conservation status

Bern Convention, Appendix II (*C. e. corsicanus* only), Appendix III.
EU Habitats & Species Directive, Annex II* & Annex IV (*C. e. corsicanus* only).
IUCN Red List, Endangered (*C. e. corsicanus* only).

Other information

May cause serious damage to forestry plantations at high population densities. Important game animal in most of Europe.

Literature

Bützler (1986) – review
Clutton-Brock *et al.* (1982)
Dolan (1988)
Lowe & Gardiner (1974)
Trense (1989)
Wermmer (1987)

P. Koubek & J. Zima

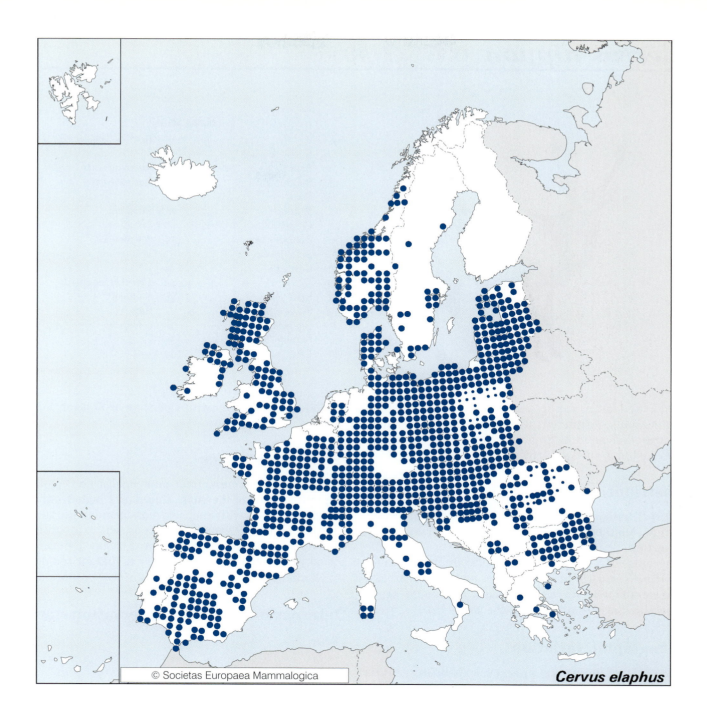

© Societas Europaea Mammalogica

Cervus elaphus

389

Cervus nippon TEMMINCK, 1838

J. Mikuletič

Regarded as a superspecies consisting of many subspecies, often with an allopatric or insular distribution pattern. Some of the subspecies may be elevated to species rank by certain authors.

Distribution

World: indigenous to eastern Asia: Taiwan, eastern China, Manchuria, Korea, Russian Far East, Japan, Vietnam. Introduced to certain parts of Europe, Caucasus, USA, New Zealand, and certain Pacific islands.
Europe: occurs in the British Isles and several areas of the continent from France to Russia. Commonly kept in parks and also established in the wild.

Geographic variation

Extremely polytypic species exhibiting sexual dimorphism, with extensive variation in size and colour among various populations. Many native populations now extinct and/or affected by translocations, introductions and semi-domestication in farms and enclosures. Native populations may differ in their diploid chromosome numbers as a result of centric autosomal fusions. Herds introduced to Europe from different parts of the native range are, consequently, polymorphic in their karyotype. Chromosomal variation may result also from hybridization with the red deer *Cervus elaphus*.

Habitat

Deciduous or mixed woodland with dense undergrowth, including plantations with clearings or adjacent open ground. Grazes and browses.

Population status

Lives in small groups, with adult males and females separated most of the year. Abundance higher only in certain locations with intensive management. European introduced populations usually represent a mixture of individuals of various geographical origin. Population density in Scotland may be similar to that for red deer. In Germany, 2.5 to 4.3 deer ind./km² were reported.

International legal & conservation status

None.

Other information

Game animal in areas where abundant. May damage forest growth. In areas of sympatric occurrence, hybridization with red deer occurs and introgression is complete in parts of the British Isles.

Literature

Feldhammer (1980) – review
Hoffmeister (1983) – review
Krapp & Niethammer (1986) – review
Lowe & Gardiner (1974)
Ratcliffe (1987)
Wermmer (1987)

J. Zima & P. Koubek

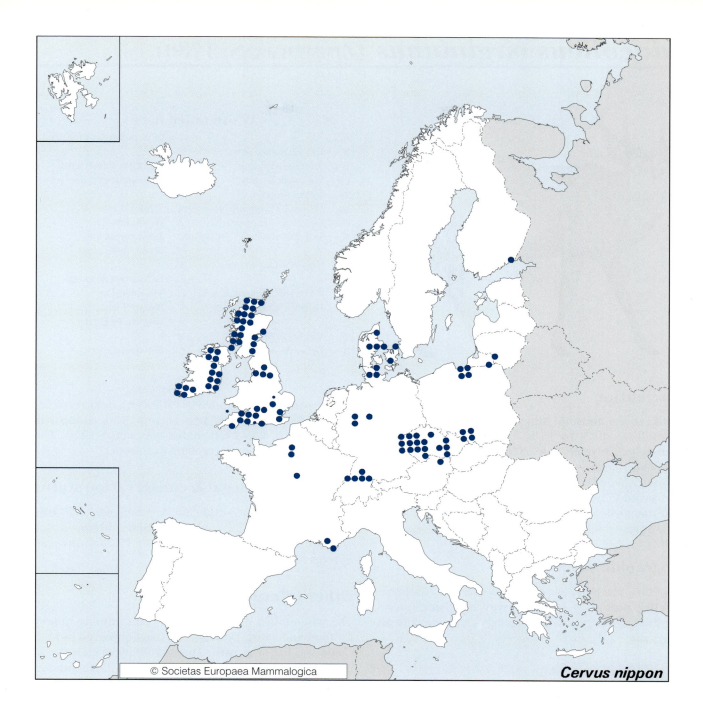

© Societas Europaea Mammalogica

Cervus nippon

Odocoileus virginianus (ZIMMERMANN, 1780)

J. Mikuletič

Distribution

World: indigenous to America, where distribution ranges from 60°N to 15°S. Introduced from North America to Europe, New Zealand, Cuba and other Caribbean Islands.

Europe: introduced to the Czech Republic, Serbia, Croatia and Finland. Later introduced to Bulgaria and the former Soviet Union from Finland. Subsequently died out in Bulgaria (G. Markov, pers. comm.).

Geographic variation

One of the most polytypic species of deer; 38 subspecies showing diversity in body weight, dimensions, coloration, antler growth, physiology and behaviour are recognized.

Habitat

As a concentrate selector, highly specialized in selecting for cell content material, the white-tailed deer is seen in a variety of forested environments. As the bulk of the indigenous population is in sub-boreal and boreal regions, the animal is well adapted to annual cycles of plant phenology and exploits such peculiarities as changes in energy contents and digestibility of different plant parts. Mean snow cover exceeding 40 cm appears to limit its resource usage and reduce survival.

Population status

In America, the population declined with the increase of human settlements in 1800–1900, but a clear recovery, following enhanced protection and scientific management, has been under way since 1900. The population has been increasing in Europe.

International legal & conservation status

None in Europe, but certain native American subspecies are included in CITES Appendix III and considered rare or endangered by IUCN (1996) or US Endangered Species Act respectively.

Other information

The white-tailed deer is an important hunting quarry for food and sport. Damage has been observed in both crops and forest growth. The possibility of infection of indigenous elk *Alces alces* populations by the meningeal worm *Parelaphostrongylus tenuis* vectored in America should be a concern. To date, European deer populations have been free of this and other major fatal causes of illness. As a species of foreign origin, the management of this animal in Europe has so far mostly been to prevent an increase in its distribution. May play an important role in revitalization of the local large predator populations of Europe.

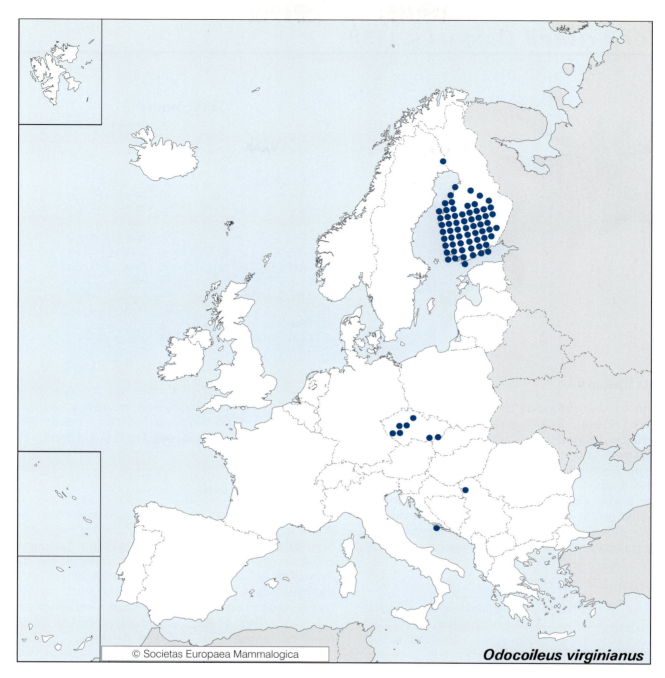

© Societas Europaea Mammalogica

Odocoileus virginianus

Literature

Hofmann (1985)
Pulliainen & Sulkava (1986) – review
Smith (1991) – review

K. Nygrén

Alces alces (LINNAEUS, 1758)

V. Ree

Elk; Moose			
AL	-	LT	Briedis
BG	Лос	LU	Elch
CZ	Los	LV	Alnis
DE	Elch	MK	Лос
DK	Elsdyr; Elg	MT	-
EE	Põder	NL	Eland
ES	Alce	NO	Elg
FI	Hirvi	PL	Łoś
FO	Elgur	PT	Alce
FR	Elan	RO	Elan
GR	Άλκη	RU	Лосъ
HR	Los	SE	Älg
HU	Jávorszarvas	SI	Los
IR	-	SK	Los mokrad'ový
IS	Elgur	TR	-
IT	Alce euroasiatico	YU	Лос

Distribution

World: Northern Holarctic from Scandinavia through northern Russia, Alaska and Canada to Newfoundland and Maine (USA). Zonally from forest tundra through taiga, locally into broadleaved forest-steppe zone.
Europe: European continuous distribution from Fennoscandia without Denmark and Russia through the Baltic States and Belarus to Poland and northern Ukraine. Local in southern Czech Republic and northern Austria. Stragglers south and west to Romania, Croatia, Hungary and southern and eastern Germany.

Geographic variation

Eight subspecies described. European-western Siberian nominate subspecies karyologically and morphologically distinct. Otherwise geographic variation in size, coloration and development of antlers largely clinal.

Habitat

A variety of forest habitats from poor coniferous taiga to eutrophic lowland hardwood and riverine forests. Prefers areas including more or less extensive aquatic and wetland habitats. Recent population explosion in Scandinavia and other parts of the range is at least partly the result of replacement of natural taiga forests by secondary growth following large-scale clearcuts. As a specialist of plant cell content, the elk monitors a wide variety of plant species of boreal forest to find the phenologically optimal season . Most of its food is derived from the tree and bush layers but dwarf shrubs, herbs and water plants are used whenever possible. Uses traditional over-wintering areas consisting of pine-growing mires, riparian willow and hardwood communities, and young mixed stands by old burns and clearings.

Population status

In the Early Holocene, range extended westwards to the British Isles, south to the northern Pyrénées and Italian Alps. By the beginning of 20th century this range had become reduced to more or less isolated populations in Norway, Sweden, Finland and northern Russia with small pockets in the Baltic countries and north-eastern Poland. Conservation and game management efforts led to large population increases and, as a result, to recent recovery of much of the early historic range.

In the last 200 years, European populations have shown long-term fluctuations which are fairly synchronous in different countries. The total world population is about 1.5 million; the European population is around 0.5 million.

International legal & conservation status

Bern Convention, Appendix III.

Other information

The entire elk population is exploited as a traditionally important source of protein. Legislation, in the main, aims at sustainable use. In the majority of European

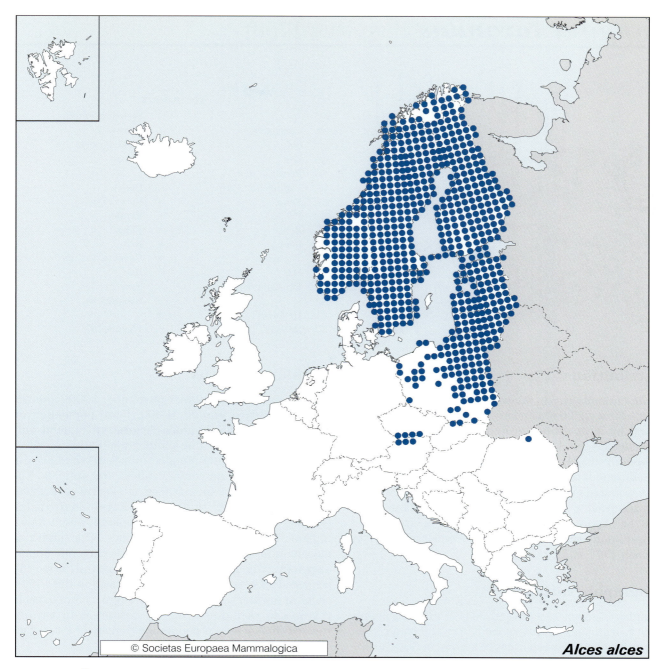

© Societas Europaea Mammalogica

Alces alces

countries, elk populations are controlled to prevent damage to both forestry and agriculture. The elk is a key species for the survival of populations of large predators, particularly in huge areas lacking other large ungulates.

Heptner & Nasimowitsch (1967) – review
Hofmann (1985)
Nygrén (1986) – review

K. Bauer & K. Nygrén

Literature

Baskin *et al.* (1997)
Bédard (1975)
Briedermann (1988) – review
Franzmann (1981) – review

Rangifer tarandus (LINNAEUS, 1758)

E. Hazebroek

Distribution

World: circumboreal in tundra and taiga, from northern Europe through Siberia and arctic America. Range much altered by local extinction and replacement by semi-domesticated reindeer.

Europe: Svalbard, Fennoscandia and northern Russia. Autochthonous wild populations on the fells of southern Norway and in northern Russia. Wild herds of the forest form returned to eastern Finland from Russia in about 1950. Feral population on Iceland originated from about 100 semi-domesticated animals introduced from Norway between 1771 and 1787.

Geographic variation

A number of subspecies recognized (10), differing mainly in the morphology of antlers, body size and coat colour. In Europe, distinct subspecies recognized in Norway (the nominate subspecies), Svalbard (*R. tarandus platyrhynchus* (Vrolik, 1829)), and eastern Finland (*R. t. fennicus* Lönnberg, 1909) respectively. Variation conspicuous particularly in domesticated herds.

Habitat

Montane and arctic tundra, open woodland. May migrate between summer (tundra) and winter (forest) feeding places. The aboriginal Finnish populations of *R. t. fennicus* confined particularly to forest habitats. The diet consists mainly of lichens, mosses, grasses, willow and polar birch leaves.

Population status

Wild herds in southern Norway number 30000 animals and on Svalbard around 10000. Feral population on Iceland about 2000 animals. In eastern Finland only about 1000 animals, but another population of forest reindeer was recently founded in a watershed area in western Finland and contains about 400 animals. The population is kept in a fenced enclosure to prevent introgression from semi-domestic reindeer. In the reindeer management areas in Lapland, about half a million semi-domesticated individuals. The tundra or mountain form of the wild reindeer is currently almost absent from the European part of Russia, and the world's largest stocks, estimated at 400000 head in the 1950s, occur in northern Asia. Population density fluctuates in relation to variation in lichen resources in various regions. In Norway, a population density of 2 ind./km² was reported.

International legal & conservation status

Bern Convention, Appendix III.
EU Habitats & Species Directive, Annex II (only *R. t. fennicus*).

Other information

The semi-domesticated form is used for meat, skin, milk, and transport as draft animals. An attractive game animal.

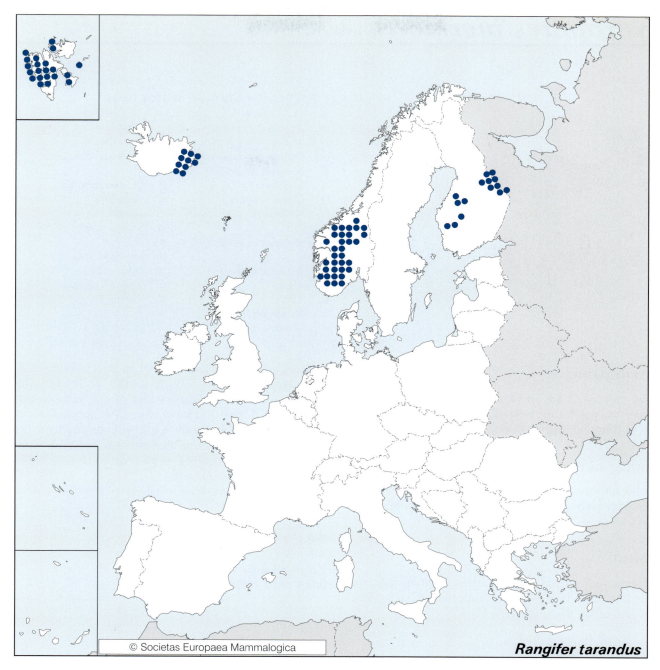

© Societas Europaea Mammalogica

Rangifer tarandus

Literature

Banfield (1961)
Herre (1955)
Herre (1986) – review
Trense (1989)
Wermmer (1987)

P. Koubek & J. Zima

Hydropotes inermis SWINHOE, 1870

P. Barrett

Distribution

World: eastern China and Korea.
Europe: released and escaped from captivity in some areas of England. Introduced to France in 1954.

Geographic variation

Only one species in genus. Two subspecies described by some authorities, the nominate subspecies being the form in Europe.

Habitat

Reedbeds, fens, grassland, broadleaved woodland and arable farmland. Prime habitat comprises open feeding areas and taller, dense cover.

Population status

Established in the wild in England since 1940s. Up to 650 adults in the wild with 600–900 free-ranging in parks. Thought to be increasing overall, but total still small with few flourishing populations. High mortality in cold, wet winters. Dispersing animals killed on roads.

International legal & conservation status

IUCN Red List, Lower Risk – near-threatened.

Other information

Rarely a pest to agriculture or other interests in England, but shot on farmland and culled in parks. Population decreases associated with dense or increasing populations of *Muntiacus reevesi*. Adult body weight comparable to that in native range for populations in areas where habitat similar, e.g. reedbeds and fens, but may be reduced where forage sub-optimal, e.g., parkland. Major mortality incident in park population in 1930s blamed on enteritis.

Literature

Cooke & Farrell (1987)
Cooke & Farrell (1995)
Farrell & Cooke (1991)
Harris *et al.* (1995)

A. S. Cooke

© Societas Europaea Mammalogica

Hydropotes inermis

Capreolus capreolus (LINNAEUS, 1758)

F. Müller

Roe deer

AL	Kaprolli	LT	Stirna
BG	Европейска сърна	LU	Réi
CZ	Srnec obecný	LV	Stirna
DE	Reh	MK	Срна
DK	Rådyr	MT	-
EE	Metskits; Kaber	NL	Ree
ES	Corzo	NO	Rådyr
FI	Metsäkauris	PL	Sarna
FO	Rádýr	PT	Corço
FR	Chevreuil européen	RO	Căprioară
GR	Ζαρκάδι	RU	Европейская косуля
HR	Srna	SE	Rådjur
HU	Európai őz	SI	Srna
IR	-	SK	Srnec lesný
IS	Rádýr	TR	Karaca
IT	Capriolo	YU	Срна; Срндаћ

There are remarkable genetic differences between European and Asiatic roe deer, so that we have an evolutionary trend towards two separate species.

Distribution

World: Palaearctic; from Spain in the west to the Paciific coast; from Norway to Italy and the Caucasus; from Asia Minor to north Syria, north Iraq, Iran, Siberia (in some parts to 65°N), Altai, Kazakhstan, north Mongolia, China and Korea. Introduced to North America.
Europe: widespread, but missing from Corsica, Sardinia and Sicily. Not indigenous to Ireland, where introduction attempted.

Geographic variation

Six subspecies recognized: in Europe the nominate subspecies is present in most of the area and *C. capreolus garganta* (Meunier, 1983) in Spain; the other subspecies are distributed in Asia.

Habitat

The species uses a wide variety of habitats. A mixture of woodland and agricultural landscapes is preferred. A new ecotype of field roe deer lives in open agricultural areas.

Population status

From the 1960s the numbers have increased to 15 million in central Europe. Population density in favourable habitats is 10–20 ind./100 ha, but it can be even higher in suburban environments. Yearly bag record for Germany about 1 million, The Netherlands 10000, Norway 50000–60000, Sweden about 300000, Hungary about 40000, Czech Republic 115000, Switzerland about 50000. Exhibits seasonal changes in territorial behaviour; larger groups are observed in winter. Predators include wolves and lynxes. High mortality by traffic.

International legal & conservation status

Bern Convention, Appendix III.

Other information

Found in nearly all hunting areas; antlers are huntsman's trophy. Hunting season different for males and females. Browses in woodlands, but does not strip bark from trees.

Literature

Heptner & Naumov (1974)
Meunier (1983)
Stubbe (1997)
Zernahle (1980)

C. Stubbe

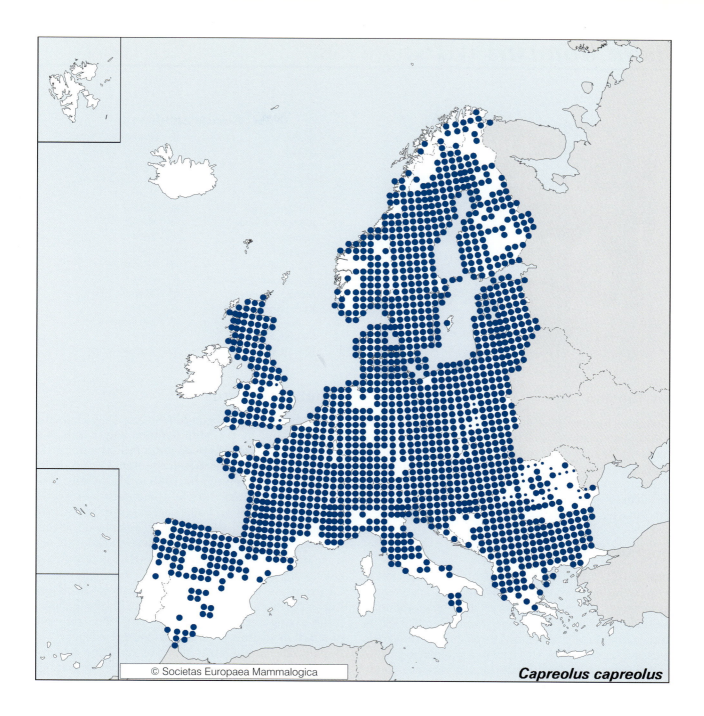

Capreolus capreolus

© Societas Europaea Mammalogica

401

Bison bonasus (Linnaeus, 1758)

F. Müller

European bison			
AL	Bizoni	LT	Stumbras
BG	Зубър	LU	-
CZ	Zubr	LV	Sumbrs
DE	Wisent	MK	Европски бизон
DK	Bison	MT	Buflu
EE	Euroopa piison; Pürg	NL	Wisent
ES	Bisonte europeo	NO	Visent
FI	Visentti	PL	Żubr
FO	Bisonur	PT	Bisão
FR	Bison d'Europe	RO	Zimbru
GR	Ευρωπαικός βίσωνας	RU	Зубр
HR	Bizon	SE	Visent
HU	Európai bölény	SI	Zober
IR	-	SK	Zubor hrivnatý
IS	Vísundur	TR	Bizon
IT	Bisonte europeo	YU	Европски бизон

Distribution

Endemic to Europe. The original geographic range of the European bison covered nearly the whole of Europe. At present, bison live in nearly 200 enclosed breeding centres and 32 free-living populations in Poland, Belarus, Lithuania, Ukraine and Russia. Roaming individuals found in eastern Slovakia, small groups in the Romanian Carpathians.

Geographic variation

In the early 19th century, two distinct subspecies of European bison occurred in two localities; the nominate lowland bison in Białowieża Forest and the montane or Caucasian bison *B. bonasus caucasicus* Turkin & Satunin, 1904 in the Caucasus. The offspring of one male Caucasian bison (which survived in a zoological garden in Germany) and female lowland bison gave rise to the line of Lowland-Caucasian bison. In the European Bison Pedigree Book, these bison are kept separate from individuals of pure Lowland line.

Habitat

The lowland bison occurred in the zone of temperate deciduous and mixed forests in Europe. The Caucasian bison inhabited forests and seasonally also mountain meadows in the north-west slopes of the Caucasus mountains.

Population status

In the 10th century the range of the bison began to shrink gradually and by the 19th century only two isolated populations survived in Białowieża Primeval Forest and in the Caucasus. The last free-living bison became extinct in the early 20th century (in 1919 in Białowieża, and in 1927 in Caucasus). Single specimens survived in zoological gardens and enclosed reserves in Germany, Poland and Sweden. All extant European bison originate from a mere 12 individuals. Białowieża Primeval Forest now harbours the largest free-living population, consisting of 569 individuals in 1995, whereas the Caucasus is inhabited by six populations of pure European bison as well as a 900-head herd of European bison x American bison hybrids. In 1995, the world population of European bison comprised over 3000 individuals; about 40% living in enclosed breeding centres and 60% in the wild. The species is no longer considered critically endangered.

International legal & conservation status

Bern Convention, Appendix III.
IUCN Red List, Endangered.

Literature

Krasiński (1994)
Pucek (1986) – review
Raczyński (1996)
Slatis (1960)

Z. A. Krasiński

Bison bonasus

Rupicapra pyrenaica BONAPARTE, 1845

D. Roth

Distribution

Endemic to Europe: the Pyrénées, north-western Spain and central Italy (Abruzzo).

Geographic variation

Three subspecies are recognized. Apennine populations: *R. pyrenaica ornata* Neumann, 1899. Iberian populations: *R. p. pyrenaica* Bonaparte, 1845 (Pyrénées) and *R. p. parva* Cabrera, 1911 (north-west Spain).

Habitat

Female groups and subadult males range over alpine meadows during the warm season. They stay at higher elevations as long as grass patches are available, otherwise they move to the forested lower slopes. Adult males seem to prefer more wooded and rugged areas all year long except during the rut. Principal environmental factors related to habitat selection are: the distribution of steep and rocky areas, aspect, distribution and quality of food, and snow depth.

Population status

Population trend and dispersion not evaluated. Southern chamois is relatively abundant, and though the Apennine chamois is technically endangered, current conservation management appears successful.

Apennine chamois have a geographically restricted distribution; very small populations, but possibly increasing trend. Densities of Iberian populations are low outside protected areas, where numbers are probably too high (30 up to 80 animals per 100 ha). About 35000 Southern chamois are estimated in Europe (Spain: >19000; France: 15000; Italy: 500).

International legal & conservation status

Bern Convention, Appendix II (*R. p. ornata* only), Appendix III (as part of *R. rupicapra sensu lato*).
EU Habitats & Species Directive, Annex II* & Annex IV (*R. p. ornata* only), Annex V (as part of *R. rupicapra sensu lato*).
CITES, Appendix I; EC 338/97, Annex A. (*R. p. ornata* only).
IUCN Red List, Endangered (*R. p. ornata* only).

Other information

A reintroduction plan for Apennine chamois has recently started (LIFE project). A group of 28 chamois was released in the Majella massif between 1991 and 1996, and more recently 26 were reintroduced into the Gran Sasso massif. About 40 individuals are kept in large breeding enclosures sited in five different areas. No studbook has been kept. All translocations took place in protected areas; further ones are suggested in the Velino Sirente Regional Park and in the Sibillini National Park.

© Societas Europaea Mammalogica

Rupicapra pyrenaica

Literature

Lovari & Cosentino (1986)
Masini & Lovari (1988)
Richard-Hansen *et al.* (1992)
Schröder *et al.* (1983)
Shackleton *et al.* (1997)

L. Pedrotti & S. Lovari

Rupicapra rupicapra (Linnaeus, 1758)

D. Roth

Alpine chamois

AL	Dhia e eger	LT	Gemzė
BG	Дива коэа	LU	Gems
CZ	Kamzík horský	LV	Eiropas ģemze
DE	Gemsé	MK	Дивокоэа
DK	Gemse	MT	Kamoxx
EE	Mägikits; Tava-mägikits	NL	Gems
ES	Rebeco alpino	NO	Gemse
FI	Gemssi	PL	Kozica
FO	Gemsa	PT	Camurça
FR	Chamois	RO	Capra-neagră
GR	Αγριόγιδο	RU	Серна
HR	Divokoza	SE	Gems
HU	Alpesi zerge	SI	Navadni gams
IR	-	SK	Kamzík vrchovský
IS	Gemsa	TR	Çengel boynuzlu dağ keçisi
IT	Camoscio	YU	Дивокоэа

Distribution

World: Mountain regions of central and southern Europe and Asia Minor between 35° and 50°N. Introduced to New Zealand and Argentina.
Europe: Chartreuse, Alps, High Tatra, Carpathians and Balkan countries. Introduced to northern Bohemia and northern Moravia, Lower Tatra, Vogeses, Massif Central, Swiss Jura, Black Forest and Schwäbische Alps.

Geographic variation

Seven subspecies are recognized (six are present in Europe and one in Asia Minor).

Habitat

Suitable habitats are steep and rocky areas. In summer, alpine and subalpine meadows above the timber line, in winter lower altitudes. Chamois are adaptable and may range from submontane, mixed broadleaved woodlands around 500 m or lower, to the alpine zone. A recent and substantial dispersal into forested areas has occurred (forest chamois ecotype).

Population status

Alpine chamois is currently widely distributed and generally increasing. Factors favouring this increase include a progressive decrease in agriculture and domestic livestock numbers in mountain areas, creation of protected areas and an improvement in biologically sound hunting regulations.

R. rupicapra carpatica Couturier, 1938: stable and fragmented population.
R. r. balcanica Bolkay, 1925: endangered in Greece, vulnerable in Albania and rare in Bulgaria; fragmented in very small populations; some populations stable, others decreasing.
R. r. tatrica Blahout, 1972: vulnerable in Poland and rare in Slovakia; geographically restricted distribution and decreasing population.
R. r. cartusiana Couturier, 1938: endangered in France; geographically restricted distribution and probably decreasing population; priority for immediate conservation action. About 150 individuals remain.
R. r. asiatica Lyddekker, 1908: insufficiently known in Turkey.
R. r. caucasica Lydekker, 1910: vulnerable; geographically restricted distribution and decreasing population in Caucasus.

About 440000 chamois estimated in Europe (excludes Caucasus populations). France: 40000; Switzerland: >100000; Austria: 157000; Italy: 100000; Germany: >10000; Czech Republic: 400; Slovenia and Croatia: >11000; Poland: 140; Slovakia: 725; Romania: 9000; Former Yugoslavia (except Slovenia and Croatia): 14400; Albania: 1050; Bulgaria: >1600; Greece: 400. Highest densities, reported for some protected areas, exceed 20/100 ha.

International legal & conservation status

Bern Convention, Appendix III.
EU Habitats & Species Directive, Annex II & Annex IV

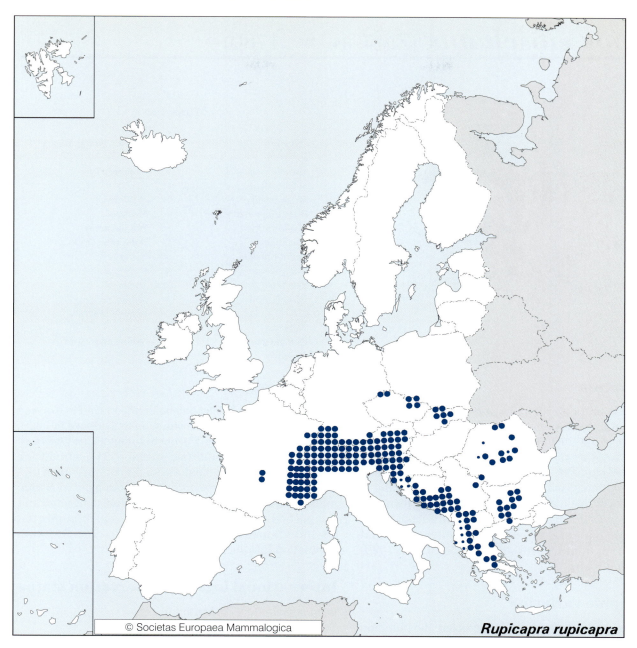

© Societas Europaea Mammalogica

Rupicapra rupicapra

(*R. r. balcanica* only).
IUCN Red List, Critically Endangered (*R. r. cartusiana* only).
IUCN Red List, Endangered (*R. r. tatrica* only).

Other information

Alpine chamois is hunted almost everywhere. Management and hunting methods vary and regional tradition is still the most important determinant. A tendency towards over-hunting outside protected areas and private hunting preserves may occur. Potential problems of chamois populations damaging their habitat should be addressed and examined in relation to human-induced disturbance (year-round tourism, hunting season, livestock grazing). In some areas recreation activities may significantly disturb chamois. Major threats for critical subspecies are poaching, domestic livestock grazing, habitat loss, and in some cases hybridization with introduced subspecies of other geographic origin.

Literature

Masini & Lovari (1988)
Sägesser & Krapp (1986) – review
Schröder *et al.* (1983)
Shackleton *et al.* (1997)

L. Pedrotti & S. Lovari

Ovibos moschatus (Zimmermann, 1780)

EO'97
E. Hazebroek

Distribution

World: circumpolar distribution in Greenland and Canada (indigenous populations), and in Alaska, Russia and Scandinavia (introduced populations).

Europe: widespread throughout Europe in prehistoric times, but disappeared about 4000 years ago, probably due to a combination of climate change and hunting by Neolithic man. No indigenous populations in historical time. Introduced several times to Norway, from where individuals have migrated and established a small population in Sweden. Introduced to Svalbard (1929), but died out there.

Geographic variation

Two subspecies are commonly recognized, the nominate subspecies on the mainland of Canada and *O. moschatus wardi* Lydekker, 1900 on the Arctic archipelago in Greenland. The introduced populations are all *O. m. wardi*.

Habitat

Confined to the alpine tundra heath in Scandinavia. During spring, however, musk oxen migrate to birch forests at lower altitudes. Following the progressing snow melt, they migrate upward to the open tundra heath above the tree-line. High winter precipitation is, particularly when combined with sequential ice-crust formation, a major factor affecting distribution and mortality patterns.

Population status

Since 1925, the musk ox has been introduced to Norway six times, including the introduction to Svalbard in 1929. Today, the only viable European population exists in Norway. This was established in 1947–53 by introducing 21 musk oxen from East Greenland. Since then the population has increased and now stabilized at a total number of 50–80. In 1971, five individuals migrated and established a population in Sweden, which numbered 38 individuals in 1987. Since then, the Swedish population has declined.

International legal & conservation status

Bern Convention, Appendix II.

Other information

The musk ox is known for its very soft and highly insulating under-wool, 'qiviut' (the Inuit term), which is shed annually in July. The American astronauts in the Apollo programme used underwear made of qiviut. Qiviut is highly expensive and, mainly for this reason, domestication programmes have been implemented in several places, including one in Norway. Due to problems with sickness and increased parasite load, the musk ox farm in Norway closed in 1976. In the High Arctic, musk oxen rarely suffer from parasites. Introduced to new habitats in Norway, however, the population quickly became infested with micro and macro parasites from the indigenous ruminant species. In Scandinavia,

Ovibos moschatus

© Societas Europaea Mammalogica

parasite-related mortality exerts a considerable influence on population dynamics. Musk ox-human interaction is a problem in Norway and, presently, steps are being taken to ensure a more intensive management of the population, including fencing, immobilization of migrating individuals and organized hunting schedules.

Literature

Alendal & Helle (1983)
Bohlken (1986) – review
Bretten (1990)
Forchhammer & Boertmann (1993)
Groves (1995)
Lent (1988) – review
Lundh (1991)

M. C. Forchhammer

Capra aegagrus ERXLEBEN, 1777

E. Hazebroek

Distribution

World: Palaearctic; Greece, southern and eastern Turkey, eastern Caucasus, Middle East, southern Turkmenistan, Afghanistan, south-western Pakistan. Introduced to USA, New Mexico and the Czech Republic. **Europe:** pure populations on Crete and its satellite islands. Feral populations of hybrids with domestic goats *Capra hircus* in other parts of Greece and in southern Moravia (Pálava).

Geographic variation

Four subspecies are recognized (one present in Europe). Their validity is still uncertain as insufficient research has been carried out to clarify the taxonomic situation. *Capra aegagrus cretica* Schinz, 1838: Cretan wild goat or agrimi, is restricted to a small area in the Lefka Mountains at the western end of Crete. A small semi-captive population of *C. a. cretica* is present on the island of Theodorou.

Habitat

Wild goats prefer to live in steep mountainous regions, particularly with shrub-covered areas, rocky outcrops with caves, overhangs and thickets, and conifer forests. They are superbly adapted to extremely varied and dry climatic conditions.

Population status

Wild goats appear safe, but require constant monitoring, because they could quickly become threatened. Wild goats usually live at low elevation in low productivity habitats that are readily accessible to humans. They live in small isolated populations, at low densities and may not be as secure as some believe. No general estimates are available for Turkey, but populations are fragmented and numbers are believed to be increasing slowly. The Agrimini population of Crete amounts to more than 600 animals with an increasing trend. In the Czech Republic, the population was removed from the original introduction area in 1997 and translocated to enclosures in various parts of the country.

International legal & conservation status

Bern Convention, Appendix II.
EU Habitats & Species Directive, Annex II & Annex IV (natural populations only).
IUCN Red List, Vulnerable.

Other information

Not native to the Mediterranean islands, as indicated by absence of fossils. Introduced by man, became feral, around the Neolithic period or later. High degree of interbreeding with domestic goats.

Conservation problems are related to the small total population size, but also to hybridization with domestic

Capra aegagrus

goats. Nearly all wild goats from Greece, except *C. a. cretica,* are interbred with domestic goats. Feral populations of domestic goat may occur in various areas; in Europe such populations are found living wild, particularly in the British Isles. Populations introduced from Mediterranean islands are kept in several enclosures in the Czech Republic. It is highly probable that they were hybridized with domestic goats in the past and so they are not shown on the map.

Literature

Husband & Davis (1984)
Nievergelt (1986) – review
Shackelton *et al.* (1997)

L. Pedrotti & S. Lovari

Capra ibex LINNAEUS, 1758

F. Müller

	Alpine ibex		
AL	-	LT	Alpių ožys
BG	Алпийски козел	LU	Steebock
CZ	Kozorožec horský	LV	Alpu kaza
DE	Alpen-Steinbock	MK	Алпски коэорог
DK	Alpestenbuk	MT	-
EE	Alpi kaljukits	NL	Steenbok
ES	Íbice de los Alpes	NO	Alpesteinbukk
FI	Alppikauris	PL	Koziorożec alpejski
FO	-	PT	-
FR	Bouquetin des Alpes	RO	-
GR	-	RU	Альпийский козёл
HR	Planinski kozorog	SE	Stenbock
HU	Kőszáli kecske	SI	Alpski kozorog
IR	-	SK	Kozorožec vrchovský
IS	Steingeit	TR	-
IT	Stambecco delle Alpi	YU	Козорог

Ibex populations occurring in northern Africa and Asia are usually treated as species distinct from *Capra ibex* (*C. nubiana, C. sibirica, C. walie*).

Distribution

Endemic to Europe: the Alps of France, Switzerland, Austria, Germany and northern Italy. Introduced to Slovenia, Bulgaria, and the USA.

Geographic variation

Only the nominate subspecies recognized.

Habitat

Rocky montane regions at altitudes between 500 and 3000 m. Ibex's preferred winter habitat is steep and south-exposed slopes with grassy vegetation and rugged, rock-interspersed relief around 1600–2800 m. Gregarious, living in herds of up to 50 and more; active predominantly during the day. Diet consists of alpine grasses and rocky plants and shrubs.

Population status

Ibex disappeared from several regions of the Alps where formerly it was abundant above the tree line. After being reduced by over-hunting to few hundred animals distributed only in Gran Paradiso Massif (Italy), in 1821–1836 it was legally protected by the creation of the Royal Hunting Preserve in the Gran Paradiso. After being rescued from the brink of extinction, Alpine ibex are now considered safe with current conservation management. Translocation programmes, combined with some natural colonization, have increased the range of ibex, but its distribution is still rather discontinuous in the Alps. Generally increasing. Mean population size still low. About 30000 ibex estimated in Europe: France: 3300; Switzerland: 15100; Austria: 3300; Italy: 10000; Germany: 300; Slovenia: 220; Liechtenstein: 430. The highest summer densities in Gran Paradiso National Park range between 15 and 24 ind./100 ha.

International legal & conservation status

Bern Convention, Appendix III.
EU Habitats & Species Directive, Annex V.

Other information

All current populations originated from translocations of ibex from Gran Paradiso National Parks (reintroduction to former habitat or introductions into areas where they were not known to occur historically) or from subsequent natural colonization. The discontinuity of occupied areas and concomitant isolation for many colonies still encourage development of reintroduction programme incentives. Although the ibex is not threatened, there is concern regarding genetic variability within colonies, founder effect and minimum viable population. Interbreeding has been reported where goat densities are high and where ibex have recently been reintroduced. Serious consideration must

© Societas Europaea Mammalogica

Capra ibex

be given to controlling free-pasture of domestic sheep and goats in alpine ranges used by ibex because of disturbance, hybridization and disease transmission.

Stüwe & Nievergelt (1991)
Tosi *et al.* (1986)

L. Pedrotti & S. Lovari

Literature

Bassano & Peracino (1994)
Giacometti (1991)
Nievergelt & Zingg (1986) – review
Pedrotti (1995)
Randi *et al.* (1990)
Ratti (1994)
Shackelton *et al.* (1997)

Capra pyrenaica Schinz, 1838

D. Roth

Spanish ibex

AL	-	LU	Spueneschen Steebock
BG	Пиренейски козел	LV	Pireneju kaza
CZ	Kozorožec iberský	MK	-
DE	Pyrenäen-Steinbock	MT	-
DK	Pyrenæisk stenbuk	NL	Iberische steenbok
EE	Pürenee kaljukits	NO	Pyreneersteinbukk
ES	Cabra montés ibérica	PL	Kozioróżec pirenejski
FI	Pyrenæidenvuorikauris	PT	Cabra-montez; Cabra do
FO	-		Gerês
FR	Bouquetin des Pyrénées	RO	-
GR	-	RU	Козёл пиренейский
HR	Pirenejski kozorog	SE	Iberisk stenbock
HU	Spanyol kecske	SI	Pirenejski kozorog
IR	-	SK	Kozorožec pyrenejský
IS	Spánargeit	TR	-
IT	Stambecco iberico	YU	Шпански козорог
LT	-		

The current classification of the Alpine and the Spanish ibex as separate species should be considered tentative. Based on allozyme electrophoresis, the genetic distance between Alpine and Spanish ibex does not exceed a value typical for ungulate subspecies.

Distribution

Endemic to Europe. In the Holocene, distributed on all the mountains of the Iberian Peninsula. At present, dispersed in isolated populations. Mountain areas of the Pyrénées, central and southern Spain.

Geographic variation

Three subspecies are recognized, the fourth, *C. pyrenaica lusitanica* Franca, 1909 became extinct in 1892. The nominate subspecies, formerly distributed in the Spanish Pyrénées, is now restricted to Ordesa National Park; *C. p. victoriae* Cabrera, 1911 is limited to a single population in the Sierra de Gredos Hunting Preserve; *C. p. hispanica* Schimper, 1848 was previously more widespread throughout southern Spain, but is now found in six main areas from Gibraltar to the mouth of Ebro river, including Sierra Morena.

Habitat

Mountain areas of the Pyrénées, central and southern Spain. Spanish ibex live on the cliffs and in the meadows above the timberline but climb down to the forested slopes, especially after snowfall and in spring. They are often found in dry areas where the sparse forests were cut down, or in oak and pine forests.

Population status

C. p. pyrenaica is at present virtually extinct; recent official reports indicate the presence of only two females in Ordesa National Park; priority for immediate conservation action.

C. p. victoriae is restricted to a single population and believed to be stable, with the last official census recording 3300 head.

C. p. hispanica suffered a serious reduction in numbers from a mange infection; today the total estimate is *c.* 7900, subdivided into very small populations.

International legal & conservation status

Bern Convention, Appendix III, but *C. p. pyrenaica* is Appendix II.
EU Habitats & Species Directive, Annex II* & Annex IV (*C. p. pyrenaica* only), Annex V.
IUCN Red List, *C. p. pyrenaica:* Critically Endangered; *C. p. victoriae:* Vulnerable; *C. p. hispanica:* Lower Risk – near-threatened.

Other information

The status of Spanish ibex could deteriorate if such factors as overgrazing and disease transmission by domestic animal occur (in Cazorla y Segura ibex density dropped more than 90% as a consequence of mange

© Societas Europaea Mammalogica

Capra pyrenaica

transmitted by domestic goats). *C.p. pyrenaica* is defined as the top priority taxon in the Conservation Action Plan for *Caprinae*. A European recovery plan (LIFE Project) has been started to capture and subsequently to captive breed the last individuals with males of other subspecies in order to recover the population and reintroduce captive-bred animals. Causes of decline are unknown, but there are a number of hypotheses, including competition for food with chamois, inbreeding depression, parasitic infections from domestic livestock, climatic conditions and poaching.

Literature

Alados & Escos (1996)
Engländer (1986) – review
Guiral *et al.* (1997)
Hartl *et al.* (1995)
Shackleton *et al.* (1997)

L. Pedrotti & S. Lovari

Ammotragus lervia (Pallas, 1777)

M. Năzăreanu

Distribution

World: native to North Africa, introduced to USA and Mexico.
Europe: introduction has been attempted in Spain, including the Canary Islands, and a small population has appeared recently in the Czech Republic after an escape from a zoo in 1976.

Geographic variation

About seven subspecies currently recognized. The origin of the European population is unclear.

Habitat

Rocky dry mountains and broken country of the Saharan zone. They are very good climbers and jumpers. Habitats occupied in the Czech Republic apparently inappropriate in the view of the species' requirements.

Population status

Lives in family groups in geographic isolates. Numbers rapidly decreasing in the northern parts of the native range and it has become extinct in certain areas (Egypt). Size of the European population only several tens to hundreds of individuals. The occurrence in the Czech Republic seems only temporary.

International legal & conservation status

CITES, Appendix II. EC 338/97, Annex B.
IUCN Red List, Vulnerable.

Other information

Hunted in the Czech Republic.

Literature

Gray & Simpson (1980)
Shackleton *et al.* (1997)

J. Zima & M. Homolka

© Societas Europaea Mammalogica

Ammotragus lervia

Ovis ammon (Linnaeus, 1758)

J. Mikuletič

Despite high phenotypic and karyotypic variation, the wild sheep which occurs from Europe to Mongolia belongs to only one species. In recent literature, the name *Ovis aries* may be used for this species. We avoid this, because the name was created for the domesticated form.

Distribution

World: Corsica, Sardinia, Cyprus, Anatolia, Armenia, northern and eastern Iraq, Iran, Turkistan, Afghanistan south of the Hindu Kush, Pakistan west of the Indus, northern India, Pamir, the highlands of Tibet, through the Tien Shan mountains to the Gobi Altai mountains in Mongolia. As well as Europe, it has also been introduced into California, Texas, Hawaii, Argentina and the Kerguelens.

Europe: from the middle of the 18th century, mouflon from Corsica and Sardinia have been brought to continental Europe. Free-ranging herds are now present in Spain, France, Belgium, Luxembourg, Germany, Denmark, Italy, Austria, Switzerland, Slovenia, Croatia, the Czech Republic, Slovakia, Poland, Finland, Romania, Bulgaria, Lithuania, Bosnia Herzegovina, Macedonia, Yugoslavia and Ukraine (Crimea).

Geographic variation

There is a remarkable increase in body size from west to east (in males: 35–180 kg; in females: 30–90 kg). Differences in body size, coat colour and the shape of the horns have led to the description of more than 20 subspecies.

Habitat

Much variation within the wide distribution range. Open hill areas, bushy landscapes, woods, semi-deserts, high mountains with cold deserts. Altitudes from 300 m up to 6100 m. The digestive system is of a grass-eating type. Different habitats and seasons produce a great adaptability to different foods: grasses, herbs, shrubs, leaves, sedges, sage, lichens, bark, wood, seeds and fruit.

Population status

Very variable. On the whole, both numbers and distribution are decreasing. The reasons include: political changes in eastern Europe, revolutions and wars in Asia, illegal persecution and the introduction of domestic livestock into protected areas. Within Europe, well protected populations live on Corsica and Sardinia. Mouflon that have been introduced into other areas have a good chance of survival.

International legal & conservation status

Bern Convention, Appendix III.
EU Habitats & Species Directive, Annex II & Annex IV (only natural populations on Corsica and Sardinia).
IUCN Red List, Vulnerable (only autochthonous populations).

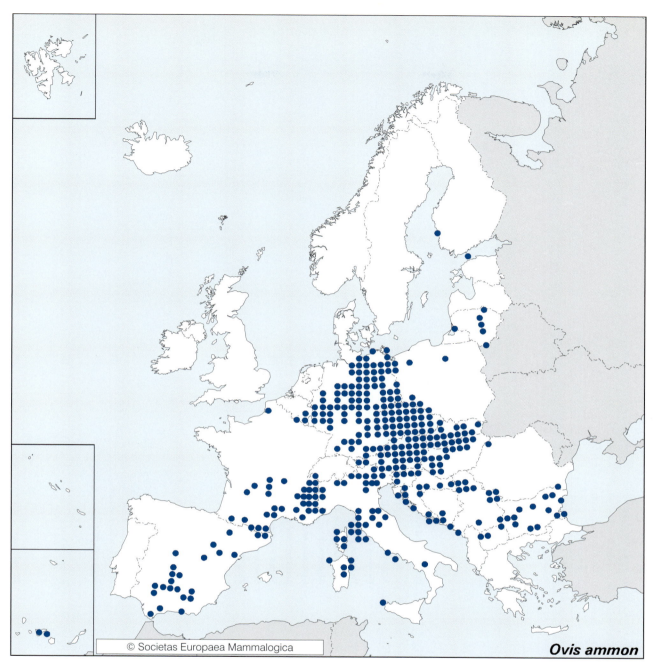

© Societas Europaea Mammalogica

Ovis ammon

Other information

Hunted for trophies and meat. Introduced mouflon
appear to have no great impact on other mammalian
species. *Ovis ammon* is the ancestor of the domestic
sheep.

Literature

Herre & Röhrs (1955)
Röhrs (1986) – review

M. Röhrs

List of European Mammal Species
with their international legal and conservation status

This list includes all extant mammal species resident in the study area of the *Fauna Europaea*.[1]
Taxonomy is based on Wilson & Reeder (1993), with the few exceptions described in the Introduction (p5).
Data for rodents and lagomorphs of European Russia have been checked with Gromov & Erbaeva (1995) and for insectivores in the Caucasus with Sokolov & Tembotov (1989)

Species in **bold** are described in this atlas.

Scientific name	Authority	English name	Habitats Directive	Bern	Bonn	CITES I,II & EC 338/97 A,B	ICRW	IUCN
Macropus rufogriseus	(Desmarest, 1817)	**Red-necked wallaby**	-	-	-	-	-	-
Atelerix algirus	(Lereboullet, 1842)	**Algerian hedgehog**	IV	II	-	-	-	-
Erinaceus concolor	Martin, 1838	**Eastern hedgehog**	-	-	-	-	-	-
Erinaceus europaeus	Linnaeus, 1758	**Western hedgehog**	-	III	-	-	-	-
Hemiechinus auritus	(Gmelin, 1770)	Long-eared hedgehog	-	-	-	-	-	-
Sorex alpinus	Schinz, 1837	**Alpine shrew**	-	III	-	-	-	-
Sorex araneus	Linnaeus, 1758	**Common shrew**	-	III	-	-	-	-
Sorex caecutiens	Laxmann, 1788	**Masked shrew**	-	III	-	-	-	-
Sorex coronatus	Millet, 1828	**Millet's shrew**	-	III	-	-	-	-
Sorex granarius	Miller, 1910	**Spanish shrew**	-	III	-	-	-	-
Sorex isodon	Turov, 1924	**Taiga shrew**	-	III	-	-	-	-
Sorex minutissimus	Zimmermann, 1780	**Least shrew**	-	III	-	-	-	-
Sorex minutus	Linnaeus, 1766	**Pygmy shrew**	-	III	-	-	-	-
Sorex raddei	Satunin, 1895		-	.	-	-	-	-
Sorex samniticus	Altobello, 1926	**Appenine shrew**	-	III	-	-	-	-
Sorex satunini	Ognev, 1922		-	.	-	-	-	-
Sorex tundrensis	Merriam, 1900	Tundra shrew	-	.	-	-	-	-
Sorex volnuchini	Ognev, 1922		-	.	-	-	-	-
Neomys anomalus	Cabrera, 1907	**Miller's water shrew**	-	III	-	-	-	-
Neomys fodiens	(Pennant, 1771)	**Water shrew**	-	III	-	-	-	-
Neomys teres	Miller, 1908		-	.	-	-	-	-
Crocidura canariensis	Hutterer, López-Jurado & Vogel, 1987	**Canary shrew**	IV	II	-	-	-	VU
Crocidura gueldenstaedtii	(Pallas, 1811)		-	-	-	-	-	-
Crocidura leucodon	(Hermann, 1780)	**Bi-coloured white-toothed shrew**	-	III	-	-	-	-

Scientific name	Authority	English name	Habitats Directive	Bern	Bonn	CITES I,II & ICRW EC 338/97 A,B	IUCN
Crocidura osorio	Molina & Hutterer, 1989	Osorio shrew	-	III	-	-	VU
Crocidura russula	(Hermann, 1780)	Greater white-toothed shrew	-	III	-	-	-
Crocidura sicula	Miller, 1900	Sicilian shrew	-	III	-	-	-
Crocidura suaveolens	(Pallas, 1811)	Lesser white-toothed shrew	-	III; II (only C.s. caneae)	-	-	-
Crocidura zimmermanni	Wettstein, 1953	Cretan white-toothed shrew	-	III	-	-	VU
Suncus etruscus	(Savi, 1822)	Pygmy white-toothed shrew	-	III	-	-	-
Desmana moschata	(Linnaeus, 1758)	Russian desman	-	II	-	-	VU
Galemys pyrenaicus	(E. Geoffroy, 1811)	Pyrenean desman	II/IV	II	-	-	VU
Talpa caeca	Savi, 1822	Blind mole	-	-	-	-	-
Talpa caucasica	Satunin, 1908	Caucasian mole	-	-	-	-	-
Talpa europaea	Linnaeus, 1758	Common mole	-	-	-	-	-
Talpa levantis	Thomas, 1906	Levant mole	-	-	-	-	-
Talpa occidentalis	Cabrera, 1907	Iberian mole	-	-	-	-	-
Talpa romana	Thomas, 1902	Roman mole	-	-	-	-	-
Talpa stankovici	V. Martino & E. Martino, 1931	Balkan mole	-	-	-	-	-
Rhinolophus blasii	Peters, 1866	Blasius' horseshoe bat	II/IV	II	II	-	LR-nt
Rhinolophus euryale	Blasius, 1853	Mediterranean horseshoe bat	II/IV	II	II	-	VU
Rhinolophus ferrumequinum	(Schreber, 1774)	Greater horseshoe bat	II/IV	II	II	-	LR-cd
Rhinolophus hipposideros	(Bechstein, 1800)	Lesser horseshoe bat	III/IV	II	II	-	VU
Rhinolophus mehelyi	Matschie, 1901	Mehely's horseshoe bat	III/IV	II	II	-	VU
Myotis bechsteinii	(Kuhl, 1817)	Bechstein's bat	III/IV	II	II	-	VU
Myotis blythii	(Tomes, 1857)	Lesser mouse-eared bat	III/IV	II	II	-	-
Myotis brandtii	(Eversmann, 1845)	Brandt's bat	IV	II	II	-	-
Myotis capaccinii	(Bonaparte, 1837)	Long-fingered bat	II/IV	II	II	-	VU
Myotis dasycneme	(Boie, 1825)	Pond bat	II/IV	II	II	-	VU
Myotis daubentonii	(Kuhl, 1817)	Daubenton's bat	IV	II	II	-	-
Myotis emarginatus	(E. Geoffroy, 1806)	Geoffroy's bat	II/IV	II	II	-	VU
Myotis myotis	(Borkhausen, 1797)	Greater mouse-eared bat	II/IV	II	II	-	LR-nt
Myotis mystacinus	(Kuhl, 1817)	Whiskered bat	IV	II	II	-	-
Myotis nattereri	(Kuhl, 1817)	Natterer's bat	IV	II	II	-	-
Pipistrellus kuhlii	(Kuhl, 1817)	Kuhl's pipistrelle	IV	II	II	-	-
Pipistrellus maderensis	(Dobson, 1878)	Madeira pipistrelle	IV	II	II	-	VU
Pipistrellus nathusii	(Keyserling & Blasius, 1839)	Nathusius' pipistrelle	IV	II	II	-	-
Pipistrellus pipistrellus	(Schreber, 1774)	Common pipistrelle	IV	III	II	-	-
Pipistrellus savii	(Bonaparte, 1837)	Savi's pipistrelle	IV	II	II	-	-

Scientific name	Authority	English name	Habitats Directive	Bern	Bonn	CITES I,II & EC 338/97 A,B	ICRW	IUCN
Nyctalus azoreum	(Thomas, 1901)	Azorean bat	IV	II	II	-	-	VU
Nyctalus lasiopterus	(Schreber, 1780)	Greater noctule	IV	II	II	-	-	LR-nt
Nyctalus leisleri	(Kuhl, 1817)	Leisler's bat	IV	II	II	-	-	LR-nt
Nyctalus noctula	(Schreber, 1774)	Noctule	IV	II	II	-	-	-
Eptesicus bottae	(Peters, 1869)	Botta's serotine	IV	II	II	-	-	-
Eptesicus nilssonii	(Keyserling & Blasius, 1839)	Northern bat	IV	II	II	-	-	-
Eptesicus serotinus	(Schreber, 1774)	Serotine	IV	II	II	-	-	-
Vespertilio murinus	Linnaeus, 1758	Parti-coloured bat	IV	II	II	-	-	-
Barbastella barbastellus	(Schreber, 1774)	Barbastelle	II/IV	II	II	-	-	VU
Plecotus auritus	(Linnaeus, 1758)	Brown long-eared bat	IV	II	II	-	-	-
Plecotus austriacus	(J. Fischer, 1829)	Grey long-eared bat	IV	II	II	-	-	-
Plecotus teneriffae	Barrett-Hamilton, 1907	Tenerife long-eared bat	IV	II	II	-	-	VU
Miniopterus schreibersii	(Kuhl, 1817)	Schreibers' bat	II/IV	II	II	-	-	LR-nt
Tadarida teniotis	(Rafinesque, 1814)	European free-tailed bat	IV	II	II	-	-	-
Macaca sylvanus	(Linnaeus, 1758)	Barbary ape	-	-	-	II, B	-	VU
Ochotona alpina	(Pallas, 1773)	Northern pika	-	-	-	-	-	-
Ochotona pusilla	(Pallas, 1769)	Steppe pika	-	-	-	-	-	VU
Lepus capensis	Linnaeus, 1758	Cape hare	-	III	-	-	-	-
Lepus castroviejoi	Palacios, 1977	Broom hare	-	III	-	-	-	VU
Lepus corsicanus	de Winton, 1898	Corsican hare	-	III	-	-	-	-
Lepus europaeus	Pallas, 1778	Brown hare	-	III	-	-	-	-
Lepus granatensis	Rosenhauer, 1856	Iberian hare	-	III	-	-	-	-
Lepus timidus	Linnaeus, 1758	Mountain hare	V	III	-	-	-	-
Lepus tolai	Pallas, 1778	(Hare)	-	-	-	-	-	-
Oryctolagus cuniculus	(Linnaeus, 1758)	Rabbit	-	-	-	-	-	-
Sylvilagus floridanus	(J. A. Allen, 1890)	Eastern cottontail rabbit	-	-	-	-	-	-
Sciurus anomalus	Güldenstaedt, 1785	Persian squirrel	IV	II	-	-	-	LR-nt
Sciurus carolinensis	Gmelin, 1788	Grey squirrel	-	-	-	-	-	-
Sciurus vulgaris	Linnaeus, 1758	Red squirrel	-	III	-	-	-	LR-nt
Callosciurus erythraeus	(Pallas, 1779)	Pallas's squirrel	-	-	-	-	-	-
Callosciurus finlaysonii	(Horsfield, 1824)	Thailand tree squirrel	-	-	-	-	-	-
Marmota bobak	Müller, 1776	Bobak marmot	-	-	-	-	-	LR-cd
Atlantoxerus getulus	(Linnaeus, 1758)	Barbary ground squirrel	-	-	-	-	-	-
Marmota marmota	(Linnaeus, 1758)	Alpine marmot	-	III	-	-	-	-
Spermophilus citellus	(Linnaeus, 1766)	European souslik	II/IV	II	-	-	-	VU

Scientific name	Authority	English name	Habitats Directive	Bern	Bonn	CITES I,II & ICRW EC 338/97 A,B	IUCN
Spermophilus fulvus	(Lichtenstein, 1823)	Large-toothed souslik	-	-	-	-	-
Spermophilus major	(Pallas, 1778)	Russet souslik	-	-	-	-	LR-nt
Spermophilus musicus	Ménétries, 1832	(souslik)	-	-	-	-	-
Spermophilus pygmaeus	(Pallas 1778)	Little souslik	-	-	-	-	-
Spermophilus suslicus	(Güldenstaedt, 1770)	Spotted souslik	-	II	-	-	VU
Tamias sibiricus	(Laxmann, 1769)	Siberian chipmunk	-	-	-	-	-
Pteromys volans	(Linnaeus, 1758)	Russian flying squirrel	II*/IV	II	-	-	LR-nt
Castor canadensis	Kuhl, 1820	American beaver	-	-	-	-	-
Castor fiber	Linnaeus, 1758	Eurasian beaver	II/IV (excl. Finnish & Swedish pops.); V	III	-	-	LR-nt
Cricetus cricetus	(Linnaeus, 1758)	Common hamster	IV	II	-	-	-
Allocricetulus eversmanni	(Brandt, 1859)	(hamster)	-	-	-	-	-
Cricetulus migratorius	(Pallas,1773)	Grey hamster	-	-	-	-	LR-nt
Mesocricetus newtoni	(Nehring, 1898)	Romanian hamster	-	II	-	-	VU
Mesocricetus raddei	(Nehring, 1894)	Ciscaucasian hamster	-	-	-	-	-
Dicrostonyx torquatus	(Pallas, 1778)	Collared lemming	-	-	-	-	-
Myopus schisticolor	(Lilljeborg, 1844)	Wood lemming	-	-	-	-	LR-nt
Lemmus lemmus	(Linnaeus, 1758)	Norway lemming	-	-	-	-	-
Lemmus sibiricus	(Kerr, 1792)	Siberian lemming	-	-	-	-	-
Clethrionomys glareolus	(Schreber, 1780)	Bank vole	-	-	-	-	-
Clethrionomys rufocanus	(Sundevall, 1846)	Grey-sided vole	-	-	-	-	-
Clethrionomys rutilus	(Pallas, 1779)	Red vole	-	-	-	-	-
Dinaromys bogdanovi	(Martino, 1922)	Balkan snow vole	-	-	-	-	LR-nt
Arvicola sapidus	Miller, 1908	Southern water vole	-	-	-	-	LR-nt
Arvicola terrestris	(Linnaeus, 1758)	Water vole	-	-	-	-	-
Ondatra zibethicus	(Linnaeus, 1766)	Muskrat	-	-	-	-	-
Microtus agrestis	(Linnaeus, 1761)	Field vole	-	-	-	-	-
Microtus arvalis	(Pallas, 1778)	Common vole	-	-	-	-	-
Microtus cabrerae	Thomas, 1906	Cabrera's vole	II/IV	III	-	-	LR-nt
Microtus daghestanicus	(Shidlovskii, 1919)	(vole)	-	-	-	-	-
Microtus duodecimcostatus	de Sélys-Longchamps, 1839	Mediterranean pine vole	-	-	-	-	-
Microtus gregalis	(Pallas, 1779)	Narrow-skulled vole	-	-	-	-	-
Microtus felteni	Malec & Storch, 1963	Balkan pine vole	-	-	-	-	LR-nt
Microtus gerbei	(Gerbe, 1879)	Pyrenean pine vole	-	-	-	-	-
Microtus guentheri	(Danford & Alston, 1880)	Guenther's vole	-	-	-	-	LR-nt
Microtus lusitanicus	(Gerbe, 1879)	Lusitanian pine vole	-	-	-	-	-

Scientific name	Authority	English name	Habitats Directive	Bern	Bonn	CITES I,II & ICRW EC 338/97 A,B	IUCN
Microtus majori	Thomas, 1906	Caucasian pine vole	-	-	-	-	-
Microtus multiplex	(Fatio, 1905)	**Alpine pine vole**	-	-	-	-	-
Microtus obscurus	(Eversmann, 1841)	(vole)					
Microtus oeconomus	(Pallas, 1776)	**Root vole**	II*/IV (only *M.o. arenicola*); IV (only *M.o. mehelyi*)	III	-	-	**LR-nt**
Microtus rossiaemeridionalis	Ognev, 1924	**Sibling vole**	-	-	-	-	-
Microtus savii	de Sélys-Longchamps, 1838	**Savi's pine vole**	-	-	-	-	-
Microtus socialis	(Pallas, 1773)	Social vole, Steppe vole	-	-	-	-	
Microtus subterraneus	de Sélys-Longchamps, 1836	**Common pine vole**	-	-	-	-	-
Microtus tatricus	Kratochvíl, 1952	**Tatra vole**	-	II	-	-	**LR-nt**
Microtus thomasi	(Barrett-Hamilton, 1903)	**Thomas's vole**	-	-	-	-	**LR-nt**
Chionomys gud	(Satunin, 1909)	Caucasian snow vole	-	-	-	-	LR-nt
Chionomys nivalis	(Martins, 1842)	**Snow vole**	-	III	-	-	**LR-nt**
Chionomys roberti	(Thomas, 1906)	Robert's snow vole	-	-	-	-	LR-nt
Lagurus lagurus	(Pallas, 1773)	Steppe lemming	-	-	-	-	-
Prometheomys schaposchnikowi	Satunin, 1901	Long-clawed mole-vole	-	-	-	-	-
Ellobius talpinus	(Pallas, 1770)	Northern mole-vole	-	-	-	-	-
Meriones meridianus	(Pallas, 1773)	Midday gerbil	-	-	-	-	-
Meriones tamariscinus	(Pallas, 1773)	Tamarisk gerbil	-	-	-	-	-
Meriones tristrami	Thomas, 1892	**Tristram's jird**	-	-	-	-	-
Spalax arenarius	Reshetnik, 1939	Sandy mole rat	-	-	-	-	VU
Spalax giganteus	Nehring, 1898	Giant mole rat	-	-	-	-	VU
Spalax graecus	Nehring, 1898	**Balkan mole rat**	-	II	-	-	**VU**
Spalax microphthalmus	Güldenstaedt, 1770	Greater mole rat	-	-	-	-	VU
Spalax zemni	Erxleben, 1777	Podolsky mole rat	-	-	-	-	-
Nannospalax leucodon	(Nordmann, 1840)	Lesser mole rat	-	-	-	-	VU
Micromys minutus	(Pallas, 1771)	**Harvest mouse**	-	-	-	-	**LR-nt**
Apodemus agrarius	(Pallas, 1771)	**Striped field mouse**	-	-	-	-	-
Apodemus alpicola	Heinrich, 1952	**Alpine-mouse**	-	-	-	-	**dd**
Apodemus flavicollis	Melchior, 1834	**Yellow-necked mouse**	-	-	-	-	-
Apodemus fulvipectus	Ognev, 1924	(mouse)	-	-	-	-	-
Apodemus mystacinus	(Danford & Alston, 1877)	**Rock mouse**	-	-	-	-	-
Apodemus ponticus	Sviridenko, 1936	(mouse)	-	-	-	-	-
Apodemus sylvaticus	(Linnaeus, 1758)	**Wood mouse**	-	-	-	-	-

Scientific name	Authority	English name	Habitats Directive	Bern	Bonn	CITES I,II & EC 338/97 A,B	ICRW	IUCN
Apodemus uralensis	(Pallas, 1811)	**Pygmy field mouse**	-	-	-	-	-	-
Rattus norvegicus	(Berkenhout, 1769)	**Brown rat**	-	-	-	-	-	-
Rattus rattus	(Linnaeus, 1758)	**Black rat, Ship rat**	-	-	-	-	-	-
Mus domesticus	Schwartz & Schwartz, 1943	**Western house mouse**	-	-	-	-	-	-
Mus macedonicus	Petrov & Ružić, 1983	**Balkan short-tailed mouse**	-	-	-	-	-	-
Mus musculus	Linnaeus, 1758	**Eastern house mouse**	-	-	-	-	-	-
Mus spicilegus	Petényi, 1882	**Steppe mouse**	-	-	-	-	-	LR-nt
Mus spretus	Lataste, 1883	**Algerian mouse**	-	-	-	-	-	-
Acomys minous	Bate, 1906	**Cretan spiny mouse**	-	-	-	-	-	VU
Glis glis	(Linnaeus, 1766)	**Fat dormouse, Edible dormouse**	-	III	-	-	-	LR-nt
Muscardinus avellanarius	Linnaeus, 1758	**Common dormouse**	IV	III	-	-	-	LR-nt
Eliomys quercinus	(Linnaeus, 1766)	**Garden dormouse**	-	III	-	-	-	VU
Dryomys nitedula	(Pallas, 1778)	**Forest dormouse**	IV	III	-	-	-	LR-nt
Myomimus roachi	(Bate, 1937)	**Mouse-tailed dormouse**	-	II	-	-	-	VU
Sicista betulina	(Pallas, 1779)	**Northern birch mouse**	IV	II	-	-	-	LR-nt
Sicista caucasica	Vinogradov, 1925	(birch mouse)	-	-	-	-	-	-
Sicista kazbegica	Sokolov, Baskevich & Kovalskaya, 1986	(birch mouse)	-	-	-	-	-	dd
Sicista kluchorica	Sokolov, Kovalskaya & Baskevich, 1980	(birch mouse)	-	-	-	-	-	dd
Sicista severtzovi	Ognev, 1935	(birch mouse)	-	-	-	-	-	-
Sicista strandi	(Formozov, 1931)	(birch mouse)	-	-	-	-	-	-
Sicista subtilis	(Pallas, 1773)	**Southern birch mouse**	-	II	-	-	-	LR-nt
Dipus sagitta	(Pallas, 1773)	Northern three-toed jerboa	-	-	-	-	-	-
Stylodipus telum	(Lichtenstein, 1823)	Thick-tailed three-toed jerboa	-	-	-	-	-	-
Allactaga elater	(Lichtenstein, 1828)	Small five-toed jerboa	-	-	-	-	-	-
Allactaga major	(Kerr, 1792)	Great jerboa	-	-	-	-	-	-
Pygeretmus pumilio	(Kerr, 1792)	(jerboa)	-	-	-	-	-	-
Hystrix cristata	Linnaeus, 1758	**Crested porcupine**	IV	II	-	-	-	LR-nt
Myocastor coypus	(Molina, 1782)	**Coypu**	-	-	-	-	-	-
Delphinapterus leucas	(Pallas, 1776)	White whale	IV	III	II	II,A	-	VU
Monodon monoceros	Linnaeus, 1758	Narwhal	IV	II	II	II,A	-	dd
Phocoena phocoena	(Linnaeus, 1758)	Harbour porpoise	II/IV	II	II only North, Baltic and Black Seas	II,A	-	VU
Steno bredanensis	(Lesson, 1828)	Rough-toothed dolphin	IV	II	-	II,A	-	dd

Scientific name	Authority	English name	Habitats Directive	Bern	Bonn	CITES I,II & EC 338/97 A,B	ICRW	IUCN
Delphinus delphis	Linnaeus, 1758	Common dolphin	IV	II	II only North, Baltic and Black Seas and western Mediterranean	-	-	-
Sousa teuszii	(Kükenthal, 1892)	Atlantic hump-backed dolphin	IV	II	II	I,A	-	dd
Stenella attenuata	(Gray, 1846)	Pantropical spotted dolphin	IV	II	-	II,A	-	LR-cd
Stenella clymene	(Gray, 1846)	Clymene dolphin	IV	II	-	II,A	-	dd
Stenella coeruleoalba	(Meyen, 1833)	Striped dolphin	IV	II	II only western Mediterranean	II,A	-	LR-cd
Stenella frontalis	(G. Cuvier, 1829)	Atlantic spotted dolphin	IV	II	-	II,A	-	dd
Lagenodelphis hosei	Fraser, 1956	Fraser's dolphin	IV	III	-	II,A	-	dd
Lagenorhynchus acutus	(Gray, 1828)	White-sided dolphin	IV	II	II only North and Baltic Seas	II,A	-	-
Lagenorhynchus albirostris	(Gray, 1846)	White-beaked dolphin	IV	II	II only North and Baltic Seas	II,A	-	-
Tursiops truncatus	(Montagu, 1821)	Bottlenose dolphin	II/IV	II	II only North, Baltic and Black Seas and western Mediterranean	II,A	-	dd
Grampus griseus	(G. Cuvier, 1812)	Risso's dolphin	IV	II	II only North and Baltic seas	II,A	-	dd
Globicephala melas	(Traill,1809)	Long-finned pilot whale	IV	II	II only North and Baltic seas	II,A	-	-
Globicephala macrorhynchus	Gray, 1846	Short-finned pilot whale	IV	II	-	II,A	-	LR- rd
Orcinus orca	(Linnaeus, 1758)	Killer whale	IV	II	II in Europe only eastern North Atlantic	II,A	-	LR-cd
Pseudorca crassidens	(Owen, 1846)	False killer whale	IV	II	-	II,A	-	-
Feresa attenuata	Gray, 1875	Pygmy killer whale	IV	III	-	II,A	-	dd
Peponocephala electra	(Gray, 1846)	Melon-headed whale	IV	III	II,A		-	-
Hyperoodon ampullatus	(Forster, 1770)	Northern bottlenose whale	IV	II	II	I,A	-	LR-cd
Ziphius cavirostris	G. Cuvier, 1823	Cuvier's beaked whale	IV	II	-	II,A	-	dd
Mesoplodon bidens	(Sowerby, 1804)	Sowerby's beaked whale	IV	II	-	II,A	-	dd

Scientific name	Authority	English name	Habitats Directive	Bern	Bonn	CITES I,II & EC 338/97 A,B	ICRW	IUCN
Mesoplodon grayi	von Haast, 1876	Gray's beaked whale	IV	III	-	II,A	-	dd
Mesoplodon mirus	True, 1913	True's beaked whale	IV	II	-	II,A	-	dd
Mesoplodon densirostris	(Blainville, 1817)	Blainville's beaked whale	IV	III, II (only Mediterranean)	-	II,A	-	dd
Mesoplodon europaeus	(Gervais, 1855)	Gervais' beaked whale	IV	III	-	II,A	-	dd
Kogia breviceps	(Blainville, 1838)	Pygmy sperm whale	IV	II	-	II,A	-	-
Kogia simus	(Owen, 1866)	Dwarf sperm whale	IV	III, II (only Mediterranean)	-	II,A	-	-
Physeter catodon	Linnaeus, 1758	Sperm whale	IV	III, II (only Mediterranean)	-	I (reservation by Norway), A	protected	VU
Eubalaena glacialis	(Müller, 1776)	Right whale	IV	-	I	I,A	protected	EN
Balaena mysticetus	Linnaeus, 1758	Bowhead whale	IV	II	I	I,A	protected	EN (only North-east Atlantic and Spitzbergen stock)
Balaenoptera acutorostrata	Lacépède, 1804	Minke whale	IV	III, II Mediterranean	-	I (reservation by Norway), A	protected	LR-nt
Balaenoptera borealis	Lesson, 1828	Sei whale	IV	III, II (only Mediterranean)	-	I (reservation by Norway), A	protected	EN
Balaenoptera edeni	Anderson, 1879	Bryde's whale	IV	II	-	I,A	protected	dd
Balaenoptera physalus	(Linnaeus, 1758)	Fin whale	IV	II	-	I (reservation by Norway), A	protected	EN
Balaenoptera musculus	(Linnaeus, 1758)	Blue whale	IV	II	I	I,A	protected	VU (only North Atlantic stock)
Megaptera novaeangliae	(Borowski, 1781)	Humpback whale	IV	II	I	I,A	protected	VU
Canis aureus	Linnaeus, 1758	**Golden jackal**	V	-	-	-	-	-
Canis lupus	Linnaeus, 1758	**Wolf**	II*/IV (except Finnish pops.: V; Spanish pops. N of Duero and Greek pops. N of the 39th parallel: IV)	II	-	II (reserv. by Switzerland); A (excluding Spanish pops. N. of Duero & Greek pops. N of the 39th parallel)	-	VU (only Italy); LR-cd (only Portugal and Spain)

Scientific name	Authority	English name	Habitats Directive	Bern	Bonn	CITES I,II & EC 338/97 A,B	ICRW	IUCN
Alopex lagopus	(Linnaeus, 1758)	**Arctic fox**	II*/IV	II	-	-	-	-
Vulpes corsac	(Linneus, 1768)	Corsac fox	-	-	-	-	-	-
Vulpes vulpes	(Linnaeus, 1758)	Red fox	-	-	-	-	-	-
Nyctereutes procyonoides	(Gray, 1834)	Raccoon dog	-	-	-	-	-	-
Ursus arctos	Linnaeus, 1758	**Brown bear**	II*(except Finnish and Swedish pops); IV	II	-	II, A	-	-
Ursus maritimus	Phipps, 1774	**Polar bear**	-	II	-	II, B	-	LR-cd
Procyon lotor	(Linnaeus, 1758)	Raccoon	-	-	-	-	-	-
Mustela erminea	Linnaeus, 1758	Stoat	-	III	-	-	-	-
Mustela eversmanii	Lesson, 1827	Steppe polecat	-	II	-	-	-	-
Mustela lutreola	(Linnaeus, 1761)	**European mink**	II/IV	II	-	-	-	EN
Mustela nivalis	Linnaeus, 1766	Weasel	-	III	-	-	-	-
Mustela putorius	Linnaeus, 1758	**Western polecat**	-	III	-	-	-	-
Mustela sibirica	Pallas, 1773	Siberian weasel	-	-	-	-	-	-
Mustela vison	Schreber, 1777	**American mink**	-	-	-	-	-	-
Vormela peregusna	(Güldenstaedt, 1770)	**Marbled polecat**	-	II	-	-	-	VU (only the European population = *V.p. peregusna*)
Martes foina	(Erxleben, 1777)	**Beech marten, Stone marten**	-	III	-	-	-	-
Martes martes	(Linnaeus, 1758)	**Pine marten**	-	III	-	-	-	-
Martes zibellina	(Linnaeus, 1758)	Sable	-	-	-	-	-	-
Gulo gulo	(Linnaeus, 1758)	**Wolverine**	II*/IV	II	-	-	-	VU
Meles meles	(Linnaeus, 1758)	**Badger**	-	III	-	-	-	-
Lutra lutra	(Linnaeus, 1758)	**Otter**	II/IV	II	-	I (reservation by Russian Federation), A	-	-
Genetta genetta	(Linnaeus, 1758)	**Common genet**	V	III	-	-	-	VU (only *G.g.isabelae*)
Herpestes auropunctatus	Hodgson, 1836	**Small Indian mongoose**	-	-	-	-	-	-
Herpestes ichneumon	(Linnaeus, 1758)	**Egyptian mongoose**	V	III	-	-	-	-
Felis chaus	Schreber, 1777	Jungle cat	-	-	-	II, B	-	-
Felis silvestris	Schreber, 1775	**Wildcat**	IV	II	-	II, A	-	VU (only *F.s. grampia*)
Lynx lynx	(Linnaeus, 1758)	**Lynx**	II (except Finnish pops); IV	III	-	II, A	-	-

Scientific name	Authority	English name	Habitats Directive	Bern	Bonn	CITES I,II & EC 338/97 A,B	ICRW	IUCN
Lynx pardinus	(Temminck, 1827)	Iberian lynx, Pardel lynx	II*/IV	II	-	I, A	-	EN
Odobenus rosmarus	(Linnaeus, 1758)	Walrus	-	II	-	B	-	-
Phoca caspica	Gmelin, 1788	Caspian seal	-	-	-	-	-	VU
Phoca groenlandica	Erxleben, 1777	Harp seal	V	III,	-	-	-	-
Phoca hispida	Schreber, 1775	Ringed seal	II (Ph. botnica); II*/IV (Ph. saimensis); V	III, II (only Ph. saimensis & Ph. ladogensis)	-	-	-	VU (only Ph. botnica & Ph. ladogensis); EN (only Ph. saimensis)
Phoca vitulina	Linnaeus, 1758	Common seal	II/V	III	II only Baltic and Wadden Sea	-	-	-
Halichoerus grypus	(Fabricius,1791)	Grey seal	II/V	III	II only Baltic Sea	-	-	EN (only Baltic Sea)
Erignathus barbatus	(Erxleben, 1777)	Bearded seal	V	III	-	-	-	-
Monachus monachus	(Hermann, 1779)	Mediterranean monk seal	II*/IV	II	I/II	I, A	-	CR
Cystophora cristata	(Erxleben, 1777)	Hooded seal	V	III	-	-	-	-
Sus scrofa	Linnaeus, 1758	Wild boar		III (only S.s. meridionalis)	-	-	-	-
Muntiacus reevesi	(Ogilby, 1839)	Reeves' muntjac	-	-	-	-	-	-
Axis axis	(Erxleben, 1777)	Axis deer	-	-	-	-	-	-
Dama dama	(Linnaeus, 1758)	Fallow deer	-	III	-	-	-	-
Cervus elaphus	Linnaeus, 1758	Red deer	II*/IV (only C. e. corsicanus)	III, II (only C. e. corsicanus)	-	-	-	EN (only C.e. corsicanus)
Cervus nippon	Temminck, 1838	Sika deer	-	-	-	-	-	-
Odocoileus virginianus	(Zimmermann, 1780)	White-tailed deer	-	-	-	-	-	-
Alces alces	(Linnaeus, 1758)	Elk, Moose	-	III	-	-	-	-
Rangifer tarandus	(Linnaeus, 1758)	Reindeer	II (only R.t. fennicus)	III	-	-	-	-
Hydropotes inermis	Swinhoe, 1870	Chinese water deer	-	-	-	-	LR-nt	est
Capreolus capreolus	(Linnaeus, 1758)	Roe deer	-	III	-	-	-	-
Capreolus pygargus	(Pallas, 1771)	Siberian roe deer	-	-	-	-	-	-

Scientific name	Authority	English name	Habitats Directive	Bern	Bonn	CITES I,II & ICRW EC 338/97 A,B	ICRW	IUCN
Bison bonasus	(Linnaeus, 1758)	**European bison**	-	III	-	-	-	EN
Saiga tatarica	(Linnaeus, 1766)	Saiga	-		-	II, B	-	VU
Rupicapra pyrenaica	Bonaparte, 1845	**Southern chamois**	V (except *Rp. ornata*: II*/IV)	II (except *Rp. ornata*: II)	-	I, A both only *R.p. ornata*	-	EN (only *R.p. ornata*)
Rupicapra rupicapra	(Linnaeus, 1758)	Alpine chamois	V (except *R.p. balcanica*: II/IV)	III	-	-	-	EN (only *R.p. tatrica*); CR (only *R.p. cartusiana*)
Ovibos moschatus	(Zimmermann, 1780)	Musk ox	-	II	-	-	-	-
Capra aegagrus	Linnaeus, 1758	Wild goat	II/IV (only natural populations)	II	-	-	-	VU
Capra caucasica	Güldenstaedt & Pallas, 1783	West caucasian tur, Kuban	-	-	-	-	EN	-
Capra cylindricornis	(Blyth, 1841)	East caucasian tur	-	-	-	-	-	VU
Capra ibex	Linnaeus, 1758	**Alpine ibex**	-	III	-	-	-	-
Capra pyrenaica	Schinz, 1838	Spanish ibex	V (except *C.p. pyrenaica*: II*/IV)	III; II (only *C.p. pyrenaica*)	-	-	-	CR (only *C.p. pyrenaica*); VU (only *C.p. victoriae*); LR-cd (only *C.p. hispanica*); LR-nt
Ammotragus lervia	(Pallas, 1777)	**Barbary sheep**	-	-	-	II, B	-	VU
Ovis ammon	(Linnaeus, 1758)	**Mouflon**	II/IV (only natural populations on Corsica and Sardinia)	III	-	-	-	VU (autochtonous populations)

HABITATS: *Council Directive (92/43/AEEC) on the Conservation of Natural Habitats and of Wild Fauna and Flora*, as amended after the accession of Austria, Sweden and Finland. URL http://www.ecnc.nl/doc/europe/legislat/habidire.html

Annex II: Animal and plant species of Community interest whose conservation requires the designation of special areas of conservation.

Annex IV: Animal and plant species of Community interest in need of strict protection.

Annex V: Animal and plant species of Community interest whose taking in the wild and exploitation may be subject to management measures

BERN: *Convention on the Conservation of Natural Habitats and of Wild Fauna and Flora*. Annexes as amended by the Conference of the Parties in 1997. URL http://www.ecnc.nl/doc/europe/legislat/bernconv.html

Appendix II: Strictly protected species.

Appendix III: Protected species.

BONN: *Convention on the Conservation of Migratory Species of Wild Animals*, Annexes as amended by the Standing Committee in 1997. URL http://www.wcmc.org.uk/CMS/

Appendix I: Endangered migratory species.

Appendix II: Migratory species to be subject to agreements.

The following agreements have been concluded under Appendix II:

- Agreement on the Conservation of Seals in the Wadden Sea

- Agreement on the Conservation of Bats in Europe.

- Agreement on the Conservation of Cetaceans of the Black Sea, Mediterranean Sea and Contiguous Atlantic Area.

- Agreement on the Conservation of Seals in the Wadden Sea

- Agreement on the Conservation of Small Cetaceans of the Baltic and North Seas.

CITES: *Convention on International Trade in Endangered Species of Wild Fauna and Flora*, Annexes as amended by the Conference of the Parties in 1997. URL http://www.wcmc.org.uk/CITES/english/appendic.htm

Appendix I contains species that the Parties have deemed to be threatened with extinction and which are, or may be, affected by trade/ Appendix II contains species that, although not necessary threatened, could become so if their trade is not properly controlled.

Appendix II also contains some species that look so similar to species already listed that their trade is monitored and regulated in order to make control easier. (Appendix III does not mention European states).

EC 338/97: *Council Regulation (EC) No 338/97 on the protection of species of wild fauna and flora by regulating trade therein.* http://europa.eu.int/eur-lex/en/lif/dat/en_397R0939.html
Annex A: species which are listed in Appendix I of CITES for which EC Member States have not entered a reservation or which are considered by the EC to be threatened by international trade.

Annex B: species which are listed in Appendix II of CITES or are in Appendix I but subject to a reservation by Member States or which are considered by the EC to require their international trade to be controlled.

ICRW: International Convention for the Regulation of Whaling

IUCN: *1996 IUCN Red List of Threatened Animals*. (Baillie & Groombridge (1996). URL http://www.wcmc.org.uk/species/animals/index.html. Compiled for Europe (excluding the categories "Lower Risk near threatened" and "Lower Risk - conservation dependent") in the European Vertebrate Red Data Book (WCMC, in press).
CR: Critically endangered; EN: Endangered; VU: Vulnerable; LR-nt: Lower Risk-near threatened; LR-cd: Lower Risk-conservation dependent; dd: data deficient.

[1] Succinct description of the boundaries of the study area of *Fauna Europaea*, starting at the North Pole, counter-clockwise (A. Legakis, in litt.). The 45°W meridian from the North Pole to the coast of Greenland, the eastern coast of Greenland, the 45°W meridian from the coast of Greenland to the south until it meets the 3000 m isobath. Thereafter, the 3000 m isobath west of the Mid-Atlantic Ridge 26°N parallel and the African Atlantic coast, the southern and eastern coast of the Mediterranean (Cyprus is excluded), the Greek-Turkish border in the Aegean, the Dardanelles, the Sea of Marmara and the Bosphorus the Black Sea coast of Asia Minor and Georgia (Transcaucasia is excluded), the Russian border in the Caucasus, the western coast of the Caspian Sea, the Kazakhstan-Russia border, the Urals, the eastern coast of Novaya Zemlya, the 70°E meridian from the tip of Novaya Zemlya to the North Pole.

Addresses of Country Co-ordinators

Albania

Dr M. Vlašín & Ing P. Koutný
Veronica
Post pr. 91
CZ–60191 BRNO 1
Czech Republic

Dr C. Prigioni
Dipartemento di Biologia Animale
Università di Pavia
I–27100 PAVIA
Italy

Austria

Dr F. Spitzenberger
Naturhistorisches Museum Wien
Burgring 7
A–1014 WIEN

Belgium

Dr R. Libois
Institut de Zoologie
Université de Liège
Quai van Beneden 22
B–4020 LIÈGE

Prof. Dr E. Van der Straeten
Universiteit Antwerpen,
Department Biologie.
Rijksuniversitair Centrum
Groenenborgerlaan 171
B–2020 ANTWERPEN

Bosnia & Herzegovina

Dr B. Kryštufek
Slovenian Museum of Natural History
Prešernova 20
pp 290
SI-1001 LJUBLJANA
Slovenia

Bulgaria

(Lagomorpha, Carnivora, Artiodactyla)
Dr G. Markov
Institute of Zoology
Bulgarian Academy of Sciences
Bul. Tzar Osvoboditel 1
BG-1000 Sofia

(Insectivora, Rodentia)
Dr V. Vohralík
Department of Zoology
Charles University
Viničná 7
CZ–128 44 PRAHA 2
Czech Republic

(Chiroptera)
Mr P. Benda
Institute of Anatomy
Department of Zoology
National Museum (Natural History)
CZ–115 79 PRAHA 1
Czech Republic

Croatia

Dr N. Tvrtković
Croatian Natural History Museum
Demetrova 1
HR–1000 ZAGREB

Dr B. Kryštufek
Slovenian Museum of Natural History
Prešernova 20
pp 290
SI–1001 LJUBLJANA
Slovenia

Czech Republic

Dr M. Anděra
Department of Zoology
National Museum (Natural History)
CZ–115 79 PRAHA 1

Dr J. Zima
Department of Zoology
Charles University
Viničná 7
CZ–128 44 PRAHA 2

Denmark

Mr T. Asferg
National Environmental Research Institute
Dept. of Landscape Ecology
Grenåvej 12
Kalø
DK–8410 RØNDE

Estonia

Mr T. Maran
Tallinn Zoo
Paldiski mnt. 145
EE–0035 TALLINN

Faeroe Islands

Dr D. Bloch
Museum of Natural History
Zoological Department
Futalag 40
FR–100 TÓRSHAVN

Finland

Dr H. Henttonen
Finnish Forest Research Institute
Dept. Forest Protection
PL 18
FIN–01301 VANTAA

France

Mr P. Haffner & Mr H. Maurin
Muséum National d'Histoire Naturelle
Institut d'Ecologie et de Gestion de la Biodiversité
Service du Patrimoine Naturel
57, rue Cuvier
F–75231 PARIS Cedex 05

Germany

Mr P. Boye
Bundesamt für Naturschutz
Konstantinstraße 110
D–53137 BONN

Dr R. Hutterer
Museum A. Koenig
Adenauerallee 160
D–53113 BONN

Prof. Dr M. Stubbe
Martin–Luther Universität
Institut für Zoologie, Tierökologie
Domplatz 4
D–06099 HALLE

Greece

(Lagomorpha, Carnivora, Artiodactyla)
Dr G. Catsadorakis
WWF Greece
26 Filellinon St
GR-105 58 ATHENS

(Chiroptera)
Prof. Dr O. von Helversen
Institut für Zoologie
Lehrstuhl II
Friedrich–Alexander–Universität Erlangen
Staudtstr. 5
D–91058 ERLANGEN
Germany

(Insectivora, Rodentia)
Dr V. Vohralík
Department of Zoology
Charles University
Viničná 7
CZ–128 44 PRAHA 2
Czech Republic

Hungary

Dr G. Csorba
Hungarian Mammalogical Society
Hungarian Natural History Museum
Baross utca 13
H–1088 BUDAPEST

Iceland

Dr P. Hersteinsson
Institute of Biology
University of Iceland
Grensásvegi 12
IS–108 REYKJAVÍK

Ireland

Dr T. Hayden
Department of Zoology
University College Dublin
Belfield
DUBLIN 4

Italy

Dr G. Amori
CNR, Centro Genetica Evoluzionistica
via Lancisi 29
I–00161 ROMA

Dr C. Prigioni
Dipartimento di Biologia Animale
Università di Pavia
I–27100 PAVIA

Kaliningrad Region, Russia

Dr G. Grishanov & Dr V. Beliakov
Department of Zoology
University of Kaliningrad
Universitetskaya str. 2
KALININGRAD 236040

Latvia

Mr V. Pilāts
Gauja National Park
Baznīcas iela 3
SIGULDA, LV 2150

Lithuania

Dr L. Balčiauskas
Institute of Ecology
Akademijos 2
VILNIUS 2600

Luxembourg

Dr E. Engel
Musée National d'Histoire Naturelle
25 Rue Münster
L–2160 LUXEMBOURG

Macedonia

Dr B. Kryštufek
Slovenian Museum of Natural History
Prešernova 20
pp 290
SI–1001 LJUBLJANA
Slovenia

Dr S. Petkovski
Macedonian Museum of Natural History
Bld. Ilinden 86
MK–91000 SKOPJE

Malta

Mr J. J. Borg
13, The Catacombs
RABAT, RBT 07

The Netherlands

Mr J. B. M. Thissen
IKC Natuurbeheer
Postbus 30
NL–6700 AA WAGENINGEN

Norway

Mr P. Shimmings & Ms A–H. Rønning
Norwegian Zoological Society
Postbox 102
Blindern
N–0314 OSLO

Poland

Dr W. Bogdanowicz
Museum & Institute of Zoology
Polish Academy of Sciences
ul. Wilcza 64
P.O. Box 1007,
PL–00–679 WARSZAWA

Dr B. W. Wołoszyn
Institute of Animal Systematics and Evolution
Polish Academy of Sciences
Sławkowska 17
PL–31–016 KRAKÓW

Portugal

Prof. M. L. Mathias
Departamento de Zoologia e Antropologia
Faculdade de Ciências
Universidade de Lisboa
P–1700 LISBOA

Dr M. G. Ramalhinho
Museu de História Natural
Rua da Escola Politécnica 58
P–1250 LISBOA

Dr M. J. Cabral
Instituto da Conservação da Natureza
Rua da Lapa 73
P–1200 LISBOA

Romania

Dr D. Murariu
Muzeul de Istorie Naturalä
"Grigore Antipa"
Soseaua Kisseleff 1
R–79744 BUCURESTI 2

Prof. Dr I. Coroiu
Babes Bolayi Chair of Zoology
Str. Kogalniceanu 1
R–3400 CLUJ–NAPOCA

Spain

Dr L. J. Palomo
SECEM
Universidad de Málaga
E–29071 MÁLAGA

Dr F. González
SECEMU
Apdo. 380,
E–33080 OVIEDO

Slovakia

(Insectivora, Rodentia)
Dr A. L. G. Dudich
Department of Biology
Technical University in Zvolen
Štúrova 3
SK–960 51 ZVOLEN

(Chiroptera)
Dr M. Uhrin
Muránska National Park
J. Král'a 12
SK–050 01 REVÚCA

(Carnivora, Artiodactyla)
Ing M. Žilinec
Institute of Forest Ecology
Štúrova 3
SK–960 53 ZVOLEN

Slovenia

Dr B. Kryštufek
Slovenian Museum of Natural History
Prešernova 20
pp 290
SI–1001 LJUBLJANA

Sweden

Prof. L. Hansson
Department of Conservation Biology, SLU
P.O. Box 7002
S–750 07 UPPSALA,

Prof. K. Fredga
Department of Genetics
Uppsala University
P.O. Box 7003
S–750 07 UPPSALA

Prof. I. Ahlén
Department of Conservation Biology, SLU
P.O. Box 7002
S–750 07 UPPSALA

Switzerland

Dr F. Saucy
Institut de Zoologie
Université de Fribourg
Bd. Pérolles
CH–1700 FRIBOURG

Dr S. Capt
Centre Suisse de Cartographie
Terreaux 14
CH–2000 NEUCHÂTEL

Turkey

Prof Dr C. Kurtonur & Dr B. Özkan
Department of Biology
Trakya University
T–22030 EDIRNE

United Kingdom

Dr A. J. Mitchell–Jones
English Nature
Northminster House
PETERBOROUGH PE1 1UA

Mr H. R. Arnold
Environmental Information Centre
Institute of Terrestrial Ecology
Monks Wood
Abbots Ripton
HUNTINGDON PE17 2LS

Prof. W. I. Montgomery
School of Biology & Biochemistry
The Queen's University of Belfast
97 Lisburn Rd
BELFAST BT9 7BL

Yugoslavia

Dr B. Kryštufek
Slovenian Museum of Natural History
Prešernova 20
pp 290
SI–1001 LJUBLJANA
Slovenia

Mr M. Paunović
Natural History Museum in Belgrade
Njegoševa 51
YU–11000 BEOGRAD

Literature

Ahlén, I. & Gerell, R. (1989). Distribution and status of bats in Sweden. Pp. 319–325, in: Hanák, V., Horáček, I. & Gaisler, J. (Eds.). *European bat research 1987*. Charles University Press, Praha, 718 pp.

Akkermann, R. (1975a). Untersuchungen zur Ökologie und Populationsdynamik des Bisams (*Ondatra zibethicus*) an einem nordwestdeutschen Verlandungssee. I. Bauten. *Zeitschrift für angewandte Zoologie*, 62: 39–81.

Akkermann, R. (1975b). Untersuchungen zur škologie und Populationsdynamik des Bisams (*Ondatra zibethicus*) an einem nordwestdeutschen Verlandungssee. II. Nahrung und Nahrungsaufnahme. *Zeitschrift für angewandte Zoologie*, 62: 173–218.

Akkermann, R. (1975c). Untersuchungen zur Ökologie und Populationsdynamik des Bisams (*Ondatra zibethicus*) an einem nordwestdeutschen Verlandungssee. III. Verhalten und Populationsdynamik. *Zeitschrift für angewandte Zoologie*, 62: 281–338.

Alados, C. L. & Escos, J. (1996). Ecologia y comportamiento de la cabra montès. Consideracion para la su gestion. *Monografias, Museo Nacional de la Ciencias Naturales*. Consejo Superior de Investigaciones Cientificas, Madrid, 332 pp.

Alendal, E. & Helle, O. (1983): Helminth parasites of muskoxen *Ovibos moschatus* in Norway incl. Spitsbergen and in Sweden, with a synopsis of parasites reported from this host. *Fauna Norvegica, Series A*, 4: 41–52.

Amori, G. & Angelici, F. M. (1992). Note on the status of crested porcupine *Hystrix cristata* in Italy. *Lutra*, 35: 44–50.

Amori, G. & Gippoliti, S. (1995). Siberian chipmunks *Tamias sibiricus* in Italy. *Mammalia*, 59: 288–289.

Amori, G. & Lapini, L. (1997). Le specie di mammiferi introdotte in Italia: il quadro della situazione attuale. *Supplemento alle Ricerche di Biologia della Selvaggina*, 27: 249–267.

Anděra, M. & Hanzal, V. (1995a). *Atlas of the mammals of the Czech Republic. A provisional version. I. Even–toed ungulates (Artiodactyla), lagomorphs (Lagomorpha)*. National Museum, Prague, 64 pp. (in Czech with English summary).

Anděra, M. & Hanzal, V. (1995b). *Atlas of the mammals of the Czech Republic. A provisional version. I. Carnivores (Carnivora)*. National Museum, Prague. 95 pp. (in Czech with English summary).

Anderson, S. S. (1992). *Halichoerus grypus* (Fabricius, 1791) – Kegelrobbe. Pp. 97–115, in: Duguy, R. & Robineau, D. (Eds.). *Handbuch der Säugetiere Europas, Band 6/II: Pinnipedia*. Aula Verlag, Wiesbaden, 309 pp.

Andrzejewski, R. & Wrocławek, H. (1961). Mass occurrence of *Apodemus agrarius* (Pallas, 1771) and variations in the number of associated Muridae. *Acta Theriologica*, 5: 173–184.

Andrzejewski, R., Babińska–Werka, J., Gliwicz, J. & Goszczyński, J. (1978). Synurbanization processes in a population of *Apodemus agrarius*. I. Characteristics of the populations in urbanization gradient. *Acta Theriologica*, 23: 341–358.

Angermann, R. (1983). The taxonomy of Old World *Lepus*. *Acta Zoologica Fennica*, 174: 17–21.

Arlettaz, R. (1990). Contribution à l'éco–éthologie du Molosse de Cestoni, *Tadarida teniotis* (Chiroptera), dans les Alpes valaisannes (sud–ouest de la Suisse). *Zeitschrift für Säugetierkunde*, 55: 28–42.

Arlettaz, R. (1995). *Tadarida teniotis* Rafinesque, 1814. Pp. 198–202, in: Hausser, J. (Ed.). *Säugetiere der Schweiz. Verbreitung – Biologie – Ökologie*. Denkschriften der Schweizerischen Akademie der Naturwissenschaften, 103: xii+1–501. Birkhäuser Verlag, Basel.

Arlettaz, R., Guibert, E., Lugon, A., Médard, P. & Sierro, A. (1993). Variability of fur colouration in Savi's bat *Hypsugo savi* (Bonaparte, 1837). *Bonner zoologische Beiträge*, 44: 293–297.

Arlettaz, R., Ruedi, M., Ibañez, C., Palmeirim, J. & Hausser, J. (1997). A new perspective on the zoogeography of the sibling mouse–eared bat species *Myotis myotis* and *Myotis blythii*: morphological, genetic and ecological evidence. *Journal of Zoology, London*, 242: 45–62.

Arnold, H. R. (1993). *Atlas of mammals in Britain.* HMSO, London, 144 pp.

Arnold, W. (1990). The evolution of marmot sociality: I. Why disperse late? *Behavioral Ecology & Sociobiology,* 27: 229–237.

Asselberg, R. (1971). De verspreiding van de kleine zoogdieren in België aan de hand van braakballenanalyse. *Bulletin de l'Institut Royal des Sciences Naturelles de Belgique,* 47(5): 1–60.

Atkinson, R. I., Bouvier, M., Hall, D. & Prigioni, C. (1990). *Albania. Environmental status report 1990.* IUCN East European Programme, Cambridge, 38 pp.

Auffray, J.–C., Marshall, J. T., Thaler, L. & Bonhomme, F. (1990a). Focus on the nomenclature of European species of *Mus. Mouse Genome,* 88: 7–8.

Auffray, J.–C., Tchernov, E., Bonhomme, F., Heth, G., Simson, S. & Nevo, E. (1990b). Presence and ecological distribution of *Mus "spretoides"* and *Mus musculus domesticus* in Israel. Circum–Mediterranean variance in the genus *Mus. Zeitschrift für Säugetierkunde,* 55: 1–10.

Avery, M. (1991). Pipistrelle. Pp. 123–128, in: Corbet, G. B. & Harris, S. (Eds.). *The handbook of British mammals.* 3rd ed. Blackwell Scientific Publications, Oxford, 588 pp.

Ayarzaguena, J. N. & López–Martínez, N. (1976). Estudio filogenético y comparativo de *Microtus cabrerae* y *Microtus brecciensis. Doñana, Acta Vertebrata,* 3(2): 181–204.

Baagøe, H. J. (1986). Summer occurrence of *Vespertilio murinus* Linné – 1758 and *Eptesicus serotinus* (Schreber – 1780) (Chiroptera, Mammalia) on Zealand, Denmark, based on records of roosts and registrations with bat detector. *Annalen des Naturhistorischen Museums in Wien,* 88–89B: 281–291.

Baagøe, H. J. (in press a). *Myotis bechsteini.* In: Niethammer, J. & Krapp, F. (Eds) *Handbuch der Säugetiere Europas. Fledermäuse.* Aula Verlag, Wiesbaden.

Baagøe, H. J. (in press b). *Vespertilio murinus.* In: Niethammer, J. & Krapp, F. (Eds.). *Handbuch der Säugetiere Europas. Fledermäuse.* Aula Verlag, Wiesbaden.

Baagøe, H. J. & Bloch, D. (1994). Bats in the Faroe Islands. *Fróðskaparrit,* 41: 69–76.

Baillie, J. & Groombridge, B. (Eds.) (1996). *1996 IUCN Red List of Threatened Animals.* IUCN, Gland, Switzerland, 448 pp.

Baker, A., Eger, J., Peterson, R. & Manning, T. (1983). Geographic variation and taxonomy of arctic hares. *Acta Zoologica Fennica,* 174: 45–48.

Banfield, A. W. F. (1961). A revision of the reindeer and caribou, genus *Rangifer. Bulletin of the National Museum of Canada,* 177: 1–137.

Bannikov, A. G. & Sokolov, V. E. (Eds.) (1985). Mlekopitayushchie. In: *Krasnaya kniga SSSR.* 2nd edition. Lesnaya promishlenost, Moscow, pp 9–97.

Barratt, E. M., Deaville, R., Burland, T. M., Bruford, M. W., Jones, G., Racey, P. A. & Wayne, R. K. (1997). DNA answers the call of pipistrelle bat species. *Nature, London,* 387:138–139.

Bašenina, N. V. (1951). Ecology of the Grey hamster (*Cricetulus migratorius* Pall.) in European part of USSR. *Fauna i Ekologija Gryzunov,* 4: 157–183 (in Russian).

Baskin L., Hjeljord O. & Elgmork K. (1997). Fluctuation in number of moose, wolf and bear in northern Europe. The Fourth International Moose Symposium, Fairbanks, Alaska.

Bassano, B. & Peracino, V. (1994). Effetti della densità sulla struttura di popolazione di stambecco (*Capra ibex ibex* L.) del Parco Nazionale del Gran Paradiso. *Ibex, Journal of Mountain Ecology,* Supp. 2: 35–38.

Bassano, B., Durio, P., Gallo Orsi, U. & Macchi E. (Eds.) (1992). First International Symposium on Alpine Marmot (*Marmota marmota*) and on the Genus *Marmota.* Proc. Saint Vincent, Aosta, Italy 1991.

Bates, P. J. J. & Harrison, D. L. (1997). *Bats of the Indian Subcontinent*. Harrison Zoological Museum, Sevenoaks, Kent, xvi + 258 pp.

Beck, A. (1995). Fecal analyses of European bat species. *Myotis,* 32–33: 109–119.

Becker, K. (1978a). *Rattus norvegicus* (Berkenhout, 1769) – Wanderratte. Pp 401–420, in: Niethammer, J. & Krapp, F. (Eds.). *Handbuch der Säugetiere Europas. Band 1/I, Rodentia I* . Aula Verlag, Wiesbaden, 476 pp.

Becker, K. (1978b). *Rattus rattus* (Linnaeus, 1758) – Hausratte. Pp 382–400, in: Niethammer J. & Krapp F. (Eds.). *Handbuch der Säugetiere Europas. Band 1/I, Rodentia I.* Aula Verlag, Wiesbaden, 476 pp.

Bédard, J. (Ed.) (1975). Alces. Moose ecology International Symposium, Québec, 26–28 March 1973. Presses Univ. Laval, Québec, 741 pp.

Belkhir, K., Britton–Davidian, J. & König, B. (1991). De nouvelles populations robertsoniennes de souris (*Mus musculus domesticus*) au nord des Alpes. *Genome,* 34: 658–660.

Beltrán, J. F., Rice, J. E. & Honeycutt, R. L. (1996). Taxonomy of the Iberian lynx. *Nature, London,* 379: 407–408.

Benda, P. & Horáček, I. (1995a). Biometrics of *Myotis myotis* and *Myotis blythi*. *Myotis*, 32–33:45–55.

Benda, P. & Horáček, I. (1995b). Geographic variation in three species of *Myotis* (Mammalia: Chiroptera) in South of the Western Palearctics. *Acta Societatis Zoologicae Bohemicae*, 59: 17–39.

Ben David, M. (1988). The biology and ecology of the marbled polecat (*Vormela peregusna syriaca*) in Israel. M.Sc. Thesis, Tel–Aviv University.

Benzal, J. & Fajardo, S. (1994). *Programa para la Protección y Conservación de los Murciélagos. Informe de la Campaña de 1994*. Gobierno de Canarias, Viceconsejería de Medio Ambiente, Santa Cruz de Tenerife (unpublished report).

Benzal, J. & Izquierdo, I. (1993). *Programa para la Protección y Conservación de los Murciélagos. Informe de la Campaña de 1993*. Gobierno de Canarias, Viceconsejería de Medio Ambiente, Santa Cruz de Tenerife (unpublished report).

Bergengren, A. (1969). On genetics, evolution and history of distribution of the heath–hare, a distinct population of the arctic hare, *Lepus timidus* Linn. *Viltrevy, Swedish Wildlife*, 6: 381–460.

Bernard, R. T. F. & Bester, G. J. (1988). Roost selection by the long–fingered bat, *Miniopterus schreibersii*, is influenced by reproductive condition, and roost microclimate and structure. *South African Journal of Science*, 84: 921–922.

Berry, R. J. (1981). Population dynamics of the house mouse. Pp 395–425, in: Berry, R. J. (Ed.) *Biology of the House Mouse*. Academic Press, London, 715 pp.

Bertrand, A. (1993). *Repartition géographique du Desman des Pyrénées Galemys pyrenaicus dans un cours d' eau des Pyrénées Françaises*. Proceedings of the Meeting on the Pyrenaen Desman, Lisboa, Sept. 1992.

Bibikov, D. I. (1988). Der Wolf: *Canis lupus*. Neue Brehm-Bücherei, No. 587. Wittenberg–Lutherstadt, 198 pp.

Bibikov, D. I. (1996). Die Murmeltiere der Welt. 2nd Edition. Neue Brehm-Bücherei, No. 388. Spektrum Akad. Verlag, Heidelberg.

Bjärvall, A. (1983). Scandinavia's response to a natural population of wolves. *Acta Zoologica Fennica,* 174: 273–275

Blanco, J. C. & González, J. L. (1992). *Libro rojo de los vertebrados de España*. ICONA, Madrid, 714 pp.

Blanco, J., Reig, S. & Cuesta, L. (1992). Distribution, status and conservation problems of the wolf *Canis lupus* in Spain. *Biological Conservation,* 60: 73–80.

Blandford, P. R. S. (1987). Biology of the Polecat *Mustela putorius*: a literature review. *Mammal Review,* 17: 155-198.

Bobak, A. W. (1970). *Das Wildkaninchen*. Neue Brehm–Bucherei, Vol. 415, Wittenberg Lutherstadt, 116 pp.

Bodenheimer, F. S. (1949). *Problems of vole populations in the Middle East*. The Research Council of Israel, Jerusalem, 77 pp.

Bogdanowicz, W. (1994). *Myotis daubentonii*. *Mammalian Species*, 475: 1–9.

Bogdanowicz, W. (in press). *Pipistrellus kuhlii*. In: Niethammer, J. & Krapp, F. (Eds.). *Handbuch der Säugetiere Europas. Fledermäuse*. Aula Verlag, Wiesbaden.

Bogdanowicz, W. & Kock, D. (1998). Quoting and spelling species names from H. Kuhl's "Die deutschen Fledermäuse". *Bat Research News,* 39(1): 4–5.

Bogdanowicz, W. & Ruprecht, A. L. (in press): *Nyctalus leisleri*. In: Niethammer, J. & Krapp, F., (Eds.). *Handbuch der Säugetiere Europas. Fledermäuse*. Aula Verlag, Wiesbaden.

Bohlken, H. (1986). *Ovibos moschatus* (Zimmermann, 1780) – Moschusochse. Pp. 349–361, in: Niethammer, J. & Krapp, F. (Eds.). *Handbuch der Säugetiere Europas. Band 2/II, Artiodactyla*. Aula Verlag, Wiesbaden, 462 pp.

Böhme, W. (1978a). *Apodemus agrarius* (Pallas, 1771) – Brandmaus. Pp. 368–381, in: Niethammer, J. & Krapp, F. (Eds.) *Handbuch der Säugetiere Europas, Band 1/I, Rodentia 1*. Aula Verlag, Wiesbaden, 476 pp.

Böhme, W. (1978b). *Micromys minutus* (Pallas, 1778) – Zwergmaus. Pp. 290–304, in: Niethammer, J. & Krapp, F. (Eds.). *Handbuch der Säugetiere Europas, Band 1, Rodentia 1*. Aula Verlag, Wiesbaden, 476 pp.

Bonhomme, F., Catalan, J., Britton–Davidian, J., Chapman, V., Moriwaki, K., Nevo, E. & Thaler, L. (1984). Biochemical diversity and evolution in the genus *Mus*. *Biochemical Genetics,* 22: 275–303.

Boonman, A. M., Bongers, W. & Twisk, P. (1997). Rosse vleermuis *Nyctalus noctula* (Schreber, 1774). Pp. 172–182, in: Limpens, H., Mostert, K. & Bongers, W., (Eds.). *Atlas van de Nederlandse vleermuizen. Onderzoek naar verspreiding en ecologie*. KNNV Uitgeverij, Utrecht, 260 pp.

Born, E.W. (1992). *Odobenus rosmarus* Linnaeus, 1758 – Walroß. Pp. 269–299, in: Duguy, R. & Robineau, D. (Eds.). *Handbuch der Säugetiere Europas, Band 6/II, Pinnipedia*. Aula Verlag, Wiesbaden, 309 pp.

Borowski, S. & Dehnel, A. (1952). Studies on the biology of the Soricidae. *Annales Universitatis Mariae Curie–Skłodowska*, C7: 305–448 (in Polish)

Borralho, R., Rego, F., Palomares, F. & Hora, A. (1996). The distribution of the Egyptian mongoose *Herpestes ichneumon* (L.) in Portugal. *Mammal Review*, 26: 1–8.

Bosma, A. A., de Haan N. A. & Macdonald A. A. (1991). The current status of cytogenetics of the Suidae. *Bongo*, 18: 258–272.

Boursot, P., Auffray, J.–C., Britton–Davidian, J. & Bonhomme, F. (1993). The evolution of house mice. *Annual Review of Ecology and Systematics,* 24: 119–152.

Boursot, P., Jacquart, T., Bonhomme, F., Britton–Davidian, J. & Thaler, L. (1985). Différentiation géographique du génome mitochondrial chez *Mus spretus* Lataste. *Comptes Rendus de l'Academie des Sciences, Paris, Ser. III, Sciences de la Vie,* 301: 161–166.

Boyce, C. C. K. (1991). Genus *Arvicola*. Pp. 212–218, in: Corbet, G. B. & Harris, S. (Eds.). *The Handbook of British Mammals*, Blackwell, Oxford, 588 pp.

Boyd, I. L., Myhill, D. G. & Mitchell–Jones, A. J. (1988). Uptake of Gamma–HCH (Lindane) by pipistrelle bats and its effect on survival. *Environmental Pollution*, 51: 95–111.

Boye, P., Pott–Dörfer, B., Dörfer, K. & Demetropoulos, A. (1990). New records of bats (Chiroptera) from Cyprus and notes on their biology. *Myotis*, 28: 93–100.

Brass, D. A. (1994). *Rabies in bats: natural history and public health implications*. Livia Press, Connecticut, 335 pp.

Braun, M. (1986). Rückstandsanalysen bei Fledermäusen. *Zeitschrift für Säugetierkunde*, 51: 212–217.

Bretten, S. (1990). Moskusfeet. Pp. 173–190, in: Semb–Johansson, A. (Ed.). *Norges dyr*. J. W. Cappelsen Forlag, Oslo (in Norwegian).

Briedermann, L. (1988). Elchwild (*Alces alces* L.). Pp. 94–104, in: Stubbe, H. (Ed.). *Das Buch der Hege. 1. Haarwild*. Verl. H. Deutsch, Thun und Frankfurt.

Bright, P. W. & Morris, P. A. (1996). Why are dormice rare? A case study in conservation biology. *Mammal Review*, 26: 157–187

Broekhuizen, S., Hoekstra, B., van Laar, V., Smeenk, C. & Thissen, J. B. M. (Eds.) (1992). *Atlas van de Nederlandse zoogdieren*. 3rd revised edition. KNNV Uitgeverij, Utrecht, 336 pp.

Brosset, A., Barbe, L., Beaucournu, J.–C., Faugier, C., Salvayre, H. & Tupinier, Y. (1988). La raréfaction du rhinolophe euryale (*Rhinolophus euryale* Blasius) en France. Recherche d'une explication. *Mammalia*, 52:101–122.

Brosset, A. & Caubère, B. (1959). Contribution à l'étude écologique des chiroptères de l'ouest de la France et du Bassin Parisien. *Mammalia*, 23:180–238.

Brunet–Lecomte, P. & Nadachowski, A. (1994). Comparative analysis of the characters of the first lower molar in *Microtus (Terricola) thomasi* (Rodentia, Arvicolidae). *Acta Zoologica Cracoviensia*, 37: 157–162.

Butet, A. & Leroux A. (1993). Polymorphisme spécifique de *Sorex coronatus* dans le marais de l'Ouest de la France. *Mammalia*, 57: 367–373.

Butet, A. & Volobouev, V. T. (1995). R–chromosome banding study of the dark form *Sorex coronatus* from western France marshes. *Mammalia*, 59: 103–107.

Bützler, W. (1986). *Cervus elaphus* Linneaus, 1758 – Rothirsch. Pp. 107–139, in: Niethammer, J. & Krapp, F. (Eds.). *Handbuch der Säugetiere Europas. Band 2/II, Artiodactyla*. Aula Verlag, Wiesbaden, 462 pp.

Calinescu, R. (1931). Mamiferele României. Repartiţia şi problemele lor biogeografice–economice. *Buletinul Ministeruliu Agriculturii, Industriei, Comerciuliu si Domeniilor, Bucuresti*, 251: 1–103.

Capanna, E. (1981). Cariotype et morphologie cranienne de *Talpa romana* de terra typica. *Mammalia*, 45: 71–82.

Capolongo, D. & Panascì, R. (1976). Le talpe dell'Italia centro–meridionale. *Rendiconti dell'Academiá delle Scienze Fische e Matematische, Napoli*, 17: 104–138.

Carpaneto, G. M. (1990). The Indian Grey Mongoose (*Herpestes edwardsi*) in the Circeo National Park: a case of incidental introduction. *Small Carnivore Conservation*, 2: 10.

Carpaneto, G. M. & Cristaldi, M. (1995). Dormice and man: a review of past and present relations. *Hystrix*, 6: 303–330.

Cassaing, J. & Crosset, H. (1985). Organisation spatiale, competition et dynamique des populations sauvages de souris (*Mus spretus* Lataste et *Mus musculus domesticus* Rutty) du Midi de la France. *Zeitschrift für Säugetierkunde*, 50: 271–284.

Castro, L. R. & Palma, L. (1996). The current status, distribution and conservation of Iberian lynx in Portugal. *Journal of Wildlife Research*, 2: 179–181.

Catalan, J., Poitevin, F., Fons, R., Gerasimov, S. & Croset, H. (1988). Biologie évolutive des populations ouest-européennes de crocidures (Mammalia, Insectivora). III. Structure génétique des populations continentales et insulaires de *Crocidura russula* (Hermann, 1780) et de *Crocidura suaveolens* (Pallas, 1811). *Mammalia*, 52: 387-400.

Catto, C. M. C., Hutson, A. M. & Racey, P. A. (1994). The diet of *Eptesicus serotinus* in southern England. *Folia Zoologica*, 43: 307–314.

Catzeflis, F. (1984). Systématique biochimique, taxonomie et phylognie des musaraignes d'Europe (Soricidae, Mammalia). Thèse, Université de Lausanne, Suisse.

Catzeflis, F., Graf, J–D., Hausser, J. & Vogel, P. (1982). Comparison biochimique des musaraignes du genre *Sorex* en Europe occidentale (Soricidae, Mammalia). *Zeitschrift für zoologische Systematik und Evolutionsforschung*, 20: 223–233.

Chaline, J. & Graf, J.–D. (1988). Phylogeny of the Arvicolidae (Rodentia): biochemical and paleontological evidence. *Journal of Mammalogy*, 69: 22–33.

Chapman, D. & Chapman, N. (1985). *Fallow deer*. Terence Dalton Ltd, Lavenham, Suffolk, 271 pp.

Chapman, J. A., Hockman, J. G. & Ojeda, M. M. C. (1980). *Sylvilagus floridanus. Mammalian species*, 106: 1–8.

Chapman, N. G., Claydon, K., Claydon, M., Forde, P. G. & Harris, S. (1993). Sympatric populations of muntjac (*Muntiacus reevesi*) and roe deer (*Capreolus capreolus*): a comparative analysis of their ranging behaviour, social organisation and activity. *Journal of Zoology, London,* 229: 623–640.

Chapman, N., Harris, A. & Harris, S. (1994a). What gardeners say about muntjac. *Deer,* 9: 302–306.

Chapman, N., Harris, S. & Stanford, A. (1994b). Reeves' muntjac *Muntiacus reevesi* in Britain: their history, spread and habitat selection, and the role of human intervention in accelerating their dispersal. *Mammal Review,* 24: 113–160.

Chotolchu, N., Stubbe, M. & Samjaa, R. (1989). Verbreitung des Tigeriltis *Vormela peregusna* (Gueldenstaedt, 1770) in Eurasien und sein Status in der Mongolischen Volksrepublik. In: Stubbe, M. (ed.). *Populationsökologie marderartiger Säugetiere. Wissenschaftliche Beiträge der Universität Halle,* 1989/ 37 (P39): 585–596.

Christov, L. (1985). *Mesocricetus newtoni*. P. 142, in: *Red Data Book of the Peoples Republic of Bulgaria. Vol. 2. Animals*. Publishing House of the Bulgarian Academy of Sciences, Sofia (in Bulgarian).

Clutton–Brock, T. H., Guinnes, E. E. & Albon, S. D. (1982). *Red deer. Behaviour and ecology of the two sexes*. Edinburgh University Press, Edinburgh,

Contoli L. (1980). Les *Pitymys* de l' Italie centrale– occidentale (Rodentia, Arvicolidae). Données craniometriques et dentaires. *Mammalia,* 44: 319–337.

Cooke, A. S. & Farrell, L. (1987). The utilisation of neighbouring farmland by Chinese water deer (*Hydropotes inermis*) at Woodwalton Fen National Nature Reserve. *Huntingdonshire Fauna & Flora Society Report for 1986,* 39: 28–38.

Cooke, A. S. & Farrell, L. (1995). Establishment and impact of muntjac (*Muntiacus reevesi*) on two National Nature Reserves. Pp 48–62, in: Mayle, B. A. (Ed.). *Muntjac deer: their biology, impact and management in Britain*. Forestry Commission, Farnham & British Deer Society, Trentham, 70 pp.

Cooke, A. S. & Lakhani, K. (1996). Damage to coppice regrowth by muntjac deer *Muntiacus reevesi* and protection with electric fencing. *Biological Conservation,* 75: 231–238.

Cooke, A. S., Farrell, L., Kirby, K. J. & Thomas, R. C. (1995). Changes in abundance and size of dog's mercury apparently associated with grazing by muntjac. *Deer,* 9: 429–433.

Cooke, A. S., Green, P. & Chapman, N. G. (1996). Mortality in a feral population of muntjac *Muntiacus reevesi* in England. *Acta Theriologica,* 41: 277–286.

Corbet, G. B. (1978). *The mammals of the Palaearctic region – a taxonomic review*. British Museum (Natural History) & Cornell University Press, London & Ithaca, 314 pp.

Corbet, G. B. (1980). *The mammals of the Palaearctic region – a taxonomic review* 2nd edition. British Museum (Natural History), London, 314 pp.

Corbet, G. B. (1988). The family *Erinaceidae*: a synthesis of its taxonomy, phylogeny, ecology and zoogeography. *Mammal Review*, 18: 117–172.

Corbet, G. B. & Hill, J. E. (1992). *The mammals of the Indomalayan region: a systematic review*. Oxford University Press, Oxford, 488 pp.

Corbet, G. B. & Southern, H. N. (Eds.) (1977). *The handbook of British mammals*. Blackwell, Oxford, 520 pp.

Cosson, J. F., Pascal, M. & Bioret, F. (1996). Origine et répartition des musaraignes du genre *Crocidura* dans les îles bretonnes. *Vie & Milieu*, 46: 233–244

Currado, I., Scarramozzino, P. L. & Brusino, G. (1987). Note sulla presenza dello scoiattolo grigio (*Sciurus carolinensis* Gmelin, 1788) in Piemonte (Rodentia: Sciuridae). *Annales della Facultá delle Scienze e Agraria, Torino,* 14: 307–331.

Dal Farra, A., Cassol, M. & Lapini, L. (1996). Status del Burunduk (*Tamias sibiricus* /Laxmann, 1769/, Rodentia, Sciuridae) nel Bellunese (Italia nord–orientale). *Bolletino del Museo civico di Storia naturale di Venezia*, 45 (1994): 189–193.

Danilov, P. I. (1995). Canadian and European Beaver in the Russian Northwest – distribution, number and comparative ecology. Pp. 10–16, in: *The Third Nordic Beaver Symposium, 1992, Finland*. Finnish Game and Fisheries Research Institute, Helsinki.

Danilov, P., Helle, P., Annenkov, V., Belkin, V., Bljudnik, L., Helle, E., Kanshiev, V., Lindén, H. & Markowsky, V. (1996). Status of game animal populations in Karelia and Finland according to winter track count data. *Finnish Game Research*, 49: 18–25.

Dannelid, E. (1989). Medial tines on the upper incisor and other dental features used as identification characters in European shrews of the genus *Sorex* (Mammalia, Soricidae). *Zeitschrift für Säugetierkunde,* 54: 205–214.

Dannelid, E. (1994). Chromosome polymorphism in *Sorex alpinus* (Mammalia, Soricidae) in the western Alps and the Swiss Jura. *Zeitschrift für Säugetierkunde*, 59: 161–168.

de Beaufort, F. & Vignon, V. (1989). *Mammiféres d'Europe; actes du séminaire technique international (Paris, 27–29 juin 1988)*. SFF/MNHN & Societas Europaea Mammalogica, Paris. 119 pp.

DeBlase, A. F. (1972). *Rhinolophus euryale* and *R. mehelyi* (Chiroptera, Rhinolophidae) in Egypt and southwest Asia. *Israel Journal of Zoology*, 21:1–12.

Degn, H. J. (1973). Systematic position, age criteria and reproduction of Danish red squirrels (*Sciurus vulgaris* L.). *Danish Review of Game Biology,* 8: 1–24.

Dehnel, A. (1949). Studies on the genus Sorex L. *Annales Universitatis Mariae Curie–Skłodowska*, C4: 17–97. (in Polish).

Delibes, M. (1980). Feeding ecology of the Spanish Lynx in the Coto Doñana (Huelva, Spain). *Acta Theriologica*, 25: 309–324.

Delibes, M. (1982). Notas sobre la distribución pasada y actual del Meloncillo, *Herpestes ichneumon* (L.) en la Península Ibérica. *Doñana, Acta Vertebrata,* 9: 341–352.

Delibes, M. & Palomares, F. (1993). *Herpestes ichneumon* (Linnaeus, 1758). Manguste. Pp. 1011–1034, in: Stubbe, M. & Krapp, F. (Eds.). *Handbuch der Säugetiere Europas, Band 5/II, Carnivora (Fissipedia)*. Aula Verlag, Wiesbaden, xv + 529–1213.

Demeter, A. & Spassov, N. (1993). *Canis aureus* Linnaeus, 1758 – Schakal, Goldschakal. Pp. 107–138, in: Stubbe, M. & Krapp, F. (Eds.). *Handbuch der Säugetiere Europas. Raubsäuger I*. Aula Verlag, Wiesbaden, 527 pp.

Denisov, V. P. (1961). Otnosheniya malogo i krapchatogo suslikov na styke ikh arealov. *Zoologicheskii Zhurnal*, 40: 1079–1085.

Denisov, V., Belianin, A., Jordan, M. & Rudek, Z. (1969). Karyological investigations of two species of *Citellus* (*Citellus pygmaeus* Pall. and *Citellus suslicus* Güld.). *Folia Biologica, Warszawa*, 17: 169–175.

Dieterlen, F. (1963). Zur Kenntnis der Kreta–Stachelmaus, *Acomys (cahirinus) minous* Bate. *Zeitschrift für Säugetierkunde,* 28: 47–57.

Dieterlen, F. (1978). *Acomys minous* (Bate, 1905) – Kreta–Stachelmaus. Pp. 452–461, in: Niethammer, J. & Krapp, F. (Eds.). *Handbuch der Säugetiere Europas. Band 1/I, Rodentia 1*. Akademische Verlagsgesellschaft, Wiesbaden, 476 pp.

Dolan, J. M. (1988). A deer of many lands – a guide to the subspecies of the red deer *Cervus elaphus* L. *Zoonoz*, 62: 4–34.

Dolgov, V. (1985). *Shrews of the Old World.* Moscow University Press, Moscow, 221 pp. (in Russian).

Doncaster, P. & Jouventin, P. (1989). Les Ragondins. *La Recherche,* 211(20): 754–761.

Doria, G. (1991). Silvilago o Minilepre *Sylvilagus floridanus* (Allen). P 68 in: Capocaccia Orsini, L. & Doria, G. (Eds). *Animali e piante dalle Americhe all'Europa.* Sagep, Genova, 326 pp.

Doude van Troostwijk, W. J. (1976). The musk–rat (*Ondatra zibethicus* L.) in the Netherlands, its ecological aspects and their consequences for man. *Rijksinstituut voor Natuurbeheer Verhandeling,* 7: 1–136.

Douma–Petridou, E. (1984). Contribution to the knowledge of *Martes foina* Erxl. (Mammalia, Carnivora) from Achaia, northern Peloponnesus Greece and rest southern Balkan Peninsula. *Mammalia,* 48: 565–572.

Duguy, R. & Marchessaux, D. (1992). *Monachus monachus* (Hermann, 1779) – Mönchsrobbe. Pp. 250–267, in: Duguy, R. & Robineau, D. (Eds.). *Handbuch der Säugetiere Europas. Band 6/II, Pinnipedia.* Aula Verlag, Wiesbaden, 309 pp.

Ðulić, B. (1989). Bats in the Red Data List of Croatia. Pp. 389–392, in: Hanák, V., Horáček, I. & Gaisler, J., (Eds) *European bat research 1987.* Charles University Press, Praha, 718 pp.

Dumitrescu, M., Tanasachi, J. & Orghidan, T. (1962–63). Răspândirea chiropterelor în R. P. Română. *Lucrările Institutului de Speologie "Emil Racoviţă" I–I2:* 509–575.

Ebersbach, H. & Stubbe, M. (1996). Vorkommen und Raumnutzung von Baummardern in Europa. Pp 37–44, in: Canters, K. & Wijsman, H. (Eds.), *Wat doen we met de Boommarter.* KNNV Uitgevery, Utrecht, 87pp.

Ejgelis, Ju. K. (1980). *Rodents of Eastern Transcaucasia and the problem of the local plague foci sanitation.* Publishing House of Saratov University, Saratov, 262 pp. (in Russian).

Ellerman, J. R. & Morrison Scott, T. C. S. (1951). *Checklist of Palearctic and Indian Mammals, 1758 to 1946.* British Museum (Natural History), London, 810 pp.

Engländer, H. (1986). *Capra pyrenaica* Schiny, 1838 – Spanischer Steinbock, Iberiensteinbock. Pp. 405–422, in: Niethammer, J. & Krapp, F. (Eds.). *Handbuch der Säugetiere Europas. Band 2/II, Artiodactyla.* Aula Verlag, Wiesbaden, 462 pp.

Entwistle, A. C., Racey, P. A. & Speakman, J. R. (1996). Habitat exploitation by a gleaning bat, *Plecotus auritus. Philosophical Transactions of the Royal Society of London,* 351B: 921–931.

Entwistle, A. C., Racey, P. A. & Speakman, J. R. (1997). Roost selection by the brown long–eared bat *Plecotus auritus. Journal of Applied Ecology,* 34: 399–408.

Erkinaro, E., Heikura, K., Lindgren, E., Pulliainen, E. & Sulkava, S. (1982). Occurrence and spread of the wild boar (*Sus scrofa*) in eastern Fennoscandia. *Memoranda Societas Fauna et Flora Fennica,* 58: 39–47.

Ermala, A. (1995). Reglering och vård av bäverstammen i Finland. Pp. 17–20, in: *The Third Nordic Beaver Symposium, 1992, Finland.* Finnish Game and Fisheries Research Institute, Helsinki.

Fa, J. E. (1981). The apes on the Rock. *Oryx,* 16: 73–76.

Fa, J. E. (1984). Structure and dynamics of the Barbary macaque population in Gibraltar. Pp. 263–306, in: Fa, J.E (Ed.). *The Barbary macaque – A Case Study in Conservation.* Plenum Press, New York & London, 369 pp.

Fa, J. E. (1992). Visitor–directed aggression in the Gibraltar Barbary macaques. *Zoo Biology,* 11: 43–52.

Fa, J. E. & Lind, R. (1996). Population management and viability of the Barbary macaques in Gibraltar. Pp. 235–262, in: Fa, J. E. & Lindburg, D. G. (Eds.), *Evolution and Ecology of Macaque Societies.* Cambridge University Press, Cambridge, 479 pp.

Fadeev, E.V. (1981). On the dynamics of the northern border of the area of the wild boar in East Europe. *Biologičeskie Nauki (Moscow),* 9: 56–64 (in Russian).

Fairon, J., Gilson, R., Jooris, R., Faber, T. & Meisch, C. (1982). Cartographie provisoire de la faune chiroptérologique belgo–luxembourgeoise. *Bulletin du Centre Baguement et de Recherche chiropterologique de Belgique*, 7: 1–125.

Farrell, L. & Cooke, A. S. (1991). Chinese water deer *Hydropotes inermis*. in: Corbet, G. B. & Harris, S. (Eds). *The Handbook of British Mammals*, Blackwell, Oxford, 588 pp.

Fayard A., Saint–Girons, M. C. & Maurin, H. (1984). *Atlas des mammiféres sauvages de France*. SFF, Paris.

Fedorov, V., Jaarola, M. & Fredga, K. (1996). Low mitochondrial DNA variation and recent colonisation of Scandinavia by the wood lemming *Myopus schisticolor*. *Molecular Ecology,* 5(4): 577–581.

Feldhammer, G. A. (1980). *Cervus nippon. Mammalian Species*, 128: 1–7.

Feldhammer, G. A., Farris–Renner, K. C. & Barker, C. M. (1988). *Dama dama. Mammalian Species*, 317: 1–8.

Felten, H. (1971). Eine neue Art der Fledermaus–Gattung *Eptesicus* aus Kleinasien (Chiroptera: Vespertilionidae). *Senckenbergiana biologica*, 52: 371–376.

Ferreras, P., Aldama, J. J., Beltrán, J. F., & Delibes, M. (1992). Rates and causes of mortality in a fragment population of Iberian lynx, *Felis pardina* (Temminck). *Biological Conservation,* 61: 197–202.

Filippucci, M. G., Civitelli, M. V. & Capanna, E. (1988). Evolutionary genetics and systematics of the garden dormouse, *Eliomys* Wagner, 1840. 1 – Karyotype divergence. *Bollettino di Zoologia,* 55: 35–45.

Filippucci, M. G., Fadda, V., Kryštufek, B., Simson, S. & Amori, G. (1991). Allozyme variation and differentiation on *Chionomys nivalis* (Martins, 1842). *Acta Theriologica,* 36: 47–62.

Filippucci, M. G. & Kotsakis, T. (1995). Biochemical systematics and evolution of Myoxidae. *Hystrix (n.s.)* 6: 77–97.

Filippucci, M. G., Kryštufek, B., Simsom, S., Kurtonur, C. & Özkan, B. (1995). Allozymic and biometric variation in *Dryomys nitedula* (Pallas, 1778). *Hystrix,* 6: 127–140.

Filippucci, M. G. & Lapini, L. (1988). First data on the genetic differentiation between *Erinaceus europaeus* Linnaeus, 1758 and *Erinaceus concolor* Martin, 1838 in north–eastern Italy (*Mammalia, Insectivora, Erinaceidae). Gortania–Atti del Museo Friulano di Storia Naturale*, 9: 227–236.

Filippucci, M. G., Nascetti, G., Capanna, E. & Bullini, L. (1987). Allozyme variation and systematics of European moles of the genus *Talpa* (Mammalia, Insectivora). *Journal of Mammalogy,* 68: 487–499.

Filippucci, M. G. & Simson, S. (1996). Allozyme variation and divergence in *Erinaceidae (Mammalia, Insectivora). Israel Journal of Zoology*, 42(4): 335–345.

Filippucci, M. G., Storch, G. & Macholán, M. (1996). Taxonomy of the genus *Sylvaemus* in western Anatolia – morphological and electrophoretic evidence (Mammalia: Rodentia: Muridae). *Senckenbergiana biologica*, 75: 1–14.

Flint, V. E. (1960). Contribution to the biology of *Sicista subtilis* Pall. *Zoologicheskii Zhurnal,* 39: 942–946 (in Russian with English summary).

Flint, W. E. (1966). *Die Zwerghamster der paläarktischen Fauna*. Neue Brehm-Bücherei, No. 366. A. Ziemsen Verlag, Wittenberg, 99 pp.

Flousek, J., Flousková, Z., Tomášová, K. (1985). To the knowledge of small mammals in the Rodnei Mts. (Rumania). *Vestnik Československé Společnosti Zoologické*, 49: 6–17.

Flowerdew, J. R. (1991). Wood mouse *Apodemus sylvaticus*. Pp. 220–229, in: Corbet, G. B. & Harris, S. (Eds.). *The handbook of British mammals*, 3rd ed. Blackwell Scientific Publications, Oxford, 588 pp.

Flowerdew, J. R., Gurnell, J. & Gipps, J. H. W. (Eds.) (1985). The ecology of woodland rodents: bank voles and wood mice. *Symposia of the Zoological Society of London*, No. 55. Academic Press, London, 418 pp.

Flux, J. E. C. & Angermann, R. (1990). The hares and jackrabbits. Pp. 61–94, in: Chapman, J. A. & Flux, J. E. C. (Eds). *Rabbits, hares and pikas*. IUCN, Gland, Switzerland, 168 pp.

Flyger, V. & Gates, J. E. (1982). *Fox and grey squirrels*. Pp. 209–229, in: Chapman, J. A. &. Feldhamer, G. A. (Eds.). *Wild Mammals of North America*. John Hopkins University Press, Baltimore, 1147 pp.

Fons, R. (1975a). Premières données sur l'écologie de la pachyure étrusque, *Suncus etruscus* (Savi, 1822) et comparaison avec deux autres Crocidurinae: *Crocidura russula* (Hermann, 1780) et *Crocidura suaveolens* (Pallas, 1811) (Insectivora, Soricidae). *Vie & Milieu,* 25C : 315-360.

Fons, R. (1975b). Contribution à la connaissance de la musaraigne étrusque *Suncus etruscus* (Savi, 1822). Thèse Doc. Univ. Paris VI, 189 pp.

Forchhammer, M. & Boertmann, D. (1993). The muskoxen in north and northeast Greenland: population trends and the influence of abiotic parameters on population dynamics. *Ecography*, 16: 299–308.

Foster–Turley, P., MacDonald, S. & Mason, C. (1990). *Otters; an action plan for their conservation*. IUCN Species Survival Commission, Gland. 126 pp.

Franzmann, A. W. (1981). *Alces alces. Mammalian Species*, 154: 1–7.

Fredga, K., Bilton, D. & Searle, J. (1995). Colonization history of the pygmy shrew, *Sorex minutus*, in Britain and Scandinavia revealed by genetic markers. P. 38, in: Gurnell, J., (Ed.), 2nd European Congress of Mammalogy, Abstracts of Oral and Poster Papers, Southhampton, 226 pp.

Gaisler, J. (1979). Results of bat census in a town (Mammalia, Chiroptera). *Vestník Československé Společnosti Zoologické*, 43: 7–21.

Gaisler, J. (1994). The bats *Pipistrellus kuhli* and *Hypsugo savii* on the island of Rab (Croatia). *Folia Zoologica*, 43: 279–280.

Gaisler, J., Hanák, V. & Dungel, J. (1979). A contribution to the population ecology of *Nyctalus noctula* (Mammalia: Chiroptera). *Acta Scientiarium Naturalium Academiae Scientiarium Bohemoslovacae Brno (N. S.)*, 13: 1–38.

Galleni, L., Stanyon, R., Contadini, L. & Tallini, A. (1998). Biogeographical and karyological data on the *Microtus savii* group (Rodentia, Arvicolidae) in Italy. *Bonner zoologische Beiträge*, 47: 277-282.

Galleni, L., Tellini, A., Stanyon, R., Cicalò, A. & Santini, L. (1994). Taxonomy of *Microtus savii* (Rodentia, Arvicolidae) in Italy: cytogenetic and hybridization data. *Journal of Mammalogy*, 75: 1040–1044.

Gasc, J.–P., Cabela, A., Crnobrnja–Isailovic, J., Dolmen, D., Grossenbacher, K., Haffner, P., Lescure, J., Martens, H., Martínez Rica, J. P., Maurin, H., Oliveira, M. E., Sofianidou, T. S., Veith, M. & Zuiderwijk, A. (Eds.) (1997) *Atlas of Amphibians and Reptiles in Europe*. Societas Europaea Herpetologica & Muséum National d'Histoire Naturelle, Paris, 496 pp.

Genoud, M. (1982). Distribution écologique de *Crocidura russula* et d'autres Soricidae (Insectivora, Mammalia) en Suisse romande. *Bulletin de la Société vaudoise des Sciences naturelles,* 76: 117–132.

Genoud, M. & Hutterer, R. (1990). *Crocidura russula* (Hermann, 1780) - Hausspitzmaus. Pp. 429-452, in: Niethammer, J. & Krapp, F. (Eds.). *Handbuch der Säugetiere Europas. Band 3/I, Insectivora & Primates*. Aula Verlag, Wiesbaden, 523 pp.

Gerasimov, S., Nikolov, H., Mihailova, V., Auffray, J.–C. & Bonhomme, F. (1990). Morphometric stepwise discriminant analysis of the five genetically determined European taxa of the genus *Mus. Biological Journal of the Linnean Society,* 41: 47–64.

Gerell, R. (1987). Distribution of *Myotis mystacinus* and *Myotis brandtii* (Chiroptera) in Sweden. *Zeitschrift für Säugetierkunde*, 52: 338–341.

Gerell, R. & Lundberg, K. G. (1993). Decline of a bat *Pipistrellus pipistrellus* population in an industrialized area in south Sweden. *Biological Conservation*, 65: 153–157.

Giacometti, M. (1991). Beitrag zur Aussiedelung-sdynamik und aktuellen Verbreitung des Alpensteinbockes (*Capra ibex ibex* L.) im Alpenraum. *Zeitschrift für Jagdwissenschaft*, 37: 157–173.

Giagia–Athanasopoulou, E. B., Chondropoulos, B. P. & Fraguedakis–Tsolis, S. E. (1995). Robertsonian chromosomal variation in subalpine voles *Microtus (Terricola)*, (Rodentia, Arvicolidae) from Greece. *Acta Theriologica*, 40: 139–143.

Gibb, J. A. (1990). The European rabbit *Oryctolagus cuniculus*. Pp. 116–120, in: Chapman, J. A. & Flux, J. E. C. (Eds). *Rabbits, hares and pikas*. IUCN, Gland, Switzerland, 168 pp.

Gisbert, J., López–Fuster, M. J. Garcia–Perea, R. & Ventura, J. (1988). Distribution and biometry of *Sorex granarius* (Miller, 1910) (Soricidae, Insectivora). *Zeitschrift für Säugetierkunde,* 53: 267–275.

Gloor, S., Stutz, H.–P. & Ziswiler, V. (1995). Nutritional habits of the noctule bat *Nyctalus noctula* (Schreber, 1774) in Switzerland. *Myotis*, 32–33: 231–242.

Glas, G. H. (1986). Atlas van de Nederlandse vleermuizen 1970–1984, alsmede een vergelijking met vroegere gegevens. *Zoologische Bijdragen,* 34: 1–97.

Gorgas, M. (1993). *Ursus (Thalarctos) maritimus (Phipps, 1774)* – Eisbär. Pp. 310–328, in: Niethammer, J. & Krapp, F. (Eds.). *Handbuch der Säugetiere Europas. Band 5/I Carnivora (Fissipedia)*. Aula Verlag, Wiesbaden, 527 pp.

Görner, M. & Hackethal, H. (1988). *Säugetiere Europas*. Neuman, Leipzig-Radebeul, 372 pp.

Gosálbez, J. (1987). *Insectívors i Rosegadors de Catalunya*. Ketres ed., Barcelona, 241 pp.

Gosling, M. (1989). Extinction to order. *New Scientist,* 121(1654): 44–49.

Gosling, L. M. & Skinner, J. R. (1984). *Coypu*. Pp. 246–251, in: Mason, I. L. (Ed.). *Evolution of domesticated animals.*, Longman, London & New York, 452 pp.

Graf, J.–D. (1982). Génétique biochimique, zoogéographie et taxonomie des Arvicolidae. *Revue Suisse de Zoologie*, 89: 749–787.

Graf, J–D., Hausser, J., Farina, A. & Vogel, P. (1979). Confirmation du status spécifique de *Sorex samniticus* Altobello 1926 (Mammalia, Insectivora). *Bonner zoologische Beiträge*, 30: 14–21.

Graf, M., Stutz, H.–P. B. & Ziswiler, V. (1992). Regionale und saisonale Unterschiede in der Nahrungszusammensetzung des Grossen Mausohrs *Myotis myotis* (Chiroptera, Vespertilionidae) in der Schweiz. *Zeitschrift für Säugetierkunde*, 57: 193–200.

Grakov, N. N. (1993). The pine marten and its harvest in Russia. *Lutreola*, 2: 7–13.

Gray, G. G. & Simpson, C. D. (1980). *Ammotragus lervia*. *Mammalian Species,* 144: 1–7.

Gromov, I. M., Bibikov, D. I., Kalabukhov, N. I., & Meier, M. N. (1965). *Fauna SSSR, Mlekopitayushchie*, 3, 2. AN SSSR Izd. Nauka, Moskva–Leningrad. 466 pp. (in Russian)

Gromov, I. M. & Polyakov, I. Y. (1992). *Fauna of the USSR: Mammals. Vol. 3/8 Voles (Microtinae)*. E. J. Brill, Leiden & New York. 725 pp.

Gromov, I. M. & Erbajeva, M. A. (1995) *The mammals of Russia and adjacent territories. Lagomorphs and rodents*. Russian Academy of Sciences, Zoological Institute, St. Petersburg, 456 pp.

Groves, C. P. (1981). Ancestors of the pigs: taxonomy and phylogeny of the genus *Sus*. Technical Bulletin No. 3, Dept of Prehistory, Research School of Pacific studies, Australian National University, 96 pp.

Groves, P. (1995). The takin and the muskox: a molecular and ecological evaluation of relationship. PhD thesis, University of Alaska, Fairbanks.

Guiral, J., Fernandez–Arias, A., Folch, J. & Hidalgo, R. (1997). The Bucardo (*Capra pyrenaica pyrenaica*) recovery plan. *Abstract of 2nd World Conference on Mountain Ungulates*: 78–79.

Gurnell, J. (1987). *The Natural History of Squirrels*. Croom Helm, London, 201 pp.

Gurnell, J. (1996). The effects of food availability and winter weather on the dynamics of a grey squirrel population in southern England. *Journal of Applied Ecology,* 33: 325–338.

Gurnell, J. & Pepper, H. (1988). Perspectives on the management of red and grey squirrels. Pp. 92-109, in: Jardine, D.C. (Ed.). *Wildlife Management in Forests*. ICF, Edinburgh.

Gurnell, J. & Pepper, H. (1993). A critical look at conserving the British red squirrel *Sciurus vulgaris*. *Mammal Review,* 23: 125–136.

Hable, E. & Spitzenberger, F. (1989). Die Birkenmaus, *Sicista betulina* Pallas, 1779 (Mammalia, Rodentia) in Österreich. Mammalia austriaca 16. *Mitteilungen der Abteilung für Zoologie des Landesmuseums Joanneum,* 43: 3–22.

Hagemeijer, E. J. M. & Blair, M. J. (Eds.) (1997). *The EBCC Atlas of European breeding birds: their distribution and abundance*. Poyser, London. cxii & 903 pp.

Hall, E. R. & Kelson, K. R. (1959). *Mammals of North America*. Ronald Press Co., New York, 1083 pp.

Hamar, M. (1967) Rozătoarle României Din viaţa rozătoarelor. *Ed. St. Bucureşti*: 1–174.

Hamar, M. & Schutowa, M. (1966). Neue Daten über die geographische Veränderlichkeit und die Entwicklung der Gattung *Mesocricetus* Nehring, 1898 (Glires, Mammalia). *Zeitschrift für Säugetierkunde,* 31: 237 – 251.

Hanák, V. & Gaisler, J. (1971). The status of *Eptesicus ognevi* Bobrinskii, 1918, and remarks on some other species of this genus (Mammalia: Chiroptera). *Vestník Československé Společnosti Zoologické*, 35:11–24.

Hanák, V. & Gaisler, J. (1983). *Nyctalus leisleri* (Kuhl, 1818), une espèce nouvelle pour le continent africain. *Mammalia*, 47: 585–587.

Hanák, V. & Horáček, I. (1986). Zur Südgrenze des Areals von *Eptesicus nilssoni* (Chiroptera: Vespertilionidae). *Annalen des Naturhistorischen Museums in Wien*, 88/89B: 377–388.

Hanák, V., Lamani, F. & Muraj, X. (1961). Te dhena nga perhapja e lakuriqeve te nates (Ordo Chiroptera) ne Shqiperi. *Buletin i Shkencave Natyrore*, 3: 124–156.

Hansson, L. (1982). Field mouse (*Microtus agrestis*). Pp. 189–190, in: Davis, D.E. (ed.) CRC handbook of census methods for terrestrial vertebrates. CRC Press, Boca Raton, Florida, 397 pp.

Hardy, C., Callou, C., Vigne, J.–D., Casane, D., Denebouy, N., Mounolou, J.C. & Monerot, M. (1995). Rabbit mitochondrial DNA diversity from prehistoric to modern times. *Journal of Molecular Evolution*, 40: 227–237.

Harris, S., Morris, P., Wray, S. & Yalden, D. (1995). *A review of British mammals: population estimates and conservation status of British mammals other than cetaceans*. Joint Nature Conservancy Committee, Peterborough, 168 pp.

Harrison, D. L. & Bates, P. J. J. (1991). *The mammals of Arabia*. Harrison Zoological Museum, Sevenoaks, Kent, UK, 354 pp.

Hartl, G. B., Meneguz, P. G., Apollonio, M., Marco–Sanchez, I., Nadlinger, K. & Suchentrunk, F. (1995). Molecular systematics of ibex in Western Europe. Pp. 21–26, in: *Proceedings of an International Congress on the Genus Capra* 1992, Ronda (Spain).

Hartl, G. B., Suchentrunk, F., Nadlinger, K. & Willing, R. (1993). An integrative analysis of genetic differentiation in the brown hare (*Lepus europaeus*). *Acta Theriologica*, Suppl. 2: 33–57.

Hausser, J. (1990). *Sorex coronatus* Millet, 1882 – Schabrackenspitzmaus. Pp. 279–286, in: Niethammer, J. & Krapp, F. (Eds.). *Handbuch der Säugetiere Europas. Band 3/1, Insectivora, Primates*. Aula Verlag, Wiesbaden, 523 pp.

Hausser, J. (Ed.) (1995). *Säugetiere der Schweiz: Verbreitung, Biologie, Ökologie*. Birkhäuser Verlag, Basel, 501p.

Hausser, J., Hutterer, R. & Vogel, P. (1990). *Sorex araneus* Linnaeus, 1758 – Waldspitzmaus. Pp. 237–277, in: Niethammer, J. & Krapp, F. (Eds.). *Handbuch der Säugetiere Europas. Band 3/1, Insectivora, Primates.* Aula Verlag, Wiesbaden, 523 pp.

Hecht–Markou, P. (1994). Beschreibung, geographische Verbreitung, Biotope und Ortswechsel des *Sciurus anomalus* Güeldenstadt, 1758, auf der Insel Lesbos (Griechenland). *Annales Musei Goulandris,* 9: 429–444.

Heidecke, D. (1986). Taxonomische Aspekte des Artenschutzes am Beispiel der Biber Eurasiens. *Hercynia,* 22: 146–161.

Heidemann, G. (1986). *Cervus dama* (Linnaeus, 1758) – Damhirsch. Pp. 140–158, in: Niethammer, J. & Krapp, F. (Eds.). *Handbuch der Säugetiere Europas. Band 2/II, Artiodactyla.* Aula Verlag, Wiesbaden, 462 pp.

Heise, G. & Schmidt, A. (1988). Beiträge zur sozialen Organisation und Ökologie des Braunen Langohrs (*Plecotus auritus*). *Nyctalus (N. F.),* 2: 445–465.

Hell, P. (1990). Der Wolf (*Canis lupus*) in den slowakischen Karpaten. *Zeitschrift für Jagdwissenschaft,* 36: 160–168.

Helle, E. (1992). *Phoca hispida* Schreber, 1775 – Ringelrobbe. Pp. 138–161, in: Duguy, R. & Robineau, D. (Eds.). *Handbuch der Säugetiere Europas. Band 6/II, Pinnipedia.* Aula Verlag, Wiesbaden, 309 pp.

Helle, E. & Kauhala, K. (1991). Distribution history and present status of the raccoon dog in Finland. *Holarctic Ecology,* 14: 278–286.

Helversen, O. von (1999). *Eptesicus bottae* (Mammalia, Chiroptera) auf der Insel Rhodos. *Bonner zoologische Beiträge,* 48: 113-121.

Hemmer, H. (1993a). *Felis silvestris* Schreber, 1777 – Wildkatze. Pp. 1076–1118, in: Stubbe, M. & Krapp, F. (Eds.). *Handbuch der Säugetiere Europas. Band 5/II, Carnivora.* Aula Verlag, Wiesbaden, xv + 529–1213.

Hemmer, H. (1993b). *Felis (Lynx) lynx* Linnaeus, 1758 – Luchs, Nordluchs. Pp. 1119–1167, in: Stubbe, M. & Krapp, F. (Eds.). *Handbuch der Säugetiere Europas.*

Band. 5/II, Carnivora. Aula Verlag, Wiesbaden, xv + 529–1213.

Henry, C., Lafontaine, L., Mouches, A. (1988). Le blaireau (*Meles meles* Linnaeus, 1758). *Encyclopédie des Carnivores de France,* 7: 1–35.

Henttonen, H., Okanen, T., Jortikka, A. & Haukisalmi, V. (1987). How much do weasels shape microtine cycles in the northern Fennoscandian taiga? *Oikos,* 50: 353–365.

Henttonen, H. & Peiponen, V. A. (1982). *Clethrionomys rutilus* (Pallas) – Polàrrötelmaus. Pp. 165–176, in: Niethammer, J. & Krapp, F. (Eds.). *Handbuch der Säugetiere Europas. Band 2/I, Rodentia II.* Akademische Verlagsgesellschaft, Wiesbaden, 649 pp.

Henttonen, H. & Viitala, J. (1982). *Clethrionomys rufocanus* (Sundevall, 1846) – Graurötelmaus. Pp. 147–164, in: Niethammer, J. & Krapp, F. (Eds.). *Handbuch der Säugetiere Europas, Band 2/I, Rodentia II.* Akademische Verlagsgesellschaft, Wiesbaden, 649 pp.

Heptner, V. G. & Nasimowitsch, A. A. (1967). *Der Elch.* Neue Brehm-Bücherei No. 386, Wittenberg Lutherstadt, 231 pp.

Heptner, V. G., Naumov, N. P., Yurgenson, P. B., Sludsky, A. A., Chirkova, A. F. & Bannikov, A. G. (1967). *Mlekopitayushchie Sovetskogo Soyuza (Mammals of the Soviet Union). Vol. 2 (Part 1): Sea cows and Carnivores.* Vysshaya Shkola Publ., Moscow, 1004 pp. (in Russian).

Heptner, V. G. & Naumov, N. P. (1974). *Die Säugetiere der Sowjetunion. Vol. II: Seekühe und Raubtiere.* Fischer Verlag, Jena, 1006 pp.

Heptner, V. G., Naumov, N. P., Jürgenson, P, B., Sludski, A. A., Cirkova, A. F. & Bannikov, A. G. (1974). Steinmarder, *Martes (Martes) foina* Erxleben 1777. Pp. 571–591, in: Heptner, V. G. & Naumov, N. P. (Eds.). *Die Säugetiere der Sowjetunion. Vol. II: Seekühe und Raubtiere.* Fischer Verlag, Jena, 1006 pp.

Herre, W. (1955). *Das Ren als Haustier: eine zoologische Monographie.* Leipzig.

Herre, W. (1986). *Rangifer tarandus* (Linnaeus, 1758) –

Ren, Rentier. Pp. 198–216, in: Niethammer, J. & Krapp, F. (Eds.). *Handbuch der Säugetiere Europas. Band 2/II, Artiodactyla.* Aula Verlag, Wiesbaden, 462 pp.

Herre, W. & Röhrs, M. (1955). Über die Formenmannigfaltigkeit des Gehörns der *Caprini* Simpson, 1945. *Der Zoologische Garten (N.F.),* 22: 85–110.

Hewson, R. (1995). Mountain hares *Lepus timidus* on Hoy, Orkney, and their habitat. *Journal of Zoology, London,* 236: 331–337.

Hille, A. & Meinig, H. (1996). The subspecific status of European populations of the striped mouse *Apodemus agrarius* (Pallas, 1771) based on morphological and biochemical characters. *Bonner zoologische Beiträge,* 46: 203–231.

Hoffmann, M. (1958). *Die Bisamratte.* Neue Brehm–Bücherei, No. 78. Akademische Verlagsgesellschaft, Leipzig, 44 pp.

Hoffmann, R. (1971). Relationships of certain holarctic shrews, genus *Sorex. Zeitschrift für Säugetierkunde,* 36: 193–200.

Hoffmann, R. (1987). A review of the systematics and distribution of Chinese red–toothed shrews (Mammalia, Soricidae). *Acta Theriologica Sinica,* 7: 100–139.

Hofmann, R. R. (1985). Digestive physiology of the deer – their morphophysiological specialisation and adaptation. In: Drew, K. & Fennessy, P. (Eds.). Biology of deer production. *Royal Society of New Zealand Bulletin,* 22: 393–407.

Hoffmeister, H. (1983). *Das Sikawild.* Landbuch Verlag, Hannover, 72 pp.

Hokkanen, H. & Fokin, I. (1997). Flying squirrel *Pteromys volans* Linnaeus. East–Fennoscandian Red Book. Helsinki.

Hokkanen, H., Törmälä, T. & Vuorinen, H. (1982). Decline of the flying squirrel *Pteromys volans* L. populations in Finland. *Biological Conservation,* 23: 273–284.

Hollander, H. & Limpens, H. G. J. A. (1997). Mopsvleermuis *Barbastella barbastellus* (Schreber, 1774). Pp 210–213, in: Limpens, H., Mostert, K. & Bongers, W. (Eds.). *Atlas van de Nederlandse vleermuizen. Onderzoek naar verspreiding en ecologie.* KNNV Uitgeverij, Utrecht, 260 pp.

Holz, H. & Niethammer, J. (1990a). *Erinaceus concolor* Martin, 1838 – Weißbrustigel, Ostigel. Pp. 50–64, in: Niethammer, J. & Krapp, F. (Eds.). *Handbuch der Säugetiere Europas. Band 3/I. Insectivora, Primates.* Aula Verlag, Wiesbaden, 523 pp.

Holz, H. & Niethammer, J. (1990b). *Erinaceus europaeus* Linnaeus, 1758 – Braunbrustigel, Westigel. Pp. 26–49, in: Niethammer, J. & Krapp, F. (Eds.) *Handbuch der Säugetiere Europas. Band 3/I. Insectivora, Primates.* Aula Verlag, Wiesbaden, 523 pp.

Holz, H. & Niethammer, J. (1990c). *Atelerix algirus* (Lereboullet, 1840) – Wanderigel. Pp 65–74, in: Niethammer, J. & Krapp, F. (Eds.). *Handbuch der Säugetiere Europas. Band 3/I. Insectivora, Primates.* Aula Verlag, Wiesbaden, 523 pp.

Horáček, I. (1984). Remarks on the causality of population decline in European bats. *Myotis,* 22: 138–147.

Horáček, I., Bogdanowicz, W. & Đulić B. (in press). *Plecotus austriacus.* In: Niethammer, J. & Krapp, F. (Eds.). *Handbuch der Säugetiere Europas. Fledermäuse.* Aula Verlag, Wiesbaden.

Horáček, I. & Hanák, V. (1984). Comments on the systematics and phylogeny of *Myotis nattereri* (Kuhl, 1818). *Myotis,* 21–22: 20–29.

Horáček, I. & Hanák, V. (1986). Generic status of *Pipistrellus savii* and comments on classification of the genus *Pipistrellus* (Chiroptera, Vespertilionidae). *Myotis,* 23–24: 9–16.

Horáček, I. & Hanák, V. (1989). Distributional status of *Myotis dasycneme.* Pp. 565–590, in: Hanák, V., Horáček, I. & Gaisler, J. (Eds.). *European bat research 1987.* Charles University Press, Praha, 718 pp.

Hůrka, L. (1989). Die Säugetiere des westlichen Teils der Tschechischen Sozialistischen Republik. II. Die Fledermäuse (Chiroptera). *Folia Musei Rerum Naturalium Bohemiae Occidentalis Plzeň, Zoologica*, 29: 1–61.

Husband, T. P. & Davis, P. B. (1984). Ecology and behaviour of the Cretan agrimi. *Canadian Journal of Zoology*, 62: 411–420.

Hutterer, R. (1990). *Sorex minutus* Linnaeus, 1766 – Zwergspitzmaus. Pp. 183–206, in: Niethammer, J. & Krapp, F. (Eds.). *Handbuch der Säugetiere Europas. Band 3/I. Insectivora, Primates.* Aula Verlag, Wiesbaden, 523 pp.

Hutterer, R. (1993). Order Insectivora. Pp. 69-130, in: Wilson, D. & Reeder, D. (Eds.). *Mammals species of the world: a taxonomic and geographic reference.* 2nd ed. Smithsonian Institution Press, Washington and London, 1206 pp.

Hutterer, R., Maddalena, T. & Molina, M. O. (1992). Origin and evolution of the endemic Canary Island shrews (Mammalia: Soricidae). *Biological Journal of the Linnean Society*, 46: 49–58.

Ibáñez, C. & Fernández, R. (1985). Systematic status of the long–eared bat *Plecotus teneriffae* Barret–Hamilton [sic], 1907 (Chiroptera: Vespertilionidae). *Säugetierkundliche Mitteilungen,* 32:143–149.

Ibáñez, C., Guillén, A. & Bogdanowicz, W. (in press). *Nyctalus lasiopterus*. In: Niethammer, J. & Krapp, F. (Eds.). *Handbuch der Säugetiere Europas. Fledermäuse.* Aula Verlag, Wiesbaden.

ICZN (1998). Opinion No. 1894. *Bulletin of Zoological Nomenclature,* 55: 64–71,

Iljin, V. Yu., Ermakov, O. A. & Lukyanov, S. B. (1996). New data on distribution of mammals in Povolzh'e and Volga–Ural River region. *Biulletin Moskovskogo Obshchestva Ispytatelei Prirody, Otdel Biologicheskii*, 101, 2: 30–37.

Ingelög, T., Andersson, R. & Tjernberg, M. (1993). *Red data book of the Baltic region. Part 1. List of threatened vascular plants and vertebrates.* Swedish Threatened Species Unit, Uppsala.

Ioannidis, Y. & Giannatos, G. (1991). Preliminary survey on the distribution and status of jackal (*Canis aureus* L., 1758) in southern Greece. *Biologia Gallo–hellenica,* 18: 67–74.

Ivanter, E. V. (1975). *Population ecology of small mammals in the north western taiga of the USSR.* Nauka, Leningrad, 248 pp. (in Russian with English synopsis).

Jabir H. A., Bajomi, D. & Demeter, A. (1985). New record of the black rat (*Rattus rattus* L.) from Hungary, and a review of its distribution in Central Europe (Mammalia). *Annales Historico–Naturales Musei Nationalis Hungarici*, 77: 263–267.

Jakubiec, Z. (1993). *Ursus arctos* Linnaeus, 1753 – Braunbär. Pp. 254–300, in: Stubbe, M. & Krapp, F. (Eds.). *Handbuch der Säugetiere Europas. Band. 5/I, Carnivora.* Aula Verlag, Wiesbaden, 527 pp.

Jalas, J. & Suominen, J. (1967). Mapping the distribution of European vascular plants. *Memoranda Societatis pro Fauna et Flora Fennica,* 43: 60–72.

Jalas, J. & Souminen, J. (Eds.) (1972). *Atlas florae Europaeae: distribution of vascular plants in Europe 1. Pteridophyta (Psilotaceae to Azollaceae).* Committee for Mapping the Flora of Europe, Helsinki, 121 pp.

Jansen, E. A. & Buys, J. C. (1997). Gewone grootoorvleermuis *Plecotus auritus* (Linnaeus, 1758). Pp 214–223, in: Limpens, H., Mostert, K. & Bongers, W. (Eds.). *Atlas van de Nederlandse vleermuizen. Onderzoek naar verspreiding en ecologie.* KNNV Uitgeverij, Utrecht, 260pp.

Jenkins, S. H. & Busher, P. E. (1979). *Castor canadensis. Mammalian Species,* 120: 1–8.

Jennersten, O. (ed.) (1995). *Meeting on lemmings.* WWF–Sweden, Stockholm.

Jensen, A. & Jensen, B. (1972). Ilderen (*Putorius putorius*) Og Ilderjagten i Danmark 1969/70. *Danske Vildtundersogelser, Vildtbiologisk Station,* 18: 1–32.

Jimenez, R., Burgos, M. & Diaz de la Guardia, R. (1984). Karyotype and chromosome banding in the mole (*Talpa occidentalis*) from the south–east of the Iberian Peninsula. Implication on its taxonomic position. *Caryologia*, 37: 253–258.

Johansen, B. S. (1995). Atlas over piggsvin i Norge 1980–1995. *Fauna,* 48: 204–207 (in Norwegian).

Jones, G. & van Parijs, S. M. (1993). Bimodal echolocation in pipistrelle bats: are cryptic species present? *Proceedings of the Royal Society of London,* 251B: 119–125.

Jones, K. E., Altringham, J. D. & Deaton, R. (1996). Distribution and population densities of seven species of bats in northern England. *Journal of Zoology, London,* 240: 788–798.

Jorga, W. (1971). Die südliche Verbreitungsgrenze der Nordischen Wühlmaus, *Microtus oeconomus*, auf dem Gebiet der DDR und Bemerkungen zu deren Grenzpopulationen. *Hercynia,* 8: 286–306.

Jounanin, C. (1990). L'ecureuil a ventre rouge d'Antibes. Pp. 277–284, in: Guerineau, M.–C. (Ed.). *Introductions et reintroductions des mammifères sauvages*. Jean Louis Senotier Nature Centre, Saint–Jean–de–Braye, France.

Jüdes, U. (1981). Some notes on population density of *Micromys minutus* in a secondary biotope. *Zeitschrift für Säugetierkunde*, 46: 266–268.

Judin, B. (1964). The geographical distribution and interspecific taxonomy of *Sorex minutissimus* Zimmermann, 1780, in West Siberia. *Acta Theriologica,* 8: 167–179.

Jurczyszyn, M. (1995). Population densities of *Myoxus glis* (L.) in some forest habitats. *Hystrix,* 6: 265–271.

Kaikusalo, A. (1993). Nisäkäsatlas 1993. Nisäkäposti 33. 70 pp. (Finnish mammal atlas, in Finnish).

Kalela, O. (1961). Seasonal changes of habitat in the Norwegian lemming, *Lemmus lemmus* (L.) *Annales Academiae Scientiarium Fennicae, Series A, Biologica,* 55: 1–72.

Kalela, O. (1963). Die geographische Verbreitung des Waldlemmings und seine Massenvorkommen in Finnland. *Archivum Societatis Zoologicae Botanicae Fennicae "Vanamo"*, 18 (suppl.): 47–55.

Kalela, O. & Koponen, T. (1971). Food consumption and movements of the Norwegian lemming in areas characterized by isolated fells. *Annales Zoologici Fennici,* 8: 80–84.

Kandefer–Szerzeń, M., Męczyński, S., Borowska, L., Szuster–Ciesielska, A. & Rzeski, W. (1994). Seasonal modulation of interferon response in the spotted sousliks (*Spermophilus suslicus*). *Archivum Immunologiae et Therapiae Experimentalis,* 42: 425–431.

Kapel, F.O. (1992a). *Erignathus barbatus* (Erxleben, 1777) – Bartrobbe. Pp. 80–96, in: Duguy, R. & Robineau, D. (Eds.). *Handbuch der Säugetiere Europas. Band 6/ II, Pinnipedia*. Aula Verlag, Wiesbaden, 309 pp.

Kapel, F. O. (1992b). *Phoca groenlandica* Erxleben, 1777 – Sattelrobbe. Pp. 196–224, in: Duguy, R. & Robineau, D. (Eds.). *Handbuch der Säugetiere Europas. Band 6/ II, Pinnipedia*. Aula Verlag, Wiesbaden, 309 pp.

Kapel, F. O. (1992c). *Cystophora cristata* (Erxleben, 1777) – Klappmütze. Pp. 225–249, in: Duguy, R. & Robineau, D. (Eds.). *Handbuch der Säugetiere Europas. Band 6/II, Pinnipedia*. Aula Verlag, Wiesbaden, 309 pp.

Kauhala, K. (1992). Ecological characteristics of the raccoon dog in Finland. Ph.D. thesis, University of Helsinki.

Kauhala, K. (1996a). Introduced carnivores in Europe with special reference to central and northern Europe. *Wildlife Biology,* 2: 197–204.

Kauhala, K. (1996b). Habitat use of raccoon dogs, *Nyctereutes procyonoides*, in southern Finland. *Zeitschrift für Säugetierkunde*, 61: 269–275.

Kauhala, K., Kaunisto, M. & Helle, E. (1993). Diet of the raccoon dog, *Nyctereutes procyonoides*, in Finland. *Zeitschrift für Säugetierkunde*, 58: 129–136.

Kefelioğlu, H. (1997). Taxonomic status and karyological characters of *Meriones tristrami* Thomas, 1892

(Mammalia: Rodentia) in Turkey. *Turkish Journal of Zoology,* 21: 57–62.

Kerth, G., Mayer, F. & König, B. (1995). Genetische Verwandtschaft unter Bechsteinfledermäusen (*Myotis bechsteini*) innerhalb und zwischen Wochenstuben. *Verhandlungen der Deutschen Zoologischen Gesellschaft,* 88: 38.

Kime, R. D. (1990). *A provisional atlas of European Myriapods, part 1. Fauna Europaea Evertebrata, Volume 1.* European Invertebrate Survey, Luxemburg, 109 pp., 50 maps.

King, C. (1989). *The Natural History of Weasels & Stoats.* Christopher Helm, London, 253 pp.

King, J. (1983). *Seals of the world.* British Museum of Natural History, London and Oxford University Press, Oxford, 240 pp.

Kock, D., Malec, F. & Storch, G. (1972). Rezente und subfossile Kleinsäuger aus dem Vilayet Elazig, Ostanatolien. *Zeitschrift für Säugetierkunde,* 37: 204–229.

Kokurewicz, T. (1990). The decrease in abundance of the lesser horseshoe bat *Rhinolophus hipposideros* Bechstein, 1800 (Chiroptera: Rhinolophidae) in winter quarters in Poland. *Myotis,* 28: 109–118.

Kokurewicz, T. (1995). Increased population of Daubenton's bat (*Myotis daubentoni* (Kuhl, 1819)) (Chiroptera: Vespertilionidae) in Poland. *Myotis,* 32–33:155–161.

König, C. (1962). Eine neue Wühlmaus aus der Umgebung von Garmisch–Partenkirchen (Oberbayern): *Pitymys bavaricus* (Mammalia, Rodentia). *Senckenbergiana biologica,* 43: 1–10.

Koopman, K. F. (1993). Order Chiroptera. Pp. 137–241, in: Wilson, D. E. & Reeder, D. M. (Eds.). *Mammal species of the world: a taxonomic and geographic reference.* Smithsonian Institution Press, Washington D.C., 1206 pp.

Koopman, K. F. (1994). Chiroptera: systematics. Pp. vii+1–217, in: Niethammer, J., Schliemann, H. & Starck, D., (Eds.) *Handbook of Zoology. Vol. VIII. Mammalia. Part 60.* Walter de Gruyter, Berlin.

Koprowski, J. L. & Gavish, L. (in press). *Sciurus anomalus. Mammalian Species .*

Kostian, E. (1970). Habitat requirements and breeding biology of the Root Vole, *Microtus oeconomus* (Pallas), on shore meadows in the Gulf of Bothnia, Finland. *Annales Zoologici Fennici,* 7: 329–340.

Kotenkova, E.V. & Bulatova, N.S. (Eds.) (1994). *The house mouse. Origin, distribution, systematics, behaviour.* Nauka, Moscow (in Russian with an English summary).

Kowalski, K. (1960). *Pitymys* McMurtrie 1831 (Microtidae, Rodentia) in the northern Carpathians. *Acta Theriologica,* 6: 230–235.

Kowalski, K., Gaisler, J., Bessam, H., Issaad, C. & Ksantini, H. (1986). Annual life cycle of cave bats in Northern Algeria. *Acta Theriologica,* 13: 185–206.

Král, B., Bel'anin, A. N., Zima, J., Malygin, V. M., Gajcenko, V. A., Orlov, V. N. (1980). Distribution of *Microtus arvalis* and *Microtus epiroticus. Acta Scientarum Naturalium Acadamae Scientarium Bohemoslovacae Brno,* 14(9): 1–30.

Kramer, F. (1956). Über die Winterbaue des Hamsters (*Cricetus cricetus* L.) auf zwei getrennten Luzerneschlägen. *Wissenschaftliche Zeitschrift der Universität Halle,* 5(4): 673–682.

Krapp, F. (1978a). *Marmota marmota* (Linnaeus, 1758) – Alpenmurmeltier. Pp. 153–181, in: Niethammer, G. & Krapp, F. (Eds.). *Handbuch der Säugetiere Europas. Band 1/I, Rodentia I.* Akademische Verlagsgesellschaft, Wiesbaden, 476 pp.

Krapp, F. (1978b). *Tamias sibiricus* (Laxmann, 1769) – Burunduk. Pp. 116–121, in: Niethammer, J. & Krapp, F. (Eds.). *Handbuch der Säugetiere Europas. Band 1/I, Rodentia I* Akademische Verlagsgesellschaft, Wiesbaden, 476 pp.

Krapp, F. (1982a). *Microtus multiplex* (Fatio, 1905) – Alpen–Kleinwühlmaus. Pp. 419–428, in: Niethammer, J. & Krapp, F. (Eds.). *Handbuch der Säugetiere Europas. Band 2/I, Rodentia II* Akademische Verlagsgesellschaft, Wiesbaden, 649 pp.

Krapp F. (1982b). *Microtus nivalis* (Martins, 1842) – Schneemaus. Pp. 261–283, in: Niethammer, J. & Krapp, F. (Eds.). *Handbuch der Säugetiere Europas. Band 2/I, Rodentia II.* Akademische Verlagsgesellschaft, Wiesbaden, 649 pp.

Krapp, F. (1982c). *Microtus pyrenaicus* (de Sélys–Longchamps, 1847) – Pyrenäen–Kleinwühlmaus. Pp. 442–446, in: Niethammer, J. & Krapp, F. (Eds.). *Handbuch der Säugetiere Europas. Band 2/I, Rodentia II.* Akademische Verlagsgesellschaft, Wiesbaden, 649 pp.

Krapp, F. (1982d). *Microtus savii* (de Sélys Longchamps 1838) – Italienische Kleinwühlmaus. Pp. 429–437, in: Niethammer, J. & Krapp, F. (Eds.). *Handbuch der Säugetiere Europas. Band 2/I, Rodentia II.* Akademische Verlagsgesellschaft, Wiesbaden, 649 pp.

Krapp, F. (1990). *Crocidura leucodon* (Hermann, 1780) – Feldspitzmaus. Pp. 465–484, in: Niethammer, J. & Krapp, F. (Eds.). *Handbuch der Säugetiere Europas. Band 3/I, Insectivora, Primates.* Aula Verlag, Wiesbaden, 523 pp.

Krapp, F. (1993). *Herpestes auropunctatus* (Hodgson, 1836) – Goldstraubmanguste, Indische Zwergmanguste, Mungo. Pp. 1035–1055, in: Stubbe, M. & Krapp, F. (Eds.). *Handbuch der Säugetiere Europas, Band 5/II, Carnivora (Fissipedia).* Aula Verlag, Wiesbaden, xv + 529–1213.

Krapp, F. & Delibes, M. (1993). *Genetta genetta* (Linnaeus, 1758). Ginsterkatze. Pp. 965–999, in: Stubbe, M. & Krapp, F. (Eds.). *Handbuch der Säugetiere Europas. Band 5/II, Carnivora (Fissipedia).* Aula Verlag, Wiesbaden, xv + 529–1213.

Krapp, F. & Niethammer, J. (1982). *Microtus agrestis* (Linnaeus, 1761) – Erdmaus. Pp. 349–373, in: Niethammer, J. & Krapp, F. (Eds.). *Handbuch der Säugetiere Europas. Band 2/I, Rodentia II.* Aula Verlag, Wiesbaden, 649 pp.

Krapp, F. & Niethammer, J. (1986). *Cervus nippon* Temminck, 1830 – Sikahirsch. Pp. 159–172, in: Niethammer, J. & Krapp, F. (Eds.) *Handbuch der Säugetiere Europas. Band 2/II, Artiodactyla.* Aula Verlag, Wiesbaden, 462 pp.

Krasiński, Z. A. (1994). Restytucja żubrów w Białowieży w latach 1929–1952. *Parki Narodowe i Rezerwaty Przyrody,* 13(4): 3–23 (in Polish with English summary).

Kratochvíl, J. (1964). Die systematische Stellung von *Pitymys tatricus* Kratochvíl, 1952. *Zeitschrift für Säugetierkunde,* 29: 230–235.

Kratochvíl, J. (1970). Pitymys–Arten aus der Hohen Tatra (Mamm., Rodentia). *Acta Scientarum Naturalium Academiae Scientarium Bohemoslovacae Brno,* 4(12): 1–63.

Kratochvíl, J. (1971). Der Status der Populationen der Gattung *Pitymys* aus Attika (Rodentia, Mamm.). *Zoologicke Listy,* 20: 107–206.

Kratochvíl, J. (Ed.) (1959). The common vole *Microtus arvalis.* CSAV Publishing House, Praha, 359 pp. (in Czech with German summary).

Kryštufek, B. (1990). Geographic variation in *Microtus nivalis* (Martins, 1842) from Austria and Yugoslavia. *Bonner zoologische Beiträge,* 41:121–139.

Kryštufek, B. (1991). Sympatry in two petricolic voles: *Dinaromys bogdanovi* and *Microtus nivalis.* First European Congress of Mammalogy, Lisboa, 18–23 March 1991, p. 60.

Kryštufek, B. (1993). Geographic variation in the greater horseshoe bat *Rhinolophus ferrumequinum* in south–eastern Europe. *Acta Theriologica,* 38: 67–79.

Kryštufek, B. (1994). The taxonomy of blind moles (*Talpa caeca* and *T. stankovici,* Insectivora, Mammalia) from south–eastern Europe. *Bonner zoologische Beiträge,* 45: 1–16.

Kryštufek, B. (1996). Phenetic variation in the European souslik, *Spermophilus citellus* (Mammalia: Rodentia). *Bonner zoologische Beiträge,* 46: 93–109.

Kryštufek, B. & Ðulić, B. (in press). *Rhinolophus blasii*. In: Niethammer, J. & Krapp, F., (Eds.). *Handbuch der Säugetiere Europas. Fledermäuse.* Aula Verlag, Wiesbaden.

Kryštufek, B., Filippucci, M. G., Macholán, M., Zima, J., Vujoševic, M. & Simson, S. (1994). Does *Microtus majori* occur in Europe? *Zeitschrift für Säugetierkunde*, 59: 349–357.

Kryštufek, B. & Hrabe, V. (1996). Variation of the baculum of the European souslik, *Spermophilus citellus. Zeitschrift für Säugetierkunde*, 61: 228–235.

Kryštufek, B. & Kovačić, D. (1989). Vertical distribution of the snow vole *Microtus nivalis* (Martins, 1842) in northwestern Yugoslavia. *Zeitschrift für Säugetierkunde*, 54: 153–156.

Kryštufek, B & Kraft, R. (1997). Cranial variation and taxonomy of garden dormice *(Eliomys* Wagner, 1840) in the circum-Mediterranean realm. *Mammalia,* 61: 411-429.

Kryštufek, B. & Macholán, M. (1998). Morphological differentiation in *Mus spicilegus* and the taxonomic status of mound–building mice from the Adriatic coast. *Journal of Zoology, London,* 245: 185-196.

Kryštufek, B., Murariu, D. & Kurtonur, C. (1997). Present distribution of the Golden Jackal *Canis aureus* in the Balkans and adjacent regions. *Mammal Review*, 27: 109–114.

Kryštufek, B. & Petrov, B. (1989). The first occurrence of Blasius's horseshoe bat (*Rhinolophus blasii*) in Serbia, with remarks on its distribution in Yugoslavia. Pp. 399–401, in: Hanák, V., Horáček, I. & Gaisler, J., (Eds.). *European bat research 1987.* Charles University Press, Praha, 718 pp.

Kryštufek, B. & Tvrtković, N. (1990a). Variability and identity of the jackals (*Canis aureus*) of Dalmatia. *Annalen des Naturhistorischen Museums Wien,* 91B: 7–25.

Kryštufek, B. & Tvrtković, N. (1990b). Range expansion by Dalmatian jackal population in the 20th century (*Canis aureus* Linnaeus, 1758). *Folia Zoologica,* 39: 291–296.

Kryštufek, B. & Tvrtković, N. (1992). New information on the introduction into Europe of the small Indian mongoose, *Herpestes auropunctatus. Small Carnivore Conservation*, 7: 16.

Kryštufek, B. & Vohralík, V. (1994). Distribution of the forest dormouse *Dryomys nitedula* (Pallas, 1779) (Rodentia, Myoxidae) in Europe. *Mammal Review*, 24: 161–177.

Kryštufek, B., Vohralík, V. & Kurtonur, C. (1998). A new look at the identity and distribution of water shrews (*Neomys* spp.) in Turkey. *Zeitschrift für Säugetierkunde*, 63: 129–136.

Kugelschafter, K., Deeg, S., Kümmerle, W & Rehm, H. (1984/85). Steinmarderschäden [*Martes foina* (Erxleben, 1777)] an Kraftfahrzeugen: Schadensanalyse und verhaltensbiologische Untersuchungsmethodik. *Säugetierkundliche Mitteilungen,* 32: 35–48.

Kurt, F., Grzimek, B. & Zhiwolschenko, V. (1988). Echte Bären. Pp. 480–501, in: *Grzimeks Enzyklopädie–Säugetiere. Vol III.* Kindler, München, 648 pp.

Kurtén, B. (1968). *Pleistocene mammals of Europe.* Weidenfeld & Nicolson, London, 377 pp.

Kurtonur, C. & Özkan, B. (1990). New records of *Myomimus roachi* (Bate, 1937) from Turkish Thrace (Mammalia: Rodentia: Gliridae). *Senckenbergiana biologica,* 71: 239–244.

Kutcheruk, V. V. (1994). The area of superspecific complex *Mus musculus* s. lato. Pp. 56–81, in: Kotenkova, E.V. & Bulatova, N.S. (Eds.). *The House Mouse. Origin, Distribution, Systematics, Behaviour.* Nauka, Moscow (in Russian, English summary).

Kuzjakin, A. P. (1950). Letucie myši (Sistematika, obraz žizni i pol'za dla sel'skogo i lesnogo chozjajstva). Sovetskaja Nauka, Moskva, 444 pp.

Kuzjakin, A. P. (1980). Gigantskaja večernica (*Nyctalus lasiopterus*) u SSSR. Pp. 55–59 in: Kuzjakin, A. P. & Panjutin, K. K. (Eds.): *Rukokrylye (Chiroptera).* Nauka, Moscow, 320 pp.

Labhardt, F. (1990). *Der Rotfuchs*. Paul Parey, Hamburg and Berlin, 158 pp.

Lahti, S. & Helminen, M. (1974). The Beaver *Castor fiber* (L.) and *Castor canadensis* (Kuhl) in Finland. *Acta Theriologica*, 19: 177–189

Lamani, F. (1970). Lloje te reja lakuriqesh nate ne vendin tone. *Buletni i Shkencave Natyrore*, 2: 143–150.

Langbein, J. & Thirgood, S. J. (1989). Variation in mating systems of fallow deer (*Dama dama*). *Ethology*, 83 : 195–214

Langley, P. J. W. & Yalden, D. W. (1977). The decline of the rarer carnivores in Great Britain. *Mammal Review*, 7: 95–116.

Lapini, L. (1989). Il riccio occidentale e il riccio orientale nel Friuli–Venezia Giulia: prima sintesi cartografico-distributiva. *Fauna*, 1: 62–63.

Lapini, L. & Perco, F. (1987). Primi dati su *Erinaceus concolor* Martin, 1838 nell'Italia nord–orientale (*Mammalia, Insectivora, Erinaceidae*). *Gortania – Atti del Museo Friulano di Storia Naturale*, 8(1986): 249–262.

Lapini, L., dall'Asta, A., Dublo, L., Spoto, M. & Vernier, E. (1996). Materiali per una teriofauna dell'Italia nord–orientale (*Mammalia*, Friuli–Venezia Giulia). *Gortania – Atti del Museo Friulano di Storia Naturale*, 17(1995): 149–248.

Larsen, T. (1980). *Die Welt der Eisbären*. Hannover, 108 pp.

Larson, J. S. & Gunson, J. R. (1983). Status of the beaver in North America. *Acta Zoologica Fennica*, 174: 91–93

Le Berre, M., Ramousse, R. & Le Guelte, L. (Eds.) (1996). Biodiversity in Marmots. Second International Symposium on Alpine Marmot (*Marmota marmota*) and on the Genus *Marmota*. Proc. Aussois, France, 1994.

Lekagul, B. & McNeely, J. A. (1988). *Mammals of Thailand*. Darnsutha Press, Bangkok, Thailand, 758 pp.

Lent, P. C. (1988). *Ovibos moschatus. Mammalian Species*, 302: 1–9.

Libois, R. M. (1982). Atlas provisoire des mammifères sauvages de Wallonie. Première partie. *Cahiers d'Ethologie appliqué*, 2, Suppl. 1–2, 207 pp.

Libois, R. M. (1984). Essai synécologique sur les mammifères d'Europe atlantique et ouest-méditerranéenne. Etude par analyse du régime alimentaire de la chouette effraie, *Tyto alba* (Scopoli). *Cahiers d'Ethologie appliqué*, 4 (2): 1–202.

Libois, R. M. (1986) Biogéographie et écologie des crossopes (genre *Neomys*, Kaup, 1889). Atlas des mammifères sauvages de Wallonie (suite). *Cahiers d'Ethologie appliqué*, 6 (1): 101–120.

Libois, R. M. (1993). Evolution de la situation des mammifères sauvages en Région wallonne au cours de la décennie 1983–1992. *Cahiers d'Ethologie appliqué*, 13: 77–92.

Ligtvoet, W. & van Wijngaarden, A. (1994). The colonization of the island of Noord–Beveland (The Netherlands) by the common vole *Microtus arvalis*, and its consequences for the root vole *M. oeconomus*. *Lutra*, 37: 1–28.

Limpens, H. J. G. A. & Feenstra, M. (1997). Franjestaart *Myotis nattereri* (Kuhl, 1818). Pp. 91–100, in: Limpens, H., Mostert, K. & Bongers, W. (Eds.). *Atlas van de Nederlandse vleermuizen. Onderzoek naar verspreiding en ecologie*. KNNV Uitgeverij, Utrecht, 260 pp.

Limpens, H., Mostert, K. & Bongers, W. (Eds.) (1997). *Atlas van de Nederlandse vleermuizen. Onderzoek naar verspreiding en ecologie*. KNNV Uitgeverij, Utrecht, 260 pp.

Lina, P. H. C. & Rheinhold, J. O. (1997). Ruige dwergvleermuis *Pipistrellus nathusii* (Keyserling & Blasius, 1839). Pp. 164–171, in: Limpens, H., Mostert, K. & Bongers, W., (Eds.). *Atlas van de Nederlandse vleermuizen. Onderzoek naar verspreiding en ecologie*. KNNV Uitgeverij, Utrecht, 260 pp.

Linn, I. & Birks, J. D. S. (1989). Mink (Mammalia; Carnivora: Mustelidae): correction of a widely quoted error. *Mammal Review,* 19: 175–179.

Lipej, L. & Kryštufek, B. (1992). Pygmy white–toothed shrew *Suncus etruscus* (Savi, 1822) in north–western Istria (Insectivora, Mammalia). *Gortania – Atti del Museo Friulano di Storia Naturale,* 13: 225–233.

Livet, F. & Roeder, J. –J. (1987). La genette (*Genetta genetta,* Linnaeus 1758). *Encyclopedie des carnivores de France,* 16: 1–33.

Loch, R. (1977). A biometrical study of karyotypes A and B of *Sorex araneus* Linnaeus 1758 in the Netherlands (Mammalia, Insectivora). *Lutra,* 19: 21–36.

Long, C. & Killingley, C. A. (1983). *The badgers of the world.* Charles C. Thomas, Springfield, 404 pp.

López–Fuster, M. J. & Ventura, J. (1996). A morphological review of the *Sorex araneus–arcticus* species group from the Iberian peninsula (Insectivora, Soricidae). *Bonner zoologische Beiträge,* 46: 327–337

Lovari, S. & Cosentino, R. (1986). Seasonal habitat selection and group size of the Abruzzo chamois. *Bolletino di Zoologia,* 53: 73–78.

Lowe, V. P. W. & Gardiner, A. S. (1974). A re–examination of the subspecies of red deer (*Cervus elaphus*) with particular reference to the stocks in Britain. *Journal of Zoology, London,* 174: 185–201.

Loy, A., Capolongo, D. & Di Martino, S. (1996). Patterns of geographic variation of *Talpa romana* Thomas (Insectivora, Talpidae). Preliminary results derived from a geometric morphometric approach. *Mammalia,* 60: 77– 89.

Lozan, M. N. (1970). *Gryzuny Moldavii. Istorija stanovlenija fauny i ekologija recentnih vidov. Tom 1 (Rodents of Moldavia. Vol. 1).* Akademia Nauk MoSSR, Kisinev (in Russian).

Lukáčová, L., Dannelid, E., Hausser, J., Macholán, M. & Zima, J. (1996). G–banded karyotype of the alpine shrew, *Sorex alpinus* (Mammalia, Soricidae), from the Sumava Mts. *Folia zoologica,* 45: 223–226.

Lundh, N. G. (1991). Home range and habitat choice of muskoxes in Sweden. *Fauna och Flora,* 86: 14–29 (in Swedish, English summary).

Lüps, P.& Wandeler, A. I. (1993). *Meles meles* (Linnaeus, 1758) – Dachs. Pp. 856–906, in: Stubbe, M. & Krapp, F. (Eds.). *Handbuch der Säugetiere Europas. Band 5/2, Carnivora (Fissipedia).* Aula Verlag, Wiesbaden, xv + 529–1213.

Lura, H., Langhelle, G., Fredriksen, T. & Byrkjedal, I. (1995). Distribution of the field mice *Apodemus flavicollis* and *A. sylvaticus* in Norway. *Fauna Norvegica, Series A.* 16: 1–10.

Lutz, W. (1984). Die Verbreitung des Waschbären (*Procyon lotor* Linné 1758) im mitteleuropäischen Raum. *Zeitschrift für Jagdwissenschaft,* 30: 218–228.

Macdonald, D. W. (1987). *Running with the Fox.* Unwin Hyman, London, 224 pp.

Macdonald, D. & Barrett, P. (1995). *The Mammals of Britain and Europe.* HarperCollins, London, 312 pp.

Macdonald, D. W., Tattersall, F. H., Brown, E. D. & Balharry, D. (1995). Reintroducing the European Beaver to Britain: nostalgic meddling or restoring biodiversity? *Mammal Review,* 25: 161–200.

Machado Carrillo A. (1985). Observaciones biologicas a la presencia de Ardilla moruna en Fuerteventura. *Estudios Canarios,* 26/27: 13–15.

Macholán, M. & Vohralík, V. (1997). Note on the distribution of *Mus spicilegus* (Mammalia, Rodentia) in the south–western Balkans. *Acta Scientiatis Zoologicae Bohemicae,* 61: 219-226.

Maddalena, T., Vogel, P. & Hutterer, R. (1990). *Crocidura sicula* Miller, 1901 – Sizilienspitzmaus. Pp. 461–464, in: Niethammer, J. & Krapp, F. (Eds.). *Handbuch der Säugetiere Europas. Band 3/I, Insectivora, Primates.* Aula Verlag, Wiesbaden, 523 pp.

Maeda, K. (1982). Studies on the classification of *Miniopterus* in Eurasia, Australia and Melanesia. *Honyurui Kagaku (=Mammalian Science),* Suppl. 1: 1–176.

Maeda, K. (1983). Classificatory study of the Japanese Large Noctule. *Nyctalus lasiopterus aviator* Thomas, 1911. *Zoological Magazine*, 92: 21–36.

Makin, D. & Mendelssohn, H. (1989). A recent mass–kill of bats: who cares? *Israel Land & Nature*, 14(2): 82–85.

Malygin, V. M. (1983). *Systematics of the common vole.* Nauka, Moscow. (in Russian).

Maran, T. (1992). The European mink, *Mustela lutreola,* in protected areas in the former Soviet Union. *Small Carnivore Conservation,* 7: 10–12.

Maran, T. (1996). Ex situ and in situ conservation of the European mink. *International Zoo News,* 43: 399–407.

Maran, T. & Henttonen, H. (1995). Why is the European mink, *Mustela lutreola* disappearing? – A review of the process and hypotheses. *Annales Zoologici Fennici,* 32: 47–54.

Marchant, J. H., Hudson, R., Carter, S. P. & Whittington, P. (1990). *Population trends in British breeding birds.* BTO, Tring, 300 pp.

Markov, G. (1960). Beitrag zur Untersuchung der Hamster (Cricetinae) in Bulgarien. *Izvestija na Zoologičeskija Institut, Sofia,* 9: 293 – 303.

Markowski, J. & Hejduk, J. (In press). Ssaki Polski środkowej – stan poznania [Mammals of central Poland – state of knowledge]. *Acta Universitatis Lodziensis, Folia Sozologica.*

Martin, R. D. & von Segesser, F. (1996). Fragmentation of natural populations, genetics and conservation biology. Pp. 311–326, in: Cortes, J. E. (Ed.). *II Jornadas de Estudio y Conservación de la Flora y Fauna del Campo de Gibraltar*, Algeciras, Mancomunidad del Campo de Gibraltar.

Masini, F. & Lovari, S. (1988). Systematics, phylogenetic relationships and dispersal of the chamois (*Rupicapra* spp.). *Quaternary Research,* 30: 339–349.

Mason, C. F. & MacDonald, S. M. (1986). *Otters: ecology and conservation.* Cambridge University Press, Cambridge. 236 pp.

Masseti, M. (1995). Quaternary biogeography of the Mustelidae family on the Mediterranean Islands. In: Prigioni, C. (Ed.). Proceedings of the II Italian Symposium on Carnivores. *Hystrix (N. S.),* 7 (1–2): 17–34.

Mathias, M. L. (1988). An annotated list of the mammals recorded from the Madeira Islands. *Boletim do Museu Municipal do Funchal*, 40(201): 111–137.

Matthey, R. (1963) Polymorphisme chromosomique intraspécifique et intraindividuel chez *Acomys minous* Bate (Mammalia–Rodentia–Muridae). *Chromosoma*, 14: 468–497.

Męczyński, S. (1985). Does the European ground squirrel, *Spermophilus citellus* Linnaeus, 1766, still occur in Poland? *Przegląd Zoologiczny,* 29: 521–526. (in Polish with English summary).

Męczyński, S. (1991). The occurrence of spotted souslik *Spermophilus suslicus* Güldenstaedt, 1770 in Poland and the conception of its protection. *Ochrona Przyrody*, 48: 208–238.

Médard, P. & Guibert, E. (1990). Disparition d'un milieu et raréfaction d'une espèce en France: le murin de Capaccini, *Myotis capaccinii* (Bonaparte, 1837). *Mammalia*, 54: 297–300.

Metsu, I. & van den Berge, K. (1987). *De otter in Vlaanderen Deel II,* Nationale Campagne Bescherming Roofdieren, Gavere, 140 pp.

Meunier K. (1983). Das spanische Reh. Pp. 147–153, in: Hoffmann R.R. (ed.) *Wildbiologische Informationen für den Jäger*, Vol. VI. Jagd & Hege Verlags AG, St Gallen, Switzerland, 168 pp.

Mezhzerin, S. V. & Lashkova, E. I. (1992). Diagnostics, geographic variation and distribution of two closely related mouse species – *Sylvaemus sylvaticus* and *S. flavicollis* (Rodentia, Muridae) in an area of their overlapping occurrence. *Vestnik Zoologii,* 3: 33–41 (in Russian with English summary).

Mezhzerin, S. V. & Zagorodnyuk, I. V. (1989). Novy vid myshey roda *Apodemus* (Rodentia, Muridae). *Vestnik Zoologii*, 4: 55–59.

Milishnikov, A. N., Lavrenchenko, L. A. & Rafiev, A. N. (1989). Orological and biochemical identification of some forms of the supraspecies complex of *Mus musculus* s. lato. Pp. 80–98, in: Sokolov, V. E., Kotenkova, E. V., Krasnov, B. R. & Meshkova, N. N. (Eds.) *House Mouse*. USSR Academy of Sciences, Moscow (in Russian with English summary).

Miller, G. S. (1912). *Catalogue of the Mammals of Western Europe (Europe exclusive of Russia)*. British Museum, London, 1019 pp.

Mitchell–Jones, A. J., Cooke, A. S., Boyd, I. L. & Stebbings, R. E. (1989). Bats and remedial timber treatment chemicals – a review. *Mammal Review*, 19: 93–110.

Mohr, E. (1965). *Altweltliche Stachelschweine*. Neue Brehm–Bücherei, No. 350, Ziemsen Verlag, Wittenberg Lutherstadt, 164 pp.

Molina, O. M. & Hutterer, R. (1989). A cryptic new species of *Crocidura* from Gran Canaria and Tenerife, Canary Islands (Mammalia: Soricidae). *Bonner zoologische Beiträge*, 40: 85–97.

Monnerot, M., Casane, D., Hardy, C., Vigne, J–D. (1994a). Evolution of *Oryctolagus*: relationships within the Lagomorpha system and access to population history by ancient DNA. *Polish Ecological Studies*, 20: 543–551.

Monnerot, M., Vigne, J.–D., Biju–Duval, C., Casane, D., Callou, C., Hardy, C., Mougel, F., Soriguer, R., Denebouy, N. & Mounolou, J. C. (1994b). Rabbit and man: genetic and historical approach. *Genetics Selection Evolution*, 26, Suppl. 1: 167s–182s.

Montgomery, W. I. (1985). Interspecific competition and the comparative ecology of two congeneric species of mice. Pp. 129–187, in: Cook, L. M. (Ed.). *Case studies in population biology*. University of Manchester Press, Manchester, UK, 218 pp.

Moore, J. C. & Tate, G. H. H. (1965). A study of the diurnal squirrels, *Sciurinae*, of the Indian and Indochinese subregions. *Fieldiana: Zoology*, 48: 1–351.

Moore, N. W. (1975). The diurnal flight of the Azorean bat (*Nyctalus azoreum*) and the avifauna of the Azores. *Journal of Zoology, London*, 177: 483–486.

Morel, J. & Meylan, A. (1970). Une pullulation de Campagnols terrestres (*Arvicola terrestris* L.) (Mammalia, Rodentia). *Revue Suisse de Zoologie*, 77: 705–712.

Mostert, K. (1997). Meervleermuis *Myotis dasycneme* (Boie, 1825). Pp. 124 & 141–150, in: Limpens, H., Mostert, K. & Bongers, W. (Eds.). *Atlas van de Nederlandse vleermuizen. Onderzoek naar verspreiding en ecologie*. KNNV Uitgeverij, Utrecht, 260 pp.

Müskens, G. J. D. M. & Broekhuizen, S. (1986). De verspreiding van de boommarter *Martes martes* (L., 1758) in Nederland. *Lutra*, 29: 81–98.

Musser, G. & Carleton, M.D. (1993). Family Muridae. Pp. 501–755, in: Wilson, D. E. & Reeder, D. M. (Eds.). *Mammals species of the world. A taxonomic and geographic reference*, 2nd ed. Smithsonian Institute Press, Washington D.C., 1206 pp.

Myllymäki, A. (1970). Population ecology and its application to the control of the field vole, *Microtus agrestis* (L.). *EPPO Publications, Series A*, 58: 27–48.

Myllymäki, A. (1977). Outbreaks and damage of the field vole, *Microtus agrestis* (L.) since World War II in Europe. *EPPO Bulletin*, 7: 177–208.

Mys, B., van der Straeten, E. & Verheyen, W. (1985). The biometrical and morphological identification and the distribution of *Sorex araneus* L., 1758 and *S. coronatus* Millet, 1828 in Belgium (Insectivora, Soricidae). *Lutra*, 28: 55–70.

Nader, I. A. & Kock, D. (1990). *Eptesicus (Eptesicus) bottae* (Peters 1869) in Saudi Arabia with notes on its subspecies and distribution (Mammalia: Chiroptera: Vespertilionidae). *Senckenbergiana biologica*, 70: 1–13.

Nechay, G., Hamar, M. & Grulich, I. (1977). The Common hamster (*Cricetus cricetus* [L.]); a review. *EPPO Bulletin,* 7: 255–276.

Neet, C. R. & Hausser, J. (1990). Habitat selection in zones of parapatric contact between the common shrew *Sorex araneus* and the Millet's shrew *S. coronatus. Journal of Animal Eco*logy, 59: 235–250.

Neet, C. R. & Hausser, J. (1991). Biochemical analysis and determination of living individuals of the Alpine races and species of the *Sorex araneus* group. *Mémoires de la Société vaudoise des Sciences naturelles,* 19: 97–106.

Nellis, D. W. (1989). *Herpestes auropunctatus. Mammalian species,* 342: 1–6.

Niethammer, G. (1963). *Die Einbürgerung von Säugetieren und Vögeln in Europa.* Paul Parey, Hamburg & Berlin, 319 p.

Niethammer, J. (1978a). *Apodemus flavicollis* (Melchior, 1834) – Gelbhalsmaus. Pp. 325–336, in: Niethammer, J. & Krapp, F. (Eds.), *Handbuch der Säugetiere Europas. Band 1, Rodentia I.* Aula Verlag, Wiesbaden, 476pp.

Niethammer, J. (1978b). *Apodemus mystacinus* (Danford & Alston, 1877) – Felsenmaus. Pp. 306–315, in: Niethammer, J. & Krapp, F. (Eds.). *Handbuch der Säugetiere Europas, Band 1, Rodentia I.* Aula Verlag, Wiesbaden, 476 pp.

Niethammer, J. (1978c). *Apodemus sylvaticus* (Linnaeus, 1758) – Waldmaus. Pp. 337–358, in: Niethammer, J. & Krapp, F. (Eds.). *Handbuch der Säugetiere Europas. Band 1, Rodentia I.* Aula Verlag, Wiesbaden., 476 pp.

Niethammer, J. (1981). Über *Microtus (Pitymys) savii* (de Sélys Longchamps, 1838) von Monte Gargano, Italien. *Säugetierkundliche Mitteilungen,* 29: 45–48.

Niethammer, J. (1982a). *Cricetulus migratorius* (Pallas, 1773) – Zwerghamster. Pp. 39 – 50, in: Niethammer, J. & Krapp, F. (Eds.). *Handbuch der Säugetiere Europas. Band. 2/I, Rodentia II.* Akademische Verlagsgesellschaft, Wiesbaden, 649 pp.

Niethammer, J. (1982b). *Cricetus cricetus* (Linnaeus, 1758) – Hamster (Feldhamster). Pp. 7–28, in: Niethammer, J. & Krapp, F. (Eds.). *Handbuch der Säugetiere Europas. Band. 2/I, Rodentia II.* Akademische Verlagsgesellschaft, Wiesbaden, 649 pp.

Niethammer, J. (1982c). *Hystrix cristata* Linnaeus, 1758 – Stachelschwein. Pp. 588–605, in: Niethammer, J. & Krapp, F. (Eds.). *Handbuch der Säugetiere Europas. Band 2/I, Rodentia II.* Akademische Verlagsgesellschaft, Wiesbaden, 649pp.

Niethammer, J. (1982d). *Mesocricetus newtoni* (Nehring, 1898) – Rumänischer Goldhamster. Pp. 29–38, in: Niethammer, J. & Krapp, F. (Eds.). *Handbuch der Säugetiere Europas. Band. 2/I, Rodentia II.* Akademische Verlagsgesellschaft, Wiesbaden, 649 pp.

Niethammer, J. (1982e). *Microtus cabrerae* Thomas, 1906 – Cabreramaus. Pp. 340–348, in: Niethammer, J. & Krapp, F. (Eds.). *Handbuch der Säugetiere Europas. Band 2/I, Rodentia II.* Akademische Verlagsgesellschaft, Wiesbaden, 649 pp.

Niethammer, J. (1982f). *Microtus duodecimcostatus* (de Sélys-Longchamps, 1839) - Mittelmeer-Kleinwühlmaus. Pp. 463-475, in: Niethammer, J. & Krapp, F. (Eds.). *Handbuch der Säugetiere Europas. Band 2/I, Rodentia II.* Akademische Verlagsgesellschaft, Wiesbaden, 649 pp.

Niethammer, J. (1982g). *Microtus felteni* (Malec & Storch, 1963). Pp. 438–441, in: Niethammer, J. & Krapp, F. (Eds.). *Handbuch der Säugetiere Europas. Band 2/I, Rodentia II.* Akademische Verlagsgesellschaft, Wiesbaden, 649 pp.

Niethammer, J. (1982h). *Microtus guentheri* Danford & Alston, 1880 – Levante–Wühlmaus. Pp. 330–339, in: Niethammer, J. & Krapp, F. (Eds.). *Handbuch der Säugetiere Europas. Band 2/I, Rodentia II.* Akademische Verlagsgesellschaft, Wiesbaden, 649 pp.

Niethammer, J. (1982i). *Microtus lusitanicus* (Gerbe, 1879) – Iberien–Wühlmaus. Pp. 476–484, in: J. Niethammer & F. Krapp (Eds.). *Handbuch der Säugetiere Europas. Band 2/I, Rodentia II.* Akademische Verlagsgesellschaft, Wiesbaden, 649 pp.

Niethammer, J. (1982j). *Microtus subterraneus* (de Sélys–Longchamps, 1836) – Kurzohrmaus. Pp. 397–418, in: Niethammer, J. & Krapp, F. (Eds.). *Handbuch der Säugetiere Europas. Band 2/I, Rodentia II.* Akademische Verlagsgesellschaft, Wiesbaden, 649 pp.

Niethammer, J. (1982k). *Microtus tatricus* (Kratochvíl, 1952)– Tatra Wühlmaus. Pp. 491–496, in: Niethammer, J. & Krapp, F. (Eds.). *Handbuch der Säugetiere Europas. Band 2/1, Rodentia II.* Akademische Verlagsgesellschaft, Wiesbaden, 649 pp.

Niethammer, J. (1982l). *Microtus thomasi* Barrett–Hamilton, 1903 – Balkan–Kurzohrmaus. Pp. 485–490, in: Niethammer, J. & Krapp, F. (Eds.). *Handbuch der Säugetiere Europas. Band 2/I, Rodentia II.* Akademische Verlagsgesellschaft, Wiesbaden, 649 pp.

Niethammer, J. (1990a). *Talpa caeca* Savi, 1822– Blindmaulwurf. Pp. 145–156, in: Niethammer, J. & Krapp, F. (Eds.). *Handbuch der Säugetiere Europas. Band 3/I, Insectivora, Primates.* Aula Verlag, Wiesbaden, 523 pp.

Niethammer, J. (1990b). *Talpa europaea* Linnaeus, 1758 – Maulwurf. Pp. 99–133, in: Niethammer, J. & Krapp, F. (Eds.). *Handbuch der Säugetiere Europas. Band 3/I, Insectivora, Primates.* Aula Verlag, Wiesbaden, 523 pp.

Niethammer, J. (1990c). *Talpa occidentalis* Cabrera, 1907 – Spanischer Maulwurf. Pp. 157–161, in: Niethammer, J. & Krapp, F. (Eds.). *Handbuch der Säugetiere Europas. Band 3/I, Insectivora, Primates.* Aula Verlag, Wiesbaden, 523 pp.

Niethammer, J. (1990d). *Talpa romana* Thomas, 1902 – Römischer Maulwurf. Pp. 134–140, in: Niethammer, J. & Krapp, F. (Eds.). *Handbuch der Säugetiere Europas. Band 3/I, Insectivora, Primates.* Aula Verlag, Wiesbaden, 523 pp.

Niethammer, J. (1990e). *Talpa stankovici* V. & E. Martino, 1931 – Balkan–Maulwurf. Pp. 141–144, in: Niethammer, J. & Krapp, F. (Eds.). *Handbuch der Säugetiere Europas. Band 3/I, Insectivora, Primates.* Aula Verlag, Wiesbaden, 523 pp.

Niethammer, J. & Henttonen, H. (1982). *Myopus schisticolor* (Lilljeborg, 1884) – Waldlemming. Pp. 70–86, in: Niethammer, J. & Krapp, F. (Eds.). *Handbuch der Säugetiere Europas. Band 2/1, Rodentia II.* Akademische Verlagsgesellschaft, Wiesbaden, 649 pp.

Niethammer, J. & Krapp, F. (1982). *Microtus arvalis* (Pallas, 1779) – Feldmaus. Pp. 284–318, in: Niethammer, J. & Krapp, F. (Eds.). *Handbuch der Säugetiere Europas. Band 2/1, Rodentia II.* Akademische Verlagsgesellschaft, Wiesbaden, 649 pp.

Nievergelt, B. (1986). *Capra aegagrus* Erxleben, 1777 – Bezoarziege. Pp. 367–383, in: Niethammer, J. & Krapp, F. (Eds.). *Handbuch der Säugetiere Europas. Band 2/II, Artiodactyla.* Aula Verlag, Wiesbaden, 462 pp.

Nievergelt, B. & Zingg, R. (1986). *Capra ibex* Linnaeus, 1758 – Steinbock. Pp. 384–404, in: Niethammer, J. & Krapp, F. (Eds.). *Handbuch der Säugetiere Europas. Band 2/II, Artiodactyla.* Aula Verlag, Wiesbaden, 462 pp.

Nolet, B. A. (1997) *Management of the beaver* (Castor fiber): *towards restoration of its former distribution and ecological function in Europe.* Nature and Environment 86, Council of Europe, Strasbourg, 32 pp.

Nolet, B. A. & Rosell, F. (1998). Comeback of the beaver *Castor fiber*: an overview of old and new conservation problems. *Biological Conservation,* 83: 165–173

Nores, C. (1991). Aproximación a la metodologia y estudio del área de distribuiçon, estatus de población y selección de habitat del desmán (*Galemys pyrenaicus*) en la Peninsula Ibérica. Informe preliminar. ICONA/Univ. Oviedo, Madrid.

Novikov, G. A. (1939). *The European mink.* Izd. Leningradskogo Gos. Univ., Leningrad, 177 pp. (in Russian).

Nowak, E. (1993). *Nyctereutes procyonoides* Gray, 1834 – Marderhund. Pp. 215–248, in: Stubbe, M. & Krapp, F. (Eds.). *Handbuch der Säugetiere Europas. Band 5/I, Carnivora (Fissipedia).* Aula Verlag, Wiesbaden, 527 pp.

Nowak, R.M. (1991). *Walker's mammals of the World.* 5th Edition. Vol. II. The John Hopkins University Press, Baltimore, 643–1629.

Nowell, K. & Jackson, P. (1996). *Wild Cats: Status Survey and Conservation Action Plan*. IUCN, Gland, Switzerland, 382 pp.

Nygrén, K. (1986). *Alces alces* (Linnaeus, 1758) – Elch. Pp. 173–197, in: Niethammer, J. & Krapp, F. (Eds.) *Handbuch der Säugetiere Europas. Band 2/II, Artiodactyla*. Aula Verlag, Wiesbaden, 462 pp.

O'Connor, T. P. (1986). The garden dormouse *Eliomys quercinus* from Roman York. *Journal of Zoology, London*, 53: 620–622.

Ognev, S. I. (1931). *Mammals of eastern Europe and northern Asia*. Glavnauka, Moskva & Leningrad, 2: 1–776 (English translation; Israel Program for Scientific Translations, Jerusalem, 1962, 590 + xv pp.).

Oksanen, L. & Oksanen, T. (1992). Long–term microtine dynamics in north Fennoscandian tundra: the vole cycle and the lemming chaos. *Ecography*, 15: 226–236.

Oksanen, T. & Henttonen, H. (1996). Dynamics of voles and small mustelids in the taiga landscape of northern Fennoscandia in relation to habitat quality. *Ecography*, 19: 432–443.

Oliver, W. L. R. (Ed.) (1993). *Status survey and conservation action plan. Pigs, peccaries and hippos*. IUCN, Gland, Switzerland, 202 pp.

Oliver, W. L. R. (1995). Taxonomy and conservation status of the Suiformes – An overview. *Ibex*, 3: 3–5.

Olsen, K. M., Gjerde, L., Klann, M., Rigstad, K., Starholm, T., Syvertsen, P. O. & Wergeland Krog, O. M. (1996). De enkelte flaggermusartene i Norge. Pp. 27–133, in: Olsen, K. M. (Ed.) *Kunnskapsstatus for flaggermus i Norge*. Norsk Zoologisk Forening, Rapport 2, 210 pp.

Özkan, B. (1995). Gökçeada ve Bozcaada Adalarinin Kemiricileri. Trakya Üniversitesi, Edirne (Unpublished Ph.D.).

Palacios, F. (1976). Descripcion de una nueva especie de liebre (*Lepus castroviejoi*) endemica de la Cordillera Cantabrica. *Doñana Acta Vertebrata*, 3(2): 205.

Palacios, F. (1978). Sistematica, distribucion geografica y ecologia de las liebres espanolas. Situacion actual de sus poblaciones. Ph.D. dissertation, Univ. Politecnica, Madrid. 150 pp.

Palacios, F. (1983). On the taxonomic status of the genus *Lepus* in Spain. *Acta Zoologica Fennica*, 174: 27–30.

Palacios, F. (1989). Biometric and morphologic features of the species of the genus *Lepus* in Spain. *Mammalia*, 73: 227–264.

Palacios, F. (1996). Systematics of the indigenous hares of Italy traditionally identified as *Lepus europaeus* Pallas, 1778 (Mammalia: Leporidae). *Bonner zoologische Beiträge*, 46: 59–61.

Palacios, F. & Fernandez, J. (1992). A new subspecies of hare from Majorca (Balearic Islands). *Mammalia*, 56: 71–85.

Palacios, F. & Meijide, M. (1979). Distribucion geografica y habitat de las liebres en la Peninsula Iberica. *Naturalia Hispanica*, 19: 1–40.

Palacios, F. & Ramos, B. (1979) Situacion actual de las liebres en Espana y medidas para su conservacion. *Boletin de la Estacion Central de Ecologia*, 15: 69–76.

Palmeirim, J. M. (1991). A morphometric assessment of the systematic position of the *Nyctalus* from Azores and Madeira (Mammalia: Chiroptera). *Mammalia*, 55: 381–388.

Palmeirim, J. M. & Rodrigues, L. (1995). Dispersal and philopatry in colonial animals: the case of *Miniopterus schreibersii*. Pp. 219–231, in: Racey, P. A. & Swift, S. M. (Eds.). Ecology, evolution and behaviour of bats. *Symposia of the Zoological Society of London*, 67, 421 pp.

Palomares, F. & Delibes, M. (1993a). Resting ecology and behaviour of Egyptian mongooses in southwestern Spain. *Journal of Zoology, London*, 230: 557–566.

Palomares, F. & Delibes, M. (1993b). Key habitats for Egyptian mongooses in Doñana National Park, southwestern Spain. *Journal of Applied Ecology*, 30: 752–758.

Palomares, F. & Delibes, M. (1994). Spatio–temporal ecology and behavior of European genets in Southwestern Spain. *Journal of Mammalogy*, 75: 714–724.

Palomares, F., Ferreras, P., Fedriani, J. M. & Delibes, M. (1996). Spatial relationship between Iberian Lynx and other carnivores in an area of south–western Spain. *Journal of Applied Ecology,* 33: 5–13.

Pandurska, R. (1996). Altitudinal distribution of bats in Bulgaria. *Myotis*, 34: 45–50.

Pasa, A. (1951). Alcuni caratteri della Mammalofauna Pugliese. *Memorie di Biogeografica Adriatica* 2: 2–21.

Pavlinov, I. J., Dubrovsky, Y. A., Rossolimo, O. L. & Potapova, E. G. (1990). *Gerbils of the world*. Nauka, Moscow, 368 pp.

Pavlov, M. P. (1973). Acclimatisation of game animals and birds in the USSR. Part 1, Kirov (in Russian)

Pedrotti, L. (1995). La reintroduzione dello Stambecco (*Capra ibex ibex*) nelle Alpi Orobie – occupazione dello spazio, utilizzo dell'habitat, dinamica dei branchi e valutazione degli home–ranges. Tesi di Dottorato di Ricerca in Scienze Naturalistiche e Ambientali, Università degli Studi di Milano.

Peters, G. (1993). *Canis lupus* Linnaeus 1758 – Wolf. Pp. 47–106, in: Niethammer, J. & Krapp, F. (Eds.). *Handbuch der Säugetiere Europas. Band 5/I, Carnivora (Fissipedia)*. Aula Verlag, Wiesbaden, 527 pp.

Petersen, ð. (1994). Leðurblökur á Íslandi. *Náttúrufræðingurinn*, 64(1): 3–12.

Petersons, G. (1990). Die Rauhhautfledermaus, *Pipistrellus nathusii* (Keyserling u. Blasius, 1839), in Lettland: Vorkommen, Phänologie und Migration. *Nyctalus (N. F.),* 3: 81–98.

Petersons, G. (1995). Erstnachweis des Mausohrs (*Myotis myotis*) in Lettland. *Nyctalus (N.F.)*, 5: 485–487.

Petrov, B. (1989). *Erinaceus europaeus* Linnaeus, 1758 – new species in the fauna of Mammals in Yugoslavia. *Glasnik Prirodnjačkog muzeja Beograd, B*, 43/44: 205–207.

Petrov, B. & Ružić, A. (1982). *Microtus epiroticus* Ondrias, 1966 – Südfeldmaus. Pp. 319–330, in: Niethammer, J. & Krapp, F. (Eds.). *Handbuch der Säugetiere Europas, Band 2/I, Rodentia II*. Akademische Verlagsgesellschaft, Wiesbaden, 649 pp.

Petrov, B. & Zivkovic, S. (1972). Zur Kenntnis der Thomas–Kleinwühlmaus, *Pitymys thomasi* (Barrett–Hamilton, 1903), eines der wenig bekannten Säugetiere Jugoslawiens. *Säugetierkundliche Mitteilungen,* 20: 249–258.

Petrov, B. & Todorović, M. (1982). *Dinaromys bogdanovi* (V. et E. Martino, 1922) – Bergmaus. Pp. 193–208, in: Niethammer, J. & Krapp, F. (Eds.). *Handbuch der Säugetiere Europas, Band 2/I, Rodentia II.* Akademische Verlagsgesellschaft, Wiesbaden, 649 pp.

Petrov, B., Zivkovic, S. & Rimsa, D. (1976). Über die Arteigenständigkeit der Kleinwühlmaus *Pitymys felteni* (Mammalia: Rodentia). *Senckenbergiana biologica,* 57: 1–10.

Petrov, B. M. (1992). Mammals of Yugoslavia. Insectivores and Rodents. *Natural History Museum in Belgrade, supplement* 37: 1–186.

Petrusewicz, K. (1983). Ecology of the bank vole. *Acta Theriologica*, 28: 1–242.

Petzsch, H. (1952). *Der Hamster*. Neue Brehm-Bücherei, No. 21. Akademische Verlagsgesellschaft Geest & Portig K.–G., Leipzig, 56 pp.

Piechocki, R. (1990). Die Wildkatze *Felis silvestris*. Neue Brehm-Bücherei, No. 189. A. Ziemsen Verlag, Wittenberg Lutherstadt, 232 pp.

Pielowski, Z. & Pucek, Z. (Eds) (1976). *Ecology and management of European hare populations*. PWRL, Warsaw, 286 pp.

Pieper, H. (1966). Über einige bemerkenswerte Kleinsäuger–Funde auf den Inseln Rhodos und Kos. *Acta Biologica Hellenica,* 1: 21–28.

Pieper, H. (1990). *Crocidura zimmermanni* Wettstein, 1953 – Kretaspitzmaus. Pp. 453–460, in: Niethammer, J. & Krapp, F. (Eds.). *Handbuch der Säugetiere Europas. Band 3/I, Insectivora, Primates.* Aula Verlag, Wiesbaden, 523 pp.

Pietsch, M. (1982). *Ondatra zibethicus* (Linnaeus, 1766) – Bisamratte, Bisam. Pp. 177–192, in: Niethammer, J. & Krapp, F. (Eds.). *Handbuch der Säugetiere Europas. Band 2/I, Rodentia II.* Akademische Verlagsgesellschaft, Wiesbaden, 649 pp.

Pir, J. B. (1996). Réparation et status des Rhinolophidés (Mammalia, Chiroptera) au Luxembourg. *Bulletin de la Société des Naturalistes luxemburgeois*, 97: 147–154.

Pisareva, M. E. (1948). On ecology and systematics of the hillock mouse. *Sbornik rabot biologicheskogo fakul'teta Gosudarstvennyi Universitet, Dnepropetrovsk,* 32: 227–248.

Popescu, A. & Barbu, P. (1979). Date privind răspândirea şi frecvenţa siricidelor (Soricidae – Insectivora) în România. *Ocrotirea Naturii si a Mediuliu Înconjurator,* 23(2): 163–168.

Prager, E. M., Tichy, H. & Sage, R. D. (1996). Mitochondrial DNA sequence variation in the Eastern house mouse, *Mus musculus*: Comparison with other house mice and report of a 75–bp tandem repeat. *Genetics*, 143: 427–446.

Preleuthner, M., Pinsker, W., Kruckenhauser, L., Miller W. J. & Prosl, H. (1995). Alpine marmots in Austria. The present population structure as a result of the postglacial distribution history. Pp. 87–100, in: Hartl, G. B. & Markowski, J. (Eds.). Ecological genetics in mammals II. *Acta Theriologica*, 40 (suppl. 3).

Prigioni, C., Bogliani, G. & Barbieri, F (1986). The otter *Lutra lutra* in Albania. *Biological Conservation,* 36: 375–383.

Pucek, Z. (Ed.) (1981). *Keys to Vertebrates of Poland.* Mammals. PWN – Polish Scientific Publishers, Warszawa, 367 pp.

Pucek, Z. (1982a). *Sicista betulina* (Pallas, 1778) – Waldbirkenmaus. Pp. 516–538, in: Niethammer, J. & Krapp, F. (Eds.). *Handbuch der Säugetiere Europas. Band 2/I, Rodentia II.* Akademische Verlagsgesellschaft, Wiesbaden, 649 pp.

Pucek, Z. (1982b). *Sicista subtilis* (Pallas, 1773) – Steppenbirkenmaus. Pp. 501–515, in: Niethammer, J. & Krapp, F. (Eds.). *Handbuch der Säugetiere Europas. Band 2/I, Rodentia II.* Akademische Verlagsgesellschaft, Wiesbaden, 649 pp.

Pucek, Z. (1986). *Bison bonasus* (Linnaeus, 1758) – Wisent. Pp. 278–315, in: Niethammer, J. & Krapp, F. (Eds.). *Handbuch der Säugetiere Europas. Band 2/II, Artiodactyla.* Aula Verlag, Wiesbaden, 462 pp.

Pucek, Z. (1992). *Sorex caecutiens* Laxmann, 1788. Pp 34–36, in: Głowaciński, Z. (Ed.) Polska czerwona księga zwierzat [Polish Red Data Book of Animals], Państwowe Wydawnictwo Rolne i Leśne, Warszawa, 351 pp. (in Polish).

Pucek, Z. & Raczyński, J. (Eds.) (1983). Atlas of Polish mammals. Państwowe Wydawnictwo Naukowe, Warszawa, 188 pp. + 90 maps.

Pulliainen, E. (1965). On the distribution and migrations of the arctic fox (*Alopex lagopus* L.) in Finland. *Aquilo, Ser. Zool,* 2: 25–40.

Pulliainen, E. (1974). *Suomen suurpedot.* Tammi, Helsinki, 263 pp.

Pulliainen, E. (1980). The status, structure and behaviour of populations of the wolf (*Canis lupus* L.) along the Fenno–Soviet border. *Annales Zoologici Fennici,* 17: 107–112.

Pulliainen, E. (1981). A transect survey of small land carnivores and red fox populations on a subarctic fell in Finnish forest Lapland over 13 winters. *Annales Zoologici Fennici*, 18: 270–278.

Pulliainen, E. (1985). The expansion mechanism of the wolf (*Canis lupus*) in northern Europe. *Revue d'Ecologie (Terre et Vie),* 40: 157–162.

Pulliainen, E. (1988). Ecology, status and management of the Finnish wolverine *Gulo gulo* populations. *Lutra,* 31: 21–28.

Pulliainen, E. (1993a). *Alopex lagopus* (Linnaeus, 1758) – Eisfuchs. Pp. 195–214, in: Stubbe, M. & Krapp, F. (Eds.). *Handbuch der Säugetiere Europas. Band 5/I, Carnivora (Fissipedia)*. Aula Verlag, Wiesbaden, 527 pp.

Pulliainen, E. (1993b). *Gulo gulo* (Linnaeus, 1758) – Vielfraß. Pp. 481–502 in: Stubbe, M. & Krapp, F. (Eds.). *Handbuch der Säugetiere Europas. Band 5/I, Carnivora (Fissipedia)*. Aula Verlag, Wiesbaden, 527 pp.

Pulliainen, E. & Sulkava, S. (1986). *Odocoileus virginianus* (Zimmermann, 1771) – Weißwedelhirsch. Pp. 217–232, in: Niethammer, J. & Krapp, F. (Eds.). *Handbuch der Säugetiere Europas. Band 2/II, Artiodactyla*. Aula Verlag, Wiesbaden, 462 pp.

Pulliainen, E. & Tunkkari, P. (1987). Winter diet, habitat selection and fluctuation of a mountain hare *Lepus timidus* population in Finnish forest Lapland. *Holarctic Ecology*, 10: 261–267.

Pyatrouski, Y. T. (1958). Raspausyudzhanne krapchataga suslika u Byalorussii i gistoryya utvaréniya yago aréala. *Vestsi AN Byalorussk SSR*, 1: 119–122.

Queiroz, A.I., Bertrand, A. & Khakhin, G. (1996). *Status and conservation of Desmaninae in Europe*. Nature and Environment, No. 76, Council of Europe, Strasbourg, 79pp.

Rachwald, A. (1992). Variation in two wing dimensions in *Pipistrellus nathusii* (Keyserling & Blasius, 1839). *Nyctalus (N.F.)*, 4: 343–346.

Raczyński, J. (Ed.) (1996). *European Bison Pedigree Book 1995*. Białowieża National Park, Białowieża, 65 pp.

Rakhmatulina, I. (1996). The bat fauna of the Caucasus and problems of its study. *Myotis*, 34: 51–57.

Randi, E. (1995). Conservation genetics of the genus *Sus. Ibex*, 3: 6–12.

Randi, E., Lucchini, V. & Diong, C.H. (1996). Evolutionary genetics of the Suiformes as reconstructed using mtDNA sequencing. *Journal of Mammalian Evolution*, 3: 163–194.

Randi, E., Tosi, G., Toso, S., Lorenzini, R. & Fusco, G. (1990). Genetic variability and conservation problems in alpine ibex, domestic and feral goat populations (genus *Capra*). *Zeitschrift für Säugetierkunde*, 55: 413–420.

Ransome, R. D. (1989). Population changes of greater horseshoe bats studied near Bristol over the past twenty-six years. *Biological Journal of the Linnean Society*, 38: 71–82.

Ransome, R. D. (1990). *The natural history of hibernating bats*. Christopher Helm, London, 235 pp.

Ransome, R. D. & McOwat, T. P. (1994). Birth timing and population changes in greater horseshoe bat colonies (*Rhinolophus ferrumequinum*) are synchronised by climatic temperature. *Zoological Journal of the Linnean Society*, 112: 337–351.

Rasmont, P. & André, J. (1989). Applications d'un logiciel de projection U. T. M. à la surveillance des Invertébrés. *Inventaire de Faune et Flore*, 53: 227–252.

Ratcliffe, P. R. (1987). Distribution and current status of sika deer, *Cervus nippon*, in Great Britain. *Mammal Review*, 17: 39–58.

Ratti, P. (1994). Stand von Hege und Erforschung des Steinwildes im Kanton Graubünden (Schweiz). *Zeitschrift für Jagdwissenschaft*, 40: 223–231.

Reggiani, G., Boitani, L., D'Antoni, S. & De Stefano, R. (1993). Biology and control of the coypu in the Mediterranean area. *Ricerche di Biologia della Selvaggina, Suppl.* 21: 67–100.

Řehák, Z. & Beneš, B. (1996). Contribution to roosting ecology of *Myotis brandti* (Mammalia: Chiroptera) in the Czech Republic and Slovakia. *Acta Societatis Zoologicae Bohemicae*, 60: 51–56.

Reichstein, H. (1958/1959). Populationsstudien an der Erdmaus, *Microtus agrestis* (Markierungsversuche). *Zoologische Jahrbücher (Systematik)*, 86: 367–382.

Reichstein, H. (1982a). *Arvicola sapidus* Miller, 1908 – Südwesteuropäische Schermaus. Pp. 211–216, in: Niethammer, J. & Krapp, F. (Eds.). *Handbuch der*

Säugetiere Europas. Band 2/I Rodentia II. Akademische Verlagsgesellschaft, Wiesbaden, 649 pp.

Reichstein, H. (1982b). *Arvicola terrestris* (Linnaeus, 1758) – Schermaus. Pp. 217–252, in: Niethammer, J. & Krapp, F. (Eds.). *Handbuch der Säugetiere Europas. Band 2/I Rodentia II*. Akademische Verlagsgesellschaft, Wiesbaden, 649 pp.

Reichstein, H. (1993a). *Mustela erminea* Linné, 1758 – Hermelin. Pp. 533–570, in: Stubbe, M. & Krapp, F. (Eds.). *Handbuch der Säugetiere Europas. Band 5/II, Carnivora (Fissipedia)*. Aula Verlag, Wiesbaden, xv + 529–1213.

Reichstein, H. (1993b). *Mustela nivalis* Linné, 1766 – Mauswiesel. Pp. 571–626, in: Stubbe, M. & Krapp, F. (Eds.). *Handbuch der Säugetiere Europas. Band 5/II, Carnivora (Fissipedia)*. Aula Verlag, Wiesbaden, xv + 529–1213.

Reijnders, P. J. H. (1992). *Phoca vitulina* Linnaeus, 1758 – Seehund. Pp.120–137, in: Duguy, R. & Robineau, D. (Eds.). *Handbuch der Säugetiere Europas. Band 6/II, Pinnipedia*. Aula Verlag, Wiesbaden, 309 pp.

Reijnders, P., Brasseur, S., van der Toorn, J., van der Wolf, P., Boyd, I., Harwood, J., Lavigne, D. & Lowry, L. (1993). *Seals, Fur Seals, Sea Lions, and Walrus: Status Survey and Conservation Action Plan*. IUCN, Gland, Switzerland, 88 pp.

Reijnders, P. J. H., Verriopoulos, G. & Brasseur, S. M. J. M. (Eds.) (1997). *Status of Pinnipeds relevant to the European Union*. IBN Scientific Contributions 8. Institute for Forestry & Nature Research (IBN), Wageningen, The Netherlands, 195 pp.

Reumer, J. W. F. (1986). Notes on the Soricidae (Insectivora, Mammalia) from Crete. I. The Pleistocene species *Crocidura zimmermanni*. *Bonner zoologische Beiträge*. 37: 161–171.

Rey, J. M. & Landin, A. (1973). Sobre la presencia de *Crocidura suavolens* en el sur de Andalucia (Mammalia, Insectivora). *Boletín de la Real Sociedad Española de Historia Natural, Seccion Biologica,* 71: 9–16.

Richard–Hansen, R., Gonzalez, G. & Gerard, J. F. (1992). Structure sociale de l'Isard (*Rupicapra pyrenaica*) dans trois sites Pyreneens. *Gibier Faune Sauvages,* 9: 137–149.

Richardson, E. G. (1977). The biology and evolution of the reproductive cycles of *Miniopterus schreibersii* and *Miniopterus australis*. *Journal of Zoology, London,* 183:353–375.

Richarz, K. (1989). Ein neuer Wochenstubennachweis der Mopsfledermaus *Barbastella barbastellus* (Schreber, 1774) in Bayern mit Bemerkungen zu Wochenstubenfunden in der BRD und DDR sowie zu Wintervorkommen und Schutzmöglichkeiten. *Myotis,* 27: 71–80.

Ridgway, S. H. & Harrison, J. R. (Eds.) (1981). *Handbook of Marine Mammals, vol. 2: Seals*. Academic Press, London, 359 pp.

Röben, P. (1975). Die Ausbreitung des Waschbären, *Procyon lotor* (Linné, 1758) und des Marderhundes, *Nyctereutes procyonoides* (Gray, 1834) in der Bundesrepublik Deutschland. *Säugetierkundliche Mitteilungen,* 23: 93–101.

Röben, P. (1976). Veränderungen des Säugetierbestandes der Bundesrepublik Deutschland und deren Ursachen. *Schriftenreihe für Vegetationskunde,* 10: 239–254.

Robinson, M. F. & Stebbings, R. E. (1994). Changing land–use in south Cambridgeshire: its effect on serotine bats. *Nature in Cambridgeshire,* 36: 62–69.

Robinson, P. (1996). European marbled polecat in need of conservation action. *Small Carnivore Conservation,* 14: 19–20.

Rodríguez, A., & Delibes, M. (1990). *El lince ibérico (Lynx pardina) en España distribución y problemas de Conservación*. ICONA, Serie Técnica, Madrid, 116 pp.

Roer, H. (1984). Zur Bestandssituation von *Rhinolophus ferrumequinum* (Schreber, 1774) und *Rhinolophus hipposideros* (Bechstein, 1800) (Chiroptera) im westlichen Mitteleuropa. *Myotis,* 21–22: 122–131.

Röhrs, M. (1986). *Ovis ammon musimon* (Pallas, 1811) – Mufflon. Pp. 435–449, in: Niethammer, J. & Krapp, F. (Eds). *Handbuch der Säugetiere Europas. Band 2/II, Artiodactyla.* Aula Verlag, Wiesbaden, 462 pp.

Ronseveil, D. E., Taylor, R. J. & Hocking, G. J. (1991). Distribution records of native terrestrial mammals in Tasmania. *Wildlife Research,* 18: 699–717.

Ruedi, M. & Arlettaz, R. (1991). Biochemical systematics of the Savi's bat (*Hypsugo savii*) (Chiroptera: Vespertilionidae). *Zeitschrift für zoologische Systematik und Evolutionsforschung*, 29: 115–122.

Ružić, A. (1978). *Citellus citellus* (Linnaeus, 1766) – Der oder das Europäische Ziesel. Pp. 123–144, in: Niethammer, J. & Krapp, F. (Eds.) *Handbuch der Säugetiere Europas. Band 1/I, Rodentia I.* Akademische Verlagsgesellschaft, Wiesbaden, 476 pp.

Rydell, J. (1992). Exploitation of insects around streetlamps by bats in Sweden. *Functional Ecology,* 6: 744–750.

Rydell, J. (1993). *Eptesicus nilssoni. Mammalian Species*, 430: 1–7.

Rydell, J. & Arlettaz, R. (1994). Low–frequency echolocation enables the bat *Tadarida teniotis* to feed on tympanate insects. *Proceedings of the Royal Society of London,* 257B: 175–178.

Rydell, J. & Baagøe, H. J. (1994). *Vespertilio murinus. Mammalian Species*, 467: 1–6.

Rydell, J. & Bogdanowicz, W. (1997). *Barbastella barbastellus. Mammalian Species*, 557: 1–8.

Rydell, J., Strann, K. B. & Speakman, J. R. (1994). First record of bats breeding above the Arctic Circle: the Northern bat at 69–70°N in Norway. *Journal of Zoology, London*, 233: 335–339.

Sablina, O.V., Zima, J., Radjabli, S.I., Kryštufek, B. & Goleniščev, F. N. (1989). New data on karyotype variation in the pine vole, *Pitymys subterraneus* (Rodentia, Arvicolidae). *Vestník Československé Společnosti Zoologické,* 53: 295–299.

Saez–Royuela, C. & Telleria, J. L. (1986). The increased population of the wild boar (*Sus scrofa* L.) in Europe. *Mammal Review*, 16: 97–101.

Sage, R. D. (1981). Wild mice. Pp. 39–90, in: Foster, H. L., Small, J. D. & Fox, J. G. (Eds.). *The Mouse in Biomedical Research,* Vol. 1. Academic Press, New York, 306 pp.

Sage, R. D., Atchley, W. R. & Capanna, E. (1993). House mice as models in systematic biology. *Systematic Biology,* 42: 523–561.

Sägesser, H. & Krapp, F. (1986). *Rupicapra rupicapra* (Linnaeus, 1758) – Gemse, Gams. Pp. 316–348, in: Niethammer, J. & Krapp, F. (Eds.). *Handbuch der Säugetiere Europas. Band 2/II, Artiodactyla.* Aula Verlag, Wiesbaden, 462 pp.

Sałata–Piłacińska, B. (1990). The southern range of the root vole in Poland. *Acta Theriologica,* 35: 53–67.

Salvioni, M. (1986). Domaines vitaux, relations sociales et rythme d' activité de trois éspèces de *Pitymys* (Mammalia, Rodentia). Thesis, Faculty of Science, University of Lausanne.

Santini, L. (1974). *Pitymys savii* (de Sel.) in Italy: zones of regular outbreaks and evaluation of the damage done to agriculture in the period 1945–1972. First Report of the Working Party on Field Rodents, Warsaw. EPPO Publ., Paris, 31: 25–35.

Sarà, M. (1996). A landmark–based morphometrics approach to the systematics of Crocidurinae. A case study on endemic shrews *Crocidura sicula* and *C. canariensis* (Soricidae, Mammalia). Pp. 335–344 in: Marcus, L. F. *et al.* (Eds.). *Advances in Morphometrics.* Plenum Press, New York, 587 pp.

Sarà, M., Lo Valvo, M. & Zanca, L. (1990). Insular variation in central Mediterranean *Crocidura* Wagler, 1832 (Mammalia, Soricidae). *Bolletino di Zoologia*, 57: 283-293.

Saucy, F. (1994). Density dependence in time series of the fossorial form of the water vole, *Arvicola terrestris*. *Oikos,* 71: 381–392.

Savić, I. R. (1982a). *Microspalax leucodon* (Nordmann, 1840) – Westblindmaus. Pp. 543–569, in: Niethammer, J. & Krapp, F. (Eds.). *Handbuch der Säugetiere Europas. Band 2/I, Rodentia II*. Akademische Verlagsgesellschaft, Wiesbaden, 649 pp.

Savić, I. R. (1982b). *Spalax graecus* Nehring, 1898 – Bukowinische Blindmaus. Pp. 577–584, in: Niethammer, J. & Krapp, F. (Eds.). *Handbuch der Säugetiere Europas. Band 2/I, Rodentia II*. Akademische Verlagsgesellschaft, Wiesbaden, 649 pp.

Savić, I. & Soldatović, B. (1984). Karyotype evolution and taxonomy of the genus *Nannospalax* Palmer, 1903, Mammalia, in Europe. *Serbian Academy of Sciences and Arts, Beograd,* 560/59: 1–104.

Scharenberg, W. (1992). Belastung schleswig-holsteinischer Fledermäuse mit Chlorkohlenwasser-stoffen. *Myotis*, 30: 85–94.

Schauenberg, P. (1966). La genette vulgaire (*Genetta genetta* L.). Répartititon géographique in Europe. *Mammalia* 30: 371–396.

Schlapp, G. (1990). Populationsdichte und Habitatansprüche der Bechsteinfledermaus *Myotis bechsteini* (Kuhl, 1818) im Steigerwald (Forstamt Ebrach). *Myotis,* 28: 39–58.

Schlawe, L (1980). Zur geographischen Verbreitung der Ginsterkatzen, Gattung *Genetta* Cuvier, 1816. *Faunistische Abhandlungen, Staatliches Museum für Tierkunde in Dresden*, 7: 147–161.

Schneider, E. (1978). *Der Feldhase. Biologie – Verhalten – Hege und Jagd*. BLV, München, Bern, Wien, 198 pp.

Schober, W. & Grimmberger, E. (1989). *A guide to bats of Britain and Europe*. Hamlyn, London, 224 pp.

Schröder, W., Elsner–Schak, I. & Schröder, J. (1983). *Die Gemsen.* Jahrbuch Verein zum Schutze der Bergwelt. e. V., München, 48: 33–70.

Serra–Cobo, J. & Balcells, E. (1991). Migraciones de quirópteros en España. Pp. 181–209, in: Benzal, J. & de Paz, O. (Eds.). *Los murciélagos de España y Portugal*. ICONA, Madrid, 330 pp.

Shackleton, D. M. (Ed.) and the IUCN/SSC Caprinae Specialist Group (1997). *Wild sheep and goats and their relatives. Status survey and conservation action plan for Caprinae*. IUCN, Gland, Switzerland and Cambridge, UK, 390 + vii pp.

Shvarts, E. A. & Vaisfeld, M. A. (1993). Problem of saving vanishing species and the islands (discussion of the introduction of the European mink *Mustela lutreola* on Kunashir Island). *Uspechi Sovremennoj Biologii,* 113: 46–59. (In Russian).

Sidorovich,V. E., Savchenko,V. V. & Bundy, V. B. (1995). Some data about the European mink *Mustela lutreola* distribution in the Lovat River Basin in Russia and Belarus: current status and retrospective analysis. *Small Carnivore Conservation,* 12: 14–18.

Siivonen, L. (1967). Pohjolan nisäkkäät (Mammals of Northern Europe). Otava, Helsinki, 181 pp.

Simak, S.V. (1997). South–Russian marbled polecat (*Vormela peregusna*) in the Samarskaya Region. In: *Rare mammals of Russia and adjacent territories*. Abstracts of the International Conference, Moscow, 9–11 April, 1997.

Simionescu, I. (1920). *Mamiferele noastre*. Tip. "România Nova", Bucureşti, 111 pp.

Simionescu, V. (1965). Contribuţii la cunoaşterea sistematicii şi răspândirii geografice a faunei de rozătoare (Glires) din Moldova. *Analene Stiintifice ale Universitatii "Al. I. Cuza". Section II,* 11: 127–142.

Simionescu, V. (1971). Contributions concernant la systematique et la variabilite des taupes de Roumanie (genre *Talpa* Linnaeus, 1758). *Analele Stiintifice ale Universitatii "Al. I. Cuza", Ser. biol.,* 17: 461–472.

Skarén, U. (1972). Fluctuations of small mammal populations in mossy forests of Kuhmo, eastern Finland, during eleven years. *Annales Zoologici Fennici,* 9: 147–151.

Slatis, H. M. (1960). An analysis of inbreeding in the European bison. *Genetics*, 45: 275–287.

Sludsky, A. A. (1964). Mutual help during hunting in predators of different species (adjutorism). *Zoologicheskii Zhurnal*, 43: 1203–1210.

Sluiter, J. W., van Heerdt, P. F. & Voûte, A. M. (1971). Contribution to the population biology of the pond bat, *Myotis dasycneme* (Boie, 1825). *Decheniana – Beihefte*, 18: 1–44.

Smith, W. P. (1991). *Odocoileus virginianus. Mammalian Species*, 388: 1–13.

Sokolov, V. E., Baskevich, M. I. & Koval'skaya, Yu. M. (1986). The karyotype variability in the southern birch mouse (*Sicista subtilis* Pallas) and substantiation of the species validity of *S. severtzovi. Zoologicheskii Zhurnal*, 65: 1684–1692 (in Russian with English summary).

Sokolov, V. J., Koval'skaja, J. M. & Baskevic, M. I. (1987). Review of karyological research and the problems of systematics in the genus *Sicista* (Zapodidae, Rodentia, Mammalia). *Folia Zoologica*, 36: 35–44.

Sokolov, V. J., Koval'skaja, J. M. & Baskevic, M. I. (1989). On species status of northern birch mice *Sicista strandi* (Rodentia, Dipodidae). *Zoologicheskii Zhurnal* 68: 95–106 (in Russian with English summary).

Sokolov, V. E. & Bashenina, N. V. (Eds.) (1994). Common vole: the sibling species *Microtus arvalis* Pallas, 1779 and *M. rossiaemeridionalis* Ognev, 1924. Nauka, Moscow (in Russian).

Sokolov, V. E. & Tembotov, A. K. (1989). *Pozvonochnye Kavkaza. Mlekopitajushchie, Nasekomojaniye*. Nauka, Moscow, 547 pp.

Sörensen, O. J. (1990). The brown bear in Europe in the mid 1980's. *Aquilo, Ser. Zool.*, 27: 3–16

Sörensen, O., Kvam, T., Wabakken, P. & Landa, A. (1986). Ulven (*Canis lupus* L.) i Norge 1948–1984. Viltrapport 3.

Spagnesi, M. & Trocchi, V. (1992). *La Lepre. Biologia, Allevamento, Patologia, Gestione*. Edagricola, Bologna.

Speakman, J. R. & Webb, P. I. (1993). Taxonomy, status and distribution of the Azorean bat (*Nyctalus azoreum*). *Journal of Zoology, London*, 231: 27–38.

Spitzenberger, F. (1986). Die Zwergmaus, *Micromys minutus* Pallas, 1771. Mammalia austriaca 12 (Mamm., Rodentia, Muridae). *Mitteilungen der Abteilung für Zoologie am Landesmuseum Joanneum*, 39: 23–40.

Spitzenberger, F. (1990a). *Neomys anomalus* Cabrera, 1907 – Sumpfspitzmaus. Pp. 317–333, in: Niethammer, J. & Krapp, F. (Eds.). *Handbuch der Säugetiere Europas. Band 3/I, Insectivora, Primates*. Aula Verlag, Wiesbaden, 523 pp.

Spitzenberger, F. (1990b). *Neomys fodiens* (Pennant, 1771) – Wasserspitzmaus. Pp. 334–374, in: Niethammer, J. & Krapp, F. (Eds.). *Handbuch der Säugetiere Europas. Band 3/1, Insectivora, Primates*. Aula Verlag, Wiesbaden, 523 pp.

Spitzenberger, F. (1990c). *Sorex alpinus* Schinz, 1837 – Alpenspitzmaus. Pp. 295–312, in: Niethammer, J. & Krapp, F. (Eds.). *Handbuch der Säugetiere Europas. Band 3/1, Insectivora, Primates*. Aula Verlag, Wiesbaden, 523 pp.

Spitzenberger, F. (1990d). *Suncus etruscus* (Savi, 1822) - Etruskerspitzmaus. Pp. 376-392, in: Niethammer, J. & Krapp, F. (Eds.). *Handbuch der Säugetiere Europas. Band 3/1, Insectivora, Primates*. Aula Verlag, Wiesbaden, 523 pp

Spitzenberger, F. (1993). Die Mopsfledermaus (*Barbastella barbastellus* Schreber, 1774) in Österreich. Mammalia austriaca 20. *Myotis*, 31:111–153.

Spitzenberger, F. (1994). The genus *Eptesicus* (Mammalia, Chiroptera) in Southern Anatolia. *Folia Zoologica*, 43: 437–454.

Spitzenberger, F. (1996). Distribution and subspecific variation of *Myotis blythi* and *Myotis myotis* in Turkey (Mamm., Vespertilionidae). *Annalen des Naturhistorischen Museums in Wien, Suppl.*, 98B: 9–23.

Spitzenberger, F. (1997a). Distribution and range expansion of Savi's bat (*Hypsugo savii*) in Austria. *Zeitschrift für Säugetierkunde*, 62: 179–181.

Spitzenberger, F. (1997b). Erstnachweis der Brandmaus *(Apodemus agrarius)* für Österreich. Mammalia austriaca 22. *Zeitschrift für Säugetierkunde,* 62: 250–252.

Spitzenberger, F. & Bauer, K. (1987). Die Wimperfledermaus, *Myotis emarginatus* Geoffroy, 1806 (Mammalia, Chiroptera) in Österreich. Mammalia austriaca 13. *Mitteilungen der Abteilung für Zoologie am Landesmuseum Joanneum*, 40: 41–64.

Spitzenberger, F. & Englisch, H. (1996). Die Alpenwaldmaus (*Apodemus alpicola* Heinrich, 1952) in Österreich. Mammalia austriaca 21. *Bonner zoologische Beiträge*, 46: 249–260.

Stebbings, R. E. & Griffith, F. (1986). *The distribution and status of bats in Europe*. Institute of Terrestrial Ecology, Abbots Ripton, UK, 142 pp.

Stebbings, R. E. (1988). *Conservation of European bats*. Christopher Helm, London, 246 pp.

Steele, M. A. Weigl, P. D. (1993). The ecological significance of body size in fox squirrels (*Sciurus niger*) and grey squirrels (*S. carolinenis*). Pp. 57–69, in: Moncreas, N. E., Edwards, J. W. & Tappe, P.A. (Eds.). *Proceedings of the Second Symposium on south–eastern fox squirrels, Sciurus niger,* Virginia Museum of Natural History Special Publication No. 1.

Stein, G. H. W. (1958). Die Feldmaus (*Microtus arvalis* Pallas). Neue Brehm–Bücherei, No. 225. A. Ziemsen Verlag, Wittenberg, 76 pp.

Stenseth, N. C. (Ed.) (1977). Population dynamics of the field vole, *Microtus agrestis*: a modelling study. Proceedings of a symposium at Tvärminne Biological Station, Finland, 22–26 March, 1976. *Oikos*, 29: 447–642.

Stenseth, N. C. & Ims, R. A., (Eds.) (1993). *The biology of lemmings*. Academic Press, London, 683 pp.

Storch, G. (1977). Die Ausbreitung der Felsenmaus (*Apodemus mystacinus*): Zur Problematik der Inselbesiedlung und Tiergeographie in der Ägäis. *Natur und Museum*, 107: 174–182.

Storch, G. (1978a). *Dryomys nitedula* (Pallas, 1779) – Baumschläfer. Pp. 227–237, in: Niethammer, J. & Krapp, F. (Eds.). *Handbuch der Säugetiere Europas. Band 1/I, Rodentia I.* Akademische Verlagsgesellschaft, Wiesbaden, 476 pp.

Storch, G. (1978b). *Eliomys quercinus* (Linnaeus, 1766) – Gartenschläfer. Pp. 208–225 in: Niethammer, J. & Krapp, F. (Eds.). *Handbuch der Säugetiere Europas. Band 1/I, Rodentia I.* Akademische Verlagsgesellschaft, Wiesbaden, 476 pp.

Storch, G. (1978c). *Glis glis* (Linnaeus, 1766) – Siebenschläfer. Pp. 243–258, in: Niethammer, J. & Krapp, F. (Eds.). *Handbuch der Säugetiere Europas. Band 1/I, Rodentia I.* Akademische Verlagsgesellschaft, Wiesbaden, 476 pp.

Storch, G. (1978d). *Muscardinus avellanarius* (Linnaeus, 1758) – Haselmaus. Pp. 259–280 in: Niethammer, J. & Krapp, F. (Eds.). *Handbuch der Säugetiere Europas. Band 1/I, Rodentia I.* Akademische Verlagsgesellschaft, Wiesbaden, 476 pp.

Storch, G. (1978e). *Myomimus roachi* (Bate, 1937) – Mausschläfer. Pp. 238–242, in: Niethammer, J. & Krapp, F. (Eds.). *Handbuch der Säugetiere Europas. Band 1/I, Rodentia I.* Akademische Verlagsgesellschaft, Wiesbaden, 476 pp.

Storch, G. & Lütt, O. (1989). Artstatus der Alpenwaldmaus, *Apodemus alpicola* Heinrich, 1952. *Zeitschrift für Säugetierkunde*, 54: 337–346.

Storch, G. & Winking, H. (1977). Zur Systematik der *Pitymys multiplex – Pitymys liechtensteini* Gruppe (Mammalia, Rodentia). *Zeitschrift für Säugetierkunde*, 42: 78–88.

Strachan, R., Birks, J. D. S., Chanin, P. R. F. & Jefferies, D. J. (1990). *Otter survey of England 1984–1986*. Nature Conservancy Council, Peterborough. 67pp.

Strachan, R. & Jefferies, D. J. (1993). *The water vole* Arvicola terrestris *in Britain 1989–1990: its distribution and changing status*. The Vincent Wildlife Trust, London, 136 pp.

Strachan, R. & Jefferies, D. J. (1996). *Otter Survey of England 1991–1994*. The Vincent Wildlife Trust, London. 223 pp.

Strelkov, P. P. (1988). Buryj ušan (*Plecotus auritus*) i seryj ušan (*P. austriacus*) (Chiroptera, Vespertilionidae) v SSSR. Soobšcenie 2. *Zoologicheskii Zhurnal*, 67: 287–292.

Strinati, P. & Aellen, V. (1958). Confirmation de la présence de *Rhinolophus mehelyi* Matschie dans le sud de la France. *Mammalia*, 22: 527–536.

Stubbe, C. (1997). *Rehwild.* 4th edition. Parey Buchverlag, Berlin.

Stubbe, M. (1975). Der Waschbär *Procyon lotor* (L., 1758) in der DDR. *Hercynia (N. F.),* 12: 80–91.

Stubbe, M. (1982a). Die europäische Fuchspopulation *Vulpes vulpes* (L., 1758) in den Jahren 1976 bis 1978. *Beiträge zur Jagd– und Wildforschung,* 12: 14–20.

Stubbe, M. (1982b). *Myocastor coypus*. Pp. 607–630, in: Niethammer J. & Krapp, F. (Eds.). *Handbuch der Säugetiere Europas. Band 2/I, Rodentia II*. Akademische Verlagsgesellschaft, Wiesbaden, 649 pp.

Stubbe, M. (1989a). Baum– und Steinmarder – *Martes martes* L., *Martes foina* (Erxleben). Pp. 478–502, in: Stubbe, M. (Ed.). *Buch der Hege, Band 1, Haarwild*. 5. Aufl., Berlin,

Stubbe, M. (1989b). Fuchs *Vulpes vulpes* (L.). Pp. 344–382, in: Stubbe, M. (Ed.). *Buch der Hege, Band 1, Haarwild*. 5. Aufl., Berlin.

Stubbe, M. (1989c). Iltis *Mustela putorius* L. Pp. 503–513, in: Stubbe, M (Ed) *Buch der Hege Band 1 Haarwild*, 5 Aufl., Berlin.

Stubbe, M. (1989d). Verbreitung und Ökologie des Fischotters *Lutra lutra* (L. 1758) in der DDR. *Populationsokologie marderartiger Säugtiere, Wissenschaftliche Beiträge der Universität Halle,* 1: 13–33.

Stubbe, M. (1990). Der Status des Waschbären *Procyon lotor* (L.) in der DDR (1975–1984). *Beiträge zur Jagd– und Wildforschung,* 17: 180–192.

Stubbe, M. (1993a). *Martes martes* (Linné, 1758) – Baum–, Edelmarder. Pp. 374–426, in: Stubbe, M. & Krapp, F. (Eds.). *Handbuch der Säugetiere Europas. Band 5/I, Carnivora (Fissipedia).* Aula Verlag, Wiesbaden, 527 pp.

Stubbe, M. (1993b). Monitoring Fischotter – Grundlagen zum überregionalen Management einer bedrohten Säugetierart in Deutschland. *Tiere im Konflikt,* 1: 3–10.

Stubbe, M. (1993c). *Procyon lotor* (Linné, 1758) – Waschbär. Pp. 331–364, in: Niethammer, J. & Krapp, F. (Eds.). *Handbuch der Säugetiere Europas. Band 5/I, Carnivora (Fissipedia).* Aula Verlag, Wiesbaden, 527 pp.

Stubbe, M. (1994d). *Mustela lutreola* (Linné, 1758) – Europäische Nerz. Pp. 627–653, in: Stubbe, M. & Krapp, F. (Eds.) *Handbuch der Säugetiere Europas. Band. 5/II, Carnivora (Fissipedia),* Aula Verlag, Wiesbaden, xv + 529–1213.

Stubbe, M. (1993e). *Mustela vison* Schreber, 1777– Mink, Amerikanischer Nerz. Pp. 654–698 in: Stubbe, M. & Krapp, F. (Eds.). *Handbuch der Säugetiere Europas. Band. 5/II, Carnivora (Fissipedia).* Aula Verlag, Wiesbaden, xv + 529–1213.

Stubbe, M. & Stubbe, A. (1994). Säugetiere und deren feldökologische Erforschung im östlichen Deutschland. *Tiere im Konflikt,* 3: 3–52.

Stubbe, M. & Stubbe, A. (1997). Das Mauswiesel – bejagt oder geschützt? – seine Stellung im Ökosystem und im Gesetz. *Beiträge zur Jagd– und Wildforschung,* 22: 257-262.

Stutz, H.–P. B. (1989). Die Höhenverteilung der Wochenstuben einiger ausgewählter schweizerischer Fledermausarten (Mammalia, Chiroptera). *Revue Suisse de Zoologie*, 96: 651–662.

Stüwe, M. & Nievergelt, B. (1991). Recovery of Alpine ibex from near extinction: the result of effective protection, captive breeding, and reintroductions. *Applied Animal Behavioral Science*, 29: 379–383.

Sulkava, S (1978). *Pteromys volans* (Linnaeus, 1758) – Flughörnchen. Pp. 71–84, in: Niethammer, J. & Krapp, F. (Eds.). *Handbuch der Säugetiere Europas. Band 1/I, Rodentia I.* Akademische Verlagsgesellschaft, Wiesbaden, 476 pp.

Sulkava, S. (1989). Resting places of the mountain hare, *Lepus timidus*, in winter. *Aquilo, Ser. Zool.*, 24: 95–98.

Sulkava, S. (1990a). *Sorex caecutiens* Laxmann, 1788 – Maskenspitzmaus. Pp. 215–224, in: Niethammer, J. & Krapp, F. (Eds.). *Handbuch der Säugetiere Europas. Band 3/I, Insectivora, Primates.* Aula Verlag. Wiesbaden, 523 pp.

Sulkava, S. (1990b). *Sorex isodon* Turov, 1924 – Taigaspitzmaus. Pp. 225–236, in: Niethammer, J. & Krapp, F. (Eds.). *Handbuch der Säugetiere Europas. Band 3/I, Insectivora, Primates.* Aula Verlag. Wiesbaden, 523 pp.

Sulkava, S. (1990c). *Sorex minutissimus* Zimmermann, 1780 – Knirpsspitzmaus. Pp. 207–214, in: Niethammer, J. & Krapp, F. (Eds.). *Handbuch der Säugetiere Europas. Band 3/I, Insectivora, Primates.* Aula Verlag. Wiesbaden, 523 pp.

Sulkava, S. (1996). "Villisiasta tunturisopuliin" – Kuusamon nisäkkäistä, niiden suojelutarpeista ja viimeaikaisista runsaudenvaihteluista. *Oulanka Reports,* 15: 67–72.

Sulkava, P. & Sulkava, R. (1993). Liito–oravan ravinnosta ja ruokailutavoista Keski–Suomessa (Feeding habits of the flying squirrel in central Finland). *Luonnon Tutkija,* 97: 136–138 (in Finnish).

Sulkava, S., Sulkava, P. & Kaikusalo, A. (1996). Selection and consumption of mosses in the food stores of the wood lemming (*Myopus schisticolor* Lillj.) in Finland. *Aquilo, Ser. Zool.,* 29: 25–32.

Sullivan, C. M., Shiel, C. B., McAney, C. M. & Fairley, J. S. (1993). Analysis of the diets of Leisler's *Nyctalus leisleri*, Daubenton's *Myotis daubentoni* and Pipistrelle *Pipistrellus pipistrellus* bats in Ireland. *Journal of Zoology, London*, 231: 656–663.

Svendsen, P. & Fibiger, M. (1992). *The distribution of European Macrolepidoptera. Faunistica Lepidopterorum Europaeorum, Volume 1. Noctuinae 1.* European Faunistical Press, Copenhagen. 293 pp., 135 maps.

Swift, S. M. (1997). Roosting and foraging behaviour of Natterer's bats (*Myotis nattereri*) close to the northern border of their distribution. *Journal of Zoology, London*, 242: 375–384.

Taake, K.–H. (1992). Strategien der Ressourcennutzung an Waldgewässern jagender Fledermäuse (Chiroptera: Vespertilionidae). *Myotis*, 30: 7–74.

Taberlet, P., Fumagalli, L. & Hausser, J. (1994). Chromosomal versus mitochondrial DNA evolution: tracking the evolutionary history of the south–western European populations of the *Sorex araneus* group (Mammalia, Insectivora). *Evolution,* 48: 623–636.

Tast, J. (1982a). *Lemmus lemmus* (Linnaeus, 1758) – Berglemming. Pp. 87–105, in: Niethammer, J. & Krapp, F. (Eds.). *Handbuch der Säugetiere Europas. Band 2/I, Rodentia II.* Akademische Verlagsgesellschaft, Wiesbaden, 649 pp.

Tast, J. (1982b). *Microtus oeconomus* (Pallas,1776) – Nordische Wühlmaus, Sumpfmaus. Pp. 374–396, in: Niethammer, J. & Krapp, F. (Eds.). *Handbuch der Säugetiere Europas. Band 2/I, Rodentia II.* Akademische Verlagsgesellschaft, Wiesbaden, 649 pp.

TEI & ELC (1992). *Environmental review and environmental strategy studies.* The World Bank, Washington & Government of Albania, 205 pp.

Topachevskii, V. A. (1969). *Fauna of the USSR: Mammals, Vol. 3, Pt. 3, mole rats (Spalacidae).* Nauka, Leningrad, 247 pp. (in Russian).

Tosi, G., Scherini, G., Apollonio, M., Ferrario, G., Pacchetti, G., Toso, S. & Guidali, F. (1986). Modello di valutazione ambientale per la reintroduzione dello Stambecco (*Capra ibex ibex* Linnaeus, 1758). *Ricerche di Biologia della Selvaggina,* 77: 1–77.

Trense, W. (1989). *The big game of the world.* Paul Parey, Hamburg and Berlin.

Trujillo, D. (1991). *Murciélagos de las Islas Canarias.* ICONA, Madrid, Spain, 167 pp.

Tvrtković, N. & Kryštufek, B. (1990). Small Indian mongoose *Herpestes auropunctatus* (Hodgson, 1836) on the Adriatic Islands of Yugoslavia. *Bonner zoologische Beiträge,* 41: 3–8.

Urbańczyk, Z. (1990). Northern Europe's most important bat hibernation site. *Oryx,* 24(1): 30–34.

Uspensky, S. M. (1989). *Belyj medved.* Agropromizdat, Moscow, 188 pp.

van den Brink, F. H. (1955). *Zoogdierengids van Europa ten westen van 30° oosterlengte.* Elsevier, Amsterdam, 231 pp.

van den Brink, F. H. (1978). *Zoogdierengids van alle in ons land en overig Europa voorkomende zoogdieren.* Elsevier, Amsterdam. 274 pp.

van der Merwe, M. (1973). Aspects of social behaviour of the Natal–clinging bat *Miniopterus schreibersii natalensis. Mammalia,* 37: 379–389.

van der Straeten, E. (1972). De verspreiding van Micromammalia in de provincië Antwerpen, België, op grond van braakballenanalysen. *Lutra,* 14: 15–22.

van der Straeten, E. & van der Straeten, B. (1977). Etude de la biométrie crânienne et de la répartition d'*Apodemus flavicollis* en Belgique. *Acta Zoologica et Pathologica Antwerpiensia,* 69: 169–182.

van Vliet, J. A. & Mostert, K. (1997). Kleine hoefijzerneus *Rhinolophus hipposideros* (Bechstein, 1800). Pp. 69–71, in: Limpens, H., Mostert, K. & Bongers, W. (Eds.). *Atlas van de Nederlandse vleermuizen. Onderzoek naar verspreiding en ecologie.* KNNV Uitgeverij, Utrecht, 260 pp.

van Wijngaarden, A., van Laar, V. & Trommel, M. D. M. (1971). De verspreiding van de Nederlandse zoogdieren. *Lutra,* 13: 1–41, map 1–64.

van Wijngaarden, A. & Zimmermann, K. (1965). Zur Kenntnis von *Microtus oeconomus arenicola* (de Sélys-Longchamps, 1841). *Zeitschrift für Säugetierkunde,* 30: 129–136.

Vargas, J. M., Palomo, L. J. & Palmquist, P. (1991). Reproduction of the Algerian mouse (*Mus spretus* Lataste, 1883) in the south of the Iberian Peninsula. *Bonner zoologische Beiträge,* 42: 1–10.

Ventura, J. & Gosàlbez, J. (1989). Taxonomic review of *Arvicola terrestris* (Linnaeus, 1758) (Rodentia, Arvicolidae) in the Iberian Peninsula. *Bonner zoologische Beiträge,* 40: 227–242.

Ventura, J., Gosàlbez, J. & López–Fuster, M. J. (1989). Trophic ecology of *Arvicola sapidus* Miller, 1908 (Rodentia, Arvicolidae) in the Ebro Delta (Spain). *Zoologischer Anzeiger,* 223: 283–290.

Ventura, J., López-Fuster, M. J. & Cabrera-Millet, M. (1998). The Cabrera vole, *Microtus cabrerae*, in Spain: a biological and morphometric approach. *Netherlands Journal of Zoology*, 48 (1): 83-100.

Vernier, E. (1993). Lo strano caso del pipistrello albolimbato, una species di chirottero in espansione. *Ambiente Risorse Salute, Padova,* 16: 54–56.

Vernier, E. (1995). Seasonal movements of *Pipistrellus kuhlii*: 18 years of observations on a single colony in Padova (N. E. Italy). *Myotis,* 32–33: 209–214.

Vesmanis, I. & Kahmann, H. (1978). Morphometrische Untersuchungen an Wimperspitzmäusen (*Crocidura*). 4. Bemerkungen über die Typusreihe der kretaischen *Crocidura russula zimmermanni* Wettstein, 1953 im Vergleich mit *Crocidura gueldenstaedti caneae* (Miller, 1909). *Säugetierkundliche Mitteilungen,* 26: 214–222.

Vibe, C. (1982). *Grønlands hvide bjørne.* Naturens Verden.

Vigne, J.–D. (1992). Zooarchaeology and the biogeographical history of the mammals of Corsica and Sardinia since the last ice age. *Mammal Review*, 22: 87–96.

Viitala, J. (1977). Social organization in cyclic subarctic populations of the vole *Clethrionomys rufocanus* (Sund.) and *Microtus agrestis* (l.). *Annales Zoologici Fennici*, 14: 53–93.

Virgós, E. & Casanovas, J. G. (1997). Habitat selection of genet *Genetta genetta* in the mountains of central Spain. *Acta Theriologica*, 42: 169–177.

Viro, P. & Niethammer, J. (1982). *Clethrionomys glareolus* (Schreber, 1780) – Rötelmaus. Pp. 109–146, in: Niethammer, J. & Krapp, F. (Eds.). *Handbuch der Säugetiere Europas. Band 2/I, Rodentia II.* Akademische Verlagsgesellschaft, Wiesbaden, 649 pp.

Vlasák, P. & Niethammer, P. (1990). *Crocidura suaveolens* (Pallas, 1811) - Gartenspitzmaus. Pp. 397-414, in: Niethammer, J. & Krapp, F. (Eds.). *Handbuch der Säugetiere Europas. Band 3/I, Insectivora, Primates.* Aula Verlag, Wiesbaden, 523 pp.

Vogel, P. (1986). Der Karyotyp der Kretaspitzmaus, *Crocidura zimmermanni* Wettstein, 1953 (Mammalia, Insectivora). *Bonner zoologische Beiträge*, 37: 35–38.

Vogel, P. (1988). Taxonomical and biogeographical problems in Mediterranean shrews of the genus *Crocidura* (Mammalia, Insectivora) with reference to a new karyotype from Sicily (Italy). *Bulletin de la Société vaudoise des Sciences naturelles,* 79: 39–48.

Vogel, P., Maddalena, T., Mabille, A. & Paquet, G. (1991). Confirmation biochimique du statut spécifique du mulot alpestre *Apodemus alpicola* Heinrich, 1952 (Mammalia, Rodentia). *Bulletin de la Société vaudoise des Sciences naturelles,* 80: 471–481.

Vogel, R. (1936). Das gegenwärtige Vorkommen des Hamsters (*Cricetus cricetus* L.) in Württemberg in seiner Abhängigkeit vom Boden. *Jahreshefte des Vereins für vaterländische Naturkunde in Württemberg,* 92: 171–180.

Vohralík, V. (1991). A record of the mole *Talpa levantis* (Mammalia, Insectivora) in Bulgaria and the distribution of the species in the Balkans. *Acta Universitatis Carolinae–Biologia,* 23: 119–127.

Vohralík, V. & Sofianidou, T. (1987). Small mammals (Insectivora, Rodentia) of Macedonia, Greece. *Acta Universitatis Carolinae–Biologica,* 1985: 319–354.

Vohralík, V. & Sofianidou, T. S. (1992). Small mammals (Insectivora, Rodentia) of Thrace, Greece. Acta *Universitatis Carolinae–Biologica,* 36: 341–369

Volobouev, V. T. & Catzeflis, F. (1989). Mechanisms of chromosomal evolution in three European species of the *Sorex araneus–arcticus* group (Insectivora, Soricidae). *Zeitschrift für zoologische Systematik und Evolutionsforschung,* 27: 252–262

von Dirk, H. (1976). Remarks on the Medieval occurrence of the Norwegian rat (*Rattus norvegicus* Berk., 1769) in Schleswig–Holstein. *Zoologischer Anzeiger,* 196 (3–4): 273–278.

Vorontsov, N. N., Boyeskorov, G. G., Mezhzherin, S. V., Lyapunova, E. A. & Kandaurov, A. S. (1992). Sistematika lesnykh myshey podroda *Sylvaemus* Kavkaza (Mammalia, Rodentia, Apodemus). *Zoologicheskii Zhurnal,* 71: 119–131.

Voskar, J. (1983). Present problems of wolf preservation in Czechoslovakia. *Acta Zoologici Fennici,* 174: 287–288.

Wandeler, A. I. & Lüps, P. (1993). *Vulpes vulpes* (Linnaeus, 1758) – Rotfuchs. Pp. 139–193, in Stubbe, M. & Krapp, F. (Eds.): *Handbuch der Säugetiere Europas. Band 5/I, Carnivora.* Aula Verlag, Wiesbaden, 527 pp.

Warburton, B. & Sadleir, R. M. F. (1990). *Bennett's Wallaby.* Pp 44–51, in: King, C. M. (Ed.) *The Handbook of New Zealand Mammals*, Blackwell, Oxford, 609 pp.

Wauters, L. A. & Lens, L. (1995). Effects of food availability and density on red squirrel (*Sciurus vulgaris*) reproduction. *Ecology,* 76: 2460–2469.

Wauters, L. A., Hutchinson, Y., Parkin, D. & Dhondt, A. A. (1994). The effects of habitat fragmentation on demography and the loss of genetic variation in the red squirrel. *Proceedings of the Royal Society of London, Series B*, 255: 107–111.

Weber, D. (1988). Die aktuelle Verbreitung des Iltisses (*Mustela putorius* L.) in der Schweiz. *Revue Suisse de Zoologie*, 95(4): 1041-1056.

Wendt, W. (1984). Chronobiologische und ökologische Untersuchungen zur Biologie des Feldhamsters (*Cricetus cricetus* L.) unter Berücksichtigung volkswirtschaftlicher Belange. Dissertation der Martin–Luther–Universität, Halle–Wittenberg.

Wermmer, C. M. (1987). *Biology and management of the Cervidae*. Smithsonian Institution, Washington D.C.

Willner, G. R., Feldhammer, G. A., Zucker, E. E., Chapman, J. A. (1980). *Ondatra zibethicus. Mammalian Species*, 141: 1–8.

Wilson, D. E. & Reeder, D. M. (Eds.) (1993). *Mammal species of the world: a taxonomic and geographic reference*. Smithsonian Institution Press, Washington D.C., 1206 pp.

Wilson, W. L., Montgomery, W. I. & Elwood, R. W. (1993). Population regulation in the Wood mouse *Apodemus sylvaticus* (L.). *Mammal Review*, 23: 73–92.

Wiltafsky, H. (1978). *Sciurus vulgaris* Linnaeus, 1758 – Eichhornchen. Pp. 86–105, in: Niethammer, J. & Krapp, F. (Eds.) *Handbuch der Säugetiere Europas, Band 1, Rodentia I*. Akademische Verlagsgesellschaft, Wiesbaden, 476 pp.

Winking, H. (1976). Karyologie und Biologie der beiden iberischen Wühlmausarten *Pitymys mariae* und *Pitymys duodecimcostatus*. *Zeitschrift für Zoologische Systematik und Evolutionsforschung* 14: 104–129.

Winking, H. & Niethammer, J. (1970). Der Karyotyp der beiden kleinen Iberischen *Pitymys* Arten (Mammalia, Rodentia). *Bonner zoologische Beiträge*, 21: 284–289.

Wójcik, J. M. & Searle, J. B. (1988). The chromosome complement of *Sorex granarius:* the ancestral karyotype of the common shrew *Sorex araneus. Heredity*, 61: 225–230.

Wolsan, M. (1993). *Mustela eversmanii* Lesson, 1827 – Steppeniltis. Pp. 770–816, in: Stubbe, M. & Krapp, F. (Eds.). *Handbuch der Säugetiere Europas. Band 5/II, Carnivora (Fissipedia)*. Aula Verlag, Wiesbaden, xv + 529–1213.

Wolz, I. (1993). Das Beutespektrum der Bechsteinfledermaus *Myotis bechsteini* (Kuhl, 1818) ermittelt aus Kotanalysen. *Myotis*, 31: 27–68.

Woods, C. A., Contreras, L, Willner–Chapman, G. &, Whidden P.H. (1992). *Myocastor coypus. Mammalian Species*, 398, 1–8.

Yalden, D.W. (1991). *Red–necked wallaby*. Pp 563–567, in: Corbet, G. B. & Harris, S. (Eds.). *The Handbook of British Mammals*. 3rd edition. Blackwell, Oxford, 588 pp.

Yoshiyuki, M. (1989). *A systematic study of Japanese Chiroptera*. National Science Museum, Tokyo, 242 pp.

Yosida, T. H. (1980). *Cytogenetics of the black rat: karyotype evolution and species differentiation*. University of Tokyo Press, Tokyo, 256 pp.

Youngman, P. M. (1982). Distribution and the systematics of the European mink *Mustela lutreola* Linnaeus 1761. *Acta Zoologica Fennica*, 166: 1–48.

Zagorodnyuk, I. V. (1989). Taxonomy, distribution, and morphological variation in the Terricola voles in eastern Europe. *Vestnik Zoologii*, 5: 3–11 (in Russian, English summary).

Zagorodnyuk, I. V. & Zima, J. (1992). *Microtus tatricus* (Kratochvíl, 1952) in the eastern Carpathians: cytogenetic evidence. *Folia Zoologica*, 41: 123–126.

Zernahle K. (1980) Zytogenetische Untersuchungen am europaischen Rehwild (*Capreolus c. capreolus* L., 1758), sibirischen Rehwild (*Capreolus c. pygargus* Pallas, 1771) und deren Bastarden. *Beiträge zur Jagd–und Wildforschung*, 9: 304–309.

Zima, J., Gaichenko, V. A., Macholán, M., Radjabli, S. I., Sablina, O. V. & Wójcik, J. M. (1990). Are Robertsonian variations a frequent phenomenon in mouse populations in Eurasia? *Biological Journal of the Linnean Society,* 41: 229–233.

Zima, J., Fedyk, S., Fredga, K., Hausser, J., Mishta, A., Searle, J., Volobuev V. T. & Wójcik, J. M. (1996). The list of the chromosome races of the common shrew (*Sorex araneus*). *Hereditas,* 125: 97–107.

Zimmermann, K., Wettstein, O. v., Siewert, H. & Pohle, H. (1953). Die Wildsauger von Kreta. *Zeitschrift für Säugetierkunde,* 17: 1–71.

Zingg, P. E. (1988). Search calls of echolocating *Nyctalus leisleri* and *Pipistrellus savii* (Mammalia: Chiroptera) recorded in Switzerland. *Zeitschrift für Säugetierkunde,* 53: 281–293.

Zingg, P. E. & Arlettaz, R. (1995). *Myotis brandti* (Eversmann, 1845). Pp. 99–103, in: Hausser, J. (Ed.). *Säugetiere der Schweiz. Verbreitung – Biologie – Ökologie*. Denkschriften der Schweizerischen Akademie der Naturwissenschaften, 103. Birkhäuser Verlag, Basel, xii+1–501.

Zörner, H. (1981). *Der Feldhase*. Neue Brehm-Bücherei, Ziemsen Verlag, Wittenberg–Lutherstadt, 172 pp.

Zuchuat, O. & Keller, A. (1995). *Myotis bechsteini* (Natterer in Kuhl, 1818). Pp. 119–121, in: Hausser, J. (Ed.). *Säugetiere der Schweiz. Verbreitung – Biologie – Ökologie*. Denkschriften der Schweizerischen Akademie der Naturwissenschaften, 103. Birkhäuser Verlag, Basel, xii+1–501.

Zukal, J. (1994). Activity, echolocation and foraging behaviour of *Myotis emarginatus*. Ph.D. dissertation, Faculty of Sciences, Masaryk University, Brno, 104 pp.

Zukal, J. & Gaisler, J. (1989). K výskytu a změnám početnosti netopýra severního, *Eptesicus nilssoni* (Keyserling et Blasius, 1839) v Československu. *Lynx (N. S.),* 25: 83–95.

Index

The main entry is to be found where there is a double page spread. Single page numbers indicate a minor reference, mainly of distinction from similar animals.

ISBN 0-85661-130-1

9 780856 611308